GREEK ATHLETICS

EDINBURGH READINGS ON THE ANCIENT WORLD

GENERAL EDITORS
Michele George, *McMaster University*
Thomas Harrison, *University of Liverpool*

ADVISORY EDITORS
Paul Cartledge, *University of Cambridge*
Richard Saller, *Stanford University*

This series introduces English-speaking students to central themes in the history of the ancient world and to the range of scholarly approaches to those themes, within and across disciplines. Each volume, edited and introduced by a leading specialist, contains a selection of the most important work, including a significant proportion of translated material. The editor also provides a guide to the history of modern scholarship on the subject. Passages in ancient languages are translated; technical terms, ancient and modern, are explained.

PUBLISHED

Sparta
Edited by Michael Whitby

Sex and Difference in Ancient Greece and Rome
Edited by Mark Golden and Peter Toohey

Greeks and Barbarians
Edited by Thomas Harrison

The Ancient Economy
Edited by Walter Scheidel and Sitta von Reden

Roman Religion
Edited by Clifford Ando

Athenian Democracy
Edited by P. J. Rhodes

The Athenian Empire
Edited by Polly Low

Augustus
Edited by Jonathan Edmondson

Greek Athletics
Edited by Jason König

GREEK ATHLETICS

Edited by
Jason König

EDINBURGH UNIVERSITY PRESS

© in this edition Edinburgh University Press, 2010, 2013
© in the individual contributions is retained by the authors

Edinburgh University Press Ltd
22 George Square, Edinburgh EH8 9LF

First published in hardback by Edinburgh University Press 2010

www.euppublishing.com

Typeset in Ehrhardt
by Koinonia, Manchester

A CIP record for this book is available from the British Library

ISBN 978 0 7486 3490 3 (hardback)
ISBN 978 0 7486 3944 1 (paperback)

The right of the contributors
to be identified as authors of this work
has been asserted in accordance with
the Copyright, Designs and Patents Act 1988.

Published with the support of Edinburgh University
Scholarly Publishing Initiatives Fund.

Contents

Illustrations	vii
Acknowledgements	ix
Note to the Reader	xi
Abbreviations	xii
Maps	xviii
Ancient Greek Athletics: An Introduction	1

PART I: OLYMPIA, THE *PERIODOS* AND PANHELLENISM

	Introduction to Part I	19
1	Sanctuaries, the State and the Individual *Catherine Morgan*	23
2	The So-called Olympic Peace in Ancient Greece *Manfred Lämmer, trans. Julietta Steinhauer*	36

PART II: *GYMNASION* EDUCATION

	Introduction to Part II	63
3	*Gymnasia* and the Democratic Values of Leisure *Nick Fisher*	66
4	Notes on the Role of the *Gymnasion* in the Hellenistic City *Philippe Gauthier, trans. Margarita Lianou*	87

PART III: FESTIVAL FOUNDATIONS

	Introduction to Part III	105
5	Opening Address: Eighth International Congress of Greek and Latin Epigraphy *Louis Robert, trans. Margarita Lianou*	108
6	Two Greek Athletic Contests in Rome *Louis Robert, trans. Margarita Lianou*	120

PART IV: COMPETITION AND VICTORY

Introduction to Part IV — 143

7   Games, Prizes, Athletes and Ideology — 145
    H. W. Pleket

8   Athletics, Festivals and Greek Identity in the Roman East — 175
    Onno van Nijf

PART V: ATHLETIC REPRESENTATIONS

Introduction to Part V — 201

9   The Economy of *Kudos* — 204
    Leslie Kurke

10 Greek Athletics as Roman Spectacle: The Mosaics from Ostia and Rome — 238
    Zahra Newby

PART VI: GREEK ATHLETICS AND THE MODERN WORLD

Introduction to Part VI — 265

11 First with the Most: Greek Athletic Records and 'Specialization' — 267
    David Young

12 E. Norman Gardiner and the Decline of Greek sport — 284
    Donald Kyle

Guide to Further Reading — 312
Chronology — 313
Glossary — 315
Works Cited — 318
Index — 324

Illustrations

Fig. 0.1 The *Diskobolos* ('Discus-thrower') of Myron. Roman copy of a bronze original of the 5th century BCE. From Hadrian's Villa in Tivoli, Lazio, Italy. London, British Museum (image no. 00034472001). (Photo courtesy of the Trustees of the British Museum).

Fig. 4.1 Plan of the *gymnasion* at Delphi (J.-Fr. Bommelaer and D. Laroche, *Guide de Delphes. Le Site*, 1991, p. 72) (© EfA).

Fig. 4.2 Plan of the *gymnasion* at Delos (G. Roux, *BCH* 104, 1980, p. 139, fig. 4) (© EfA).

Fig. 6.1 Agonistic inscription from Delphi.

Fig. 8.1 The origins of Olympic victors 600 BCE–300 BCE.

Fig. 8.2 The origins of Olympic victors 300 BCE–400 CE.

Fig. 9.1 Herald announcing the victor in the horse race, as a youth approaches with tripod and crown. Black-figure amphora of Panathenaic shape, ca 570 BCE. London, British Museum B144. (Photo courtesy of the Trustees of the British Museum).

Fig. 9.2 Crowning of athletic victor wreathed in fillets. Black-figure amphora of Panathenaic shape. London, British Museum B138. (Photo courtesy of the Trustees of the British Museum).

Fig. 10.1 Room D (off palaestra), Baths of Neptune, Ostia. (Archivio Fotografico della Soprintendenza Archeologica di Ostia neg. no. C787). (Reproduced courtesy of the Soprintendenza Archeologica di Ostia).

Fig. 10.2 Room D (heated). Baths of the Trinacria, Ostia. (Archivio Fotografico della Soprintendenza Archeologica di Ostia neg. no. B3229). (Reproduced courtesy of the Soprintendenza Archeologica di Ostia).

Fig. 10.3 Room B (heated), Terme Marittime, Ostia. (Fototeca Unione neg. no. F7260). (Reproduced courtesy of the Fototeca Unione, at the American Academy in Rome).

Fig. 10.4 Room A, Terme Marittime, Ostia. (Archivio Fotografico della Soprintendenza Archeologica di Ostia neg. no. A1558). (Reproduced courtesy of the Soprintendenza Archeologica di Ostia).

Fig. 10.5 Apodyterium near the palaestra, Baths of Porta Marina, Ostia. (Image oriented to show the view from the entrance to the room). (Author's photograph).

Fig. 10.6 Inn of Alexander Helix, Ostia. (Archivio Fotografico della Soprintendenza Archeologica di Ostia neg. no. B888). (Reproduced courtesy of the Soprintendenza Archeologica di Ostia).

Fig. 10.7 Cassegiato del Lottatore, Ostia. (Author's photograph).
Fig. 10.8 Heated room, baths on the Via Severiana, Ostia. (Archivio Fotografico della Soprintendenza Archeologica di Ostia neg. no. R3269, 16). (Reproduced courtesy of the Soprintendenza Archeologica di Ostia).
Fig. 10.9 Mosaic from the baths on the Via Portuense, Rome. (Servizio di Fotoriproduzione, Soprintendenza Archeologica di Roma inv. 125523). (Reproduced courtesy of the Soprintendenza Archeologica di Roma).
Fig. 10.10 Mosaic from the baths on the Via Portuense, Rome. (Servizio di Fotoriproduzione, Soprintendenza Archeologica di Roma inv. 125521). (Reproduced courtesy of the Soprintendenza Archeologica di Roma).

Acknowledgements

For permission to reprint the essays and chapters in this volume I am grateful to the following: Professor Catherine Morgan, Cambridge University Press and the Faculty of Classics Board, University of Cambridge (for chapter 1); Professor Manfred Lämmer and Academia Verlag (for chapter 2); Professor Nick Fisher and Cambridge University Press (for chapter 3); Professor Philippe Gauthier and Verlag C.H. Beck (for chapter 4); the Epigraphical Museum of Athens and the heirs to Louis Robert's estate (for chapter 5); the Académie des Inscriptions et Belles-Lettres and the heirs to Louis Robert's estate (for chapter 6); Professor H.W. Pleket and Academia Verlag (for chapter 7); Professor Onno van Nijf (for chapter 8); Professor Leslie Kurke and Oxford University Press (for chapter 9); Dr Zahra Newby and the British School at Rome (for chapter 10); Professor David Young (for chapter 11); Professor Donald Kyle and Texas A&M University Press (for chapter 12). In all cases full details of original publication are given in the first footnote of the chapter.

For permission to reproduce the images in the volume, I am grateful to the following: the Trustees of the British Museum (for the images in the introduction and on the cover); the Ecole française d'Athènes (for the maps in chapter 4); Professor Glen Bowersock, on behalf of the Fond Louis Robert at the Académie des Inscriptions et Belles Lettres (for the image in chapter 6); The Random House Group Ltd (for the maps in chapter 8, reproduced from H.A. Harris, *Greek Athletes and Athletics*, Hutchinson); the Trustees of the British Museum (for the images in chapter 9); Dr Zahra Newby (for images 10.5 and 10.7), the Soprintendenza Archeologica di Ostia (for images 10.1, 10.2, 10.4, 10.6, 10.8), the Fototeca Unione at the American Academy in Rome (for image 10.3) and the Ministero per i Beni e le Attività Culturali--Soprintendenza Speciale per i Beni Archeologici di Roma (for images 10.9 and 10.10) (N.B. in the case of images 10.9 and 10.10 original copies could not be traced; the images have therefore been reproduced, at lower quality than others in the chapter, from the original article).

I am also grateful to the many people who have offered help and advice at various stages, especially the following: the series editors, especially Tom Harrison, for suggesting this volume in the first place; Don Kyle and Mark Golden, for advice on the choice of articles; the anonymous readers for EUP for many helpful suggestions; Tom Scanlon, for generously sharing the choice of articles for his forthcoming *Oxford Readings in Greek Sport* – I have done my best at all stages to make this selection complementary to his; Onno van Nijf and Denis Rousset for advice on permissions, especially Denis Rousset for his generous assistance with permissions for the two translated articles by Louis Robert; Margarita Lianou and Julietta Steinhauer for translations; Glen Bowersock and Zahra Newby for help with images; Carol MacDonald and Máiréad McElligott at EUP for their help with countless enquiries; and all those St Andrews students who have studied in my honours module on 'Greek Athletics in the Ancient World', which has allowed me to think through the ideas and article choices in this volume.

Note to the Reader

The articles and excerpts included in this book were originally published in a range of different journals and books. A degree of uniformity has been imposed (for example in the abbreviations used), but many of the conventions of the original pieces have been preserved. This applies to spelling and punctuation (UK or US) and to different modes of referencing: chapters using the Harvard (i.e. name and date) system are followed by individual bibliographies; those using 'short titles' usually have footnotes and no bibliographies. The final bibliography contains works referred to in my various introductory sections. Some Greek terms, especially those in use in English, have been transliterated. Translations have been added for all quotations not in English. All editorial additions, apart from very minor adjustments and corrections, are in square brackets.

All abbreviations of ancient texts, modern collections, books and journals, used either in the chapters or in the editorial material, are listed and explained on pp. xii–xvii. Other abbreviations have, in general, been avoided. The following abbreviations are contained within the republished articles: *ad loc./ad locc.* (in the relevant place, used of a commentary on a particular text), *ap.* (quoted by), c. or ca. (about, used of approximate dates and figures), cf. (compare), ch./chs (chapter/s), ed./eds (editor/s), ibid. (the same work or text), id. (the same author), fr./frs (fragment/s), f./ff. (and following line/s or page/s), *loc. cit.* (passage cited above), *op. cit.* (work cited above), p./pp. (page/s), *pace* (with due respect to, i.e. contradicting), s.v. (under the word, i.e. used of dictionaries).

There is no consensus about the most desirable spelling of Greek names and titles. In my own introductory sections I have generally preferred to stick closely to the original Greek form in transliterating, except where a Latinate spelling is so familiar that it would look peculiar in its Greek form, but there is inevitably a considerable amount of variation between the various articles and extracts reprinted here.

In my introductory sections I have followed standard periodizations for Greek history and literature: archaic (roughly 800–479 BCE); classical (479–323 BCE); Hellenistic (323–31 BCE); imperial (31 BCE to roughly 300 CE).

The maps reproduced on pp. xviii–xix do not include every city mentioned in the text, but I have aimed to include all major athletic festival centres, as well as all other cities which are discussed at any length.

Abbreviations

1 ANCIENT AUTHORS, TEXTS AND CORPORA

ABV	J.D. Beazley, *Attic Black-figure Vase-Painters* (Oxford 1956)
Aeschin[es]	
Aesch[ylus]	*Eum[enides]*
Aineias Takt[ikos]	*Poliork[etika]=Siegecraft*
Andoc[ides]	
Anth[ologia] Pal[atina]	
Ar[istophanes]	*Ach[arnians]*
	Eccl[esiazousae]=Assemblywomen
	Kn[ights]
	Lys[istrata]
Aristotle	*Ath[ênaiôn] Pol[iteia]=On the Constitution of the Athenians*
	Pol[itics]
	Rhet[oric]
Artemidorus	*Oneir[ocritica]=Dream Interpretation*
Athen[aeus] or Ath[enaeus]	
Bacch[ylides] or Bacchyl[ides]	
BMC Galatia Syria	*British Museum Catalogue of Greek Coins*, vol. 20: *Galatia, Cappadocia and Syria*
B.M. Papyri	*British Museum Papyri*
Callim[achus] Pfeiffer	R. Pfeiffer, *Callimachus*
CEG	*Carmina Epigraphica Graeca*
CIA	*Corpus Inscriptionum Atticarum*
Cicero	*ad Fam[iliares]*
	Tusc[ulan Disputations]
CIG	*Corpus Inscriptionum Graecarum*
CIL	*Corpus Inscriptionum Latinarum*
Dem[osthenes]	
Dio Cass[ius]	
Dio Chrys[ostom]	*Or[ation]*
Diod[orus Siculus] or Diod[orus] Sic[ulus]	
Diog[enes] Laert[ius]	

Abbreviations xiii

Dion[ysius of] Hal[icarnassus]	
DK	H. Diels and W. Kranz, *Die Fragmente der Vorsokratiker*
Ebert	J. Ebert, *Griechische Epigramme auf Sieger an gymnischen und hippischen Agonen*
Eur[ipides]	*Bacch[ae]*
	Tro[jan Women]
Euseb[ius]	*Praep[aratio] Evang[elica]*
FGH or *FGrHist*	F. Jacoby, *Die Fragmente der griechischen Historiker*
FHG	*Fragmenta Historicorum Graecorum*
GGA	*Göttingische gelehrte Anzeiger*
H[ero]d[o]t[us]	
Homer	*Il[iad]*
	Od[yssey]
I.Délos	*Inscriptions de Délos*
I. Ephesos	*Die Inschriften von Ephesos*
IG	*Inscriptiones Graecae*
IGR	*Inscriptiones Graecae ad res Romanas pertinentes*
IGUR	*Inscriptiones Graecae Urbis Romae*
IK	*Inschriften griechischer Städte aus Kleinasien*
I. Lampsakos	*Die Inschriften von Lampsakos*
IM	Isthmia Miscellaneous
I. Magnesia	*Die Inschriften von Magnesia am Maeander*
I.Milet	*Inschriften von Milet*
I. Mylasa	*Die Inschriften von Mylasa*
I. Priene	*Inschriften von Priene*
Isocr[ates]	
I. Sardis	W.H. Buckler, D.M. Robinson, *Sardis, VII. Greek and Latin Inscriptions*
I. Syrie	*Inscriptions Grecques et Latines de la Syrie*
I. Tralleis	*Die Inschriften von Tralleis und Nysa*
IvO or *I.Olympia* or Dittenberger and Purgold	W. Dittenberger and J. Purgold, *Die Inschriften von Olympia*
Josephus	*A[ntiquitates] J[udaicae]*
K/A	R. Kassel, and C. Austin, *Poetae Comici Graeci*
Laum	B. Laum, *Stiftungen in der griechischen und römischen Antike. Ein Beitrag zur antiken Kulturgeschichte*, I-II
Libanius	*Ep[istle]*
Lucian	*Deor[um] Conc[ilium]*
	Pro imag[inibus]
Lys[ias]	N.B. Th=Teubner edition by Thalheim; G-B=Budé edition by Gernet and Bizos
Michel, *Recueil*	C. Michel, *Recueil d'inscriptions grecques*
Milet	*Milet. Ergebnisse der Ausgrabungen und Untersuchungen seit dem Jahre 1899*

Moretti	L. Moretti, 'Olympionikai, i vincitori negli antichi agoni olimpici', *Memoria della Classe di Scienze morali e storiche dell' Accademia dei Lincei* 8.2 (1957): 55–198.
Moretti, *Iscr. agon. gr.*	L. Moretti, *Iscrizioni agonistiche greche*
Nauck	A. Nauck, *Tragicorum Graecorum Fragmenta*
OGI	*Orientis Graecae Inscriptiones Selectae*
Page	D.L. Page, *Further Greek Epigrams*
Paus[anias]	
Phil[ostratus]	*Gymn[asticus]*=On Athletic Training
Phot[ius]	*Bibl[iotheca]*
Pind[ar]	*Nem[ean]*
	Ol[ympian]
	Isthm[ian]
	Pyth[ian]
Pl[ato] or Plat[o]	*Apol[ogy]*
	Charm[ides]
	Crat[ylus]
	Phaedr[us]
	Prot[agoras]
	Symp[osium]
Plato Com[icus]	
P[o]l[y]b[ius]	
Pliny (the Elder)	*H[istoria] N[aturalis]*=Natural History
Pliny (the Younger)	*Ep[istles]*
Plut[arch]	*Ages[ilaus]*
	Lys[ander]
	[De] malign[itate] Herod[oti]
	Quaest[iones] Conv[ivales]=Sympotic Questions
	Solon
PMG	D.L. Page, *Poetae Melici Graeci*
P.Zenon	*Zenon Papyri*
Sammlung Aulock	*Sylloge Nummorum Graecorum, Sammlung Hans Von Aulock*
Schol[ia] or Sch[olia]	
SEG	*Supplementum Epigraphicum Graecum*
SIG³ or Syll.³	*Sylloge Inscriptionum Graecarum* (third edition)
Simon[ides]	*Ep[igram]*
S[criptores] H[istoriae] A[ugustae]	*Hadr[ian]*
Strab[o]	
Suetonius	*Ner[o]*
Suppl. Epigr. Rodio	Pugliese Carratelli, G. 'Supplemento epigrafico rodio', in *ASAA* 30–32 (1952–1954): 247–316.
TAM	*Tituli Asiae Minoris*
Thuc[ydides]	
Virgil	*Aen[eid]*

Vitr[uvius]
W   M.L. West, *Iambi et Elegi Graeci*
Xenoph[anes]
Xen[ophon]   *Anab[asis]*
                         Hell[enica]
                         [Peri] Hipp[ikês]=*On Horsemanship*
                         Mem[orabilia]
                         Oik[onomikos]
                         Symp[osium]

2 PERIODICALS, MONOGRAPHS AND WORKS OF REFERENCE

À travers l'Asie Mineure	Robert, L. (1980) *A travers l'Asie Mineure. Poètes et prosateurs, monnaies grecques, voyageurs et géographie*, Paris.
ABSA	*Annual of the British School at Athens*
AC or *Ant. Class.*	*L'Antiquité classique*
AE	*Archaiologike Ephemeris*
AJA	*American Journal of Archaeology*
AJP	*American Journal of Philology*
Annales ESC	*Annales. Économies, Sociétés, Civilisations*
AnzWien	*Anzeiger. Österreichische Akademie der Wissenschaften, Wien, Philologisch-historische Klasse*
AR	*Archaeological Reports*
ASAA	*Annuario della Scuola Archeologica di Atene a delle Missioni Italiane in Oriente*
ASAW	*Abhandlungen der Sächsischen Akademie der Wissenschaften zu Leipzig*
BCH	*Bulletin de correspondance hellénique*
BICS	*Bulletin of the Institute of Classical Studies*
BSA	*Annual of the British School at Athens*
Bull. épigr.	'Bulletin épigraphique', in *Revue des études grecques*
CA	*Classical Antiquity*
CAH	*Cambridge Ancient History*
Choix d'écrits	Robert, L. (2007) *Choix d'écrits* (ed. D. Rousset, avec la collaboration de Ph. Gauthier et I. Savalli-Lestrade), Paris.
CJ	*Classical Journal*
CQ	*Classical Quarterly*
CR	*Classical Review*
CRAI	*Comptes rendus de l'Academie des Inscriptions et Belles-Lettres*
CSCA	*University of California Studies in Classical Antiquity*
Dict. Saglio-Pottier	*Dictionnaire des antiquités grecques et romaines* (ed. Pottier, E. and Saglio, E.)

Documents de l'Asie Mineure méridionale	Robert, L. (1966) *Documents de l'Asie Mineure méridionale*, Paris
EMC/CV	*Échos du monde classique/Classical Views*
Ét. épigr.	Robert, L. (1938) *Etudes épigraphiques et philologiques*, Paris.
Études anatoliennes	Robert, L. (1937) *Etudes anatoliennes. Recherches sur les inscriptions grecques de l'Asie mineure*, Paris.
Festschrift Zepos	Caemmerer, E. von (ed.) (1973) *Xenion. Festschrift für Pan. J. Zepos anlässlich seines 65. Geburtstages am 1. Dezember 1973*, Athens (3 vols).
G&R	*Greece and Rome*
GIBM	*The Collection of Ancient Greek Inscriptions in the British Museum* (Oxford 1874–1916)
GRBS	*Greek, Roman and Byzantine Studies*
HTR	*Harvard Theological Review*
HSCP	*Harvard Studies in Classical Philology*
Ist. Mitt.	*Istanbuler Mitteilungen*
JHS	*Journal of Hellenic Studies*
JÖAI	*Jahreshefte des Österreichischen Archäologischen Instituts*
KBSW	*Kölner Beiträge zur Sportwissenschaft*
La déesse de Castabala	Robert, L. (1964) *La déesse de Hiérapolis Castabala*, Paris.
L'épigramme grecque	*L'épigramme grecque* (Entretiens sur l'antiquité classique, Fondation Hardt 14)
LSJ	H.G. Liddell, R. Scott, and H. Stuart Jones, *Greek-English Lexicon*
MAL	*Memoria della Classe di Scienze morali e storiche dell' Accademia dei Lincei*
MDAI(A)	*Mitteilungen des Deutschen Archäologischen Instituts (Athen. Abt.)*
Monnaies grecques	Robert, L. (1967) *Monnaies grecques*, Paris
OMS or *Opera Minora* or *Opera Minora Selecta*	Robert, L. *Opera Minora Selecta* (7 volumes)
P&P	*Past and Present*
PCPhS	*Proceedings of the Cambridge Philological Society*
PLLS	*Papers of the Liverpool Latin Seminar*
RA	*Revue archéologique*
RE	*Paulys Realencyclopedie der Classischen Altertumswissenschaft*
REA	*Revue des études anciennes*
REG	*Revue des études grecques*
Rev. Arch.	*Revue archéologique*
Rev. Num.	*Revue numismatique*
Rev. Phil.	*Revue de philologie, de littérature et d'histoire anciennes*
Riv. Fil.	*Rivista di filologia e d'istruzione classica*

SBAW	*Sitzungsberichte der Bayerischen Akademie der Wissenschaften, Philologisch-historische Klasse*
ThPKK	*Theorie und Praxis der Körperkultur*
YCS	*Yale Classical Studies*
ZPE	*Zeitschrift für Papyrologie und Epigraphik*

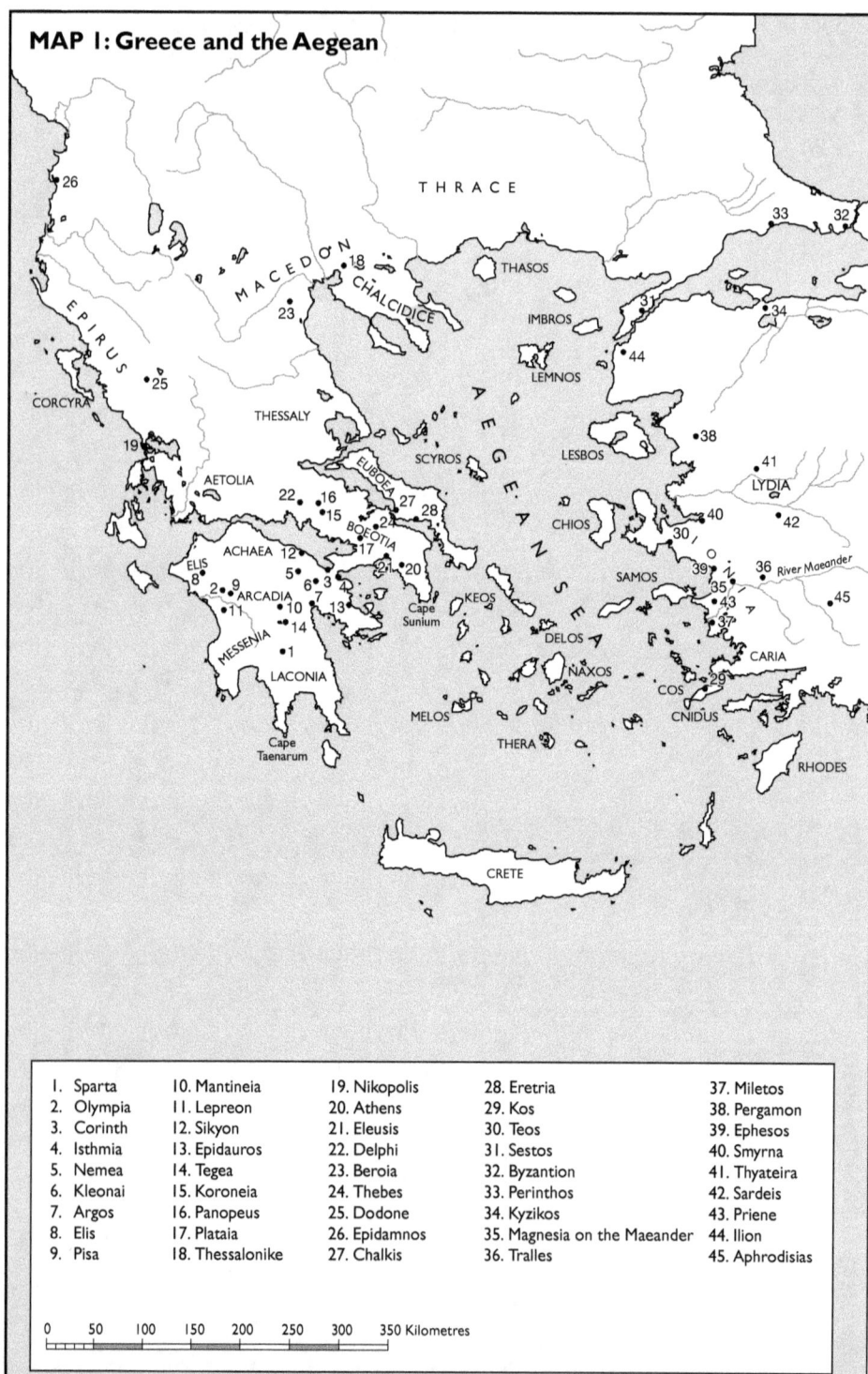

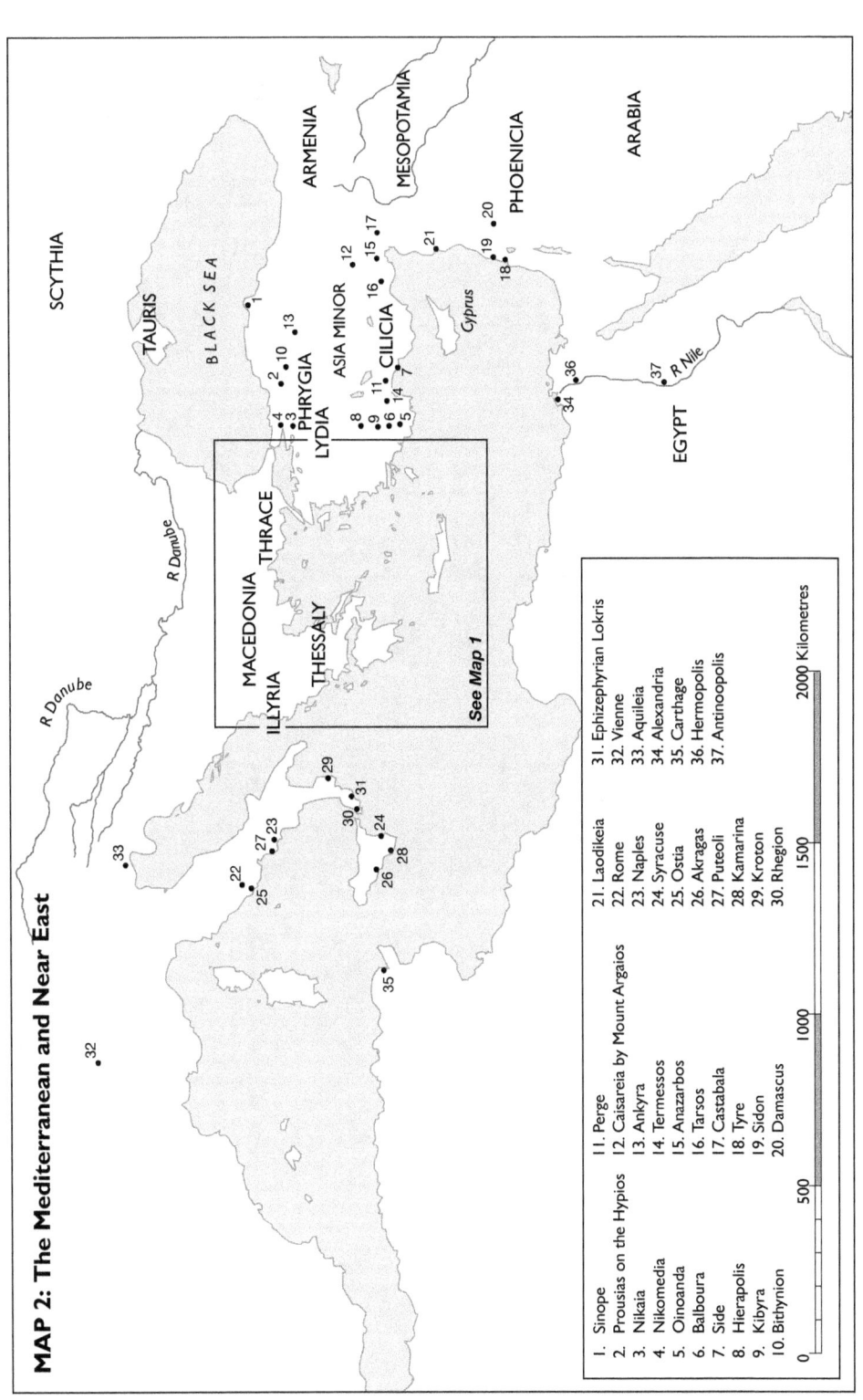

Ancient Greek Athletics: An Introduction

WHY STUDY ANCIENT SPORT?

There are no doubt many different ways of responding to that question, and many different hooks which attract people to the subject. Personal enthusiasm for sport and curiosity about understanding and imagining the similarities and differences between ancient and modern experience must be a key motivation for many (more on that below). But the answer I want to stress first of all in this introduction is simply the fact that sporting activity played a central role within many different areas of ancient Greek society. For that reason it offers us a powerful vehicle through which to approach an understanding of the classical world as a whole.

One way of bringing out that centrality is through a history of athletic institutions. The festivals of the Greek-speaking Mediterranean world, from the eighth century BCE right through to at least the fourth century CE regularly included athletic and indeed musical and equestrian competitions. These were institutions through which individual cities celebrated their history and identity, as well as their membership of a wider Greek community. Victory could be enormously prestigious: victorious athletes brought great prominence to their own cities and were viewed as representatives of discipline and excellence, held up as role models for others to follow. On a more day-to-day level, the *gymnasion* was, from the Hellenistic period onwards, one of the key institutions of higher education in the ancient world, a place for male members of the Greek elites to receive the military and physical education which marked out high social status. The office of gymnasiarch, head of the *gymnasion*, with responsibility for funding and in some cases also running the *gymnasion*, was accordingly viewed as one of the most prestigious benefactions a wealthy man or woman could undertake for his or her city – as indeed was the position of agonothete, with responsibility for funding and running the festivals already mentioned. Festival and *gymnasion* culture were viewed as key components of the Greek heritage. They also spread far beyond the traditional centres of the Greek world, as communities both in the east and in the west (including Rome itself) attempted to appropriate some of the prestige of traditional Greek culture.

The centrality of athletics in the ancient world was also a conceptual, symbolic centrality. Images of athletic competition and athletic training saturate ancient art and literature. They offered important vehicles through which to conceptualise human virtues and social status, and through which to stage debates about identity

I

and education. And they were often linked with the agonistic virtues which were prized so much in other areas of life, particularly in military activity.[1] The idealised (and often eroticised) athletic body was a familiar image, not only in statues erected in honour of athletic victors, but also in literary texts, where the figure of the athlete appears at every turn.[2] For example, athletic training resurfaces repeatedly as an image of the struggle for spiritual enlightenment in philosophical writing, and that metaphor is in turn taken up by Christian writers, most famously St Paul, to describe the disciplines of the new Christian faith.[3]

Many of the articles reprinted in this volume explore those institutional and conceptual centralities. One of the themes which emerges from them repeatedly is the role of athletics in perceptions of both individual and communal identity, in other words the way in which athletics, with all of the idealising (and conversely satirical) connotations attached to it, affected the way in which the inhabitants of the ancient world saw themselves. That insight leads us back to the issue of modern sporting enthusiasm as a motivating force for study. One of the greatest attractions of all in studying ancient athletics is the promise of reaching an understanding of bodily experience in ancient Greek culture. Inevitably we are distant from the ancient world. Our reliance on all-too-often fragmentary texts and images can make the lived, physical experience of the ancient Greece and Rome seem impossibly hard to access. But the fascination of ancient athletics lies at least in part in the fantasy that it might help us to overcome that sense of distance. Through painstaking reconstruction of the contexts within which the athletic body was used and the meanings which were attached to it, we can perhaps start to reconstruct a sense of how it might have felt and what it might have meant to step out into the stadium to compete, to train in the *gymnasion*, even to sit in the audience at a great festival.

Inevitably our reconstructions have elements of fantasy or at least conjecture. But we might also comfort ourselves with the knowledge that the ancient authors too did not always understand the history and significance of current athletic practice. This was especially so within the Roman period, the great heyday of Greek athletic culture, from when so much of our surviving evidence dates. To take just one example: Greek athletes exercised and competed naked, and that nakedness was itself taken as a marker of distinctively Greek culture, and yet the reasons for this custom were themselves lost in the mists of time, the subject of endless speculation for ancient authors, just as they have been within modern scholarship.[4] One might even suspect that this kind of inscrutability and mystery was itself one of the key contributing factors in ancient fascination with the athletic body. In that sense the essays reprinted here take part in an enterprise of debate and exploration which has

---

[1] The stereotype of ancient Greek society as uniquely competitive still has some force, even if we need to be careful to avoid oversimplification in using it: e.g., see Golden (1998) 28–33, Spivey (2004) 4–16. On agonistic vocabulary in Greek, see Scanlon (1983).

[2] See Scanlon (2002) for extensive discussion.

[3] Cf. very brief further discussion of Christian engagement with athletics at the end of the introduction to section 3.

[4] E.g., see Arieti (1974–5), Crowther (1982), Mouratidis (1985), Bonfante (1989), McDonnell (1991), Golden (1998) 65–9, Miller (2000), Scanlon (2002) 205–10, Christesen (2002).

powerful roots in the ancient world itself, even if the idioms by which they approach that task are very different from anything we find in ancient texts.

SIMILARITIES AND DIFFERENCES

Where, then, should we locate the most significant similarities and differences between modern and ancient sport? There is, I want to suggest, an odd tension between familiarity and difference in ancient athletics, and being aware of that tension is an important starting-point for assessing the ancient evidence. Clearly there are some areas where the two have much in common: most obviously, many events from the ancient games are still central to the modern Olympics. The massive festival calendar of the athletics of the Hellenistic and Roman periods has much in common with modern sporting organisation, in its globalised scale and complex organisation, as have ancient record-keeping practices, which are discussed by David Young in chapter 11. At the same time, however, many features of ancient sport do indeed look quite peculiar by modern standards.

One important reference point for understanding that odd combination of similarity and difference is the way in which the early Olympic movement in the late nineteenth and twentieth centuries used ancient evidence, copying some things very closely, but also in other ways using very distorted pictures of ancient athletics in order to justify modern practice. One important example is the 1936 games in Berlin,[5] and especially Leni Riefenstahl's famous film of those games, *Olympia*.[6] These games were notable among other things for their systematic appropriation of classical imagery and ideology. Ceremonial details invented for the 1936 games continue to play a role in the Olympics of the twenty-first century, most notably the carrying of the Olympic torch from Olympia to the venue of the games: it seems remarkable that the Nazi origins of that ritual are not more widely known and more warily treated today. In many ways Riefenstahl's film feels like a very modern piece – and it was in fact very influential on the formation of modern techniques of sports photography – but it also drew a sustained and highly idealised link between modern sport and the ancient world. For example, the film repeatedly suggests links between ancient athletic statues and the modern athletic physique, especially in the breathtaking opening scene which shows an ancient statue in a ruined temple setting coming to life and turning into a modern discus thrower on screen. The film also paints Nazi Germany as inheritor of ancient athletic ideals, for example in the early sections where the Olympic torch is represented travelling across a map of Europe, over territory which Germany would invade very soon afterwards. There is considerable debate about the degree to which Riefenstahl was linked with the Nazi party: clearly her directing was not a straightforward piece of official propaganda, but the links with Nazi ideology are nevertheless hard to miss.

---

[5] There has been an enormous rush of recent journalistic and popular-scholarly publications, many of them almost identically titled and covering almost exactly the same ground as each other, on the 1936 games in Berlin: good older accounts include Hart-Davis (1986) and Mandell (1987); more recently see esp. Bachrach (2000), Kruger and Murray (2003), Hilton (2006), Rippon (2006), Walters (2007), Large (2007).
[6] On Riefenstahl, see, among others, Graham (2001).

Fig. 0.1. The *Diskobolos* ('Discus-thrower') of Myron. Roman copy of a bronze original of the 5th century BCE. From Hadrian's Villa in Tivoli, Lazio, Italy. London, British Museum (image no. 0034472001). (Photo courtesy of the Trustees of the British Museum).

Modern sport thus owes a great deal to the ancient games, but there are also enormous differences, which are sometimes hard to see at first glance because inaccurate ideas about ancient sport have become so familiar to us over the last century. One of the most obvious points to make here is about the intertwining of sport and religion in the ancient world. The great festivals of Greece were not simply occasions for entertainment, they were also religious events: occasions for processions and sacrifices to the gods. But I want to focus here on a rather different issue – the link between sport and violence – as a brief case study for understanding how fundamentally different sport was in ancient culture. That link was much more deeply embedded than it is in modern culture.

The history of athletic institutions which I have sketched out above offers us a good starting-point for thinking about athletics and violence. The *gymnasion*, particularly in the Hellenistic world, was a place among other things for training in warfare. Often military trainers would be employed alongside athletic instructors. According to some accounts it was the rise of hoplite warfare in the sixth century which necessitated the development of the *gymnasion* as a place for training.[7] The context of warfare was also crucial to the great festivals of the Greek world. These were indeed times for the whole of the Greek world to come together, but the modern image of universal Olympic peace and harmony is nevertheless a misleading one:[8] competition between citizens of different cities seems to have been viewed as much as anything as a substitute or continuation of the rivalries which were played out on the battlefield. Admittedly that is much less the case in the Roman period, when the whole of the Greek world was effectively united under Roman peace. Nevertheless, even in that period, the violence of the Greek past was there for everyone to see, with the temples at Olympia full of dedications by cities celebrating victories in battle – in many cases victories over other Greek cities which themselves sent competitors to the festival – from many centuries before.

It is important also to stress the violence of much athletic competition itself: we have to work quite hard at putting aside our preconceptions about the ancient games in order to recapture that.[9] Violence is of course not entirely alien to modern sport, but we might nevertheless be shocked, if we were transported to a ringside seat in the Olympic stadium for the men's boxing contest, by the blatant enjoyment of violence among spectators, watching competitors fighting without boxing gloves, with only hardened leather strips wound around their hands, designed not only for protection but also to inflict more damage on their opponents.

One reason why this very violent strand in ancient sport is so easy to forget is simply because of the dominance of idealised, statuesque athletic images celebrating unscarred, quasi-divine athletic beauty (cf. Fig. 0.1), the kind of image which Riefenstahl's *Olympia* celebrates. Statues like these would often be put up as thank offerings to the gods in celebration of athletic victory. However, most of those which survive are actually copies from the Roman period: many wealthy Romans

---

[7] On the links between athletics and warfare, see Golden (1998) 23–8, Spivey (2004).
[8] Cf. Lämmer, chapter 2 of this volume.
[9] Cf. Scanlon (2002) 299–322 on the symbolic importance of the risk of death in athletic and equestrian contests; Crowther (1994b) on the attractions of violence for spectators of the equestrian events.

collected athletic statues, along with other Greek art, as a sign of their sophistication, rather than through any particular interest in athletic contest. With that fact in mind, the links between real-life contest and idealising commemorative statuary come to seem rather less self-evident than we might initially expect.

There is, however, another strand in the surviving images – especially in the mosaics but also in some statues – which is less familiar in the modern world. These are images of heavily scarred, brutal athletic figures, sometimes created with satirical intent, but more often with a kind of idealisation of that brutality and strength for its own sake, very different from the kind of idealisation of bodily perfection and virtue just outlined (as we will see in chapter 10). The "unscarred" and "scarred" types of athletic image were both highly prevalent in the ancient world, sometimes on show side-by-side. We should not ignore the existence of the latter in forming our own images of ancient sport: they reflect the prevalence and ubiquity of violence in the ancient stadium.

The closeness of gladiators and athletes is also important here.[10] One stereotype which still holds sway is the contrast between civilised Greek athletics and bloodthirsty Roman gladiatorial games. Gladiatorial games certainly never lost their capacity to be viewed as stereotypically Roman, just as athletic contest never lost its capacity to be viewed as stereotypically Greek. But in practice there was very widespread cross-fertilisation between the two. Rome had its own athletic festivals, and was a key city in the Greek festival calendar; and gladiatorial games were enormously popular in the Greek-speaking east of the empire, and often took place in the same spaces as traditional Greek athletic or theatrical spectacle. Similarly, monuments celebrating gladiators often use the language of athletics to describe gladiatorial victory. The pleasures experienced by the audience of a boxing match may not have been so clearly separated from the pleasures offered to the crowd at the arena as we sometimes assume.

HISTORY OF ATHLETIC SCHOLARSHIP

Understanding how modern preconceptions about the ancient games have been formed, and how they have changed over time, requires attention not only to twentieth-century sporting history, but also at the same time to the changing landscape of modern scholarship on ancient athletics. I want in this section to lay out briefly some of the key landmarks in these developments over the last hundred years or more.[11] Many of the late nineteenth- and early twentieth-century attempts to explore ancient athletic practice and ideology were written by scholars who were in some way involved with the early Olympic movement. That movement had been stimulated in part by the excavations at the site of Olympia, which was not rediscovered until 1766, and not excavated systematically until the 1870s, by a team from the German Archaeological Institute at Athens. Important also was the context of increasing Greek national feeling after independence in the 1820s, which led to calls

---

[10] The key study is Robert (1940), in French.
[11] More detailed discussion of key bibliography on many of the issues discussed here follows in the section introductions.

for a refounding of the Olympic games, and indeed a number of attempts at revival in Greece through the nineteenth century. But the modern series of Olympics, which began with the 1896 games in Athens, quickly turned into a much more international affair, partly thanks to the involvement of the French aristocrat Pierre de Coubertin, who himself left behind many thousands of pages of writing on how ancient athletic practices should be reshaped for new uses in the modern age, and whose work represents another important testimony – along with Riefenstahl's *Olympia* – to the way in which ancient practices were both imitated and distorted in equal measure within the modern Olympic tradition.[12] The story of the 1896 games has often been told. The best accounts acknowledge the complexity of the processes which led to their foundation: we should not necessarily follow Coubertin's own self-aggrandising version of events, given the importance of others (in particular a number of Coubertin's Greek contemporaries) in the negotiations which led up to those games and in the setting-up of similar events in previous decades. Particularly important in this respect were the "Olympic" games held in Greece during the earlier nineteenth century, under the sponsorship of the wealthy Greek Evangelis Zappas, which were consistently ignored by Coubertin in his writing.[13]

One of the ideological keystones for the early Olympic movement was the belief in the importance of keeping sport amateur: any hint of involvement in professional sport led to exclusion from the games. That determination was based in part on the belief that amateurism was central to ancient sport too, a belief which informs much of the scholarship on ancient athletics from the first half of the twentieth century. Particularly important here is the work of E. Norman Gardiner (whose links with the amateur movement are discussed by Donald Kyle in the final chapter of this book), and who posited a decline from the early days of archaic and early-classical amateurism to increasing degeneracy and corruption and professionalism in later centuries.[14] He was followed in that respect by H. A. Harris. Harris' main contribution, in addition to a monograph on Greek athletics and Jewish culture in the ancient world, was the reconstruction of specific events, often with quite an incautious use of specific literary sources.[15] It was not until David Young's landmark book, *The Olympic Myth of Greek Amateur Athletics*, published in 1984, that the falsity of ascribing ideals of amateurism to ancient sport was really exposed in full.[16]

The 1980s and 1990s saw a major expansion of interest in ancient athletic history, with an increasingly wide range of publications. Nevertheless, it is important not to underestimate the significance of some of the key work which predates that expansion. In particular, key articles by H. W. Pleket and Louis Robert (both of them represented in this volume) did a great deal to bring a new rigour to our understanding of the vast body of epigraphical texts from which so much of our

---

[12] On Coubertin, see among others MacAloon (1981) and Biddiss (1999); and for his writings, see Coubertin (2000).
[13] See esp. Young (1987) and (1996) and Llewelyn Smith (2004).
[14] Gardiner (1910), (1925) and (1930).
[15] Harris (1964), (1972) and (1976).
[16] Young (1984); see also Young (1988) for further discussion. Young's work has been widely welcomed, although the details of his argument have attracted some disagreement, on the grounds that he is too eager to identify non-elite athletes without sufficient evidence: see Pritchard (2003) 193–9.

evidence for ancient festivals comes. Robert's work in particular is still oddly neglected even within recent athletic scholarship, partly perhaps because of its inaccessibility (most of his work remains untranslated into English).

It is only in the last two decades, however, that the study of ancient sport has really come into its own. For example, Donald Kyle's 1987 monograph on athletics in classical Athens offered an important model for showing the advantages of a very detailed focus on one particular location.[17] Underlying the shared, Mediterranean-wide athletic practice was a vast range of different local cultures, each with its own priorities and its own debates. There is still, I suggest, more work to be done along similar lines on examination of the festival and *gymnasion* culture of particular cities or particular regions. Thomas Scanlon, Joachim Ebert and Nigel Crowther, among many others, all published many important articles in the same period (in all three cases, their articles are now published as collections, and for that reason I have reluctantly chosen not to include any of them in this selection).[18] Stephen Miller's sourcebook of athletic texts in translation, *Arete*, is a key starting-point for anyone coming to the subject for the first time;[19] and his archaeological work on Nemea made important contributions in supplementing our understanding of the four traditional *periodos* games of Greece (see introduction to section 1 for explanation of that phrase), which had in the past been heavily focused on Olympia.[20] In addition, two scholarly journals devoted to ancient sport, *Stadion* and *Nikephoros*, have published many detailed studies, too many to catalogue here (Pleket's article in chapter 7 was written for the first issue of *Stadion*, the foundation of which he discusses briefly early in the opening pages). Both Nigel Crowther and Thomas Scanlon also published in the 1980s important bibliographical catalogues, listing previous work on athletic topics at great length.[21]

More recently, building on this foundation, there has been a sudden proliferation of excellent introductory works,[22] and a number of excellent collected volumes of essays.[23] At the same time there has also been an increasing tendency towards large-scale single-authored monographs which aim for in-depth discussion of particular bodies of material. Some of these texts focus on archaic and classical athletic culture: for example, Catherine Morgan's archaeological take on the early

---

[17] Kyle (1987).

[18] Scanlon (2002), Ebert (1997), Crowther (2004); Scanlon's volume, unlike the other two, contains heavily revised versions of the original articles, woven together within an overarching thesis on the relationship between sport and sexuality.

[19] Miller (2004a); the numberings in this third, revised edition do not correspond with those in the first and second editions; other sourcebooks with English translation are Robinson (1955) and Sweet (1987); important also are Moretti (1953), a collection of victory inscriptions, with Italian commentary (and cf. his catalogue of Olympic victors – Moretti (1957)); and Ebert (1972), a collection of victory epigrams, with commentary in German.

[20] See, most accessibly, Miller (2004c).

[21] Scanlon (1984) and Crowther (1984–5) and (1985–6); see also Crowther (1990) and Kyle (1983a) and (1983b) for survey discussions.

[22] See esp. Golden (1998) and (2004), Tyrrell (2004), Miller (2004b), Young (2004), Spivey (2004), Newby (2006), Kyle (2007); also (in German) Decker (1995). Of these, Miller (2004b) has a particularly impressive selection of images, as does Valavanis (2004), which focuses on festivals only, rather than ancient athletic culture more broadly.

[23] See esp. Phillips and Pritchard (2003), Papakonstantinou (2010).

history of the Panhellenic festivals, an extract from which appears in section 1;[24] Nigel Nicholson's work on representations of social status in the victory odes of Pindar and Bacchylides;[25] or Paul Christesen's work on the genre of the Olympic victor list.[26] Others have begun to draw out the richness of the later history of athletics in the Roman Empire (the athletics of the Hellenistic world still await similarly sustained treatment). For example, my own 2005 book discusses practices and literary representations of athletics in the Greek culture of the Roman Empire,[27] while Zahra Newby's *Victory and Virtue* offers a complementary analysis of similar questions but with a particular focus on visual evidence.[28]

That expansion of interest has been marked by increasing sophistication in the analysis of what is at stake in particular representations of athletic activity. In addition, traditional interest in questions of social status and in the events and institutions of ancient athletics have been supplemented by a more theoretically informed understanding of the links between athletics and identity, which help us to nuance simplistic generalisations about (for example) the role of athletic festivals and *gymnasion* education as vehicles for expressing and performing Greek affiliation. Here the field of Sports Studies, with its interest in sport and cultural identity or sport and the experience of the human body, has provided important stimuli, although there is still more work to do in addressing classical sport with these approaches in mind.[29] Jeremy MacClancy, amongst others, has written about modern sport very illuminatingly in these terms, offering us models for thinking about how sport both allows the expression and performance of selfhood and at the same time necessarily leaves identities and self-imaginings open to contestation. "Sports," he suggests, "are ways of fabricating in a potentially complex manner a space for oneself in their social world ... A sport is an embodied practice in which meanings are generated, and whose representation and interpretation are open to negotiation and contest."[30]

This volume aims to give a first taste of all of these many developments by reprinting some of the key articles published on athletic subjects over the last forty years. It aims to complement Thomas Scanlon's forthcoming volume of collected articles on ancient sport, which has a slightly wider focus, including a number of articles on gladiatorial contests, and also on the equestrian events which were often paired with athletic competition in Greek agonistic festivals.[31] Each of the six sections which follow addresses one key area of ancient athletic culture, and each is accompanied by an introductory essay, which offers a brief framing analysis, and further reading suggestions, to supplement the bibliographical starting-points offered in this introduction. Read together, the twelve essays reprinted here are intended to give a fairly comprehensive introduction to the field. Sections 1–3

---

[24] Morgan (1990).
[25] Nicholson (2005).
[26] Christesen (2007).
[27] König (2005).
[28] Newby (2005).
[29] Good starting-points include Hargreaves (1986), McPherson (1989), MacClancy (1996).
[30] MacClancy (1996) 4.
[31] Scanlon (forthcoming).

address in turn the early history of the Olympic festival, the development of *gymnasion* education in classical Athens and its spread in the Hellenistic period and after, and the development of the Greek festival calendar from the fifth century BCE right through to the Roman period. Section 4 then pauses to examine a little more closely the representation and idealisation of victory and competition, with further discussion of debates about ancient athletics and social status; section 5 follows on, looking at literary and artistic representations of athletic victory; section 6, finally, jumps forward by many centuries to look at the reception of ancient athletics in the nineteenth and twentieth centuries.

Each article has been chosen for its capacity to raise new questions in a vivid and accessible form. Some of these pieces are very much of their time, monuments to particular moments in the development of athletic scholarship and modern sporting history, as well as lasting and important contributions to our understanding of the ancient world (note especially Manfred Lämmer's engagement with post-war Olympic ideology up to the early 1980s in chapter 2, although many of his points undoubtedly still apply). Some, moreover, are undeniably dense and difficult in their details, through their engagement with the complex epigraphical record (especially in sections 3 and 4); some of them also overlap a little in the ground they cover – for example, in the way they repeatedly go over the question of how different types of festivals were categorised in the ancient world. However, it seemed to me important to present these more complex articles in their full difficulty, in order to give a taste of the painstaking and rigorous epigraphical work on which our understanding of ancient athletics is based. They also demonstrate vividly, despite the difficulty of that task, the unrivalled capacity of epigraphical evidence to bring to life particular snapshots of ancient athletic practice. An additional reason for selecting some of them has been their inaccessibility as originally published: much of the important athletic scholarship of recent decades has been published in journals which are relatively hard to access within the average university library. Above all, however, my hope is that all of the articles here will help to show how studying ancient athletics has to be, at its best, inextricably linked to the exploration of ancient culture more broadly.

TWO CASE STUDIES

Gaining a sense of the contours of recent scholarship on ancient sport is no substitute, however, for getting to grips with the original sources. The texts of ancient athletics, both literary and epigraphical, hold enormous fascination. They are often spectacular and passionate, inspirational in intent, and wonderfully vivid in their capacity to open up windows onto details of ancient life; they are also often odd and puzzling, for the reasons already stated above, because ancient athletics is often far removed from anything with which we are familiar, connected with other areas of life in ways we would not necessarily expect. They are also fascinating, I suggest, for their variety. Athletics was a much debated subject. Any writer on the subject has to navigate through many competing conceptions and valuations of ancient sport. Many ancient representations of athletics are marked by that process of dispute, attacking or defending themselves against alternative viewpoints. Some of the athletic scholarship of the twentieth century tended to be rather literal-minded about the interpretation of ancient athletic sources. More recently, however, the full richness of these sources has come to be more appreciated, not simply as repositories for evidence about specific kinds of athletic activity, but also as documents which shed light on the complex process by which ancient sporting ideals were created and sustained and debated, and on the different authorial agendas and priorities of their authors.[32]

Accordingly I want to conclude this introduction with a pair of case studies which between them should give at least a preliminary taste of this richness, and of the variety of ways in which ancient athletic activity could be represented. My first example is from Philostratus' *Imagines* 2.6,[33] a text composed in the first half of the third century CE. Philostratus was a multi-faceted author, a rhetorician and biographer. Several of his works take an interest in athletic subjects, most notably his work *On Training* (*Gymnasticus*), a manual for athletic trainers, which is not so much a detailed practical guide as a repository for athletic history and an idealising portrait of the athletic body and the general principles required for training.[34] His *Imagines* is a work on visual art, describing in succession a great range of different paintings, as if to an imaginary interlocutor in an art gallery, and drawing on ancient literary techniques of *ekphrasis*, the process of written description of art works. The attraction of *ekphrasis* for ancient authors lay in part in its capacity to bring works of art to life, to conjure them up before the mind's eye of their readers. Many of the chapters of the *Imagines* describe athletic subjects.

Imagines 2.6 is one of the most breathtaking of all these creations. It transports us to precisely the place I referred to above, to a seat among the banks of spectators lining the sides of the Olympic stadium, although in this case we are watching not the Olympic boxing, but instead the equally violent *pankration*, a kind of all-in wrestling event. The opening lines of the portrait – "Now you have come to the Olympic Games, and to the best of the contests at Olympia" – with its direct, second-person address, draws the reader immediately into the scene. One of the many things that makes ancient spectacle distinctive from our own versions of it is the idea that being a member of the audience can actively involve one in the spectacle or contest on display, either because one lives through the experience of the competitors, or because the audience is felt to be able to influence the action by their own involvement and their own reactions, or else simply because being present in the audience was a way of displaying one's own status or affiliation. All of those phenomena are no doubt familiar in some form to modern sports fans, but the active role of the audience in the ancient world was distinguished by being much more explicitly discussed and acknowledged. These active conceptions of audience resurface later in the Philostratus account too, combining neatly with his own ekphrastic aim of bringing the picture to life, making us feel as if we were there.

---

[32] See König (2005) for longer discussion along these lines.
[33] Full translation available in Miller (2004a) no. 45; the translations here are my own.
[34] For further discussion of Philostratus' writing on athletics, see König (2005) 301–44, (2007) and (2009).

The painting depicts the famous Olympic victory of the pankratiast Arrichion, who is said to have died at the moment of victory, strangled by his defeated opponent, but so fixated on winning the glory of victory that he is unwilling to give up his winning hold to save his own life. Philostratus brings the audience into the scene:

> He seems to have overpowered not only his opponent, but the Greeks in the audience as well. They are jumping up from their seats and shouting, some waving their hands, some leaping from the ground, and others slapping one another on the back. His astonishing feat has left the spectators beside themselves. Who is so stolid as not to shriek aloud at this athlete.

One of the other immediately striking things about Philostratus' description is its idealisation of violence, and its transformation of death into glory. That transformation paints Arrichion as a modern-day version of Homer's heroes, for whom death in battle is compensated for by becoming the subject of song. One function of the athletic victor statue in Greek culture was to perpetuate the glory of the victor.[35] Philostratus' *ekphrasis*, with its capacity to breathe life into the scenes it describes, performs much the same function. That is clear most of all from the final lines of the chapter:

> The one who is strangling Arrichion is painted to look like a corpse as he signals with his hand that he is giving up. But Arrichion is painted as are all victors. His blood is in full flower, and sweat still glistens, and he smiles like a living man who sees his victory.

We see Arrichion here not only being crowned by the Olympic officials at the moment of his death, but also being transformed and kept alive by Philostratus' artistry. That transformation parallels the act of statuesque commemoration which will follow his death and his victory. Moreover, Arrichion's glory is made all the more vivid by the anonymity of his unnamed, corpse-like opponent. That breathing-of-life into Arrichion at the moment of his death is all the more extraordinary if we consider the time gap between Philostratus' present-day world and the Olympic festival he describes, eight centuries before. The massive renaissance of Greek athletics under Roman rule, in the first to third centuries CE, was fuelled in part, in a society which valued links with the classical heritage, by the way in which athletic traditions could act as performances of continuity between past and present. Philostratus here celebrates the power of his own writing to maintain those links in particularly powerful form, keeping the past alive, although of course this scene has a certain exotic quality too, which reminds us that we are in a timeless, almost mythical fantasy moment far removed from the realities of day-to-day life. In that sense Philostratus, like so many other ancient writers, uses the imagery of athletic activity and athletic commemoration to reflect on and advertise his own very different type of cultural ambitions.

What exactly is Arrichion's achievement, however? It is striking that there is no specific mention of what emotions the audience are feeling: they seem to be experiencing intense excitement, and even pleasure, but it is not immediately clear why. One possibility is that the audience may be excited above all by the pleasure of

---

[35] Cf. Kurke's article, chapter 9.

watching violence. Certainly Philostratus goes out of his way to stress the brutality of the combat:

> The pankratiasts, my boy, practise a dangerous brand of wrestling ... They must be skilful in various ways of strangulation. They bend ankles and twist arms and throw punches and jump on their opponents ... Arrichion's opponent, having already a grip around his waist, thought to kill him, and put an arm around his neck and choked off his breath ... But Arrichion was not done yet, for as his opponent began to relax the pressure of his legs, Arrichion kicked away his own right foot and fell heavily on his left, holding his opponent at the groin, with his left knee still holding the opponent's foot firmly. So violent was the fall that the opponent's left ankle was wrenched from the socket.

This is not, however, simply a bloodthirsty satisfaction of voyeuristic appetites, for it is clear that Arrichion is also himself an object of admiration. Should we see Arrichion as a representative of athletic virtue? Philostratus stresses the cultural affiliation of the audience – this is an audience of Greeks. Is Arrichion's victory therefore to be seen as a display of archetypal Greek manliness? Certainly it is common for athletes to be presented as archetypes of virtue, and similar implications must be lying behind this representation. Philostratus, however, says nothing which would explicitly lead us to that conclusion. Even more important than Arrichion's virtue, perhaps, may be the uniqueness of his achievement. Philostratus tells us, for example, that "The present accomplishment surpasses the already great record of two previous victories at Olympia, for this one has lost him his life ..." It is a common theme of Greek literature and the Greek culture of commemoration that unique and astonishing events are worthy of being recorded for their own sake. Herodotus, for example, in the much-imitated preface to his *Histories*, writes that one of his aims is to record "great and amazing deeds'. Athletic victory inscriptions regularly proclaim the uniqueness of the particular combination of victories an athlete has won. Arrichion's victory here seems to be a supreme example of unique athletic achievement, which marks out the limits of human achievement. More shockingly still, Philostratus suggests that Arrichion's death may have been premeditated:

> This present accomplishment surpasses his already great record of two previous victories at Olympia, for this one has cost his life and he departs for the land of the blessed with the dust still on him. But do not think that this is accidental, for he has planned his victory very cleverly.

That claim is not explained here in detail, but the implication is that Arrichion may have engineered his death-in-victory as the thing most likely to win him notoriety, as a unique, and so more memorable, way of winning victory.

My second text, or rather group of texts, is Pliny, *Letters* 10.39, 10.40, 10.118 and 10.119.[36] Here we have a vastly different vision of the athletic world.[37] Pliny the Younger (his uncle, conventionally named Pliny the Elder in classical scholarship, wrote the great encyclopaedic work of the Roman Empire, the *Natural History*) was a distinguished senator, at the height of his career in the last decades

---

[36] Full translation available in Miller (2004a) no. 151; the translations here are my own.
[37] For further discussion of Pliny's representation of athletics in his *Letters*, see Woolf (2006).

of the first century CE and the first decade of the second. He was also one of the great letter writers of the ancient world. Ten books of his letters survive. The first nine books contain an assortment of letters to friends and colleagues and family. Book 10, by contrast, consists entirely of letters between Pliny and the emperor Trajan during Pliny's time as governor of the province of Bithynia-Pontus, almost certainly published posthumously. Most of these letters involve Pliny reporting on the progress of his governorship and asking for advice on specific problems, with brief replies from the emperor. A number of these texts deal with athletic subjects. The priorities of government and financial management which preoccupy Pliny and Trajan mean that their approach is very far removed from what we have seen for Philostratus, and indeed from most other Greek writing on the subject.

In 10.39, first of all, Pliny writes as follows:

> The citizens of Nikaia, sir, had their *gymnasion* burnt down before my arrival. They have begun to rebuild it on a larger scale than it was before, and have voted funds for the purpose which are in danger of being wasted. The structure is poorly planned and unorganised. Furthermore the present architect (who is admittedly a rival of the architect who began the work) says that the walls, even though they are twenty-two feet thick, cannot support the load placed on them, because they are rubble at the core and have no brick facing.

Here we see immediately the centrality of the *gymnasion* to civic life: repairing the *gymnasion* seems to be a matter of public concern for the Nikaians. To that extent the letter reinforces the impression we receive from inscriptions concerning *gymnasia*. However, Pliny's letter is also remarkable for giving a glimpse behind the celebratory façade of inscriptions recording *gymnasion* benefactions and other public building projects. It shows us signs of shoddy building work, as well as internal squabbling between those involved. By contrast, honorific inscriptions, set up in honour of the benefactors who have paid for public building projects, tend to emphasise (not surprisingly) the glory of the buildings and the unanimity of opinion within the cities they describe.

In addition, the letters offer us a vivid view of Roman involvement in and attitudes towards the games. Trajan's reply, 10.40, is short and dismissive: "Those little Greeks have a weakness for *gymnasia*. Perhaps, therefore, the citizens of Nikaia were overly ambitious in undertaking the construction of their *gymnasion*. But they will have to be content with one which is adequate for their city." Once again, this contradicts the impression of civic independence we find in honorific inscriptions. While those inscriptions do sometimes mention Rome, for example by offering lip-service to the honour which is due to the emperor, they tend to represent their own decisions about public building and festival programming as more or less autonomous ones, freely and unanimously taken. Here, by contrast, the deadening hand of Roman control is utterly dominant, all the more so for the brevity of Trajan's dismissal. One motive for Roman interference in civic policy on the *gymnasion* or on festival foundations was financial, and that seems to be a priority here: Pliny and Trajan are anxious about the consequences of overly liberal use of the city's funds. Those practical, financial considerations give the letter a very functional quality, utterly free of any interest in the athletic idealisation which looms so large for Philostratus. And Trajan's use of stereotypically Roman contempt for Greek athletics reinforces that impression, painting him once again as a pragmatic administrator, free of sentimental attachment to any glorification of Greek tradition. Even so, we may feel that Trajan is being a little disingenuous, and that in other contexts he, and certainly some of his predecessors and successors as emperor, would have been rather more likely to play along with the idealisation of festival culture and athletic education: Roman emperors were after all routinely honoured as part of agonistic festival foundations. Moreover, Trajan's comments also overemphasise the difference between Greek and Roman views of athletics: we know that *gymnasion* culture held considerable attraction for members of the Roman elite by this time. That dissociation of himself from the interests of his Greek-speaking subjects plays an ideologically charged role in Trajan's self-representation, which is carefully tailored for this particular context in order to portray him as a pragmatic and unsentimental ruler, and so very different from some of his more Hellenophilic predecessors. Trajan deliberately offers a stereotypically Roman response, ideally suited for a context where the emperor's responses need to be marked out as representatively and authoritatively Roman.

The second pair of letters, 10.118 and 10.119, covers similar ground, insisting on financial prudence, but in this case in relation to Greek festival culture. Trajan, it seems, has recently ruled that a specific pension should be granted to all victors in festivals with eiselastic status, i.e. top rank games, whose status was under the gift of the emperor, and which gave victors the right to be escorted home in triumph into their native cities. The athletes' petition asks for the pension to be payable from the moment of victory; Pliny suggests that it should be payable instead from the moment of the eiselastic ceremony. The athletes have also asked that victories at games recently granted eisalastic status by Trajan should be rewarded with a pension even where the victory took place before Trajan's ruling on the change of status. Pliny recommends rejecting this petition too; Trajan endorses all of Pliny's recommendations with characteristic brevity.

Once again, financial saving is clearly an important motive for Pliny and Trajan's reluctance. In that sense, these letters remind us of the vast expenditure given to maintaining the festival calendar of the Greek world. They also remind us of the enormous administrative complexity of it, in a world where athletic participation was increasingly globalised: presumably the petition made to Pliny here has come from one of the athletic guilds, powerful Mediterranean-wide bodies formed to protect the interests of athletes. Perhaps even more importantly for our perceptions of ancient Greek athletics, the letters remind us of the importance of financial rewards for victory. Financial rewards were not entirely hidden from view, but they tended to take quite a low profile in honorific texts, which give their main attention to athletic virtue and record-breaking prowess.[38] Here we see a rather different, more pragmatic picture of athletes fighting to maximise their financial rewards. In the process the letters touch on theoretical questions, of the kind which have interested modern scholars,[39] about where exactly athletic glory is to be located –

---

[38] See Pleket, chapter 7 of this volume.
[39] As we shall see in Kurke's article in chapter 9.

at the moment of victory? the moment of crowning? the moment when the athlete brings his victory home and dedicates it to his home city? However, Trajan's blunt, functional reply shuts out any possibility of debate on the issue, and deliberately avoids any engagement with ancient scholarly accounts of athletic history or athletic custom.

The letters of Pliny and Trajan thus offer us a picture which corrects or at least modifies the much more idealised vision we find in many literary or epigraphic representations of athletic victory and *gymnasion* education. It is not the case that either view – the idealistic or the pragmatic – is more accurate. Rather, what we are seeing is a sign of the great range of different and often competing perspectives on athletic activity. Any representation of athletic activity is necessarily a tendentious attempt to impose a particular viewpoint. And even these apparently very functional administrative letters turn out on closer inspection to have an ideological function, serving to reinforce the public self-presentation of Trajan as emperor and Pliny as prudent provincial governor. The passion and struggle and disagreement that ancient athletics inspired is clear even here, even in this at first sight entirely dispassionate text, just as much as it is for Philostratus' *Imagines*, which stands right at the other end of the spectrum in terms of its idealism. Clear, too, is the way in which talking about athletic activity is so often an exercise of self-representation and self-definition for ancient writers.

PART I

Olympia, the *Periodos* and Panhellenism

Introduction to Part I

The origins and early history of the Greek festival calendar have held an enduring fascination for modern scholarship, as indeed they did for the ancient Greeks and Romans. We share with them, too, the difficulty of accurately understanding these things: much of our information about the early history of the games is overlaid with mythical detail and with the ideological trappings of later periods. Ancient histories of the early games, most of them composed many centuries after the traditional date of foundation for the Olympics, 776 BCE, need to be examined with the agendas of their authors firmly in mind, rather than as transparent windows onto the past. The evidence of archaeology has been crucial in forcing us to rethink traditional assumptions, and to look beyond our reliance on these difficult texts.[1]

Despite those problems of interpretation, however, it may be worth stepping back for a moment to offer a few general observations about the development and content of the Olympic games and the other great festivals of Greece.[2] The commonly accepted Olympic foundation date of 776 BCE already mentioned may not in itself be precisely right, but it does seem to be the case that the eighth century BCE saw an intensification of activity at the site. The second important landmark period comes some 200 years later (in the 580s and 570s BCE) when festivals at Delphi (the Pythian Games), Isthmia (controlled by Corinth) and Nemea (controlled by the city of Kleonai, with the backing of Argos) were given the same "sacred" status as the Olympic festival. Between them these four festivals made up the *periodos* or "circuit", the most prestigious of all places to win victory (several other games joined these four in the *periodos* in the Roman period – see further discussion in the introduction to Part 3, below). The Delphic and Olympic festivals, first in prestige, were held every four years, Isthmia and Nemea every two.

It is undeniable, despite the caveats which follow below, that Olympia and the other games came to be viewed as gathering places for the assembled community of Greeks – they are often referred to in modern scholarship as "panhellenic",

---

[1] See (in addition to the work by Morgan discussed here) Mallwitz (1988) and Kyrielis (2003) for summary accounts of excavations and their conclusions over the last 150 years.

[2] There are many introductory accounts of the Olympics available: e.g., see Drees (1968), Finley and Pleket (1976), Swaddling (1980), Sinn (2000), Young (2004), Spivey (2004); valuable collections of essays are available in Coulson and Kyrielis (1992) and Raschke (1988); of the many internet resources on ancient Olympia by far the best, at the time of writing, are those at http://ancientolympics.arts.kuleuven.be/

that is, involving the whole of Greece – as well as venues for civic self-assertion and for competition between cities.[3] Attending the games must have been a major event in the life of any inhabitant of the ancient Mediterranean. The festival was vastly popular, so far as we can tell, despite the difficulties of the journey and the hardship of relatively primitive accommodation at the site.[4] These were not simply sporting occasions, but showcases for other kinds of cultural activity in addition: for example, we have many stories of renowned intellectuals giving speeches or readings of their work to the assembled Greek community at Olympia and Delphi.[5] Moreover, spectatorship and tourism at Olympia and at other festival sites tended to be overlaid with elements of pilgrimage, not just for the many ambassadors who attended the festivals as representatives of particular cities and participated in sacrifices, but also for ordinary spectators.[6] Religious observance loomed large in the games, in ways which would seem bewildering at first to a modern viewer.[7] The temple buildings, which housed dedications from cities across the Greek world, became increasingly spectacular as new buildings were added through the thousand years of Olympic history, none more so than the central temple of Zeus, with its massive statue of the god Zeus, sculpted by the famous artist Pheidias. Athletes swore sacred oaths to abide by the rules, and processions, culminating in sacrifices, threaded their way through the rich temples of the Olympic site, interspersed between the three days of competition.[8]

What of the sports themselves?[9] Spectators would see boxing, wrestling, *pankration*, running – the short (roughly 200m) *stadion*, the *diaulos*, twice that length, the longer *dolichos* race and the *hoplitês*, or race in armour – and the pentathlon (comprising the *stadion*, wrestling, long jump, javelin and discus), all of these in both boys' and mens' categories; also a range of equestrian events in the hippodrome on the edge of the site; and, most peculiarly from a modern perspective, contests in heraldry and trumpeting.[10] All of these events were under the supervision of the official referees, the *Hellanodikai*, literally "Greek judges", a name which points once again to the role of Olympia as an iconic centre of Greek culture. The Olympic programme developed gradually, with addition of different events at successive festivals, but the ancient evidence suggests that the bulk of the athletic events were in place by the late seventh century BCE. This template was roughly followed in other Greek agonistic festivals, although with many local variations. But Olympia was relatively unusual in not holding musical events: victory at the Pythian Games was the greatest goal for musical competitors, with contests in

---

[3] See Nielsen (2007) for the argument that one of the roles of the Olympic festival in antiquity was to allow the participation and self-advertisement of individual cities within a communal framework.

[4] See Crowther (2001)

[5] E.g., see Tell (2007).

[6] See Rutherford (2000).

[7] On the religious character of ancient sport, see Golden (1998) 10–23 and Pemberton (2000); cf. also (controversially) Sansone (1988).

[8] See Lämmer (1993).

[9] For good accounts of the ancient events, see Lee (2001), Spivey (2004) 86–117 and Miller (2004b) 31–86 (with extensive further bibliography on pp. 258–60); on the combat sports specifically, see Poliakoff (1987).

[10] On heraldry and trumpeting contests, see Crowther (1994a).

(amongst other things) instrument playing and singing, tragic acting, poetry and prose writing.

The details of how the festivals developed, especially in their earliest days, or what led to the decision to formalise these festivals both individually and as a circuit, are very hard to pin down.[11] The genre of Olympic history was a very popular one in the ancient world. Most often it took the form of lists of victors at the various Olympiads, which were used in part as resources for establishing and standardising dates: different cities tended to have their own local dating systems, and this overarching Hellenic dating framework made it easier to translate between them.[12] In some cases these accounts are overlaid with longer accounts of the mythical origins of the games. Many writers record traditions about an earlier version of the festival, of which the newly instituted games were a revival. According to some, Pelops was responsible for the foundation of those previous games; others ascribed them to Herakles. These stories may have some basis in truth, but it is also clear that they served particular contemporary agendas, justifying the dominance of particular cities over the games, or reinforcing ideals of peace and co-operation which may have been more relevant to the world of the fifth century BCE, or even to the second century CE, from when many of our late accounts date, with its habit of celebrating the harmony of a world united under the influence of Roman rule and Greek culture, than to the archaic Greek world of the eighth century BCE and before. In addition, the idea of a mythical origin for the games of course helped to paint present-day athletes as living manifestations of virtues which had their origin in the heroic past.

Both of the chapters in this section make important progress in questioning our assumptions about the early games. Catherine Morgan, first, uses archaeological evidence, in particular evidence for dedications by individuals and states, in order to trace the history of Olympia, Delphi, Isthmia and Nemea. It is important to stress that the outline reproduced here is part of a very wide-ranging book, and is backed in addition by Morgan's other publications on related subjects.[13] One of the implications of her work is that we should be wary of imagining that these sites had a uniformly panhellenic character throughout their history. Instead, she suggests, the evidence points to a very gradual development, coincident with the consolidation of *polis* (i.e. city) culture in the same period. Olympia, for example, seems to have been primarily a meeting place for west-Greek chiefs in the early eighth century and before, slowly expanding through the eighth and seventh centuries (with a particularly significant intensification of activity in the late eighth century) to attract participation from a wider geographical range, with city dedications eventually displacing the dedications of individuals. However, it seems to have been not until the sixth century, with the formation of the *periodos*, that we see the devel-

---

[11] For good summary discussion of the origins and mythologisation of the early games, see Lee (1988a and 1998); Golden (1998) 40–45; Spivey (2004) 206–37; Kyle (2007) 94–109; and see Lee (2001) on development of the Olympic programme.

[12] See Christesen (2007).

[13] See also (among others) Morgan (1993) for further discussion of Olympia and Delphi, and Morgan (1994) and (2002) on Isthmia; also on the archaeology of Isthmia see Gebhard (1993); and various chapters in Raschke (1988).

opment of the formalised city participation which was so central to the panhellenic character of the games throughout the later centuries of Greek history. Many of the idealising accounts of the mythical origins of the games date from this later period, aimed at bolstering the present-day importance of panhellenic festival traditions by the impression of antiquity.[14] Morgan's work illustrates powerfully the way in which archaeology can bring a new complexity to athletic history, taking us far beyond the story as it appears in our literary sources. She stresses, too, the importance of rigorous attention to the difference between different festival contexts, suggesting, for example, that the contours of development at Delphi during the same period are in many ways very different from those sketched for Olympia above.

Manfred Lämmer's article, secondly, challenges the idea of a worldwide peace during the period of the Olympic games, and shows that the concept of an Olympic truce was a much narrower one, directed only at the host territory, and those travelling to and from the games. That idea of worldwide peace has had a powerful influence over twentieth-century Olympic history. Lämmer's article thus offers not only an impressively rigorous and exhaustive reading of key sources on the ancient games, but also a striking illustration of the way in which misinterpretations of the ancient games continue to influence modern sporting practice and ideology.

---

[14] See esp. Morgan (1993).

1 Sanctuaries, the State and the Individual*

CATHERINE MORGAN

In the introductory chapter [Morgan (1990) 1–25] I discussed the way in which patterns of cult activity reflect the variety of forms of community organisation which emerged in different regions of Greece from the eighth century onwards. There is a clear distinction between the development of sanctuaries within state borders and those beyond the boundaries of the major participant states, sanctuaries which were later to develop inter-state functions. This latter group forms an especially valuable source of information about the changes in the balance between collective and individual interests which were characteristic of state formation. I shall return to such general issues in this concluding chapter; first, though, I should briefly summarise my conclusions on the development of Olympia and Delphi during the Iron Age.

OLYMPIA AND DELPHI

From the late tenth or early ninth century onwards, a rural cult shrine existed at Olympia and served as a meeting place for the petty chiefs of Messenia and Arkadia. The dedication of monumental bronze tripods attests to participation by members of local aristocracies, perhaps forming part of a cycle of conspicuous consumption involving the display of wealth (and possibly also athletic prowess) by which aristocrats may have maintained their personal status within their individual communities. Even at this early date, therefore, the location of the sanctuary at some distance from the major participant communities may be a reflection of Olympia's social and political role as a neutral meeting place. During the Early Iron Age, the dedication of bronze and terracotta figurines, many of which have clear agricultural connotations, suggests that some form of rustic celebration may have formed part of the festival. Furthermore, the presence of a large quantity of ash and burnt bone from an altar in the Altis area suggests that some form of sacrificial activity took place, perhaps with ritual meals. Otherwise, however, there is scant evidence for the nature of early activity, and although the idea of an early athletic contest may seem attractive, there is no evidence with which to test this hypothesis.

---

* Originally published in Catherine Morgan, *Athletes and Oracles: The Transformation of Olympia and Delphi in the Eighth Century* (Cambridge: Cambridge University Press 1990), pp. 191–4, 212–23.

During the eighth century, we can trace in two stages an increase in the range of sanctuary activities. From c. 800, changes in dedicatory practice reflect not only an intensification of existing patterns of activity by west Peloponnesian communities, but also the beginning of participation by the elites of other emerging states. Athletic events may have been instituted at this time also, if they did not already exist. Secondly, from c. 725, the resettlement of Elis, and consequently the beginning of participation by the inhabitants of these newly founded communities, marks the start of Olympia's local role, a role of lasting significance in the development of the sanctuary and the region alike. Elite individuals from an increasing number of emerging states began to participate in sanctuary activity, and western dominance was finally ended; at this time also the games expanded to include four events in addition to the original stade race. By the last quarter of the eighth century, therefore, there is clear evidence, especially in the pattern of tripod dedication, to show that competition between aristocrats within emerging states had begun to spill over state boundaries. The changes which took place during the last quarter of the eighth century set the pattern for the subsequent development of Olympia, and although during the Archaic period it is possible to trace the gradual harnessing of investment and competition at inter-state sanctuaries to the advantage of the participant states, the nature of cult activity changed little after c. 700.

The eighth century was thus a crucial phase in the transformation of Olympia from rural cult place, serving the petty chiefs of the western Peloponnese, to inter-state sanctuary under Elean control, and, by acting as a catalyst for the breakdown of western domination, Sparta played a particularly significant role in this process. The participation of Spartan craftsmen and visitors at Olympia was in itself an important factor in the maintenance and expansion of the sanctuary, especially during the earlier part of the eighth century; yet it is also possible that a desire to gain information about neighbouring regions in the west and central Peloponnese led to increased Spartan activity at the sanctuary which they shared. The subsequent Spartan conquest of Messenia marked the end of independent activity by one of the most important early participants at Olympia, and may also have been followed by a break in the visits of itinerant Spartan metal-workers. Yet the long-term prosperity of Olympia was ensured by the fact that changes in the political circumstances of the early participant regions of the western Peloponnese coincided with the appearance at the sanctuary of dedications made by the elites of emerging states further afield, and thus this potentially difficult transition from western to future Panhellenic sanctuary was bridged by Spartan activity.

Certain similarities in the development of sanctuary activity are evident at Olympia and Delphi, especially during the last quarter of the eighth century. Similar changes in the pattern of dedication of figurines and tripods are particularly striking, even though the identity of participant states varied according to the relative locations of the two sanctuaries. Yet one major difference was the presence of a village at Delphi which predated the establishment of the sanctuary, and which had its own independent connections and interests, not necessarily corresponding with those of the sanctuary and its participants. The Delphic sanctuary did not have a long history of cult activity to compare with that of Olympia, nor did it share any of Olympia's rustic traditions; instead, it was the creation of the emergent states of the eastern Greek mainland and Thessaly, and from its inception, therefore, cult activity reflected closely the interests of the elites of these early states. Furthermore, the establishment of the Delphic oracle marked the relatively early beginning of *state* participation at the sanctuary, and indeed, the process of state domination of activity appears to have advanced more quickly than at Olympia, and to have been achieved more comprehensively. To a great extent this was probably owing to the nature of the relationship between the sanctuary and the local population, since the ending of local intervention in sanctuary affairs by means of force, military or diplomatic, must have required concerted effort at a state level. Thus the First Sacred War (whatever its form) may be regarded as *terminus ante quem* for complete state control of Delphic sanctuary activity.

In the introductory chapter [Morgan (1990) 1–25], I commented on our general failure to consider the methodological question of how we interpret archaeological evidence found in sanctuary contexts, and since my approach to analysis of the archaeological record has, I hope, become clear in the course of the previous chapters, I have little to add to those remarks. I would, however, emphasise that almost all of the arguments which I have presented in this book rest upon consideration of material evidence, and although literary sources provide invaluable information about the system of values which governed dedicatory behaviour, ancient authors rarely discuss the trends and processes with which I have been concerned. The autonomy of the material record is here clearly illustrated: not only can material evidence provide answers to questions which were not considered by ancient authors, but it can also provide invaluable assistance in untangling the mass of myth and legend which surrounds the early history of many Greek sanctuaries

[...]

THE FORMATION OF THE FESTIVAL CIRCUIT

By the eighth century at the latest, an athletic contest was held at Olympia, and it is possible that a similar, informal competition may have existed at Delphi also. Examination of eighth- and seventh-century evidence from Athens has highlighted the relationship between activity at inter-state sanctuaries and private, aristocratic celebrations such as funeral games, which may have been held whenever appropriate occasions arose. From early in the fifth century, however, Delphi, Olympia, Isthmia and Nemea came to form the heart of an institutionalised festival circuit on the Greek mainland (known as the *periodos*), which also included many local events of which little or no archaeological trace survives. Pindar, writing in the mid-fifth century, named some thirty other contests and implied that many more existed.[1] I have so far concentrated discussion upon the main theme of this book, namely the change in the nature of activity at Olympia and Delphi during the eighth century, and how this established the pattern for the subsequent development of both sanctuaries through the early Archaic period. However, since the formation

[1] Pleket (1975).

of the *periodos* marked a turning point in the histories of participant sanctuaries, and is also directly related to the questions of the chronology, nature and purpose of the institutionalisation of activity at inter-state sanctuaries which I raised in the introductory chapter [Morgan (1990) 1–25], it is worth pausing to consider it in more detail.

Of the four sanctuaries central to the *periodos*, the senior pair, Delphi and Olympia, attracted participation from more than one region of Greece from the time of their foundation, whereas the junior pair, Nemea and Isthmia, were both the creations of single states, and were relatively late to acquire inter-state functions. Indeed, the Isthmian and Nemean festivals were, from their inception, timed to avoid Olympic and Pythian years, and their foundation therefore reflects the idea of a festival cycle.

From early Protogeometric times, a cult place had existed at Isthmia, some 1400 m. from the Saronic Gulf, just outside the Mycenaean trans-Isthmus fortification wall. Here, too, the Iron Age sanctuary was located beside a Mycenaean site, but there is no evidence for continuity of activity from the Bronze Age, let alone continuity of function. From the mid-eleventh century into the Archaic period, ritual activity, feasting and drinking, was practised continuously, and it seems likely that an ash altar, similar to that at Olympia, was established during the Iron Age and continued in use into the sixth century. Yet there is nothing to suggest that this cult place was of more than local significance during the Iron Age, and Isthmia undoubtedly remained in Corinthian control from the time of its foundation.[2]

Despite an increase in the level of cult activity during the eighth century, the sanctuary at Isthmia remained poor by comparison with the two main centres of Corinthian investment, at Delphi and Perachora. Few metal dedications of any kind are earlier than c. 700 and, apart from a late eighth-century terrace wall at the edge of the sacrificial area, there is no evidence of building before the construction of the first temple in the latter half of the seventh century.[3] Indeed, the selection of Isthmia as the location of a second Corinthian monumental temple may have been due not only to its accessibility, since it was located beside the main route from Corinth to Athens and the north, but also to its lack of association with any

---

[2] Gebhard (1987). Cf. Broneer (1973) 6–7. The following summary is based upon my study of the Mycenaean and Iron Age remains from the sanctuary, the publication of which is in preparation [now published as *Isthmia VIII: The Mycenaean Settlement and Early Iron Age Sanctuary*, Princeton, 1999]. I thank the excavation director, Prof. E. R. Gebhard, for long discussion of the early history of the site. Examples of local prehistoric material: Smith (1955). The Bronze Age pottery sequence extends into LHIIIC (i.e. Late Helladic IIIC), but then ceases until the earliest Protogeometric, c. 1050, and there is nothing to parallel the Submycenaean styles known from Corinth, cf. Rutter (1979).

[3] I thank Prof. I. Raubitschek and Dr A. Jackson for permission to study unpublished metal finds, and for access to the manuscripts of their forthcoming volumes in the "Isthmia" series. [The first of those is now published as Raubitschek, I. (1998) *Isthmia VII, The Metal Objects (1952–1989)* Princeton. Relevant also are two chapters in *Isthmia VIII*, chapter 1.3 (by I. Raubitschek) on "The metal objects' and chapter 1.4 (by A. Jackson) on "Three possible early dedications of arms and armor at Isthmia". See also Jackson, A. (1992) "Arms and armour in the panhellenic sanctuary of Poseidon at Isthmia", in Coulson, W. and Kyrielis, H. (eds) *Proceedings of an International Symposium on the Olympic Games, 5–9 September 1988*, Athens: 141–4]. Only about a dozen items are closely datable to the period pre-700 (although much apparently early material is too fragmentary to date precisely); of these, the majority are 8thC, and are paralleled at Corinth. Terrace wall: Gebhard (1987) 475.

particular aspect of Corinthian domestic or foreign development (as, for example, the prosperity of Perachora reflected activity in the west). It was thus an ideal location for a symbol of the overall achievements of the Corinthian state. The first temple at Isthmia was a major Corinthian investment and a strikingly early example of the Doric order. Its construction was a purely Corinthian political statement, and most probably an early Kypselid answer to the Bacchiad temple on Temple Hill at Corinth, since traits such as its slightly larger size, painted decoration on the cella walls, and possibly also a colonnade, make it a rather more elaborate construction than its predecessor.[4]

There is no evidence of early settlement at Isthmia, and the temple stood in splendid isolation, at least during the early years of its life until the traditional date of the foundation of the Isthmian Games, c. 582/580.[5] Whether 582/580 refers to the foundation of the games, or, as Solinus (7.14 [*On the Wonders of the World*]) indicates, their re-establishment after a lapse during tyrannical rule, has long been a matter of debate. It does, however, coincide approximately with the appearance at the sanctuary of athletic equipment (strigils, weights, etc.), and it is hard to see where races could have been run before the construction of the first stadium during the sixth century, since the topography of the sanctuary area must have been highly irregular at this time.[6] Furthermore, since the demise of the Kypselid tyranny occurred early in the sixth century, it is possible that the games were instituted to celebrate the new order at Corinth, just as the construction of the temple may have marked Kypselos's rise. Until then, Isthmia remained an isolated, if architecturally splendid, sanctuary near the borders of Corinthian territory, which closely reflected the formation of the Corinthian state. Even after the establishment of the festival, Isthmia, of all inter-state sanctuaries, seems to have been most completely dominated by its controlling state; indeed, Pindar frequently referred to it as synonymous, or intimately associated, with Corinth (e.g. *Nem.* 4.88; *Ol.* 9.86, 13.4–5). It is striking that no major monuments, such as treasuries, erected by other participant states have yet been discovered, even though one should take into account limitations of excavation.

Early evidence from Nemea is much less plentiful, and there is nothing to suggest that cult activity began before the seventh century at the earliest. A very

---

[4] Broneer (1971) 3–56; Broneer (*ibid.* 55) dates the temple to the first half of the seventh century, and the last stages of Bacchiad rule. I prefer a rather later date, not before 650, on the grounds of the dating of an associated perirrhanterion (ibid. plate 7). Pliny the Elder (*Natural History* 35.5.15–16) notes that the art of wallpainting was a Corinthian development.

[5] Broneer (1974). The first burials occur west of the sanctuary, near the fork of the modern road to Hexamilia. The beginning of activity here is dated by fragments of an Attic komast cup by the KY Painter (c. 580–70), and some 119 graves span the 6th and 5thC, extending slightly into the 4thC.

[6] E.g. Broneer (1973) 3–4 expresses the contrary view that the institution of the games coincided with the construction of the Archaic temple. Athletic equipmnt: e.g. inscribed jumping weight dating c. 580–75, Broneer (1959) 322–3, plate 73a. Stadium: Broneer (1973) 46–7; Gebhard (1987) 476. Despite Broneer's statement that the area of the sanctuary must have been almost level in antiquity (ibid. 1), reappraisal of the stratigraphy of the eastern part of the *temenos* and electromagnetic conductivity survey, conducted by Prof. F. Hemans in 1987–8, have revealed that the area around the edge of the rock plateau upon which the temple stands was cut by stream beds and gullies, and the area of the stadium must therefore have required considerable levelling. I thank Prof. Hemans and the excavation director, Prof. Gebhard, for information about the 1987–8 survey.

small quantity of eighth-century material from the sanctuary area most probably represents settlement, and there is scant evidence of Iron Age activity in any part of the Nemea valley.[7] While the first temple of Zeus at Nemea is certainly earlier than the traditional date of the foundation of the Nemean Games, c. 573, its exact date remains a matter of debate. A date around 600 seems most likely, and would accord well with the chronology of temple construction at Olympia and Delphi, and indeed, the site excavators do not believe that the temple could be significantly earlier. Of the four major inter-state sanctuaries on the Greek mainland, the architectural development of the sanctuary at Nemea was therefore most closely related to the foundation of its festival.[8] Although the surviving stadium dates to the fourth century, earlier material evidence for athletics comes from a large votive deposit in the sanctuary area, and includes items such as an inscribed discus of the third quarter of the sixth century, a bronze strigil and a lead jumping weight.[9] The sanctuary and festival were originally under the control of Kleonai, but were formally transferred to Argos before the violent destruction of the sanctuary at the end of the fifth century. By this time, Kleonai must have been at least overshadowed by Argos, and the limited Iron Age material evidence available from the Nemea valley is either of Argive manufacture or shows strong Argive influence.[10] So although Nemea had no long history of local cult activity to match that at Isthmia, it was similarly controlled by a single powerful state, even if relations between Argos and Nemea were at least nominally looser than those between Corinth and Isthmia during the Archaic period.

Further parallels in mythology and sanctuary organisation indicate a mutual self-awareness on the part of Isthmia and Nemea, which may relate to rivalry between the neighbouring states of Corinth and Argos. Both festivals were biennial, for example, and primarily athletic from their inception. At both sites, young heroes were worshipped at shrines very similar in form (open rocky areas within *temenos* walls), and in both cases, funeral games for these dead heroes formed the mythical origins of later athletic contests. The first shrine of Opheltes at Nemea dates to the sixth century, and that of Melikertes-Palaimon at Isthmia was established in the middle of that century.[11] The legends surrounding the two children also appear very similar in their received versions. Opheltes, son of Lykourgos and Eurydice, was placed by his nurse Hypsipyle in a bed of wild celery, where he was killed by a serpent; the Seven against Thebes, who were travelling through Nemea on their way to Boiotia, found the dead child, renamed him Archemoros, and celebrated the original Nemean Games at his funeral, to propitiate the gods. Melikertes-Palaimon, the son of Ino, daughter of Kadmos of Thebes, and Athamas, king of Orchomenos,

---

[7] *AR* 33 (1986–7) 17 notes a cemetery disturbed by ploughing, with Protogeometric and Early Geometric burials, in the area of the Phlious acropolis. I thank the directors of the Nemea Valley Archaeological Project for discussion of material from survey of this area. Sanctuary: Stephen Miller (1979) 82; (1982) plate 9e, g, h.

[8] Blegen (1927); Stephen Miller (1980) 183–7; (1981) 51–5. Stella Miller (1983) 71–5; Rhodes (1987). Stella Miller (1988) for summary account of the development of the sanctuary.

[9] Stella Miller (1983) 78–80. Stadium: Stephen Miller (1976) 193–202; (1978) 84–8; (1979) 93–103; (1980) 198–203; (1981) 65–7; Romano (1977).

[10] Kelly (1976) 124–8. *RE* XVI 2322–7. Cf. Miller (1988) 144 n. 25 for bibliography.

[11] Nemea: Stephen Miller (1981) 60–5. Stella Miller (1984) 173–4. Isthmia: Gebhard (1987) 476.

was drowned when his father went mad and pursued his wife to the shore of the Saronic Gulf, where she plunged into the sea with her child in her arms. Ino was transformed into the nymph Leukothea, and Melikertes was borne by a dolphin to the Isthmus of Corinth, where he was discovered and buried by Sisyphos, king of Corinth (or by Theseus in an alternative Athenian version). The funeral games celebrated in his honour formed the first Isthmian festival, and thenceforth, he was worshipped as a hero at Isthmia.[12]

On a more general level, similar political considerations may have played a significant role in the establishment of the *periodos* also. It is interesting to note that athletic contests were founded at around the same time at the two sites most closely connected with Corinth, Isthmia and Delphi, in emulation of Olympia. These were then copied at Nemea, a political creation like Isthmia, which was at least indirectly controlled by Argos, a rival polis to Corinth and probably therefore eager to copy Corinthian achievements. The relative chronology of these four festivals is clear, even though precise details are available only from late sources: Eusebius (Eusebius, *Chronicle* 101d), for example, notes the establishment of the Isthmian and Pythian Games in a single synchronistic entry dated to the third or fourth year of the forty-ninth Olympiad (i.e. 583–581), although Euphorion puts Isthmia slightly earlier than Nemea.[13] I would therefore emphasise the importance of the role played by Corinth, as a major investor in sanctuary activity at Delphi, as the creator and controller of Isthmia, and as a prominent and powerful state, inviting emulation of its achievements by its rivals.

In considering the question of the pace and nature of changes in the balance between state and individual interests evident at the future inter-state sanctuaries, I have stressed the value of monumental architecture and formalised festivals as indices of institutionalisation. Yet there are certain kinds of votive, which, whilst not strictly "state" dedications, do particularly reflect the role of the individual as citizen. Armour dedications are especially important, since, as I have indicated, the creation of a monopoly of force must be one of the first acts of any emergent state. At both Olympia and Delphi, the appearance, late in the eighth century, of arms and armour in any quantity coincides with their transfer from the personal context of the grave to the public one of the sanctuary within the borders of individual participant states.[14] Thus there was no significant chronological discrepancy in the dedication of arms and armour at sanctuaries inside and outside state borders, and both reflect equally the preoccupations of the elites of emergent states. At least on the Greek mainland, however, armour dedications occurred in quantity only at those inter-state sanctuaries which were already in existence by the end of the eighth century, namely Delphi, Olympia and Dodona. Nemea received comparatively few dedications of arms and armour of any period, and such finds as have been made have tended to be associated with occasional violent disturbances rather

---

[12] Opheltes-Archemoros: Pausanias 2.15.2–3. Melikertes-Palaimon: Pindar (Snell (1964) frag. 6.5(1)); Aeschylus, *Athamas*. Euripides, *Iphigeneia in Aulis* 625–6. Pausanias 1.44.7–8. Ovid, *Fasti* 6.493–503, *Metamorphoses* 4.511–42, *Heroides* 18.159–60.

[13] Powell (1925) frag. 84.

[14] Snodgrass (1964) *passim*; (1980) 53–4 on transfer from graves to sanctuaries.

than with regular dedicatory practice. The role of Isthmia as a Corinthian sanctuary is rather more complex, but here also, despite a small quantity of seventh- and sixth-century material, finds are few before the fifth century. Although material evidence is insufficient to allow firm conclusions to be drawn, the presence of votives such as ship models reinforces Isthmia's role as a primarily maritime sanctuary, and it therefore seems possible that different aspects of Corinthian activity were celebrated at her two most prestigious sanctuaries, with armour dedications concentrated upon Temple Hill.[15] Furthermore, Poseidon played an important role in the Greek world as patron of federal gatherings, as shown by his patronage of the seventh-century Kalaurian Amphictyony, and also of the Ionian League, which met at his sanctuary on Mount Mykale. It is thus possible that Isthmia's role in the *periodos* was developed around these two features, the patronage of Poseidon over an inter-state gathering, and the maritime interests which were of great importance to many participant states. During the late eighth century, however, when the elites of a number of emerging states were beginning to participate at Olympia and Delphi, Isthmia was just a Corinthian rural cult place, and therefore hardly an appropriate recipient of elaborate, politically significant dedications.

In considering the more general issue of the role of inter-state festivals in aristocratic culture, it is interesting to assess the continuity of values from the earlier Iron Age into the sixth century. As I remarked in the introductory chapter [Morgan (1990) 1–25] the institution of *xenia* (loosely translatable as ritualised personal relations or, more specifically and perhaps less accurately, guest friendship) not only survived alongside citizenship, the rules of which were formulated early in the life of most emerging states, but thrived and was exploited from time to time for purposes of state. When the Epidaurians were seeking to obtain materials and services for the construction of their temple of Apollo during the fourth century, they encouraged individual citizens to exploit their personal ties of *xenia*, and in establishing *proxeniai*, or diplomatic connections, states often employed individuals who had *xenoi* in the host community.[16] *Xenia* was an ancient institution, as Gabriel Herman has shown, much older than the city states who superimposed their values upon it, but did not dissolve it.[17] Although the city state officially disapproved of *xenia*, the resulting conflict of values required some accommodation, especially as *xenia* was primarily an elite institution, and the state had, as far as possible, to find an appropriate role for it. The various ways in which this was achieved have been explored fully by Gabriel Herman, but I would emphasise that the conduct of activity at inter-state sanctuaries, and especially the practice of athletics, reflects many of the ideals of *xenia* expressed in a fashion acceptable to the state. The

---

[15] I thank Dr Alastar Jackson for information about early arms and armour from Isthmia, and for access to the manuscript of his forthcoming volume on the subject in the "Isthmia" series. In Dr Jackson's opinion, IM 2616, a bronze spearhead dating to the late 8th/early 7thC, and IM 2450, a fragment of Kegelhelm dating c. 700, are amongst the earliest dedications. A tiny quantity of 7thC material is closely paralleled at Olympia and Delphi, and also at Corinth itself, although it is impossible to identify the place of their manufacture. Ship models: I thank Prof. D. G. Mitton for discussion of these finds and for information from his unpublished Ph.D. dissertation. In his opinion, the sequence of terracotta ships begins early in the 7thC. Arms and armour at Corinth: Snodgrass (1964) *passim*.

[16] Epidauros: Burford (1969) 21–4, 35–9. *Proxenia*: Herman (1987) 130–42.

[17] Herman (1987) 1–9.

exchange of material goods was an essential part of the establishment and maintenance of ritualised personal relations, and as we have seen, in the course of the seventh century the tripod, an early symbol of *xenia*, was either adopted for state purposes (as at Delphi) or, in the case of Olympia, abandoned.[18]

The formalisation of the *periodos* thus served to accommodate the interests both of the elite and of the state, and as the process of state formation advanced, the establishment and renewal of *xenia* relations must have become increasingly dependent upon meetings at neutral sites such as inter-state sanctuaries. Pindar praises *xenoi* alongside the achievements of individuals as citizens (e.g. *Pyth.*, 3.70-1, 9.82, 10.64-72), and chariot racing, instituted at Olympia early in the sixth century, was always regarded as an elite preserve [Morgan (1990) 90-1], to the point of being satirised as an extravagance contrary to the values of the good citizen (Aristophanes, *Clouds*). Isokrates included in the speech delivered by Alcibiades in his own defence against charges of treason (Isokrates, *On the Team of Horses*, 31-3) the claim that his Olympic chariot victory of 416 redounded to the credit of Athens, and that he was therefore worthy of praise for spending so much time and money to the glory of the city. This was undoubtedly special pleading which must have strained credulity, and in general, such expenditure would have been regarded, at least officially, with disapproval or even distrust by state authorities.[19]

Nonetheless the extent to which the comparative values of *xenia* and citizenship were emphasised at different inter-state sanctuaries varied greatly. Olympia remained perhaps the most open to the personal interests of the elite, and certainly, it was never encumbered with state concerns of the kind embodied in enquiries presented to the Delphic oracle; indeed, the institutionalisation of the *periodos* appears to have had very little impact upon the conduct of sanctuary activity. Yet Olympia was in many ways exceptional, and its significance as a model for later festivals should not be underestimated. The pattern of investment in temple building at the four sanctuaries is equally informative. The actual materials used at Isthmia, Nemea and Olympia are unremarkable, and in fact the temple of Zeus at Olympia was built in a most unprepossessing local shelly limestone. However, as I noted in the introductory chapter [Morgan (1990) 1-25], the difference in the level of investment evident in state and sanctuary projects was particularly marked at Delphi, which retained no strong local function after the early sixth century. When the temple of Apollo was rebuilt after the fire of 548, the Alkmaeonidai, a leading Athenian family, not only accepted the contract for the project, but improved upon the original plan by providing marble for the façade, a gift for which they were praised by Pindar (*Pyth.* 7).[20] Since the Alkmaeonidai were in exile from Athens at that time, the gift may have been an attempt to demonstrate their status and right to power, and to gain favour amongst participant states, and it was thus a political statement closer in nature to state building projects than to the more personal elite dedications evident at contemporary Olympia.

---

[18] Delphi: Amandry (1987). Cf. Delos: Amandry and Ducat (1973). Olympia: Herrmann (1966); (1979). Herman (1987) ch. 4

[19] Kyle (1987) 136-7. Herman (1987) 116-18. Seager (1967).

[20] Coulton (1977) 22, 57, 162 n. 43 for bibliography. Herodotos 5.62.2.

Clearly, there was considerable variation in the nature of activity at the four great inter-state sanctuaries at the heart of the *periodos*, and a detailed knowledge of their origins and early development is essential in order to appreciate how and why this should have been so. It is also the case that the formalisation of a festival circuit, in which each sanctuary had its own particular role, influenced the way in which sanctuaries were presented in myth and legend. The odes of Pindar are particularly valuable sources of evidence for the way in which mythology was used to emphasise connections or similarities between sanctuaries, and to reinforce the unity of the *periodos*, since, of all our extant sources, he was most concerned with the mythology and histories of the participant sanctuaries and states. Although each sanctuary retained its own individual repertoire of local legends (Pindar, *Ol*. 1, for example, described the role of Pelops at Olympia), especially from the sixth century onwards, it is possible to trace a number of parallels between sanctuaries. I have already commented upon similarities in the mythology and ritual organisation surrounding hero cults at Isthmia and Nemea, but I suggest that Herakles also played a significant, and more general, role at inter-state sanctuaries. Pindar refers to Herakles' slaying of the Nemean lion (*Isth*. 6.35–49) and his foundation of the Olympic games (e.g. *Ol*. 10.24–59; *Ol*. 2.1–4). A month in the Delphic calendar was named after him, in celebration of his unsuccessful struggle with Apollo for control of the Delphic tripod. What may be the earliest depiction of this struggle, on a tripod leg from Olympia, dates from the late eighth century (although this identification is by no means secure), but, as John Boardman and Herbert Parke have shown, the story only achieved wide circulation at around the time of the First Sacred War and the institution of the Pythian festival.[21]

The figure of Herakles is therefore common to all four sanctuaries, and had the additional advantage of playing an important role in the mythology of many participant states. Thus depiction of an episode from Herakles's life could be seen as a compliment to the sanctuary in question, as well as emphasising the identity of the donor state. The depiction of the struggle for the Delphic tripod on the east pediment of the Siphnian treasury (c. 525), along with the inclusion of a figure often identified as Herakles in a gigantomachy on its north frieze, is a well-known example, and one which had a considerable impact upon the presentation of these subjects in other media (including vase painting).[22] A more complicated case resulted from the Athenian attempt, early in the fifth century, to stress the importance of the city's "founding father", Theseus, and to present him as a latter-day Herakles: from the last quarter of the sixth century, there was a marked increase in the number

---

[21] Galinsky (1972) ch. 2. Adshead (1986) ch. 3, esp. 51–2. Defradas (1954) pt 2, ch. 1, on Herakles at Delphi. Tripod: Kunze (1950) plate 8.1, OM B1730. Parke and Boardman (1957); Boardman (1978b); Williams (1983).

[22] Ridgeway (1965). Cf. Watrous (1982) for bibliography. Brinkmann (1985) for alternative identification of figures depicted on the north and east friezes on the basis of inscriptional evidence: Brinkmann identifies the "Herakles" figures as Hermes and Dionysos. Vase painting: von Bothmer (1977). Herakles also appears among the statues of the kings of Argos on the Argive semi-circular monument: Bourguet (1929) 54–6. Cf. Carpenter (1986) ch. 4, esp. 68–73. The labours of Herakles form the subject of the frieze on the temple of Zeus at Olympia, in this case emphasising that Herakles, son of Zeus was also grandson of the local hero and founding father of the games, Pelops: Ashmole and Yalouris (1967) 22–9.

of depictions of Theseus in Athenian vase painting, and perhaps the high point of Theseus's popularity was reached when, in c. 475, Kimon removed what was claimed to be his bones from Skyros (Plutarch, *Theseus* 36.1–2; *Kimon* 8.3–6). This association is made explicit with the depiction of the deeds of both Herakles and Theseus on the frieze of the Treasury of the Athenians at Delphi (c. 490 or slightly earlier). Furthermore, a third theme on this frieze, an Amazonomachy, may refer to the battle at the Amazons' city of Themiskyra when Theseus accompanied Herakles on his quest for the girdle of Hippolyta.[23] The sculptural programme of the treasury was part of a general trend in Athenian propaganda, but it also accorded with the popularity of Herakles at Delphi. Isthmia also played an important role in the mythology surrounding Theseus, and here too, we find a clear reference to the exploits of Herakles. In an early version of the story of Sinis the pinebender, who lived beside the road to Athens close to the Isthmus, Sinis challenged his victims to test their strength by bending a pine tree to the ground, and killed those who failed at this task until he finally met his match in Theseus. This story is very similar to the version of the Olympic myth in which Oinomaos slew the losers in a chariot race until he in turn was slain by Herakles, and thus the parallels between Theseus and Herakles, and Isthmia and Olympia are strong.[24] Clearly, therefore, connections between the four main sanctuaries of the *periodos* were reinforced by parallel elements of mythology, many of which were created, or elaborated, at the time of the formation of the circuit early in the sixth century.

Yet such emphasis upon the unity of the *periodos* was complemented by stress upon the identity of individual sanctuaries within the framework of the circuit, often by means of mutual rivalry. It is, for example, not unusual for foundation legends to refer to the re-establishment of festivals after earlier competitions had lapsed, in an attempt to stress, or to fake, their antiquity. Olympia and Delphi are two such cases where, even though mutual self-awareness seems to have had early origins (with the development of the myth of the Delphic succession which put the origins of the sanctuary and the oracle far back in the primeval past, even before the arrival of the Olympian gods), it was certainly exacerbated by the formalisation of their relationship within the *periodos*. The creation of fake responses sanctioning the establishment of the Olympic games may also be seen as an attempt to assert Delphi's seniority and authority (although the exact date of their creation remains uncertain since they are mentioned only in late sources). Such rivalry was not, of course, confined to the four main inter-state sanctuaries; in the previous chapter [Morgan (1990) 148–90] I noted an apparent alliance between the oracles of Zeus at Dodona and Zeus Ammon at Siwa against that of Apollo at Delphi, and I suggested that competition between the oracles at Delphi and Dodona may have been partly responsible for the elaboration of the mythology surrounding the Delphic succession.[25] Examples of this kind are numerous, and since different aspects of sanctuary

---

[23] Boardman (1978a) 156–60, fig. 213; (1982) 3–15.

[24] Broneer (1973) 1. Plutarch (*Theseus* 3.1) refers to Theseus's descent from Pelops in the female line, and also to his emulation of Herakles in founding the Isthmian Games (25.4-5).

[25] Sourvinou-Inwood (1987) on the formation of the Delphic succession. Delphic responses sanctioning Olympia games: Fontenrose (1978) 268–70 for sources. Parks (1967) on inter-sanctuary rivalry.

activity led to different patterns of interaction, consideration of a sanctuary's role in the *periodos* alone must inevitably present an incomplete picture. Nevertheless, the establishment of an institutionalised festival circuit created a much firmer, formal framework within which sanctuaries might interact, and thus encouraged the development of increasingly close, but more sharply defined, relations between them.

The establishment of a formal festival circuit may therefore be seen as a watershed in the development of the four major interstate sanctuaries on the Greek mainland, formalising the relationship between state and individual activity at each site, and ending the period of fluctuation which had originated during the eighth century, as the nature of activity came to reflect the process of state formation in participant regions. During the seventh century, activity at Olympia and Delphi (and also at Isthmia) had continued to follow the pattern established by the end of the eighth. From the very end of the seventh century, however, with the construction of monumental temples at all four of the major sanctuaries, and the beginnings of treasury building especially at Olympia and Delphi, the great age of state activity began.

[...]

WORKS CITED

Adshead, K. (1986), *Politics of the Archaic Peloponnese. The Transition from Archaic to Classical Politics*, Aldershot.
Amandry, P. (1987), "Trépieds de Delphes et du Péloponnèse", *BCH* 111: 79–131.
Amandry, P. and Ducat, J. (1973) "Trépieds Déliens", in *BCH* Supp. 1, *Études Déliens*: 17–64.
Ashmole, B. and Yalouris, N. (1967) *Olympia. The Sculpture of the Temple of Zeus*, London.
Blegen, C. (1927) "Excavations at Nemea, 1926", *AJA* 31: 421–40.
Boardman, J. (1978a) *Greek Sculpture. The Archaic Period*, London.
  (1978b) "Herakles, Delphi and Kleisthenes of Sikyon", *RA*: 227–34.
  (1982) "Herakles, Theseus and Amazons", in Kurtz, D. C. and Sparkes, B. A. (eds), *The Eye of Greece. Studies in the Art of Athens*: 1–28, Cambridge.
Bourguet, E. (1929) *Fouilles de Delphes, vol. 3(1): Epigraphie. Inscriptions de l'entrée du Sanctuaire au Trésor des Athéniens*, Paris.
Brinkmann, V. (1985) "Die aufgemalten Namensbeischriften an Nord- und Ostfries des Siphnier-schatzhauses", *BCH* 109: 77–130.
Broneer, O. (1959) "Excavations at Isthmia, fourth campaign 1957–1958", *Hesperia* 28: 298–343.
  (1971) *Isthmia, vol. 1: Temple of Poseidon*, Princeton.
  (1973) *Isthmia, vol. 2: Topography and Architecture*, Princeton.
  (1974) "From the West Cemetery at Isthmia", *Hesperia* 43: 401–11.
Burford, A. (1969) *The Greek Temple Builders at Epidauros*, London.
Carpenter, T. (1986) *Dionysian Imagery in Archaic Greek Art. Its Development in Black-Figure Vase Painting*, Oxford.
Coulton, J. J. (1977) *Greek Architects at Work*, London.
Defradas, J. (1954) *Les Thèmes de la propagande delphique*, Paris.
Fontenrose, J. (1978) *The Delphic Oracle*, Berkeley.
Galinsky, G. K. (1972) *The Herakles Theme*, Oxford.

Gebhard, E. R. (1987) "The early sanctuary of Poseidon at Isthmia", *AJA* 91: 475–6.
Herman, G. (1987) *Ritualised Friendship and the Greek City*, Cambridge.
Herrmann, H. V. (1966) *Olympische Forschungen*, vol. 6: *Die Kessel der Orientalisierenden Zeit*, pt 1, Berlin.
  (1979) *Olympische Forschungen*, vol. 11: *Die Kessel der Orientalisierenden Zeit*, pt 2, Berlin.
Kelly, T. (1976) *A History of Argos to 500 BC*, Minneapolis.
Kunze, E. (1950) *Olympische Forschungen*, vol. 2: *Archaische Schildbänder*, Berlin.
Kyle, D. G. (1987) *Athletics in Ancient Athens*, Leiden.
Miller, Stella G. (1983) "Excavations at Nemea, 1982", *Hesperia* 52: 70–95.
  (1984) "Excavations at Nemea, 1983", *Hesperia* 53: 171–92.
  (1988) "Excavations at the panhellenic site of Nemea", in Raschke, W. J. (1988) *The Archaeology of the Olympics. The Olympics and Other Festivals in Antiquity*, Madison: 141–5.
Miller, Stephen G. (1976) "Excavations at Nemea, 1975", *Hesperia* 45: 174–202.
  (1978) "Excavations at Nemea, 1977", *Hesperia* 47: 58–88.
  (1979) "Excavations at Nemea, 1978", *Hesperia* 48: 73–103.
  (1980) "Excavations at Nemea, 1979", *Hesperia* 49: 178–205.
  (1981) "Excavations at Nemea, 1980", *Hesperia* 50: 45–67.
  (1982) "Excavations at Nemea, 1981", *Hesperia* 51: 19–40.
Parke, H. W. (1967) *Greek Oracles*, London.
Parke, H. W. and Boardman, J. (1957) "The struggle for the tripod and the first Sacred War", *JHS* 77: 276–82.
Pleket, H. W. (1975) "Games, prizes, athletes and ideology", *Stadion* 1: 49–89.
Powell, J. U. (1925) *Collectanea Alexandrina*, Oxford.
Rhodes, R. F. (1987) "Early Corinthian architecture and the origins of the Doric order", *AJA* 91: 477–80.
Ridgway, B. S. (1965) "The east pediment of the Siphnian treasure. A reinterpretation", *AJA* 69: 1–5.
Romano, D. G. (1977) "An early stadium at Nemea", *Hesperia* 46: 27–31.
Rutter, J. B. (1979) "The last Mycenaeans at Corinth", *Hesperia* 48: 348–92.
Seager, R. (1967) "Alcibiades and the charge of aiming at tyranny", *Historia* 16: 6–18.
Smith, E. (1955) "Prehistoric pottery from the Isthmia", *Hesperia* 24: 142–6.
Snell, B. (ed.) (1964) *Pindari Carmina cum fragmentis*, vol. 2, 3rd edn, Leipzig.
Snodgrass, A. M. (1964) *Early Greek Armour and Weapons from the End of the Bronze Age to 600 B.C.*, Edinburgh.
  (1980) *Archaic Greece. The Age of Experiment*, London.
Sourvinou-Inwood, C. (1987) "Myth as history: the previous owners of the Delphic oracle", in Bremmer, J. (ed.), *Interpretations of Greek Mythology*: 215–41, London.
Von Bothmer, D. (1977) "The struggle for the tripod", in Höckman, U. and Krug, A. (eds), *Festschrift für Frank Brommer*: 51–63, Mainz.
Watrous, L. V. (1982) "The sculptural program of the Siphnian treasurey at Delphi", *AJA* 86: 156–72.
Williams, D. J. R. (1983) "Herakles, Peisistratos and the Alcmaeonids" in Lissarrague, F. and Thelamon, F. (eds), *Image et céramique grecque*: 131–40, Rouen.

2 The So-Called Olympic Peace in Ancient Greece[*]

MANFRED LÄMMER
(translated by Julietta Steinhauer)

The modern Olympic movement, founded ninety years ago by the Frenchman Baron Pierre de Coubertin, has always claimed to make a special contribution towards understanding between nations and world peace.[1] However, it has not to date been possible for the movement to claim any historically tangible success in this respect, nor has it been able to explain by what concrete means it plans to achieve these things. Even the Olympic Charter contains only some short and general phrases[2] that have for some time now been viewed as insufficient. And yet, a critical engagement with the Olympic Charter has begun only very recently, after the events at the 1980 Olympic Games in Moscow and at the 11th Olympic congress held in 1981 in Baden-Baden.[3]

During recent decades, the relevant representatives of the IOC and of international sport have always supported the peace-bringing intention of the Olympic Games by referring to ancient Olympia, claiming that the ancient festival at Olympia too had served the pursuit of peace. Furthermore, they have argued that the compulsory truce observed throughout the whole Greek world during the period of the Games should be seen as a symbolic expression of the idea of an Olympic peace. This claim has surfaced repeatedly in treatises on the ancient festival, particularly

---

[*] Originally published in *Stadion* 8–9 (1982–3), pp. 47–83.

[1] A representative selection can be found in H. Lenk, *Werte, Ziele, Wirklichkeit der modernen Olympischen Spiele*, 2nd ed., Schorndorf 1972, pp. 119–77. A comprehensive investigation of this topic has not yet been published (but cf. the preliminary survey by A. Höfer, *Der Friedensgedanke in der Geschichte der modernen Olympischen Bewegung*, Diplomarbeit, Deutsche Sporthochschule Köln, Köln 1984). However, in recent years some research concerning the general relationship between sports and peace-politics in its historical dimension has been conducted, especially in German academic circles, e.g. see S. Güldenpfennig/H. Meyer (eds), *Sportler für den Frieden. Argumente und Dokumente für eine sportliche Bewußtseinsbildung. Mit einem Vorwort von Willi Daume*, Köln 1983 [=Sport – Arbeit – Gesellschaft, Vol. 22]; H. Becker, "Berichte über Friedensinitiativen im Sport", in *Sportunterricht* 33 (1984), pp. 65–7; Evangelische Akademie Bad Boll (eds), *Olympische Spiele in Los Angeles – ein Beitrag des Sports in internationalen Friedensarbeit? Tagung vom 28.-30. März 1984 in der Evangelischen Akademie Bad Boll*, Bad Boll 1984 [=Protokolldienst 19/84].

[2] Cf. Comité International Olympique, *Olympic Charter 1984*, Lausanne 1984, Rule 1, p. 6: "The aims of the Olympic movement are: [...] to educate young people through sport in a spirit of better understanding between each other and of friendship, thereby helping to build a better and more peaceful world [...]".

[3] Cf. Comité International Olympique (eds), *11th Olympic Congress Baden-Baden 1981*, 3 vols, Lausanne 1982. The IOC has appointed a special committee to update the Olympic Charter, in particular its principles. The new version will be adopted at the 90th IOC-Session in October 1986 in Lausanne.

within the field of sport studies. It has led to impassioned speeches by sporting officials and euphoric visions in the feature-sections of newspapers. Tiresome reproduction of a long list of relevant quotations can be dispensed with in this article.[4] One of the most impressive examples was uttered by P. de Coubertin himself in his famous speech on "the philosophical foundations of modern Olympism" broadcast before the Games of 1936, held in Berlin. The speech clearly refers to conditions in Greek antiquity and Coubertin, convinced of the fact that war will always be part of politics, states: "I myself would welcome it if enemies, in warfare, would interrupt their conflict and instead fight with the power of their muscles in a loyal and chivalrous way."[5] The French baron and many other leading theoreticians of Olympism clearly stood in the tradition of neohumanistic educational ideals. This included the unlimited enthusiasm for Greece that was widespread within certain circles of nineteenth-century bourgeoisie and only subsequently entered the field of sport – for particular reasons that cannot be elaborated upon here in detail – much later, with a lasting effect that exceeded its impact in any other area. The ideas and principles of action practised by the ancient Hellenes in many areas of life, particularly the arts and education, were both obligatory and unattainable models for Coubertin's contemporaries. We should not judge this enthusiasm for Greece from our own "enlightened" point of view and belittle it as a cultural or historical oddity. Many renowned scholars in other relevant areas such as Archaeology, Ancient History, Philology and Art History agreed with the ideologues of Olympism and painted the same romanticised image of Greece over a long period of time.[6] This enthusiasm also aroused a great deal of energy, and contributed to the fulfilment of ideas which influenced education and the development of sport in our century in a crucial way, and with lasting effect.[7]

Since the beginning of the seventies a more critical and sophisticated approach towards athletics and the Olympic Games in ancient times has emerged within academic circles. Accordingly, a new succession of general surveys and individual studies has been published, characterised by a closer engagement with primary sources, as well as by inclusion of new evidence and a stronger emphasis on socio-historical aspects. These publications have shown convincingly that enthusiastic leaders and ideologues in the sporting world often distorted antiquity in inappropriate ways by projecting the images and role-models of the modern onto the

---

[4] A representative selection is provided by Lenk [see n. 1], pp. 109–19.

[5] P. de Coubertin, *Der Olympische Gedanke. Reden und Aufsätze*, ed. by the Carl-Diem-Institut of the German Academy of Sports Köln, Lausanne/Stuttgart 1966, p. 153. See in the same speech (p. 154): "celebrating the Olympic Games means referring to history. It (history) is the thing best suited to secure peace."

[6] Cf. e.g. the Loeb-edition of Plutarch, *Lykourgos* 1, 1 p. 205, n. 1: "A stay of hostilities was observed all over Greece during the festival"; H.-V. Herrmann, *Olympia. Heiligtum und Wettkampfstätte*, Stuttgart 1972, p. 12: "Before, during and after the Games there was a cease-fire all over Greece, the "Ekecheiria". During the period of this Olympic truce, no war was allowed to begin and all battles within Greece were put on hold"; R. Patrucco, *Lo sport nella Grecia Antica*, Florence 1972, pp. 7–8: "the sacred truce, which was marked by a complete willingness for peace among all the cities of the Greek world". In 1981, P. SIEWERT defended this view again. See also the discussion below in n. 66.

[7] Cf. e.g. E. Grüner, *Das hellenistische Bildungsideal in der Geschichte der deutschen Leibeserziehung*, Diss., Leipzig 1941; J. Gerstenberg, *Die Wiedergewinnung Olympias als Stätte und Idee, Ein Beitrag zur Geistesgeschichte*, Baden-Baden 1949 [Diss. Tübingen 1947].

ancient world in order to authorise their own claims and to support the theory of an ageless "Olympic idea" with certain constant values. These revisions of received opinion deal with key issues like the ideal of the amateur, women in sports, the importance of victory, violence and fairness, the origin of Greek athletics and the reasons for its decline – in other words they deal with questions about the meaning of the Games.[8] This paper will pursue a similar goal. Its aim is systematically to collect and analyse the available sources concerning the so-called "Olympic peace" in order to describe its character and function. Furthermore, the evidence will be analysed with reference to the idea, widespread in the world of sports and until recent years widely accepted, that the modern interpretation of the "Olympic peace" corresponds to the reality of the ancient world.[9]

Of central importance as a starting-point for the subsequent line of my argument is the fact that the Greeks themselves never used the word peace (*eirênê*) to describe the regulation under discussion, but instead made use of the word *ekecheiria*, literally translated as "a state in which the hands are held back".[10] Although Thucydides uses this term in the sense of a (usually short) truce,[11] it more often signifies an officially proclaimed and formally agreed *inviolability* of people, territories and objects on the occasion of religious festivals and their associated contests.[12] The word *immunity*, which is Latin in origin, is probably closest to the meaning of *ekecheiria*. As there is no distinct definition of *ekecheiria* handed down to us,[13] we must try to gain a clear image by scrutinising the evidence, which lies far away in time and space.[14]

---

[8] This new dimension is particularly reflected in: M. I. Finley/H. W. Pleket, *Die Olympischen Spiele der Antike*, Tübingen 1976 [originally published in English as *The Olympic Games. The First Thousand Years*, London 1976]; J. Ebert, *Olympia. Von den Anfängen bis Coubertin*, Leipzig 1980. Concerning this problem see also: M. Lämmer, "The future of the Olympic Games does not lie in its past", in: *11. Olympischer Kongreß Baden-Baden 1981*, Bulletin 6, pp. 12–15, 42–8.

[9] The first detailed analysis with broad use of sources is: L. Weniger, "Das Hochfest des Zeus in Olympia. III. Der Gottesfriede", in *Klio* 5 (1905), pp. 184–218. In addition L. Ziehen, "Olympia", in *RE* XVIII (1939), cols 3–6; H. Popp, *Die Einwirkung von Vorzeichen, Opfern und Festen auf die Kriegsführung der Griechen im 5. und 4. Jahrhundert v. Chr.*, Diss. Erlangen 1957, pp. 125–44; L. Drees, *Olympia. Götter, Künstler und Athleten*, Stuttgart 1967, pp. 39–41; G. Rougement, "La hiéromenie des Pythia et les trêves sacrées d'Eleusis, de Delphes et d'Olympie", in *BCH* 97 (1973), pp. 75–106. See also L. Robert in *REG* 86 (1973), pp. 65–6, no. 71; R. Muth, "Olympia – Idee und Wirklichkeit" in *Serta Philologica Aenipontana III*, ed. R. Muth and G. Pfohl, Innsbruck 1979, pp. 168–74 [= *Innsbrucker Beiträge zur Kulturwissenschaft vol. 20*]; Ebert, *Olympia* [see n. 8], pp. 14–18.

[10] Cf. H. Frisk, *Griechisches Etymologisches Wörterbuch*, Vol. I, Heidelberg 1960, p. 476. Questions concerning the origin and meaning of the word cannot be discussed here in any depth.

[11] Thucydides IV, 58, 1; 117, 3; 118, 11; 118, 12; 118, 13; 119, 3; V, 15, 2. See H. Bengtson, *Die Staatsverträge des Altertums vol. 2: Die Verträge der griechisch-römischen Welt von 700 bis 338 v. Chr.*, München/Basel 1962, numbers 179, 185, 196.

[12] The term can also mean a break from activity in the courtroom: see L. Robert, "Décrets d'Ilion", in *Études Anatoliennes. Recherches sur les inscriptions grecques de l'Asie mineur*, Paris 1937 [reprint Amsterdam 1970], pp. 172–79 ; cf. n. 53. The meaning of *ekecheiria* remains unclear in Himerios, *Oratio* 14, 6: see L. Robert, "Épigramme d'Égine" in *Hellenica. Recueil d'épigraphie, de numismatique et d'antiquités grecques*, vol. IV: Épigrammes du Bas-Empire, Paris 1948, p. 25.

[13] Gellius I, 25, 8–9 is unclear: "Moreover the Greeks, more significantly and pointedly, have called that agreed cessation from fighting an *ekecheiria* ... For since there is no fighting at that time and their hands are held back, they call it an *ekecheiria*.'

[14] It should be stressed that the aim here is not to follow every nuance of the term's meaning in the legal life of antiquity or to trace back the controversial traditions of the word's origin in its most complex intricacies. Both problems are of only limited importance for the question of a proper characterisation of the Games in classical times.

Within the ancient tradition it is unanimously agreed that the word *ekecheiria* is as old as the Games themselves, even though different accounts give different versions of the chronology of the early Olympics, and a reconstruction of their true origins seems almost impossible due to the contradictory character of the different mythical stories.[15] According to the "official" version that was spread by the Eleans, Iphitos of Elis, Kleosthenes of Pisa and Lykourgos of Sparta got together at some point in the 8th century BC and decided to celebrate a festival with contests every four years within the sanctuary of Zeus at Olympia.[16] Accordingly, a declaration was said to have been written on a bronze discus that was stored afterwards in the rear of the temple of Hera. Both Aristotle (384–322 BC) and the travel writer Pausanias who visited Olympia in AD 174 are supposed to have seen the original artefact.[17] However, the shape of the letters and the "old-fashioned" way in which they are arranged on the discus cannot hide the fact that the discus is more likely to have been a later forgery crafted in order to legitimate the Elean claim of being in charge of the sanctuary and the Games. For exactly the same reason, the Eleans argued that the three kings were led to the act of foundation through instruction by the Delphic oracle.[18] The agreement contained three main provisions:

1. The area of the sanctuary of Zeus at Olympia was declared *holy* (Greek: *hieros*) and therefore sacrosanct.[19] Like other Greek cultic centres within sacral communities, it now received a recognised status of inviolability (Greek: *asylia*). The unusual part of the agreement was the fact that the inviolability was extended throughout the *whole state* of Elis, to which Olympia belonged.[20] The impact of that regulation amounted to political and military neutralisation of the area, and its inhabitants were thus seen as "holy people" of Zeus. The Delphic oracle is said to have ordered the Eleans to stay out of internal Greek quarrels and exclusively to look after the sanctuary and Games.[21] This is obviously a subsequent construction drawn up to strengthen Elean authority and to legitimise their right to host the Games, a privilege they were able to secure only in 570 BC, after continuous battles against the Pisatans. This privilege presupposes panhellenic acceptance of the Games, which is out of the question for the time of the foundation of the Games. Nevertheless, this legend reflects the role attributed to the Eleans by the Greek city-states during the classical period.

According to Strabo, the armies of Greek city-states had the right to march through Elis but they had to hand in their weapons to the relevant authorities at the borders and would receive them again when leaving the country.[22] This provision was presumably significant almost exclusively for Sparta: on the whole,

---

[15] A discussion of chronological problems cannot be provided here.
[16] Phlegon of Tralles, *FGrHist* 257, 1.
[17] Plutarch, *Lykourgos* 1, 1; Pausanias V, 20, 1.
[18] See Phlegon, *FGrHist* 257, 1. The authenticity of the discus was already doubted by Ziehen [see n. 9], col. 4. The same judgement was made by H. Bengtson, *Die Olympischen Spiele in der Antike*, 3rd edition, Zürich/München 1983, p. 13.
[19] Strabo VIII, 358.
[20] Phlegon, *FGrHist* 257, 1. See E. Caillemer, "Asylia", in Ch. Daremberg/E. Saglio, *Dictionnaire des Antiquités Grecques et Romaines*, Vol. 1, Paris 1877, [Reprint Graz 1969], p. 505.
[21] Phlegon, *FGrHist* 257, 1: πολέμου δ' ἀπέχεσθε.
[22] Strabo VIII, 358.

the neutralisation of Elis was in the interest of the Spartans, as they were now relatively protected against surprise attacks from the north. Not only the alleged participation of Lykourgos at the realisation of the agreement but also the large number of Spartan Olympic winners in the seventh century BC show clearly the dominant influence of the leading Peloponnesian power in the archaic period.[23]

The historian Polybius describes the special development of Elis, protected by panhellenic guarantees: its inhabitants neither considered it necessary to fortify their city nor did they have an army actually ready for action. They were seen as "unwarlike" and neither participated in internal Greek quarrels nor made any effort in matters of colonisation. Even in threatening situations they would not join panhellenic ventures, or if so then only half-heartedly.[24]

Because of their wealth in people, farmland and livestock, their rural settlements and their security from looting, they are thought to have had a high standard of living and relatively few tensions in their social structure.[25] The claim that they were not averse to drinking and had an unrestrained lifestyle is a product of cliched fantasies. However, in their experience of surviving the perpetual Greek struggles without any harm and sometimes even with gains,[26] the Eleans, in their "Phaeacian existence", can be compared to some of the European neutrals during the great wars of our century.

Apart from the quarrels mentioned above between Elis and Pisa and the battle against Dyme[27] – which is more likely to have been legendary – the sanctity of Olympia was generally respected. In any case, only one violation is known between the reorganisation of the Games which, according to the ancient tradition, took place in 776 BC, and the end of the fifth century: Pheidon of Argos conquered the sanctuary of Olympia in the seventh century probably during an expedition against the Spartans, and organised the Olympic Games together with the Pisatans. He was, however, forced to leave under pressure from the Spartans and Eleans shortly afterwards.[28] The latter are said to have regarded the Olympiad as invalid (Greek: *anolumpias*), the first time that had happened.[29] The enlargement of the status of inviolability from the sanctuary to the whole state-territory might have been a consequence of a Spartan guarantee that was made after these events. According to Strabo, this intervention of Pheidon demonstrated that the *ekecheiria* was ineffective if a leading power refused to adhere to it.[30] After this bitter experience, the Eleans decided to build up their own army for security purposes. This did not, however, change their exceptional position within the Greek world: the first

---

23 See also L. Moretti, *Olympionikai. I vincitori negli antichi agoni olympici*, Rome 1957. A. Hönle, *Olympia in der Politik der griechischen Staatenwelt von 776 bis zum Ende des 5. Jahrhunderts*, Bebenhausen 1972 [Diss., Tübingen 1968], pp. 128 ff.

24 Polybius IV, 73–4.

25 However, the rivalry between the Eleans and the Pisatans might be rooted not only in ethnic but also in social reasons.

26 Drees [see n. 9], p. 41.

27 Philostratus, *Gymnastikos* 7.

28 Strabo VIII, 358; Herodotus VI, 127; Pausanias VI, 22,2.

29 Pausanias VI, 22, 2. Hönle [see n. 23] doubts this as the lists of victors do not include any annotation.

30 Strabo VIII, 358.

and main component of the Olympic *ekecheiria* was and remained the commonly accepted sanctity of the sanctuary of Zeus and the neutrality of the state of Elis.

2. In order to guarantee the continuous celebration of the Games and the participation of all Greeks who wished, the three kings named above, whose agreement obviously reflects the real convention of the late archaic period, offered special protection during and after the time of the Games: athletes and their coaches, members of festival delegations and even spectators could travel to, stay at and return from Olympia without fear for their lives or possessions, even if they had to cross the territory of states with which their homelands were at war. It is nowhere explained how this guarantee was actually put into practice. "It is likely that the athletes of the particular cities, including escorts and "fans", travelled in closed groups whose travel-purposes were easily identifiable".[31] This *temporary protection of festival participants* was the much-cited "peace of the gods", often evoked but at the same time often misunderstood. It took effect whenever the so-called *theôroi* and *spondophoroi* – heralds who were specially sent by the Eleans to the cities and cultic centres of Greece – declared it and confirmed it with a common sacrifice.[32] In theory, any Greek city could have refused to adhere to the *ekecheiria*, particularly in times of war, but it seems as if that almost never happened, due to the high esteem of the Olympic Games.[33]

A recent study by Stephen Miller has shed new light on the much-discussed question of the dating of the Olympic festival.[34] The starting-point of his calculation was midsummer's day, which in antiquity was located in the last ten days of June. The athletes had to arrive at Elis before the first full moon after that, and had to start their preparations under the supervision of the *hellanodikai*. The second full moon marked the date of the actual Games. Miller's indices of the years 500 BC–AD 97 show that the Games were held, consequently, at the end of July or the beginning of August. The *ekecheiria* of earlier times, when only Peloponnesian tribes participated at the Games, might have been shorter than the *ekecheiria* in the fifth century BC when people from all over Greece participated and the athletes had to be in Olympia for the compulsory probation period as much as four weeks before the official start of the Games. The only precise information concerning the duration of this period of divine protection is given by Lucian who mentions a period of four months.[35] This statement has not been given much attention for it is found

---

[31] Muth [see n. 9], p. 171.

[32] This is clearly demonstrated by Thucydides V, 49. See also [E.] Szanto, Ἐκεχειρία in *RE* X, 2 (1905), cols 2162–3. The heralds in the literary sources are called *spondophoroi* (Pindar, *Isthm.* 2, 23) or *theôroi* (*I. Olympia* 39): see Weniger [see n. 9], pp. 214–18; Ziehen [see n. 9], cols 3–4; P. Boesch, *Theoros. Zur Epangelie griechischer Feste*, Diss., Berlin 1908; L. Ziehen, "*Theoroi*", in *RE* V A, 2 (1934), cols 2239–44.

[33] In times of political tension or military conflict the acceptance of the *ekecheiria* of an important festival could certainly be refused. According to Aischines, *De falsa legatione* 2, 133–4 the Phocian tyrants were the only Greeks to deny the acceptance of the "divine protection" to the *spondophoroi* from Athens who proclaimed the beginning of the Eleusinian mysteries. The acceptance remained an voluntary act, so Harris, p. 15 is wrong in saying: "[...] the herald proclaiming the Games used to demand safe conduct through all territories for those attending the festival either as competitors or spectators, and invoked the anger of the god in whose honour the festival was held *on any who refused* it" [my emphasis – ML].

[34] Stephen G. Miller, "The date of Olympic Festivals", in *MDAI(A)* 90 (1975), pp. 215–31.

[35] Lucian, *Ikaromenippos* 33. Zeus has to delay the execution of a philosopher due to the Olympic

not in a historical context but in a fictional, satirical dialogue. However, the author's competence concerning agonistic questions allows no doubt regarding the accuracy of his statement for the fourth century BC.[36] Contemporary literature dealing with the topic suggests that most modern authors are of the opinion that the *ekecheiria* lasted for three months during the classical epoch.[37] They all refer to L. Weniger, who in 1905 analysed the surviving fragments of lists of Elean cult-officials from the Roman period.[38]

Although separate groups of Elean heralds departed at the same time for the different regions of the Greek world, the official ceremony of accepting the *ekecheiria* did not take place at the same time in the different cities on account of varying distances and itineraries. This, and another episode[39] that will be discussed below, led Rougement to the conclusion that the obligation to adhere to the *ekecheiria* took legal effect at different times in different cities.[40] Under these circumstances, misunderstandings and conflicts occurring at the outset of the period cannot be ruled out. The end of the period of *ekecheiria*, however, must have been determinable in terms of precise dates in order to prevent legal insecurity.[41] Each city that had once sworn to uphold the *ekecheiria* was in effect admitted to the Olympic festival-community. After the city's agreement had been given once, it was probably subsequently taken for granted, since we cannot assume that the Eleans announced the dates of the *ekecheiria* itself every four years again in all states of the Greek world. They probably restricted the announcement to the most important cities and cultic centres.[42]

---

ekecheiria: "It is not right for anyone to be punished, since it is now the "sacred period" (*hieroménia*), as you know, for four months, and I have already proclaimed the *ekecheiria*".

[36] Lucian not only visited Olympia five times and witnessed the death of Peregrinus the philosopher there in AD 165 but he also had precise knowledge in the fields of gymnastics and athletics. The action of the *Ikaromenippos* is deliberately set in the fourth century BC, in which Menippos of Gadara lived. As he has put these words into Zeus' mouth I virtually rule out a mistake.

[37] J. Ebert, *Griechische Epigramme auf Sieger an gymnischen und hippischen Agonen*, Berlin [East] 1972, p. 153, even seems to consider a two-month period based upon Thucydides V, 47, 10.

[38] See n. 9.

[39] Thucydides V, 49–50.

[40] Rougement [see n. 9], p. 94.

[41] The solution to this problem is made even harder by the fact that in relation to the Olympic Games as well as other important festivals the word *hieroménia* is used as well as *ekecheiria*. According to Rougement [see n. 9], p. 81, it is crucial to keep the two terms completely separate: the *hieroménia* signifies the whole period of celebrations and sacrifices, which were separated off from everyday life, and during which most public activities of the city in which the festival was held were suspended. Hence, during this time no decisions were made in the Council, no trials were conducted in court, legal enforcements and executions were postponed etc. The *ekecheiria* on the other hand meant the special protection offered to those coming from outside; its length could differ from that of *hieroménia*. Nevertheless, Rougement's hypothesis includes discrepancies and contradictions. When checking the appropriate pieces of evidence one gets the impression that these two terms were used differently in different places, sometimes with the same meaning as each other and sometimes with different meanings. In addition, their meaning may have changed over the course of time: thus Aeschines, *De falsa legatione* 12, clearly uses *spondai* ("treaty") in the sense of *ekecheiria*, whereas Libanios, *Hypothesis* 2 to Demosthenes XIX (ed. W. Dindorf, 4th edn, revised by F. Blass, Leipzig 1908) p. 335, speaks of *hieroménia* in the sense of *ekecheiria*.

[42] Cf. *I. Magnesia* 50, l. 36: The people's assembly of Paros recognises the newly founded *agôn* of the *Leukophryeneia* in Magnesia and confirms also in the name of other communities of the Aegean islands that the *asylia* and *ekecheiria* will be respected "for all time" (εἰς τὸν ἅπαντα χρόνον). Therefore a four-yearly repetition of the announcement becomes unnecessary. This may have been due in part to practical difficulties of travel and to economic reasons.

3. The third provision of the agreement was also of great importance: all partners of the contract gave assurance to one another that they would oppose by all means necessary anyone who ignored the inviolability of the sanctuary or the participants in the Games.[43] In practice this amounted to a Spartan guarantee in the early years. In later times all the other Greek states that came to participate in the festival were obliged to show solidarity in their opposition to those breaking the law.

The *ekecheiria* – an indispensable precondition for continuous and undisturbed holding of the Olympic Games – was, however, no arbitrary human institution, but divine law. Because it was decreed by the Delphic oracle, Apollon Thesmios was its guarantor.[44] The Greeks, however, portrayed the *Ekecheiria* as a personification closely connected with Zeus, in a way similar to the personification *Agôn* ("Contest"). In 460 BC Mikythos, the treasurer of the tyrant Anaxilas of Rhegion, donated a group of statues made by Glaukos of Argos. These were placed to the right of the temple of Zeus at Olympia and showed the personified *Ekecheiria* crowning king Iphitos.[45] These facts indicate that anybody breaking the rules would certainly have to fear the revenge of Zeus. But it was not only the threatening power of the two gods mentioned above that acted as a deterrent: "at least as powerful a guarantee of the truce was the universal interest in the Games, coupled with the economic, military and political insignificance of Elis as a state".[46]

The historical origin of the *ekecheiria* may lie in a convention of the early Greek nobility according to which breaks during long-lasting battles were arranged in order to collect and bury the corpses.[47] Related rituals, for example funeral Games, were probably covered by the same guarantee, "not to lay hands on". In later times, in the event of the death of a relative, the often feuding noble families arranged an *ekecheiria* even in relatively peaceful times in order to guarantee a secure journey for relatives and friends to and from the burial and the accompanying Games. This custom was expanded so as to apply to periodically repeated celebrations in memory of dead heroic ancestors. After all, the four main panhellenic Games had their roots in funerary cults.[48] The founders of the Olympic *ekecheiria* were probably members of the extensive noble family of the "Heraklids", who despite internal quarrels always remained conscious of their communal spirit and also possessed the capability to enforce these rules.

In opposition to the widely held view, especially prevalent in the sporting world, that the *ekecheiria* constituted a complete and binding truce for the whole of the Greek world, one can point to three substantial facts:

---

[43] Strabo VIII, 358.
[44] According to Plutarch, *Lykourgos* 23, the Spartan king's action was commanded by a "divine voice".
[45] Pausanias V, 10, 10; 26, 2–3; Herodotus VII, 170; Diodorus IX, 48, 66. Cf. Weniger [see n. 9], p. 185.
[46] Finley/Pleket [see n. 8], p. 161.
[47] Cf. Homer, *Iliad* VII, 375–7; XXIV, 657–70 (and cf. the mistrust of the Trojans: XXIV, 777–81). As late as after the battle at Leuctra in 371 BC the Spartans and Boeotians came to an arrangement of this sort: Diodorus XV, 56, 4. There was a similar agreement between the Spartans and Thebans in 394 BC at Koroneia: Plutarch, *Agesilaos* 19, 3.
[48] Cf. Drees [see n. 9], p. 32. The Pelopion in the centre of the Altis was seen as the grave of Pelops in whose honour the Games were held. Cf. also the oath of the suitors in connection with the boxing fight of the beggar Iros and Odysseus, which reads like a parody of the *ekecheiria*: Homer, *Odyssey* XVIII, 55–8.

1. The *ekecheiria* of the Olympic Games was not, as is frequently assumed, a unique institution, although it was certainly the first of its kind to be recognised by all Greeks.[49] Many other festivals provided similar protection for athletes and spectators as well. The Pythian *ekecheiria* of the Games at Delphi, for instance, presumably lasted four months as well.[50] The Nemean and Isthmian Games, for which we have clear evidence, surely lasted for a similar period of time due to their Panhellenic character.[51] By contrast, the *ekecheiria* of the famous Attic Eleusinia lasted fifty-five days, that of the Panathenaia only one month.[52] A safe-passage arrangement was also guaranteed to participants of many other regional and local festivals.[53]

Since the dates of the important periodic festivals lay some distance apart from one another in order to avoid clashes, and were moreover held in different years, the *ekecheiriai* of the important festivals alone already covered most of the summer, and so almost the whole period in which shipping and military expeditions took

---

[49] See E. N. Gardiner, *Athletics of the Ancient World*, 4th edn, Oxford 1967, p. 34. A. Raubitschek has expressed the same opinion in a letter to the author dated 30 July 1983. Cf. on the other hand Herrmann [see n. 6], p. 12. See also Patrucco [see n. 6], p. 78, n. 1, who calls the *ekecheiria* "a concept truly unique in the history of humanity[!]".

[50] Rougement [see n. 9], p. 88. Concerning the *ekecheiria* of the Pythian Games: Thucydides V, 1; Plutarch *Moralia* 413d. By contrast according to Rougement the "local time of celebration" of the Pythian Games, the *hieromênia*, lasted one year! Cf. *IG* II², 1126.

[51] On the *ekecheiria* of the Nemean Games see: Pindar, *Nemean* 3,2; Xenophon, *Hellenika* IV, 7, 2; Plutarch, *Philopoimen*, 11, 1 and *Aratos* 28, 3–4. On the *ekecheiria* of the Isthmian Games see: Thucydides V, 9, 10; Xenophon, *Hellenika* IV, 5, 1; Plutarch *De Pythiae Oraculis* 3; Pausanias V, 2, 1; cf. II, 15, 1. See also Weniger [see n. 9], p. 204.

[52] *SIG*³ 42b gives evidence for the duration of the Eleusinian *ekecheiria*; other sources are to be found in Rougement [see n. 9], p. 88. Thucydides V, 47, 10 appears to give an indication of the duration of the "period of divine protection" (Gottesschutz) for the Panathenaean festival.

[53] I do not intend to demonstrate these arrangements systematically here, nor to analyse them individually. However, the statement of G. Busolt and H. Swoboda (*Griechische Staatskunde* vol. 2., 3rd reprint, München 1926, p. 1263), claiming that until the end of the fourth century BC the *ekecheiria* was put into effect only in connection with the important panhellenic Games, the Eleusinian Mysteries and the Asklepieia of Epidaurus, is not correct. Xenophon gives evidence for *ekecheiriai* in connection with the festivals at Phlius (*Hellenika* IV, 2, 16) and Mantineia (V, 2, 2) already at the beginning of the fourth century BC In the year 376 BC (according to others 330 BC) the Athenians (for the first time) held biennial Games on the occasion of a victory or a peace treaty (in honour of the goddess *Eirênê* ("Peace")) including an *ekecheiria* lasting ten days for inhabitants and visitors. Cf. L. Robert, "Une fête de la paix à Athènes au IVème siècle", in *AE* 1977, pp. 211–16; J. and L. Robert, "Bulletin Épigraphique" in *REG* 93 (1980), p. 390, no. 193. On the *ekecheiria* of Kos cf. *SEG* 12 (1955), no. 371; W. Blümel, *Die Inschriften von Iasos*, vol. I, Bonn [1984], no. 21. In about 200 BC the city of Magnesia ad Meandrum established a festival in honour of Artemis Leukophryene including an Isopythian Games that was supposed to be held every four years. The resolutions of the cities of Megalopolis and Paros, in which they explicitly accept the *ekecheiria* proclaimed by festival envoys, are still preserved: *I. Magnesia* no. 38, lines 14, 32–3, 39, 44, 48; no. 50, l. 53. An *ekecheiria* also existed at the Asklepieia of Lampsakos: cf. P. Frisch, *Die Inschriften von Lampsakos*, Bonn 1978, no. 9 [= *IK* vol. 6]. The interesting wording of an "*ekecheiria* by all people towards each other (πάσι προ ς πάντων)", found in connection with the festival celebrated at Sparta during the months Agrianos and Hyakinthos (*IG* V, 1, 18B, 8 ff = Laum II, 20) as well as with the initiation of a statue of Artemis at Magnesia (*I. Magnesia* 100, ll. 25–6), makes clear that this was a question of a renunciation, by all festival participants, of any claims against each other. It is clear that the term *ekecheiria* in later times mainly described a "legal truce"; cf. n. 41. An inscription from Ephesos (*SIG*³ 867, 3–16; 63–4) shows that the *ekecheiria* of the Artemisia was extended to last one month in 160 AD. Under the reign of Gordian III (238–244 AD) the city of Side/Pamphylia established an Isopythian Games in honour of Apollo *Epicheirios*; cf. on that point G. E. Bean/ T.B. Mitford, *Journeys in Rough Cilicia 1964–1968*, Vienna 1970, no. 21b and the relevant commentary on p. 45; P. Weiss, "Ein agonistisches Bema und die isopythischen Spiele von Side", in *Chiron* 11 (1981), pp. 317–46; cf. J. and L. Robert, "Bulletin Épigraphique", in *REG* 95 (1982), no. 450, pp. 417–22.

place. Had the *ekecheiriai* implemented a complete truce throughout the whole of Greece, one festival-peace would have been followed by the next and no miliary conflicts between the different city-states would have been possible. Those who read Thucydides' detailed description of the Peloponnesian war (431–404 BC) carefully will notice that the so-called "peaceful" years of the Olympic Games were by no means different in respect to military campaigning from the years in between the Games.[54]

2. We have three pieces of evidence which attest explicitly to significant military activities – some actually carried out, others only planned – during the *ekecheiriai* of panhellenic festivals:

a) In the summer of 422 BC the Athenians attacked the island of Delos during the *ekecheiria* of the Pythian Games and expelled all inhabitants under the pretext of cleansing the place for cultic reasons. No disapproval or active response by the Greeks assembled in Delphi is mentioned by Thucydides.[55]

b) In 412 BC during the *ekecheiria* of the Isthmian Games, King Agis of Sparta requested that the allied Corinthians take part in a naval landing operation on the island of Chios, then situated within the Athenian sphere of influence. The Corinthians, however, refused to get involved before the end of the *ekecheiria*, given the attendance of the Athenian athletes, spectators and in particular the presence of an official Athenian legation. Even though Agis, in view of the rather late stage of the season, offered to present the operation as a purely Spartan one, while nevertheless using Corinthian ships, he was not able to change the Corinthians' decision.[56] It is remarkable that the Athenians participated in the Isthmian Games in 412 BC even though they were engaged in an acrimonious war with the host nation of Corinth, which threatened their very existence. On the one hand this was certainly due to the traditional position of honour that the Athenians occupied at these Games. On the other hand they might also have been trying to "find out more about a suspicious rumour about treacherous plans of the Chians, who were at that time allies of Corinth …".[57] Moreover it is clear that during the period of an *ekecheira* military operations were not generally prohibited. They were simply incompatible with the duties of the hosts, who had agreed to a special relationship with all participants of the celebration for a certain period of time.

c) In August 394 BC the Spartan king Agesilaos defeated the Thebans and their allies at Koroneia in Boeotia. Immediately after the battle he went to Delphi, only 40 kilometres away, where the Pythian Games were being held. At Delphi he honoured Apollo with an ostentatious procession and sacrificed a tithe of the spoils they had previously gained in Asia Minor. The battle at Koroneia must therefore have taken place during the period of the *ekecheiria* of the Pythian Games.[58]

---

[54] Cf. H. A. Harris, *Greek Athletes and Athletics*, London 1964, pp. 155–6; Muth [see n. 9] pp. 170–1.

[55] Thucydides V, 1 (although the text is problematic at this point); cf. Rougement [see n. 9] p. 104.

[56] Thucydides, VIII, 5. The Mantineans too refused to help their Spartan allies at the beginning of the 4th century, referring to an *ekecheiria*-obligation: Xenophon, *Hellenika* V, 2, 2. The same reason – upholding the obligation of an *ekecheiria* – was given as an excuse by the Phliasians in 394 BC for their refusal to participate in an operation of the Spartans against the Athenians and Argives: Xenophon, *Hellenika* IV, 2, 16.

[57] Muth [see n. 9], p. 174. On the special position of the Athenians cf. Popp [see n. 9], p. 140.

58 Plutarch, *Agesilaos* 19, 3.

3. All written evidence presented by ancient authors on offences against the Olympic *ekecheiria* either refers to direct attacks on Elis or to hostilities against visitors to the Games. No literary source, however, mentions "illegal" war-activities among third parties[59] or even against "barbarians".[60] This will become clearer in examples elaborated upon below. According to mythological tradition, the most prominent violator of the Isthmian *ekecheiria* was Herakles, who killed his enemies, the sons of Aktor the Elean, on their way to the Games. As neither Herakles nor the Argives were held responsible for this violation, the Eleans decided to boycott the Isthmian Games in the future.[61] It is of no importance whether this legend – obviously aimed at explaining a refusal to participate which was at first presumably

---

[59] This outdated opinion was recently defended again by P. Siewert, "Eine Bronze-Urkunde mit elischen Urteilen über Böoter, Thessaler, Athen und Thespiai", in A. Mallwitz (ed.), *X. Bericht über die Ausgrabungen in Olympia*, Berlin 1981, p. 244, n. 100. He particularly refers to an event that even Rougement [see n. 9], pp. 105–6 could not bring into line with his own hypothesis: in the summer of 382 BC the Spartan Phoibidas occupied the *Kadmeia*, the castle-sanctuary of Thebes, with help from leading members of the local oligarchic party and established a Spartan-friendly vassal state. Xenophon, the most important contemporary witness (*Hellenika* V, 2, 25–31; V, 4, 1), as well as other authors, describes and judges this incident from a purely strategic and military point of view; cf. Isokrates, *Panegyrikos* 126; Diodorus XV, 20, 1–2; XVI, 29, 2; Plutarch, *Pelopidas* V, 2–3; *Moralia* 576a; Cornelius Nepos, *Pelopidas* 1, 2–3; Polybius IV, 27, 4; Iustinus, *Epitome historiarum Philippicarum Pompei Trogi* VIII, 1, 5. After the defeat of the Spartans at Leuktra in 371 BC, they were condemned to pay a large fine by the court of the Amphyktionic council at Delphi, which, however, they refused to do. Diodorus XVI, 29, 2 simply names the occupation as the reason for the court-case. According to Xenophon, *Hellenika* V, 4, 1, Phoibidas had broken the solemn promise to secure freedom and autonomy for the regional city-states. In the view of the complaining party, this was clearly a breach of a political contract (cf. Polybius IV, 27, 4: "Phoibidas having broken the treaty" (Φοιβίδου παρασπονδήσαντος) whereas the Spartans saw the changeover of power as a domestic matter, denying any influence of their troops in Thebes on the independence of the city. The conflict probably became even more problematic since Phoibidas infringed the inviolability (*asylia*) of the *Kadmeia*, where the festival of the Thesmophoria was being held at the time of the occupation, as Xenophon reports. However, none of the above mentioned texts names the Pythian Games and their *ekecheiria*. The interpretation of Rougement and Siewert is based on a misunderstanding of a passage of the orator Publius Aelius Aristides (AD 117–180). He refers to the incidents of the year 382 BC and adds that they took place "during the Pythian festival". This formulation confirms and makes more precise the timing – "during the summer" – given by Xenophon. One can assume that Aristides gained the information from a source different from those mentioned above. If the co-operation of the Spartans and local oligarchs in fact took place during the Pythian Games, which would fit perfectly with its surprise character (cf. below on the similar action of Kylon in Athens), and yet all the sources mention only the breaking of the political contract as the reason for the indignation of the Spartan enemies, the fact that the Pythian Games were held at the same time cannot have played an important role. Otherwise, one would have expected that at least one of the eight authors would have mentioned them explicitly in one of the eleven passages referring to the events. In my view, the Spartan operation in 382 BC did not constitute a breach of the Pythian *ekecheiria*. Moreover, military action against a third party was obviously allowed during that period. Hence, the only support for Siewert's interpretation of a total peace during panhellenic festivals, on which he based his hypothesis of a breaking of the Olympic *ekecheiria* in 480 BC, falls away.

[60] Popp's claim [see n. 9] (p. 127) that the *ekecheiria* in 480 BC prevented the deployment of the Greeks against the attacking Persians is unsustainable. If there had been a fundamental ban on war-operations the Spartans could not have sent Leonidas and his 300 troops ahead and would have tried to excuse their own hesitation by giving the festival of the *Karneia* as reason. Most of the Greeks postponed their mobilisation to the time after the Olympic Games, according to Herodotus VIII, 206, because they did not believe that the battle at Thermopylae would be decided so quickly; their behaviour was therefore based on an interpretation of the military situation rather than on the Olympic *ekecheiria*. Many cities obviously took advantage of the Olympic Games to learn more about the attitude of the other Greeks, especially of those that were seen as being "Persian-friendly".

[61] Pausanias V, 2 ; Plutarch, *De Pythiae Oraculis* 3. Because Tiryns was seen as the home of Herakles, he was an Argive.

The So-Called Olympic Peace in Ancient Greece   47

ritually motivated but had by a later date become unintelligible – is based on a true historical event. Friedrich Schiller interpreted the breach of the Isthmian *ekecheiria* in poetic fashion: the singer Ibycus is killed on his way to the Isthmian Games by robbers at the Isthmus of Corinth. When the murderers visit the Games later on, Apollo ensures their exposure and punishment.[62]

As mentioned above, the *ekecheiria* of the Olympic Games was by and large observed during the archaic and classical periods. Two incidents from this period are, however, remarkable. When the leading Athenians of the ruling family of Alkmeonids took part in the Games in 636 or 632 BC, the young Kylon, a victorious athlete at the Olympic Games, took advantage of their absence and staged a *coup d'état*. Nevertheless, nowhere in the relevant sources is he ever accused of a breach of the *ekecheiria*. Rather, the actions of the returning Alkmeonid Megakles who quelled the *coup d'état* and apprehended and executed Kylon's followers, thereby disregarding their right to asylum after finding refuge in the sanctuaries of the Acropolis, made their way into the historical records under the label of the "Kylonian sacrilege".[63]

During the Olympic Games in 476 BC the much acclaimed Themistocles, glorious victor at Salamis, openly agitated against the presence of Hieron, tyrant of Syracuse, demanding his exclusion from the Games and calling on the assembled Greeks to attack his palatial tents as he had refused to participate in the Hellenic struggle for freedom against the Persians. But the *hellanodikai* stayed calm and the audience kept its discipline. Hieron emerged as winner from the horse-races and his success was glamorously celebrated by the poet Pindar.[64] Even if one sympathises with the emotions driving Themistocles, it nevertheless seems disconcerting that a man like him, belonging as he did to the official Athenian delegation,[65] would willingly incite the festive crowd and call for a break of the *ekecheiria* for reasons of political propaganda.[66]

---

[62] The ancient sources of this legend are established in W. Schmid, *Geschichte der griechischen Literatur*, Vol. I, 1, München 1929, p. 492, n. 10 [= *Handbuch der Altertumswissenschaft* VII, 1, 1]. On the poem of Schiller cf. E. Jokl, "Pax Olympica", in: *Proceedings of the First International Seminar on the History of Physical Education and Sport, Wingate Institute for Physical Education, Netanya (Israel), April 9–11, 1968*, Wingate Institute 1969, pp. 3/2–3/3.

[63] Thucydides I, 126. Cf. Moretti, *Ol.*, no. 56, p. 65, where additional evidence can be found.

[64] Plutarch, *Themistocles* 25 (cf. 5, 4 and 17, 4); Pausanias VIII, 50, 3.

[65] Aristotle, *Ethica Eudemia* 1233b.

[66] It is not surprising that Ziehen [see n. 9], col. 36 views Plutarch's report as fictitious! Siewert [see n. 59], p. 247, n. 123 describes it as "presumably unhistorical". Hence, Finley/Pleket's claim [see n. 8] (p. 161) that because of the *ekecheiria* no violence ever occurred during the Olympic Games is wrong. According to Siewert an inscription found in 1965 in Olympia refers to an event during the same Olympic Games. It says that the Elean *mastroi*, a sort of court of appeal, partly revised a judgement of two judges made in a first court case on fines for damages that had to be paid by the Boeotians and Thessalians to the Athenians and Thespians. According to Siewert both Greek tribes were punished because they broke the *ekecheiria* in the summer of 480 BC by fighting side-by-side with the Persians against Athens and Thespiai. In 476 BC the first court case was held in the presence of Themistocles at Olympia but the judgement was revised in 472 BC. Together with the occupation of the *Kadmeia* in Thebes by Spartan troops (discussed above), Siewert interprets this court case as another proof of the absolute prohibition of warfare during the *ekecheiria* of a panhellenic festival. But his whole argument is based on unproven assumptions and is circular. There is no reason to see the two judges of the first court case as *Hellanodikai* nor can we discern the reason for the punishment. Siewert seems to conclude, on the basis of the undated inscription, that the number of *Hellanodikai* in 476 BC was two simply because he assumed the men to be *Hellanodikai* in the first place! This document of Olympia might well have

A completely new situation emerged due to the events of the Peloponnesian war of 431–404 BC. Even in the early days of the war, Pericles considered the possibility that the enemies of Athens, despite the traditional inviolability, could loot the temple-treasures of Olympia and Delphi in order to finance their increasing military expenditure.[67] This fear, however, proved unfounded. In 428 BC Mytilene, after breaking the alliance with Athens, sent for help to Sparta, asking for membership of the Peloponnesian League. The Spartans ordered the representatives of Mytilene to travel to Olympia, protected by the *ekecheiria*, in order to discuss strategy and to plan their next steps after the Games.[68] Whereas the Olympic festival of the sixth and fifth centuries BC surely served as a neutral place for quarrelling parties to discuss rivalries and to find solutions, the festive assembly in this case provided the opportunity for one Greek party to hatch war-plans against another.[69]

The temporary inviolability of a state hosting the panhellenic Games could even consciously be used as a means of military strategy. Facing an approaching Spartan army in the spring of 388 BC, the Argives spontaneously called for the *ekecheiria* of the Nemean festival, that was actually supposed to be held again in 387, much earlier than usual, probably through a manipulation of the calendar, in order to ensure their safety from being attacked. The Spartan commander, King Agesipolis, refused to give his approval but as a precaution consulted the oracles of Delphi and Olympia to affirm the invalidity of this arbitrary arrangement before attacking Nemea and Argos.[70]

But let us go back now to the Peloponnesian war: in April 421 BC the first part of the quarrel between Athens and Sparta, the so-called Archidamian war, came to an end through the peace of Nikias, which aimed at an equitable balance between the great powers. In spring 420 BC, however, the party of Alkibiades, which was hostile to Sparta, was in control in Athens. A pact of non-aggression and mutual assistance was agreed between Athens, Argos, Mantineia and the so far neutral Elis.[71] Sparta felt encircled by enemies, especially on its Messenian northern flank, and carried out a pre-emptive strike immediately before the beginning of the Olympic Games against Triphylia, the southern part of Elis, in order to secure control over the city of Lepreon and the fortress of Phyrkos.[72] The further events are described by Thucydides as follows:[73]

---

something to do with the Persian wars but a connection with the *ekecheiria* of the Olympics is unlikely; cf. Ebert [see n. 8], p. 90.

[67] Thucydides I, 121; 143.

[68] Thucydides III, 8.

[69] One could not imagine NATO in 1980 giving Olympic-Passports to its legates and sending them off to Moscow in order to discuss with the Romanian delegation the Romanian withdrawal from the "Warsaw Pact" and the subsequent deployment of western troops to their country!

[70] Xenophon, *Hellenika* IV, 7, 2; cf. Popp [see n. 9] p. 144.

[71] Thucydides V, 47. Others say that Elis was already in 431 BC a member of the Peloponnesian League. It is hard to say what reasons caused the Eleans to give up their neutral role. Siewert [see n. 59] p. 237 assumes that the protection of Lepreon demanded by the Spartans was the main reason; cf. Drees [see n. 9], p. 184: "Elis may have abandoned its traditional neutrality because it realised that the Greek powers could no longer maintain this state of total war and that religious law no longer had enough force to protect the territory. Elis had been involved in internal Greek struggles since the Peloponnesian War.'

[72] It is not quite clear whether Lepreon and Phyrkos belonged to Elis but this was obviously not questioned by the Spartans.

[73] Thucydides V, 49–50; cf. Xenophon, *Hellenika* III, 2, 21; Pausanias VI, 2, 1–3.

The Olympic festival was held this summer, and the Arcadian Androsthenes was victor for the first time in the wrestling and boxing. In addition, the Spartans were excluded from the temple by the Eleans, and thus prevented from sacrificing or competing, for having refused to pay the fine specified in the Olympic law imposed upon them by the Eleans, who alleged that they had attacked Fort Phyrkos, and sent heavy infantry into Lepreon during the Olympic truce. The amount of the fine was two thousand *minai*, two for each heavy-armed soldier, as the law prescribes. The Spartans sent envoys, and pleaded that the judgement was unjust, saying that the truce had not yet been proclaimed at Sparta when the heavy infantry were sent off to Lepreon. But the Eleans affirmed that the *ekecheiria* had already begun for them (they proclaim it first among themselves), and that the aggression of the Spartans had taken them by surprise while they were living quietly as in a period of truce, and not expecting anything. Upon this the Spartans submitted that if the Eleans really believed that they had committed an aggression, it was useless after that to proclaim the truce at Lakedaimon; but they had proclaimed it notwithstanding, as though believing nothing of the kind, and from that moment the Spartans had made no attack upon their country. Nevertheless the Eleans adhered to what they had said, that nothing would persuade them that an aggression had not been committed; if, however, the Spartans would restore Lepreon, they would give up their own share of the money and pay that of the god for them. As this proposal was not accepted, the Eleans tried a second proposal: instead of restoring Lepreon, if this was objected to, the Spartans should ascend the altar of the Olympian Zeus, as they were anxious to have access to the temple, and swear before the Hellenes that they would pay the fine at a later date. This being also refused, the Spartans were excluded from the temple, the sacrifice, and the Games, and sacrificed at home; the Lepreans being the only other Hellenes who did not attend. Still the Eleans were afraid of the Spartans sacrificing by force, and kept guard with a heavy-armed company of their young men, being also joined by a thousand Argives, the same number of Mantineans, and by some Athenian cavalry who were waiting for the festival at Harpina. Great fear was felt, during the festival, about the prospect of the Spartans coming in arms, especially after Lichas, son of Arkesilaos, a Spartan, had been whipped on the course by the umpires. This happened because, upon his horses being the winners, and the Boeotian people being proclaimed the victor on account of his having no right to enter, he came forward on the course and crowned the charioteer, in order to show that the chariot was his. After this incident all were more afraid than ever, and firmly expected a disturbance: the Spartans, however, kept quiet, and let the festival pass by, as we have seen ...

Thucydides' report allows for some interesting conclusions on the character and handling of the *ekecheiria*:

a) The observance of the *ekecheiria* was ensured by the so-called "Olympic law" (Greek: *Olympiakos nomos*), which apparently contained detailed provisions regarding its execution and punishment for misconduct. Every person or state that violated it had to compensate for the damage caused. In this particular instance the Spartans were required to give back the occupied territory and to compensate the aggrieved party, in this case the Eleans, with one *mina* plus an additional one for the temple. This matched exactly the sum that had to be paid in the Peloponnese as a ransom in times of war.[74] The transgressors were thus seen as prisoners of the Olympic Zeus and a ransom had to be paid for their "release".

---

[74] Cf. Weniger [see n. 9], p. 196; Herodotus VI, 79. According to Drees [see n. 9], p. 46, the 2000 *minai* demanded by the Eleans were worth 6,600 cows.

b) The regulations concerning the entry into force of the *ekecheiria* evidently contained a loophole, which was probably exploited deliberately by the Spartans: within the short period of time between its proclamation in Elis itself and its announcement in Sparta, the Spartans attacked two strategically important fortresses[75] while the Eleans, completely unsuspecting, were already enjoying the peace of the festival truce. This discussion shows that it was not the operation as such but the time at which it took place that constituted a violation of the *ekecheiria*. From that time onwards the Eleans could no longer rely on a general inviolability as they had given up their traditional neutrality for an alliance with Athens and its allies.

c) The course of the subsequent intractable discussions shows that the Eleans did not seek justice, nor were they even concerned with the return of their territories or the ransom.[76] Rather they intended, in accordance with Athenian interests, to inflict a diplomatic defeat on the Spartans in front of the assembly of all Greeks, thereby aiming at politically isolating Sparta and bringing it into disrepute. It was irrelevant whether the Spartans would admit their guilt and accept the punishment or decide to refuse and subsequently be excluded from the panhellenic cultic community. Once more, Olympia became a field of propaganda for the great powers and its Games a continuation of war by other means.

d) Sparta's reaction was a prudent one: although in formal terms they were in the right,[77] they accepted the exclusion and held their own festival in honour of Zeus back home in Sparta.[78] Only Lichas, who did not want to miss the opportunity of winning the Olympic horse-race with his excellent chariot, resorted to trickery. He entered the competition under the flag of Boeotia, which was taking part in the Games despite being allied with Sparta. His team won and instead of quietly enjoying the victory, he revealed himself as Spartan in order to gain the honour in his own and Sparta's name. Unexpectedly, his compatriots did not take revenge for his disgraceful treatment afterwards. This might be attributed to the fact that he acted without the authorisation of the Spartan politicians who had decided beforehand to accept the exclusion and instead hold their own festival. The Spartans did not think to force their way into the area of the Games either, since it was secured by thousands of allied soldiers that had come to support Elis.[79]

e) The episode of 420 BC also shows that adherence to the rules of the *ekecheiria* was a rather tiresome duty for both warring parties. It was formally observed, but – as the Spartan example shows – judicially pushed to its limits.[80]

---

[75] The distance between Elis and Sparta amounts to about 140 kilometres as the crow flies but given the roads used at that time it probably came at least to 160 kilometres. The Elean heralds probably needed at minimum five days to reach Sparta.

[76] At this point one cannot agree with Muth [see n. 9], p. 173 who claims that the Eleans showed "great pliability".

[77] Cf. Popp [see n. 9], p. 130. Weniger [see n. 9] is of the opposite opinion, p. 196.

[78] Cf. Hönle [see n. 23], pp. 155–6.

[79] Pausanias claims (VI, 2, 1–3) that the Spartans did resort to violence.

[80] However, Muth's conclusion [see n. 9] (p. 176) seems too pessimistic. According to him the Greeks were inclined "to break the "peace of the gods" (*Gottesfrieden*) for reasons of political opportunism; to the Eleans, the Spartans and the politicians of other states it was a political tool".

After its total defeat in 404 BC, Athens for the time being lost its political influence in the Peloponnese. Its former ally Elis was conquered by the Spartan kings Agis and Pausanias (402–400 BC) and had to come to an arrangement with them.[81] The Eleans lost a part of their territory and by a formal declaration had to concede to the Spartans the right to sacrifice at Olympia and to participate in the Games. They thereby publicly confessed the "unlawfulness" of the sanctions of 420 BC.[82] Incidentally, in the light of their refusal to pay the fine for allegedly breaking the *ekecheiria*, the question of whether the Spartans competed at the Olympic Games in the years 416, 412, 408 and 404 remains controversial.[83] Aside from some lootings, however, the victorious Spartans resisted the temptation to take revenge for the suffered humiliation. They even explicitly confirmed Elean authority over the sanctuary and the Games as they had doubts about the ability of the rural population – who similarly claimed that right for themselves – to carry it out competently, as Xenophon remarks.[84] The astonishing fact that the Athenians, who had only just been defeated, took part in the Games of 400 BC and in Minos even provided the winner of the stadium race, shows how little a war which had lasted thirty years had affected the cast of mind of all participants.[85]

However, the *chronique scandaleuse* of Olympia continued soon afterwards, revealing the increasing decline of political culture and religious respect: in 388 BC, Dionysius of Syracuse conquered the united Greek cities of southern Italy, destroyed Rhegion and enslaved its inhabitants, at a time when the Greek motherland had to face the threat of another Persian invasion.[86] Some weeks later he sent his brother Thearides to the Olympic Games, escorted by a distinguished delegation. Not only did they bring several promising *quadrigae*, but they resided in golden tents decorated with precious carpets, and had the best contemporary singers recite the tyrant's poems in front of them. At that moment the orator Lysias, an émigré of Syracuse, stirred up the crowd by hinting at the absence in the tyrant of panhellenic spirit concerning the Persian threat, and enraged the people so much that they attacked the tyrant's tents and humiliated the delegation.[87] Unlike the audience of Themistocles' time, in this case the crowd let itself get carried away and broke the *ekecheiria*. It seems, however, that the Eleans took measures neither against Lysias nor against the violent crowd.

---

[81] Xenophon, *Hellenika* III, 2, 22–31; Diodorus XIV, 17, 34; Pausanias III, 8, 3–5. Cf. Popp [see n. 9] p. 133, n. 178.

[82] Xenophon, *Hellenika* III, 2, 21–31; cf. Pausanias III, 8, 5. When Agis tried to conquer Elis for the first time an earthquake made him withdraw, out of respect for the sanctity of the site.

[83] Moretti, no. 342, p. 109 dates the Olympic victory of the Spartan Lakrates, killed on military service at Athens (Xenophon, *Hellenika* II, 4, 33) to the year 416. Hönle [see n. 23], p. 130 by contrast argues that the Spartans were not able to take part in the Olympic Games between 420 and 400 BC However, it is rather unlikely that the Eleans were able to maintain the exclusion of Sparta, particularly as the military situation of Athens and its allies deteriorated. When King Agis some years later wanted to sacrifice to Zeus at Olympia, following an oracle's advice, his wish was refused by the Eleans, not because of the fine still to be paid but because of an old custom that the Greeks were not allowed to consult the oracle when they intended to march against other Greeks: Xenophon, *Hellenika* III, 2, 22. This shows that the Spartans were generally allowed to enter the sanctuary again.

[84] Xenophon, *Hellenika* III, 2, 31.

[85] Diodorus XIV, 35; Africanus in Eusebius: Minon; cf. Moretti, no. 357, p. 112.

[86] Dionysius of Halicarnassus, *De Lysia* 29.

[87] Diodorus XIV, 109.

In the year 365 BC the Arcadians, who had founded a confederation only a few years earlier, wrested the region of Triphylia and within it the area of Olympia from the Eleans, who were by this time in alliance with Sparta again, with the help of an Athenian cavalry contingent, and established a Pisatan vassal state. They occupied the sanctuary of Zeus and exacted a mandatory loan in order to pay their mercenaries. The Greek historian Xenophon (430–345 BC), living on an estate close to Olympia at the time, reports dramatic events which he may have witnessed himself:[88]

> When the Arcadians were no longer busy with Kromnos, they turned their attention again to the Eleans, and they not only kept Olympia garrisoned more strongly, but also, because the Olympic year was approaching, prepared to hold the Olympic festival together with the Pisatans, who claimed to have been the first to have charge of the sanctuary. However, when the month came in which the Olympic festival takes place and the days in which the festal assembly gathers, the Eleans, having prepared themselves openly and having called the Achaians to their aid, set off on the route to Olympia. The Arcadians had never imagined that the Eleans would march against them, and were themselves directing the festival together with the Pisatans. They had already held the horse race and the running events of the pentathlon, and those competitors who had got as far as the pentathlon wrestling event were wrestling no longer in the stadium, but instead in the space between the stadium and the altar, for the Eleans, under arms, had by this stage reached the sanctuary. The Arcadians did not advance to meet them, but drew up their forces at the river Kladaos, which flows past the Altis and empties into the Alpheios. They had allies with them, about 2,000 Argive hoplites and 400 Athenian horsemen. And the Eleans lined up on the other side of the river, and having sacrificed, immediately advanced. And although they had in the past been looked down upon in military terms by the Arcadians and the Argives, the Achaians and the Athenians, nevertheless on that day they led their allies as men who were most valiant, and they not only routed the Arcadians at once – for it was with them that they first came into contact – but also engaged with the Argives who had come to help and defeated them. However, when they had pursued them into the space which lay between the Council chamber and the temple of Hestia and the theatre next to these buildings, despite the fact that they fought no less bravely and kept pushing the enemy towards the altar, nevertheless some of the Eleans were killed because they were being pelted from the roofs of the porticoes and the Council chamber and the great temple, including Stratolas himself, who was leader of the Three Hundred. At this point they withdrew to their own camp. However, the Arcadians and those who were with them were so afraid of what might happen the next day that they did not sleep during the night, but instead demolished the carefully constructed booths and built a stockade. As for the Eleans, when they approached the next day and saw that the stockade was strong and that many men had climbed up onto the temples, they withdrew to their city ...

This event, which made its way into the history books as the "battle in the Altis", was certainly the most spectacular breach of the Olympic *ekecheiria*. Naturally, the Eleans saw themselves as acting legitimately in their role as the traditional keepers of the sanctuary and the Games, and they refrained from adding the Olympiad of 364 BC to their lists, for the second time in the festival's history.[89] Shortly after-

---

[88] Xenophon, *Hellenika* VII, 4, 28–32; cf. Pausanias IV, 22, 3. According to Diodorus XV, 78, 3 the Arcadians and Pisatans were the aggressors.

[89] Pausanias VI, 22, 3; cf. Moretti, no. 419, p. 121.

wards, the Arcadian conquerors and particularly the Mantinean soldiers began to doubt their own behaviour. To avoid going down in history as wrongdoers they finally withdrew and reinstated the Eleans in their rightful position.[90]

Another spectacular breach of the *ekecheiria*, during the reign of Philip II of Macedonia (359–336 BC), stirred up much trouble in Athenian domestic politics. In the year 348 BC Macedonian soldiers took an Attic citizen named Phrynon of Rhamnus prisoner while he was on his way to the Olympic Games as an athlete, visitor or delegate. They set him free only after a ransom had been paid. The pro-Macedonian party in Athens, led by Aischines, tried to play the case down, speaking of "highwaymen", referring to a comment supposedly made by the victim himself. The supporters of Demosthenes, however, hostile to Macedonia, took full advantage of the event for their own propaganda. Philip, when asked by an Athenian delegation containing the victim Phrynon himself to pay back the ransom, did not deny the incident but gave the excuse that his soldiers had not been aware that the holy period of the festival (*hieromênia*) had already come into effect.[91] The king, who was himself a three-times winner in the equestrian contests at the Olympic Games, the last time probably at the 108th Olympiad which is in question here, and who was not only looking for acknowledgement as leader of the Greeks in their struggle against the Persians, but also facing important negotiations with the Athenians, settled the matter immediately: he restored the victim's property and moreover presented him with expensive gifts from his own private fortune.[92] We have no information about any Elean reaction in this case, unlike the case of 420 BC when they excluded the Spartans, conscious of total public support. Ziehen is probably right in accusing them of lacking courage in the face of the rising great power of Macedonia, which defeated the united Greeks ten years later at Chaironeia thereby ending the period of the autonomous polis.[93]

Assessing other acts of violence in the fourth and third centuries BC is not unproblematic. This is due to the fact that after Elis gave up its neutrality only the temple area remained protected, rather than the whole territory of the state in charge of it. The *ekecheiria* was therefore breached only in cases of direct attacks either on the Olympic site itself or on the participants on their way to or from Olympia. Such a breach occurred for instance in 312 BC when the Macedonian general Telesphoros in the course of the wars of the successors following Alexander's death, took fifty silver talents from the temple-treasury in Olympia.[94]

Similarly, a quarrel arose in 230 BC concerning the Nemean *ekecheiria*: during the celebration in Argos, Aratos, the military leader of the Achaian league held an "anti-Nemean-festival" in the neighbouring city of Kleonai and sold into slavery all participants in the "official" Nemean festival of Argos that he could get hold of. He would certainly have rejected Plutarch's accusation of breaching the *ekecheiria*

---

[90] Xenophon, *Hellenika* VII, 4, 33–5; cf. Drees [see n. 9], p. 184.

[91] Aischines, *De falsa legatione* 12; Libanios, *Hypothesis* 2 on Demosthenes XIX, p. 335. Since Phrynon also belonged to another important delegation, he had probably been an Attic legate.

[92] Cf. the slightly inaccurate account given by Gardiner [see n. 49], p. 34. "Philip [...] was compelled to apologize and to pay the fine.'

[93] Ziehen [see n. 9], col. 6.

[94] Diodorus XIX, 87, 2.

first since for him his own festival was the only legitimate one. As a matter of course, he proclaimed a period of divine protection for the visitors to his festival and observed it.[95] Shortly afterwards, Elis was again drawn into military quarrels. During the so-called war of allies (220–217 BC) it sided with the Aitolians against Philip V of Macedonia and was temporarily occupied by the latter. Polybius, in his report, explicitly regrets that the Eleans were not able to regain their traditional neutral position among the Greeks.[96] A final violation of the Olympic *ekecheiria* occurred when, shortly before the beginning of the Games in 208 BC, Machanidas the Spartan attempted to conquer the sanctuary of Zeus and to lead the festival himself, but then had to withdraw in the face of the approaching troops of Philip V.[97]

When Greece eventually became a Roman province in 146 BC, the *ekecheiriai* of panhellenic festivals, especially of the Olympic Games, lost importance. This was due to the fact that the right to use force against other city-states or private persons passed from the former sovereign and autonomous *poleis* or alliances into the hands of the Roman Empire whose systems of security and administration secured the course of the Games and the safe travel of participants and visitors from the whole Greco-Roman *oikoumenē*. Admittedly, the Elean heralds continued to announce the official date of the Games, inviting the cities to participate and declaring the *ekecheiria*, which was reaffirmed by representatives of the independent cities through sacrifices. This whole procedure, however, was merely a continuation of an old tradition without any political meaning.

Even in these times, however, especially during the Roman civil wars, capricious offences against the cultic site of Olympia occurred. Sulla, for example, raided the temple treasure again, gave the order for the transport of precious votive donations to Rome, and moved the 175th Olympic Games in 80 BC to Rome in order to commemorate the triumph over Marius and Mithridates a year earlier.[98] Similarly, the arrogant and extremely embarrassing manner in which the eccentric philhellene Nero ignored all traditional rules concerning the date and programme of the contest in AD 67 was certainly seen as a rude breaking of the *ekecheiria* by quite a few tradition-conscious Eleans – although, needless to say, the emperor enforced all his wishes without recourse to military action. After Nero's death, this Olympiad, the date of which had been changed by about two years, became the third to be declared invalid.[99] When the *Pax Romana* collapsed under the pressures of mass

---

[95] Plutarch, *Aratos* 28, 3–4. In 390 BC a similar case had occurred. The Argives, who had agreed to a *sympoliteia* with the Corinthians, became formal holders of the Isthmian Games, which had earlier been held exclusively by the Corinthians. Shortly before the festival, the Spartan king Agesilaos and the oligarchic immigrants who had left Corinth when the federation was established approached, and demanded that the Corinthian refugees should hold the festival under Spartan protection. The invaders, in their view, did not break the *ekecheiria* because they saw themselves as the legitimate organisers and as champions of the restoration of religious order: Xenophon, *Hellenika* IV, 5, 1–2. After the withdrawal of the Spartan troops the Argive "cowards" who had fled, held the Games again, deeming the prior Games illegitimate (Plutarch, *Agesilaos* 21, 3). Cf. Diodorus XIX, 36, 5 (with wrong assignment to the year 394 BC).

[96] Polybius IV, 73–4.

[97] Livy XXVIII, 7, 14–17.

[98] Appian, *Bellum Civile* I, 99; cf. V. J. Matthews, "Sulla and the Games of the 175th Olympiad (80 BC)", in *Stadion* 5 (1979), pp. 239–43.

[99] Cf. Moretti, p. 158.

migration during the third century AD and the Herulians in AD 267 even managed to advance to the gates of Olympia, the chain of continuous, historically provable Olympiads came to an end. The Olympic Games are said to have been officially prohibited by the emperor Theodosius I in AD 394.[100]

After critical scrutiny of the historical sources, the dogma of a total truce in connection with the Olympic Games obligating all of Greece in antiquity, which has been maintained by the Olympic movement for generations and traditionally viewed as irrefutable, proves to be far from the historical reality. As shown in detail above, the ancient *ekecheiria* merely involved the mutual promise of all members of the Olympic community to accept the inviolability of the sanctuary and to secure the safe and undisturbed journey of all athletes or spectators within a particular time period, even if their route led them through the territory of a state with which their own country was then at war. Because the *ekecheiria* describes an *immunity of those immediately involved in the festival activities* and not a state of affairs affecting the whole Greek world in general, one should speak of *divine protection* (*Gottesschutz*) rather than of *a peace of gods* (*Gottesfrieden*). This "divine protection" can be compared to the medieval *treuga Dei*, a guarantee for knights that they could travel to and from tournaments even though this might have necessitated crossing hostile territories.[101] For that reason the term *ekecheiria* is translated in English and French respectively as *truce* and *trêve*, terms which capture its meaning in a more precise way than the German equivalents, and prevent far-fetched interpretations. This is underlined by the level-headed way in which this topic is dealt with in Anglo-Saxon literature.[102]

Adherence to the *ekecheiria* was ensured by sanctions that could be imposed by the Eleans with the agreement of all participants. As we have seen, this did not always take place in an impartial and unselfish manner. However, the continuity of the Games in a Greek world of permanent warfare was guaranteed and that in turn led to the growing importance and general acceptance of the Games themselves. The origins of the *ekecheiria* can be found in the close and organically evolved connection between ancient contests and divine cult. At the same time, it reflects the Greek sense of realism and pragmatism. The *ekecheiria* was not an "ideal" but an agreement. It did not have the effect of interrupting ongoing wars but rather guaranteed that the Olympic Games would be held despite these ongoing wars. It presented a form of "particular" and "temporary" peace which H. Schelsky, following the horrible events of 1972 in Munich, realistically identified as the only achievable minimal goal for the Olympic society.[103]

---

[100] Cf. Ebert, *Olympia* [see n. 8], pp. 125–9.

[101] A similar idea is mentioned by Rougement [see n. 9], p. 101 in his "Note complémentaire: Une hypothèse sur la nature des "trêves sacrées" panhelleniques". On the *treuga Dei* cf. L. K. Ruhl, "Das Turnier als friedfertiger Krieg", in H. Becker (ed.), *Sport im Spannungsfeld zwischen Krieg und Frieden*, Clausthal-Zellerfeld 1985, pp. 31–53 (= *Deutsche Vereinigung für Sportwissenschaft, Protokoll* 15).

[102] A good example is to be found in the commentary of Harris on the paper of E. Jokl, quoted in n. 62. See also Finley/Pleket [see n. 8], p. 161.

[103] H. Schelsky, *Friede auf Zeit. Die Zukunft der Olympischen Spiele*, Osnabrück 1973, p. 11. Szanto [see no. 32], cols 2162–3 already recognised the true character of the *ekecheiria*. Cf. Bengtson [see n. 18], *Olympische Spiele*, p. 31; I. Weiler, *Der Sport bei den Völkern der alten Welt*, Darmstadt 1981, p. 109; Ebert, *Olympia* [see n. 8], p. 17; Muth [see n. 9], pp. 170–1; cf. the characterisation of F. Enz, "Die

As a result of the boycott and exclusions in connection with the Games of 1976 in Montreal, 1980 in Moscow and 1984 in Los Angeles, the IOC seriously considered a modern form of *ekecheiria* in order to guarantee safe and undisturbed Games and the chance of participation for all teams. The suggestion of the Hellenic Olympic committee that the Games should be held permanently in an area with extraterritorial status close to the ancient site of Olympia was refused by an overwhelming majority of the national Olympic Committees and the international Sport-associations.[104] Likewise, the attempt to guarantee the inviolability of the Olympic Games via a resolution or declaration passed by the UN General Assembly, which might even have established a legally binding convention in international law over time, failed in much the same way.[105]

In the light of the insights presented so far, one question arises, the answer to which is important for an adequate appreciation of the political meaning and significance of the ancient Olympic Games: is it the case that the main motivation for assembling all Greeks every four years at the shores of the River Alpheios was to unite the whole Greek world politically under a comprehensive and lasting state of peace and if so, was the *ekecheiria* a conscious manifestation of this goal, as is claimed not only by modern ideologues but also by a number of authors of late antiquity?[106] A detailed analysis and discussion of the sources in question is an attractive and desirable prospect but cannot be done within the confines of this article. The results of recent relevant research, however, which are in agreement with this author's long held conviction, will be summarised here briefly. They

---

Kirche und die Idee des Friedens im Sport. Aufgaben und Möglichkeiten", in P. Jakobi/H.-E. Rösch (eds), *Sport-Dienst an der Gesellschaft. Kirche, Frieden und Sport*, Mainz 1977, p. 35. The *ekecheiria* is one of the few ancient Olympic arrangements worth adopting nowadays. If something similar had been put into effect in the past, the terrorist attack in Munich would not have happened because no country in the world would have given refuge to the terrorists. The refusal of entry for the Soviet Olympian legate Oleg Jurmischkin by the US administration before the Olympic Games in Los Angeles was likewise incompatible with a modern *ekecheiria* no matter what he was guilty of according to American law. Whether such regulations would have saved the Games of 1916, 1940 and 1944 as Pierre de Coubertin had wished must be seriously doubted.

[104] Cf. K. Fricke, *Die Idee der ständigen Austragung der Olympischen Spiele in Griechenland*, Diplomarbeit, Deutsche Sporthochschule Köln, Köln 1982, pp. 76–84.

[105] The IOC is still determined to push the idea through despite this failure.

[106] In the course of correspondence A. E. Raubitschek has pointed out that the older witnesses of the history of the early Olympic Games, namely Pindar and Herodotus, did not mention Olympia as a "symbol of common Greek kinship and unity". Even Thucydides, chronicler of Greek self-destruction during the Peloponnesian war, did not make that connection. The very first signs can be seen in Aristophanes' *Lysistrata*, 1128–34. From 400 BC onwards, poets and thinkers were inspired by wars and by the Persian threat to create connections between the Games and the idea of a panhellenic union. Lysias, *Olympikos* 3, states that Herakles had established the *ekecheiria* of the Olympic Games in order to strengthen the friendship amongst the Greeks so as to be able to defeat the Persians. Similar thoughts are expressed by Isokrates, *Panegyrikos* IV, 43. Cf. Herakleides Pontikos (*FHG* II, 610) and later authors like Phlegon, *FGrHist* 257, 1; Pausanias V, 4, 6; Eusebios *Chronika* I, 194; Scholia to Plato, *Republic* 465d. Philostratos' claim (*Gymnastikos* 7) that the hoplite race came last in the Olympic programme in order to represent the end of the *ekecheiria* and the resumption of warfare must be seen in the same context. Cf. the commentary of J. Jüthner, *Philostratos über die Gymnastik*, Leipzig/Berlin 1909 [reprint Amsterdam 1969], p. 198, note on 138, 12. Muth [see n. 9], not as critical as usual, calls the hoplite race of the Olympic Games an "alien element" which had a very contradictory relationship with the *ekecheiria* (p. 175). In doing so he underestimates the natural and traditional closeness of athletics and war for the Greeks.

clearly contradict the traditional conception, which originated in nineteenth-century enthusiasm for Greece, and which proved to be especially persistent in Germany against the background of its long struggle to form a single nation-state. Only Greeks were allowed to participate at the Olympic Games. Although they came from microstates which were often quarrelling among themselves, they still celebrated the Games as an expression of an already existing community of cult and culture. This was most prevalent in archaic and classical times (750–400 BC) when an aristocratic attitude to life and values defined not only the character of the Games but the general spirit of contests. The Games, however, did not serve the purpose of politically uniting all Greeks and certainly were not aimed at fraternisation with non-Greek "barbarians", who were excluded from the Games and from whom the Greeks differentiated themselves proudly and clearly. Beyond the immediate religious-cultic and sporting experience, the Olympic Games did not have any further purpose.

Despite this categorical assumption, however, some issues (often overestimated in the past) must be mentioned here. The celebration, for instance, offered – like any other cultic event – "opportunities for a mutual rapprochement" and "to discuss political issues and ease upcoming conflicts".[107] Likewise, the presence of many important politicians in Olympia automatically led to a decrease or postponement of military operations during the celebration period. On the other hand, Olympia served as a stage for the self-promotion of quarrelling noble families and city-states, an environment "in which discord was often sown instead of concord".[108] Admittedly, during the Peloponnesian war and particularly in the fourth century BC some attempts were made to rouse the Greeks to united political and military action. In particular, the orators Gorgias (c. 436–380 BC), Lysias (c. 445–380 BC) and Isokrates (436–338 BC) engaged in such attempts. But one must bear in mind that this happened only when Greece was in life-threatening states of emergency. The *ekecheiria* was not a conscious expression of a panhellenic programme, but it did inspire orators, who argued for a temporary unity in order to counter the Persian, Carthaginian or Macedonian attacks effectively.[109]

The establishment of a unified Greek state with a centralised authority that would have brought to an end what seems to us to be the economically unproductive fragmentation of the Greek world as well as the military conflicts among the city states was never achieved, not because the politicians were not able but because they were not willing to bring it into being. The central aspect of their political thinking and action was the autonomous *polis* – the small, autonomous city-state. Had the Greeks viewed Olympia as a place of panhellenic community, they would not have built so many votive objects and monuments remembering military victories of some Greeks over others. In this respect, the Altis perfectly embodies inner Greek disunity. Even the Eleans partly financed the building works

---

[107] Ebert, *Olympia* [see n. 8], p. 103.
[108] Ebert, *Olympia* [see n. 8], p. 104.
[109] Cf. Ebert, *Olympia* [see n. 8], p. 105; H. C. Baldry, *The Unity of Mankind in Greek Thought*, Cambridge 1965, p. 22; G. Dobesch, *Der Panhellenische Gedanke im 4. Jahrhundert v. Chr. und der „Philippos" des Isokrates. Untersuchungen zum Korinthischen Bund* I, Wien 1968.

of the great temple of Zeus, the united Greek sanctuary, with reparations they received from the Pisatans after crushing a revolt in 470 BC.[110] Shortly after the building works were finished, the Spartans placed a golden shield on the ridge of the temple's roof to commemorate their successful battle at Tanagra against the Argives, Athenians and their Ionian allies.[111] The Naupactians and Messenians also erected a statue of the famous Nikê of Paionios on the occasion of their victory against the Spartans in the Archidamian war around 421 BC, unusually without naming the defeated party in the inscription on the statue base.[112] "Contemporaries as well as future generations certainly knew who was meant by "the enemies" and the Spartans generously tolerated the monument even though they could have ordered its removal some years later."[113]

Particularism and separatism, originating in the tribal structures and clan orders of Indo-European tribes and strengthened by geographical conditions, were not simply deficient preliminary stages but basic categories of Greek political thinking. A union of Greek states became objectively even more unlikely in later times due to the differing developments within particular states, especially in Athens and Sparta. Accordingly, all alliances were merely temporary partnerships of convenience.[114]

In archaic and classical times a comprehensive state of peace (*koinê eirênê*), discussed by various philosophers, orators and historians after the Peloponnesian war,[115] would not have been a desirable aim for the Greek aristocracy, which was central to the value-systems of the time. Their class-based ethic effectively demanded the self-realisation and trial of young members of the elite through contest, either in the form of bloody battles for life and death or during uncompromising athletic competition. For the aristocracy, war was not just a "normal" part of life and a "beneficial challenge for the able man"[116] but a noteworthy, in some cases even welcome, and certainly legitimate, means of politics. The idea that the nobility, whose highest educational ideal was the warrior-athlete, actively tried to combine the idea of peace with the Olympic Games is self-contradictory. The Olympic Games of antiquity differ completely from the modern Games of Pierre de Coubertin in which the basic ideas of internationality and the promotion of peace play a central role. In some aspects, the festivals of the ancient Hellenes can be compared to the *Deutsche Turnfeste* in Germany (especially before the foundation

---

[110] Pausanias V, 10, 2. It is not important whether this story is true or not – whether it is or not, the Eleans spread the news proudly and without any feeling of embarrassment at all.

[111] Pausanias V, 10, 4. A small piece of the inscription has been found: *I. Olympia* 253.

[112] *I. Olympia* 259. Cf. Pausanias V, 26, 1.

[113] Herrmann [see n. 6], p. 160.

[114] Cf. H. Bengtson, *Griechische Geschichte von den Anfängen bis in die römische Kaiserzeit*, 5th edn, München 1977, pp. 285–6.

[115] Cf. above n. 106. It was not until 374 BC that the first public statue of *Eirênê* ("Peace"), the work of Kephisodotos, was erected in Athens: Cornelius Nepos, *Timotheus* 2, 2. See on that question W. Nestle, *Der Friedensgedanke in der antiken Welt*, Leipzig 1938 [= *Philologus-Supplementband* 31.1].

116 I. Scheibler, "Götter des Friedens in Hellas und Rom", in *Antike Welt* 15/1 (1984), p. 39. Cf. M. Lämmer, "Die Zukunft der olympischen Spiele", pp. 42–4. Cf. W.-D. Eberwein/P. Reichel, *Friedens- und Konfliktforschung. Eine Einführung*, München 1976, p. 15: "To a certain extent, war was understood to be normal and necessary ... it was even described as the 'father of all things' (Heraclitus), and accordingly considered a chief motivating factor in any cultural investigation of mankind, while peace was perceived to be the interruption of the normal state of war."

of the German Reich in 1871), the *Sokol-Festivals* of the Slavic national movement, the Jewish *Makkabiades*, or the communist *Spartakiades*, in the sense that they represented and furthered the unity of a specific group while explicitly excluding others, but did not serve any organised political movement.

If this study had been published some years ago it would come to an end at this point. But some experiences have made me add the following remarks especially for those who might deliberately or unconsciously misinterpret my argument. In the run-up to the 11th Olympic congress 1981 in Baden-Baden, I drew up an essay on the character and function of the "divine protection" (*Gottesschutz*), basically consisting of the same thoughts and evidence as presented in this paper, in order to emphasise the differences in meaning between the ancient and modern Olympic Games, in the light of the so-called "Hellas-Plan", i.e. the idea of holding the Olympic Games permanently in Greece.[117] As a result I was vehemently attacked by a periodical called *Sportecho*, published in the GDR, as well as by the *Olympische Panorama*, the international propaganda-institution of the Soviet NOK, arguing that anyone writing something like this was a "bomber" trying to "break up the Olympic movement" in a particularly sophisticated way under the guise of historical revisionism.[118] The polemical reaction shows that I hit a nerve for a particular group within the Olympic movement which still holds onto an anachronistic image of the ancient Olympic Games and sees their much-loved clichés, which are so easy to use in day-to-day journalism, threatened by my corrections. There is a certain piquancy to the fact that representatives of socialist states of all people evoke the norms and values of a period of slavery as an ideal worth emulating. This is neither the place for a detailed public discussion of the accusations – some of which are abstruse – nor for an elaboration of the political motivations involved. This would be especially unnecessary for all those who read my deliberations presented at the time. However, after the results presented here were explicitly confirmed by internationally acknowledged scholars working in the GDR[119] and, moreover, found their way into the new GDR standard publication on the History of Sports[120] it became possible for W. Schroeder in his recently published paper to utter the following thoughts (not fully accurate but still almost revolutionary compared to the former *communis opinio* of these circles) in the leading periodical of GDR sports-science: "the often praised Olympic peace, the so-called *ekecheiria*, was only a temporary truce, in territory which was steeped in conflict, without which an undisturbed journey to and from the sacred site of Olympia was impossible."[121] It seems that the bomb has been defused by socialist firefighters. The author is relieved.

The aims of the Olympic movement – to achieve world peace and international understanding – deserve the appreciation and the support of everyone in a position

[117] Cf. n. 7 on the so-called "Hellas-Plan" and the publication of Fricke [see n. 104].

[118] D. Wales, "Im Gespräch", in *Deutsches Sportecho*, 96, 19th May 1981, p.2; J. Gringaut, "Coubertin hat doch Recht gehabt", in *Olympisches Panorama* 2 (1982), p. 39.

[119] Cf. J. Ebert, *Olympia* [see n. 8], pp. 14–19.

[120] W. Eichel, *Illustrierte Geschichte der Körperkultur*. Vol. I: *Körperkultur in der Urgesellschaft und in der Antike. Körperkultur in Deutschland bis 1917*. Berlin [Ost] 1983, p. 37.

[121] W. Schroeder, "Olympismus als Bestandteil der Weltkultur und verpflichtendes historisches Erbe", in *ThPKK* 33 (1984), p. 804.

of responsibility, in and outside the world of sport. But this aim must be achieved in the same way as the other principles and demands of Olympism: by reliance on the universally recognised norms and values of our modern society rather than vague and inaccurate claims about the ancient Greeks. In that sense, my research is intended both to correct the often misunderstood historical facts and also, as a constructive critique of ideology, to serve as a point of reference in solving contemporary Olympic problems.

NOTES

For some time now I have been conducting comparative research on the meaning of the Olympic Games in antiquity and modern times. After the terrorist attack on the Israeli Olympic team in 1972 in Munich, frequent reference to the Olympic peace was made in public discourse. At that point I turned my attention to the problem of the Olympic truce, and in autumn 1974 gave a paper presenting some initial conclusions, outlining a new perspective and a new assessment of the issue, at the Deutsche Sporthochschule Köln. The subsequent publication was repeatedly postponed but a short version was published in English: "The nature and function of the so-called Olympic Truce in Greek Antiquity", in Uriel Simri (ed.) *1974 Proceedings of the Society on the History of Physical Education and Sport in Asia and Pacific Area*. Tel Aviv 1975, pp. 95–106, and under the title "The nature and function of the Olympic truce in ancient Greece", in History Committee of the International Council of Sport and Physical Education (ed.), *History of Physical Education and Sport. Research and Studies* 3, Tokyo 1975–6, pp. 37–52.

In the following years I discussed various aspects of my research with colleagues who encouraged me to publish my work in a unified form. A realisation of that aim, however, became impossible owing to administrative and organisational duties after taking over the directorship of the Institute for Sport History at the Deutsche Sporthochschule Köln. I did, however, make my first German outline available to I. Weiler (Graz), J. Ebert (Halle), R. Muth (Innsbruck) and A. E. Raubitschek (Palo Alto) who referred to my work in various papers and books in the years 1975–80, in which they mostly agreed with my arguments, but also corrected or added material which I had not been able to include or which I had overlooked. This leads to a rather odd situation where the authors I am referring to in this article relied in their own work on a first and incomplete version of my article. That becomes clear every so often in trains of thought and specific expressions in their work which I recognised as my own, but which I have not modified for this article. I want to thank the above-named colleagues, many of whom I have been friends with for many years now, for their inspiration and critique and even more for their patience. In addition, I especially thank H. Langenfeld (Münster) and H. Lee (College Park, Maryland) for reading the manuscript and pointing out a number of mistakes. I would also like to thank Y. Kempen for clarifying particular content-related questions with great knowledge and enthusiasm as well as helping to draw up the notes.

PART II

Gymnasion Education

Introduction to Part II

The history of athletic education runs in parallel with the history of athletic festivals on which section one has made a start. Here the iconic starting-point is Athens.[1] The *gymnasion* as a place of education and exercise was by no means unique to Athens, but the development of a systematic education system – the *ephebeia* – in the late classical period, where young men were trained in their late teens, was nevertheless a very distinctively Athenian invention. In addition, the Athenian art and literature of the fifth and fourth centuries, which lay at the heart of later imaginings of the Greek cultural heritage, is saturated with references to the *gymnasion* culture of the city. One might contrast the rigorous systems of Spartan physical education, which included, most notoriously, a public whipping contest. Spartan educational practice was renowned for its capacity to produce soldiers, but was nevertheless always viewed as an oddity, outside the Athenian-style mainstream of later athletic culture.[2]

Like Olympia, then, Athens was highly influential as a model for athletic practice in future ages, although it too had elements in its athletic culture which were quite unusual. Here we need to step back from the *gymnasion* for a moment to look at the city's festivals, in particular the great Athenian festival of the Panathenaia.[3] On one level this seems to have been intended to rival the *periodos* festivals outlined in the previous section, since it was founded in 566 BCE, just a few years after the *periodos* was formed. However, it also had unusual and distinctively Athenian features. For example it included team events, which were not part of standard athletic, Olympic practice, most importantly the torch race held between teams representing the various tribes of the city.[4] The four festivals of the *periodos* were held in relatively marginal, neutral spaces, not within powerful individual cities, and that seems to have been one of the things which made them so attractive as Greece-wide gathering spaces; the festivals of Athens, by contrast, were resolutely part of the city's wider democratic culture.

I mention the Panathenaia here partly because it is an important reference-point in placing the social role of the *gymnasion* in classical Athens, which is itself a much

---

[1] See Kyle (1987).
[2] See Kennell (1995), Hodkinson (1999), Kyle (2007) 180–97.
[3] See Neils (1992) and (1996); and for good summary, see Miller (2004b) 132–45 and Kyle (2007) 152–66.
[4] For further discussion of other distinctive features, see Fisher in chapter 3.

debated subject. On some accounts, the *gymnasion* was a highly elitist institution which stood apart from the more democratic culture of the Panathenaia, rather like the institution of the symposium or "drinking party". Nick Fisher's article in this section challenges that assumption, arguing that the *gymnasion* gradually became more socially inclusive, during the fifth and fourth centuries, than has previously been thought. Not all later commentators have agreed with his analysis,[5] but his work is nevertheless an important attempt to qualify over-simplistic generalisations about Athenian *gymnasion* culture, and one of the best statements of resistance to the model of Greek athletic participation as overwhelmingly elitist in this and later ages, which still holds sway in recent scholarship.[6] In the process, Fisher offers a wonderfully rich and vivid reading of the enormous body of evidence for Athenian athletics. He also discusses at length the links between *gymnasion* culture and homosexual eroticism which were so ingrained in Athenian culture.

The spread of *gymnasion* culture and ephebic education outside Athens is part of a broader story of the spread of Greek culture across the Mediterranean world and beyond in the early Hellenistic period, following the conquests of Alexander, and into the Roman world.[7] For example we have numerous inscriptions from imperial-period Athens which show that the *ephebeia* there was still going strong.[8] The expansion of the agonistic festival calendar, which is part of the same process, will be discussed in the introduction to section 3.

The role of the *gymnasion* in the Hellenistic and imperial periods is not an easy one to summarise. For example, the degree to which the *gymnasion* was an important venue for military education is a controversial subject. Current scholarly consensus is that the military element of *gymnasion* training was generally a key feature, especially in the Hellenistic period, but *gymnasion* training was not for the most part *exclusively* military. It could even include literate education, since we know of lectures held in *gymnasia* in many different cities. More importantly, the *gymnasion* was a place for young men to learn their role as citizens. It is no accident that ephebes were often allocated specific places within festival processions and auditoria, for their participation was viewed as important for the health of the city.[9] It is important also to pay some attention to the physical structure of *gymnasion* buildings.[10] Many cities built very elaborate *gymnasia*, at great expense, as we saw in the letters of Pliny and Trajan discussed in the introduction, another sign of their civic importance. Even if we accept Fisher's arguments for a more inclusive *gymnasion* culture in classical Athens, it is undeniable that social status was one of the rewards of a *gymnasion* education in the later Greek world. In Egypt (admittedly an unusual case) that status was codified through official membership of the "gymnasial class", which involved tax breaks.

How important was the *gymnasion* for those outside the *ephebeia*? Certainly the end of the *ephebeia* did not bring an end to *gymnasion* participation, since older

---

[5] See esp. Pritchard (2003) for disagreement.
[6] See the introduction to section 4 for further discussion.
[7] The most comprehensive recent treatment of the Hellenistic *gymnasion* is Kah and Scholz (2004), with essays mainly in German.
[8] See Newby (2005) 168–201.
[9] E.g. see Rogers (1991), esp. 58–60, 67–9, 114–15 on Ephesos in the Roman Empire.
[10] For good introductory discussion see Miller (2004b) 176–85.

men continued to exercise in the *gymnasion*. The most important category here is the category of the *neoi*, or "young men", older than ephebes, but still maintaining an official involvement with the *gymnasion* after the end of their *ephebeia*. It is also worth stressing that the highly focused, official uses of the *gymnasion* just outlined – for military and citizen training, and for preparation for participation in festival contests – were not the only ones which mattered. There is also a large amount evidence for exercise as a way of maintaining good health.[11] Medical writing on athletics is important here. For example, the great medical writer of the second century CE, Galen, denounces the way in which the extremes of athletic training for competition, encouraged by athletic trainers, damage the human body, while also in other works giving his own recommendations for healthy *gymnasion* exercise.[12] Most of the evidence we have even for this type of training is for men. We do see occasional signs of female participation in athletic training and also competition but the most striking thing about it is its rarity.[13] The *gymnasion* was overwhelmingly a masculine place in the ancient imagination, as indeed was the average agonistic festival.

Philippe Gauthier's article offers an outstanding introduction to these complex developments. He traces the spread and social role of the *gymnasion* in the Hellenistic world, and delves into the complex question of the educational activity which took place inside them. In doing so, he navigates with wonderful clarity through the large body of epigraphic material, with close attention to local variations. One particularly important text in that respect (edited and published by Gauthier elsewhere) is the *gymnasion* law of Beroia in Macedonia, dating probably from the early second century BCE, which outlines at length the regulations for the city's *gymnasion*, and gives us a vivid glimpse into the world of ancient politics and education in the process.[14] However, Gauthier also stresses the importance of looking beyond it to the many other, briefer *gymnasion* inscriptions which survive. Most importantly, he explores the tension between tradition and innovation which was inherent in these developments, showing that the *gymnasion* continued to be used as a venue for elite education and in the process became more embedded in the institutional landscape of the Greek city and brought with increasing frequency under civic control.[15] It was also an increasingly important vehicle for benefaction on the part of wealthy citizens, who would win honour from the city in exchange for their contribution to the enormous expenses of running and maintaining the building and its educational programmes.[16]

---

[11] E.g., see Dickie (1993).

[12] See König (2005) 254–300.

[13] See Scanlon (2002), esp. 98–198 for detailed discussion; also Lee (1984) and (1988b); and see Golden (1998) 123–40, Miller (2004b) 150–9 and Kyle (2007) 217–28 for good introductory synthesis.

[14] Gauthier and Hatzopoulos (1993), with commentary in French; the inscription is translated into English as text no. 185 in Miller (2004a).

[15] For further discussion of the *gymnasion* as institution, and of its close counterpart the *palaistra* or wrestling-school (which tended to be private institutions, rather than under control of the city), see Glass (1988); and for good introductory discussion, see Miller (2004b) 176–95.

[16] Aside from the physical fabric of the buildings and the wages of instructors, one key expense was the provision of olive oil: it was standard practice in the Greek *gymnasion* to cover oneself with oil prior to exercising (hence the repeated references "anointing" and "those who anoint themselves", that is, "those who exercise" in chapter 4).

3 Gymnasia *and the Democratic Values of Leisure**

NICK FISHER

INTRODUCTION

Elites define themselves in part by the fact that they have more time for leisure activities than the lower orders and have more wealth to spend on more highly valued and pleasurable activities and consumables; and they tend to pride themselves, and like to be envied, for the luxuriousness, taste, sophistication or intellectual superiority of whatever they choose to spend their time or money on. Attitudes of the less rich can vary significantly. The study of leisure has its history and its debates; a perceptive and useful survey, with application to the ancient world, is provided by Toner (1995). I wish to make two preliminary points. Many sociologists and historians have sought to restrict the notion of "mass leisure", or even "leisure" itself, to industrial societies, on the grounds that previously there was little or no consciousness of "free time" as opposed to work, and that the communally organised rituals of shared enjoyments lacked the elements, essential for "leisure", of self-determined, freely chosen pleasurable activities.[1] Such views seem unduly modernist and patronising, and fail to take account of sophisticated pre-industrial societies such as those of Greece and Rome, where, on the one hand, the philosophical elite developed an idealised view of *scholê* or *otium* (Greek and Latin respectively for "leisure"), the "best way to live", located above all in the reflective activities of high culture such as Aristotelian *theoria* ("contemplation");[2] and where, on the other, the people in Athens or Rome undeniably had choices of where to spend some free time (for example, in bars, at private parties or meetings of associations and clubs, in barbers' shops or cockfighting and gambling dens) as well as how far to participate in or observe a variety of collective enjoyments at festivals and games. Secondly, following the Aristotelian tradition, and the modern pioneer Veblen (1925), there is often an intellectualist assumption that leisure, or at least the more "important" elements of a culture's leisure activities, are exclusively the preserve of the propertied or "leisure" class. This equally patronising assumption should be challenged, and in studying the ancient world, and especially an ancient democratic society, we should avoid excessive concentration on

---

* Originally published in Cartledge, P., Millett, P. and von Reden, S. (eds) *Kosmos: Essays in Order, Conflict and Community in Classical Athens* (Cambridge: Cambridge University Press, 1998), pp. 84–108.
[1] Cf. Toner 1995, especially chs 1–4; also Burke 1995.
[2] On Aristotelian *scholê* cf. Stocks 1936; de Ste Croix 1981: especially 114–17.

elite perceptions and activities; there is an associated risk of failing to question another assumption, namely that ancient societies operated with a sharp and largely unbroken division between elite social activities, which needed wealth, style and *savoir faire*, and a more common or mass culture.[3] In fact Aristotle did not concern himself exclusively with the contemplative and restrainedly sympotic activities of the Academy or the Lyceum, the very activities which produced in time the linguistic switch from "leisure" to "school". In his treatment of friendship in both the *Eudemian* and the *Nicomachean Ethics*, he recognised the social importance for the community and for the overall health of the political system of the solidarity enjoyed by many voluntary religious and social organisations such as *thiasoi* or *eranoi* and of the collective sacrifices and festivals, which as he says both honoured the gods and provided relaxation and pleasure, and often coincided with the periods of the agricultural year when the people had most free time (*escholazon*).[4]

The relations between classes of citizens in Athenian society, and especially between the mass and the elite (in Ober's over-simple phrase), have been the subject of many analyses recently: in particular, the questions of the relationship between involvements and attitudes of Athenian citizens towards athletics, sex, food and drink and the democracy's success as a functioning and cohesive, and not too violent, community, are now receiving sustained treatment, if general agreement on central questions is far from in sight.[5] Gymnastic training and competition, and formal commensality, seem to have been the two central components of the traditional life-style of the archaic aristocrats, and there are undoubtedly many cases where democratic Athenian discourse expresses strong hostility and envy towards conspicuous, contemptuous or conspiratorial behaviour by elite members at *gymnasia* or *symposia*.[6] But here, as in most areas of the relations between social classes in Athens, both systematic contradictions and considerable change are to be expected. This paper suggests that significant aspects of these leisure activities and their rituals became more accessible to wider groups of citizens; that participation in such things became part of democratic expectations, at least for those roughly of hoplite status; and that such participation had both positive and negative effects, in the promotion of social order and social mobility, and in the creation of fresh forms of social and individual tensions.

In the archaic period in Athens, and similarly elsewhere in many Greek cities, a distinctive "aristocratic life-style" has been plausibly identified, derived from comparable institutions observable in the Homeric poems, and focused above all on male athletic and gymnastic activities during the hours of daylight, and in the evenings on the predominantly male convivial, potatory and sexual activities at *symposia* and *komoi*.[7] Yet how exclusively aristocratic these activities were even in

---

[3] Cf. Toner 1995: 26–33, Purcell 1995: 3–37, on the ambiguities of the Roman elites' attitudes: simultaneously extending leisure activities to their urban poor, worrying about the moral effects, and maintaining hierarchical divisions.

[4] Cf. on the difficulties and relationships of these two accounts to Aristotle, Schofield 1998 and on the associations of the *polis*, Arnaoutoglou 1998: 69.

[5] Cf. e.g. Ober 1989; Kyle 1987; Murray 1990; Davidson 1993 and 1997; Braund 1994; Luke 1994.

[6] E.g. Ar. *Kn.* 579–80, Dem. 54 *passim*. On the latter, see also Millett 1998: 203–4, 227–8.

[7] Murray 1994; 1983a and b; 1990; Kurke 1991; van Wees 1995.

archaic states is disputable. Young's provocative book on the professionalisation of the panhellenic athletics circuit argued that even in the archaic period less aristocratic but talented youths may have won victories and become wealthy and powerful, largely thanks to the value of the prizes on offer at some of the non-cyclical festivals; he suggested that some of the famous archaic and classical athletes found in the sources will in fact not have been of noble birth, or inherited wealth.[8] But strong counter-arguments have been urged, that while the prizes were significant, it is difficult to see how youths from unleisured backgrounds could find the time, support and training to compete at that level.[9]

My concern is rather with classical Athens, the most democratic and best attested city and period. Here Kyle has argued for a strictly limited increase in professionalism and lower-class involvement in serious athletics, but there is room for more argument.[10] Similarly differing views have been expressed on the extent of non-elite involvement in any forms of *symposia*.[11] This paper will concentrate on the issues of athletic competitions and training, while further work will reconsider settings of shared food and drink. The uniting aim will be to argue that attitudes of many ordinary Athenians to such things were much more varied and complex than merely feelings of exclusion, envy, resentment and hostility.

ATHLETIC AND GYMNASTIC PARTICIPATION

Young was able to point to a number of instances even in the archaic period of successful athletes who were originally poor and of non-noble birth: for example Glaukos the alleged plough-boy from Carystos who became first a champion boxer, then a governor of Camarina (Moretti no. 134; Paus. 6.10, Aeschin. 3.189–90 and *Scholia*), the goat herding hare-courser Polymestor of Miletos (Phil. *Gymn.* 13, Moretti no. 79), or the Olympic victor for whom, allegedly, Simonides wrote an epigram, celebrating how he had previously carried fresh fish from Argos to Tegea in a rough basket on his shoulders (Aristotle, *Rhet.* 1365a20–6, Simon. *Ep.* 41 Page).[12] All these cases, if they reflect even rare occurrences, offer hints that certain low-grade occupations might, despite anti-*banausic* prejudices, provide a good basic training, whether for strength or stamina, which contributed to later success in boxing or long distance running.

For Athens three texts, it can be argued, suggest a consciousness of increased non-elite athletic activity at least from the later fifth century. First, Isocrates' defence given to the younger Alcibiades includes an alleged justification of Alcibiades *père* for his decision to concentrate on the most expensive and exclusive form of Olympic competition, the chariot-races (*hippotrophia*), because he saw

---

[8] Young 1984; some support in Golden 1990: 71–2, and N. Richardson in *CAH* v² 1994: 232–6.
[9] E.g. Instone 1986; Dickie 1984; Kyle 1985; also Kurke 1991: 3.
[10] Kyle 1987: 113–15, 127–9.
[11] E.g. Murray in Murray (ed.) 1990: 149–53; and Cooper/Morris ibid. 66–81, see them as essentially elitist, while Schmitt-Pantel and Pellizer in Murray 1990: 14–26 and 177–84, and E. Bowie 1995 contemplate wider participation.
[12] As Kyle points out (1984: 141), the (mythologising) details of some of these cases arouse doubts, and Aristotle explicitly adduces the fish-porter's achievement as an exceptional case.

that in gymnastic events "some of the athletes were low born, lived in small *poleis* ("cities") and were poorly educated" (16.33–4). For some, this is good evidence that at least from the late fifth century on some non-elite and poorly educated youths – and probably in Athens as well as in "smaller cities" – entered Olympic competition.[13] But others dismiss this text from consideration, on the grounds that Alcibiades could look down on almost anyone, and this was the sort of thing that any noble athletes would say in justifying their concentration on chariot-racing.[14] But we should focus attention not so much on whether, or why, Alcibiades might have thought this, as on why Isocrates thought it an appropriate sentiment to have young Alcibiades ascribe to his father in a court case. It was probably an effective gambit to give Alcibiades an authentic aristocratic and uppity tone, and elaborate on his desire to be envied for his actions of extravagance which benefited the city, such as his liturgies and chariot-victories, the ones that brought the most extreme form of athletic *kudos* ("glory") to victor and city.[15] But it would harm the case to attribute to him a statement that was totally misleading as well as somewhat arrogant. One could yet argue that the three terms used in these alleged sneers by the elder Alcibiades were intended to be applied equally to all his supposed instances, who were all alike ill-born, from more insignificant cities and badly-educated. In this case he was presented as, perhaps more excusably, if no less snobbishly, attacking exclusively non-Athenians, and the passage, strictly speaking, provides information about social mobility in other, smaller states, where perhaps greater state effort was put into encouraging victors. But one could still argue that it would be unlikely that nothing comparable to the rise of a Glaukos could happen in democratic Athens, and that awareness of some such cases nearer to home would add plausibility to the sneers.[16] Thus the text in its context may imply more about Athenian athletics than, strictly speaking, it claims.

Two other general texts may further advance the suggestion that athletics might lead directly to wealth accretion and social mobility. In the anti-athlete tirade found in Euripides' satyr-play *First Autolykos* (fr. 441N², quoted by Athenaeus 413c–f), the first criticisms are that athletes "do not learn how to live well, nor could they: how could a man who is a slave to his jaw and defeated by his belly, attain wealth superior to his father's? Nor are they able to cope with being poor, nor can they adapt to ill fortune; not accustomed themselves to proper habits, they find it hard to change to fit difficult times." This line of argument –no doubt exaggerated, and not necessarily of course reflecting Euripides' own view, but still a serio-comic presentation in an Athenian festival – seems to assume that some serious athletes went into the game expecting to get richer, and found it hard to cope with their winnings, or still harder to cope with relative failure. This text thus seems to assume that panhellenic athletics could be perceived as a major source of new wealth and of social mobility, as well as a route to city-given honours – such as crowns, statues,

---

[13] Cf. Young 1984: 154ff.; Pleket 1975: 49–89, and (a direct response to Young) 1988: 147–60.
[14] Dickie 1984: 248–9; Kyle 1987: 136.
[15] Cf. on this *kudos*, Kurke 1993.
[16] Cf. Young 1984: 100–2; Golden (1990: 72) adds the possibility that Melesias, the father of Thucydides, founded the reputation and high marriage connections of his distinguished family through his skill as an athlete and trainer.

dining at the Prytaneion – and perhaps political influence.[17]

Secondly, the Old Oligarch takes up – characteristically – different positions on gymnastic activity in Athens, and appears also to attribute – again characteristically – contradictory attitudes to the people. At 1.13 he appears to say that the *demos* ("people") "has put down those who train and practise culture, thinking that it is not a fine activity, but realising that they are not capable of engaging in these studies";[18] but immediately afterwards he comments that the people, the recipients of the expenditure of the *choregoi*, *gymnasiarchoi* and *trierarchoi*, not only enjoy the money, but participate, sing, run, dance and row in the ships.[19] And later, at 2.10, he claims first, as before, that the *demos* enjoys the benefits of the sacrifices and the festivals without paying for them; and then argues that "while the rich have some of their own private *gymnasia*, baths and changing rooms, the *demos* has built for itself exclusively many wrestling grounds (*palaistrai*), changing rooms and public baths, and get more benefit from those than do the few and the prosperous".[20] So according to this text, probably of the 420s, members of the Athenian *demos* are simultaneously sneering at those of the rich who spend a good deal of their leisure in athletics, music and the arts;[21] while also themselves engaging enthusiastically in choruses and races, and acquiring training facilities where they (men and boys, presumably) can practise their gymnastics and wrestling, and can change and bathe. Since the Old Oligarch might have preferred to represent the *demos* as idle, sneering, or cheering spectators of the cultural and athletic activities of the elite, passive beneficiaries of their liturgical expenditures, it seems better to suppose that there is some substance at least to the more unusual of his remarks, that there was widespread participation at festivals and a growth of new *gymnasia* and *palaistrai* aimed at a much wider clientele.[22]

The growth of athletic training in Athens has been well described by Kyle. Already for Pindar and Bacchylides, Athens was notable for providing excellent

---

[17] On the frequency of athletic themes and discussions in satyr-plays, cf. Seaford's 1984 edition of Eur. *Cyclops* 39–40; Sutton 1980: 60; Kyle 1987: 128–30. Seaford's explanation, that men and boys dressed as satyrs may have competed in races at the Anthesteria, is perhaps too specific to be satisfying. Also relevant may be that naked, cavorting and phallic satyrs were the ideal figures to parody athletes' concern with exaggerated and self-obsessed public displays of the body beautiful. It is tempting to suppose a subtle connection, in the title of Euripides' satyr play, with the currently notorious young athlete Autolykos – with an ambiguous effect rather like that which could be achieved by denoting an attractive youth as "pretty" (*kalos*) on a pot (cf. Kyle 1987: 128, and below n. 60).

[18] τοὺς δὲ γυμναζομένους αὐτόθι καὶ τὴν μουσικὴν ἐπιτηδεύοντας κατελέλυκεν ὁ δῆμος: the verb seems to mean, unusually, "strongly disparage", rather than "destroy" or "abolish".

[19] The contradiction is observed by Ridley 1979: 541–3; Kyle in Neils (ed.) 1992: 98. Cf. also Schmitt Pantel 1992: 231–3.

[20] Cf. Delorme 1960: 258; Kyle 1987: 68, 134; it is puzzling that the author emphasises private *gymnasia* and public *palaistrai* rather than the other way round; but perhaps he is being deliberately paradoxical, and exaggerating the self-assertiveness and participation, at least in wrestling activities, of the "people".

[21] Cf. the pleas of the chorus in Ar. *Knights* 580 that, provided that they are seen to fight nobly for the city, the audience should not show envy towards them with their long hair and their strigilled bodies.

[22] Cf. Kyle 1987: ch. 3, with a useful survey of the evidence for the growth of athletic facilities; also Kyle in Neils (ed.) 1992: 77–101. Cf. also the Old Oligarch's similar observations at 2.7, and 2.9, where the author implies that the luxury imports – "kinds of festive fare" (*tropous euochion*) – can be experienced by the *demos* in general, not just by the rich, and that the *demos* enjoys being feasted while the rich pay, with Braund 1994; and below p. 74.

trainers for panhellenic athletes, especially wrestlers (Bacch. 12. 190–8; Pind. *Nem.* 5. 48–9, *Ol.* 8. 54–66, *Nem.* 4.93–6, 6. 66–9: the two big names were Menandros and Melesias, the father of the politician Thucydides). From the mid-fifth century on, increasing numbers of trainers and owners of *palaistrai* can be named; by the early fourth century, educational discussions in Plato, Isocrates and Aristotle suggest that elaborate training techniques have become standard and widespread, designed alike to maintain levels of general fitness, to suit the needs of boys, or older athletes, to prepare competitors for the running and other contests, or to provide advanced individual programmes for those seeking to win at the highest, panhellenic, level (see especially Pl. *Prot*, 326b, *Politicus* 294d–e; Isocr. 15. 183; Arist. *Pol.* 1288b 10–20, 1338b 39–1339a 10).[23]

Consideration of the manpower demands of Athenian festivals and games can strengthen the case that athletic competition and training, at these less elevated levels, did involve very extensive participation, parallel indeed to participation in political life. Three points emerge. First, while one cannot calculate with exactitude the number of competitors needed in all the athletic or gymnastic events in the Athenian calendar, from the Panathenaea onwards, such calculation as can be done confirms that so many were needed (certainly thousands rather than hundreds) that competitors, especially for the closed events, must have been drawn from far beyond the elite families. Second, as Osborne argues, the proliferation of competitions and their tribal organisation, involving large numbers, with prizes given not just to the winners but to the first four places, were felt to be highly valuable to the *polis*; they offered training for the young, mitigated the effects of excessive competition, and built up community spirit within age-classes and within the Kleisthenic tribes.[24] Third, a great many of the competitors were boys and youths, learning how to be citizens.

A particular issue concerns the involvement of the ephebes. This is not the place to enter the long debates on the existence and form of the early *ephebeia*, the nature of the changes introduced c. 335, and the question of whether it was, at different times, restricted to those in the hoplite census and above.[25] But it seems most likely that from the early to mid-fourth century, if not earlier, there was a two-year cycle of relatively low-key and limited competitive and military activities, involving many, perhaps most, of the eighteen- to nineteen-year-old new citizens (there were between 450 and 550 ephebes a year in the 334–332 period; how many in the pre-Lycurgan period is unclear).[26] Sekunda has recently argued, with much plausibility, that a major feature of the first year of training was preparation for and participation in the tribal torch races, most importantly at the Panathenaea, organised by the *gymnasiarchoi*, and that this activity may well have involved all the ephebes. These torch races certainly involved contestants of widely varying fitness and speed; fatter and slower runners might apparently find themselves mocked and hit

[23] Kyle 1987: 141–5.
[24] The notoriously packed programme of festivals with varied athletic competitions has been recently and helpfully surveyed and discussed by Osborne 1993: 20–37; also Kyle, in Neils (ed.) 1992: 80–3, 98–9, who is again perhaps a little dismissive of the possibility of wider participation in the "mass" events. On the prizes, also Kyle in Neils (ed.) 1996: 106–36.
[25] Cf. e.g. Reinmuth 1971; Vidal-Naquet 1986a: chs 5 and 6; Winkler 1990b: 25–8.
[26] Hansen 1985: 47ff.

by the spectators for their lack of fitness (Ar. *Frogs* 1087ff.). Important evidence is provided by Xenophon's pamphlet of the mid-fourth century, which gives advice to "those instructed to exercise ... in the gymnasia", and to those "instructed to guard in the garrisons and to serve as peltasts" (*Poroi* 4. 51–2). These young men engaged in some form of organised youth training can only be the ephebes as they existed in this period (and Aeschines 1. 49 and 2. 167 is good evidence for two-year service for youths explicitly called *epheboi*).[27] Sekunda's attractive suggestion is that sons of hoplites served in the garrisons, and sons of thetes as peltasts; probably neither group involved compulsory service in this period, which is certainly unlikely for sons of thetes, but social pressures and awareness of future military demands are likely to have produced quite a high percentage of able-bodied hoplite youths in the *ephebeia*.

Xenophon's advice that their levels of fitness would be much higher in the *gymnasia* if they were regularly supplied with maintenance, rather than, as at this time, being trained for the torch races under the command of the gymnasiarchs (*Poroi* 4. 5–2: cf. also the general advice to the young to keep fit in Xen. *Mem.* 3.12), suggests that some training, if perhaps rudimentary, for torch races was the essential athletic element of the first of the two years of ephebic activities. These ephebes were probably also involved in other ritual and athletic events, as they certainly were, more intensively, from the Lycurgan period onwards; from the earlier fourth century at least they probably not only participated in the torch-races, but also entered the Panathenaic and other games in the beardless category.[28]

Also at the Panathenaea there were other liturgically organised events for young citizens and future citizens, which also carried evident ideological associations with the acquisition of allegedly "transferable" skills which would be of use in a hoplite battle, and more generally with proofs of manhood. The pyrrhic dances were for boys, beardless youths and men, offered high prizes, and may or may not have been tribally organised, but involved at least three teams, and maybe many more, in each of the three categories.[29] They were forms of military "ballet", at which nude males danced with spears and shields, in imitation of the defensive and aggressive moves of fighters (see, for example, Pl. *Laws* 815a). Various aetiologies for the *pyrrhichê* were in use, in different parts of Greece, including a cluster associated with Achilles and Neoptolemos/Pyrrhos, leaping at Patroclos's pyre, in triumph after defeating Eurypylos, or down from the Wooden Horse.[30] In relation to the Panathenaea, however, Athenians thought above all of acts of Athena, at her birth, or more significantly at her victories in the Gigantomachia; the derivation of Pallas, the "leaper", from *pallesthai* ("to leap") is found in Plato (*Laws* 796b, *Crat.* 406d–7a), and conveyed, in all probability, as well by her pose on many Panathenaic vases, flanked on their columns by those powerful symbols of manhood, the

---

[27] Sekunda 1990, in a new interpretation of *IG* II² 1250; see also Whitehead 1991: 42–4 for improved restorations, but accepting the ephebes' involvement; earlier, Gauthier 1976 ad loc. had properly emphasised the importance of the Xenophon passage for the mid-fourth century *ephebeia*.

[28] Cf. Lonsdale 1993: 162–8; e.g. *IG* II² 2311.

[29] Davies 1967: 36–7; Osborne includes them in his list of tribal competitions, without argument, in Sommerstein et al., 1993: 30–1.

[30] Borthwick 1967: 18–23; Vidal-Naquet 1986b: 136; Lonsdale 1993: 140–9.

fighting cocks.³¹ The sources (especially Plato, *Laws* 796) explicitly emphasise the importance in training programmes of future and current fighters of the defensive and offensive moves made by pyrrhic dancers;³² its importance in the *polis* rituals is exemplified by the outrage displayed by the old fashioned Stronger Argument of the *Clouds*, who is upset that modern youth cannot adequately raise their shields when they are called on (*deon autous*) to perform the dance for Athene at the Panathenaea (988–9 – and so, as a side effect, deprive the boy-obsessed old man "of his favourite sight" [Dover 1968b: *ad loc.*]). Connections between the training activities in *gymnasia* and military preparations were strongly reinforced by use of the Lyceum, established or rebuilt by Pericles, and to a lesser extent of the Academy, as training and parade grounds for the hoplites and the cavalry.³³

Youthful physical promise was probably central to the "manhood" contest, the *euandria* at the Panathenaea: this contest was restricted to Athenians, organised tribally, with prizes of an ox (for the tribe) and a shield (probably for the winner).³⁴ It is described as a contest of "physical size and strength" (Xen. *Mem.* 3.3.13: *megethos* and *rhomē*) and also of the appropriate young men's beauty (Athen. 565f.: "they choose the most beautiful men and instruct them to carry first" (*protophorein*)). No source explictly mentions the ages of the contestants, but possible parallels from Crete or Elis, and the plausible iconographic examples proposed by Neils (in Coulson et al., 1994: 154ff., cf. below), suggest youths, either pre-ephebe or more probably ephebes; and the shield-prize would be, as in Crete, a proof of especial readiness for military service.³⁵ In *Mem.* 3.3.12–13 Xenophon's Sokrates suggests, encouraging a young cavalry commander, that the Athenians did especially well in musical choruses at Delos, or in *euandria* contests, not so much thanks to their inherently greater musical or physical qualities, as to their keenness for honour (*philotimia*), meaning in this context the collective drive to win the honour of victory which motivated them all and above all their gymnasiarch, who provides the parallel for Sokrates' advisee.³⁶

Summing up on the question of numbers of participants, on Davies' calculations (1967: 33–40) in years of the quadrennial Great Panathenaea, about fifty *gymnasiarchoi*, and about thirty in other years, were charged with financing, and organising the training of teams of athletes, war-like dancers or posing beauties, through the central liturgy-system; one might mention also the *choregoi* who trained singers and dancers in dramatic choruses, many of whom were youths or boys, and needed to attain considerable levels of fitness and endurance.³⁷ This is probably

---

[31] Poursat 1968; Ridley 1979: 543–8; Pinney 1988; Lonsdale 1993: 150–2. On fighting cocks, Csapo 1993.
[32] See especially Lonsdale 1993: 137–9.
[33] Cf. Kyle 1987: 75, 80; Ogden in Lloyd (ed.) 1996: 128–9. Humphreys 1974: 90 is perhaps oversceptical.
[34] *IG* II² 2311.75–6; Arist. *Ath. Pol.* 60.3; Rhodes 1981 ad loc. There was a *euandria* contest also at the Thesea, at least in the second century, *IG* II² 956, 48ff.; on the classical Thesea, cf. also Calame 1996: 153–5; Schmitt Pantel 1992: 136ff.
[35] Ephoros *FGH* 70F140; Pl. *Symp.* 182a–b.
[36] Cf. also Crowther 1985; Neils, in Coulson et al., 1994: 154ff; Goldhill 1998: 108; and, with a different suggestion, Boegehold, in Neils (ed.) 1996: 95–105. Cf. also Xen. *Hipp.* 1.26.
[37] Winkler's bold hypothesis (1990b) that all dramatic *choreutai* ("chorus members") were ephebes, though attractive, seems to lack sufficient evidence; cf. Vidal-Naquet 1986b: 137.

an underestimate, as we hear of some further city festivals involving competitions such as torch-races (cf. the list of torch-races in Rhodes 1981: *ad Ath.Pol.* 57.1); and there were other competitions too at more localised festivals such as those held in the demes.[38] Each year, then, perhaps about fifty elite rich men went looking to make up their teams for these competitions, seeking the thousands of athletic and fit boys, youths and men they needed. In part selectors would have been guided by past form, but they must also have felt a constant concern to seek out new talent, by speaking to relations, fellow-demesmen and friends, and keeping their eyes open at the various *gymnasia* and training grounds and consulting those who ran and trained at them. Possible glimpses of conversations at these settings can be found in Theophrastos' *Characters*: the disruptive chatterer, the *lalos*, hangs round schools and *palaistrai*, interrupting the boys' learning processes (7.4); the unnamed show-off who takes up the second half of 5 liked to be seen in the places where the greatest crowds and excitement were to be found, in the *agora* by the bankers, in the *gymnasia* in the places where the ephebes worked out, and in the theatre, in the seats next to the generals (he also has his own little wrestling ground with real sand, and ball-park, which he hires out to sophists, weapons-trainers and musicians) (5.7, 9).[39] Once gymnasiarchs had formed their teams, and, when dealing with boys, had persuaded their fathers that all would be organised properly and with decorum (cf. Antiphon 6. 11ff.), their own *philotimia* would encourage them to see that keen co-operation in pursuit of the prize held the group together and developed the collective training and levels of fitness.

In these ways then, after the establishment of these elaborate festival competitions, at the time of Kleisthenes or soon after, the democratic system gradually, but positively, encouraged much wider participation in athletics and gymnastics, at least among the hoplite class and perhaps further. The liturgical organisation fostered the constant co-operation, in athletics and in choruses (and even more clearly on the ships), of elite leaders, with large numbers of collective teams, usually from the same tribe, engaged in intense and physically taxing competition. This will have helped to increase tribal solidarity and to break down class suspicions and hostilities. Against the grumbles of the Old Oligarch (1.13, 2.9–10) and Socrates in Xenophon's *Oikonomikos* (2.4–9), one can place Ischomachos' different view at Xen. *Oik.* 11.9, or Xenophon's Socrates in *Mem.* 3.5. 16ff., where the indiscipline in the infantry and cavalry is contrasted with the discipline and attention to orders in the navy, and the athletic and choral teams, or, more impressively yet, the powerful speech by Cleocritos the herald of the mysteries at *Hell.* 2.4.19–22, appealing to shared festival and military experience. Nor should one forget the alleged generosity and consideration of the young long-haired Mantitheos, countering the suspicion against him for his participation in the cavalry under the Thirty (*Lysias* 16).[40] The prizes on offer for these competitions, and the concomitant rewards and honours

---

[38] Cf. also Whitehead 1986: 224.

[39] On this unidentifiable character, see J. S. Rusten in the Loeb volume (1993). Theophrastos' *Characters* is a valuable source for many aspects of Athenian society at various social levels, though one must remember its date, towards the end of the classical democracy (c. late 320s?), its concentration on undesirable social types, and its author's somewhat elitist and snobbish viewpoint: see Rusten's Introduction, and Millett 1991: 5–6 and *passim*, and now also Lane Fox 1996.

[40] Cf. Cartledge in Easterling and Muir 1985: 116–18; Whitehead 1986: 234–52.

and general fame in the community, must have made it easier for young, not very rich, athletes, to train, become known, and proceed to the open individual events, and hence to increase their wealth and renown. Thus this need to attract more competitors helps to explain the growth of *gymnasia*, *palaistrai* and trainers, and the rush of youths eager to get trained; it also suggests that poor but able young athletes could well have found support and forms of patronage to develop their careers.

EROTIC PURSUITS

One vitally important aspect of the activities and the atmosphere at the *gymnasia* demands attention at this point. *Gymnasia* and *palaistrai* were perhaps the single most important settings for arousal of erotic interest – doubtless at various levels of intensity – and for the formation and development of pederastic relationships: "Happy is he who exercises in the *gymnasion* when in love, and going home sleeps all day with the lovely boy", as the "Theognis" couplet has it (1335–6).[41] Less explicitly, there is often a strongly felt erotic charge in Pindar's praise of the beauty and strength of youthful victors; his odes play elegantly, through his mythical narratives as well as with his direct praise, with the ideas of the beautiful athletes as objects of desire both for older lovers and for girls for whom marriages might be arranged.[42] For Athens, late archaic and early classical vases (roughly from 560 to 470) repeatedly associate scenes of homosexual courtship and play with gymnastic settings and accessories;[43] from the mid-fifth century abundant literary evidence attests pervasive opportunities for ogling comments, pick-ups and the development of serious relationships, and the tensions and problematic decisions thereby produced; one can find also hints that some social mobility might be involved.[44] Platonic settings reveal best the general excitement at attractive new boys at the *palaistrai*; most attention is aroused, it is true, when the beautiful new youth who attracts a crowd of *erastai* ("lovers") succeeds in matching up his lovely body with a noble family tree, and a soul apt for learning and philosophy, as in both the *Charmides* and the *Lysis*; but it seems possible that the relief and pleasure with which "Socrates" learns that the new lovely is also of known and good family may reflect an awareness that he might well not be (*Lysis* 204e, *Charm.* 154a–b). Most importantly, the *Phaedrus*, the *Symposium* and other protreptic documents demonstrate the intensity of competition between would-be lovers for pretty boys and youths, and boys' competition to attract attention from famous young or not so young men; and they illustrate the dangers of teasing, exploitation and betrayal, on both sides (Pl. *Phaedr.* and *Symp. passim*; Dem. 60). The theme is equally central to Xenophon's *Symposium*: its setting is a grand party given for Autolykos the son of Lykon, who has just won the boy's *pancration*, by his lover Callias, the richest of the

---

[41] Cf. also e.g. Pl. *Laws* 636f., *Phaedr.* 255b; with Dover 1978: 54–7, 154–160; Buffière 1980; Ogden in Lloyd ed. 1996: 129–31. For the intimate associations on vases of *palaistrai* and homosexual courtship and activity, see e.g. Shapiro 1981; Kilmer 1993a: 12, 16–17, 88–9, 93–7.
[42] This is well brought out by Instone 1990: 34–9.
[43] Cf. e.g. Bérard et al. 1989: 81ff.; Bremmer in Murray 1990: 143–5; Koch-Harnack 1983; Kilmer 1993a: 81–6.
[44] Cf. Dover 1978: 44–9, 53–7; Foucault 1985: 231–7; Vlastos 1987: 95–6.

Athenians. The party serves to display Autolykos' very considerable attractiveness as a catch to their fellow-Athenians, and then to the readers (Xen. *Symp. passim*).

Laws – in operation at least by the fourth century, and naturally described as Solonian by Aeschines – protected boys at *gymnasia* as well as at schools (Aeschin. 1.9–11), and in the developed Lycurgan *ephebeia* specified officials, over forty, regulated the morality of the youths (Arist. *Ath. Pol.* 42). Old Comedy liked to play with the running joke that newly successful individuals, including comic poets, might use their fame for sexual conquests. Aristophanes repeated his claim that he never used his position as a successful poet to try to pick up boys down at the *palaistrai* (*Wasps* 1023–5, *Peace* 762–3); there was apparently, according to the *Scholia* on both passages, a dig here at his rival Eupolis, who responded – to what may well have been a running series of gags – with shameless boasts, allegedly in his *Autolykos* (on which see also below). These jokes rest on the assumption that any member of the social elite, especially a new member, might choose to use his increased pulling power to advantage to persuade an especially attractive and athletically renowned boy to sleep with him. Some of the dangers and propensity for violence in these relationships were paraded before the courts in the lawsuit between Archippos and Teisis, our fragments of Lysias' speech for the case suggest that the initial insults, involving aspersions about Teisis' relationship with his guardian and lover Pytheas, took place at a *palaistra*, and the outcome was, allegedly, a particularly sadistic and degrading whipping inflicted by the "couple" on Archippos (Lys. fr. 75Th = XVII G–B).[45]

Our sources naturally concentrate on spectacularly pretty boys, the real beauties like Lysis or Charmides, or on famous lovers, such as Callias or Eupolis. If such boys had to cope with a pack of pursuers, led by the old rich, or famous new arrivals on the scene, each hoping to be able to boast of enjoying the beauty, then meanwhile other less favoured boys might have to choose between less numerous, and less glamorous, and in many cases perhaps older, suitors. The simple "pederasty model" of Greek homosexuality, involving an "educational" relationship between a beardless (or downy) adolescent and an unmarried youth in his twenties appears indeed to have been the culturally dominant norm; but the dominance of these "protocols" in reality has been overestimated in much recent work. The vase evidence shows a range of age differences, and occasionally apparent contemporaries involved, and may perhaps hint at, rather than display, anal pleasures; and literary evidence too attests age variations, and above all, perhaps, suggests that many men continued to pursue, casually or seriously, boys, adolescents, or older youths, throughout their later (usually married) lives.[46]

---

[45] Cf. Fisher 1992: 39–40; Cohen 1995: 137–9.

[46] For the model, cf. e.g. Halperin 1990: 130–7; Buffière 1980: 123–48; Bremmer 1980; important qualifications in Hupperts in Christiansen et al. 1988: 255–68; Ogden in Lloyd ed. 1996: 107–11; Osborne and Frontisi-Ducroux, in Kampen (ed.) 1996: 65–6, 81–95; and Davidson 1997: especially 167–82, 250–63. A long fragment from a fourth-century comic poet, Mnesimachos, instructs a slave to go to the "Herms", in the North-West of the Agora, where the cavalry-Phylarchs, and in particular one Pheidon, will be instructing the "attractive students" (i.e. new, young and rich members of the cavalry) in mounting and dismounting, and invite them to a highly (and fantastically) elaborate dinner, *symposion* and rave-up (fr. 4K–A = Athen. 402e–3d).

Now in all these circumstances of social and sexual opportunities and tensions, it seems likely that boys who showed some athletic talent (for example in a tribal competition) but lacked wealthy backgrounds (say sons of comfortable hoplites), could have been helped to train, and encouraged to go in for further, more ambitious, contests, by liturgists, or trainers; and if they were at all attractive as well, some hangers-on at the gym might try to help in the training process, as part of their claims to be accepted as lovers, or equally might help them diversify into politics, rhetoric or philosophy. Thus in principle such concurrences of interests should have created increased opportunities for athletic, gymnastic or political competition for those of new families, forged bonds of friendship across social divides, and helped to create erotic relationships.[47] In many cases these could have passed from the intensity, or pain, of love or strong desire, to a more lasting friendship, mutual pledges and reciprocal assistance (as many of the speeches of the *Phaedrus* anticipate: 232e–234c – in the Lysianic speech; 256a–b, and 256c–d, the more and the less philosophical pairs in Socrates' later, serious analysis).[48] In other cases, love and admiration may have turned to distaste or hatred, especially if fed by jealousy, gossip or fear of gossip. One may adduce here the "paradoxical" but in many ways plausible remarks in favour of relationships involving the non-lover in the *Phaedrus*, emphasising the damage that can be done by a boastful, jealous or resentful lover (231a, 232a–234a–b); and also the other disclaimer in the *parabasis* from the *Wasps*, that:

> nor, if any lover full of hatred at his boyfriend pressed him to make the boy the butt of his comedy, has he ever gone along with anyone like that, keeping always his purpose straight, so as not to make pimps of the Muses with whom he has his dealings.[49] (1025–8)

Further evidence to support the idea that such athletic relationships, with erotic overtones, attracted public attention and may have led to the advancement of poorer Athenian youths as well as involving dangers, may be tentatively sought both in iconography and in speeches, above all in Aeschines' speech against Timarchos. First, this idea may help the explorations of some obscure details in early-fifth-century Athenian artistic representation, discussed interestingly by Sitta von Reden and by Jennifer Neils. Von Reden considers a number of late archaic and early classical red-figure vases which seem to portray interaction between young adult males and younger men and boys, and include a money pouch being offered by the *erastes* to the *paidika* ("beloved") in gymnastic contexts;[50] on the other hand, sympotic scenes do not show gifts of money being offered. Von Reden (1995: ch. 9)

---

[47] On these issues of the nature of friendships in Athens, cf. Foxhall 1998: 52–67; my sympathies will be seen to be with Foxhall in emphasising the possibilities of strongly affectionate or passionate elements, as well as instrumental ones, in many such relationships.

[48] At 256b one might suggest that the reference to the noblest couple, those who have grown full wings and subdued the vice-ridden parts of their souls, "winning the first of three falls in the real Olympics" includes an allusion to the earthly Olympics that were a goal for many a more ordinary pair of lovers.

[49] Perhaps here too there is intended to be understood a joke at Eupolis' expense, as the scholia imply.

[50] Indications of gymnastic contexts, such as strigils, sponges and oil flasks may also themselves have sexual connotations, and many perhaps often hint at anal possibilities, as Kilmer 1993a: ch. 6 suggests (cf. also Frontisi-Ducroux in Kampen ed. 1996: 90, 96).

suggests that the relevant difference may be that the *gymnasia* were seen as settings of more public male control, appropriate leisure for the community, and displays of manly virtue (*aretē*), while sympotic contexts speak of private enjoyment, mutual pleasures and the possibility of excess; hence she argues that money is acceptable in the context of gymnastic and athletic contests because it "had a positive image in the exchanges that linked victor, poet and audience, as the choral lyric of the same period suggests" (1995: 205f.). The analysis seems to me to gain force if we suppose that at least in the archaic period vase painters could suggest a precise function of money in this exchange (as in the exchanges between city and victor, or praise-poet and victor's family), as a direct and positive part in the relationship between trainer/lover and young athlete; it was acceptable for members of the elite in athletic contexts to offer "sponsorship" money at the preparatory stage, as well as "friendship" and support, as it was recognised that money helped the young achieve excellence in these vital areas of male competition. Money-pouches at the *symposion*, on the other hand, might suggest much too strongly that money was being directly exchanged for sexual favours.

Neils (in Coulson et al., 1994: 154–9), in a search for images of victors in the *euandria*, focuses on a series of vases showing beautiful youths, often specifically designated as *kaloi* ("beautiful") being crowned by older men (and admired by other men), and often carrying branches, wearing red sashes or ribbons round their arms and thighs, sometimes "liberty caps", and nothing else. In one such cup, by Douris, whose work contains an unusually large number of gymnastic and athletic scenes, we see on the outside a youth with the cap being admired by older bearded men, while on the interior such an older man holds out a money pouch. Neils suggests this might be understood as the gymnasiarch financing the youth for the tribal contest of the *euandria*. But equally here too the idea may be that the viewer, reaching the interior of the cup, may suspect the hint of an erotic relationship behind the idea of *euandria* "sponsorship".[51] Scenes of homosexual courtship and activities diminish almost to nothing on Athenian vases from about 470 BCE, for reasons that are still far from clear. One might suggest that among the reasons may have been that homosexual relationships, based on *gymnasia*, athletic and military training, and then on training for rhetoric and other more directly political activities, became simultaneously more widespread among wider circles of Athenians and more problematised, both morally and in terms of threats of legal proceedings, and so representations of them came to be avoided. If so, scenes combining money and *gymnasia* seem particularly sensitive, if they implied relationships indicating unequal "patronage" involving cash between older and younger citizens, as youths had to be careful for their reputations.[52]

---

[51] While it is tempting to follow Ogden's view (1996), that homosexual activity was institutionalised and important (rather than just casual and common as in many armies) in the Athenian land army, as it probably was in the Spartan and Theban armies, a major problem is the lack of any obious connection between the principles of organisation of the army, based on the Kleisthenic structures of tribes, trittyes and demes, and the main settings for the formation of serious relationships in the *gymnasia*, frequented largely on an indivdual, not a deme, basis. Tribally organised contests might seem to go some way to fill this gap, but not far enough.

[52] On the relative absence of patronage-relations in general in Athens, Millett in Wallace-Hadrill ed.

One might have hoped that Athenian prosopography would help this approach. Kyle's useful survey of known Athenian athletes presents a number of cases, from the mid-fifth century on, where panhellenic victors or otherwise famous athletes come from otherwise unknown families, or from those attested as "new-rich", or as belonging to wealthy but non-aristocratic families. Kyle (1987: 113ff.) observed, fairly enough, that where we have no information about the sources of these men's wealth, or no information at all, it may yet be the case that they all had acquired wealth independently of their athletic careers; but equally previous anonymity may actually reflect such social mobility rather than simply our ignorance of their forebears.

Here I discuss just two cases. Evidence for Lykon's wealth and status before his son took up with Callias is ambiguous. There are faint suggestions in Xenophon's *Symposion* that, while the relationships are entirely proper, Lykon is considerably less rich than his son's lover Callias (3.13), who generally spreads his money about generously, had already helped Autolykos to find the best trainer, inspired him with *philotimia* and endurance, and was next going to train him for the next stage in his career, to go into politics (2.7, 8.36ff.); though there is also a flattering allusion to Autolykos, like Callias, having a notable (*onomastos*) father (8.7).[53] There is also an allegation that Cratinus satirised Lykon as a poor man in *Pytine* (*Schol*. Plat. *Apol*. 23e = Cratinus 214 K/A), along with other indications that the whole family was much attacked in the later 420s by comic poets, for alleged domestic irregularities – featuring a wife Rhodia (or possibly the "Rhodian woman", not his wife) as well as the son Autolykos; and Lykon himself was apparently stigmatiscd as effeminate (*malakos*). Autolykos, his parents, and lover were the prime targets in Eupolis' two plays named *Autolykos*, the first performed in 420, and the second some years later.[54] This may reflect comic perceptions that the super-rich Callias had been instrumental in raising the wealth and political chances of the pair, already members of the elite (thus making the father a superior form of *kolax* ("flatterer"), like the many others, including high-quality sophists, satirised also by Eupolis in his *Kolakes* of 421), while the son acquired the demeaning nickname "Eutresios" or "well-bored" (Athen. 216d, 64K/A); or it may be that Lykon's assets were, or had suddenly become, below normal elite levels, and Callias' support of them both was crucial to their rise. Aurolykos' success was apparently marked by a famous statue by Leochares (Pliny *HN* 34.79), and apparently led to a later political career, ended by the Thirty (Plut. *Lys*. 15.5); it is disputed whether Lykon then became one of Socrates' accusers, or whether that "defender of orators" (Plat. *Apol*. 23e) was a different man. I am less sure than others that Xenophon was incapable of the ironic anticipation that would follow from the closing praise by Lykon of Socrates (9.1), if he had indeed turned out to be his prosecutor.[55]

1989: 15–47. On changes in artistic representation, see e.g. Dover 1968: lxiv–lxvi; Shapiro 1981; Kilmer 1993a: 1ff.

[53] Unless there is a subtle joke here, and we are meant to think that they were both "named" in comedy.

[54] Eupolis, *Autolykos* frr. K/A; Ar. *Lys*. 270 and Sch.; Sch. Ar. *Wasps* 1169; Storey 1985: 322–3.

[55] The identification is doubted by Storey 1985: 323; but similar ironies may be seen in the presentation of Ischomachos' ideal marriage in the light of the public scandals retailed in Andoc. 1.124–9; cf. the exposition of views in S. B. Pomeroy's edition (1994: 259–64).

A more interesting case may be Aeschines' family. Demosthenes' increasingly vicious and wild attacks are mostly lies, but from Aeschines' defence (2. 147) it is clear that nothing in the way of noble birth and no liturgies could be claimed for his father Atrometos.[56] What Aeschines does claim is that when his father was young, and before he lost property in the war, he trained as an athlete;[57] then, in exile from the Thirty, he served as a hoplite in Asia, and came back in support of the returning democracy. There are further reasons to suppose that his sons, including the orator, had gymnastic or athletic experience, as well as making successful careers, as Aeschines worked his way via clerking and acting into serious politics, and his brothers achieved positions of military leadership, embassies and administrative jobs (2.147–150). Above all, we have Aeschines' own admission that by middle age he (and his brothers and other relations) had long been habitués of *gymnasia* and Aeschines had long pursued, and still did pursue, boys he met there, and got into many fights (1.135–140). So one might suppose that Atrometos, when an ordinary hoplite, had started to build more respectable wealth and a military and perhaps also a political career in part through athletic competition, suffered a financial setback in the war, and had to rebuild, but brought up his sons with burning ambitions to join the gymnastic, rhetorical and political elite; however, allegations of erotic connections are absent from the record of the father, unlike the sons.[58]

More generally, Aeschines' speech against Timarchos shows repeatedly the acceptability to a formal democratic audience of talking, decorously, about a collective and popular interest in admiring the bodies of talented and beautiful boys, and hoping for later glittering careers for them. First, Aeschines concentrates on the issue of the function of *gymnasia* and pederasty in the education of boys, as he anticipates the opposing view of a "famous general": elements in what he will allegedly say, not controverted by Aeschines himself, include the statement that "all of you, when about to have children, pray that your unborn sons may be *kaloi kagathoi* (literally translated "beautiful and good" (i.e. "gentlemen", "members of the elite")) in appearance, and worthy of the *polis*". He then suggests, and Aeschines is especially quick to make it clear that he agrees, that it would be very unfair if young men of exceptional beauty and youthful perfection (*kallos* and *hora*), whose attractiveness to men inevitably provokes desires and fights, were to find their citizen status challenged by such prosecutions (1.133–4). This "agreement" between opponents constitutes some evidence that many citizens at least saw physical attractiveness, fame at the *gymnasia*, and an "educationally beneficial" affair with an older man as major benefits for youths they cared for, presumably

---

[56] Cf. most recently on Aeschines' early career Harris 1995: 21–33; Lane Fox 1994: 137–43; neither makes much of early gymnastic connections.

[57] So Kyle 1987: 216; against Young's unnecessary doubts (1984: 156), on the phrase *athlein toi somati*.

[58] Kyle 1987: 150 n. 160 reports that Atrometos was an athlete "before he lost his property" and was therefore well-off at that stage, but, as he argued earlier, Aeschines was not apparently able to claim substantial wealth for his father at any stage. Deinarchos (fr. VI.14 Conomis), prosecuting much later the apparently self-made, and eventually pro-Macedonian, politician Pytheas, appears to have claimed that he had spent time with Aeschines (as Timarchos had with his disreputable lovers), before moving to another man with whom he learnt to "mine gold", i.e. made money, but not to do or suffer whatever was proposed to him (i.e as he had with Aeschines).

in part as sources of future wealth, reputation and career opportunities: given the necessary qualification that "you" addressed to Athenian jurors need not have equal application to all citizens, including the poorest thetes, this does no harm to the supposition that gymnastic success could lead to mobility.

This picture is strikingly reinforced by a later passage, in which Aeschines gives a short list of spectacularly beautiful boys, both of those in the previous generation and of those now in their best time of life (*hêlikia*), most of whom have evaded damaging accusations of self-*hetairêsis* ("self-prostitution"), while some, like Timarchos, have not (1.155–9). Among the respectable older men, one may note, one, Timesitheos, is identified as the runner (as Kyle notes, probably the grandfather of the later liturgist Timesitheos)[59] and among the younger ones, Antikles the *stadion*-runner (who may be the Olympic winner of 340, Diod. 16.77, Moretti 451), as well as the other Timarchos, the nephew of Iphicrates (himself a self-made man, Arist. *Rhet.* 1367b18). The whole passage makes the assumption that there was among the citizens a general admiration for, and interest in, the young athletes and others who proudly displayed their beautiful young naked bodies before the popular gaze, in one competition or exercise or another; no doubt they took a gossipy and malicious interest in who their lovers were, and what they did, and simultaneously if contradictorily nourished hopes that they would proceed, without too much of a scandal becoming attached to them, to other activities in the public arena.[60] As Winkler suggests (without linking the point to social mobility),[61] this is the positive counterpoint to the jokes of the Old Comedy poets (and Plato's Aristophanes) that it is the willingly buggered and anally flexible, the *euryprôktoi*, who are the real men and the future leaders; some of these passages suggest that the number of debauched new politicians is increasing exponentially (like Hydra heads: cf. Plato Com. 202K/A). Thus both these and the Aeschines passages imply that popular expectations were that extremely beautiful and promising young were often born to other than elite fathers, and proceeded to later careers.

I hope these arguments strengthen the case that the focus of the public gaze towards the ideal boy, youth or adult male as equally athlete and warrior steadily expanded downwards from the aristocratic or elite members at least as far as those in the hoplite class. These citizens were thus admired (and perhaps pursued) in the *gymnasion* or running down the competition routes in the streets of the city, reliant on their bodily inviolability, strength, beauty or speed; on other occasions they were grouped collectively, and tribally, clad in their anonymous armour; they might even be – unusually – represented in high art, as in the apparent representation of the Panathenaea procession on the Parthenon frieze the naked hoplite seems to have

---

[59] Kyle 1987: 116, 226–7. If so, he is the father of the first member of the family identified as a liturgist, Demainetos (Davies 1971: 102–3), and it is at least possible that his beauty and victories helped to establish the family's wealth.

[60] On the remarkable public "gaze" and admiration for naked youths, cf. also the illuminating article of Larissa Bonfante 1989: 543–70, though she seems to describe the youths portrayed alternately as aristocratic or as hoplite, without facing the issue of any explanation. Another element is probably the constant habit of labelling and/or showing pretty youths as *kaloi* on pots; cf. Lissarrague 1990: 106; but interpretation of this practice is very elusive, cf. Dover 1978: 111–24; Kilmer 1993b.

[61] Ar. *Ach.* 716–17, *Knights* 877–80, *Clouds* 1089–104, *Wasps* 1068–70, *Eccl.* 111–14, fr. 677; Eupolis fr. 100; Plat. Com. 202 K/A; Pl. *Symp.* 191e–2a. See Winkler 1990a: 64; also Dover 1978: 141–2.

become an idealised, or even heroised, cavalryman.[62]

On the other side of the coin, the gravest danger for the young boyfriends in or around the *palaistrai* and their associated intellectual schools was that they might lose their reputations, as had, allegedly, Timarchos and the rest of the bad ones enumerated by Aeschines, if the mercenary/sexual nature of the relationship(s) became too evident. Such individuals are notably identified by Aeschines through stigmatising nicknames – "Diophantos the so-called orphan", "Cephisodoros known as the son of Molon, who ruined his most be beautiful youthful perfection (*kallistan horan*) most disgracefully",[63] and "Mnesitheos known as the *mageiros*' ("butcher's") son" (1.158–9). In practice, the reputations of a great many attractive youths are likely to have been much more uncertain and ambiguous than the white or black picture painted here, as the speeches in the *Phaedrus* suggest, and as one can observe in the cases of those later politicians against whom allegations of self-*hetairêsis* were paraded in the courts, though not as far as we know prosecuted, such as Epichares (one of the prosecutors of Andocides: Andoc.1.99–100), Androtion (Dem. 22.30–6), or Hegesandros (Aesch. 1.64).

In practice too, the more intellectual activities around the *gymnasia* and *palaistrai*, the rhetorical and philosophical discussions and schools, provided a more direct route to elite activities. Many cases of relations between elite teachers, or practising orators and politicians, and their young pupils could be listed; many accounts are hostile and designed to wound (for example, Aeschines' attacks on Demosthenes' relations with Aristarchos, 1.171–2, 2.148, 166, or Deinarchos' against Aeschines and Pytheas, fr. VI.13, or Androtion and Anticles, Dem. 22. 30–6; Aeschin 1.165–6). The picture in comedy, where it is constantly assumed, in general and in particular, that new young politicians, especially from suspicious backgrounds, had all been *paidika* and *euryprôktoi*, tends to suggest they left the discipline of the wrestling grounds for the easier pleasures of (hot) baths, expensive foods, wine and sex, and the more directly relevant training offered by sophists and rhetoricians. This pattern has the added advantage of enabling comic poets to abuse the new men for their unfit flabby bodies, pallor, thin chests, small or worn-away bottoms, as opposed to the muscular, and militarily useful, young athletes (for example Ar. *Daitaleis* 214 K/A, *Ach.* 716, and above all the *agôn* of the *Clouds passim*).[64] The subtle portrait of the "Stronger Argument" in the *Clouds*, however, with its obsession with haunting the *gymnasia* and ogling boys' genitals, the fantasy fondling at *Birds* 137–41, like the later pictures in Aeschines' speech and in Theophrastos, make it clear that erotic interest, and serious, and potentially dangerous, relationships remained equally likely to develop between keen and fit young athletes and their elders.

Some of these relationships, as suggested above, may have developed into lasting and important friendships, in which sexual desire played less of a part (an apparently rare case of a long-standing, still homoerotic, relationship is presented in

---

[62] Cf. Humphreys 1993: xvi–xvii; Osborne 1987: 103–4.

[63] I hope to say more about nicknames elsewhere.

[64] Those who signed up with the specialist philosophers were supposed to give up both gymnastics and wine, and become pale and thin (*Clouds* 103, 419–21, 440).

Plato's *Symposion*, between Pausanias and Agathon). Aeschines' speech against Timarchos, in a different way, may possibly testify to the strength of these friendships. Those accused of associations with Timarchos (whatever the nature of their relationships in fact) appear to have stayed "loyal" to him and refused to testify or agree to Aeschines' challenges (though they are likely to have had other motives as well). Aeschines' account of Hegesandros' manipulation of the arbitration procedure in his case against the state-slave Pittalakos, involving an old friend and alleged lover Diopeithes as a most helpful arbitrator, points in a similar direction (1. 63–4). Gossip and scandal were very frequent, but prosecutions for *hetairêsis* perhaps very rare, though the two we hear of were apparently successful, Cleon's of Gryllos (referred to in Ar. *Knights* 875–8) and Aeschines' of Timarchos. Reluctance to give evidence by the accused's alleged partners and perhaps still friends would have been a constant problem for any potential prosecutors.[65]

It seems likely, then, that gymnastic and festival needs, military ambitions, and the desire among many non-elite Athenians to shine, to rise socially and to share aspects of the good life, produced a great expansion of athletic and gymnastic activity, as I believe comparable desires and opportunities produced a markedly greater spread of elements of "sympotic" style in the many occasions of shared eating and drinking, at festivals, in religious and social associations, and among groups of friends. The interests alike of the state, the tribe, and the individual liturgist and performing group, in attaining success at varying levels of the games, permitted perhaps patterns of support or patronage for young athletes and other competitors; social pressures, however, may have necessitated that such patterns become increasingly circumspect or covert. Such support may in turn have aided social mobility and provided brief or lasting friendships for ambitious youths; some of these friendships may have had temporary or more extended erotic elements. On the other hand, such relationships were regarded with deep ambivalence, and carried multiple dangers, above all for the upwardly mobile younger men; fear of gossip, or even fear of prosecutions (or at least the threat of prosecutions) may well have inhibited or destroyed some such relationships. Thus these complex patterns of athletic and social activities will, contradictorily, either have increased opportunities for many Athenians for advancement, close relationships and consensus, or, on the other hand, have produced further grounds for tensions and hatreds.

WORKS CITED

Arnaoutoglou, I. (1998) "Between *koinon* and *idion*: legal and social dimension of religious associations in ancient Athens" in Cartledge, Millett and von Reden 1998: 68–83.
Bérard, C. et al. (1989) *A City of Images* (French orig. Paris 1984), Princeton.
Boegehold, A. L. (1996) "Group and single competitions at the Panathenaia" in Neils 1996: 95–105.
Bonfante, L. (1989) "Nudity as a costume in classical art" *AJA* 93: 543–70.
Borthwick, E. K. (1967) "Trojan leap and Pyrrhic dance in Euripides' *Andromache* 1129–41", *JHS* 87: 18–23.
Bowie, E. L. (1995) "Wine in old comedy" in Murray and Tecusan 1995: 113–25.

---

[65] Cf. also Foxhall 1998: 60. Cf. also on these prosecutions, Winkler 1990a: 54–6.

Braund, D. (1994) "The luxuries of Athenian democracy", *G&R* 41: 41–4.
Bremmer, J. (1980) "An enigmatic Indo-European rite: pederasty", *Arethusa* 13: 279–98.
— (1990) "Adolescents, *symposion* and pederasty" in Murray 1990: 135–48.
Buffière, F. (1980) *Eros adolescent*, Paris.
Burke, P. (1995) "The invention of leisure in early modern Europe", *P&P* 146: 136–50.
Calame, C. (1996) *Thésée et l'imaginaire athénien*, Lausanne.
Cartledge, P. (1985) "The Greek religious festivals" in Easterling and Muir 1985: 98–127.
Cartledge, P., Millett, P. C. and von Reden, S. (1998) eds, *Kosmos: Essays in Order, Conflict and Community in Classical Athens*, Cambridge.
Christiansen, J. and Melander, T. (1988), eds, *Proceedings of the 3rd Symposium on Ancient Greek and Related Pottery*, Copenhagen.
Cohen, D. (1995) "The rule of law and democratic ideology in Classical Athens" in Eder 1995: 227–44
Cooper, F. and Morris, S. (1990) "Dining in round buildings" in Murray 1990: 66–85.
Coulson, W. D. E. et al. (1994), eds, *The Archaeology of Athens and Attica under the Democracy*, Oxford.
Crielaard, J. P. (1995), ed., *Homeric Questions*, Amsterdam.
Crowther, N. B. (1985) "Male beauty contests in Greece: the *Euandria* and *Euexia*", *CA* 54: 285–91.
Csapo, E. (1993) "Deep ambivalence? Notes on a Greek cockfight", *Phoenix* 47: 1–28, 115–24.
Davidson, J. (1993) "Fish, sex and revolution", *CQ* 43: 53–66.
— (1997) *Courtesans and Fishcakes: the consuming passions of Classical Athens*, London.
Davies, J. K. (1967) "Demosthenes on liturgies: a note", *JHS* 87: 33–40.
— (1971) *Athenian Propertied Families 600–300 BC*, Oxford
Delorme, J. (1960) *Gymnasium: Étude sur les monuments consacrés à l'éducation en Grèce*, Paris.
Dickie, M. (1984) "Phaeacian Athletes", *PLLS* 4: 237–52.
Dougherty, C. and Kurke, L. (1993), eds, *Cultural Poetics in Archaic Greece. Cult, Performance, Politics*, Cambridge.
Dover, K. I, (1968) *Aristophanes "Clouds"*, Oxford.
— (1978) *Greek Homosexuality* (2nd edn. Cambridge, 1989), London.
Easterling, P. E. and Muir, J. V. (1985), eds, *Greek Religion and Society*, Cambridge.
Eder, W. (1995), ed., *Die athenische Demokratie im 4. Jahrhundert v. Chr.: Vollendung oder Verfall einer Verfassungsform?*, Stuttgart.
Fisher, N. (1992) *Hybris. A Study in the Values of Honour and Shame in Ancient Greece*, Warminster.
Foucault, M. (1985) *The Use of Pleasure. The History of Sexuality* II (French orig. Paris 1984), London and New York.
Foxhall, L. (1998) "The politics of affection: emotional attachments in Athenian society" in Cartledge, Millett and von Reden 1998: 52–67.
Frontisi-Ducroux, F. (1996) "Eros, desire and the gaze" in Kampen 1996: 81–100.
Gabba, E. (1983), ed., *Tria Corda. Scritti in onore di Arnaldo Momigliano*, Como.
Gauthier, Ph. (1976) *Un commentaire historique des Poroi de Xénophon*, Geneva.
Golden, M. (1990) *Children and Childhood in Classical Athens*, Baltimore and London.
Goldhill, S. (1998) "The seductions of the gaze: Socrates and his girlfriends" in Cartledge, Millett and von Reden 1998: 105–24.
Hägg, R. (1983), ed., *The Greek Renaissance of the 8th century BC: Tradition and Innovation*, Stockholm.
Halperin, D. M. (1990) *One Hundred Years of Homosexuality and other essays on Greek love*, New York and London.

Hansen, M. H. (1985) *Demography and Democracy: the Number of Athenian Citizens in the Fourth Century BC*, Herning.
Harris, E. M. (1995) *Aeschines and Athenian Politics*, Oxford.
Hornblower, S. and Osborne, R. (1994), eds, *Ritual, Finance, Politics. Athenian Democratic Accounts presented to David Lewis*, Oxford.
Humphreys, S. C. (1974) "The Nothoi of Kynosarges", *JHS* 94: 88–95.
— (1993) *The Family, Women and Death*, 2nd edn, Ann Arbor.
Hupperts, C. A. M. (1988) "Greek love: homosexuality or pederasty? Greek love in black figure vase-painting" in Christiansen and Melander 1988: 255-65.
Instone, S. (1986) Review of Young 1984, *JHS* 106: 238–9.
— (1990) "Love in Pindar: some practical thrusts", *BICS* 37: 34-42.
Kampen, N. B. (1996), ed, *Sexuality in Ancient Art*, Cambridge.
Kilmer, M. F. (1993a) *Greek Erotica*, London.
— (1993b) "In search of the wild *kalos*-name", *EMC/CV* n.s. 12: 173–99.
Koch-Harnack, G. (1983) *Knabenliebe und Tiergeschenke*, Berlin.
Kurke, L. (1991) *The Traffic in Praise. Pindar and the Poetics of Social Economy*, Ithaca.
— (1993) "The economy of *kudos*" in Dougherty and Kurke 1993: 131–63.
Kyle, D. G. (1985) Review of Young 1984: *EMC/CV* 4 134-44.
— (1987) *Athletics in Ancient Athens*, Leiden.
Lane-Fox, H. (1994) "Aeschines and Athenian politics" in Hornblower and Osborne 1994: 137–55
— (1996) "Theophrastos' Characters and the historian" *PCPS* 42: 127–70.
Lissarrague, F. (1990) *The Aesthetics of the Greek Banquet* (French orig. 1987), Princeton.
Lloyd, A. (1996), ed., *Battle in Antiquity*, London.
Lonsdale, S. H. (1993) *Dance and Ritual Play in Greek Religion*, Baltimore and London.
Luke, J. (1994) "The krater, *kratos* and the *polis*", *G&R* 41: 23–32.
Millett, P. C. (1989) "Patronage and its avoidance in classical Athens" in Wallace-Hadrill 1989: 15–47, London.
— (1991) *Lending and Borrowing in Ancient Athens*, Cambridge.
— (1998) "Encounter in the agora" in Cartledge, Millett and von Reden 1998: 203–28.
Murray, O. (1983a) "The Greek symposium in history" in Gabba 1983: 257–93.
— (1983b) "The symposium as social organisation" in Hägg 1983: 195–9.
— (1990), ed., *Sympotica. A Symposium on the Symposion*, Oxford.
— (1996) "Nestor's cup and the origins of the symposion" in *Apoikia: Scritti in onore di Giorgio Buchner*, *AION* n.s. 1 (1996): 47–54.
Murray, O. and Tecusan, M. (1995), eds, *In vino veritas*, London
Neils, J. et al. (1992) *Goddess and Polis: The Panathenaic festival in Ancient Athens*, Princeton.
— (1994) "The Panathenaia and Kleisthenic ideology" in Coulson et al. 1994: 151–60.
— (1996), ed., *Worshipping Athena: Panathenaia and Parthenon*, Madison.
Ober, J. (1989) *Mass and Elite in Democratic Athens: Rhetoric, Ideology and the Power of the People*, Princeton.
Ogden, D. (1996) "Homosexuality and warfare in ancient Greece" in Lloyd 1996: 107–68.
Osborne, R. (1987) The viewing and obscuring of the Parthenon frieze", *JHS* 107: 98–105.
— (1993) "Competitive festivals and the *polis*: a context for dramatic festivals at Athens" in Sommerstein et al. 1993: 21–38.
— (1996) "Desiring women on Athenian pottery" in Kampen 1996: 65–80.
Pellizer, E. (1990) "Outlines of a morphology of sympotic entertainment" in Murray 1990: 177–84.
Pinney, G. F. (1988) "Athena and the Panathenaea" in Christiansen and Melander 1988: 465–77.

Pleket H. W. (1975) "Games, prizes, athletes and ideology", *Stadion* 1: 49–89.
— (1988) "The participants in the ancient Olympic Games" in Coulson, W. D. E. and Kyrieleis, H., eds, *Proceedings of an International Symposium on the Olympic Games* (1992): 147–52, Athens.
Pomeroy, S. (1994), ed., *The Oeconomicus of Xenophon*, Oxford.
Poursat, F. (1968) "Danse armée dans la céramique attique", *BCH* 92: 550–615.
Purcell, N. (1995) "Literate games: Roman society and the game of *alea*", *P&P* 147: 3–37.
Reinmuth, O. W. (1961) *The Ephebic Inscriptions of the Fourth Century BC*, Leiden.
Rhodes, P. J. (1981) *A Commentary on the Aristotelian Athēnaiōn Politeia*, Oxford [repr. with corr. and add. 1993].
Ridley, R. T. (1979) "The hoplite as citizen", *AC* 48: 508–49.
Ste Croix, G. E. M. de (1981) *The Class Struggle in the Ancient Greek World. From the Archaic Age to the Arab Conquest*, London [corr. repr. 1983].
Schmitt-Pantel, P. (1990) "Sacrificial meal and *symposion*: two models of civic insitutions in the archaic city?" in Murray 1990: 14–26.
— (1992) *La cité au banquet: histoire des repas publics dans les cités grecques*. Publications de l'école française de Rome 157, Rome.
Schofield M. (1998) "Political friendship and the ideology of reciprocity" in Cartledge, Millett and von Reden 1998: 37–51.
Seaford, R. (1984), ed., Euripides, *Cyclops*, Oxford.
Sekunda N. V. (1990) "IG II^2 1250: A decree concerning the *Lampadephoroi* of the tribe Aiantis", *ZPE* 83: 149–82.
Shapiro, H. A. (1981) "Courtship scenes in Attie vase painting", *AJA* 85: 131–43.
Sommerstein, A. H. et al. (1993), eds, *Tragedy, Comedy and the Polis*, Bari.
Stocks, J. L. (1936) "*Scholê*", *CQ* 30: 177–87.
Storey, I. C. (1985) "The symposium at *Wasps* 1299ff.", *Phoenix* 39: 317–33.
Sutton, D. (1980) *The Greek Satyr Play*, Meisenheim.
Toner, J. P. (1995) *Leisure in Ancient Rome*, Cambridge.
Van Wees, H. (1995) "Princes at dinner" in Crielaard 1995: 147–81.
Veblen, T. (1925) *The Theory of the Leisure Class*, London.
Vidal-Naquet, P. (1986a) *The Black Hunter. Forms of Thought and Forms of Society in the Greek World* (French orig. Paris 1981), Baltimore and London.
— (1986b) "The Black Hunter revisited", *PCPhS* 32: 126–44.
Vlastos, G. (1987) "Socratic irony", *CQ* 37: 79–96.
Von Reden, S. (1995) *Exchange in Ancient Greece*, London.
Wallace-Hadrill, A. (1989), ed., *Patronage in Ancient Society*, London.
Whitehead, D. (1986) *The Demes of Attica, 508/7–ca. 250 BC: a social and political study*, Princeton.
— (1991) "The Lampadephoroi of Aiantis again", *ZPE* 87: 42–4.
Winkler, J. J. (1990a) *The Constaints of Desire: The Anthropology of Sex and Gender in Ancient Greece*, New York and London.
— (1990b) "The ephebes' song: *tragōidia* and the *polis*" in Winkler and Zeitlin 1990: 20–62.
Winkler J. J. and Zeitlin F. (1990), eds, *Nothing to Do With Dionysos? Athenian Drama in its Social Context*, Princeton.
Young, D. C. (1984) *The Olympic Myth of Greek Amateur Athletics*, Chicago.

4 Notes on the Role of the Gymnasion in the Hellenistic City*

PHILIPPE GAUTHIER
(translated by Margarita Lianou)

As a building and an institution, the *gymnasion* is typical of the Hellenistic towns and cities. We know next to nothing about the *gymnasia* of the fifth and fourth centuries BC (before 330 BCE), which were more or less rustic sanctuaries isolated from the cities. The earliest *gymnasion* known to us through its ruins is that of Delphi, constructed roughly between 337 and 327 BC.[1] Even then, this is an exceptional case, since the construction and maintenance of the building reveal more about the Amphictiony [i.e. the league responsible for administration of the sanctuary] than the Delphians themselves, who had the use of the building only in the intervals between successive occurrences of the Pythian festival.[2] Later on, the urban *gymnasia* multiplied and ruins of *gymnasia* have been discovered in many sites, not only in mainland Greece, but also even more so on the islands, in Asia and in Cyrenaica.[3]

Writing in the reign of Augustus, Diodoros cites the *gymnasion* among the buildings that "contribute to the happiness of human life."[4] Later on, Pausanias hesitates to categorise the Phocidian community of the Phanoteans (from Phanoteus, or Panopeus) as a city "because they have no buildings for the magistrates, no *gymnasion*, no theatre, no agora, no fountain bringing up water ... However", he adds, "their territory does have boundaries that separate them from their neighbours, and they also despatch representatives to the Phocidian Assembly."[5]

This remark of Pausanias should alert us against generalisations. As the example of Phanoteus shows, many small cities situated in isolated regions, scarcely populated and deprived of resources, probably used rudimentary installations as

---

* Originally published in M. Wörrle and P. Zanker (eds), *Stadtbild und Bürgerbild im Hellenismus* (Munich: Beck, 1995), pp. 1–11.

[1] J. Bousquet, *Études sur les comptes de Delphes*, 1988, 170 n. 10. Cf. J. Jannoray, *Fouilles de Delphes II. Le Gymnase*, 1953; J.-Fr. Bommalaer, *Guide de Delphes. Le site*, 1991, 73–9.

[2] See below regarding the accounts of Dion.

[3] Cf. J. Delorme, *Gymnasion*, 1960, whose list, despite needing corrections and additions, remains useful.

[4] Diod. 5.15.2; cf. 4.30.1; 15.13.5.

[5] Paus. 10.4.1. This text was invoked by J. Delorme, op. cit., 254; by M. P. Nilsson (see following note); also, in regard to the borders, by D. Rousset, *BCH* 116, 1992, 197 (with references and discussion, at the end of the article, on the city of Phanoteus and its territory). The reference to borders and representation in the Phokikon [i.e. the Phocidian assembly] shows that Pausanias alludes to the *city* in general, and not just the *town*.

opposed to real buildings.[6] Equally, in Makedonia, according to the Gymnasiarchal Law of Beroia, which was adopted around 180 BC, there was not a *gymnasion* in every city.[7] Nevertheless, this remark of Pausanias shows us that in his time the *gymnasion* had long become a typical component of the urban landscape. One of the novelties of the Hellenistic period was precisely this flourishing of *gymnasia*, which was encouraged in particular by the numerous foundations and re-foundations of towns and cities, as well as by the self-serving munificence of the Hellenistic kings.

Inscriptions are very informative for the Hellenistic *gymnasia*. I want to make just three specific points, engaging also with archaeological scholarship.[8]

I. THE *GYMNASION* AS A BUILDING IN INSCRIPTIONS

For this topic, the nature of the documents matters more than their length. For example, the gymnasiarchal law of Beroia, detailed as it is in certain points, tells us almost nothing about the location, the layout and the planning of the *gymnasion* of the city. It is only indirectly and by implication that one or another sentence allows us to catch a glimpse of the entrance, the *palaistra* and its porticoes, the altar of Hermes, the area where the prizes of the victors in the Hermaia were consecrated, and finally the baths.[9] There is nothing unnatural in this lack of precise details. The law was made in order to define the rights and obligations of the gymnasiarch and his assistants. The authors, therefore, did not need to refer, except by allusion, to a building that they and the citizen body as a whole knew very well.

More instructive are honorific decrees (and also dedications). In the Hellenistic period – and I will return to this point below – the cities took responsibility for the *gymnasia*, in some places quite early in the Hellenistic period. But the construction, the restoration and the regular maintenance of a *gymnasion* were expensive. It is therefore not surprising to note that the cities had frequent recourse

---

[6] We cannot agree with M. P. Nilsson, *Die hellenistische Schule*, 1955, 30–1, when he writes: "One may assume with certainty that there was at least one *gymnasion* in every Greek city. What Pausanias says in 10.4.1 of the miserable town of Panopeus in Phokis is typical," (followed by partial citation of the passage of Pausanias). In every city, even the smallest ones, there were, without a doubt, places for the training in physical exercise, which were more or less well managed, but not necessarily buildings that merited the name of *gymnasion*.

[7] Ph. Gauthier-M. B. Hatzopoulos, *La loi gymnasiarchique de Béroia*, 1993. Cf. A, 5–8: "given that the other magistrates of the city exercise their functions according to a law and that in the cities (sc. of Makedonia) where there are *gymnasia* and where anointing is practised the gymnasiarchal laws are registered in public archives," etc. Therefore, at the date of the adoption of the law, there was not a *gymnasion* in *every* Makedonian city. See also J. and L. Robert, *Bull. épigr.* 1978, 274 (p. 432).

[8] I leave aside, among other things, one essential point, which numerous inscriptions shed light on: the *gymnasion* as a place of cult – for the traditional divinities (Hermes, Herakles), but also for the kings, and then later for citizen-benefactors, who were considered as new founders – with its altars, its cult statues and its tombs. The studies devoted to this subject by M. P. Nilsson (n. 6), 61–7, and by J. Delorme (n. 3), 337–61, are in need of revision and additions. See the critique of J. and L. Robert, *Bull. épigr.* 1956, no. 36 (criticising M. P. Nilsson) and of L. Robert, *Ant. Class.* 35, 1966, 422–3 n. 7 (*Opera Minora Selecta* VI, 46–7), in regard to the honours reserved for citizen-benefactors in the *gymnasia* (criticising J. Delorme). This interesting question deserves a synoptic study.

[9] *La loi* (n. 7), B 2 (the signal at the entrance), 10–26 (training of ephebes and boys), 46 and 54 (Hermes), 62–7 (banquet in the *gymnasion*), 67–8 (consecration of prizes), 97–9 (the official in charge of the *palaistra*, the *gloios* (i.e. scraped-off oil) and the bath). See the commentary on these different passages, ad locc.; and on the subject of the location of the *gymnasion* of Beroia (outside the ramparts), see pp. 152–3.

to the munificence of kings and of the wealthiest citizens. In spite of – or rather because of – their importance, the benefactions of the kings will not detain us here: whether they consisted of donations in silver (or of grain intended for sale) for the construction of buildings, of endowments intended to secure either the supply of oil (for anointing before exercise) or wood (for heating), or the regular payment of teachers, they provide little information on the layout and planning of the *gymnasia*.[10]

On the other hand, decrees in honour of gymnasiarchs leaving office (or on the point of leaving office) and dedications made by those magistrates themselves provide interesting details. Indeed, many gymnasiarchs built, restored, or completed at their own expense sections of the *gymnasion*: the entrance "porch" (*pylôn* or *propylon*); the "portico" (*stoa*) around the palaestra; the *exedra*, or "auditorium" (*akroatêrion*), an elongated rectangular room opening on to a portico; the "anointing room" (*aleiptêrion*); the "sand room" for wrestling (*konistêrion, konisma*); "bathing room" (*loutrôn, loutron*); the "steam room" (*puriatêrion*); and so on.[11]

Although these inscriptions allow us to appreciate the euergetism of the magistrates and to catch a glimpse of the different functions of the *gymnasion*, these details can rarely be identified today on the ground, either because the *gymnasia* of the cities concerned are unknown to us, or because the excavated buildings exhibit significant modifications dating from the imperial period,[12] or even, finally and most significantly, because the specialised use of certain rooms had very little impact on their shape, which is the only visible part today, but instead affected mainly their fittings, equipment or decoration.

We need to leave some room for a set of documents which are all the more precious because they are rare, that is to say for the accounts and inventories. In Delphi, the accounts engraved under the archon Dion (247/6? BC) reveal the works undertaken during that year in the *gymnasion* on account of the approaching Pythia.[13] Today, the location of some of these works on the excavated site poses

---

[10] E.g. on the Attalid donations in this area, see L. Robert, *Études anatoliennes*, 1937, 85 and n. 3; P. Herrmann, *Ist. Mitt.* 15, 1965, 71–117, esp. 79–82.

[11] Several examples already in E. Ziebarth, *Aus dem griechischen Schulwesen*, ²1914, 68–73; C. A. Forbes, *Neoi*, 1933, 26–9. More recently, Fr. Quaß, *Die Honoratiorenschicht des griechischen Ostens*, 1993, 206–8 (with notes), has gathered the references to the decrees, which saves me from reproducing them here. In regard to constructions undertaken by gymnasiarchs and known by their dedications, see in particular L. Robert, *Études anatoliennes*, 77–9, with some examples not mentioned by Quaß (Aigai, Iasos, Halikarnassos, Melos, Thisbe); *A travers l'Asie Mineure*, 1980, 368 (Bargasa). The majority of the terms enumerated above are fruitfully discussed by M.-Chr. Hellmann, *Recherches sur le vocabulaire de l'architecture grecque d'après les inscriptions de Délos*, 1992, s.v.; on the subject of the *aleiptêrion* and the evolution in the use of this term, cf. C. Foss, *GRBS* 16, 1975, 217–26 (*Bull. épigr.* 1976, 133; 1981, 503); P. Herrmann, *Chiron* 23, 1993, 234–5 n. 5.

[12] This is the most frequent case (cf. Delphi, Pergamon, etc.), with the increasing importance, under Roman influence, of the installations necessary for the baths (in regard to the monument excavated in Sardeis, the American archaeologists chose the name "Bath-Gymnasium Complex"). In some cases a building changed function. In Arneai in Lykia, under Trajan, a *gymnasion* was transformed to a hotel, a development which its shape made it particularly suitable for: *TAM* II, 759; cf. L. Robert, *Hellenica*, XI-XII, 1960, 16 n. 4.

[13] The inscription was re-edited, with revisions, by J. Pouilloux, in *Études delphiques*, *BCH* Suppl. IV, 1977, 103–23, with translation and commentary; picked up later by J. Bousquet, *Corpus des Inscriptions de Delphes* II n° 139 (with a correction in l. 16, κατάρασιν in place of κατάψασιν).

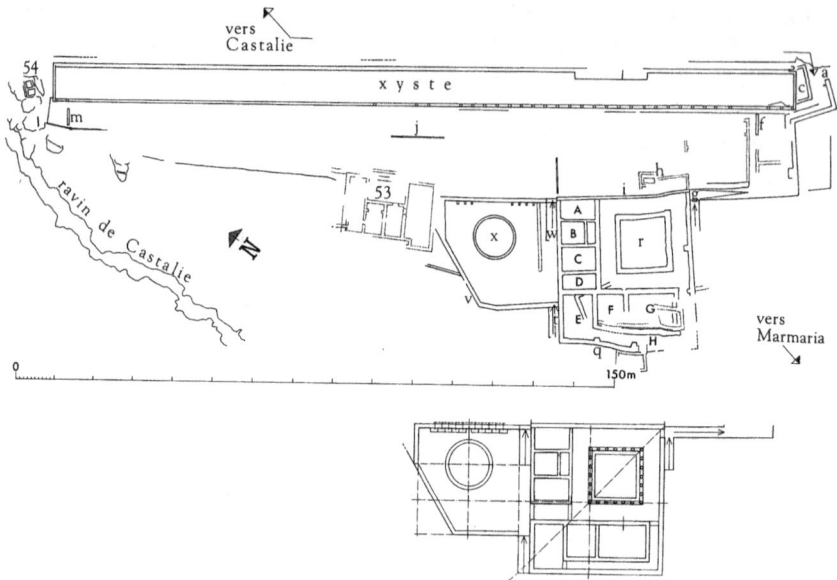

Fig. 4.1 Plan of the *gymnasion* at Delphi. (J.-Fr. Bommelaer and D. Laroche, *Guide de Delphes. La Site*, 1991, p. 72) (© EfA)
Gymnasion: plan of the site, with partial reconstruction (scale: 1:1000). a: southern entrance; c: tank?; f and m: furthest limits of the *paradromis* (practice running track); r: peristyle court of the *palaistra*; x: tank of the *loutron* (bathing room); 53: Roman baths; 54: *Damatrion*?

very few problems (see Fig. 4.1). The same goes for the digging and levelling of the covered track (*xystos*), the open-air track (*paradromis*) and the peristyle of the *palaistra*. On the other hand, when it comes to the *sphairistêrion*, probably a boxing room,[14] the wall of which had been repaired (l. 14), the wrestling hall (*konima*, l. 15), where the soil had been sifted, and the changing room (*apodytêrion*, ll. 19–20), whose walls had to be plastered, it is very difficult to identify which of the rooms that open onto the *palaistra* is which.[15]

These difficulties have been alleviated for Delos, ever since J. Tréheux provided an excellent account of the inventory of the *gymnasion* in 156/5.[16] It is sufficient to summarise his conclusions (see Fig. 4.2). In making an inventory of the bronzes, the Athenian administrators entered through the peristyle and, noting the objects they found in each place, starting from the right, they passed successively through the East, North and South galleries. Then, by making a half-circle and advancing clockwise from then on, they inventoried the bronze objects situated in the interior of the rooms. Consequently, we know with certainty the location, in the following

---

[14] On the subject of this term, which we have discussed at some length, it seems that we have to adhere to the conclusions of J. Delorme, *BCH* 106, 1982, 53–73 (who argues for the meaning "boxing room" in opposition to G. Roux, *BCH* 104, 1980, 127–49, and includes a discussion of the earlier literature on the subject); cf. below in relation to Delos.
[15] Cf. J. Jannoray, *Fouilles de Delphes II. Le Gymnase*, 1953, 77–8; J. Delorme (n. 3), 297.
[16] *I. Delos* 1417 A, ll. 118–54. J. Tréheux, *BCH* 112, 1988, 583–9. For the location of the *epistasion*, see Ph. Bruneau, *BCH* 114, 1990, 580–1.

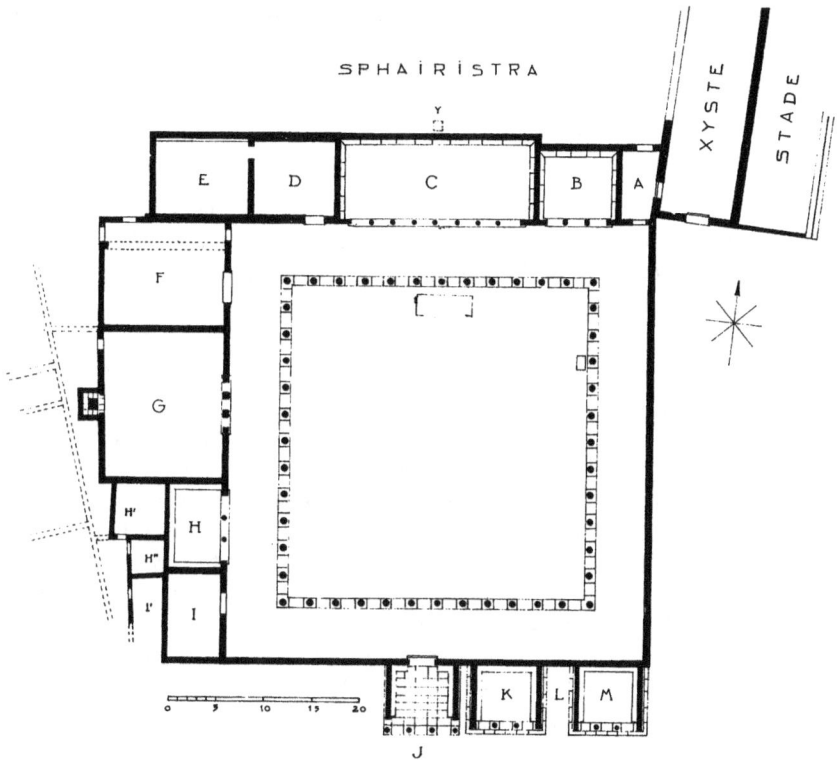

Fig. 4.2 Plan of the *gymnasion* at Delos.
(G. Roux, *BCH* 104, 1980, p. 139, fig. 4) (©EfA

order, of the great *exedrion* G, which was "a trophy room, preceded by a triple-vaulted door, richly decorated with an above-lifesize statue in the back niche, as well as other smaller statues";[17] the bath E, to which D gives access, with its brick pavement; the changing room C, endowed with a bench running on three sides; the *sphairistra* B, a small boxing room;[18] and, finally the *epistasion* A: "equipped with a beautiful marble door and placed at the junction between the *gymnasion* proper and the *xystos-stadion* complex, this room would be suitable for the supervisors of the establishment."[19]

This is an exceptional case: a detailed inventory (firmly dated to 156/5) which is now correctly explained, and corresponds to a well-excavated building, whose final state is precisely the one described in the inventory.[20] The plan and the engraved inventory of the building, which is supplemented by various epigraphic testimonies (in particular the dedications of victors in the torch race), establish in a striking

---

[17] M.-Chr. Hellmann (n. 11), 128.
[18] Cf. J. Tréheux, loc. cit., 589 and n. 35 "Our identification of the *sphairistra* with room B confirms the thesis of J. Delorme" (cf. above in relation to Delphi).
[19] Ph. Bruneau (n. 16), 581.
[20] The *gymnasion* of Delos seems to have been abandoned after the destruction that was wrought on the city in the first half of the first century BC.

way that the *gymnasion* of Delos, like the other Hellenistic *gymnasia*, was essentially intended for physical activities.

II. THE *GYMNASION* AS A PLACE OF TRAINING AND EDUCATION

If we leave Ptolemaic Egypt on one side, where the political and social context was idiosyncratic, the bulk of our documentation on the activities that took place in the Hellenistic *gymnasia* and on the teachers who taught there comes from inscriptions (decrees, dedications, victory lists of "contests", *agônes*, and of "examinations", *apodeixeis*). Based on the pioneering, and still useful, work of E. Ziebarth, M. P. Nilsson presented, a few decades ago, a clear synthesis of this evidence.[21] This is not the place to revisit or summarise the conclusions of these scholars. However, since this is a study of the *gymnasion*, and the *gymnasion* alone, we need to address, without pretending to resolve it for all the cities (since the situation varied from one city to the next and our evidence is often insufficient) a largely neglected question (neglected on account of having being subsumed into wider discussion of the "Hellenistic school"): what was the place and the role of the *gymnasion* (under the authority of the gymnasiarch) in the education of the different age groups?

We certainly should not conflate *gymnasion* with "school", as M. P. Nilsson has done.[22] This is for a very simple reason that is evident from the reading of very many inscriptions: the *gymnasion* in the Hellenistic period was essentially the domain of the *ephêboi* and the *neoi*, that is to say of youths aged approximately 18 to 30 years. The *paides*, meaning the adolescents of about 12 to 18 years, did not have access to the *gymnasion*, except in extraordinary circumstances or because of particular situations, to which I will return. As for the younger children, these did not enter at all.

Open to *ephêboi* and *neoi*, the *gymnasion* remained principally a place of training in physical and military activities. This is why the great festival of the *gymnasion*, the Hermaia, consisted only of athletic contests, to which were added unfailingly the typical examinations of the *gymnasion*, "good-condition", "discipline" and "diligence".[23] The victory list in the *gymnasion* in Samos (third-second century BC) mentions only military contests (catapult shooting, javelin throwing, bow shooting, armed combat – *hoplomachia* (i.e. fighting with weapons) and *thyreamachia* (i.e. fighting with shields)) and athletic ones (*stadion*, long-distance race, wrestling, *pankration*, etc.).[24] The same applies for Tralles, in Caria.[25] Identical or similar events are found in the contests organised annually by the gymnasiarch of Koresia in Keos from the beginning of the third century BC.[26]

---

[21] E. Ziebarth (n. 11), 79–147; M. P. Nilsson (n. 6), in particular 42–53 and 60–1.

[22] M. P. Nilsson (n. 6), 1: "The word, by which the school was known, a word, which still describes the modern high school, is the *gymnasion* ..."

[23] On the three examinations, see *La loi*, (n. 7), 102–8.

[24] Michel, *Recueil* 899 (monthly or bimonthly contests); *Syll.*³ 1061; cf. E. Preneur, *MDAI(A)* 29, 1903, 353–70; M. Launey, *Recherches sur les armées hellénistiques* II, 1950, 817, 820–1; M. P. Nilsson (n. 6), 43–4.

[25] *Syll.*³ 1060 and 1062 (*I. Tralleis* 106 and 107).

[26] *Syll.*³ 958; cf. further discussion below.

Role of the Gymnasion 93

At Sestos, within the detailed stipulations (forty lines) relating to the two gymnasiarchies of Menas (around 135–130 BC), almost everything (except for the sections which deal with the sacrifices and the banquets) points to contests of the same type, racing and torch races, javelin throwing and bow shooting, and armed combat, without forgetting of course the trials of "discipline", "diligence" and "good condition".[27]

The gymnasiarchal law of Beroia (from around 180 BC) offers an arresting image of the military specialisation of the *gymnasion* in Makedonia under the last of the Antigonid rulers.[28] In this long text, of which 130 lines are legible, there is not one single allusion to intellectual activities, or to teachers of literature, rhetoric or music. If, as seems logical, such subjects were taught one way or the other in Beroia, then they were taught outside the *gymnasion*. The *gymnasion* was entirely dedicated to athletic and military training. I summarise here the principal information (omitting for the present that which concerns the *paides*).

1. The *ephêboi* (aged probably between 18 and 20 years), as well as those "less than 22 years old", trained daily in bow shooting, javelin throwing, and in every other (military) discipline deemed necessary.
2. The *neoi* (youths of less than 30 years of age), principal users of the *gymnasion*, came there to "undress" (B 1 and 27) and to "anoint themselves" (B 4, 30, 38, 57), in other words to train in the *palaistra*, before using the bath.
3. The only contests mentioned, on the occasion of the Hermaia, concern the typical events of the *gymnasion* – "discipline", "diligence" and "good condition" (cf. above) – and the athletic events of the long-distance race and the torch race.
4. The gymnasiarch, at one point called "the leader",[29] was the sole master of the institution. It was he (or his representative) who had the signal indicating the opening and closing of the *gymnasion* raised and lowered. It was he who punished lack of discipline with fines, who chased out undesirables, in particular youths unfit for exercising in the *palaistra*, who offered prizes for the contests, and so on. It appears from reading the law that the *gymnasion* of Beroia was more of an army barracks than a university.

The example of Beroia represents, without doubt, an extreme case. During the course of the Hellenistic period, the *gymnasia* of numerous cities opened themselves up, to a greater or lesser degree, to "courses of study" (*mathêmata*). From there comes the importance of the auditorium, referred to above (part I). In the second century, the decree of Kolophon for Polemaios summarises in the following manner his formative years: "While he was still an ephebe, a regular attendee at the *gymnasion*, having nourished his soul with the most excellent studies and trained his body by the habit of physical exercises, he won crowns in the sacred contests."[30]

---

[27] *OGI* 339, 30–43 (first gymnasiarchy, before 133) and 61–86 (second gymnasiarchy, during the term of which the honorific decree under discussion here was adopted).
[28] *La loi* (n. 7), passim: see especially the conclusion, 173–6, and the index s. v. éphèbes, garçons, jeunes.
[29] A 13 (ὁ ἡγούμενος); his associate is called ὁ ἀφηγούμενος (B 3–4); cf. *La loi* (n. 7), 62–5.
[30] L. and J. Robert, *Claros I*, 1, 1989, p. 10, col. I, 1–7, with a classic commentary, pp. 19–20, on the association between "physical exercise" and "studies".

In Pergamon and Priene, around the same period, the *gymnasion* was also a place of literary "studies" (the decrees mention a *grammatikos* and contests of *philologia* – i.e. "love of learning").[31] The same was the case for Sestos. Even if the decree for the gymnasiarch Menas, already cited above, speaks only of athletic and military contests, we nevertheless find an allusion (the only one in the decree) to activities of another kind: "(Menas) also behaved generously towards all those who had given (sc. in the *gymnasion*) *akroaseis* (lectures or performances)."[32]

Let us summarise. For the *ephêboi* and the *neoi*, the *gymnasion* represented the privileged space where they pursued and completed their general education, physical (athletic) and intellectual. The content of this education, however, differed between cities and periods. And it was only the most prosperous and prestigious cities, like Athens and Rhodes, that had renowned schools of philosophy or rhetoric situated in or close to the *gymnasia* and which attracted foreign youths.[33]

On the subject of the presence of "boys" in the gymnasia, it seems to me that we can imagine two scenarios. On the one hand, under certain circumstances, notably during sacrifices and contests celebrated in the *gymnasion* in honour of Hermes and Herakles, who were the deities of the *gymnasion par excellence*, the youths (*neoi*), the ephebes and the *paides* were united momentarily under the authority of the gymnasiarch in order to participate in the athletic contests.[34] Naturally, the two groups competed in distinct categories; similarly during the banquets that followed the sacrifices later on, the boys were separated from the young men. The same happened in Beroia, during the Hermaia, and certainly also in Chalkis (although certain details are lacking), during the Herakleia and the Hermaia.[35]

Equally revealing is a detail from the decree of Sestos for Menas (cf. above). As a gymnasiarch, he was regularly praised because he "kept watch over the discipline of the *ephêboi* and the *neoi*" (l. 31), organised monthly races "for the *ephêboi* and the *neoi*" (ll. 36–7), performed sacrifices for the well-being of the people and the *neoi* (ll. 63–4), and, in general, because of his care for the physical and moral education of the "young men".[36] These groups therefore constituted the "population" ordinarily put under his authority. However, during the festivals and contests celebrated in honour of Herakles and Hermes at the end of the year, Menas, we are informed, offered prizes not only for the ephebes and the young men who were victorious,

---

[31] See L. and J. Robert, loc. cit.

[32] *OGI* 339, 74–5. "Generously" translated from φιλανθρώπως, which suggests courtesies of different kinds; the φιλανθρωπία mentioned in the preceding line refers to the opportunity given to participants to take away pieces of the sacrifice for consumption at home. Similarly, in the decree of Pergamon for the gymnasiarch Agias, it is stated that he intended to gain the loyalty of the teachers of the ephebes "through suitable rewards (φιλανθρωπίαι)": P. Jacobsthal, *MDAI(A)* 33, 1908, 380, 17–19, with the correction and the parallels indicated by H. Hepding, *MDAI(A)* 35, 1910, 492–3.

[33] On Athens at the end of the second and the beginning of the first century BC, see J.-L. Ferrary, *Philhellénisme et imperialisme*, 1988, 435–86; on Rhodes, L. and J. Robert, *Claros I*, 1, 1989, 23–5.

[34] The situation, it seems, was different in Délos, where the Hermaia, not attested at the period of independence, was, after 167/6, a "festival for children": cf. P. Bruneau, *Recherches sur les cultes de Délos*, 1970, 352.

[35] Beroia: see *La loi* (n. 7), 110–14 and 117–22. Chalkis: *IG* XII 9,952 (Herakleia); D. Knoepfler, *BCH* 103, 1979, 165–88 (Hermaia, and general commentary).

[36] *OGI* 339, 69, 71 (twice), 76, 79.

but also for the "boys".³⁷ On the occasion of the *Herakleia kai Hermaia*, then, as in Beroia or Chalkis, the *paides* in Sestos mingled with the other age groups in the *gymnasion*, under the authority of the gymnasiarch.

On the other hand, the law could oblige the "boys", at least in certain cities, to come and train in the *gymnasion*. This probably depended on the presence or absence of magistrates responsible for the education of the "boys", on the existence of the so-called *paidonomoi*, who had to abide by a "paidonomic law", and on the existence or lack of a civic *palaistra* reserved for the "boys".³⁸ Thus, in Beroia, the *paides* had to visit the *gymnasion*, accompanied by their *paidagôgoi*, twice a day, at a particular time fixed by the gymnasiarch, when the *palaistra* would be reserved for them, and where they could train under the direction of *paidotribai*.³⁹ There is no mention of *paidonomoi*; and, apparently, there was no public *palaistra* in Beroia reserved for the *paides*.⁴⁰

We catch a glimpse of a comparable situation in Eretria, but without the degree of detail we would like. A decree in honour of Elpinikos (end of second century BC) informs us that he had employed from his expenses a teacher of rhetoric (*rhêtor*) and an instructor in armed combat (*hoplomachos*), and that these two teachers "gave their lessons in the *gymnasion* to boys, *ephêboi* and, generally, to whoever wished to reap the benefits of their expertise in these fields."⁴¹ There is similar evidence in relation to another gymnasiarch in Eretria, who had obtained the services of a grammarian.⁴²

Employed and recompensed by the gymnasiarch himself, these itinerant teachers remained in Eretria for a few months.⁴³ The magistrate-benefactors wanted to allow the greatest possible number of interested parties to take advantage of their lessons. Thus, the *gymnasion* was open to all, in particular to the *paides*. However, it seems that neither the instructor in armed combat nor the *rhêtor* would have been able to teach succesfully, if several groups had not been set up, divided according to level and age and coming to the *gymnasion* at different times. Apparently, the "boys" did not possess a civic *palaistra* in Eretria that was reserved for their use.

Conversely, in Miletos, around the time when the endowment of Eudemos was established (206/5 BC), things were simpler. Under the responsibility of *paidonomoi*, the arts teachers and the *paidotribai* could instruct the "free boys" not in the *gymnasion*, which was reserved for the young men, but in the "*palaistra* of the boys" and in the rooms around it.⁴⁴

In this respect, the situation must have varied from one city to the next and, in the same city, from one period to the next. Thus, in Halikarnassos during the third

---

³⁷ Ibid., 79–83; cf. *La loi* (n. 7), 100–1. M. P. Nilsson (n. 6), 57 and n. 6, has not put this detail into the context of the end-of-the-year festival.

³⁸ On the *paidonomoi*, known mostly (but not exclusively) from the cities of Asia, see E. Ziebarth (n. 11), 19 and 39–41; M. P. Nilsson (n. 6), 57–9.

³⁹ *La loi* (n. 7), 72–6.

⁴⁰ That said, the law seems to contain an allusion to private *palaistrai* (in a sentence of dubious meaning – B 4–5); cf. *La loi* (n. 7), 59.

⁴¹ *IG* XII 9, 234 (*Syll.*³ 714), 8–12.

⁴² *IG* XII 9, 235, 10–13 (Mantidoros).

⁴³ "Wanderlehrer", E. Ziebarth (n. 11), 122, in regard to Eretria, along with other examples.

⁴⁴ *Syll.*³ 577, 32 and 83–6 (endowment of Eudemos); *Milet* I, 7 (Der Südmarkt), 292–3, n° 203 (Fr. Sokolowski, *Lois sacrées de l'Asie Mineure*, 1955, n° 49), 13–14 (the *palaistra* of the *paides*), 10–11 and 20–1 (*gymnasion* and gymnasiarch of the *neoi*).

century BC, the *gymnasion* of the *neoi* was to be reconstructed or restored in such a way that the young men made use of the "*palaistra* of the boys" (undoubtedly for specific hours). Thanks to the loans and subscriptions of the citizens (and also perhaps to a grant by the Ptolemaic king), the reconstruction was completed succesfully and the boys and young men could, from then on, train in two distinct establishments.[45] In Hydai, close to Mylasa, the decree of the late Hellenistic period honouring the *paidonomos* Chrysippos would undoubtedly permit us, had it not been mutilated, to define the conditions of use of the *gymnasion* by the boys in a small city. It seems "training in physical activities" (τὴν ἐν ταῖς γυμνασίαις ἄσκησιν, l. 7) and "the contests organised in the *palaistra*, the races, wrestling, boxing and *pankration*" (ll. 15–17) took place for the *paides* in the *gymnasion*, which is mentioned in ll. 23 and 56 (the context is lost). But surely the "studies" (l. 6) and the contests in "reading", "good writing" and *philomathia* (love of learning), (ll. 18–19) would have taken place under the direction of the *paidonomos* in other locations?[46] The same question arises for the "studies", as well as the "contests" and the "examinations" of the *paides*, in relation to their literary and musical training and their athletic exercises, as these are revealed to us in inscriptions from Ephesos or Teos.[47]

In general, it seems to me that the young children and adolescents spent their time in their schools and *palaistrai*, private or public (in the latter, under the guidance of *paidonomoi* elected by the city). The "boys" had access to the *gymnasion* at times, but this establishment remained the space where the *ephêboi* and the *neoi* took priority.

III. THE *GYMNASION* AS AN INSTITUTION

Having become an integral part of the Hellenistic *towns*, did the *gymnasion* belong to those requisite *civic* institutions that were, for that reason, located usually in the centre of the towns, close to the *agora*?[48] The answer to this question is less simple than it appears.[49] Here again, one must surely distinguish between cities; we can perhaps also detect an evolution throughout the Hellenistic period. I will limit myself to two observations.

In the first place, the control exercised by the city on the *gymnasion*, through the

---

[45] L. Migeotte, *L'Emprunt public*, 1984, n° 101, 7–13, and n° 102 (decree in honour of Diodotos, reporting on the completion of works); for the first of these texts see equally L. Migeotte, *Les Souscriptions publiques*, 1992, no. 77. One could compare also the case of Kolophon where it seems, around 200 BC, the *palaistra* of the *paides* was to be constructed or restored: M. Holleaux, *Études d'épigraphie et d'histoire grecques* II, 1938, 51–60, in particular 55 and n. 1. M. P. Nilsson (n. 6), 34, who does not cite the revision by Holleaux, is guilty of a confusion regarding this text.

[46] W. Blümel, *I. Mylasa* II, 909 (cf. *Bull. épigr.* 1987, 14); on *philomathia*, see L. Robert, *Hellenica* XI–XII, 1960, 586 (and 587), n. 7; XIII, 1965, 47 n. 3.

[47] Ephesos: J. Keil, *AnzWien* 1951, 331–5 (under the reign of Eumenes II); cf. J. and L. Robert, *Bull. épigr.* 1953, 178 (the inscription has been picked up again in *I. Ephesos* IV, 1101). Teos: *CIG* III, 3088 (Michel, *Recueil* 913); cf. E. Ziebarth (n. 11), 139–41.

[48] See H. von Hesberg, "Das griechische Gymnasion im 2.Jh.v.Chr.", in M. Wörrle and P. Zanker, *Stadtbild und Bürgerbild im Hellenismus*, 1995, 13–27.

[49] The few lines written on the subject by J. Delorme (n. 3), 254–5, are hasty and at times erroneous (in regard to the *epistatês* and the ephebarchs).

mediation of one or more magistrates elected by the people annually, was probably instituted at a great variety of different dates in the Greek world. I note that Aristotle, in his *Politics*, does not cite the gymnasiarchy among the "indispensable" civic magistracies and only briefly mentions it in the group of offices "typical of cities that enjoy more leisure and greater prosperity."[50] Such an opinion, no doubt acceptable around 335–330 BC, would not be so a couple of centuries later.

In Pherai, a list engraved shortly before the end of the third century BC and completed afterwards has revealed the names of acting gymnasiarchs in this city from 334/3.[51] There may have existed in Troizen as well, from the fourth century, a regularly elected gymnasiarch.[52] A law from Koresia in Keos, engraved around the beginning of the third century BC (the date, based on the style of the letter-cutting, is very approximate) decrees that: "a gymnasiarch should also be elected at the same time as the rest of the magistrates, aged at least thirty years old."[53] In this case, as shown by the context, it was the creation or reorganisation of a great annual festival, consisting of different contests open to young men and boys (cf. above), which gave the opportunity to the city to institute this annual magistracy. It was decided that the elected person had to: "organise a torch race for the young men to take place during the festival and, in general, keep an eye over the *gymnasion* and take the young men to the field in order to train in javelin and catapult throwing and arrow-shooting three times per month".[54] In Delos, during the period of independence, it was only around 249–247, it seems, that the office of the gymnasiarchy was instituted.[55]

In Makedonia, the gymnasiarchal law of Beroia (around 180 BC) stipulated and made provision for the election of an accountable gymnasiarch: "that the city should elect a gymnasiarch at the same time as the rest of the magistrates, aged at least thirty years old and not more than sixty, and that the elected gymnasiarch should exercise these functions after having taken the following oath," and so on (A 22–5). We are definitely dealing in this case with an innovation. Yet, the decree engraved underneath the text of the law mentions "Zopyros, son of Amyntas, the gymnasiarch": this individual had collaborated in writing the draft of the gymnasiarchal law. Thus, before the adoption of this law, the *gymnasion* of Beroia was already directed by a gymnasiarch, but one who was doubtless appointed by "those who frequented the place," under conditions and for a length of time of which we are ignorant.[56] Having their own revenues at their disposal, the *aleiphomenoi* (i.e. "those who anoint themselves", "those who exercise") of Beroia administered

---

[50] *Politics* 6.8, 1323a1.
[51] Chr. Habicht, *Demetrias I*, 1976, 181–97 (and plate XLIII), in particular 185–7. The re-edition and commentary of this inscription by Br. Helly, G. J. Te Riele and J. A. van Rossum, in *Thessalie*, 1979, 220–55, has brought out useful details on the letter-cutting, the prosopography and the relative chronology. However, the proposed restitution of the heading of the list does not appear acceptable; in that we follow Chr. Habicht.
[52] However, the mutilated decrees *IG* IV, 749 and 753 (+ Addenda p. 381), attributed to the fourth century based on the letter-cutting, could well be later (in particular because of the formula).
[53] *Syll.*³ 958, 21–2.
[54] Cf. E. Ziebarth (n. 11), 41–2.
[55] Cl. Vial, *Délos indépendante*, 1984, 242.
[56] We can state the same hypothesis for the *gymnasion* of Amphipolis, which seems not to have come under the jurisdiction of the city until the end of the third century BC; *La loi* (n. 7), 160.

themselves; the city did not intervene.[57]

In a very different context, a second-century BC inscription from Thera demonstrates how a *gymnasion* could function outside the framework of the *polis*. The decree of the *aleiphomenoi* in honour of Baton unquestionably emanated from the soldiers of the Ptolemaic garrisons (or at least from the youngest among them, that is, those who regularly frequented the *gymnasion*), stationed in the city during the reign of Ptolemy VI Philometor.[58] Another more or less contemporary inscription informs us, on the one hand, that at the request of those stationed in the garrison the king had granted them revenues from several properties, "so that they should have funds with which to meet the expenses of the sacrifices and the anointing", and on the other hand, that the soldiers themselves paid a contribution "for the restoration of the *gymnasion*".[59] This composite community, thus endowed with revenues, administered itself, elected its gymnasiarch (Baton had been active for five years when he was honoured and the regulars of the *gymnasion* asked him to extend his term of office), and participated in athletic contests[60] celebrated "for Hermes and Herakles in the name of the king".

In the Hellenistic cities, there were undoubtedly varying and at times unanticipated circumstances that determined the Assembly of the people to establish its control over the *gymnasion*, or else restricted them from doing so. In Beroia, the proclaimed objectives of the law (A 11–16) suggest that it was adopted in the aftermath of disorder and embezzlement. Elsewhere, the construction, reconstruction or restoration of a *gymnasion*, the awarding of royal funds or the allocation of revenues coming from private sources,[61] and the creation or reorganisation of festivals could all constitute occasions for the cities to take charge of the administration of the *gymnasion* through the mediation of regularly elected magistrates.

Second observation: if the *gymnasion* was essentially intended to accommodate and educate young and future citizens, it was nevertheless neither frequented by every single citizen nor by citizens alone. As an urban building, the *gymnasion* was *de facto* reserved for the city-dwellers and was open primarily to young men who, as part of that citizen population, enjoyed the same pastimes and resources and shared the same vision of life. In addition, from the classical period onwards, in Athens and elsewhere, the incorporation of philosophical schools and other disciplines in the *gymnasia* (or in their proximity) opened the way for the attendance, along with foreign teachers, of foreign students as well.[62] The young foreigners, who resided

---

[57] Cf. L. Moretti, *Riv. Fil.* 110, 1982, 45–63, in particular 46–9.

[58] *IG* XIII 3, 331; L. Robert, *Collection Froehner. Inscriptions grecques*, 1936, 141–3, no. 95.

[59] *IG* XIII 3, 327 + Addenda p. 283. See especially M. Launey, *Recherches sur les armées hellénistiques II*, 1950, 847–8; L. Robert, *Noms indigènes dans l'Asie Mineure gréco-romaine*, 1963, 388–9 and 411–20 (on the garrisoned soldiers of Pamphylian origin); R. S. Bagnall, *The Administration of the Ptolemaic Possessions outside Egypt*, 1976, 127–8. Compare the subscription of the Ptolemaic soldiers in the garrison of Paphos, T. B. Mitford, *ABSA* 56, 1961, 6, n° 8.

[60] As did the Greek mercenaries in 400 BC, when they reached Trapezus, Xenophon, *Anab.* 4.8.25–8.

[61] There is an informative example in a nearby territory: in Teos, the academic foundation of Polythrous provided the opportunity for the city to regulate the education of children and to proceed from then on to the annual election of a *paidonomos*, aged at least forty years old: *Syll.*³ 578, 1–3 and following.

[62] See e.g. P. Vidal-Naquet "La Société platonicienne des dialogues", in *Aux origines de l'hellénisme: la Crète et la Grèce: hommage à Henri Van Effenterre* (1984), 273–93, who notes that numerous individuals in the dialogues are foreigners and that their role became more prominent as Plato's oeuvre developed.

in a city "for their education" (*kata paideusin*), as in Lampsakos around 300 BC, certainly frequented not just the schools and the lecture halls, but also occasionally or regularly, the *palaistrai* of the *gymnasia*.[63] This development continued and became more marked in the course of the Hellenistic period: one need only recall, in this respect, the multiplication of local and "sacred" contests, which attracted numerous competitors from near and far. It was not the status of "citizen", but the adherence of "free" young men to the values of education *à la grecque*, that was the open-sesame to the doors of the *gymnasion*.

The law of Beroia provides very significant testimony on the subject. Let us not forget that the *gymnasion* of that city appears to have been exclusively devoted to athletic and military training. The law was clear that slaves and freedmen (as well as their sons), the *apalaistros* (most probably the young man "unfit for the exercises of the *palaistra*"), male prostitutes, anyone who exercised a profession in the *agora* and men in a state of drunkenness or seized by a fit of insanity were excluded. None of these criteria concerns citizenship. All are based on notions of liberty, way of life and ideals.[64]

Similarly, the academic establishments of Miletos and Teos were intended for the education of "free children".[65] On the same principle, the citizens of Astypalaia, who in the second century took in Ephesians, both "free and slaves", who had been kidnapped by pirates, treated the citizens of Ephesos "as their own fellow citizens" and looked after the education of the "free children".[66]

In civic decrees voted for gymnasiarchs, "foreigners" (*xenoi*), or as they are called "the foreigners who participate in public affairs" or "who play a part in the anointing" are sometimes mentioned in relation to the benefactions granted by the magistrates; at other times, they join with other *neoi* in paying homage to the qualities of the honoured magistrate.[67]

The presence of foreigners, who were certainly a minority, in the *gymnasia* of the cities is recorded in, or in some cases can be deduced from other inscriptions. Thus,

---

This phenomenon reflected the character of the "Academy as an international centre of study and knowledge" (p. 293). See in particular the *Euthydemos*, whose entire beginning is set in the Lykeion and gives a vibrant image of the *gymnasion* and its public.

[63] Foreigners coming to live in a city *kata paideusin* ("for the purposes of education"): Aineias Takt. *Poliork.* 10.10. In Lampsakos, exemption from tax is granted to students and to resident teachers, *I. Lampsakos* 8; cf. in general E. Ziebarth (n. 11), 87–8.

[64] See *La loi* (n. 7), 78–87.

[65] *Syll.*³ 577, 4 (Miletos); 578, 3–4 (Teos); cf. IG II², 896, 59–61 (Athens).

[66] IG XII 3, 1286; *I. Ephesos* Ia, 5, 30–9; cf. Ph. Gauthier, *Rev. Phil.* 64, 1990, 65–7. We can also compare the decree of Theangelos, son of Kosmiades, for the Delian Semos: *IG* XI 4, 1054a, with the supplement of Ad. Wilhelm, *Anzeiger Wien* 1924, 133–4 (Akademieschrift II, 177–8).

[67] "Foreigners who participated in public affairs" or "at the anointing": *OGI* 339, 73–4 and 85 (Sestos); *Syll.*3 714, 24–8 (Eretria); cf. Ph. Gauthier, *Rev. Phil.* 56, 1982, 229–31 (a sentence must be corrected in this article, p. 230, which should read, after the citation in ll. 24–8 of the decree of Eretria: "Further down, it is made clear that the gymnasiarch invited the citizens and the Romans present at the time, on the fourth day dealt with "those who participated in the *koina*", then, on the fifth day, with numerous other individuals, citizens and foreigners"). Foreigners in the *gymnasion* of Pergamon: H. Hepding, *MDAI(A)* 32, 1907, 275 (l. 19) and 277; 35, 1910, 422 (ll. 10–12) and 424; cf. J. and L. Robert, *Bull. épigr.* 1980, no. 94 (p. 377); in Themisonion in Phrygia: Michel, *Recueil* 544, 19–20; cf. Ad. Wilhelm, *GGA* 1900, 97–8; E. Ziebarth (n. 11), 112 n. 1. Ex-*ephēboi paroikoi* (i.e. "resident-aliens") in Priene: *I. Priene* 123, 8.

in Chalkis in the second century BC, the victory lists of the *gymnasion* at the time of the Herakleia and the Hermaia, allow us to identify a certain number of foreigners, notably Antiocheians (no doubt from the Orontes).[68] In two of his studies dedicated to athletes and to "sacred" (panhellenic) contests, L. Robert has gathered examples of victors announced by the herald, not with reference to their city of origin, but to another city. Around 300 BC, an adolescent winner in boxing at the Nemean contest was proclaimed an "Ephesian" and crowned the city of Ephesos, which in recognition bestowed on him the right of citizenship. This young man was the son of a foreign resident, who had the status of *isotelês* [i.e. having the same tax status as full citizens]. It is thus almost certain that the young man himself had grown up in Ephesos and that he had trained in the *gymnasion* of that city, next to the sons of citizens.[69] One could list other similar cases.[70]

The preceding remarks might lead us to believe that the *gymnasion*, more than an exclusively civic institution, was the setting where the fundamental values of Hellenism were expressed. But can we define "the" Hellenistic *gymnasion*? Would it not be better to limit ourselves to listing and presenting the many different types of situation, with the help of a body of evidence that continuously grows more abundant? What was there in common (in terms of buildings, number and status of users, content of teachings) between the *gymnasia* of the big maritime cities, which were populous and prosperous (like Rhodes, Miletos or Ephesos) and those of small cities, which were isolated and poor? Between the situation in the ancient cities of the Aegean world and that in the recent foundations of Asia Minor and the East? Between the needs (or aspirations) of the subject-cities occupied by royal garrisons and those of autonomous cities, which made use of civic militias to defend their territory, and, on occasion, despatched contingents intended for a common army within the framework of a confederation (as in Boiotia in the third century BC) or of a kingdom (as in Makedonia)? A careful study of "the" Hellenistic *gymnasia* will surely reveal many interesting particularities according to region (as demonstrated, in regard to Makedonia, by the publication of the law of Beroia) and according to period.

Thus, in conclusion, we can note with certain reservations both the maintenance of traditions and the appearance of innovation. On the one hand, as the heir of an aristocratic tradition, agonistic and military, the *gymnasion* fundamentally remained in the Hellenistic age the place where young men would train in athletic and military activities, although room was also made for intellectual and musical disciplines, albeit differently in different cities and in some cases earlier in the period than others. Open to "free" men who shared the same way of life and the same ideal of *aretê* it became the bastion and symbol of Hellenism.

On the other hand, a significant innovation that took place during the high

---

[68] D. Knoepfler, *BCH* 103, 1979, 179–81.
[69] L. Robert, *Rev. Phil.* 41, 1967, 14–32 (*Opera Minora* V, 354–72, in particular 358).
[70] In regard to a possible case, once more in Ephesos, cf. L. Robert, loc. cit., 27 n.3 (*Opera Minora* V, 367). I point out, without invoking them here (since victors in chariot-racing, "who had raced their carriages", were foreigners to the world of the *gymnasion*), the similar examples picked out and analysed by L. Robert in the catalogue of the *Romaia* of Xanthos, *Rev. Arch.* 1978, 277–90 (*Opera Minora* VII, 681–694, notably 691).

Hellenistic period, in parallel to the flourishing of *gymnasia*-buildings in the towns, was the fact that control of the *gymnasion* by the city became widespread. Placed under the authority of a magistrate elected by the people, whose obligation was to respect the law and to handle the funds himself (while at the same time often having to prove his own munificence), the *gymnasion* became, in the strict sense of the term, a civic institution – something that was fairly rarely the case with schools that accommodated young children. Catering above all for the education of the citizen-soldier, in places where a civic army remained (testimonies abound in this respect), the *gymnasion* became more generally speaking the crucible from which emerged the administrative class of the cities. Moreover, it is not an accident if later on (in the late Hellenistic period) the *gymnasion* served, according to the expression of L. Robert, as a "second *agora*" where, following the example of the kings, the cult of the great citizen benefactors, honoured as new founders, would develop.[71]

---

[71] See especially L. Robert, *REA* 62, 1960, 296–8 (*Opera Minora* II, 812–14, with the summary of his thesis and the expression "second *agora*" p. 814 n. 3); *Ant. Class.* 35, 1966, 419–25 (*Opera Minora* VI, 43–9). The examples are not earlier than the first century BC.

PART III
Festival Foundations

Introduction to Part III

Even more so than for the spread of *gymnasion* culture, the expansion of the Greek agonistic festival calendar is remarkable for its enormous scale, first in the early Hellenistic period, and then, after a quieter period during the first century BCE, in the Roman world of the first, second and third centuries CE. The first of Louis Robert's pieces in this section, dating from nearer the end of his career, offers a sweeping and vivid overview of this extraordinary Hellenistic proliferation and its further intensification in the Roman period. There is no need to duplicate in this introduction the outline he provides. The article represents an ideal introduction to Robert's important oeuvre. Robert has done more than anyone else in the last century to expand our understanding of the ancient festival calendar and the epigraphic representation of athletic victory through his enormous number of publications on agonistic inscriptions.[1] His elegant but compressed language and his dense referencing style (apparent especially in chapter 6) are often difficult, but the reward is a wonderfully vivid glimpse of the most intricate details of festival organisation and commemoration in the ancient world. Each individual epigraphic text comes to life, under Robert's treatment, through being contextualised as part of a much wider series of similar inscriptions.

The Olympics, and the other *periodos* Games, continued to matter in the Roman world – in fact the Olympics in particular seem to have undergone a revival in prestige after a relative decline in the late Hellenistic world. But they also increasingly came to be challenged and supplemented by others. There is evidence for an enormously large and administratively complex calendar of contests.[2] There was a great variation in the scale of agonistic festivals, ranging from the biggest of the *periodos* games, to small local festivals. Athletic guilds – and their musical counterparts – developed in the Hellenistic period, but became particularly prominent and powerful in the Roman empire as large, Mediterranean-wide bodies representing

---

[1] Reprinted in Robert (1969–90); see also the bibliography to König (2005) for a list of many of his key articles on agonistic culture; and more recently Robert (2007) for reprinting of many of Robert's most important works in the original French.

[2] See esp. Pleket (1998), who sketches out the complex infrastructure of ancient athletic cultures; for other overviews of the development of the festival calendar, in addition to the first of the Robert articles translated here, see also Mitchell (1990) (a review of Wörrle's (1988) publication, with German commentary, of the important festival foundation inscription for the festival of the Demostheneia in the city of Oinoanda); Parker (2004) on the Hellenistic period; Scanlon (2002) 40–63 on the Roman period; Spawforth (1989) on festivals in the Roman province of Achaia.

the interests of victors and competitors.³ We also see a shift to Asia Minor and other eastern provinces, which held increasingly large numbers of important athletic festivals, and which provided vast numbers of Olympic victors in this later period.⁴ Those developments come across particularly vividly if we look at the proliferation of other agonistic festivals which took the Olympic name, and imitated some but often not all features of the administration and programming of the original festival, as if in an attempt to share something of the prestige of the original Games. We know of large numbers of these imitation Olympics (more than thirty are attested), some of which were themselves important landmarks in the festival calendar, as well as a number of imitation Pythian festivals along similar lines (some of them discussed in passing by Robert in the chapters which follow).⁵

One aspect of this spreading festival calendar which deserves particular attention is the question of how it spread beyond the traditional centres of the Greek world, beyond even the wealthy cities of Asia Minor just mentioned. Onno van Nijf's article in Part 4 deals with the role of athletic culture in Lycia, an area whose Greek credentials were not at all secure, and the issue gains a brief mention in Robert's piece reprinted in chapter 5. In chapter 6, by contrast, we look more towards Rome. The west of the Roman Empire developed its own distinctive engagement with Greek agonistic culture, not only in the cities of south Italy, which were Greek-speaking cities, and not only in the sense that much of the Greek athletic revival of this period was stimulated by the sponsorship and foundation of particular festivals within Greek territory by the emperors, but also in the city of Rome itself, which as Robert shows held important Greek-style festivals from the first century CE onwards.⁶ Like Robert's work on gladiators,⁷ which reveals the enormous popularity of gladiatorial games in the Greek-speaking cities of the Roman Empire, this article is important for bringing home the inadequacy of the traditional split between Roman liking for brutal arena games and Greek love of civilised athletics. Not only were the athletic events themselves, particularly the combat sports of wrestling and boxing and pankration, very brutal, as I suggested in the introduction, but the wide geographical spread of both reveals that many elements of Greek and Roman taste were interchangeable. That said, Robert is also keen to stress that the traditional Roman arena games were never confused with Greek-style contests: the two were always clearly distinguished from each other.

Chapter 5, finally, also glances very briefly ahead to the history of athletics in the Christian era. There are many signs of Christian engagement with and knowledge of athletic culture, for example in the regular use of athletic metaphor.⁸ Despite that, however, athletic festivals and indeed the culture of the *gymnasion* began to

---

³ E.g., see Pleket (1973); and cf. Potter (1999) 258–83 for useful discussion of athletes and actors in the Roman Empire, including an outline of the athletic guilds.
⁴ See Farrington (1997) 16–32 for the increasing dominance of victors from the east at Olympia.
⁵ See Farrington (1997) 32–43.
⁶ See also König (2005) 205–35; Newby (2005) 21–140, covering *gymnasion* culture as well as festivals in the west, and further discussion of Newby's work in the introduction to section 5, below. On the festival of the Capitolia, founded by the emperor Domitian, see (in addition to the second of Robert's articles translated here) Caldelli (1993), in Italian.
⁷ Robert (1940).
⁸ See Pfitzner (1967); Seesengood (2006).

die out from the third century onwards. One important landmark is the banning of pagan festivals by the emperor Theodosius in the 390s. Nevertheless, this was not a sudden change. Even well after this, the athletic life of many Greek cities continued. One telling example comes from the city of Antioch, whose Olympic festival is attested well into the fifth century, and mentioned repeatedly in the fourth-century writings of the pagan orator Libanius.[9]

---

[9] See Downey (1939); Millon and Schouler (1988).

5 Opening Address: Eighth International Congress of Greek and Latin Epigraphy*

LOUIS ROBERT
(translated by Margarita Lianou)

My subject here is the Greek contests of the Hellenistic and Imperial periods. It is a topic that has been with me since my very young days as a student and my first publications. My aim in this treatment is to create some paths and clearings in this forest by reminding you of some essential facts, still too often neglected; also by adding some personal reflections, and referring to some documents which are new in a number of their features.

Let me make clear first of all that it is absurd to follow the lifeless, outdated tradition of using the term Olympic "Games" and Pythian "Games". The "games" (*paidiai*) of the Greeks were the spinning-top, the hoop, jacks, dice and everything that Becq de Fouquières gathered under this title [i.e. in his work *Jeux des anciens*] more than a century ago. The contests of Olympia and elsewhere were serious and testing affairs. They were not for laughs; one fought to win, to be declared and proclaimed "the first"; more often than not, there was no second place. The very word *agôn* referred to battles in war where one risked one's life, trials in court that could cost one's fortune and one's life. Athletic endeavour was the opposite of a playful activity. The *agôn*, the contest, was fundamentally distinct from the *epideixis*, which was a recital, a performance without competitors. When the Greek contest spread to Roman territory, the *ludus* ("public games") became distinct from the *certamen* (Latin: "competition") or *agôn*.

Among the Greek contests there existed a crucial distinction – one which still often goes unnoticed – between local contests and those we can call panhellenic, or more precisely, "sacred". It was not a matter of access; the local contests normally attracted foreigners as well, who were not excluded.[1] It was a matter of reward: in the sacred contests the crown alone, without money, was the prize of victory.

In the classical period, the contests that stood above all others in the hierarchy were the contests of the *periodos*: at Olympia, Delphi, Isthmia and Nemea. In the Hellenistic period, a process of continual development allowed numerous contests

---

* Originally published in *Actes du VIIIe congrès international d'épigraphie grecque et latine à Athènes, 1982* (Athens, 1982), pp. 35–45 (=*Opera Minora Selecta* 6: 709–19) (=*Choix d'écrits* 267–78). The first page of the publication, reproducing Robert's introductory remarks to his speech, is not translated here.

[1] *REA* 1936, 21–2 (*Opera Minora*, II, 784–5) [cf. also *Laodicée et Lycos. Le Nymphée* (1969) 253].

– until that time local or newly created – to obtain the status of sacred contests, stephanitic, isolympic, isopythian and so on. From the second half of the third century BC, and even more so in the second century, there were many cities that celebrated such contests: the Asklepieia in Kos, the Didymeia in Miletos, the Heliaia in Rhodes, the Eleutheria in the Thessalian Confederacy, the Leukophryeneia in Magnesia-on-the-Meander. The evidence for this last contest, which is the most abundant, and is found engraved on the walls of the *agora*, reveals in detail the mechanism of that transformation. In the beginning there was an oracle, then the agreement of the cities, as well as the kings, who were called upon by *theôroi*-ambassadors and who in turn despatched *theôroi*-representatives charged with offering a sacrifice in the name of the city. In Kos, we possess responses from the cities of Sicily and Magna Graecia all the way to Makedonia and Thrace and the kings of Bithynia and Cimmerian Bosporus.

How did this system come into being? What were the first manifestations of this process of creating new sacred contests? The question has been misunderstood for a long time on account of what was believed regarding the Soteria of Delphi, which commemorated the defeat of the Gauls in 279 BC. The creation of the Soteria immediately after this victory duplicated the Pythia by setting up a second contest in the same place. The innovative, perceptive and definitive work of Pierre Roussel has taught us that the Soteria created after the victory was an amphictyonic festival without panhellenic and stephanitic pretensions, and that the contest of the Soteria which associated Zeus Soter with Apollo Pythios and which had a stephanitic character, was a creation of the Aitolians only in the middle of the third century, when they were all-powerful in Delphi. Therefore, the first creation of a new stephanitic contest, some thirty years earlier [i.e. than the stephanitic Soteria], was that of the Ptolemaia of Ptolemy Philadelphos in honour of his father. The motive for founding a contest equal to those of the *periodos* was a display of power by the Ptolemaic monarchy, the most stable and rich of the new monarchies. It was a reflection of the centre of Greek culture which was most distant from the cities of Greece and most ambitious, the new beacon of science and the arts, the court of Alexandria with its scholarly and literary institutions. It must be noted that in its first appearance, when it was accepted by the League of the Islanders, the contest of the Ptolemaia in Alexandria was designated isolympic in its athletic and musical program, even though there was no musical contest in Olympia.

Epigraphic documents of various categories are numerous enough to allow us to draw up a list of stephanitic contests in the Hellenistic period from the third century BC to the first. The proclamation and acceptance of these contests and their celebration attest to the economic prosperity of the cities and regions where they took place. Festivals could not flourish except in conditions of peace and security. Wars brought stagnation and the interruption of the contests, as well as of other expressions of the divine cult, and much more besides. Their resumption, their renewal, *ananeôsis*, testifies both to their interruption and to the breath of air that revitalised them again, towards the end of the second century in Greece, as established first by Adolf Wilhelm.

The proliferation and density of stephanitic games in Hellenistic Greece in the second and first centuries is well attested in the Peloponnese, for example. Together with the contests of Olympia, the Isthmus, Nemea and also Argos, we have the Pythia of Sikyon, the Asklepieia of Epidaurus, the Poseidaia of Mantineia, the Aleaia of Alea Athena in Tegea, the Hemerasia of Artemis in Lousoi, the Koriasia of Artemis in Cleitor, the Lykaia of Zeus Lykaios by Mount Lykeion, the Chthoneia of Demeter in Hermione. Sparta, by contrast, retained its unique xenophobia. In Boiotia, we could juxtapose with nearly every city the name of its stephanitic contest. This tight network of small civic units became, each for a few days every four years, a panhellenic centre. In the deserted Plataiai, for more than seven centuries, throughout the Hellenistic and the Imperial periods until the eve of the third century AD, the Hellenes as one nation remembered the victory of the Hellenic armies and invoked at the same time Zeus the Liberator and the Concord of the Hellenes, divine figures which stood for their dreams of liberation and harmony, pursued through ordeals, servitude and internecine struggles.

Let us now turn our attention to the small town of Priene, which despatched *theôroi* in the third and second centuries BC to Athens, which it considered its *mêtropolis*, and to Samothrake. The town had the contests in honour of its patron deity, the Athenaia, recognised as stephanitic. Around the middle of the second century, the city's great detailed decrees for the benefactors Moschion and Herodes mention their missions as *theôroi* several times. They were *theôroi*, from time to time, to the contests celebrated in Pergamon for the victory of Perperna against Eumenes III; also to the assembly of the Ionian Confederation at the Panionion at Mykale and to the Seleukid Demetrios II. Moschion had also been a *theôros* in Magnesia and in Tralles, both of which were neighbouring towns in the valley of the Meander and, further away, in Kibyra. The contests were the Leukophryeneia in Magnesia, either the Olympia or the Pythia in Tralles, and in Kibyra, the Romaia. In an inscription from Halikarnassos, a runner is recorded as having won victory not in the Romaia of Kerkyra (Κε[ρκύρ]αι), as previously read, but of Kibyra.[2] Further, in the valley of the Meander there existed a stephanitic contest in Nysa, the Theogamia, in honour of the nuptials of Plouton and Kore.

It is also worth marking the geographical limits of this proliferation of festivals. In the region of Epiros and Illyria, the Naia of Zeus Naios in Dodone had become a stephanitic contest around the end of the third century BC, coinciding with the renaissance of the sanctuary after 218 BC (not earlier, in the times of Pyrrhus, nor later, only in the second century). Further to the North, Apollonia in Illyria and Epidamnos provided a good link with the rest of the Greek world; these two towns had received and accepted the invitation for the contests of Magnesia and their citizens were victors in various contests in Greece. The contest of the Apollonia in honour of the Nymphs of the bitumen springs was accepted in the second century as stephanitic. Further away, the Greek cities of the Dalmatian coast and its islands were too weak to institute a contest of this rank.

There were no stephanitic contests in Crete. There must have been a contest of the *koinon*, as in most places, under the Empire. For the earlier period, this absence

---

[2] In this athletic inscription from Halikarnassos *Syll.*³, 1064, Jeanne Robert has read ἐν Κιβύραι ["in Kibyra"] in the place of Ῥωμαῖα τὰ ἐν Κε[ρκύραι] ["at the Romaia of Kerkyra"].

is explicable as a consequence of the social situation in Crete and the character of its inhabitants. One could not ask the Cretan pirates not to attack those who were to participate or assist in the contests, in other words to give them *asylia*. There were no stephanitic contests in the Black Sea either, as the cities there were often under threat.

As for Magna Graecia and Sicily, their history was in much turmoil in the third century BC due to both the Carthaginians and the Romans. At the time when the status of the stephanitic contests expanded, the Greek cities were under Roman influence. They accepted the contests of Greece and the Aegean (also Kos and Magnesia); but did not create any to invite them to in turn.

Under the Empire, there was a proliferation of new contests. The Augustan peace spread everywhere and for the majority of the Greek provinces it extended well into the third century AD. This triggered an athletic explosion. Augustus created a contest, the Aktia in Nikopolis, which was not only stephanitic but was added to the *periodos*, the "circuit" of four original contests. He allowed the celebration of the Sebasta in Pergamon in his honour for the benefit of the Greeks in the province of Asia, and the Italian Sebasta in the Greek town of Neapolis. From then on, there might sometimes be several stephanitic contests in the same town. The body of evidence is dramatically expanded, from that moment on, by coins bearing the names of festivals and symbols of contests and prizes.

Also from that point on, the authorisation to celebrate one of the great contests stemmed from the emperor and was called *dôrea*, a gift. This was not a gift of money. The word appears in inscriptions, in papyri in Egypt and on coins. In certain regions the Senate could be involved in this process as well, an example being in the authorisation of a city's official titulature. In addition, consultation took place in the cities of the Greek world, which had to consent to the acceptance of the new contests. The two processes appear in the text of Tertullian, *Scorpiace* 6: at the beginning of the reign of Septimius Severus, Carthage "received the gift of a Pythian contest" for the first time (*donata Pythico agone*). The town then received the congratulations of the cities of the Greek world (*Carthaginem singulae civitates gratulando inquietant*). The Greek cities took part in the panhellenic contests by despatching their delegations of sacrificers. Thus, the term *theôroi* was usually replaced by that of *synthutai*, which clearly marks in common parlance the religious character of the ceremony; it is a *synthusia*, a communal sacrifice, and the entire universe is involved through its representatives (i.e. it is a *synthusia oikoumenês* – "common sacrifice of the entire world") as proclaimed proudly by the coins of Anazarbos.

I will quickly go through the other highlights of this period of great contests in the Roman Empire: the reign of Augustus and the Julio-Claudian period was marked by a throng of contests, with names like Sebasta, Kaisareia, Tibereia, Claudieia and so on (we find the name Augusteia only much later). Let us not speak of servitude on the part of the provinces, for these contests were the manifestations of the joy of finally living in peace – after a very harsh period – and stability. Domitian – after the short-lived attempt of the Neroneia – took the decisive step of creating a Greek contest in Rome in honour of the patron Roman deities, the Capitoline

Triad. Under the Flavians, there were few initiations of contests in the provinces; only the Barbilleia-Balbilleia in honour of the astrologer Barbillus in Ephesos and other cities of the province. Under Hadrian, there was a rich blossoming of contests in honour of the Emperor and various divinities; the Panathenaia and the Panhellenia in Athens are particularly notable. This trend was continued by Antoninus, who created the Eusebeia at Puteoli in honour of Hadrian. There were lots of Commodeia festivals. There was a similar blossoming of contests under the Severans: Severeia, Antonineia or Antoneia and so on, especially along the routes of the Roman army marching against the Persian enemy, in Propontis and Bithynia in the North, and Kilikia in the South. We should also note the prosperity of the cities in Asia Minor under the Severans, which gives no sign of the disasters and stagnation to come: contests, construction of buildings, foundations of all sorts, all attested by an extreme abundance of inscriptions in small as well as large cities. One might think that it was there, under the aegis of Rome, that Hellenism reached its high-point.

Even more, one discerns the torch of Hellenism and the classical tradition burning under the philhellenic emperors of the mid third century AD: Gordian with his wife Tranquillina, Philip the Arab with Otacilia, Valerian, and Gallienus with Salonina. Many stephanitic contests were created, mostly in Asia Minor: notably, linked to Delphi, Pythian festivals in Thessalonike, in Magnesia, in Miletos, in Ephesos, in Perge and, especially well documented, those of Side in Pamphylia. The inscription, in Athens, of a herald from Sinope[3] offers a comprehensive catalogue of the existing contests at that point in time, the fifth decade of the century. This double *periodonikēs* was a victor at the Panathenaia as well as the Panhellenia, in Argos, at the Capitolia in Rome, three times victor at the contest in honour of Athena Promachos instituted in Rome by Gordian III on the eve of his departure to war against the Persians, in the Millenial contest in Rome (τὸν χειλιέτη ἐν Ῥώμῃ; called Ῥώμης αἰώνια in the document from Olympia) celebrated by Philip in 248 AD. This Valerius Eclectus won seventy-nine victories in thirty different cities and his travels covered, including Italy (Rome, Naples and Puteoli), the Peloponnese (Argos, Epidauros), Nikopolis, Boiotia (contests existed only in Thebes and Lebadeia), Beroia in Makedonia, Thrace (including Philippoupolis, Byzantion), Bithynia (Nikaia and Nikomedeia), Kyzikos, Pergamon, Smyrna, Ephesos, Miletos, Sardeis, Tralles and Hierapolis, and then in Syria, Tyre, Sidon and Damascus, to which we must add the rare case of Aphrodisias. This list of victories resembles a catalogue of the great urban centres of the world of the late-Imperial period, which was just coming into being, an outline of the cities of the Greek world that would play a part in the Late Empire.

The proliferation of contests in Asia Minor is a sign – in contrast with the decline observed in the Greek mainland – of the ostentatious prosperity of the peninsula, of its economic and cultural development and the deepening hold of Hellenism there. Thus Syria, which probably in previous times had not known any contests other than those of Herakles in Tyre and of Apollo in Sidon, is adorned

---

[3] *IG*, II², 3169 and *I. Olympia*, 243 (Moretti, *Iscr. agon. gr.*, 90) [cf. below, chapter 6].

with multiple contests, as testified by victor inscriptions and coin legends. Even the Roman province of Arabia or Bostra celebrated Greek contests in honour of the Arab god Dousares. The limits of Hellenism were marked by the absence of such great contests. For instance, Palmyra: one finds hundreds of Greek inscriptions there, but the city is not hellenised; there is no grand stephanitic contest to which the Greek cities would be invited.

In the Latin or Romanised West, the Greek stephanitic contest also exercised its charms. It is found in Italy, from Augustus to Philip the Arab and Constantine. Under the reign of the latter, the contest of Athena Promachos was still celebrated. I have already discussed elsewhere these Greek contests in Italy.[4]

At this point I turn to a novelty, the Greek contests in Roman Carthage, that metropolis of Punic-Greek civilisation. I have recently presented elsewhere the relevant evidence, with detailed illustrations.[5] Two Greek contests took place regularly in the third century. The second celebrated Asklepios, a Greek god, who had always remained Greek without any mixtures and was the protector of the acropolis. He is attested in an inscription from Ostia and on an athletic crown with the Greek inscription *Asklepeia*, and also depicted on a mosaic from Althiburos, whose significance has been misunderstood.

The Pythia of Carthage is known by an inscription from Ostia and by the mention *Pythia en Karthagennêi* in a victory inscription from Perinthos in the Propontis. Tertullian – as I have mentioned before – recalls the creation of this Pythian contest by Septimius Severus. The impact of the foundation of such a contest is revealed in a sentence by this Christian writer: "the fervour with which people celebrate these *agônes*, festivals of wrestling and superstitious contests of ceremonies and Greek pleasures, has become known in Africa as well." In this way, the chain of the world's great stephanitic contests stretched all the way to Carthage, and was proud of this new link.

Still more. We read a description of the athletic contest and its ceremony in the narrative of the martyrdom of Vibia Perpetua, Felicitas and their companions in the amphitheatre of Carthage in 203 AD. Two days before her death, Perpetua had her last vision, from which she concluded that she would have to fight with the Devil and that she would emerge victorious. The account of her visions, and her life in prison, was written by her hand, in Greek, and forms the first part of the *Passion*, whereas the account of the scenes in the amphitheatre was written in Latin by a witness, apparently Tertullian himself. The last vision is the one which describes the fight against the Egyptian. Perpetua, anointed with oil by her trainers, wrestles in the *pankration* and overthrows the Egyptian with his face against the ground. The agonothete, who presides over the contest, is dressed in an outfit with purple stripes and wears shoes embroidered with gold and silver threads. As a prize for victory he gives Perpetua a bough with golden apples. It has been stated before that the imagery of the vision is pagan. To be more precise, it is specifically reminiscent of the first celebration of the Pythia in Carthage, which Perpetua had attended (she had been only recently converted at the time of her death, and it was only in prison

---

[4] *CRAI* 1970, 6–27: "Deux concours grecs à Rome" [=chapter 6, below].
[5] *CRAI* 1982, 228–76: "Une vision de Perpétue martyre à Carthage en 203".

that she received baptism). Indeed, in the Imperial period, the prize of the Pythia in Delphi was apples. As demonstrated by coins from Thessalonike, Perinthos, Tralles and many other cities, apples were, in strict imitation of Delphi, the prize of contests celebrated under the name of Pythia. The Egyptian pancratiast is a memory of those heavy athletes from Egypt, a great number of whom fought in the contests. Thus, a glimpse of the Pythia in Carthage is revealed to us through this wonderful text of the Christian period, with its *agonothetês* in his purple robe and the young *eisagôgeus*, the official in charge of introducing the events, in his white robe and his embroidered shoes; a text which has the feel of artlessness and truth. And it is only our very precise knowledge of the history of the stephanitic contests which, for the first time, permits us fully to comprehend the last vision of Perpetua, the one which allowed her to face the beasts in the amphitheatre without fear.

But let us return to a wider view of the stephanitic contests in the Imperial period. The deities to whom they were consecrated were, of course, the emperors of Rome, but first and foremost the principal and traditional divinity of the city, the patron deity. Studying the social history of the Hellenistic and Roman period one can discern at least two conventional narratives, two myths. The first is the death of the Greek city at Chaeroneia and, from then on, the exclusive dominance of the Hellenistic monarchs. A distinguished Italian archaeologist has claimed in print that the setting-up of honorific statues in that period was no longer the concern of the cities, but of the monarchs. That is an example of how important questions have been distorted through ignorance of the real evidence. Have confidence, however; the wind of change is blowing (οὖρος ἀνέστη).

Secondly, we are also widely mistaken on the religious sentiment and the cults of this period. We tend to think either that the Greeks were all tolerant sceptics, or that they had recourse only to mystical divinities, oriental or otherwise; that true piety manifested itself only within the isolated individual, according to his/her choice, or within religious associations; that the official ceremonies of the city can no longer have attracted the allegiance of the citizens, being devoid of meaning. I do not want to downplay the highly personal character of the evidence for worship and prayer to Asklepios or Dionysos (on which more below). But what we are dealing with here is the patron deities of these cities being honoured by the holding of contests: Athena in Priene and in Tegea, and also in Pergamon, in Ilion and in Sardeis, Helios in Rhodes, Poseidon in Mantineia, and so on. Quite often, the acceptance of a stephanitic contest is linked with the recognition of a city and its entire surrounding territory as "sacred and inviolable". One can frequently observe in this practice a simple political attempt, concealed beneath a religious pretext, to ensure some form of neutrality. Of course, this type of consecration was not effective against the force of arms. Let us emphasise an example overlooked in studies of this topic. The great town of Kyzikos honoured, above all deities, the goddess Korê.[6] The stephanitic contest of the city was the festival of Korê, an isopythian contest called the Pherephassia. Once, when the city was besieged by Mithridates around the time

---

[6] On the cult of Korê and its contest in Kyzikos, *BCH* 1978, 461–77: "Une fête de Cyzique et un oracle de Delphes à Délos et à Delphes". The two miracles during the siege of the city by Mithridates are mentioned in Plutarch, *Life of Lucullus* 10, and in Appian 12, 75, 323.

of the festival of the Korê, the citizens of Kyzikos, cut off from their countryside, did not have a black heifer for the traditional sacrifice. Out of piety they attempted to replace it by fashioning an animal out of dough. The presence of the patron deity was manifested through a first miracle: the animal that was being fattened for the purpose of the sacrifice left its pasture on its own, threw itself in the water and managed to reach the harbour. Then the goddess appeared to the secretary of the people in a dream and gave him this message: "I come bringing the *aulêtês* of Libya against the trumpeter of Pontos (ἥκω τὸν Λιβυκὸν αὐλητὴν ἐπὶ τὸν Ποντικὸν σαλπιγκτὴν ἐπάγουσα). Tell the citizens to have courage." In this phrase preserved by Plutarch, the verb "I come" (ἥκω), like "I am present" (πάρειμι), is customary for describing the public manifestation of a deity. Examples can be found in the stories of Priapos of Lampsakos coming to Thera and bringing wealth, the prophet and healing god Glykon coming to Abounouteichos in an egg, or in the gods of the prologues of Euripides and the Aristophanic parodies. It is the typical formula for the apparition of a deity, for his or her presence. The following day, a storm destroyed the siege engines of the King of Pontos. The friends of Mithridates, writes Appian, advised the King to lift the siege, "as the city was sacred" (ὡς ἱερᾶς τῆς πόλεως); this meant that it was recognised as consecrated to Korê and as inviolable. An oracle from Delphi, preserved in Delos, had indeed sanctioned the citizens of Kyzikos "to announce to men that the city was sacred". The officials of Mithridates acknowledged the validity of this consecration and the support given by the deity. The patron deity thus protects the city when it is in danger. These divinities continued to play that traditional role for the city. The city-homeland was an entity for which one would risk even death, as the citizens of Kyzikos did against Mithridates; and the citizens continued to believe in the divinity's intervention at critical moments. The god appears in epiphanies as a saviour from danger; this is the case with the origins of the Theophania in Chios, for Artemis Hyakinthotrophos in Knidos and the creation of a stephanitic contest there, for Hecate of Lagina in Stratonikeia in Caria and the contest of the Hekatesia. Piety towards these gods is not a routine matter, but a call for help when survival and preservation is at stake. This would remain the case until the end of the ancient world: Athena Promachos would appear on the ramparts of Athens during the siege by Alaric. The patron deity is never addressed in the same personal way as Asklepios or Isis, but she has her place and role in the religious consciousness of the city and is still a vivid reality for the citizens.

What are the motives lying behind the activity of those who participate in the contests? The motives are both money and glory. Let us consult once again the disinterested testimony of Tertullian. Regarding the Pythia of Carthage, he offers his thoughts on the brutality of the athletic contest in short, colourful and scathing sentences:

> their fists shake, their heels stun [i.e. the kicks allowed in the *pankration*], the boxing gloves are ripped up, the whips tear; but no one will accuse the president of the contest for exposing men to violence; at the stadium the bruises and the blood count not, what counts are the crowns, the glory, the endowment, the public privileges, the civic pensions, the portraits, the statues; the boxer himself does not complain of suffering, because he wants it; the crown soothes the wounds, the prize masks the blood. (Tertullian, *Scorpiace* 6)

The crowning glory, as in classical times, was always the proclamation of the winner by the herald and the trumpeter – a good subject for artists. This glory reflected back on the homeland. The old rule of the supreme Olympic ethic remained in force: to die in Olympia, if one must, rather than give up. This is what a 35-year-old boxer from Alexandria chose; his name was Agathos Daimon, but his epitaph in Olympia tells us that he was nicknamed the Camel. One might be tempted to think of him as a stubborn and furious brute, like an aggressive, rutting camel.[7] But we should not forget that this sport trained real men: think of the tone of the moralist Dio of Prusa in his two short works on the death of the athlete Melancomas in Naples. The runner Mnasiboulos of Elateia was *olympionikês* in 161, two times *periodonikês*, and also "best of the Greeks" (ἄριστος Ἑλλήνων), which means that he had won in the armed race of the Eleutheria in Plataiai, running heavily burdened with full armour for nearly three kilometres. Pausanias writes (X.34.5) that when the Costobocci invaded Greece (in 175 AD) and arrived in Elateia, "Mnasiboulos gathered around him a band of troops and killed many barbarians before he fell in the battle." His victories in the race-in-armour at Olympia and at Plataiai were not the vain display of a professional athlete. Here, the athletic title of Plataiai [i.e. "best of the Greeks"] regains its political and military significance. Before expressing scorn for the professional athletes of the Imperial period outright, as is common, let us think of Mnasiboulos of Elateia.

Another glorious moment – even more glorious – was the return of the victor to his homeland. He would "bring his crown into the city" (εἰσάγειν τὸν στέφανον), as did Pausimachos in Alabanda, Polemaios in Colophon, Xenombrotos in Kos. This entry took place in a chariot, hence the term to "drive in" (*eiselaunein*). In Teos, a decree in honour of Antiochos III ordained that the victors of stephanitic contests, upon entry to the city, should go directly from the gate to the *bouleutêrion* in order to crown the cult statue of the king and offer a sacrifice.[8] Nero revived an ancient privilege when upon entry into Rome, returning from his victories in Greece, he made a breach in the city walls.

The importance of this ceremonial entry explains the creation and diffusion in the Imperial period of the title *eiselastikos* in relation to the stephanitic contests; it granted the right for such an entry into one's home city.

At this point let us return to the issue of money. Not only did victory in the sacred contests enhance one's chances of walking off with large sums from the more humble contests where money was the prize, or being paid generously by the benefactors of private athletic demonstrations; in addition, the custom of granting meals in the *prytaneion* to victors in the contests of the *periodos* had survived from classical times. This privilege was extended to all the *hieronikai* (i.e. victors in sacred games), each in his home city. There was also the payment of a pension, the civic endowment that we find in Tertullian. Throughout the Hellenistic period we

---

[7] 'Les épigrammes satiriques de Lucillius sur les athlètes", dans *L'épigramme grecque* (*Entretiens sur l'antiquité classique*, Fondation Hardt, XIV), 199–201 [=*Choix d'écrits* 186–7].

[8] ὅσοι δ'ἂν νικήσαντες τοὺς στεφανίτας ἀγῶνας εἰσελαύνωσιν εἰς τὴμ πόλιν παραγίνεσθαι - ἀπὸ τῆς πύλης πρῶτον εἰς τὸ βουλευτήριον κτλ.: P. Hermann, *Antiochos III und Teos* (*Anadolu*, IX, 1967), 38, 1. 46–50; 68.

may note the privileged place given to the pensions of the *hieronikai* in the city's budget, as in Miletos.⁹ Under the Empire, papyri from Hermoupolis – a city, which according to the orator Menandros, was rich in athletes in the heavy (i.e. combat) events – concern the payment of pensions to athletes who had been victorious in Olympia and Nemea, and also in Alexandria, Sidon, Gaza and Bostra.

The term *eiselastikos* was also the subject of a consultation between Pliny the Younger, governor of Bithynia, and Trajan.¹⁰ A group of *hieronikai* had claimed pensions for victory in a contest that was not *eiselastikos*, but that subsequently acquired that honour – a claim which was blatantly improper; but why not give it a try? In Sardeis, the very distinguished pankratiast Demostratos Damas, victor in almost seventy sacred contests, put together a list of contests classed as *thematikoi*; then, after the name of some of them, he would add the phrase "now sacred", which raised their status.¹¹ Pliny's letters also contain reference to another similar question: is the pension, *obsonia*, effective from the day of entry into the homeland or from the day of the victory that warranted this entry? Trajan confirms Pliny's choice in favour of the first solution.

The reason for this was the fact that a victor's return to the homeland could be delayed until months after the victory, or longer. Athletes would go on tour. One text expresses surprise that many athletes have not stopped to compete in Athens (they "sailed past" – παρέπλευσαν).¹² When fixing the date for a new contest, a major concern was its integration with the athletic calendar. One might seek to avoid, for example, the moment when the rush towards the Capitolia in Rome,¹³ capital of Greek athletics along with Naples and Alexandria, was taking place. The absences, before victors were "brought back" (*reduces*),¹⁴ were long, sometimes very long. The athletes" association bore the title *peripolistikos* ("travelling" or "wandering"). Athletes and musicians were caught up in the enormous movements of travellers across the Empire, across the known world. Like wandering entertainers, like fairground strongmen and tightrope walkers, they were devotees of the goddess of travellers, Hekate Enodia; like them, according to the expression of the astrologer Manetho, they were "birds of the land" (ὄρνεα γῆς).

A little-known example which illustrates well the duration of these journeys is provided by the will of an athlete from Hermoupolis, whose name has not been preserved, under the reign of Antoninus Pius (papyrus of John Rylands Library, II, n. 153, published in 1915). He thanks a relative for having done him great favours back home during his absence abroad (εἰς τοὺς ἔξω τόπους). His heir, he says, will be his son, who was born while travelling with his wife Claudia Leontis – a detail which shows that the family travelled together – and was "left in the care of a wet-nurse in Smyrna" (κατέλιψα ἐν Ζμύρνῃ τῆς Ἀσίας παρὰ τροφῷ θηλάζοντα). When he comes of age, the son is to decide whether or not he will return to Hermoupolis. His guardians will be in charge of recouping for him the pensions (*opsônia*), that

---

⁹ Milet, *Delphinion*, 147, l. 18–21.
¹⁰ *Ep.* 10, 118–19.
¹¹ *I. Sardis*, 79 (Moretti, *loc. cit.*, 84).
¹² N. M. Verdelis, *BCH* 1947–8, 40–2.
¹³ *Rev. Phil.* 1930, 30–1 (*Opera Minora*, II, 1130–1).
¹⁴ P. Hermann, *Ist. Mitt.*, 25 (1975), 150, l. 31.

will be due for the span of time that the testator had the athletic crown (ὑπὲρ οὗ [χρόνου] ἔσχον ἀθλητικοῦ στεφάνου).

This text is testimony to the shifting and – if the child remained in Smyrna – the mixing of populations in the Empire: we can imagine the young Hermopolitan raised in Smyrna and settling there. Smyrna may have been either the goal of the athlete's trip, or else just a stopover point. We have seen already that, according to *CIG*, there existed in Smyrna contests of the Asian League (*Koina Asias*); there were also many others there during this period. It is noteworthy that the athlete, instead of taking the toddler with him, and with his wife, left the child for a long period of time, possibly even for ever, in that radiant capital of the festive land of Ionia, the jewel of the Muses and the heart of Hellenism. Beautiful Smyrna had exercised its charms over this athlete from deep in the valley of the Nile. We should also note the meaning of the name given to this son born in Smyrna during the trip: Hellanikos. No choice of name is more conspicuous, one might say, for aspiring to pure Hellenism.

After the title *eiselastikos*, the addition of "for the whole inhabited world" (εἰς ἅπασαν τὴν οἰκουμένην) indicates that the privileges acquired through victory were valid in the homeland of the victor, wherever it might be, across the world. Another very frequent title for a contest is *oikoumenikos*, that is, "worldwide". This is not a matter of the ethnic origin of the contestants. The contest itself, to which are invited the cities of the Greek world, becomes, through the delegations of the cities, a microcosm of the whole universe. Here we must return to a coin legend already mentioned. The town of Anazarbos, capital of Kilikia Secunda, and in constant and painstaking rivalry with Tarsos, struck several coins in the name of Elagabal, Severus Alexander, Maximinus and Decius bearing the legend *Synthusia Oikoumenês* ("Sacrifice common to the whole inhabited world"). These words, more often than not hard to read, were identified by the numismatist Hill. They have recently been deciphered with difficulty on a specimen from the reign of Maximinus.[15] The image is of a woman with an intricate hairstyle holding the double axe of the executioner in her right hand; behind her a bull, on whose neck she places her left hand. The decipherer of the legend has rightly commented: "the woman is possibly the goddess of the city on the point of sacrificing the bull with the double axe; or else a personification of the Oikoumene?" It is this latter personification that seems to me to correspond to the legend. The image is, to my eyes, that of an "ecumenical contest". It makes one appreciate the importance of the sacrifice in these festivals and, through the presence of the *synthutai*, of universal participation. This is the occasion where the unity of the Roman world becomes apparent in its most lively form, together with the harmony between all cities and provinces. In each of these contests the city holding the festival does not present only a sumptuous parade of muscles, songs and speeches; for the duration of the event it yields to the dream of universality; it stands for the *oikoumenê*, the world. The Roman Empire manifests its cohesion through the markers of Hellenism, in the excitement of a panhellenic crowd.

[15] G. F. Hill, in *Anatolian Studies presented to Sir W.M. Ramsay* (1923), 222–3 and pl. IX, 14. Neglected inscription on the coins of Maximinus *Sammlung Aulock*, 5500: Γερουσίας ἔτους ΕΝΣ.

Inscriptions and coins place before our eyes the joy and luxury of those festivals which were organised according to the form of the Greek panhellenic contests. It is not only star-athletes, their crowns and their monuments and the portraits that we see on certain mosaics that should come to mind. We should also muse on the infrastructure required for their activities; not only the athletes' and musicians' associations, but the education in these two fields provided in the *gymnasion*. In this regard, I should say that I do not agree with the theory according to which physical education was displaced by the taste for literature and the "man of letters". It is not only in Athens that gymnastics were cultivated in the *gymnasia* for the duration of antiquity. In the mountains of Pisidia and Kilikia, life in the *gymnasia* flourished and the local contests, the *themides*, attracted youths from the area and its surroundings. The late ephebic monuments in Odessos, on the west coast of the Black Sea, in the late third century AD, bore brilliant decorations. Interest in athletic culture had penetrated public life and the people understood its technical vocabulary. The Church Fathers of the fourth century, like Saint Paul, Clement of Alexandria and the Alexandrian Jewish writer Philo before them, made use of athletic imagery in their moral exhortations.

At the same time, musical contests – which have remained slightly in the background in my paper – brought about the spread of music, which was constantly evolving, and literature, from epic and elegy all the way to the myths performed in pantomime. Hellenism, still vibrant and persistent after so many conquests, was manifested through voices as well as through bodies; under the Roman Empire it experienced its greatest expansion and cultural triumph.

6 Two Greek Athletic Contests in Rome*

LOUIS ROBERT
(translated by Margarita Lianou)

I

This paper deals with two Greek athletic contests in Rome. I begin by reminding the reader, very briefly, of the order of priority of the contests (athletic, equestrian and musical) in the Greek cities of the Roman Empire. Over and above the multitude of local athletic contests – which were regulated by the city and were for the most part held in conformity with long-standing tradition, sometimes restricting participation to citizens only, sometimes allowing anyone to compete – there existed a category of contests of the first rank that we frequently call "panhellenic". The Greeks called them "sacred" (*hieroi*), and "crown" games (*stephanitai*) because, quite apart from any material reward, their prize was a crown. For a long time the only contests in this category were those which made up the *periodos*. These were the penteteric (i.e. four-yearly) contests of Olympia and Delphi and the trieteric (i.e. two-yearly) contests of Isthmia and of Nemea. However, after the expansion of the Greek world by Alexander, kings and cities were very keen to organise their own stephanitic contests modelled on these "great contests", designed so as to resemble them (and so given the titles isolympic, i.e. "equal to the Olympic festival", isopythian, "equal to the Pythian festival" etc.), and celebrated every fourth or second year. It was necessary to have such festivals "recognised" (*apodechesthai*) by the Greek cities. The holders would send out religious ambassadors (*theôroi*) to those cities. In return, the Greek cities dispatched their own representatives, also called *theôroi*, to participate in the sacrifice (in the Roman period they would be known as *synthytai* – "common sacrificers") and to bestow upon whichever of their citizens won victories the same honours as to victors in the great contests of the *periodos*. These honours essentially entailed ceremonial entry into the city and meals in the *prytaneion* or a corresponding daily allowance.[1] From the end of the first quarter of

---

* Originally published in *CRAI* (1970), pp. 6–27 (=*Opera Minora Selecta* 5: 647–68) (=*Choix d'écrits* 247–66).

[1] For our purposes, the richest example remains the series of seventy decrees of foreign cities or kings accepting the Leukophryeneia, instituted at the end of the third century BC by Magnesia-on-the-Meander. In geographic terms, these decrees stretch from Syracuse and Epidamnos and from Apollonia in Illyria to Antioch in Pisidia, as well as to the Greek cities of the Tigris and the Euphrates (*I. Magnesia*, n. 17–87). Cf. also the recently published rich documentation for the Asklepieia at Kos, dating from the middle of the third century and found in decrees from Kos (R. Herzog-G. Klaffenbach, *Asylieurkunden aus Kos, Abhandlungen der Deutschen Akademie der Wissenschaften zu Berlin, Klasse für Sprachen* 1952,

the third century BC up until the end of the Hellenistic period, these great contests, acknowledged by all of the Greeks, did not cease to multiply, to the extent that almost every city ended up having its own great panhellenic celebration. Under the Empire, this type of contest was accepted (or "granted" (δοθείς) or given as a "gift" (δωρεά), according to the formula, by the emperor).² Certain reigns exhibit a pronounced rise in the number of these contests: for example, Augustus and the Julio-Claudian dynasty in general, Hadrian, Commodus and the Severans. It is, thus, possible to build up a fairly complete picture and to follow the evolution of the contests, which is revealing for the general situation of each city, big or small. It is into this system of the great contests of Greece that Rome and Italy entered, each at a different phase. They participated in this Greek system and introduced themselves – brilliantly one might argue – into the network of events attended by athletes and Greek musicians, who toured the world from city to city in order to compete and earn the ultimate prize in their field: the crown of wild olive, laurel, pine, ash, oak, ivy, reed and so on. These contests were entirely distinct from the traditional competitions of Rome and the Roman world; that is to say the *ludi* ("games") and *munera* consisting of gladiators and hunts in the amphitheatre.³

The one Greek contest in Rome that was permanent and of the first rank was the Capitolia, created by Domitian. Suetonius (*Domitian*, 4.4)⁴ informs us:

> He instituted also, in honour of Jupiter Capitolinus, a triple quinquennial contest, musical, equestrian and athletic, with a number of prizes [i.e. a number of events] considerably larger than today ... He presided in the contests, wearing Greek shoes⁵ and dressed in a purple cloak according to the Greek manner.⁶ On his head he wore a golden crown with the figures of Jupiter, Juno and Minerva.⁷ He was surrounded by the priest of Jupiter and the collegium of the Flavians, all in the same costume except that their crowns also bore his own image.

This Greek contest in honour of the gods of the Roman capital attained universal success in the Greek world that endured until the end of the Empire. The contest is named with extreme frequency in the inscriptions of athletes and musicians throughout the Greek world. Every great athlete or musician of worldwide

---

n. 1). For a useful general study see the dissertation of P. Boesch, Θεωρός, *Untersuchung zur Epangelie der griechischer Feste* (1908).

² The official term was δωρεά; cf. notably *Études Anatoliennes*, 119–23; *Rev. Num.* 1936, 278 (*Opera Minora*, II, chap. 66); *Bull. Épigr.* 1952, 180, p. 195; *La déesse de Castabala*, p. 90 [cf. also chapter 5, above].

³ This important distinction is well made by G. Wissowa, *Die Religion der Römer* (1912), 464–6. Great confusion on the subject can be found in the article by I. C. Ringwood, *AJA* 1960, 245–51: "Agonistic festivals in Italy and Sicily" (cf. *Bull. Épigr.* 1961, 193).

⁴ *Instituit et quinquennale certamen Capitolino Ioui triplex, musicum equestre gymnicum, et aliquanto plurium quam nunc est coronatorum ... Certamini praesedit crepidatus purpureaque amictus toga Graecanica, capite gestans coronam auream cum effigie Iouis ac Iunonis Mineruaquae, adsidentibus Diali sacerdote et collegio Flauialium pari habitu, nisi quod illorum coronis inerat et ipsius imago.*

⁵ These were the shoes of the Greek agonothetes. I will return to this topic in the future in discussing the martyrdom of Perpetua and Felicitas in Carthage [cf. "Une vision de Perpétue martyre à Carthage" (*CRAI* 1982: 228–76), pp. 259–61].

⁶ This was also part of the costume of the agonothetes [cf. ibid.].

⁷ Cf. my commentary on these crowns as shown in portraits, *BCH* 1930, 262–7 (*Opera Minora*, II, chap. 60), followed by multiple addenda (cf. *CRAI* 1967, 284, n. 1; *Bull. Épigr.* 1969, 541).

reputation had earned a victory there.[8] Wherever athletic inscriptions are composed following a hierarchical order, the Capitolia appears immediately after the four contests of the *periodos*; that is, those of Olympia, Delphi, Isthmia and Nemea. In order to demonstrate the universality of his victories a musician relates to us that he has won in the sacred contests "from the Capitolia all the way to Antioch in Syria" (ἀπὸ Καπετολίων ἕως μέχρι Ἀντιοχείας τῆς Συρίας).[9] In regulating the running of a new athletic contest in Aphrodisias in Karia, another inscription takes special care in fixing its date "before the departure of the contestants for Rome".[10] At that moment, all the great agonistic champions would embark on their journey to Rome, to compete for one of the most prestigious crowns, the oak crown of Jupiter Capitolinus.[11] This contest had introduced Rome to the athletic life of the Greek world and had turned it into one of its capitals. The city of Rome brilliantly played the part of a Greek city.

This is exactly what Nero had already tried to achieve by instituting the Neroneia. "He also instituted, before anyone else, in Rome a contest according to the Greek triad, musical, athletic and equestrian, that he called Neroneia."[12] This contest, however, did not survive him and we do not yet possess any traces of it[13] in the inscriptions of Greek athletes or musicians.[14]

The Capetolia or Capitolia in Rome are, as I have already said, mentioned in a multitude of Greek athletic inscriptions. They are often referred to simply as Capitolia – as it was impossible to confuse them with other contests known as Capitolia, which were celebrated elsewhere and only in the later Imperial period – or else by the simple designation "in Rome" (Ῥώμην), which is also very frequent.[15] The Capitolia, as we shall see, was the only permanent Greek athletic contest in Rome until the times of Gordian. It was previously believed that another set of athletic contests existed in Rome: the Hadrianeia.[16] These are contests that took place in Athens and in Smyrna. The error of assuming their existence in Rome was due to inaccurate punctuation by the editors of victory lists.[17]

Before the Capitolia and the Neroneia, there existed Greek athletic contests

---

[8] See the list of L. Friedländer, *Sittengeschichte Roms*[10], IV, pp. 276–80: "Zur Geschichte des kapitolinischen Agons", which could be amply supplemented today without, however, that making it any more interesting.

[9] *CIG*, 3425 (*IGR*, IV, 1636); however, the inscription does not concern a "singer" and does not originate from Philadelphia in Lydia; cf. L. Robert in *L'épigramme grecque*, p. 184 [cf. *Choix d'écrits* p. 177].

[10] I have already established that point in *Rev. Phil.* 1930, 30–1 (*Opera Minora*, II, chap. 70).

[11] For details on the oak crown and on the epigram *Anth. Pal.* XI, 128, see *L'épigramme grecque*, 267 [cf. *Choix d'écrits* p. 229].

[12] Suetonius, Nero, 12.7: *Instituit et quinquennale certamen primus omnium Romae more Graeco triplex, musicum gymnicum equestre, quod appelavit Neronia.*

[13] See especially the article *Neronia* by W. Hartke in *PW* (1936), 42–8, and the English articles cited in *L'épigramme grecque*, 209, n. 1 [cf. *Choix d'écrits* p. 192, n. 99].

[14] The agonistic inscription of Rome L. Moretti, *Iscr. agon. gr.*, no. 65 (*IGUR* no. 249) refers to Nero, but not to his athletic contests.

[15] The reservations of G. Wissowa in L. Friedländer, loc. cit., IV, 277, are unfounded.

[16] Still in L. Friedländer, *Sittengeschichte Roms*[10], II, 151, as in *Dict. Saglio-Pottier*, s.v. *Hadrianeia* (L. Couve) and in *PW* (Stengel).

[17] I have established this in *Rev. Phil.* 1930, 37–8: "Concours grecs en Italie" (*Opera Minora*, II, chap. 79, XXIV).

related to the imperial cult in Magna Grecia, that is, Greek Italy. This is a vital fact for the history of Greek athletic contests: at the very beginning of the Empire, in 2 AD, a great quinquennial contest had been instituted in the Greek town of Neapolis in honour of Augustus, under the name of Sebasta.[18] It formed the counterpart to the contest of the Romaia Sebasta, celebrated by the province of Asia in Pergamon in honour of Augustus and Rome. The references to the Neapolis contest in the athletic inscriptions are as numerous as those to the Capitolia. The standard formula used to designate them was *Sebasta en Neapolei* or simply *Sebasta* or *Nean Polin*, since there were no other "sacred" contests in Neapolis for the entire Imperial period.[19] The crowds of contestants that thronged from every corner of the Greek world are richly attested in the victory lists of athletes and musicians, as well as in the fragments of the victor catalogues that have been found *in situ*.[20] Based on the model provided by the titles of *olympionikês*, *pythionikês*, *nemeonikês*, *isthmionikês*, *hieronikês*, *halionikês* and so on, the victor took the title of *Sebastonikês*, which has the very precise denotation of winning a victory in the Sebasta of Neapolis.[21] The founding decree, along with the regulations for the contests, has been recovered, albeit mutilated, on a stele from Olympia. Such a display in Olympia was to be expected given that the new contest, being "isolympic", that is, "equal to the Olympic Games", was placed under the patronage of the contests in Olympia.[22]

Almost a century and a half later, another city in Greek Italy acquired an important Greek contest. In 138, Antoninus Pius honoured the memory of his adoptive father by instituting for the late Hadrian a contest called the Eusebeia.[23] It was the counterpart to the Sebasta of Neapolis. This Greek contest immediately acquired a reputation that placed it alongside the Capitolia and the Sebasta on the lists.[24] It was known as *Eusebeia en Potiolois* or *Eusebeia* or *Potiolous*. This was

---

[18] Cf. provisionally (following on from scattered references elsewhere in my work), *Ant. Class.* 1968, 407–10; *L'épigramme grecque*, 207, 286–7 [cf. *Choix d'écrits* pp. 192 and 241–2].

[19] There were no Hadrianeia in Naples, nor Eusebeia (in the texts alleged to contain relevant information there is nothing more than errors in punctuation or of reading; cf. *Rev. Phil.* 1930, 37–8; *Opera Minora*, II, chap. 79, XXIV), nor Actia (cf. *Rev. Phil.* 1930, 45 or *Opera Minora*, II, 1145; *Anatolian Studies presented to W.H. Buckler* (1939), 244, n. 2 or *Opera Minora*, I. chap. 41). The same goes for the Eusebeia of Neapolis claimed by A. M. Woodward, *ABSA*, 29 (1925–6), 227, who mistakenly discusses a συνθύτης Νέαν Πόλιν [*synthutês* sent to Neapolis] from Sparta as follows: "presumably to the Augustalia (Σεβαστά). Founded in AD 2; cf. *IG* III, 129, l.17 and *IG*, VII, 49, l. 24; but in *IG*, III, 128, l. 12f., we hear of a victory won Νέαν Πόλιν-[Εὐ]σέ[β]εια [this is an incorrect reading rectified by P. Wolters in 1900 – L. R.]. See also Strabo, V, p. 246 etc".

[20] The majority of the evidence is united in *IG* XIV, but more has been found since: see *Notizie degli scavi di antichità*.

[21] Rather than "victors in the imperial contests"; cf. *Opera Minora*, I, 645. n. 8; *Ét. épigr.* 93, n. 6, with reference to Dessau, *ILS*, 5232. Partial correction in the Supplement of Liddell-Scott-Jones (1968), p. 132, but without having ascertained that the Sebasta in question were those of Neapolis and not some other Sebasta from somewhere else.

[22] *I. Olympia*, n. 56, with a good commentary by Dittenberger (originally it was believed that this document recorded musical contests in Olympia). I am not certain, however, as is G. W. Bowersock, *Augustus and the Greek World* (1965), 84, that this inscription "reveals the efforts of the Neapolitan council to attract the Olympic spectators to the isolympic Sebasta."

[23] Classical texts: Artemidoros of Daldis, *Oneir.*, I, 26; *IG*, XIV, 737, l. 7; SHA *Hadr.* 27. Cf. *Rev. Phil.* 1930, 37, n. 5 (*Opera Minora*, II, chap. 70, XXIV).

[24] Cf. provisionally the victor lists in Ch. Dubois, *Pouzzoles antique* (1907), 146; M.W. Frederiksen, *PW* s.v. *Puteoli* (1959), 2052.

because, as was also the case in Neapolis, it was the only sacred Greek contest in Puteoli.²⁵ When, in an inscription from Sparta,²⁶ an individual is presented as "having acted at his own expense as *synthutês* in Puteoli and Neapolis" (συνθύτης Ποτιόλους, Νέαν Πόλιν προῖκα),²⁷ it meant that he had represented his homeland by participating in the sacrifice of the Eusebeia in Puteoli²⁸ and of the Sebasta in Naples.

There were no Greek contests in Italy, either in Rome or in the Greek lands in Campania, created by Hadrian, the great philhellene. This was a consequence of his extended absences from Italy. His repeated voyages brought him to the sources of Hellenism and its agonistic life. He created, or ordered the creation of two international festivals – an Olympia and a Panhellenia – in Athens itself. Everywhere in his footsteps sprung up Hadrianeia and Olympia, in Ephesos, in Athens and in so many other places in the Greek world. Even his most beloved protegé, Antinous, was honoured not with a contest in Rome, but in Egypt, the place of his death and deification, and in Mantineia in Arkadia, traditionally thought to be the homeland of the Bithynians of Bithynion in Bithynia, which was the place of his birth.²⁹ It was only after Hadrian's final return and his death that his successor dedicated to his *manes* ("spirit") a great contest in the land of Italy, close to the place of his death. It was one of those Greek contests that were so close to the heart of the philhellenic emperor-traveller, and it took place in a busy and rapidly developing harbour – Puteoli – which was a gateway to the east, a place where Greek colonists mixed with Hellenised easterners.³⁰

Here, I will not linger for long on the Greek contests that were celebrated in Rome occasionally, as unique and unrepeated occurrences. In this category were the Epinikia for the victory of Marcus Aurelius and Commodus against the Parthians in 176.³¹ Epinikia were similarly celebrated in Ephesos for the return of the army

---

²⁵ Cf. *Rev. Phil.* 1930, 37–8 (*Opera Minora*, II, chap. 79, XXIV): there was no Hadrianeia.

²⁶ A. M. Woodward, *ABSA*, 27, 226 (*SEG* XI, 500); *ibid.*, 234 (*SEG* XI, 501): συνθύτης εἰς Νέαν Πόλιν ὑπερχρονίαν μὴ λαβών ["having travelled as *synthutês* to Neapolis without receiving any overtime payment"] (for an explanation of the last part of the phrase, see *Rev. Phil.* 1934, 283; *Opera Minora*, II, chap. 72); A. M. Woodward, *ABSA* 26 (1923–5), 166 (*SEG*, XI, 494): ἐγένετο δὲ καὶ Ἀκτίων συνθύτης ["he was a *synthutês* also at the Aktia"]. For a *synthutês* of Rhodes in Neapolis, see *Bull. Épigr.* 1942, 115.

²⁷ This term seems not to have replaced the term *theôros* until the Imperial period; cf. notably *Fouilles de Laodicée du Lycos*, 278, esp. n. 4.

²⁸ For Puteoli, A.M. Woodward, loc. cit., 227, explains: "The references are presumably to the Εὐσέβεια ἐν Ποτιόλοις ["Eusebeia in Puteoli"] founded by Antoninus Pius in memory of Hadrian; cf. *IG* III, 119, l. 16. This seems more likely than the Βουθ(υ)σία [*Bouthusia*] mentioned in the letter from the Tyrian residents of Puteoli (*IG* XIV, 830 = *OGI* 595 = *IGR* I, 411, l. 11)." He is certain that the representatives of the city of Lakedaimon were sent to the panhellenic Eusebeia celebrated in Puteoli and not to a private celebration of an association of Tyrians established in the city. Such differences in the nature and hierarchy of Greek festivals are often ignored by the editors of inscriptions and by historians.

²⁹ On the Antinoeia in Antinoopolis, a newly founded city, and on the *isantoneioi* contests in Egypt, see my study in *Bull. Épigr.* 1952, 180. For the cult of Antinoos in the Hadrianeia at Bithynion, see *Rev. Phil.* 1943, 184, n. 9; *Bull. Épigr.* 1950, 192, p. 199; 1953, 194. Antinoeia contests took place in Mantineia in Arkadia, as well as in the *gymnasion* at Athens [cf. *À travers l'Asie Mineure* (1980) 132–46].

³⁰ See Ch. Dubois, "Histoire commerciale de Pouzzoles" in *Pouzzoles antique* (1907), 64–110, and M. W. Frederiksen, *PW* s.v. *Puteoli* (1959), 2045–53.

³¹ Inscription of the pancratiast M. Aurelius Demostratos Damas from Sardeis (*I. Sardis*, 79; L. Moretti, *Iscr. agon. gr.*, no. 84), ll. 14–16: "at the Epinikia in Rome in honour of the sovereign emperors Antoninus and Commodus he was crowned with a gold crown and was awarded a prize of gold" ([Ῥώ]

of Lucius Verus and elsewhere in honour of other victories.³² In the same vein, a Herakleia might have been celebrated in Rome during the reign of Trajan, but evidence for this is far from conclusive.³³ The Secular Games of Philip the Arab in 248 were also one-off contests that have left their traces on the victory lists of Greece, as in the case of the herald Valerius Eclectus of Sinope, victor there in addition to two other contests in Rome, where "(he won victory also at) the festival for the thousandth anniversary of the founding of Rome, where he was honoured with a prize of gold, the first and only herald of all time to be so honoured," (τὸν χειλιετῆ ἐν Ῥώμῃ, ἐφ' ᾧ ἐτιμήθη χρυσῷ βραβείῳ μόνος καὶ πρῶτος τῶν ἀπ' αἰῶνος κηρύκων): that is the wording of his inscription from Athens;³⁴ another fragmentary inscription in his honour from Olympia lists this same festival instead as the "*Aionia* at Rome".³⁵ Before that had been held the Secular Games of Septimus Severus.³⁶

Two other Greek contests from Rome are little known since they belong to the late Imperial period and, for that reason are attested to only rarely. First, Aurelian instituted a contest in 274 in honour of his great patron deity, the Sun. At the same time he was involved in the building of a temple and the organisation of a priesthood consecrated to that god. This four-yearly contest was still celebrated in the times of Julian.³⁷

Let me move on though to the second contest that remains to be discussed. According to the Chronography of 354 AD: *Gordianus imper. ann. v, m. v, d. v. Cong. dedit (denariorum) CCCL. Hoc imp. mula hominem comedit. Agonem Minervae instituit. Excessit finibus Parthiae.* ["Gordianus ruled as emperor for five years, five months and five days. He gave a largess of 350 *denarii*. During his reign a she-mule ate a man. He founded a contest to Minerva. He died in Parthia"].³⁸ Thus, Gordian instituted a "contest to Minerva" before his departure on a campaign against the Persians, where he died. This means that the contest was instituted before 243.³⁹

We must add here an inscription from Rome⁴⁰ dating to the fourth century of our era, shortly after 313. It concerns a foundation in which the members of an athletic association, "a sacred, athletic, travelling company open to the whole world" (ἱερὰ

μὴν ἐπινείκια τῶν κυρίων αὐτοκρα[τόρων] Ἀντωνίνου καὶ Κομμόδου ἐστεφα[νώθη] χρυσῶι στεφάνωι καὶ ἔλαβε χρυσοῦν βραβεῖον).

³² Cf. *Rev. Phil.* 1930, 39–41; *Bull. Épigr.* 1959, 448 (with discussion of the Greek contests of Rome).

³³ There is an inscription from Neapolis *IG*, XIV, 747 (L. Moretti, *Iscr. agon. gr.*, no. 68). Following victories in two Olympic Games and four Capitolian, l. 12 ff.: "he was the first of mankind to be crowned in the men's *pankration* in the Herakleia Epinikia in [...] in honour of Nerva Trajan Caesar Augustus Germanicus Dacicus" (πρῶτον ἀνθρώπω[ν τὰ ἐν...] Ἡράκλεια ἐπινίκια αὐτοκράτορος Νέρουα Τραιανοῦ Κ[αίσαρος Σεβαστοῦ] Γερμανικοῦ Δακικοῦ στεφανωθέντα ἀνδρῶν παγκράτιον); then the contests of the *periodos*, the Pythia, Nemea, Isthmia, Aktia, then Neapolis and so on. L. Moretti, *loc. cit.*, 188, denies convincingly the restoration of the name of the city to Iasos (where Herakleia are attested; see also *IGR* I, 446; O. Fink, *YCS*, 8 (1942), "Victoria Parthica", 83, n. 10) or Ephesos. I would be happy to accept that we are dealing with an irregular festival in Rome honouring the return of the victorious Trajan, but I cannot prove it (cf. *Bull. Épigr.* 1959, 448).

³⁴ *IG* II², 3169–70 (L. Moretti, *Iscr. ag. gr.*, no. 90) [cf. chapter 5, above].

³⁵ *I. Olympia*, n. 243.

³⁶ *Hellenica* XI–XII, 11–14.

³⁷ Cf. notably L. Homo, *Aurélien* (1904), 185–6; Marbach, *PW* s.v. *Sol* (1927), 907–11.

³⁸ *Chronica Minora*, I. ed. Mommsen, 147; Mommsen, *Gesammelte Schriften*, VII, p. 576.

³⁹ Cf. W. Ensslin, *Zu den Kriegen des Sassaniden Shapur I* (*SBAW* 1947, V).

⁴⁰ *IG* XIV, 956 (Laum II, no. 213).

ξυστικὴ περιπολιστικὴ οἰκουμενικὴ σύνοδος) are involved. In a mutilated section of the inscription, we learn (A 16) of a sum intended for a contest: "for each contest twenty five denarii, that is of Athena Pr-", ([εἰς ἕκασ]τον ἀγῶνα δηνάρια εἴκοσι πέντε, τουτέστιν Ἀθηνᾶς Πρ-). G. Kaibel suggested "of Athena Prokathegetis" (Ἀθηνᾶς Προ[καθηγέτιδος ?]) and B. Laum copied this conjecture. It has been nearly forty years since I restored this text, though without having published my restoration: the correct reading is "Athena Promachos" (Ἀθηνᾶς Πρ[ομάχου]), identifying in this context the contest instituted by Gordian III, a contest whose precise Greek name was already known to us in three inscriptions from Old Greece. I have had the pleasure of seeing the same emendation proposed independently in the recent past by L. Moretti in his corpus of Greek inscriptions from Rome.[41] In that volume the inscription is no. 246.[42]

This contest is listed among the great contests in three Greek inscriptions.[43] An inscription from Megara, known since the seventeenth century by Spon, was re-edited by Boeckh, who drew on the former's views, in *CIG* 1068 and Dittenberger in *IG* VII, 49.[44] The contests belonging to the *periodos*[45] and those of Athens are followed by numerous contests of Greece and Asia Minor,[46] and finally those of Italy: "three victories in the Capitolia in Rome (Καπετώλια ἐν Ῥώμῃ γ☒), four in the contest in honour of Athena Promachos in Rome (Ἀθηνᾶς Προμάχου ἐν Ῥώμῃ δ☒),[47] one at the Eusebeia in Puteoli (Εὐσέβεια ἐν Ποτιόλοις), one at the Sebasta in Neapolis (Σεβαστά ἐν Νέᾳ Πόλει)". With the four victories in the contests of

---

[41] *Inscriptiones Graecae Urbis Romae*, I (Rome 1968), 246. On the volume, cf. *Bull. Épigr.* 1969, 625.

[42] Moretti writes as follows: "Ἀθηνᾶς Προ[καθηγέτιδος], Kaibel [L.R.: we should not disregard the presence of a question mark that accompanied Kaibel's conjecture]; Ἀθηνᾶς Πρ[ομάχου], ego. Romae nullum Ἀθηνᾶς Προκαθηγέτιδος certamen fuit; contra Gordianus III *agonem Minervae instituit* (*Chronica Minora*, p. 147, 31 Mommsen) quem tituli nonnulli memorant (*Iscr. agon. greche*, nos. 88, 90)" ["Kaibel reads "Athena Prokathegetis"; my reading is "Athena Promachos". There was no contest of Athena Prokathegetis at Rome; instead Gordian III "instituted a contest of Minerva", listed by several inscriptions"]. In the very small fragment C, thought to have been found in Aquileia and which must belong to that same inscription, Moretti suggests "Athena Promachos" (Ἀθηνᾶς Πρ[ομάχου]).

[43] The first is already quoted in L. Friedländer, *loc. cit.*, II, 149, n. 9.

[44] Also in L. Moretti, *Iscr. agon. gr.*, n. 88. K. Hannell, *Die Inschriftensammlung des Konstantinos Laskaris* (*Bulletin de la Société Royale des Lettres de Lund* 1934-5, IV) pointed out, p. 4, the variant readings in a copy taken in Megara by Konstantinos Laskaris (middle of the fifteenth century), according to the edition of the Greek manuscripts of Madrid by J. Iriarte. P. Moraux has informed me (1967) of the presence of copies of this inscription and of *IG*, II², 13209 in a manuscript from Bern containing the opuscula of Theophrastos and Aristotle. The difference of this sixteenth-century manuscript lies predominantly in the numerals; see the following note.

[45] "The Olympia in Pisa, the Pythia in Delphi twice, the Nemea in Argos twice, the Isthmia twice" (Ὀλύμπια ἐν Πείσῃ, Πύθια ἐν Δελφοῖς β', Νέμεια ἐν Ἄργει γ',Ἴσθμια β'). For the victory in Olympia, where Spon proposes "Olympia" (Ὀλύμπια), Lascaris renders "in Pisa" (ἐν Πίσσῃ) with the number "twice" (β'), and *Bernensis* "in Pisa" (ἐν Πείσῃ) with the number "three times" (γ').

[46] Many of these later contests are open to debate. Cf. *REA* 1928, 15, n. 1 (*Opera Minora*, 11, chap. 51) with commentary on the date; *Et. épigr.*, 59, n. 7; *Rev. Num.* 1936, 277 (*Opera Minora*, II, chap. 66).

[47] Moretti:

> The contest of Athena Promachos (cf. 90) was instituted, in Rome, by Gordianus III (*Chronica minora*, p. 147, 31 Mommsen): *agonem Minervae instituit*. The inscription ... belongs therefore to a date very close to the middle of the third century AD, given the date of the institution of the Pythia of Thessalonike (240) [cf. *Ét. épigr.* 53-61] and the four consecutive victories... in the contests of Athena Promachos in Rome. Of these victories the first was attained in 238 at the earliest and the fourth, at any rate, several years later.

We will see that the first *terminus post quem* is not 238, but 242 AD.

Athena in Rome, the monument must be dated after 254 or 255 AD. It dates from the same period as the monument of the herald Valerius Eclectus of Sinope, who is known both from Olympia[48] and from Athens.[49] This herald was twice *periodonikês* (κῆρυξ δισπερίοδος). He had won in three different contests in Rome: "three times in the Capetolia in Rome (Καπετώλια ἐν Ῥώμῃ γ☒), three times in the contest of Athena Promachos in Rome (Ἀθηνᾶς Προμάχου ἐν Ῥώμῃ γ☒), and once at the "millennial contest" in Rome (τόν χειλιετῆ ἐν Ῥώμῃ)". This last contest was, as we have seen, the Secular Games celebrated by Philip the Arab in 248 AD, which the inscription from Olympia names as Ῥώμης Αἰών[ια]. In this fragmentary inscription our herald is *trisperiodos*, in other words three times *periodonikês*, and has won four times in Olympia during the 256th, 258th, 259th and 260th Olympiads, namely in 245, 253, 257 and 261 AD.

Thus, the inscriptions of the two victors, possibly both heralds, provide express evidence that the "contest of Minerva" instituted by Gordian III was not an episodic festival, but one that was celebrated at least four times; that is, until 254 AD, for it was apparently a penteteric festival like the Capitolia. The death of Gordian III in 245 AD did not interrupt it; it was still celebrated under Valerian and Gallienus. What is more, the reconstructed inscription from Rome informs us that the festival persisted into the first quarter of the fourth century; it had taken root in the religious life of Rome.

But there is another conclusion to be drawn from the complete name revealed by the inscriptions from Greece.[50] In the brief summary of events in the Chronography, the institution of the contest immediately precedes the departure for the war against the Persians and its fatal outcome for the king. The connection between the two events is very straightforward in Aurelius Victor, 27.7: "In that year of lustration, having expanded and strengthened the contest introduced into Rome by Nero, he left against the Persians, having first opened the doors of the temple of Janus, in the traditional manner."[51] This last phrase will be elucidated below.

The victories of Gordian and Timesitheus in Syria and Mesopotamia, the recapture of Carrhae and Nisibis, the submission of Mesopotamia along with Singara, all had a special resonance not only in the official Roman coinage, but also in Asia Minor, which was exposed to Persian raids.[52] Plenty of inscriptions from the

---

[48] *I. Olympia*, no. 243 and, in conjunction with the other inscription, see O. Liermann, *Dissertationes philologicae halenses* 10 (1899), p. 154.

[49] *CIA*, III, 129 (Liermann, loc. cit., pp. 153–4); *IG*, II², 3169–70 (Moretti, loc. cit., n. 90), ll. 34–5. L. Moretti understands, p. 267, that the elocution teacher M. Aurelius Mousaios, known as Eortasios, had "the honorific obligations of a member of the *gerousia* ("council of elders") in Sardeis, of a *bouleutês* (i.e. member of the Council) in Delphi, an *archigrammateus* (i.e. chief secretary (of the athletic association)) in Elis and Aphrodisias". I have shown, *BCH* 1928, 412–22: "Ἀρχιγραμματεύς" (*Opera Minora*, II, chap. 54, IX), that we should punctuate: καὶ Ἠλεῖον καὶ Ἀφροδισιέα, ἀρχιγραμματέα, which translates as: "citizen of Elis and Aphrodisias, chief secretary (of the athletic association)" [cf. chapter 5, above].

[50] Nothing relevant in Moretti, *loc. cit.*, 261. Equally, the institution of the festival has not been mentioned in the detailed exposition of the reign of Gordianus III by P. von Rodhen, in *PW* s. v. *Antonius*, nor in *CAH* XII, 86 (W. Ensslin).

[51] *eoque anno lustri, certamine quod Nero Romam induxerat aucto firmatoque, in Persas profectus est, cum prius Iani aedes patentes more veterum fecisset.* See below n. 67.

[52] Cf. Mattingly, Sydenham and Sutherland, *The Roman Imperial Coinage*, IV 3 (1919), especially pp. 51–2, and p. 7.

Eastern Empire, like the coins, commemorate victories,[53] as well as accessions to the throne and marriages. From this standpoint, one could make a complete inventory of the municipal coins.[54]

A testimony to the contentment of the populations in Asia Minor –eloquent, but neglected – can be found in three inscriptions from Ephesos that have practically the same content.[55] The metropolis honours "the master of the earth and the sea and the human race,[56] the emperor Caesar Marcus Antonius Gordianus Pius Felix Augustus, new Helios (i.e. Sun)"[57] the good and pious king,[58] "who has restored and increased the ancient peace of life in his own world (ἀποκαταστήσαντα καὶ ἐπαυξήσαντα[59] τῷ ἰδίῳ κόσμῳ[60] τὴν ἀρχαίαν τοῦ βίου εἰρήνην)." The bringing of peace is an ancient object of praise for sovereigns.[61] Is it not in this case a just object of eulogy for the king, well-deserved and accurate, given that he had driven back the Persian incursions and the threat they posed to Antioch, and had conquered Nisibis and beyond? Given that he had eliminated the danger of Persia subduing Asia Minor, as had happened in the times of Labienus and as would happen again under this same king Chapour?[62] The emperor had secured peace in "his own world", a peace for which the adjective "ancient" (ἀρχαία) evokes the remembrance of the happy times of the past, a past forever perfect and innocent, a joyful age. The young emperor shines over this newly-found antique happiness like a "new Helios". In his turn, he becomes the inheritor of this title.

The solemn *profectio* (preparation for departure) of the Roman emperor, leaving Rome for the war, took place after he had opened the Gates of the Temple

---

[53] Cf. P. W. Townsend, *YCS* 4 (1934), "The administration of Gordian III", pp. 93–97, with the conclusion:

> It is evident that the rule of Gordian III was particularly well received in the Greek-speaking provinces in Asia, especially after the accession of Timesitheus to the praetorian prefecture. As the inscriptions and coins indicate, this was due in very large part to the decisive victory over the Persians which delivered these provinces of the danger of foreign conquest.

For an explanation of the abundant coinage of Gordian in Antioch of Pisidia and on its types, see Aleksandra Krzyżanowska, "Les monnaies de Gordien III frappées à Colonia Caesarea Antioche", in *Wiadomości Numizmatyczne*, 8 (1963), 1–18 with tables and thirteen plates.

[54] In addition to what has been pointed out by P. W. Townsend. It is an interesting subject to research the place of "Roman subjects" in the coinage of the cities of Asia Minor. In particular, it would be interesting to see what role images and inscriptions relating to the victories of the imperial armies play in the coinage and in which territories they appear. This topic was first taken up by Mr. François Rebuffat.

[55] O. Benndorf, *Forschungen in Ephesos* (1906), I, pp. 210–11, n. 2, from the Artemision. Benndorf pointed towards an identical specimen built high in the aqueduct. A third one was found in the basilica of Saint John: J. Keil, *JÖAI*, 25 (1929), Beiblatt 17–18 (*SEG*, IV, 523); *Forschungen in Ephesos*, IV, 3, *Johanneskirche* (1951), n. 36.

[56] Τὸν γῆς καὶ θαλάσσης καὶ τοῦ τῶν ἀνθρώπων ἔθνους δεσπότην.

[57] In the specimen of Benndorf.

[58] Τὸν ἀγαθὸν καὶ εὐσεβῆ βασιλέα in the specimen of Keil, replacing the official epithets of the titulature Εὐσεβῆ Εὐτυχῆ.

[59] Inverse order in the specimen of Benndorf.

[60] The word ἴδιος ("his own") is not included in the specimen of Benndorf.

[61] As shown by the decree of Halicarnassus in honour of Augustus: "the land and the sea are at peace, and the cities blossom with good order and harmony and prosperity" (εἰρηνεύθη μὲν γὰρ γῆ καὶ θάλαττα, πόλεις δὲ ἀνθοῦσιν εὐνομίαι ὁμονίαι τε καὶ εὐετηρίαι) (*GIBM*, 891; W. H. Buckler, *Rev. Phil.* 1935, l. 8–10).

[62] Cf. my thoughts on the "adulation" by the populations of Asia Minor of the emperors who had defeated the Persians, *La déesse de Castabala*, pp. 77–8.

of Janus *more veterum* ("according to the ancient customs"). Gordian conformed piously to the ancient Roman traditions – for the last time, one might add. It is within the context of this departure for the Eastern war that the creation of the contest in honour of Minerva is to be placed. It was a Greek contest, not only by virtue of its place in the category and hierarchy of contests like the Capitolia (evident from the Greek inscriptions), but also from its very name and the deity to whom it was consecrated. Athena Promachos was the Athenian goddess that had defeated the Persians at Marathon, the goddess of whom Pheidias had cast a bronze statue on the Athenian Akropolis. The testimonies regarding the name of this statue are all from later periods.[63] But even if this poses problems for those who study the statue of Pheidias, the extant later testimonies frame the period of Gordian and bear witness that in the dying days of the Empire the Athenian Athena Promachos was considered as a protectress against the Persians. More important than the reference in Alciphron is the scholion on the colossal statue found in Demosthenes:[64] "secondly, the statue made solely from bronze which was made by the victors at Marathon and named as the statue of Promachos Athena" (δεύτερον δὲ τὸ ἀπὸ χαλκοῦ μόνου ὅπερ ἐποίησαν νικήσαντες οἱ ἐν Μαραθῶνι, ἐκαλεῖτο δὲ τοῦτο Προμάχου Ἀθηνᾶς). Equally important is an epigram from the beginning of the fifth century AD, according to which the orator Apronianus erected in Athens the statue of the court prefect Herculius next to that of Athena Promachos: "the champion of the laws (τὸν πρόμαχον θεσμῶν) next to Pallas champion of the Kekropidai" (στῆσε παρὰ Προμάχῳ Παλλάδι Κεκροπί[ης]).[65] Further evidence is provided by the narrative of Zosimus (V.6.2) on the siege of Athens by the Visigoth Alaric. He recoiled from taking the city by sheer force when he experienced the following spectacle: "on the ramparts there walked Athena Promachos, as she is known from her statues, fully armed and as if ready to oppose the assailants. And in front of the ramparts stood Achilles ..."[66]

Thus, it is Athena Promachos, the protectress of the Athenians against the Persians at Marathon, who is invoked by the Emperor Gordian through the creation of a Greek athletic contest on the eve of his departure for the war against the Persians.[67] This bears testimony to the philhellenism of the young emperor,

---

[63] I refer only to O. Gruppe, *Griechische Mythologie und Religionsgeschichte* (1906), II, 1222, n. 1; H. Höfer, *Roschers Lexicon*, s. v. *Promachos*, 3028–9 (G. Radke, *PW* s.v. *Promachos* (1957), no. 5). The oldest testimony is without a doubt that of Pausanias IX.4.1 (regarding Athena Areia of Plataiai, erected from the booty from Marathon distributed by the Athenians): "the statue is hardly any bigger than the bronze statue in the Akropolis that the Athenians have consecrated also as loot from the Battle of Marathon" (μέγεθος μὲν οὐ πολύ δή τι ἀποδεῖ τῆς ἐν ἀκροπόλει χαλκῆς ἣν καὶ αὐτὴν Ἀθηναῖοι τοῦ Μαραθῶνι ἀπαρχὴν ἀγῶνος ἀνέθηκαν). It was Pheidias who made the cult statue of Athena for the Plataians. The epithet Promachos is not mentioned.

[64] Demosthenes 22.13.

[65] Kaibel, *Epigrammata Graeca* 912; *IG*, II², 4225; *Hellenica* IV, 41–2, with cross-reference to a photograph.

[66] Τὸ μὲν τεῖχος ἑώρα περινοστοῦσαν τὴν Πρόμαχον Ἀθηνᾶν, ὡς ἔστιν αὐτὴν ὁρᾶν ἐν τοῖς ἀγάλμασιν, ὡπλισμένην καὶ οἷον τοῖς ἐπιοῦσιν ἀνθίστασθαι μέλλουσαν, τοῖς δὲ τείχεσιν προεστῶτα τὸν Ἀχιλλέα τὸν ἥρω...

[67] I have noted above the connection established by Aurelius Victor between the creation of this contest and the death of the emperor in the war against the Persians, 27.7: "In that year of lustration, having expanded and strengthened the contest introduced into Rome by Nero, he left against the Persians, having first opened the doors of the temple of Janus, in the traditional manner" (*eoque anno*

who originated from a cultivated senatorial family, *nobilis in litteris*;[68] to the Greco-Roman symbiosis in the Roman Empire; to the vivacity of archaic classicism in this late period. In such a world, the teachers of oratory belt out declamations on the Persian wars and on heroes. These are not just vain exercises of scholarly rhetoric. The classical past, with its old memories of the most glorious times of Athens, still inspired the society of the mid third century. Against the unmistakable threat posed by the Persians under Chapour, the emperor of Rome, the emperor of the Graeco-Roman world, would expose himself personally and place his campaign and his state under the divine protection of Athena of Athens; the deity who had repelled the barbarians – those same Persians – at Marathon.[69]

---

lustri certamine, quod Nero Romam induxerat, aucto firmatoque in Persas profectus est, cum prius Iani aedes patentes more veterum fecisset). I do not wish to revisit all the discussions prompted by this text. I will only comment on what W. Ensslin had to say on the matter, *Zu den Kriegen des Sassaniden Schapur* I, 11. He states that *eo anno* refers to the fall of Balbienus in the summer of 238 AD, who was assassinated at the time of the Capitoline contest: "this is an impossible date for the start of the war against the Persians and it is certainly an error of our historian." And yet, "the mention of the introduction by Nero brings to mind the Neronia, which Gordianus would revive at a later date and which might have been identical with the *Agon Minervae* instituted by him". In making that claim Ensslin makes reference to the Chronography and to Mommsen, *Gesammelte Schriften* VII, 516, 7 (he should have written 576, 7). [Mommsen is, in fact, concerned there with the texts on the Neronia and not the Greek inscriptions on the "contest of Athena Promachos in Rome" (ἀγὼν Ἀθηνᾶς Προμάχου ἐν Ῥώμῃ)]. The date would then be 210, as suggested by Wissowa [see below n. 69]. But W. Hartke (*PW* XVII, [s. v. *Neronia*], 46) believes that we should approach the passage differently. He thinks that Victor, with his choice of words, did not wish to provide a periphrasis for the Neronia, but simply to state that Nero was the first to introduce in Rome a penteteric contest of the Greek type, and by that he might well have meant the Capitolia. Hartke's hypothesis has a lot going for it; however, we have to admit on the other hand that Victor has confused the Capitolia of 242 AD with those of 238 AD. In addition, it would agree with the date given in the SHA *Life of Gordianus*, which states that he still celebrated the contest in the summer, after the opening of the Temple of Janus and left immediately after with his army. In fact, I think, Gordian did not "augment and reinforce" the Neronia; this contest had definitely disappeared after the death of Nero. What Victor wanted to remind his readers, according to some source, was that this type of Greek contest was introduced in Rome for the first time by Nero. I believe this, and so does Hartke. J. D. P. Bolton, *CQ* 1948, 89–90 thought as well that Aurelius had confused Nero with Domitian, both of whom had introduced "Greek contests" to Rome. However, there was no link between the Neronia and the Capitolia other than the fact that both were Greek contests, just like the new Agon Minervae, the *agôn* of Athena Promachos. On the other hand, there was no association, or transformation, or revitalisation, and so on, between the Capitolia and the contest of Athena, as W. Hartke would suggest. Indeed, on the victory lists of Athens, Olympia and Megara the Capitolia are named alongside the contest of Athena and, hence, have not been replaced by it. The new contest, whose ideological nature I have revealed here, must have been celebrated for the first time in 242 AD, just before the entry into war.

[68] For the literary occupations of Gordian I, see P. von Rohden, *PW*, s. v. *Antonius* 61, 2629: a poem "Antoninias" in thirty books and other poetic exercises, a eulogy to the Antonines in prose, declamations, study in Antioch with Philostratus, who dedicated to him his *Lives of the Sophists*. For Gordian III, the words *in litteris nobilis* ("distinguished in learning"): SHA, *Life of Gordian* 31.4.

[69] The article *Promachos* 6 in *PW* (1957) owes a series of perpetuated confusions to G. Radke: "The Athena Promachos in No. 5 [that of Athens] is to be marginally identified with an Athena Promachos "in Rome" (ἐν Ῥώμῃ) [naturally not the statue, but rather the cult and the model], which is mentioned in later Greek inscriptions [the date is very vague] (Dittenberger, *Inscriptiones Megaridis, Oropiae, Boeotiae* [read: *IG*, VII], 49; *CIA*, III, 129 [yet another old borrowed reference, replaced by *IG*, II², 4225, published in 1935], Dittenberger-Purgold, *I. Olympia* 243 b, p. 355 f.). This Roman Promachos of Juno [*sic*] Quiritis must have resembled the visual image that conformed to the prototype of the Attic Promachos; it is helpful for this interpretation that the Roman "Quirinus" is translated by Lydus, *De mensibus* IV 1 as "Promachos" (sic N. 7)." There is no connection made with the Agon Minervae of Gordian, which was already established a long time ago. No link is established either between the Agon Minervae and the Greek inscriptions in W. Ensslin, *loc. cit.*, 11. To the contrary, already in G. Wissowa, *Religion und Kultus der Römer* (1912), 465, n. 4 we find the following: "here belong the inscriptions *IG*,

The contest of Athena Promachos in Rome, as we have seen, persisted until the reign of Constantine. It had durable political and religious success. In this final period in the history of Greek contests, the forces of the distant classical historical tradition were still alive and full of creative potential. This new Greek contest instituted in the capital of the Empire was a memorial to the Battle of Marathon, used to invoke the protection of Athena Promachos in favour of the legions that fought against the descendants of Darius and Xerxes.

Much later, under Gallienus and in a much-threatened Empire, the cities of Asia Minor and Makedonia, Thessalonike, Side, Perge, Magnesia-on-the-Meander, would institute new Pythian contests in honour of Apollo at Delphi, after requesting an oracle from Delphi.[70] In the twilight of the Empire, amidst the brutality of wars and revolutions, Minerva of Athens and Apollo of Delphi still brightened and touched the consciousness of the people in what was one of the last reflections of the classical Greek faith.

II

Another Greek contest in Rome is revealed to us by a still unedited inscription, which I will present here. During my first stay in Delphi, in the spring of 1928, and by agreement with the director of the School at Athens, Pierre Roussel, I took as my principal subject of study those inscriptions relating to agonistic life: contests and performances, musicians and athletes.[71] I assembled at the time a series of documents, which would form the subject of my second year dissertation, assessed by Maurice Holleaux in association with Edmond Pottier.[72] In the following decade, I published some of the unedited inscriptions and revisited several others published in 1929 by Émile Bourguet in an instalment of *Fouilles de Delphes*.[73] I made known and analysed, among others, documents concerning athletes,[74] flute players,[75] a female harpist and other musicians,[76] pantomimes,[77] a *magôdos* [i.e. a particular type of pantomime dancer], a lyric mime,[78] authors of elegies,[79] a Roman orator,[80] a

---

I [read III], 129, l. 13; VII 49, l. 21; Dittenberger-Purgold, *I. Olympia*, n. 243, l. 7 f. (Ἀθηνᾶς Προμάχου ἐν Ῥώμῃ)"; but they date from 240 AD and are not connected with the occasion of the foundation and with the Athenian model, no more so than in the other authors.

[70] For the creation of these last late festivals, cf. provisionally *Fouilles de Laodicée du Lycos*, 291, n. 2; *L'épigramme grecque*, 189, n. 1 [cf. *Choix d'écrits* p. 180, n. 24].

[71] Cf. *BCH* 1929, 34–41 (*Opera Minora*, I, chap. 16); G. Daux, *Actes du II.e Congrès Épigraphie Paris 1952* (1953), 270.

[72] Cf. *CRAI* 1930, 78–80.

[73] Volume III, *Épigraphie*, issue 1, *De l'entrée du sanctuaire au trésor des Athéniens*, 2nd part (numbers 352 to 578).

[74] Thus the pancratiast Demostratos Damas from Sardeis, *Rev. Phil.* 1930, n. XXVIII (*Opera Minora*, II, chap. 70); cf. *Rev. Arch.* 1934, I, 58–61 (*Opera Minora*, II, chap. 65, IV).

[75] *Rev. Phil.* 1930, n. XXX (*Opera Minora*, II, chap. 70). For the flute player (*aulêtês*) of Laodikeia in Syria p. 57, cf. *Fouilles de Laodicée du Lycos*, 288, n. 5.

[76] *BCH* 1929 (*Opera Minora*, I, chap. 16). Cf. *Ét. épigr.* 36–38.

[77] *Hermes* 1930 (*Opera Minora*, I. chap. 44; cf. *REG* 1966, 756–9); *Ét. épigr.* pp. 11–13 (cf. *Bull. Épigr.* 1942, 83).

[78] *Ét. épigr.* pp. 7–11.

[79] *Ét. épigr.* pp. 17–30.

[80] *Ét. épigr.* pp. 13–17.

Fig. 6.1 Agonistic inscription from Delphi.

trumpeter,[81] acrobats, a "strong man" and a dancer.[82] There remained a few more inscriptions.[83] Here is one of those.[84]

In the Roman Agora, just before the entrance to the sanctuary, a limestone base was found, bearing the following inscription in 23 lines (Inv. 3805; 82 cm. x 47 x 39; letters of 11 mm. Photograph Fig. 6.1):[85]

[In honour of] [L.?] Septimios Aurelianos, citizen of Nikomedeia and Athens, having won victories in all the contests listed below: the Olympia at Pisa, the Pythia twice, the Isthmia twice, the Nemea twice, the Capitolia in Rome, the Antoneinia Pythia in Rome, the Eusebeia in Puteoli twice, the Sebasta in Naples, the Panhellenia in Athens twice, the Olympeia in Athens, the Panathenaia, the Hadrianeia in Athens, the Dionyseia Herakleia Antoneineia in Thebes, the Olympia in Smyrna twice, the Balbilleia in Ephesos, the Olympia in Ephesos, the Augousteia in Pergamon twice, the Traianeia in Pergamon, the League games of Bithynia in Nikomedeia twice, and the general contest (τὸν διὰ πάντων) at the Severeia in Nikomedeia twice, and the general contest at the Antoneineia in Neikea twice, and the general contest at the Aktia in Perinthos twice, and the general contest at the Olympia in Kyzikos, and the general contest at the Antoneineia in Byzantion, and the Antoneineia in Caisareia-by-Mount-Argaios.[86]

---

[81] *Rev. Phil.* 1930, n. XXIX (*Opera Minora*, II, chap. 70).

[82] *BCH* 1928, 420–3 (*Opera Minora*, II, chap. 54, X); *REG* 1929, 433–8 (*Opera Minora*, I, chap. 13, VIII; cf. *Ét. épigr.* 102–8).

[83] Thus, the revision of the inscription regarding a flute player from Gortyn, known by Cyriacus of Ancona, *CIG* 1719, and an inscription for the athlete Demostratos Damas from Sardeis; Daux has taken responsibility for that, *BCH* 1944–5, p. 124 and p. 126; cf. *Bull. Épigr.* 1946–7, 119, p. 329. One should add in this agonistic group my studies on the Soteria of Delphi and the Nikephoria of Pergamon, *BCH* 1930 (*Opera Minora*, I, chap. 7; cf. *REA* 1936 = *Opera Minora*, II, chap. 52), as well as on the festivals of Sardeis in an inscription from Delphi (*REG* 1929, 430–2; *Opera Minora*, I, chap. 13, VII).

[84] The inscription was mentioned in *BCH* 1935, 194, n. 4 (for the festivals of Thebes; also *Hellenica*, XIII, 148); *Bull. Épigr.* 1952, 180, p. 192; *La déese de Castabala*, 81, n. 8, especially for the festival of Rome.

[85] Of all the photographs in my possession, I use one credited to J. Pouilloux.

[86]
[Λ. ?] Σεπτίμιος Αὐρηλιανὸς Νει-
κομηδεὺς κ(αὶ) Ἀθηναῖος νεικήσας ἀγῶνας τοὺς ὑπογεγραμμένους·
[Ὀλ]ύμπια τὰ ἐν Πείσῃ, Πύθια β′,
[Ἰσ]θμια β′, Νέμεια β′, Καπιτώλια ἐν Ῥώμῃ,
[Ἀ]ντωνείνια Πύθια ἐν Ῥώμῃ, Εὐσέβεια
ἐν Ποτιόλοις β′, Σεβαστὰ ἐν Νέᾳ Πόλει,
Πανελλήνια ἐν Ἀθήναις β′, Ὀλύμπεια
ἐν Ἀθήναις, Παναθήναια, Ἀδριάνεια
ἐν Ἀθήναις, Διονύσεια Ἡράκλεια
Ἀντωνείνεια ἐν Θήβαις, Ὀλύμπια
ἐν Σμύρνῃ β′, Βαλβίλληα ἐν Ἐφέσῳ,
Ὀλύμπια ἐν Ἐφέσῳ, Αὐγούστεια ἐν
Περγάμῳ β′, Τραιάνεια ἐν Περγάμῳ,
κοινὰ Βειθυνίας ἐν Νεικομηδείᾳ β′,
κ(αὶ) τὸν διὰ πάντων Σεουήρεια ἐν Νεικομηδείᾳ β′ καὶ τὸν διὰ πάντων
Ἀντωνείνια ἐν Νεικέᾳ β′ κ(αὶ) τὸν
διὰ πάντων Ἄκτια ἐν Περίνθῳ β′,
κ(αὶ) τὸν διὰ πάντων Ὀλύμπια ἐν Κυζίκῳ,
κ(αὶ) τὸν διὰ πάντων Ἀντωνείνια ἐν
Βυζαντίῳ, Ἀντωνείνεια ἐν Καισαρείᾳ
τῇ πρὸς τῷ Ἀργαίῳ.

Nothing in the text indicates the category of this victor, not even whether this citizen of Nikomedeia was an athlete or a musician.[87] At the head of the inscription, this individual has noted the most illustrious of all his victories, l. 4, "the Olympia at Pisa". This clarification, which we encounter in other monuments of the same category, is used to prevent confusion between the famous Olympic Games and the rest of the Olympic contests celebrated in Athens, Ephesos and elsewhere.[88] In cases where the only information we are given is "Olympia" or "*olympionikês*" it is not always easy to say whether we are dealing with the Olympic Games of Elis or with some other "Olympic" contest.[89] Here, this mention would encourage us at first glance to consider our Nikomedeian as an athlete, since there was no musical contest in Olympia.[90] However, the formula that recurs in lines 16, 17, 19, 20 and 21 suggests otherwise: "the general contest" (τὸν διὰ πάντων [ἀγῶνα]). This "general event" is typical of musical contests. Whatever the precise rules might have been, this type of event brought together in competition the victors from the different contests of a musical festival.[91] We are, therefore, dealing with one or other category of competitors who participated in the opening of the athletic events, as well as the beginning of the musical events: the trumpeters and the heralds.[92] The heralds could also practise other types of vocal arts, namely acting, or even *kitharôdia* (the playing of a cithara or lyre while singing).[93] If our individual was a herald, he would have been able to win the victories he lists in a range of different categories. According to the list he gives, the number of victories is thirty-four, of which seven were in the general event.[94] In any case, he could only have won in Olympia as either a herald or as a trumpeter (*salpingktês*, *salpistês*).

As regards the date, a *terminus post quem* seems to be given by the Roman citizen-name of the victor, Septimius. Better still, the same *terminus* or another even earlier one is indicated by the dynastic names of the contests; to begin with, the Severeia

---

[87] Cyriacus of Ancona had copied an inscription of an *aulêtês* from Nikomedeia from the theatre of Delphi, Titus Aelius Aurelius Theodotos, *CIG* 1720 (cf. *Rev. Phil.* 1930, 55–6); *Fouilles de Delphes*, III, 6, n. 143. His father was one Rufus, son of Philadelphos.

[88] Cf. for example the assembled series *REA* 1929, 17–18 (*Opera Minora*, II, chap. 51); *Hellenica* V, p. 63, n. 1; the list could be significantly supplemented today. Of equal value is the expression *Olympionikês Peisaios*, in the inscription from Philadelpheia in Lydia *Rev. Arch.* 1934, I, 55 (*Opera Minora*, II, chap. 65).

[89] For example, see the case of an *olympionikês* in Tralles (*Eos*, 48, II, 233, n. 28 = *Opera Minora*, I, chap. 43); for the Olympia in an inscription of an athlete from Anazarbos (*L'épigramme grecque*, 185, n. 1). Equally, the officials who presided over the Olympia in Ephesos have been mistaken for the *hellanodikai* of Olympia (cf. *Hellenica*, V, 59–63). The *kômôidos olympioneikês*, found in an inscription of the association of musicians in Ancyra (*SEG* VI, 59, l. 42), had won his title in one or other of the Olympic contests celebrated outside Pisa.

[90] We know that a musical contest in Olympia was, extraordinarily, put in place in honour of Nero. This involved a modification in the year of the Olympiad.

[91] Cf. notably A. Mie, *MDAI(A)* 1909, 1–17 and the vague article of E. J. Jory along with my discussion in *Bull. Épigr.* 1968, 254.

[92] Cf. essentially J. Frei, *De certaminibus thymelicis* (Diss. Bâle 1900), 43–4 (heralds), 65–7 (trumpeters). See also *Rev. Phil.* 1930, 50, n. 3 (*Opera Minora* II, 1150) for the trumpeters; my *Monnaies grecques* (1967), 106–15 ("La trompette de Périnthe"), where the type of trumpet along with the athletic crown depicted on the coins of Perinthos is explained.

[93] Cf. *Ét. épigr.* 92–3; *Bull. Épigr.* 1958, 160, p. 223.

[94] We can recognise the "general event" beyond doubt since he defines it as such on every occasion. However, he has not indicated his category at the beginning.

of Nikomedeia;⁹⁵ then, the Antonineia celebrated at the same time in Thebes in Boeotia,⁹⁶ Nikaia,⁹⁷ Byzantium and Caisareia in Cappadocia.

This list gives us a good idea of the activities and voyages of Aurelianos. The list is compiled in descending order of prestige. This is common for the first part of inscriptions of this type. At the head, the Olympia of Olympia supersedes the Pythia of Delphi.⁹⁸ Then, the two other contests of the *periodos* follow, the minor trieteric contests of the Isthmus and Nemea. Next, according to the order of prestige frequently adhered to, follow the great contests of Italy: the Capitolia of Rome, to which we can add here another contest in Rome, the Eusebeia of Puteoli and the Sebasta of Neapolis. The contests are then grouped according to city. It is not by accident that the three grandest contests of the illustrious city of Athens come first: the Panhellenia, Hadrianeia and Panathenaia, the first two created by Hadrian. This choice explains the reference to the second ethnic of the individual: Athenian. It is very probable that all these victories have granted him the right of citizenship in other cities;⁹⁹ but he has made a choice.¹⁰⁰ After that, a geographical order appears: a city of Old Greece, neighbour of Athens, Thebes.¹⁰¹

We then move on to the two most illustrious cities of Ionia, with their celebrated festivals of the imperial period, the Olympia of Smyrna¹⁰² and the Barbilleia or Balbilleia in Ephesos in honour of the astrologer Balbillus under Vespasian,¹⁰³ and the Olympia.¹⁰⁴ Then, also in the province of Asia, the great city of Pergamon with its Augousteia, which was the late name for the Sebasta of the province created in honour of Augustus,¹⁰⁵ and the Traianeia. Then comes Bithynia, homeland of our man, with four victories in Nikomedeia and two in Nikaia. It seems natural that this

---

⁹⁵ Cf. several inscriptions and coins in C. Bosch, *Die kleinas. Münzen der römischen Kaiserzeit*, II 1, *Bithynien* (1935), 232–3 [cf. *Choix d'écrits*, p. 696].

⁹⁶ The name is added to that of the Dionyseia and Herakleia; see below.

⁹⁷ For Nikaia, cf. E. Bosch, *Belleten Türk Tarih Kurumu* 12 (1918), 325–48: "Nikaia (Iznik) bayram oyunlar", an article which is very much open to debate; cf. already on the apples given as prizes at the Pythia, *Hellenica*, VII, pp. 93–104; VIII, 77–8, and also, for Perinthos, *Monnaies grecques*, 107, n. 5 [cf. n. 106, below].

⁹⁸ Very frequently, the contest which provided the occasion to erect the monument in the city was placed at the head, as the most recent victory.

⁹⁹ For the connection between a victory in a given city and the right of citizenship in that city, compare the remarkable expression in an inscription from Anazarbos (L. Moretti, *Iscr. agon. gr.*, no. 86; cf. *L'épigramme grecque*, 185 and n. 1): "having won ... in all the contests listed below, in which the prize is a talent or half a talent, in every region of the world, forty-seven in total, where he has also gained citizenships" (νικήσας ... τοὺς ὑποτεταγμένους ἀγῶνας παντὸς κλίματος τῆς οἰκουμένης ταλαντιαίους καὶ ἡμιταλαντιαίους μζ′ ὧν καὶ τὰς πολιτείας ἔχει). The only ethnic that this Demetrios has given is his original one, Salaminian (of Cyprus).

¹⁰⁰ There is almost always a choice, and the lists of ethnics allocated to the same individual do not always match in all their details. Cf. for example *Rev. Phil.* 1930, 47, n. 4 (*Opera Minora*, II, chap. 70); *REG* 1966, 756.

¹⁰¹ On the two contests of Thebes, the Dionyseia and Herakleia, cf. most recently *Hellenica*, XIII, 148–9; *Documents de l'Asie Mineure méridionale*, 104, n. 8.

¹⁰² Cf. *Rev. Phil.* 1930, 32, n. 8; 33; 38; 58 (*Opera Minora*, II, chap. 69); *BCH* 1933, 542 (*Opera Minora*, chap. 33).

¹⁰³ Cf. *ibid.* 1930, 30, n. 6; 58, n. 1 (*Opera Minora*, II, chap. 69); A. Stein, *Aegyptus*, 13 (1933), 125, n. 4.

¹⁰⁴ Cf. *Hellenica*, VII, 84–6; *Rev. Phil.* 1967, 40–4.

¹⁰⁵ This name for the contest is late, common especially in the third century AD or the late second century. Cf. *Rev. Phil.* 1938, 25, n. 2. On the name Augousteia in relation to the festival in Pergamon, cf. notably *Rev. Phil.* 1927, 23, 136; 1930, 33 (*Opera Minora* II, chaps 60 and 70).

citizen of Nikomedeia would set out from the gulf of Nikomedeia in the Propontis to compete in the three great cities of the Propontis: Perinthos on the north coast, with its Aktia,[106] Kyzikos on the south coast, with its Olympia,[107] Byzantion at the entrance of the Bosporus, with its Antoninia.[108] Some distance away from this circle of cities, Aurelianos competed in the great city of Cappadocia, Caisareia-by-Mount-Argaios, which was situated on the important commercial and military route towards Syria and the frontiers of the East.[109]

The festivals of the Antoninia – or, by contraction, the Antonia[110] – are frequently attested contests in many cities.[111] They could have been created to honour either Caracalla, or Elagabal, as they shared the names of Marcus Aurelius Antoninus. In many cases I think they were created under Caracalla and then carried on in the reign of Elagabal.[112] Already by that stage the contests in honour of Septimius Severus, the Severeia (Σεβήρεια, Σευήρεια) were widely attested. The Severan era marked a forward leap in the multiplication of sacred contests in the Greek cities. But this process was not equally distributed in all areas of the *pars orientalis* of the Empire. Three regions are particularly rich in such festivals in honour of Septimius Severus, Caracalla and Elagabal:[113] first of all, Bithynia with Nikaia, Nikomedeia, Prousias on the river Hypios, and also Byzantion and Perinthos; then, on the other side of the peninsula, Tarsos, Anazarbos, Castabala; and also, in the centre of Asia Minor, Ankyra in Galatia[114] and Caisareia in Cappadocia.[115] I have already indicated elsewhere[116] that these regions formed departure points, crossings and bases for the Roman armies operating against the Parthians and protecting Asia Minor against their threat; the emperors and their armies passed through these areas. The arrival and sojourn (ἐπιδημία) of Septimius Severus himself was celebrated in the

---

[106] The numismatic evidence for this contest is discussed in E. Schönert, *Die Münzprägung von Perinthos* (1965). For the apples given as prizes in the Pythia of the city, cf. *Hellenica* VII, 100; *Monnaies grecques* 107, n. 5.

[107] Cf. *Rev. Phil.* 1930, 153 (*Opera Minora* II, chap. 69).

[108] These festivals are known from elsewhere, from coins and inscriptions; I will deal with them in a work on Byzantium.

[109] I will assemble the evidence on the contest in Caisareia-by-Mount-Argaios elsewhere in publishing an inscription from Kyzikos regarding a pancratiast, which is decorated with monumental athletic crowns that are very frequently misidentified on the monuments (for example, in the relief from the theatre of Hierapolis in Phrygia published by D. Bernardi Ferrero, *Teatri classici in Asia Minore*, I (1966), p. 59, fig. 97; cf. *Bull. Épigr.* 1970); cf. *Bull. Épigr.* 1969, 579 [cf. *CRAI* 1982, 230, n. 5]. For the identification of the city, cf. for example, in this region, an inscription from Theadelpheia in Lydia: "the confederationn of Cappadocians in Caisareia-by-Mount-Argaios" (ἐν Καισαρείᾳ τῇ πρὸς Ἀργαίῳ κοινὸν Καππαδόκων) (*CIG*, 3428; *IGR*, IV, 1645). For all the coin types with athletic motifs cf. E. A. Sydenham, *The Coinage of Caesarea in Cappadocia* (London, 1933).

[110] On this second form, that has nothing to do with Antonius or with an Antonia, cf. principally *Bull. Épigr.* 1938, 477, pp. 327–8; *Fouilles de Laodicée du Lycos*, 283, 293, 294 [*Bull. Épigr.* 1974, p. 577].

[111] Cf. especially *Bull. Épigr.* 1938, 180, pp. 192 and 195.

[112] For those of Ancyra in Galatia, see *Hellenica*, XI–XII, chap. 18; "Inscription agonistique d'Ancyre", "Concours d'Ancyre", pp. 350–68.

[113] For the Antonineia, see above. For the Severeia, see the provisional lists of Hartmann, RE s. v. Sebereia (1921) (add Oinoanda and remove Thyateira, where the subject is Alexander Severus); also D. Magie, *Roman Rule in Asia Minor*, II, p. 1940 [cf. *Choix d'écrits* p. 696].

[114] See *Hellenica*, XI–XII, chap. 18: "Concours d'Ancyre".

[115] See preceding notes.

[116] Cf. *La déesse de Castabala*, 92.

coinage of Perinthos,[117] and the coins of Tarsos have revealed to us the existence of the Σεβήρεια ἐπινείκια ἐν Κοτρίγαις [Severeia Epinikia in Kotrigai].[118] This was a frequent transit route for Septimius Severus and Caracalla, and was also the route used by Elagabal coming back from Syria on his way to settle himself in Rome.[119]

Caracalla and Elagabal shared the same names and the Antoninia could equally honour the one or the other, or both. One way of judging is by the deletion of the imperial name, since this happened only in the case of Elagabal and not for Caracalla. A good example comes from an inscription from Thyateira,[120] according to which an ambassador of the city

> went on an embassy to our lord the invincible Emperor Caesar M. Aurelius [Antoninus: this name is deleted] Pius Felix Augustus on behalf of his dearest homeland and obtained, from the divine generosity of the emperor, a sacred contest for the entire world, celebrated by the triumphal entry of the victors, Augustean and equal to the Pythia.[121]

The term "Augustean" (Augousteios, Augousteia) is the one that tends to supplant *Sebasta* during this period.[122] The ambassador who achieved the recognition of this isopythian contest, Gaius Perelius Aurelius Alexander, had completed, according to the editors, an embassy "regarding the roads" (*peri hodôn*) (τὸν περὶ ὁδῶν πρεσβεύσαντα), from which he returned with the recognition of the sacred contest. I have shown, a long time ago, that this was an athlete with the status of *periodonikês* (περίοδον) and that this last word has been misread in several inscriptions[123] from Rome, Athens, Olympia and Ephesos, where it was corrected to περιοδον(είκην), supposing either an error of the stone-cutter, or an internal abbreviation.[124]

The Nikomedeian mentions his victory in the Antoninia Pythia of Rome in the privileged category of the Italian contests, following the contests of the *periodos* and just after the Capitolia of Rome. This is enough to illustrate the eminent place of the new contest in the universal hierarchy: it is the only permanent contest celebrated in Rome alongside the Capitolia of Domitian and was destined to remain so until Gordian instituted the contest of Athena Promachos. It is remarkable that, in the great abundance of our documents and victory lists from the third century, we possess only this one solitary mention. It is for this reason that I believe the Antoninia were connected not with Antoninus Caracalla, but with his namesake, Antoninus Elagabal. The choice of the Pythia, a contest associated with or assimilated to the Antoninia, is better suited to the latter. It is not only in Thyateira that

---

[117] In the north-west of Asia Minor, Severus was involved in the war against Pescennius Niger and the long siege of Byzantium.

[118] Cf. provisionally *Hellenica*, VIII, 92.

[119] On Elagabal's itinerary and its traces in several cities, cf. *La déesse de Castabala*, 57, n. 3; 79–82; 99.

[120] J. Keff and A. von Premerstein, *IIe Reise in Lydien*, no. 64 (*IGR*, IV, 1251). Entirely completed, and discussed in *Études Anatoliennes*, 119–23: "Une ambassade auprès d'Élagabal".

[121] Πρεσβεύσαντα πρὸς τὸν κύριον ἡμῶν ἀήττητον Αὐτοκράτορα Καίσαρα Μ. Αὐρ. [Ἀντωνεῖνον, deleted word] Εὐσεβῆ Εὐτυχῆ Σεβαστὸν ὑπὲρ τῆς γλυκητάτης πατρίδος καὶ ἐπιτυχόντα παρὰ τῆς θείας τύχης αὐτοῦ ἱερὸν [ἀγῶ]να εἰσελαστικὸν Αὐγούστ[ειον ἰσο]πύθιον εἰς ἅπασαν [τὴν οἰκουμένην].

[122] Cf. above, n. 105.

[123] *Études Anatoliennes, loc. cit.*

[124] Also, with reference to the text from Rome, in E. Nachmanson, *Eranos*, 10 (1910) 116–17; W. Larfeld, *Handbuch der Griechischen Epigraphik* (1914) 280. The article in the recent *Supplément* (1965) of LSJ, περίοδος = περιοδονίκης, as in the preceding supplement, is very odd.

Elagabal had "granted" Pythia.[125] In Emesa in Syria, his hometown, he granted the creation of Helia Pythia, a contest in honour of the Sun based on the model of the Pythia.[126] A coin type presents us with the words *Hêlia* and *Pythia* above and below an athletic crown[127] with two palm leaves. But the odds are, from the silence of the documents, that this Greek contest did not last in Rome. It shared the fate of all the religious institutions of Elagabal. The cult of the god Elagabal disappeared in the cities where it had been established.[128] The contest Elagabalia in Sardeis is known only by one issue of coinage.[129] The neokorates granted by this emperor to cities like Ephesos or Sardeis were abolished and the cities which, thanks to him, had become "four times *neokoroi*" slid back down to the rank of "three times *neokoroi*".[130] The temple erected to the emperor by the province was done away with. It is a completely different story with Caracalla, whose memory never suffered any official injury. A festival created by him would have persisted, as did Gordian's contest of Athena Promachos and Aurelian's contest of the Sun.

Herodian talks about the plethora of festivals that took place after the settling of Elagabal in Rome and the construction of the temple of his god: "he generously and lavishly funded many different kinds of spectacle" (φιλοτίμως καὶ πολυτελῶς ἐπιτελέσας παντοδαπὰς θεάς).[131] Having constructed a very big and very luxurious temple, every year in midsummer he would lead his god there in procession.[132] He "devised all sorts of celebrations" (πανηγύρεις τε παντοδαπὰς συνεκρότει), constructing hippodromes and theatres, and "through chariot races and various kinds of spectacle and numerous performers" (διά τε ἡνιοχείας καὶ πάντων θεαμάτων τε καὶ ἀκροαμάτων), "he thought he would amuse the people, who feasted and spent their nights in celebration" (εὐωχούμενον τὸν δῆμον καὶ παννυχίζοντα εὐφραίνειν ᾤετο). We now know the name of the festival introduced by Elagabal: the Antoninia Pythia.

Cassius Dio too speaks accurately and interestingly about the contests granted by Elagabal, 80.10.2–3:

> Sardanapalus [Dio calls him by that name, along with "pseudo-Antoninus" or "the Assyrian" etc.] held a great number of contests and spectacles, (ἀγῶνας ἐποίει καὶ θέας συχνάς), in which the athlete Aurelius Helix won success (εὐδοκίμησεν).[133] This man so much surpassed his competitors that he wanted to compete at the same time in both the wrestling and the *pankration* events in Olympia and also at the Capitolia, and won there in both events.

Dio then narrates the ploy by which the Eleans prevented his double victory in

---

[125] See above, n. 121. There the protector god of the city was Apollo Tyrimnos or Tyrimnaios.

[126] See *BMC Galatia Syria*, p. lxv and p. 240, n. 21.

[127] In line with an error which was common at the period of the catalogue (W. Wroth [1899] *Catlogue of the Greek Coins of Cappadocia, Syria and Galatea*), the coin is described as bearing "an athletic urn". See n. 109.

[128] Cf. *La déesse de Castabala*, 81–2.

[129] I will discuss this festival elsewhere; see below n. 138.

[130] Cf. *Rev. Phil.* 1967, 49.

[131] Herodian 5.5.8 and see also everything following regarding the rites.

[132] Herodian 5.6.6 and following.

[133] This is a common term in the technical vocabulary for athletes and musicians throughout the history of contests.

Olympia.¹³⁴ "But in Rome he won in both events, a feat no one else had accomplished." The inscription from Delphi elucidates the beginning of this passage. The "great number of contests and spectacles" (ἀγῶνες καὶ θεαὶ συχναί) celebrated by Elagabal are not the Capitolia of 218 AD.¹³⁵ This would not explain the statement. In fact, the inscription adds to the Capitolia of 218 AD the new great festival of Antoninia Pythia. It seems reasonable to date the festival to 219 AD or 220 at the very latest. Dio speaks of the "success" won by Helix in the contest granted by Elagabal. What he has to say later on, on the brilliant victories at the Capitolia and on the injustice the athlete suffered at the Olympia, is not directly linked to Elagabal. Rather, it is intended to be a reminder of the great fame and achievements of this particular athlete, also well known from two passages in Philostratus.

The new inscription from Delphi informs us that a new Greek contest was instituted in Rome by Elagabal. It also bears testimony to the eminent place it held in the hierarchy of these festivals, being in the midst of contests of the first rank. A brilliant future for it was in store. This festival had a double name. It was very different from the contests the list of which it supplemented. The Capitolia of Domitian glorified the three great protecting divinities of Rome, the Capitoline Triad, and took on the cult of light-hearted luxury typical of the great sacred contests of Greece, along with their splendour, their variety and their celebratory atmosphere, shared by contestants and spectators alike. A century and a half later, following the evolution in royal power, religion and public sensibility, the Syrian Elagabal honoured himself through the Antoninia contest, in the same way that the Neronia honoured Nero. Elagabal attached to his name the cult of Apollo Pythios, through the name Pythia. This god was a very suitable choice for Elagabal, being analogous to his ancestral god, to whom he was a priest and servant; a god whom he married with partner goddesses (*paredrai*) like Venus Caelestis of Carthage,¹³⁶ and whom he "led in procession in front of Jupiter Capitolinus".¹³⁷ It is remarkable that this contest was never at any point called directly by the name of the god from Emesa, Elagabalia, as was the case in Sardeis.¹³⁸ It was not even called Helia, as was the contest in Emesa,¹³⁹ which was celebrated by the Antonine whose name is preserved on the coin issues of the mints of Rome and Antioch: "undefeated priest Augustus" (*invictus sacerdos Aug(ustus)*) and "priest of the Sun god Elgabal" (*sacerdos dei Solis Elagabal(i)*).¹⁴⁰ In Emesa the contests simultaneously celebrated and brought closer together the Sun and Pythian Apollo, who at this time had

---

¹³⁴ The same Helix from Phoenicia is named in the *Heroicus* of Philostratus and in the *Gymnasticus*. For his career and his dates, see especially F. Münscher, *Philologus*, Suppl. X (1907) "Die Philostrate", 497–8 and J. Jüthner, *Philostratos über Gymnastik* (1909), pp. 87–9 and 284.

¹³⁵ Cf. L. Moretti, *Olympionikai, I vincitori negli antichi agoni olimpici* (*MAL* series VIII, vol. VIII, iss. 2; 1957), n° 9: "in 219 AD according to the current consensus (in actuality the Capitolia must have been held in 218 AD)".

¹³⁶ Cf. provisionally *La déesse de Castabala*, 79–82; 99; *Rev. Phil.* 1967, 49 [cf. *Choix d'écrits*, p. 669].

¹³⁷ Cf. Dio Cassius 79.11: καὶ πρὸ τοῦ Διὸς αὐτοῦ (Jupiter Capitolinus) ἤγαγεν αὐτόν.

¹³⁸ I have drawn attention on different occasions to the Elagabalia of Sardeis (cf. above), while waiting for the publication and commentary of the bronze of the Cabinet of Paris, which attests to this contest [cf. *Choix d'écrits*, pp. 666–70].

¹³⁹ See above, n. 126.

140 Mattingly, Sydenham and Sutherland, *The Roman Imperial Coinage* IV, 2, *Macrinus to Pupienus* (1938), pp. 24, 34, 37, 43.

become a solar deity. In Rome, the Hellenism of the new contest was marked more forcefully by mentioning only the Pythia alongside the Antoninia.[141] The creation in Rome of a contest in honour of the Sun is the result of a different set of religious changes; and for that we must wait for Aurelian. In any case, Elagabal brought a very original touch to his creation of this Greek-style contest in Rome. It would disappear with him. Thirty years later, Gordian III, senatorial emperor, appeared wholly "classical", traditional and archaicising, when, just before his departure against the "Persians", the Sassanids, he had the temple of Janus opened and created in Rome a new contest *à la grecque*, placing himself and his army under the protection of Athena Promachos, the goddess who had saved the Athenians at Marathon.

141 The contest Pythia Antoneinia under Elagabal in Laodikeia in Syria, *I. Syrie*, 1265.

PART IV

Competition and Victory

Introduction to Part IV

Both of the pieces in this section build on the discussions of festival programming and competitive participation in previous chapters. Both, I hope, will bring new dimensions and additional depth to those issues.

H. W. Pleket's article, first of all, addresses the problem of prize-giving practices in order to shed light on questions of social status and athletic ideology.[1] We have seen already, from the first of Robert's articles in section 3, that one of the key distinctions often drawn within modern scholarship on the agonistic festival calendar is the distinction between crown games and prize games, the latter of which had money prizes rather than wreaths. Pleket's achievement in the long first section of the article is to show the difficulty of maintaining that distinction in practice: he demonstrates that many crown games also gave monetary prizes; as well as laying out more often quoted evidence for the monetary rewards given to successful athletes, especially those successful at the great *periodos* games, by their home cities. From there he moves on to questions of athletic ideals. He rejects the idea that ancient athletics was dominated by an amateur ideology, while also arguing that the category of professionalism is not relevant either. A great many competitive athletes in the ancient world, he suggests, continued to be from very wealthy backgrounds even long after the classical period. Aristocratic ideals also still dominated: most athletes were happy to accumulate monetary rewards, but also keen to go out of their way to dissociate themselves from the stigma of earning money. In his rejection of the idea of ancient amateurism Pleket is in line with the influential conclusions of David Young already mentioned in this volume's introduction, although Young nevertheless in a number of works suggests that Pleket has failed to banish entirely Gardiner's claims about the elistist ideals of ancient athletics and about the decline of ancient athletics due to encroaching professionalism.[2] Many other scholars in turn have been sceptical about Young's belief that

---

[1] Other good discussions of sport and social status include Golden (1998) 141–75 and (2008); and Crowther (1991) and (1993), who suggests that the numbers of athletes competing at Olympia and elsewhere would have been relatively low, and made up mainly of wealthy competitors, partly because of the financial burden of travel and training time. See also Fisher in chapter 3 of this volume and Young (1984) for a more egalitarian view of athletic participation. A number of Pleket's other publications – esp. Pleket (1974) (in German, but republished in English translation in Scanlon (forthcoming)) and (1992) – deal further with related issues; see also the author's brief addenda, added especially for this volume, to several of the footnotes in chapter 7.

[2] See, e.g., Young (1988) 89–103.

there were large numbers of non-elite athletes even from the early days of Greek athletics.³

Onno van Nijf's view is close to Pleket's in his stress on the continuing dominance of elite athletes, but to some extent he cuts through the problems which both Pleket and Young have to grapple with in aiming for a generalised view of the question by paying close attention to the local context of games in the province of Lycia. He shows very vividly, through discussion of the epigraphic record for these cities, the involvement of members of the local elites in competition and benefaction. He also demonstrates that festivals functioned partly as opportunities to act out a vision of social order and hierarchy within the city, not only through the victory of members of the elite trained in the *gymnasion*, but also through the processions and distributions which formed such an important part of festival life. The other aspect of van Nijf's article which deserves particular attention here is his interest in the role of athletic festivals as opportunities for a city to construct and act out a Greek identity (as well as to accommodate Roman rule within a Greek cultural framework). As he makes clear, athletic participation had long been linked with Greek affiliation, but increasingly a kind of honorary Greek status seems to have become available even to non-Greeks for the purposes of competing in agonistic festivals. The area van Nijf focuses on, Lycia, was reinventing itself in the Roman period as a Greek region, and the Lycians' commitment to the archetypally Greek pursuit of athletics – an "invented tradition", in the context of Lycian culture – seems to have contributed to that process. Not only that, but it is intriguing, van Nijf suggests, that athletic contests in Lycia seem to have attracted much more attention than musical competition and literary achievement. It may be, on that basis, that we should rethink the idea of Greek culture under Roman rule dominated by literary and rhetorical means of expressing Greek identity, as the overused phrase "Second Sophistic" implies, and be more ready to accept the cultural centrality and prestige of the *gymnasion* and the athletic festival.⁴

---

³ For a summary of the debate, see Pritchard (2003) 293–300, and further discussion in relation to the work of Nick Fisher in the introduction to section 3.

⁴ For further discussion, and further detailed study of the athletic festival culture of the Imperial period, see van Nijf (2001), (2003a), (2003b), (2005) and (2006); also König (2005).

7 Games, Prizes, Athletes and Ideology: some aspects of the history of sport in the Greco-Roman world*

H. W. PLEKET

INTRODUCTION

Ancient History, that is, the history of Greco-Roman societies in their economic, social and mental aspects, is frequently felt by modern historians to be more "ancient" than "history": in their choice of themes, problems and concepts ancient historians too often do not adapt themselves to major developments in modern – especially social, economic and intellectual history. To be sure, notable and welcome exceptions exist. Problems of social structure and stratification, of economic organisation and behaviour are increasingly dealt with.

Nevertheless, regular inspection of some leading periodicals in the field will show that too many ancient historians fail to link their studies up with what goes on in the leading periodicals devoted to modern history such as the *Annales* (Économies, Sociétés, Civilisations), *Past and Present* and *Comparative Studies in Society and History*.

Fortunately, and exceptionally, there is at least one theme on which the leading schools of modern history are comparatively weak, whereas the ground has been covered quite thoroughly for the ancient world: the history of physical education and sport. The history of early and modern European sport cannot of course be called a neglected field but one gets the impression that the lion's share of the work has been done by amateur historians, themselves frequently connected with and/or active in the world of gymnastics and sport, rather than by the professional historians who people Clio's realm and her periodicals. Brailsford's *Sport and Society. Elizabeth to Anne* (London 1969) and E. Weber's recent articles on *Pierre de Coubertin and the Introduction of Organized Sport in France,*[1] and *Gymnastics and Sports in Fin-de-Siècle France: Opium of the Classes*[2] are extremely welcome contributions to the study of the organisation and ideology of sport in the past, but they are, if not exceptional, at least far too isolated. Even in the *Annales*, in which the expansive, almost imperialistic, character of history manifests itself clearly, the subject gets little attention. G. Boquet, who recently reviewed Brailsford's book in

---

* Originally published in *Stadion* 1 (1975), 49–89.
[1] *Journal of Contemporary History*, 5 (1970), 2, 3–26.
[2] *American Historical Review*, 76 (1971), 70–98.

that periodical,[3] admittedly considered Brailsford's theme a worth-while subject of historical research but his review is singularly devoid of references to similar studies on the subject.[4]

Consequently the creation of a new scholarly periodical devoted to the study of physical education and sport both in the world of today and in the past cannot be welcomed too warmly; this happy initiative has been taken by two members of the Institut für Sportgeschichte of the German Sporthochschule in Cologne. Members of this Institute have recently done much useful and solid work in the field of the history of sport in various periods, with special (though by no means exclusive) reference to problems of the ideology of sport both now and at earlier times.[5]

It is perhaps not entirely inappropriate that a study of certain aspects of sport in the Greco-Roman world should appear in the very first volume of this periodical. In Greco-Roman antiquity sport (i.e. athletics, boxing, wrestling, and equestrian games) was an essential ingredient in the educational system in the cities; and with its hundreds of *agônes*, "contests", it permeated public life. Moreover, as implied above, a long list can be made of distinguished scholars who have contributed to the history of physical education and sport in antiquity and who have founded this branch of scholarship on the solid rock of the literary, epigraphical and archaeological sources: J. H. Krause,[6] E. N. Gardiner[7] and in the last decades L. Moretti,[8] L. Robert,[9] H. A. Harris,[10] R. Patrucco[11] and I. Weiler.[12]

However, in this branch of *Altertumswissenschaft* certain dangers lurk under the wealth of material produced by the scholarly world: 1) an overdose of "antiquarianism", i.e. too much of "*antiquitates agonisticae*" (neatly classified agonistic

---

[3] G. Bocquet, "Théatre, Sport et Politique dans l'Angleterre Stuart", in: *Annales, Économies, Sociétés, Civilisations* 27 (1972), 456-72, esp. 464-72. There is no chapter on physical education and sport in J. le Goff-P. Nora, *Faire de l"Histoire* (3 vol. 1974; vol. 3 is on "nouveaux objets").

[4] But see now R. W. Malcolmson, *Popular Recreation in English Society, 1700-1850* (Cambridge 1973).

[5] Cf. e.g. the contributions of M. Lämmer, "Eine Propaganda-Aktion des Königs Herodes in Olympia", in: *Perspektiven der Sportwissenschaft, Jahrbuch der Deutschen Sporthochschule* (Köln 1972) (= Kölner Beiträge zur Sportwissenschaft (abbr. *KBSW*) I), 160-73; "Griechische Wettkämpfe in Jerusalem und ihre politischen Hintergründe", in: *KBSW* 2 (1973), 182-227; "Die Kaiserspiele von Caesarea im Dienste der Politik des Königs Herodes", in: *KBSW* 3 (1974), 95-164; of W. Decker, *Die physische Leistung Pharaos. Untersuchungen zu Heldentum, Jagd und Leibesübungen der ägyptischen Könige* (Köln 1971); of W. Körbs, "Interpretationsansätze der antiken Gymnastik und Agonistik", in: *Fachtagung vom 15. bis 17. Dezember 1967 anlässlich des 20-jährigen Bestehens der Deutschen Sporthochschule Köln*, 1-11; "Gymnasiale Mitteilungen in hellenistischen Papyri der frühen Ptolemäerzeit", in: *Festscrift C. Diem*, 1962), 88-99.

[6] J. H. Krause, *Die Gymnastik und Agonistik der Hellenen* (Leipzig 1841; reprint in 1971).

[7] E. N. Gardiner, *Athletics of the Ancient World* (Oxford 1930).

[8] L. Moretti, *Iscrizioni Agonistiche Greche* (Rome 1953).

[9] See his articles on agonistic problems in his *Opera Minora Selecta* (abbreviated *OMS*), vol. I-IV (Amsterdam 1969-74); for the numerous articles published by Robert during the last ten years one should consult the *Bulletins Épigraphiques*, which appear annually in the *Revue des Études Grecques* (by Jeanne and Louis Robert); see also his *Hellenica* I-XIII (Paris 1940-65), for various chapters on agonistic matters.

[10] H. A. Harris, *Sport in Greece and Rome* (London 1972); cf. my review in *Spiegel Historiael* 9 (1974), 630-2.

[11] R. Patrucco, *Lo Sport nella Grecia antica* (Florence 1972), with a good bibliography on 407-16.

[12] I. Weiler, *Der Agon im Mythos. Zur Einstellung der Griechen zum Wettkampf* (Darmstadt 1974).

phenomena) and not enough questions about the functions of the classified phenomena in ancient society and about their development or non-development during a very long period of time (for our purposes, ca 800 BC–ca. 400 AD). 2) the inevitable classicist "bias", evident in the late H. A. Harris' works but also occasionally even in L. Robert's fundamental contributions. Harris called himself "an old-fashioned don":[13] he liked his college-boys, i.e. amateurs, and disliked professionals – which was his good right – but he retrojected his own views and sympathies into the ancient world, with the predictable result: the rise and fall of the Roman Empire gets its little brother, the rise and fall of Greek athletics: "when money comes in at the door, sport flies out of the window".[14] From the beginning of Greek sport (ca. 800 BC) until somewhere in the fifth century BC the image is positive; afterwards a gradual but persistent decay sets in: true amateurs, recruited from the wealthy elite and considering sport their leisure occupation, not interested in "value-prizes", exercising their sport just for the sake of sport and trying to gain the victory just for the sake of victory and nothing else, *versus* well-paid professional performers, recruited from the lower classes, merely interested in money and prizes and vastly over-specialised and one-sided. Needless to say this conception of the noble Greek amateur closely resembled the views cherished by Pierre Baron de Coubertin and his followers about the athletes who in 1896 were scheduled to participate in the first modern Olympic Games in Athens: "The point of the Olympic Games lies not in winning, but in taking part; not to conquer but to struggle nobly is what matters in life."[15] It is hard to find a phrase that would have shocked the ancient Greeks more than the modern Olympic credo "to participate is more important than to win". I. Weiler has recently and successfully defended the view that the Greeks all through their history have manifested a strong agonistic mentality and that this mentality never separated participation from the urge to win and to gather prizes and prestige through victory.[16]

As for L. Robert – it is not always easy to know what he thinks about the really big issues because above all he wants to straighten out the facts, and those who have some experience of the vast amount of epigraphic evidence know what an enormous and demanding scholarly task that is. However, he once defended the post-classical "professionals" against the contempt felt for them by modern scholars, by pointing out that they had the same ideology as the classical "amateurs".[17] Though this implicitly seems to establish an exclusive link between on the one side "amateurism" and the classical period and on the other "professionalism" and later periods, it at least says something positive about the latter, thereby rejecting the very simple "black" and "white" picture. But elsewhere Robert suggests that aristocrats who had dominated the field in the archaic period (800–400 BC) admittedly continued to perform in the numerous athletic contests in the Hellenistic-Roman period, but

[13] *Op. cit.*, 73.
[14] *Op. cit.*, 40.
[15] I. Weiler, *op. cit.*, 265, note 63.
[16] *Op. cit., passim*.
[17] 'Les épigrammes satiriques de Lucillius sur les athlètes. Parodie et réalités", in: *L'Épigramme Grecque, Entretiens sur l'Antiquité Classique* (publiés par Olivier Reverdin), XIV (1968), 181–295, esp. 288.

increasingly withdrew from "Schwerathletik": the assumption is that the brutality of the latter no longer appealed to them but rather to young men of a lower class:[18] a vague sort of social bias, then, implying that Hellenistic-Roman *kaloikagathoi* (well-born gentlemen) were too well-educated and too refined to go in for brutal boxing or the *pankration*, and a variation (comparatively innocent) on the by-no-means innocent theme, recently sung by Olof Gigon when he wrote about the "Glanz" (splendour) of Pindar's late sixth/early fifth century BC *kaloikagathoi*, who in his view never trained systematically and whose achievements simply were "the result of a heroic lifestyle".[19] Gigon could probably not find any brutality at all in the Pindaric *kaloikagathoi*. Robert will have to play down the brutality of the Pindaric "Schwerathletik"; for in his view it is only in later times that it became really brutal and induced the withdrawal of aristocrats. Both points of view are very questionable: Pindaric athletics were tough and bloody, later athletics were equally tough and bloody,[20] and in both stages *kaloikagathoi*, i.e. members of the social elite, are attested as participants.

"Antiquarianism" and "bias" can perhaps be avoided if one starts by posing a number of central questions and subsequently tries to answer them on the basis of a maximum of source material. In doing so one is inevitably confronted with the problem of how much development there actually was in antiquity and what sort of development; that is to say: do we get qualitatively *new* situations, which gradually evolved out of – and in the process superseded – old situations or would it be wiser to think in terms of further elaboration of what was already available in substance in earlier times?

I would like to ask three main questions and to derive an answer to the general question about the extent of development from the answers to the first three.

They are:

I what categories of *agônes* (contests) were open to the athletes? What criteria were used to distinguish these categories? To what extent did the presence or absence of prizes serve as a distinctive feature?

II what do we know about the social background of the athletes?

III what were the main elements in the athletes' ideology?

I shall make my general starting-point the late-archaic sixth century BC and subsequently try to cover the next 800 years in outline.

I. GAMES AND PRIZES

In early-archaic times (eighth–sixth century BC) there was not much of an institutionalised agonistic systerm. The agonistic "market" offered the Olympic Games (held in every fourth summer,[21] from 776 BC, as tradition has it) and an unknown

---

[18] L. Robert, *OMS*, vol. II, 56; cf. my article "Zur Soziologie des antiken Sports", in: *Mededelingen van het Nederlands Instituut te Rome* 36 (1974), 57–87, esp. 82, note 77, 83, note 108, and 87, note 190.
[19] *Propyläen Weltgeschichte* III, 601.
[20] Cf. L. Robert, *art. cit.*, (cf. note 17), 234.
[21] Cf. Stephen G. Miller, "The Date of Olympic Festivals", in: *Mitt. Deutschen Arch. Instituts* (Athenische Abteilung) 90 (1975), 215-31 ("[It] seems safe to suggest that the Olympia took place every four years at the second full moon after the summer solstice" (p. 231), i.e. in July (end)–August).

number of contests, organised in honour of deceased noblemen and on the occasion of their funerals. One thinks immediately in this connection of Homer's elaborate description of Patroclus' funeral games, in which the noble participants received precious objects as prizes. At Olympia the reward was purely symbolic, i.e. an olive-wreath. In the course of the seventh century BC important changes took place in military matters. The predominance of the nobles on the battlefield was impaired by the rise of the so-called hoplite phalanx, a massive phalanx of middle-class peasants who had become just wealthy enough to pay for their own arms and could therefore serve in the army. J. Delorme[22] has argued that the rise of this hoplite force in its turn brought about the rise of the *gymnasion*: the latter functioned as an institute in which the hoplites, who unlike their noble predecessors, laboured most of the day on their fields, could satisfy their growing need for physical training. S. C. Humphreys[23] has recently questioned the validity of this theory and suggested a return to the view, explicitly rejected by Delorme, that the "origins of the gymnasium" should be associated "with increases in the popularity and number of athletic competitions in the sixth century". However, Delorme pointed out that the increase in the number of athletic competitions was a result rather than the cause of the rise of the *gymnasion*, his main argument being that this increase was a sixth-century BC phenomenon and that the *gymnasion* and/or the existence of gymnastics as systematic training already existed by that time. Humphreys points out that in Athens the earliest *gymnasia* seem to have been founded in the mid-sixth century BC, but in all fairness it should be said that the archaeological evidence for the existence of *gymnasia* is almost non-existent. Some sources attribute measures about management of *gymnasia* to Solon (ca. 600 BC).[24] Humphreys' further point that the lay-out and surroundings of *gymnasia* were not very suitable for hoplite manoeuvres seems irrelevant. Physical training is not identical with training in tactical manoeuvres; as to the latter – there is no way of disproving that the *gymnasion* may have functioned as a rallying place for hoplites. In later times the *gymnasion* was frequently used as a centre for the exercise and military drill of hoplites; perhaps a continuation of an earlier tradition. All in all it seems preferable to argue with W. K. Pritchett[25] that Delorme "may well be right, although there existed in antiquity nothing like our modern need for physical fitness in a civilization in which few people walk or till the fields".

Whatever the truth of the matter, the experts seem to agree that in the sixth century BC the agonistic "market" expanded; this century has been called the period of "athletic organisation". Athletic contests were added to the Pythian, Nemean and Isthmian Games which had previously been restricted to music and now constituted together with the Olympic Games the international *periodos* (the "circuit").[26] In addition an unknown number of local games, inferior in their lack

---

[22] J. Delorme, *Gymnasion*, 24; cf. also M. Détienne, "La Phalange, problèmes et controverses", in: J.-P. Vernant, *Problèmes de la guerre en Grèce ancienne* (Paris-Le Hague 1968), 119 ff., esp. 123.
[23] S. C. Humphreys, "The Nothoi of Kynosarges", in: *Journal of Hellenic Studies* 94 (1974), 88–95, esp. 90–1.
[24] Cf. my article "Zur Soziologie ..." (cf. note 18), 62.
[25] W. K. Pritchett, *The Greek State at War*, Part II (Berkeley 1974), 219, note 44.
[26] Cf. my article "Zur Soziologie ..." (cf. note 18), 61.

of international status to the *periodos*, seem to have been founded in honour of local deities or deceased aristocrats. Gardiner mentions a sixth-century BC bronze vase from Cyme in Italy, with the following inscription: "I was offered as a prize in the contests of Onomastos"; presumably contests financed by and perhaps after his death regularly celebrated in honour of a certain Onomastos.[27]

We can form no clear notion of the numbers. Pindar, who wrote odes for victors in the *periodos* ca. 500–460 BC (and *not* a manual for later sport historians), casually mentions around thirty local games, in addition to the "Big Four" of the *periodos*,[28] but in several passages he clearly implies that a great many other local games existed and were visited by his athletic clients. In his 13th Olympian ode (l. 44–6) Pindar concludes a list of major victories of members of the aristocratic clan of the Oligarthids with the words: "I am (as one) struggling with a crowd for the multitude of your honour; as indeed I should not know how to give a clear account of the pebbles of the sea"; and further down in the same ode: "Search in fine throughout all Hellas, and thou wilt find the tale too long for a single glance" (l. 112–13). In the second Nemean ode he celebrates victories of members of the Timodemids from Aegina, gained in three of the *periodos* games: "They have been encircled with eight crowns already and seven at Nemea (crowns at home past number)" (l. 23–4).[29]

As to the problem of the different categories of game – the accepted theory is that two basic types should be distinguished: the *agônes hieroi kai stephanitai* (sacred crown games) and the *agônes thematikoi* (games in which money-prizes (*themata*) were given). The former were modelled on the penteteric (Olympia, Pythia) or trieteric (Isthmia, Nemea) *periodos* games; they were officially announced by the organising cities to the world of Greek city-states and kings, who in turn accepted these games as *hieros* and consequently dispatched official representatives to the organising city; the latter were local games, neither announced to the world at large nor shaped after the *periodos*. The organising city could decide whether the games were open to citizens only or to both citizens and foreigners.[30]

This terminology, used by the ancients themselves,[31] seems at first sight to suggest that for them the basic difference was the nature of the prize awarded to the victor: sacred games provided a wreath, thematic games a money prize. However, the reality is more complicated, as appears from the fact that "even in the thematic

---

[27] E. N. Gardiner (cf. note 7), 38 ff.; cf. also W. Rudolph, "Zu den Formen des Berufssports zur Zeit der Poliskrise", in: E. Ch. Welskopf, *Hellenische Poleis* (vol. 3, Berlin 1974), 1472–83, esp. 1474.

[28] Cf. Klaus Kramer, *Studien zur griechischen Agonistik nach den Epinikien Pindars* (Diss. Köln 1970), 24–63, esp. 62–3.

[29] L. R. Farnell, *The Works of Pindar* (London 1930), 67, 70, 164; cf. also Kramer, *op. cit.*, 14–15, 16, 19; cf. also L. Robert, *art. cit.* (cf. note 17), 266.

[30] Cf. e.g. L. Robert, "Deux concours grecs à Rome", in: *Comptes Rendus Académie des Inscriptions et Belles Lettres*, 1970, 6 ff., esp. 6–8 (with further references); id.: *AE*, 1969, 49, note 1; 55, note 9. In two cities in Asia Minor (Laertes and Side) we hear of local games, in which only citizens could participate (G. E. Bean–T. B. Mitford, *Journeys in Rough Cilicia 1964–1968*, Denkschriften Akademie Wien, Phil.-Hist. Klasse 102 (1970), 103, no. 88).

[31] W. Rudolph, *art. cit.*, (cf. note 27), 1477–8, correctly pointed out that the technical terminology, used to denote these local prize-games (*arguritai, chrêmatitai, thematikoi* etc.), dates from the post-classical period. This does not mean that the custom of awarding value-prizes (*in natura* or in cash) did not exist earlier; see L. Moretti (cf. note 8), 195.

games wreaths were awarded; conversely, even *in the crown games valuable rewards and privileges were not lacking*" (my italics, H. W. P.).[32] The formula *hieros kai stephanitês* is essentially a piece of sanctifying ideology. It is used of the "Big Four" of the *periodos*, in which olive-wreaths functioned (and throughout antiquity continued to function) as prizes for the winner.

In the oldest literary and epigraphic sources the *periodos* games are mentioned in one and the same breath with other sacred games, in which both a wreath *and a material prize* were given to the winner. Victories of an unknown athlete are mentioned in Nemea, Tegea, Kleitor and Pellene (all cities on the Peloponnese) in a late sixth century BC inscription.[33] Pindar's tenth Nemean Ode (l. 39–48) refers indiscriminately to victories in the *periodos* and in games in Kleitor (the Koriasia), Tegea (the Aleaia) and Pellene (the Theoxenia). The poet mentions cloaks (Pellene) and bronze objects (Kleitor, Tegea) as prizes for the victors.[34] The games in these Peloponnesian cities certainly belonged to the same category as the Olympic Games, i.e. to that of the sacred crown games, but more tangible prizes have been added to the wreath. In Hellenistic-Roman times the games in Kleitor[35] and Tegea[36] are explicitly attested as *agônes stephanitai*. Similarly in a fifth-century BC epigram for the runner Nikoladas from Corinth[37] the *periodos* victories are mentioned on a par with the Athenian Panathenaia, the Arcadian Lykaia, with victories in Pellene and Tegea. The poem explicitly refers to the crowns *and* the amphoras, filled with oil, of the Panathenian Games. From Pindar we know that at the Lykaia bronze tripods were awarded to the victors.[38] In a second century BC catalogue of victories of the Athenian wrestler and pankratiast Menodorus victories "in the *periodos* and in the other sacred contests" are mentioned: among the latter the Panathenaia and the Lykaia appear.[39]

The conclusion seems unavoidable that originally the so-called sacred games in fact consisted of two categories: those in which the prizes were symbolic, i.e. wreaths (to be compared with our "medals") and those in which both a wreath and a "value prize"[40] were given.[41] Prior to the emergence and expansion of monetary economies (i.e. before the sixth/fifth century BC) bronze tripods and related objects

[32] E. Reisch, s.v. ἄθλον, in: *Paulys Realencyclopädie der Classischen Altertumswissenschaft* (abbreviated *RE*), II, 2 (1896), 2059.
[33] J. Ebert, *Griechische Epigramme auf Sieger an gymnischen und hippischen Agonen* (*ASAW*, Phil.-Hist. Kl. 63, no. 2, 1972), 54–5, no. 10.
[34] Cf. J. Ebert, *op. cit.*, 55.
[35] L. Robert, *OMS*, II, 1095 and 1135–36.
[36] L. Robert, *OMS*, II, 1136.
[37] J. Ebert, *op. cit.*, (cf. note 33), 92–6, no. 26.
[38] Cf. Kl. Kramer, *op. cit.*, (cf. note 28), 30; cf. also L. Robert, *art. cit.* (cf. note 17), 267.
[39] L. Moretti, *op. cit.*, (cf. note 8), 131–8, no. 51.
[40] "Value prize" is here used as the equivalent of the German "Wertpreis". I have not been able to find a good English equivalent.
[41] L. Robert, *Hellenica* VII, 107 note 5, argues that "It was only in special circumstances that an amphora was given as a prize – at the Panathenaia in Athens this was because the amphora would be filled with oil from the sacred olive trees of Athena – or that a bronze vase was given to the victors, as at the Heraia in Argos." From Kl. Kramer, *op. cit.*, (cf. note 28), 24–63, esp. 62–3. I get the impression that the "circumstances" were less "special" than R. suggests. But we shall have to wait for his "detailed study on the subject of crowns and prizes at the different contests" (Les épigrammes satiriques ... (cf. note 17), 267, note 5).

constituted a source of wealth and prestige for the victors. One may compare these prizes with those won by Homer's aristocrats in the funeral games in honour of Patroclos and explicitly equated with so-and-so-many oxen. The fact that the above-mentioned two categories of games could be subsumed under the one heading "sacred crown games" shows that at least in origin the notion of "economic value" was not considered to be fundamentally incompatible with that of the crown game.

It is perhaps not insignificant that there is a tradition according to which Olympia started with "value prizes" but after six Olympiads decided to substitute "wreaths".[42] Unfortunately the value of the tradition is questionable. It is a late story; one could argue that it was concocted as a parallel to the story about the Pythian Games which are said to have substituted wreaths for prizes in 582 BC; perhaps it was an attempt to bring the early Olympic Games in line with what happened in Patroclos' games. Speculation seems idle here. Two points should be made: a) if the story is a late, Hellenistic-Roman invention, it testifies to the feeling that in later times there was no insurmountable barrier between *agônes stephanitai* and material prizes: games which in later times were undeniably sacred-crown games could be regarded as thematic in origin. b) if the story reflects historical truth the obvious question is why the change was introduced. This is a knotty problem. The ancients put forward religious explanations: the wreath, made from the sacred olive-tree in Zeus' precinct in Olympia, is said to have been suggested to the Eleans by Apollo at Delphi; modern scholars argue: "The religious character of a contest is also often made clear by the fact that the prize of victory is taken directly from the holy precinct of the divinity."[43]

Whatever the truth is, the introduction of the change (or the awarding of wreaths from the very beginning) was not a matter of Coubertinian ideology *avant la lettre*: archaic nobles are not known to have rejected remuneration for athletic successes either in theory or in practice. Perhaps it was the Elean way of distinguishing Olympia from other contemporary *agônes*, funerary or local, which (if we assume that Homer's description of Patroclos' games reflects contemporary practice) knew tripods, cauldrons and women as prizes. Elean and other archaic nobles were certainly the kind of people who could afford to make this "sacrifice": they possessed landed wealth and though the accumulation of wealth is an never-ending process for many people, the accumulation of prestige through an Olympic wreath may have provided sufficient compensation for the members of this highly competitive society. Incidentally, participation at Olympia did not prevent them from participation in games with "value prizes" (coupled with crowns or not); and from ca. 600 BC onwards cities are known to have awarded money or bullion to their victorious athletes for their wreaths.[44]

In addition to the two types of sacred, international games (wreaths with and without material prizes) there existed of old a third category of contests, local in

---

[42] Cf. L. Ziehen, *RE* XVIII (1939), 31–2.
[43] E. Reisch, *RE* II, 2 (1896), 2059 (s.v. ἄθλον).
[44] Cf. my article "Zur Soziologie ..." (cf. note 18), 67; W. Rudolph, *art. cit.* (cf. note 27), 1475, 1477; see also H. Buhmann, *Der Sieg in Olympia und in den anderen panhellenischen Spielen* (Diss. München 1972), 104–36.

scope and with heavy emphasis on the material prize: funeral games, games in honour of local heroes and gods. I take it that among the "innumerable" games mentioned by Pindar a good many belonged to this category of minor, local prize-games; and when in the first half of the fifth century BC the pugilist and pankratiast Theogenes of Thasos is said to have gained 1,300 victories in twenty-two years, local prize-games will again have played an important part.[45] It is difficult to say what the prizes would have been like; in the pre-monetary period undoubtedly precious objects or gifts *in natura*; from 500 BC onwards coins are attested that served as prizes (the so-called "prize-coins");[46] in the Hellenistic-Roman period prizes of 3,000 and 6,000 drachmas were normal enough for the *thematikoi agônes*, to be called *hêmitalantiaioi* (half-talent) or *talantiaioi* (talent) *agônes* (one talent being 6,000 dr.).

From the above it appears that the concept "sacred crown games" had a certain ambiguity: the *periodos*-games did not have material prizes, whereas other sacred games, mentioned on a par with the *periodos* in literary and epigraphic texts, knew both crowns and material prizes. In the post-classical, Hellenistic-Roman period (ca. 300 BC–ca. 300 AD) a number of important developments took place. Firstly, the number of games increased greatly. In the Roman period the agonistic "market" offered well over 300 *agônes*, though a *precise* list does not as yet seem to have been compiled. "Export" of Greek athletics to the numerous and increasingly prosperous cities of Asia Minor and Syria explains the increase of agonistic possibilities for the athletes.[47] Secondly, athletes are increasingly (though by no means exclusively: see below) recruited from the non-aristocratic lower classes. This means that money, i.e. money prizes, became increasingly important for those athletes, who were not in a position to consider "value prizes" merely as a welcome addition to available wealth; on the contrary, prizes became an indispensable source of income for people who had no ancestral wealth. This is reflected in the documents by the fact that it is precisely in late-Hellenistic-Roman sources[48] that the "sacred crown games" and the thematic games are recorded as two distinct categories of games. As we saw above large cash-prizes ousted earlier prizes *in natura* (precious objects, oil, corn etc.).[49] In a full-blown monetary economy "professional" athletes, who had

[45] So L. Moretti, *op. cit.*, (cf. note 8), 195; W. Rudolph, *art. cit.*, 1474.

[46] See my article "Zur Soziologie ..." (cf. note 18), 61; but even in the fourth century BC, amphoras with oil (50, 40 or 18) were awarded as prizes in the Panathenaia in Athens; cf. W. Rudolph, *art. cit.*, 1478.

[47] Cf. "Zur Soziologie ...", 71.

[48] See the inscriptions in Moretti, *op. cit.* (cf. note 8), Index, 284, s.v.

[49] The victors in the sacred Theoxenia at Pellene (cf. above p. 151) originally received cloaks (χλαῖναι) as prizes; at some time in the Hellenistic period the Theoxenia lost their status of sacred contest; they became an unimportant, local "money" game (*chrêmatitês agôn*), the cloaks having been replaced by cash prizes. Similarly games which were thematic and local in origin, may well have substituted cash prizes for the original prizes-*in-natura*. Incidentally, the example of the Theoxenia shows that when an *agôn* lost its international, sacred status in the Hellenistic-Roman period, its prizes tended to become monetary. In its international phase the contest combined material prizes (cloaks) with wreaths. This does not mean that in the international phase money prizes could not already have replaced the cloaks. *Chrêmatitês* denotes loss of international status and subsequent *restriction* to money prizes; it does not imply the incompatibility of "value prizes" (cloaks or money) with the wreath in the previous stage. In fact in a Rhodian inscription (see below p. 159) we find a category of *themateitai stephanitai agônes*. For the Theoxenia cf. L. Moretti, *op. cit.*, 14 and 195–6; J. Ebert, *op. cit.* (cf. note 33), 55; E. Meyer, in: *RE* XIX (1937), 365 (s.v. Pellene).

to make a living out of their sport, were not to be satisfied with prizes, which had subsequently to be sold for cash.

As for the "sacred" games – many cities successfully tried to elevate their games to the category of sacred crown games in this post-classical period.[50] Since the *periodos* unmistakably constituted the crème-de-la-crème of the sacred games, many games outside Olympia were remodelled after the "Big Four": they became *isolympios*, *isopythios* and so on, which meant that the programme, age-classes, organisation and prizes were identical with those of the *periodos* games. Strictly speaking this meant that in a great many games – for the number of sacred, isolympian (and so on) games is vast – the athletes could not win "value prizes". The prestige of the Olympic and similar games was so enormous[51] and prestige was rated so highly among the urban aristocrats who organised the contests, that they preferred imitating Olympia to organising thematic games with cash prizes but of inferior status. Even the poorer athletes could afford to accept this "Olympic" ideology. Firstly, nothing prevented them from participating both in (iso)Olympic and in thematic games. Secondly, mother cities rewarded their victorious athletes with fixed amounts of money and with pensions.[52] Of old a victory in one of the *periodos* games meant that the victor enjoyed the right to enter (*eiselaunein*) his city in a solemn procession. In Hellenistic times the privilege of *eiselasis* (solemn entry) was extended to victors at the imitations of the original *periodos* games and, more important, special monetary rewards were given to those who had won in an *agôn eiselastikos*.[53] Incidentally this financial aspect explains why the Roman authorities wanted to control the number of eiselastic games: Greek cities were never renowned for sound budget-policy.[54] Thirdly, there is *perhaps* some evidence to show that later imitations of the old *periodos* games, in spite of the *periodos* ideology of the wreath, in actual fact added material prizes to the symbolic ones.

In Pergamum a local benefactor founded a sacred, eiselastic contest in honour of Zeus Philios and the Emperor Trajan at the beginning of the second century AD.[55] The Roman senate decided that this *agôn* should have the same legal status as another *hieros agôn* in Pergamum (the *Romaia Sebasta* in honour of Augustus and Rome).[56] The emperor wrote to the provincial governor that the victors in the new contest should receive the same rewards as those in the existing games. Unfortunately the crucial word (*praemia*: rewards) is a restoration. One could argue that the emperor wrote to the provincial governor precisely because he had in mind

---

[50] Cf. L. Robert, *art. cit.*, (cf. note 30).

[51] In the catalogues of victories the Olympic Games often come first; in some cases a victory in one of the great games of the mother city of the victor comes first; cf. L. Robert, Deux inscriptions agonistiques de Rhodes, in; *AE* 1966, 109; cf. in general for the Olympic Games: M. I. Finley–H. W. Pleket, *The Olympic Games. The first Thousand Years* (London 1976).

[52] See my article "Zur Soziologie ..." (cf. note 18), 70.

[53] Cf. P. Herrmann, "Eine Kaiserurkunde der Zeit Marc Aurels aus Milet", in: *Istanbuler Mitteilungen* 25 (1975), 149–66, esp. 156, with note 23.

[54] Cf. e.g. Pliny the Younger, *Ep.* X, 118, 119 and the new inscription from Miletus in: P. Herrmann, *art. cit.*

[55] Cf. P. Herrmann, *art. cit.*, 157 with full references.

[56] On the Romaia Sebasta cf. L. Robert, *art. cit.* (cf. note 17), 267; the victors received "a crown of oak".

the rewards given by the mother cities to athletes who had gained a victory in an *eiselastikos agôn*; the governor was in a position to see to it that the cities did not pay more than the amount given to the victors in the other Pergamene sacred contests. But the tenor of the admittedly mutilated sentence ("since this contest has the same status as the other *hieros agôn* in Pergamum, it is appropriate that the same [reward] be given in this eiselastic *agôn* as in the other")[57] suggests to me that the emperor is referring to the *praemium* given by the city of Pergamum to the victors. It is inconceivable that the emperor fixed one and the same amount of money for the *praemia* to be given by hundreds of cities to their victorious home-coming athletes. The emperor Trajan is known to have interfered in a dispute about the *obsonia* ("allowances") that cities gave their athletes for a victory in *eiselastikoi agônes* but he merely determined *the moment from which* the *obsonia* were to be paid out, not the *amount*.[58] It is hard to believe that the Roman authorities would have prescribed *one* and the same *obsonium* for all provincial cities, irrespective of the great differences in wealth among them.[59]

L. Robert has recently discussed a number of coins from cities in Asia Minor. These coins mention sacred, eiselastic, isolympic (or isopythian) games. On these coins we find representations of wreaths (and other immaterial prizes) and of "bags of coins", sometimes placed on a table next to a wreath, sometimes under the table. Robert does not discuss these purses but since at one place he writes about a "table of prizes" I take it that these "bags of coins" symbolised money prizes added to the wreaths by the organising cities.[60] At the isolympic Sebasta in Naples, founded in 2 BC the winners received both *epathla*, *athla* ("rewards, prizes) and *opsônia* (daily allowances, also for the other athletes). Under the heading *timai* (honour) the wreath is mentioned. Unfortunately the document that contains the charter of these games is mutilated so that we do not know the nature of the *(ep)athla*.[61]

During the Great Artemisia in Ephesus the "president and head of the festival (*agonothetês kai panêguriarchês*) is said to have "enlarged the prizes (*athla*) for the athletes and to have financed the erection of statues of the victors".[62] The text

---

[57] *Huius quoque iselas[tici idem quod in altero] certamine custoditur dari oportebit [victoribus praemium]*.
[58] See note 54 and my article "Zur Soziologie ..." (cf. note 18), 70;
[59] P. Herrmann translates "praemia" by "prizes", *art. cit.*, 157, 158; but in note 31 he compares the *praemia* with the *obsonia* and in the new inscription from Miletus he tentatively restores *praemia* (157, note 27) with the meaning of *obsonia*. This new inscription tells us that the Milesians asked the Roman authorities to raise the status of a sacred *agôn* to that of an *eiselastikos agôn*. The emperor gives a definition of that type of *agôn*, "contests whose victors receive prizes in their home cities, having been returned there in procession" (*certam[ina ex quibus victores reduces patriam suam [invecti praemia (ibi) capiunt ...]*). He also refers to the burdens imposed upon the budgets of other cities but he does not seem to fix the amount of money.
[60] L. Robert, *Hellenica* VII, 90 (on the Deia Kommodeia, on which see also L. Robert, *Laodicée du Lycos. Le nymphée* (1969), 283–4), 93 ff., esp. 104; id.: *Monnaies Grecques* (Paris 1967), 108 ("a decorated bag of coins").
[61] *Inschriften von Olympia* (Berlin 1896), no. 56; on the Sebasta cf. L. Robert, *L'Antiquité Classique* 37 (1968), 408–9 and *Les Épigrammes satiriques* (cf. note 17), 209, note 3.
[62] W. Dittenberger, *SIG*³, no. 867, l. 60 ff. (cf. L. Robert, *OMS*, I, 627). In *Greek Inscriptions British Museum* (Oxford 1890), III 618 we hear about an Ephesian who gave *epathla* to actors and athletes; the man had been *panegyriarchês* of the Artemisia and *agonothetês* of the Great Pythian Games; it is uncertain in which games he gave the *epathla*, though the GIBM-editor Hicks tentatively suggests that it might have been in the Artemisia and/or Pythia.

dates from c. 160 AD. In other inscriptions, dating from the mid second century AD and from c. 170 AD the Artemisia are included among the sacred contests and explicitly distinguished from the "money" games. They are called either Artemisia or *Artemisia hiera eiselastika*.[63] In the first inscription (from 160 AD) the *megala Artemisia* are annual games; on the other hand sacred contests (*hieroi agônes*) do not seem to be annual.[64]

Perhaps the *Artemisia hiera eiselastika* replaced the annual Artemisia every fourth year. The above-mentioned president of the annual Artemisia introduced a special age-category for boys, the so-called *Artemisiakoi paides*, "similar to the Πυθικοί and Ἀκτιακοὶ παῖδες",[65] i.e. to age-categories in the Pythian and Actian games, both part of the *periodos* (the Aktia being a later addition to the old *periodos*). This strongly suggests that the Artemisia were to be considered on a par with the category of sacred contests. The fact that they were called the Great Artemisia (*ta megala Artemisia*) distinguishes them from ordinary annual games. The latter were often styled "the Lesser" (*ta mikra*) in contrast with "the Great". The Great Panathenaia are mentioned together with the Olympic and similar games, the Lesser Panathenaia were only of local importance.

In fourth-century AD Antioch in Syria athletes were attracted to participate in the Olympics in that city by the prospect both of the glory of a victory in such well-known games and of the money distributed among them. The athletes came from Ionia, Bithynia and Egypt, and the *agonothetês* induced them to come "by referring to the glory, to be derived from the wreath and by adding money to it"(τῇ παρὰ τοῦ στεφάνου δόξῃ καὶ χρήματα προστιθείς). In another letter there is question of "exhortation [to come to Ant.] by means of money" (τῆς ... διὰ χρημάτων παρακλήσεως).[66] Is this a reference to money prizes, awarded to the winner, or to money given to the athletes in order to induce them to come to Antioch? In the latter case there is a parallel in a story, told by the rhetor Dion of Prusa (ca. 100 AD), about a local politician who hired a famous Olympic champion for a local contest.[67] It is hard to decide, though P. Petit seems to opt for the former solution.[68]

It is possible to argue that cities decided to add "value prizes" to the wreath in order to attract those professional athletes who, as pointed out above, had to make a living out of their sport; or that the "bags of coins" are a reminiscence of earlier times in which the games in question were not yet sacred and isolympic but

---

[63] *Greek Inscriptions British Museum*, III 605 (cf. L. Robert, *OMS*, II, 1138–9); L. Robert, *Études épigraphiques et philologiques* (Paris 1938), 23 (= *Forschungen Ephesos*, IV, i, 91, no. 14).

[64] L. Robert, *OMS*, II, 1152.

[65] L. Robert, *OMS*, I, 627; J. Ebert, Παῖδες πυθικοί, in: *Philologus* 109 (1965), 152–6.

[66] Libanius, *Ep.* 1180 and 1182 (ed. R. Foerster, vol. XI, p. 265); cf. what Flavius Josephus, *Jewish Antiquities* XV, 269 writes about the first Greek contests, organised in Jerusalem by King Herod: "the athletes and the rest of the competitors were encouraged to come from every land by the desire to win the prizes and by the glory of victory" (οἱ δ' ἀθληταὶ καὶ τὰ λοιπὰ τῶν ἀγωνισμάτων ἀπὸ πάσης γῆς ἐκαλοῦντο κατ'ἐλπίδα τῶν προκειμένων καὶ τῆς νίκης εὐδοξίᾳ); cf. M. Lämmer, *Jerusalem* (cf. note 5), 189–90.

[67] Or, LXVI (De gloria), 11.

[68] P. Petit, *Libanius et la vie municipale à Antioche au IVᵉ siècle aprés J.C.* (Paris 1955) 125–6 "According to these letters, one can see that they trained in their own cities and were then invited to the games, drawn both by the desire for glory, symbolised by a crown (*Ep.* 1179, 1180), and by the desire to win money, because prizes were given to the victors."

thematic. We know that games could rise in status from "thematic" to "sacred".[69] However, it remains true that the original ambiguity, inherent in the category of "the *periodos* and the other sacred contests" (i.e. crown games and "crown and prize games" subsumed under one heading), will have facilitated the introduction of money prizes even into the realm of the sacred, eiselastic, i.e. *periodos*-like, contests. This ambiguity was intensified by the addition to the original *periodos* of games such as the Argive Heraia, in which of old a wreath and *a bronze shield* (or vase) were given to the winner. The Heraia "belong to the category of contests which were ranked just after the four panhellenic games in importance".[70]

Prior to this enlargement of the *periodos*, the Heraia belonged to a group of sacred contests, a number of which had crowns and prizes. Now the *periodos* itself contained a contest which combined a wreath with a "value prize". Admittedly in comparison with pre-monetary archaic times the value of a precious bronze object would have been somewhat different in the Hellenistic-Roman monetary economy. Nevertheless I doubt whether these objects were ever considered to have had only a symbolic value (like our "medals"). This is certainly not true of the gold *brabeia* (prizes, rewards) which victors in a number of sacred contests are known to have received in addition to a crown.[71] The "contents" of the notion of "value" may have changed in the course of time, the notion itself was never incompatible with the nature of the sacred contests. A third century AD *agonothetês* (president) of games in the Macedonian city of Beroea probably took the most drastic step. He is praised for "having announced (καταγγείλαντα) and organised (ἀγαγόντα) *eisaktious agônas talantiaious thymelikous kai gymnikous*.[72] *Eisaktios*[73] is of course a parallel to isolympios, isopythios and so on. The Aktia were founded in commemoration of Augustus' victory over Antony in 31 BC at Actium; they were incorporated in the

---

[69] See L. Moretti, *op. cit.* (cf. note 8), 196, 245 (no. 84b), 246.

[70] For the *periodos* see J.-L. Robert, "Bulletin épigraphique", in: *Revue des études grecques* 67 (1954), no. 57, p. 114 (there is an "old *periodos*" (*archaia periodos*) and a new, enlarged *periodos* (consisting of the "Big Four" and the Aktia (in Actium), Heraia (in Argos) and Kapitolia (in Rome)); Kl. Kramer, *op. cit.* (cf. note 28), 29.

[71] For the *brabeia* ("certainly this was an object made of precious metal, almost always of gold") see L. Moretti, *op. cit.* (cf. note 8), 247. Golden *brabeia* were awarded to victors in Epinikia, i.e. sacred crown contests, which were celebrated irregularly, i.e. on the occasion of a victory of the emperor(s) over e.g. the Parthians; during the contest celebrated on the occasion of Rome's millenium (τὸν χειλιετῆ ἐν Ῥώμῃ or *ta Aiônia*) and grouped with other regular *agônas hieros oikoumenikous*, a herald was honoured with a golden *brabeion*. Both the Epinikia and the Aiônia were "exceedingly rare and distinctive" (J.-L. Robert, "Bulletin épigraphique", in: *Revue des études grecques* 72 (1959), no. 448, p. 257). Nevertheless they were sacred crown games and combined crowns as prizes (in the Epinikia in 176 AD in Rome even a golden wreath, Moretti, *op. cit.* (cf. note 8), no. 84), with a precious golden object. In the Sebasta in Naples a *brabeion* was given to the winner in the *tagma* (*IGR*, I, 449). This was probably a team race and therefore not representative of the Sebasta as such. In J. Ebert, *Griechische Epigramme* ... (cf. note 33), no. 79 the runner M. Aurelius Heras is said to have won δὶς δὲ βρ[αβ]εῖ' Ἐφέσου (prizes in Ephesos twice) but here the term may have been used in the general, metaphorical sense ("Kampfpreis"): see Ebert, p. 242 and R. Merkelbach in *ZPE* 18 (1975), 127. On the Epinikia cf. L. Robert, *art. cit.* (cf. note 30).

[72] L. Robert, *Les Gladiateurs dans l'orient grec* (Paris 1940) (reprint Amsterdam 1971), 81, no. 15, l. 12 ff.; cf. also id.: *OMS*, II, 1284–5; M. Lämmer, "Griechische Wettkämpfe in Jerusalem ...", in: *Kölner Beiträge zur Sportwissenschaft* 2 (1973), 215, note 31.

[73] Cf. L. Robert, "Enterrements et épitaphes", in: *L'Antiquité classique* 37 (1968), 406–8, esp. 417, with note 3.

periodos, in the same way as the Heraia.⁷⁴ Games which are presented as *eisaktoi*, lay claim to be on the *periodos* level. They are by definition *hieroi agônês* and among those they have pretentions to the highest category. The Aktia had both musical and athletic contests. I suggest the following translation: our president "announced and organised games (musical and athletic) which were both sacred (= *eisaktious*) and thematic". The text seems to mention *one* category, that of *eisaktioi agônes*; this category is further qualified by three adjectives. As far as I know the inscription as a whole has been discussed by a number of scholars but this particular passage has never received proper attention.⁷⁵ Others may prefer to interpret this passage as *eisaktious* (and) *talantiaious* and to argue that we have the familiar distinction between *hieroi agônes* and *talantiaioi agônes*. I tend to believe that our *agonothetês* has broken through this dichotomy, which was strongly ideological and based upon the enormous prestige of Olympia, and has adapted his terminology to reality.

Not all presidents were as blunt as their Macedonian colleague. The Athenians continued to pay lip-service to the "pure" Olympic ideology when in 131 AD under the emperor Hadrian's patronage they founded the Panhellenia, both a competitor of and homage to the old panhellenic Olympia. A recently published inscription shows that they awarded *suntaxies* ("contributions") to the victor in this sacred contest.⁷⁶ The term is revealing: prizes (*themata, epathla*) were out of the question in a pure Olympic imitation. "Contributions" were supposedly something else. Nowadays terms like "labour-reserve" are intended to convey a message different from that of "unemployment".

From the above it should not be concluded that *the hieroi agônes* and especially the imitations of the *periodos, as such* abjured Olympic practice and all adopted the habit of adding "value prizes" to the wreaths. Some organisations may have argued that victories in at least a number of sacred games were actually rewarded with a wreath plus a "value prize" and that on the basis of this fact their decision to introduce such prizes into *periodos*-like contests also was justified; others perhaps focused on the fact that of old the original *periodos* knew only wreaths as rewards for the victors and they therefore began to *distinguish* between on the one hand the

---

⁷⁴ Cf. above note 70.

⁷⁵ L. Robert, *OMS*, II, 1284–5 drew attention to Rostovtzeff's neglected reading εἰσακτίους (instead of the incomprehensible εἰς Ἀκτίους) but did not comment upon the passage.

⁷⁶ Cf. J. H. Oliver, *Marcus Aurelius, Aspects of Civic and Cultural Policy in the East*, in: *Hesperia*, Suppl. vol. 13, (1970), 107–9, no. 21–2; cf. my forthcoming article "Olympic Benefactors", in: *Zeitschrift für Papyrologie und Epigraphik* 1976. [Addendum: for συντάξεις see now G. Petzl and E. Schwertheim, *Hadrian und die dionysischen Künstler: Drei in Alexandria Troas neugefundene Briefe des Kaisers an die Künstler-Vereinigung* (Bonn 2006) p. 8, l. 10 (συντάξεις τοῖς νεικήσασιν) and p. 9 ll. 25–26 (συντάξεις διδόσθωσαν τοῖς ἱερονίκαις κατὰ τὰς ὡρισμένας προθεσμίας: "allowances for sacred victors according to the defined time-periods"; the latter are further specified on p. 12 ll. 49–51 and are related to the moment of entry (εἰσέλασις) into the hometown). These συντάξεις are identical with the *obsonia* mentioned by Pliny, *Ep.* X 118–119, and are to be paid by the hometowns of the victors, not by the cities which organised the games and paid the prizes (ἆθλα) to the victors. W. J. Slater (*JRA* 21 (2008) 616-18), suggests identifying these *syntaxeis* with life-time pensions and discards the connection between "entry into one's hometown" and the *syntaxeis*. However, this connection is evident in all the sources; it seems that the συντάξεις to be paid by the hometowns are one-off rather than life-time pensions. In the case of the Athenian inscription I assumed that the συντάξεις were paid by the organising city rather than by the victor's hometown; this assumption seems questionable in the light of the new text from Alexandria Troas.]

periodos and similar sacred and truly international games and on the other hand equally sacred but less famous games in which in addition to wreaths material prizes were given to the victors. It is the latter attitude which, I believe, is recorded in a recent Rhodian inscription.

In this honorary decree for a successful Syrian athlete who after a great many victories settled down in Rhodes and became a great benefactor, we find, in a mutilated context, two categories of contests: after isolated references to an *eisaktios agôn* in Syrian Antioch, to *Soteria Kapetolia isokapetolia* and to the Hadriania Olympia in Tarsus the achievements of the athlete are summarised in the words "and the *agônes* <in which he gained these victories> were sacred and eiselastic, ecumenical". A new paragraph probably followed beginning with the words "and he also won <the following> thematic crown-games" (καὶ τούτους ἱεροὺς καὶ εἰσελαστικοὺς οἰκουμε | [νικοὺς ἀγῶνας ...] νεικήσαντα δὲ καὶ θεματείτας στεφανείτας ἀγῶ | [νας...])

In the following lines a number of games seem to be mentioned which belong to this second category (games in Ephesus, *inter alia* the sacred contests celebrated by the Commonalty of the province of Asia). Finally victories in Rhodes and the athlete's mother city are recorded. Among the Rhodian victories there is one in an isolympic *agôn*, tentatively identified with the Great Halieia. This victory should have been mentioned at the beginning of the inscription in the first rubric but it stands to reason that in a Rhodian decree victories in Rhodian games have been singled out.[77]

I suggest that the *themateitas stepheneitas agônes* constitute one concept; in other words no comma (or no "and") should be read between the two adjectives. The first category comprises the (extended) *periodos* and *periodos*-like games which were *isolympios* (or *isokapetôlios* etc.), iselastic (like Olympia) and truly ecumenical, i.e. international, and meant for athletes from all over the world (*oikoumenê*). The combination of epithets (*hieros, eisalastikos, oikoumenikos*) is familiar. In Thyatira we find a *hieron agona eiselastikon Augousteion isopythion* for the whole inhabited world (εἰς ἅπασαν τὴν οἰκουμένην), in Side an *agôn hieros oikoumenikos isopythios eiselastikos*.[78] The second class comprises games which were equally "sacred" but nevertheless less famous than the *periodos*. Whereas in the above-mentioned (cf. p. 151) inscription from Delos "the *periodos* and the other sacred games" constituted one class, in this text we have a clear distinction between *periodos*(like)-games[79] and

---

[77] The inscription has been published in: *Suppl. Epigr. Rodio*, in: *ASAA* 30-2 (1952-1954), no. 67; cf. L. Robert, *Hellenica* XI/XII, 446 ff. and E. Erxleben, "Zu einer rhodischen Inschrift für einen Hierokeryx" (*Suppl. Epig. Rodio*, 67), in: *Klio* 52 (1970), 87 ff.; see also my article "Zur Soziologie ..." (cf. note 18), 85, note 140. Neither the original editor of the text nor Robert and Erxleben have discussed the passage quoted in the text.

[78] Cf. P. Herrmann, *art. cit.* (cf. note 53), 158, note 30; *Journal of Hellenic Studies* 28 (1908), 191, no. 20; cf. also J.-L. Robert, "Bulletin épigraphique", in: *Revue des études grecques* 85 (1972), no. 500 on p. 490.

[79] In Sidon we find in late imperial times an *agôn hieros eiselastikos oikoumenikos isolympios periporphyros*. The third-century BC *agôn periporphyros* is known to have been sacred. L. Robert supposes that *periporphyros* (i.e. "purple") denotes the original prize: "a cloth of purple from Sidon", *AE* 1966, 115, note 8). I take it that in the Hellenistic period the contest was a *sacred* contest which combined a wreath and a purple garment (in origin it may have been a *local game* with only a garment as prize). In the Roman period it had pretension to the *periodos*-level (*isolympios, eiselastikos, oikoumenikos*) and did not

those sacred games which of old had added "value prizes" to the crowns. I take it that somewhere between the classical and the Roman period the precious objects were replaced by cash-prizes (*themata*).[80] The basic attitude did *not* change: it is wrong to believe that sacred games were ever separated strictly from the notion of "value prize". It remains possible that the Rhodian "thematic crown games" were originally thematic games promoted to the status of sacred games without losing their previous *themata*;[81] however, this aspect is irrelevant for my purpose: the crucial point remains that the continuation of the prize is not a late, decadent phenomenon, caused by the emergence of greedy, lower-class professionals but rather an elaboration and articulation of what *in nuce* already existed in earlier times.

Perhaps the existence of sacred games with crowns and prizes is also implied by an epigram in honour of the Athenian gentleman T. Domitius Prometheus, deputy-director of the Athenian ephebes ca. 250 AD. First his manifold equestrian victories in the *periodos* are mentioned, then victories in other contests follow; in J. Ebert's German translation the text runs as follows: "der (ich) dem Vaterland brachte mühevoll erworbene Siegespreise aus sechzig heiligen (Agonen) deren Kranz ich errang, und bei zahlreichen heiligen (Agonen), bei denen nur ein Wertpreis ausgesetzt war" ("I who brought back to my home city laboriously won victory prizes, from sixty sacred contests where I won a crown, and from very many other sacred contests where only a money-prize was offered.")[82] Two points should be made: (a) the last category of games, in which only "value prizes" were offered to the victors, is in fact what in technical agonistic language is called the category of the *thematic* games. When Domitius calls these games "sacred", his aim is undoubtedly to raise their status, to suggest that they really were not all that different from the sacred contests *par excellence*. Nobody and nothing compelled him to say that he restricted himself to "sacred" games (in the technical sense of the expression) and rejected participation in prize games. It is typical of the wealthy gentleman of leisure not to reject attractive money prizes but to wrap them up in a sanctifying ideology. He could present thematic games as being "sacred" the more easily since (1) quite a few thematic games were organised in honour of a deity and on that score could with some justification be called sacred[83] and (2) sacred games (in the technical sense: *agônes hieroi*) are now known to have combined *themata* (prizes) with *stephanoi* (wreaths) (see above). b) Ebert infers from the emphatic reference to "sacred games in which *only themata* were awarded" that by implication sacred

---

substitute a cash-prize for the purple. If it had done the latter, it would have belonged to the *themeteitai stepheneitai agônes*. As a contest of the *periodos*-type it could safely keep the garment as a prize, since the Heraia, an *official* member of the *periodos*, also had a "value prize" (bronze vase) in addition to the wreath.

[80] Cf. above note 49.

[81] Cf. above note 69; for *themeta* in thematic games cf. L. Robert, *Hellenica* VI, 72–9

[82] J. Ebert, *Griechische Epigramme* (cf. note 33), 247–50, no. 81; Ebert's text runs as follows: [εὔμ]οχθα νείκης ἆθλα | [φέ]ροντα [π]άτρῃ [ἑ]ξήκονθ' ἱ[ε]ρῶν ὧν ἔλαβον στέφαν<ο>ν, | [κἀν] πλείστοις ἱεροῖς, | οἷς [θ]έμα κεῖτο μόνον.

[83] Cf. J. Ebert: "[O]ne should remember, however, that *hieros* refers strictly speaking only to the linking of contest with a divinity" (*op. cit.*, 250); for thematic games, organised in honour of a deity cf. e.g. L. Robert, *Hellenica* VI, 43 and 72–9.

games may possibly have been presupposed in which not only *themata* but also wreaths were given.[84]

I must add that Ebert's version of the text differs from that adopted by Moretti and Harris. Moretti restored the text to mean that Domitius won sixty sacred wreaths in very many sacred games, in which the wreath was the only prize to be awarded.[85] Here we surely have interesting philology, witness Harris' moving exclamation: "Across the centuries Titus Domitius reaches out a hand to Mr. Avery Brundage".[86] That is no longer acceptable. Domitius accumulated wealth with his sport and though he produced a nice piece of sanctifying ideology his hands would not have been good enough for Brundage (nor for his successor Lord Killanin for that matter).

Quite apart from the case of Domitius and the text of his epigram, the whole tenor of my argument so far has been that the formal and undeniable distinction made between sacred and thematic games should not induce us to believe that "sacred games" had nothing to do with "value prizes" in antiquity. In some cases crowns plus prizes were awarded at sacred games. Though the old *periodos* is not known to have awarded "value prizes" and though only in a few cases later imitations of the *periodos* can perhaps be shown to have done so, it remains true that those who participated at Olympia and so on on the one hand freely participated in thematic games and on the other were rewarded lavishly and officially by their mother-cities.

II. THE ATHLETES AND THEIR SOCIAL BACKGROUND

Domitius' case leads up to the remaining two questions (see p. 148 above), those concerning the *social background of ancient athletes* and *their ideology*.

It does not really matter with which question we start because my thesis is that from Pindar's time until Roman Imperial times members of the upper class were never absent in sport (neither in the running events nor in the body-contact sports) and that the prevailing ideology of Greek sport always was a product of that same

---

[84] "which by the way suggests that in some of the contests mentioned in line 5 a money prize (*thema*) was awarded in addition to a crown, while in the less important contests the victory prize consisted only of a *thema*" (*op. cit.*, 250). [Addendum: For some modifications in my views on the relation between sport and money and in my interpretation of some of the inscriptions discussed in this section, see my article "Einige Betrachtungen zum Thema "Geld und Sport"" in *Nikephoros* 17 (2004) [2006] 77–89. For the relation between "crowns" (*stephanoi*) and material value, see B. Le Guen, "Le palmarès de l'acteur-athlète: retours sur Syll.³ 1080 (Tégee)" in *ZPE* 160 (2007) 97–107, esp. 102–4, and W. J. Slater and D. Summa, "Crowns at Magnesia" in *GRBS* 46 (2006) 275–99.]

[85] Moretti's text runs: [εὐμ]όχθ[ου] νείκης ἆθλα | [φέ]ροντα [π]άτρῃ [ἑ]ξήκονθ᾽ ἱ[ερ]ῶν ὧν ἔλα|βον στέφανων, | [ἐν] πλείστοις ἱεροῖς, | οἷς [θέ]μα κεῖτο μόνον ("I who brought back to my home city the prizes of laboriously won victory, prizes consisting of sixty wreaths, which I won, in very many sacred contests where a wreath was the only prize"). Moretti's interpretation implies that in the final line the wreath is to be understood as subject of κεῖτο and is to be identified with θέμα. This strains credulity. Ebert's restoration [κἀν] (= καὶ ἐν) instead of [ἐν] does justice to the requirements of symmetry between the lines, as his drawing clearly shows; moreover it enables us to translate the final words in a more natural way: "in which a θέμα (*thema*) was the only prize". Ebert's emendation of στέφανων (which is on the stone) does not seem to be necessary: a translation "prizes <consisting of> sixty sacred wreaths, which I took" is not very elegant but makes sufficient sense.

[86] H. A. Harris, *op. cit.* (cf. above note 10), 175.

class. Let us first take the *problem of the participants*. There is no prosopography of ancient athletes, but there is a decent substitute, L. Moretti's list of Olympic victors (*Olympionikai*).[87]

All these *Olympionikai* are either known to have participated in many other games or may be assumed to have done so. A statistical approach is unwise. First – the record provides only a very small percentage of the total actual winners; second – it is only in relatively few cases that the social background of the athlete is more or less clear. General considerations, a few specific pieces of evidence, and a number of solid examples of upper-class athletes enable us to determine the main trends. For reasons of space I refer the reader to my article "Zur Soziologie des antiken Sports" for a short list of those upper-class athletes who are known to have performed successfully in a great many contests and who, because of the participation of highly specialised, "professional", lower-class athletes, must have been equally specialised and "professional".[88] The general considerations are as follows:

1. It is improbable that before the rise of the *gymnasion*, which occurred after 650 BC, non-nobles participated at Olympia or in the other, still rare, athletic contests;

2. It is also improbable that immediately after the rise of the *gymnasion* non-nobles penetrated into the Olympic realm. Training requirements, travel costs, the obligation to stay a month in Olympia before the beginning of the games and the resulting loss of income were decisive obstacles for the poor. Subsidisation would have been indispensable, but the earliest evidence for that is much later: an inscription from Ephesus (ca. 300 BC), which tells us that the trainer of an obviously promising but not wealthy young athlete asked the city to subsidise his client's "training and travelling abroad".[89] A well-known passage from Isocrates' *On the Team of Horses* says that, according to the well-to-do Athenian politician Alcibiades, ca. 400 BC some (ἐνίους) of the athletes who performed at Olympia were of low birth and mean education. Obviously *most* participants still belonged to the upper-class; it looks as if the recruitment of lower-class Olympic athletes was a relatively recent phenomenon on the basis of which Alcibiades began to disdain the gymnastic contests and turned to the breeding of race-horses and to the equestrian contests "possible only for those most blest by Fortune and not to be pursued by one of low estate". Alcibiades would have been happier in Pindar's time when the true *kaloikagathoi* still predominated at Olympia.

3. It is probably in the local contests, which increased rapidly from the sixth century onwards, that the hoplite middle class got its first chance to participate but we cannot substantiate this probability because of the usual lack of evidence.

What deserves to be emphasised is that after 400 BC there is no question of lower class athletes monopolizing the athletic scene and of upper-class athletes withdrawing from athletics and restricting themselves to the equestrian games. In

---

[87] L. Moretti, "Olympionikai, I vincitori negli antichi agoni olimpici", in: *Memorie Accad. Lincei*, Sc. Mor., serie VIII, vol. VIII, fasc. 2, 1957, 53–198 (with J.-L. Robert, "Bulletin épigraphique", in: *Revue des études grecques* 71 (1958), no. 160, 221–3); cf. also L. Moretti, "Supplemento al catalogo degli Olympionikai", in: *Klio* 52 (1970), 295–303.

[88] Cf. above note 18; in this article one also finds the necessary references for what follows.

[89] L. Robert, "Décrets d'Éphèse pour des athlètes", in: *Revue de Philologie* 1967, 14–32; cf. id. in: *Comptes rendus académie des inscriptions et belles lettres*, 1974, 524.

the Hellenistic-Roman material it is often impossible to determine the social background of an athlete: sometimes we have only a name; in other cases we happen to know that an athlete received honorary citizenship or a political function in his own city but we can rarely decide whether the man was a product of social mobility or belonged to a municipal elite family *ab origine*.

Fortunately we do have a number of certain and a number of very probable examples of members of the city bourgeoisie who after 400 BC and before 300 AD continued to practise high sport on a high level. In my article "Zur Soziologie des antiken Sports" (p. 72–3) I emphasised the importance of the *ephebeia*, that is, the urban youth-organisation of the scions of the municipal upper-ten who in their *gymnasia* devoted considerable time to physical education and games and on the basis of the ephebic training ventured to go in for the very specialised and (at least from our point of view) professionalised sport of the public contests, sacred and thematic alike. The ephebic training was basically a physical and para-military training, to which in the Hellenistic-Roman period some cultural activities (lectures by itinerant rhetoricians and philosophers) were added.[90] This *ephebeia* functioned as a bridge for members of the urban elite between gymnasium sport and the world of the public contests. How many crossed that bridge we do not know; but we may be certain that a number did. At present it is much harder to give a list of athletes who were lower class certainly than one of those from the upper class. For the former we have to rely on the following evidence: (1) the above-mentioned Isocrates-passage; (2) some passages in the second century AD physician Galen (born in Pergamum and practising as a doctor in Rome) in which he criticises the lack of education of trainers (and since trainers were generally ex-athletes, his statement may be taken to be valid for athletes as well);[91] (3) the fact that in the so-called Herminus papyrus – the membership certificate of an Egyptian boxer Herminus issued by the oecumenical association of professional athletes[92] – some officials and athletes happen to be *a-grammatos* (illiterate), which, at least for Asia Minor and Greece, would seem to imply that they did not belong to the *jeunesse dorée* of the city elite.[93]

It cannot be doubted that from Pindar's time onwards there was one very important constant in Greek athletics: the participation of members of the urban elite. There is another constant and that is that these aristocrats did not restrict themselves to the running events (200 metres, 400 metres and the long-distance race (4,800 metres)): among the certain instances of upper-class athletes there are boxers, wrestlers and pankratiasts, from Pindar's time until Roman imperial times.[94]

---

[90] Cf. my article: "Collegium Iuvenum Nemesiorum. A Note on Ancient Youth-Organizations", in: *Mnemosyne* 1969, 281-98, esp. 286.
[91] Cf. J. Jüthner, *Philostratos über Gymnastik* (Leipzig-Berlin 1909; reprint Amsterdam 1969), 7 and 236.
[92] For these cf. my article: "Some Aspects of the History of the Athletic Guilds", in: *Zeitschrift für Papyrologie und Epigraphik* 10 (1973), 197–227.
[93] See "Zur Soziologie ...", 76–7.
[94] See above p. 53, with note 18. [Addendum: For some "second thoughts" on the problem of the social status and the ideology of athletes see my article "Athleten im Altertum: soziale Herkunft und Ideologie" in *Nikephoros* 18 (2005) [2006] 151–63.]

III. THE IDEOLOGY OF THE ATHLETES

A third constant leads us straight into our third main question: *the ideology of athletics*. There is a clear ideological constant from the time of Pindar's athletes onwards. A full analysis would require detailed discussion of Pindar's odes, of Dio of Prusa's two essays on the Carian boxer Melancomas who died during the Sebasta in Naples in the first century AD,[95] of Lucian's dialogue *Anacharsis* (second century AD, containing a fictitious discussion between Solon and the Scythian prince Anacharsis about the use and value of athletics both in the gymnasium and in the public games), of Philostratus' manual *On Gymnastics* (early third century AD)[96] and of the various honorary decrees and epigrams for successful athletes.[97] This would clearly take us too far and moreover would entail an accumulation of rather monotonous ideological language. I shall restrict myself to a few essentials. Firstly, relatively trivial values like physical beauty and strength receive due and constant attention. Pindar describes an Olympic wrestler as καλὸς ἐσορᾶν ("comely he was to look upon"); elsewhere he describes an athlete as εὔχειρ, δεξιόγυιος and ὀρῶντα ἀλκάν ("with deftness of hands and litheness of limbs and with valour in his glance").[98] If reality happened to be different, he tactfully called an aristocratic boxer πελώριος ("a giant").[99] Melancomas is praised for being the most handsome boxer;[100] and in Lucian's *Anacharsis* the beauty of the athletes' bodies is duly emphasised by Solon.[101] In the world of the practising athletes themselves the pankratiast Kallikrates is praised by his colleagues for the natural qualities of his body which were admired all over the world.[102] A colleague, M. Alfidius, a promising champion in one of the body-contact sports, is said to have had *euphueia* (beauty and talent) and to have died in his *kallistê akmê* ("the finest prime of his life").[103]

There were at least two official interpretations of beauty. Philostratos preached the message of the beautiful young ephebe, idealised product of the gymnasium, "with a light and lean physique and with his neck held high and free". The Heracles-statues from the ephebic gymnasium exemplified this type: it is the ἐλευθέριον ἄγαλμα (the statue which befits a gentleman).[104] The association of professional athletes also chose Heracles as its patron but that Heracles showed "a colossal musculature, a powerful base of the neck with a relatively small head and a short neck", i.e. Heracles with a bull's neck.[105] Significantly the Milesian boxer and Olympic victor Nicophon, high-priest and magistrate in his city (Miletus) and probably a member

---

[95] Dio, *Or.* 28 and 29, with L. Robert, *Hellenica* XI/XII, 338, note 4; id. *L'Antiquité Classique* 37 (1968), 409 f.
[96] To be consulted in J. Jüthner's magnificent edition (see above note 91).
[97] See the list in L. Robert, *OMS*, I, 614–17; id.: *Hellenica* XIII, 134–54; add the decree for M. Alfidius published by G. E. Bean in: *Belleten, Türk Tarih Kurumu* 29 (1965), 588–93 and commented upon by L. Robert, in: *L'Antiquité Classique* 37 (1968), 406–17.
[98] Pindar, *Olympian Odes* 8, v. 19; 9, v. 94, 111; 10, v. 100–5.
[99] *Ol.*, 7, 15; cf. C. M. Bowra, *Pindar* (Oxford 1964), 167 f.
[100] Dio, *Or.* 28, § 2–3 (on Melancomas' opponent); 5; 12; *Or.* 29, § 3.
[101] Lucian, *Anacharsis* (Loeb-edition vol. IV) § 12.
[102] L. Robert, *Hellenica* XIII, 134 ff., l. 15–17.
[103] Cf. above note 97.
[104] Cf. J. Jüthner, *Philostratos über Gymnastik*, 253 and ch. 35 of Philostratus' text.
[105] J. Jüthner, ibidem.

of the urban elite, is explicitly praised in an epigram for having the heavy neck of a bull, the iron shoulders of Atlas, the beard and hair of Heracles and the eyes of a lion.[106] This emphasis on physical beauty is the more remarkable if we realise that in reality sports like boxing and *pankration* were notorious for the blood and the injuries of the contestants. To win *atraumatistos* (unwounded) was exceptional.[107]

Much more interesting is the strong and continuous emphasis on the manly and military values of sport. In Homer Nestor's son is both the fastest runner and a warrior.[108] Pindar frequently compares athletes with old heroes and identifies the athlete's *aretê* (courage) with that of the warrior.[109] Dion of Prusa and Lucian regard athletics as an ideal preparation for war. Dion argues that an athlete is even superior to a warrior.[110] Keywords in this respect are *andreia* (courage), *ponos* (toil) and *karteria* (endurance). These words have been studied in detail by L. Robert who has showed that they are to be found both in the authors and the documents from the fifth century BC onwards.[111] A special feature of the *karteria* (endurance) is that the athlete who "endures" wants *either to win or to die*. This "philosophy" is on record from the sixth century BC onwards, when the renowned pankratiast Arrichion was exhorted by his trainer with the memorable words: "what a beautiful funeral it is not to give up at Olympia". In the first century AD another pankratiast is said to have continued fighting in the final at Olympia, until it became dark because he "thought that it was better to sacrifice one's life than to give up hope of winning the wreath". A second century AD Olympic boxer prayed to Zeus for "either the wreath or death". We know from his epitaph that the poor unfortunate died. L. Robert has pointed out that precisely the same ideology is on record in an epitaph for a *citizen soldier* from Thyrreion in Acarnania.[112] The epitaph of the Olympic boxer has a splendid parallel in a funerary epigram on a *warrior* from Elis (i.e. the area round Olympia). The first two lines run as follows: "In the front-line, Charonides, you stand praying, 'Zeus, give me now *victory or death* in battle.'"[113] Robert's words deserve quotation: "The ideal of the athletes is the glory of the crown. One speaks scornfully of the "professional" athletes of the Roman Empire. But it is necessary to acknowledge that they adopted the ideal of "amateurs" and *of Greek citizens*" (italics are mine, H.W.P.).[114]

---

[106] Cf. L. Robert, "Les Épigrammes satiriques ..." (cf. note 17), 268–73.
[107] L. Robert, *art. cit.* (cf. note 106), 234–6; 204.
[108] Homer, *Odysseia*, 3, 111–12.
[109] C. M. Bowra, *Pindar* (Oxford 1964), 164 f. and 177; D. C. Young, *Pindar Isthmian 7, Myth and Exempla* (Leiden 1971), 18–19.
[110] Dio, *Or.* 29, § 9 and 15; Lucian, *Anacharsis* (cf. above note 101), § 24; cf. also J. Ebert, *Griechische Epigramme* (cf. above note 33), 21.
[111] "Les Épigrammes satiriques ..." (cf. note 17), 235, note 2; id., in: *L'Antiquité Classique* 35 (1966), 429 (*andreia*); for *ponos* cf. L. Robert, *Hellenica* XI–XII, 344–9; XIII, 140 f.; Kl. Kramer, *op. cit.* (cf. note 28), 135 (*ponos*); L. Robert, "Les Épigrammes ...", 288, with note 4; in Lucian's *Anacharsis* (§ 24) *karteria* is recommended as a boxer's virtue; cf. also L. Moretti, *op. cit.* (cf. note 8), no. 21 (fourth century BC), l. 3; cf. also R. Merkelbach, "Der griechische Wortschatz und die Christen", in *Zeitschrift für Papyrologie und Epigraphik* 18 (1975), 101–48, esp. 116, 123 (*karteria*), 118–19 (*andreia*), 100–1, 116 (*ponos*).
[112] L. Robert, "Les Épigrammes ...", 198–9, 288; cf. Merkelbach, *art. cit.*, 122–3.
[113] H. Beckby, *Anthologia Graeca*, München 1957, vol. II, 320/1 (+ Bk VII, 541 = W. Peek: *Griechische Versinschriften*, Berlin 1955, no. 1503).
[114] "Les Épigrammes ...", 288.

The continuity in the value systems of Pindaric *kaloikagathoi* and of Hellenistic-Roman athletes is, I think, to be explained by the simple fact that aristocrats continued to function in athletics after the breakdown of the monopoly of the nobles. The ephebes of the Hellenistic-Roman gymnasium provided the channel through which the old values could be transported to later periods.[115] The ideology and mentality of the urban elites of the Hellenistic-Roman polis, that is, of the *leisure class* of the cities, reminds one of the value system of the modern leisure class, as described by Th. Veblen in his famous *The Theory of the Leisure Class*. The leisure class is a group of wealthy citizens who know how to accumulate wealth but do not actually *work* themselves in the physical sense of the word. R. MacMullen's characterisation of the Roman upper class seems applicable both to the elites of the Greco-Roman cities and to Veblen's modern American "leisure class": "At one end lay the very best thing of all, wealth without a person's having to get it himself, that is, inherited. The active pursuit of it aroused certain misgivings, at least among the topmost nobility. They simply *had* money. Next along the spectrum lay wealth enjoyed in retirement; and verging towards the unrespectable, wealth still in the process of accumulation".[116] The Hellenistic-Roman city elite had hardly anything to do with war in the period of the Pax Augusta and in an empire where Roman legions had ousted the old citizen militiae. This leisure class could afford to spend their lives in comfortable idleness: "[T]he scheme of life of the class is in large part a heritage from the past, and embodies much of the habits and ideals of the earlier barbarian period."[117] In the para-military atmosphere of the gymnasium and in the athletic contests, which were adorned with the old warrior's ideology, the leisure class re-enacted the civilisation of the archaic warriors who did not bother about production but lived as gentlemen of leisure, that is, as warriors on the battlefield and as athletes between battles: "From being an honourable employment handed down from the predatory culture as the highest form of everyday leisure, sports have come to be the only form of outdoor activity[118] that has the full sanction of decorum."[119] Veblen's remark about modern athletics ("The slang of athletics ... is in great part made up of extremely *sanguinary* locutions borrowed from the terminology of *warfare*")[120] can be applied with a good deal of justification to the world of sport of the ancient leisure class.

An overriding value was the everlasting *glory* of the victorious athlete. "To participate is more important than to win" – the slogan of the Coubertinians in 1896 and of their successors at the present day – is probably the most un-Greek statement that can be made, as I. Weiler has recently emphasised once again with a

---

[115] Cf. above p. 73 f.

[116] R. MacMullen, *Roman Social Relations, 50 BC to AD 284* (New Haven and London 1974), 117.

[117] Th. Veblen, *The Theory of the Leisure Class. An Economic Study of Institutions* (London 1924), 246.

[118] The last five words do not seem to be applicable to the ancient city-elites. They acted as local politicians and benefactors and as ambassadors to the Roman authorities; as heads of the local city police (*eirênarchos, paraphylax*) they also came into touch with para-military activities. In general it may be said that violence was much more endemic in the ancient societies: cf. N. Elias, "The Genesis of Sport as a Sociological Problem", in E. Dunning (ed.), *The Sociology of Sport. A Selection of Readings* (London 1971), 88 ff; cf. also my "Zur Soziologie ...", 85, note 148a.

[119] Veblen, *op. cit.*, 258.

[120] Veblen, *op. cit.*, 256; cf. note 107 above.

wealth of details.¹²¹ It would be boring to quote passages from Pindar to Philostratus about the profound importance of *kleos*, *kudos* and *eukleia* (fame, reputation). The epigraphic documents reflect the monotony of the literary sources in this respect. Victory in itself was not enough. There is a tendency to add, so to speak, a "surplus-value" to that of the victory in itself. I shall not give a long list of these "surplus-values" here; I have in mind athletes who won *akoniti*¹²² (i.e. without having to fight, because all opponents withdrew before the beginning of the games out of fear of the superstar) and *aptôtos*¹²³ (without having fallen on one's knee; a surplus-value for wrestlers, who had won when they had thrown their opponents on the floor three times) or who achieved a series of victories *on one day* or *for the first* time; in the latter case he could be *first of all human beings* or *first of his fellow-citizens* or *first of his fellow-provincials*. It would be wrong to think that such statements were a product of lying, arrogant athletes. There is no reason "to take as lies or exaggerations the mention of victories won as first of the Milesians (*prôtos Milêsiôn*), first of the Ionians (*prôtos Iônôn*), first of all (*prôtos pantôn*) and so on, and to treat them with a tone of sarcastic and suspicious humour".¹²⁴

Incidentally, the continuous emphasis on these surplus-values shows how wrong it is to think that Greek athletes were only interested in harmony and beauty or that Greek sport was "pure". What matters above all is that this tendency not to be satisfied with the victory as such but to amplify it is already on record in Pindar's poems (see *Ol.* 13, 37–8; 11, 92). In later sources it may have become stronger, sometimes even exuberant, but basically the development is one from the vanity of a small group of archaic aristocratic winners to the more-loudly-proclaimed vanity of a larger number of athletes, aristocrats and non-aristocrats alike.¹²⁵ When in Roman imperial times the anonymous author of a *Protreptikos* for athletes writes that the winner will be praised and "pointed at with the finger in the whole world",¹²⁶ the words may be new and the vocabulary certainly has become more verbose but the attitude reflected in the words is the same as that behind Pindar's poetry.

Let us finally turn to the most important ideological problem of our time: that of "professionalism" versus "amateurism". These are modern, almost anachronistic concepts, but this does not imply that they cannot be useful heuristic tools in the hands of the historian who must anyway always try to manoeuvre between the Scylla of the reconstruction of a completely anachronistic past and the Charybdis of the servile retelling of the stories of the past themselves.

Nowadays by professionals we mean sportsmen who make money out of their sport. Full professionals are those who devote all their time to their sport and make a living out of it;¹²⁷ semi-professionals devote a certain percentage of their time to

---

¹²¹ Cf. also p. 147 with note 16.
¹²² L. Robert, "Deux Inscriptions agonistiques de Rhodes", in: *AE* 1966, 110; cf. id.: "Les Épigrammes ...", 247.
¹²³ L. Robert, "Les Épigrammes ...", 249–51.
¹²⁴ L. Robert, "Les Épigrammes ...", 183, note 2; id.: *AE* 1966, 112–18; id.: *Monnaies Grecques*, Paris 1967, 114–15.
¹²⁵ See e.g. L. Moretti, *op. cit.* (cf. note 8), no. 79, l. 10–17.
¹²⁶ Dion. Hal., vol. VI (Teubner), *Opuscula* vol. II, 1, p. 283–92, esp. 288, ch. 4, l. 9 (εὐφημεῖσθαι καὶ δακτυλοδεικτεῖσθαι); cf. also R. Merkelbach, in: *ZPE* 18 (1975), 125.
¹²⁷ Cf. W. Rudolph, *art. cit.* (cf. note 27 above).

sport and derive only part of their daily bread from it. In antiquity as far as I know there was never disapproval of the fact that successful athletes received material rewards for their victories. *Olympionikai* (Olympic victors) were not debarred from participation in thematic games and we know (cf. above p. 154) that from the sixth century onwards they received official rewards from their mother cities for their Olympic wreaths. A recent inscription from Sybaris (in southern Italy) implies that *Olympionikai* received a substantial amount of money from their home city.[128] Eight centuries later the above-mentioned Anonymous writes, without the slightest trace of criticism, that successful athletes (Olympic and otherwise) could count, after their retirement, "on a life of affluence and on the fruits of their victories".[129]

Does this mean that all ancient athletes were basically professionals? By no means: firstly, it would be unwarranted to assume that all recorded athletes devoted all their time and their entire youth to training and games. A recent text from Hellenistic (first century BC) Colophon in Asia Minor tells us about a certain Polemaios who as an ephebe trained in the gymnasium and won prizes in many sacred contests abroad but soon afterwards gave up athletics and decided to devote himself to the study of rhetoric and philosophy in Rhodes. During a short span of time he must have devoted all his energy to sport because he would otherwise have been unable to win in *hieroi agônes* at a time when competition was very strong and full-time professionals active.[130] The same may be true of some of Pindar's clients. Others went further. In the fifth century BC Theogenes of Thasos practised boxing and *pankration* during twenty-two years and gained 1,300 victories: 1,300 may be a suspiciously round figure but I do not see why this should lead us to reject the fact that we have here an athlete who for twenty-two years won on an average a victory a week.[131] This need not be exceptional. In Pindar's poems we have (admittedly poetical) parallels: some of his heroes are said to have won "innumerable" victories, or "victories as numerous as the grains of sand on the beach" (cf. also above p. 150).

It is undoubtedly among late archaic aristocrats like Theogenes of Thasos that the first professionals are to be found.[132] They would have accepted the title of professional if one defines it as a man who does nothing but athletics during a longer or shorter period of time; they would have rejected this label, if we had given the following definition: a professional is a man who derives *his income* from his sport. They would have objected because they did not earn or did not have to earn their daily bread; they *were* wealthy; they did not have a *profession*. They embody "the truth that in antiquity land ownership on a sufficient scale marks "the absence of any occupation"".[133] What they in fact did was to accumulate wealth in a honourable way. That was such a normal part of their way of life that they neither talked about it nor expected Pindar to mention it. They took it for granted.

Sometime in the Hellenistic period, at any rate before 50 BC, an association of

---

[128] J. Ebert, *Griechische Epigramme* (cf. above note 33), 251–5.
[129] *Op. cit.* (cf. note 126), p. 288, ch. 4, l. 19–20 (οἱ καρποὶ <οἱ> ἀπὸ τῆς νίκης, τὴν περιουσίαν τοῦ βίου ἄφθονον).
[130] L. Robert, in: *Revue de philologie* 1967, 17; id., "Les Juges étrangers dans la cité grecque", in: *Festschr, P. J. Zépos* (Athens 1971), 778–9.
[131] J. Ebert, *Griechische Epigramme* (cf. above note 33), no. 27, p. 118–26.
[132] Cf. my "Zur Soziologie ..." (cf. note 18 above), 63–7.
[133] M. I. Finley, *The Ancient Economy* (London 1973), 44.

ecumenical athletes came into existence. It is customary, and from our point of view correct, to speak about the association of *professional* athletes;[134] however, there is not a single document in which it is said that the members exercised a *profession* (*technê, epitêdeuma*) and made a living out of it: "The documents mostly contain monotonous lists of victories, first those in the *hieroi agones* (and among them the *periodos* on the first place) and at the end as a single total the thematic victories, as if apologising to the reader that they participated in such pedestrian, material events. It is a variant on the above-mentioned (cf. p. 160) attitude of the Athenian gentleman T. Domitius who tried to make the thematic games less thematic by calling them *hieroi*. The anonymous Roman author talks about περιουσία ἄφθονος and καρποὶ <οἱ> ἀπὸ τῆς νίκης, i.e. about "affluence" and "fruits of the victories", not about professional moneymaking.

It is *the critics* who apply the word *technê* or *epitêdeuma* (with the meaning of "profession") to athletics. Galen used it for contemporary athletics and he also writes that "the profession of the athletes" (*to tôn athlêtôn epitêdeuma*) came into existence in the early fourth century BC. In a Pseudo-Platonic text athletics are compared with other banausic crafts.[135] We do find the word *technê* in a few agonistic documents but it there pertains to a boxer or wrestler who relies on his technical skill rather than on brutal strength: *technê* denotes a specific skill or style in boxing, not boxing as such, let alone athletics in general.[136] Galen does not criticise athletics because it is a *technê* but rather because it is an example of *kakotechnia* ("base art").[137] Galen was himself a *technitês* but he called his *technê* a manifestation of well-doing; his *technê* was a "*logikê technê*" (intellectual art) and a "*semnê technê*" (honourable art) and as such superior to a banausic *technê*, but in Galen's view even the last of these can be useful to society and to the person who exercises it.[138] Professional athletics is neither a *semnê* nor a banausic *technê*; it is *kakotechnia*, not so much because this profession enables people to collect large sums of money but because these people fail to achieve an honourable way of life with their wealth: it is a *phaulon epitêdeuma* (a "mean, base profession"); it destroys body and soul.[139] It does not produce beautiful bodies; on the contrary, over-specialisation and one-sided diets bring about ugly *polusarkia* ("fleshiness", "plumpness").[140] Galen admits (and apparently accepts it) that athletic achievements provide the athletes with glory among the masses and with money, but he argues that they are unable to administer their wealth correctly: during and after their career the athletes are in debt and just as poor as an *oikonomos* (steward, manager) of a wealthy gentleman's estate picked at random.[141]

---

[134] Cf. note 92 above.
[135] Cf. *Zeitschrift für Papyrologie und Epigraphik* 10 (1973), 197; for *epitêdeuma* cf. Fl. Josephus, *Jewish Antiquities*, XV, 269 "the most outstanding in all the professions (*epitêdeumasin*) were gathered together" (συνελεγησάν τε οἱ κορυφαιότατοι τῶν ἐν τοῖς ἐπιτηδεύμασιν). See Lämmer, "Griechische Wettkämpfe in Jerusalem" (cf. note 5), 188.
[136] Cf. J. Ebert, *Griechische Epigramme*, Index, 278, s.v. τέχνη.
[137] Galen, *Protreptikos* (Teubner; ed. I. Marquardt, *Scripta Minora* I), cap. 9 § 20.
[138] Galen, ibidem, cap. 14, § 38–9; for an analysis of Galen's view on τέχναι cf. J. Christes, *Bildung und Gesellschaft* (Darmstadt 1975), 77–8, 123–5.
[139] Galen, *ibidem*, cap. 10, § 25.
[140] Galen, *ibidem*, cap. 12, § 32.
[141] Galen, *ibidem*, cap. 14, § 37.

Galen joins in with and explicitly quotes Euripides who in a fragment of his *Autolykos* set the tone for later critics of athletics: "For when there are ten thousand ills in Greece, there's none that's worse than the whole race of athletes. For, first of all, they learn not to live well, nor could they do so; for could any man being a slave to his own jaws and appetite acquire more prosperity than that of his father?".[142] There is a distinct undertone of class-prejudice in both authors. Euripides points out that the athletes of his time never manage to acquire more prosperity than their fathers had. This is perhaps another way of saying that they end their life in poverty which in turn implies that their fathers were poor as well. When lower-class athletes begin to perform successfully in athletics, both on the local and the international level, misery starts. Euripides was contemporary with Alcibiades (cf. above p. 162) who noticed and sharply criticised the presence of lower-class athletes at Olympia. Euripides is known to have celebrated Alcibiades' equestrian victories ca. 416–415 BC (though I must add that after the Sicilian expedition, launched on the initiative of Alcibiades, Euripides' sympathy for Alcibiades seems to have cooled).[143] Galen's comparison of an ex-athlete with the manager of a rich man's estate suggests that athletes were despicable: "management throughout the classical period, Greek as well as Roman, urban as well as rural, was the preserve of slaves and freedmen, at least in those larger undertakings in which the owner himself did not normally take an active part".[144] Galen does not condemn people who exercise a *technê* in order to earn their living; he condemns people who exercise a dishonorable *technê*. He distinguishes between good and bad *technai* because as a doctor he is also considered a *technitês* and because he wants to raise the status of his *technê* (*epitêdeuma*).

In the athlete's counter-ideology – a combined product of Pindaric *kaloikagathoi* and the Hellenistic-Roman aristocracy (the εὐγενεῖς[145] = well-born, noble) – athletics is never called a *technê*. It is significant that *technê* (profession, "métier") was however used of the profession of *trainer*. In an inscription from Bouthrôtos (in ancient Epirus, now in Albania) we hear of a certain Chaireas, son of Dioskourides, who was employed as *epistatês* by a young member of the urban elite, Antipatros, son of Archias. As L. Robert has brilliantly shown, Chaireas was not a magistrate (as the editor of the inscription supposed) but a trainer, a teacher of gymnastics. Ἐπιστάτης is the *terminus technicus* for this profession. Chaireas is praised because "τὰν πᾶσαν ἐπιμέλειαν μετ' εὐνοίας ἔν τε τᾶι τέχναι καὶ τᾶι ἄλλαι ἀναστροφᾶι εἰς Ἀντίπατρον ποιεῖται" ("in his "métier" and in his behaviour in general he shows all good care and goodwill towards Antipatros"). In Robert's paraphrase: "He has given eagerly to this young member of the elite all the assistance of his profession, of his art, of his technical knowledge – the *paidotribês*, the *gymnastês*, the *epistatês* is a *technitês* ("skilled worker") – towards the training and athletic and physical development of his pupil, while at the same time being, more generally speaking, a

---

[142] Euripides, fr. 282 (ed. Nauck); cf. my "Zur Soziologie ...", 68; 80, note 3; 83, note 105.
[143] C. M. Bowra, "Euripides' Epinician for Alcibiades", in: *Historia* 9 (1960), 68–79.
[144] M. I. Finley, *op. cit.* (cf. note 133), 76.
[145] For *eugeneia* cf. my "Zur Soziogie ...", 87, note 193. Aristotle, *Politica* 1294a, 22–3 writes that "nobility" (*eugeneia*) means ancient wealth (*archaios ploutos*) and virtue; cf. also G. E. M. de Ste. Croix, *The Origins of the Peloponnesian War* (London 1973), 373 ff. and D. Loenen, *Eugeneia. Adel en Adeldom binnen de Atheense Demokratie* (Amsterdam 1965), *passim*.

master and teacher and pleasant companion."[146]

A trainer had a profession, just like a sculptor, an architect, a doctor or an actor. They are contracted, hired by an individual or a community for a specific job at a specific salary (*misthos*: wage). Wage-labour had a low social status in Greco-Roman antiquity:'[I]lliberal and mean are the employments of all who work for wages, whom we pay for their labour and not for their art; for in their case their very wages are the warrant of their slavery." That is the view of Cicero who in the same paragraph condemns all craftsmen who work in their workshops for clients.[147] Though the category of those who "worked for clients (private or public) has a higher status than the man who worked for wages",[148] in the last resort the categories are held by the upper class to be of inferior status. In the second century AD Lucian vehemently attacked literary men who accepted salaried positions in the homes of wealthy Romans: "[T]heir slavery is manifest and they differ little from purchased or bred slaves."[149]

By avoiding the words *technê* and *epitêdeuma* the athletes avoided giving the impression that obtaining money through their sport was tantamount to professional work for one's daily bread. In its origin the world of athletics was dominated by aristocrats who introduced their value-system; members of the urban aristocracies continued to dominate, if not the sports, at any rate the ideology of sport. *Technê* was inferior; as a successful athlete one did not receive a *misthos* – that was reserved for trainers – but prizes or gifts. Galen actually writes that in his days athletes were daily honoured with *gifts* of money;[150] prize games were even called *agônes dôritai* (gift games).[151] "Greeks of high station and hereditary wealth" did not wish to obtain "an income overtly from professional earnings".[152] Even what we nowadays call the intellectual professions – medicine, architecture, teaching – are admittedly called "occupations in which either a higher degree of intelligence is required or from which society derives no small benefit" but they are "respectable for those whose status they befit".[153] The latter were of "evidently inferior social status",[154] not only for Cicero but for the entire Greco-Roman upper class. Significantly those intellectuals who are known to have charged fees for their teaching or services show a "tendency to treat fees as *gifts*"[155] (my italics, H.W.P.).

[146] L. Robert, "Un citoyen de Téos à Bouthrôtos d'Épire", in: *Comptes rendus académie des inscriptions et belles lettres* 1974, 508–9, esp. 517, 519–20, 528–9.
[147] Cicero, *De officiis* I, 150–1; M. I. Finley, *op. cit.*, 41–2.
[148] M. I. Finley, *op. cit.*, 75.
[149] M. I. Finley, *op. cit.*, 76; P. A. Brunt, "Aspects of the Social Thought of Dio Chrysostom and of the Stoics", in: *Proceedings Cambridge Philological Society* 199 (1973), 9–34, esp. 32.
[150] Galen, *Protreptikos* ... (cf. note 137), cap, 9, § 21 ("honoured with daily, public gifts of money from the elders of the city"; δημοσίᾳ παρὰ τοῖς πατράσι τετιμημένον ἀργυρίου δόσεσιν).
[151] J. H. Krause, *Olympia*, Wien 1838, 6, note 3 (on p. 7).
[152] P. A. Brunt, *art. cit.* (cf. note 149), 33.
[153] Cicero, *De officiis* I, 150–1; M. I. Finley, *op. cit.*, 42.
[154] P. A. Brunt, *art. cit.* (cf. note 149), 30; in inscriptions, physicians, teachers and *city-councillors* sometimes receive the same gifts from a local benefactor; nevertheless the doctors and teachers are carefully distinguished from the councillors, who constituted the city elite; see my *Epigraphica*, II (Leiden 1969), no. 21 (with further references).
[155] P. A. Brunt, *art. cit.*, 33. It is worthy of note that in Homer, Iliad X, 303–4 *misthos* is used as an equivalent of *dôron* (gift). The gift, promised by the Trojan prince Hector to the man who was prepared to spy in the Greek camp, is called a *misthos* in the next line. The meaning is "celui d'un don, d'un

The prevailing ideology was against fees, wages, salaries: these words smacked too much of "professional earnings": a gentleman "had no occupation"; nor had those gentlemen who specialised in athletics.

From the above it appears that our definition of professionalism would have appalled the ancient athlete, precisely because it starts from a positive attitude to people having a paid job. The ancient aristocrats simply *had* money, "the active pursuit of it aroused certain misgivings";[156] "work was no disgrace to a Greek of high status, provided that he was not compelled to resort to it to earn his daily bread".[157] The athletes had their own *ponos* ("toil", "hard work"); but that was honourable *ponos*, not to be confused with the *ponos* of the *penêtes*, that is, of those who had to work for their daily bread.[158] The question will be asked whether and to what extent lower-class athletes complied with this ideology; there is no way of knowing whether a successful lower-class Egyptian athlete talked openly with his colleagues in terms of *misthos* about the fees he received as a result of being "contracted" by a wealthy local politician to take part in one of the municipal contests. In fact Dion of Prusa uses the verb μισθοῦσθαι (to hire for *misthos*) in the above-mentioned (see p. 156) story to denote nothing more nor less than the agreement by a local benefactor and a renowned Olympic victor. However, what matters is that in the official ideology, as shown by the documents left by the athletes themselves, there is no question at all of money, wages, rewards or anything similar. On the contrary, in all extant catalogues of victories the victors list their victories in sacred games in detail whereas the prize games are mentioned almost casually at the end of the text, and then merely as a total, not by name, The "closed" ideology of the athletic world is in accord with what P. A. Brunt has suggested about the relation between aristocratic values and the views of the lower classes in general: "Aristocratic conceptions may have been pervasive and dominant because the lower classes were not sufficiently reflective or articulate to criticize them or to substitute something different. Nor must we underrate the inherent attractiveness of the aristocratic ideal of independence and leisure."[159] Sociologists call this attitude *imitatio domini*.[160]

One final point: why is it that, in contrast with the conceptions of de Coubertin and others, there was never a movement in antiquity to ban monetary rewards and

---

prix, d'une récompense rémunérant un exploit" (Ed. Will, Notes sur ΜΙΣΘΟΣ in: *Hommages à Cl. Préaux* (Brussels 1975), 426–38). Nevertheless, Achilles does not call the prizes offered by him to the winners in the funeral games for Patroclus *misthoi* but *aethla*. The aristocratic, elitist interpretation of *misthos*, on record in Iliad X, 303–4, can also be found in Plato's *Politeia* (613^e–14^a: the righteous receive the *athla*, *misthoi* and the *dôra* from the gods; 345^e–7^d: magistrates should receive a *misthos* consisting either of money or of *timê* (honour)) and in Aristotle's Nicomachean Ethics (1134^b l. 6 ff.: magistrates should receive *misthos*, consisting of *timê* and *geras* (gift of honour, prerogative; all these examples *apud* Will)). Due to a long process of democratisation and increasing societal differentiation the word *misthos* had acquired such a pejorative meaning for aristocrats in the Hellenistic-Roman period that it could no longer be used as an innocent equivalent of *athla* (prizes) or *dôra* (gifts). The tendency to interpret "wages" and prizes (cf. note 150 and 151) as "gifts", of course, betrays an age-old aristocratic mentality.

[156] Cf. above p. 78, with note 116.
[157] P. A. Brunt, *art. cit.*, 12.
[158] M. I. Finley, *op. cit.*, 41.
[159] *Art. cit.*, 14.
[160] J. S. Wigboldus, "Ontwikkelingen van de stratificatietheorie in geschiedsociologisch perspectief", in: *Tijdschrijt voor Geschiedenis* 84 (1971), 179–215, esp. 190; cf. also in the same periodical p. 245.

prizes completely from sport? It would be too simple to argue that throughout antiquity wealth *as such* was *unequivocally good* and *always* respectable. Admittedly, to borrow a few significant words from the emperor Claudius in a speech to the Roman senate,[161] all the "good men" (*boni*) were "wealthy" (*locupletes*) but the converse would not necessarily be true. The concept of *nouveaux riches* is a Greek invention (νεόπλουτος; ἀρτίπλουτος). Aristotle criticizes contemporary Athenian *nouveaux riches* as follows: "and since that which is old seems closely to resemble that which is natural, it follows that, if two parties have the same good, men are more indignant with the one who has recently acquired it and owes his prosperity to it".[162] The term has especially been applied to people who have seen fit to acquire wealth in trade, commerce and "industry". The same phenomenon and the same prejudice is on record in first century BC Rome, as T. P. Wiseman has shown in his *New Man in the Roman Senate, 139 BC–AD 14*.[163] In short, there was good wealth and bad wealth; consequently one cannot say that wealth as such was beyond criticism and that therefore there was no reason to separate sport and money.

In a recent article the Dutch sociologist R. Stokvis pointed out that in seventeenth- and eighteenth-century England the old landowning aristocracy had no objection to participating in contests with "professionals", or to competing for money-prizes.[164] It was not until the nineteenth century – he argues – that it became aristocratic to separate sport and money: why? His answer is that in that same nineteenth century new social groups, whose wealth was movable, based on cash, commerce, and operations on the markets, threatened the position of the landowning nobility: new-rich, entrepreneurs as opposed to the old nobility. The latter formerly combined honour and status with wealth;[165] from the very moment that people who "had nothing but money", rose to prominence, the old nobility focused on its code of honour, as being its *exclusive* preserve, and refused to participate in contests for money prizes. Let us assume that this hypothesis is acceptable; we can perhaps then understand why the old public school code and that of de Coubertin who, incidentally, was strongly impressed by Thomas Arnold's system, had no predecessor in antiquity.

---

[161] M. P. Charlesworth, *Documents Illustrating the Reigns of Claudius and Nero* (Cambridge 1939, 10, col. 2, l. 3.

[162] Cf. W. R. Connor, *The Local Politicians of Fifth Century Athens* (Princeton 1971), 155. In Athenian comedy the νεόπλουτοι are chracterised as νεοπλουτοπόνηροι, "nouveaux riches die hun welstand aan de uitbreiding en consolidatie van het Atheens imperium te danken hadden" (J. Th. M. F. Pieters, "Pericles en het Toneel", in: *Hermeneus* 46 (1975), 242); cf. also note 145 (nobility-*ancient* wealth) and Ed. Will, "Fonctions de la monnaie dans les cités grecques de l'époque classique" in: *Numismatique antique: problèmes et méthodes (Études d'archéologie classique*, IV, Annales de l'Est; Univ. de Nancy, II, 1975), 233–46, esp. 238–9, note 18 on the *archaioploutoi* and the positive picture of these given by Cratinus in his comedy *Ploutoi*.

[163] (Oxford 1971), 70–94.

[164] R. Stokvis, "Traditionalisme in de Sportwereld", in: *Mens en Maatschappij* 49 (1974), 185–207, esp. 191.

[165] Just as their ancient predecessors did, both in agonistic life and in society at large. They combined the glory (*doxa*) of the wreath with the "profit" (*kerdos*) of the prize games (cf. J. H. Krause, *op. cit.* (cf. note 151), 6, note 3; *kerdos* is the word used by a late scholiast on Pindar; it is, of course, not to be found in athletes' language). They even combined wreaths with "value prizes", but in their ideology they emphasized the *doxa* of the wreath: they could do so, because they could afford to compete for wreaths from time to time and because participation in thematic games could produce "profit" (*kerdos*) anyway.

Admittedly, as pointed out above, the phenomenon of "nouveaux riches" was not unknown in Greco-Roman antiquity but I doubt very much whether they ever seriously *threatened* the predominance of the landowning elite.[166] In this respect the recent books by M. I. Finley and R. MacMullen mentioned above leave no doubt about the fundamental predominance of the landowning elite in the ancient world.[167] In other words: in antiquity the aristocracy never ceased to accept monetary rewards for their sporting achievements, because their position was never threatened by a commercial business oligarchy, whose only merit, in the eyes of their adversaries, was wealth, and *new* wealth at that. It is clear that only a comparative analysis of the economic roles and attitudes of ancient and early-modern European aristocracies can corroborate or refute this hypothesis, which has been advanced here mainly to encourage further research. It is of course obvious that the history of sport cannot be separated from the history of society at large.

---

[166] I doubt whether R. Seager is right when he writes: "The old association between birth and wealth had first been seriously *undermined* (italics are mine, H.W.P.) at about the time of the outbreak of the Peloponnesian War, when a new type of politician began to appear: the son of a wealthy factory-owner ..." ("Elitism and Democracy in Classical Athens", in: F. Cople Jaher, *The Rich, The Well Born and the Powerful. Elites and Upper Classes in History* (Urbana 1973), 7–26, esp. 11). New politicians admittedly appeared but they were hardly numerous enough to transform *the* urban elite into an industrial-commercial group. For a vigorous and sound attack on theories about the existence or rise of "commercial aristocracies" and "industrial and merchant classes" both in the Greek city-states and in Rome see G. E. M. de Ste. Croix, "Karl Marx and the History of Classical Antiquity", in: *Arethusa* 8 (1975), 7–41, esp. 17–18.

[167] Cf. my review article: "Afscheid van Rostovtzeff", in: *Lampas* 8 (1975), 267–84; see also my forthcoming review of Finley's book in *Mnemosyne* 1976 or 1977. J. Andreau, "Le tremblement de terre de Pompée", in: *Annales. Économies, sociétés, civilisations* 28 (1973), 369–95, esp. 370–1 draws attention to the weakness of Rostovtzeff's thesis about the rise of an industrial and commercial bourgeoisie in the Roman Empire, which is supposed to have threatened the dominant position of the landowning aristocracy.

8 Athletics, Festivals and Greek Identity in the Roman East[*]

ONNO VAN NIJF

INTRODUCTION

Ceremonial life (contests and festivals) was a major preoccupation of the inhabitants of the cities of the Roman East in general and of Roman Asia Minor in particular. Processions meandered through the streets every week, and perhaps even every day, carrying processional statues and driving along sacrificial animals. The air was frequently filled with the smells and sounds of sacrificial banquets. In public places benches were set up, on which people sat to drink and eat together. On some days flocks of people could be seen rushing towards the theatre or the stadium, eager to take up their places in the auditorium, from where they could watch traditional Greek athletic or artistic contests. It must have seemed as though at any given time some part or other of the population was involved in some public ritual. The Greek city in the Roman period was – to borrow a phrase of Walter Burkert – a *Festgemeinschaft*, a festive community.[1] Greek festive life was not the last resort of traditionalists, however, trying to insulate themselves from new and unpleasant social and political realities. Traditional Greek festivals were very much part of the contemporary world. I shall argue here that Greek festivals played a central part in civic life under Roman rule. I also intend to discuss how they were reformed and adapted to fit into a world where the centre of power was located in Rome. And finally, I want to assess their importance for the self-identification of the local élites.

GREEK FESTIVALS

Agonistic festivals, i.e. festivals with athletic or artistic competitions, had been a central element of Greek culture since the earliest recorded times. Their pedigree was impeccable. The oldest Greek literature contains vivid descriptions of athletic

---

[*] An earlier version of this paper was presented to the Lampeter Classical Association. I should like to thank my audiences in Lampeter and in Cambridge, as well as the anonymous reader for the Cambridge Philological Society for their comments. I would also like to thank Christopher Kelly for allowing me to develop the thoughts presented here in his lecture series on the Second Sophistic, and for comments on style and content. I am much indebted to Sofia Voutsaki who had to read several versions of this paper, and to Paul Cartledge, H.W. Pleket and Michael Williams who read and commented upon it at the shortest of notice. The research for this paper has been made possible by a fellowship of the Royal Netherlands Academy of Arts and Sciences. Originally published in *Proceedings of the Cambridge Philological Society* 45 (1999): 176–200.

[1] Burkert: 1987.

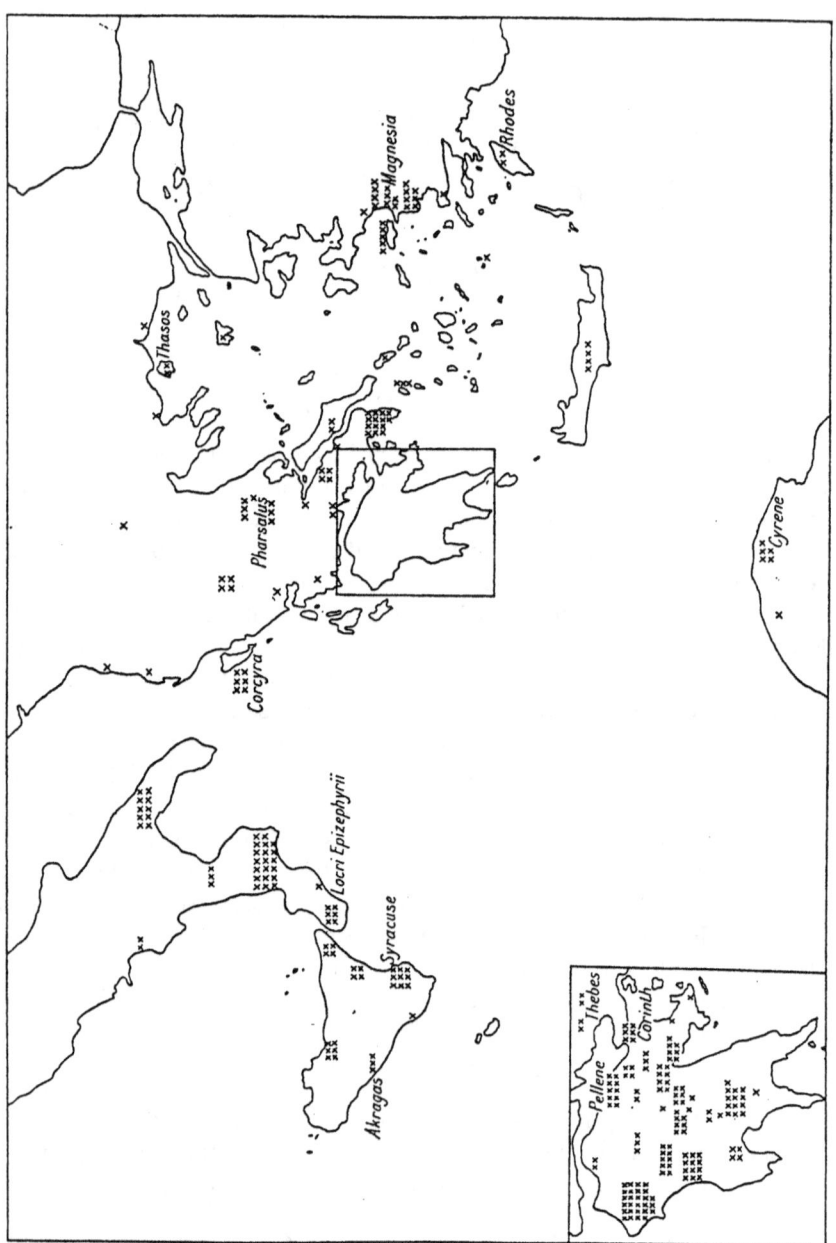

Fig. 8.1 The origins of Olympic victors 600 BCE–300 BCE.

contests in the framework of funeral games, athletic victory in panhellenic contests informed some of the finest poetry, and we should not forget that the entire corpus of Greek drama originated in an agonistic context. As Cartledge wrote: "Festivals were perhaps the single most important feature of classical Greek religion in its public aspect."[2] All over the Greek world city officials organised remarkably similar festivals in honour of their gods with processions, sacrifices, banquets and above all, contests.

The most famous of these were of course the panhellenic festivals at Olympia, Delphi, Isthmia and Nemea.[3] It is sometimes thought that over time these games gradually lost their appeal, and that they had almost petered out when a Christian emperor delivered the final blow in CE 393. But this image of slow decline is wrong. A recently discovered bronze plaque from Olympia listing athletic victors as late as CE 385, suggests a continuing popularity right up to the very end of the fourth century.[4] Some things did change, however, and a study of the place of origin of the Olympic victors yields some interesting results (Fig. 8.1 and Fig. 8.2).[5]

These maps show at least two things. In the first place they illustrate the shifting boundaries of Greekness. The panhellenic games had by definition been open only to people of Greek descent, but the boundary between Greek and non-Greek was not exactly impermeable. For example, the kings of Macedon had been allowed to compete from the fifth century onwards, but other non-royal Macedonians were made to wait until Philip and Alexander had drastically remapped the Greek world. In the Hellenistic and Roman periods, increasingly large concentric circles were drawn to include Hellenised Anatolians, Syrians, Egyptians and even Romans.[6] The permission given to the latter to participate in the Isthmian Games of 228 BCE effectively declared them to be Greek.[7] Greek identity was apparently something that could be acquired not just through language or learning but also (and perhaps more easily) through athletic training in the *gymnasion*.

Secondly, given the fact that these maps are to a large extent based on epigraphic evidence, they show that commemoration of Olympic victory became increasingly important in the eastern part of the Greek world. I shall return to this observation later.[8]

The enthusiasm for traditional Greek agonistic festivals in the Roman period is also evident elsewhere. Alongside these four major international festivals, there had always been numerous local festivals and competitions of varying standing. Some cities organised *hieroi stephanitai agônes* (sacred crown games) of their own, and the number of these increased over time. More numerous, however, were the

---

[2] Cartledge: 1985, 98.
[3] For a handy and up-to-date survey see Decker: 1995, 39–59; also Finley and Pleket: 1976.
[4] Ebert: 1997.
[5] The maps are taken from Harris: 1964. They do not represent recent additions to the list of known *Olympionikai*, but these confirm the trends visible here. Lists of Olympic victors can be found in: Moretti: 1957; Moretti: 1970; Moretti: 1992. For a more detailed study see Farrington: 1997.
[6] Finley and Pleket: 1976, 90 ff.
[7] Rigsby: 1996, 26. Cf. Polybius, 2.12.8.
[8] What these maps do not show, of course, is that the majority of the victors came from the East. Commemoration was a function in part of the rise and fall of epigraphic habits, as is noted by Farrington: 1997.

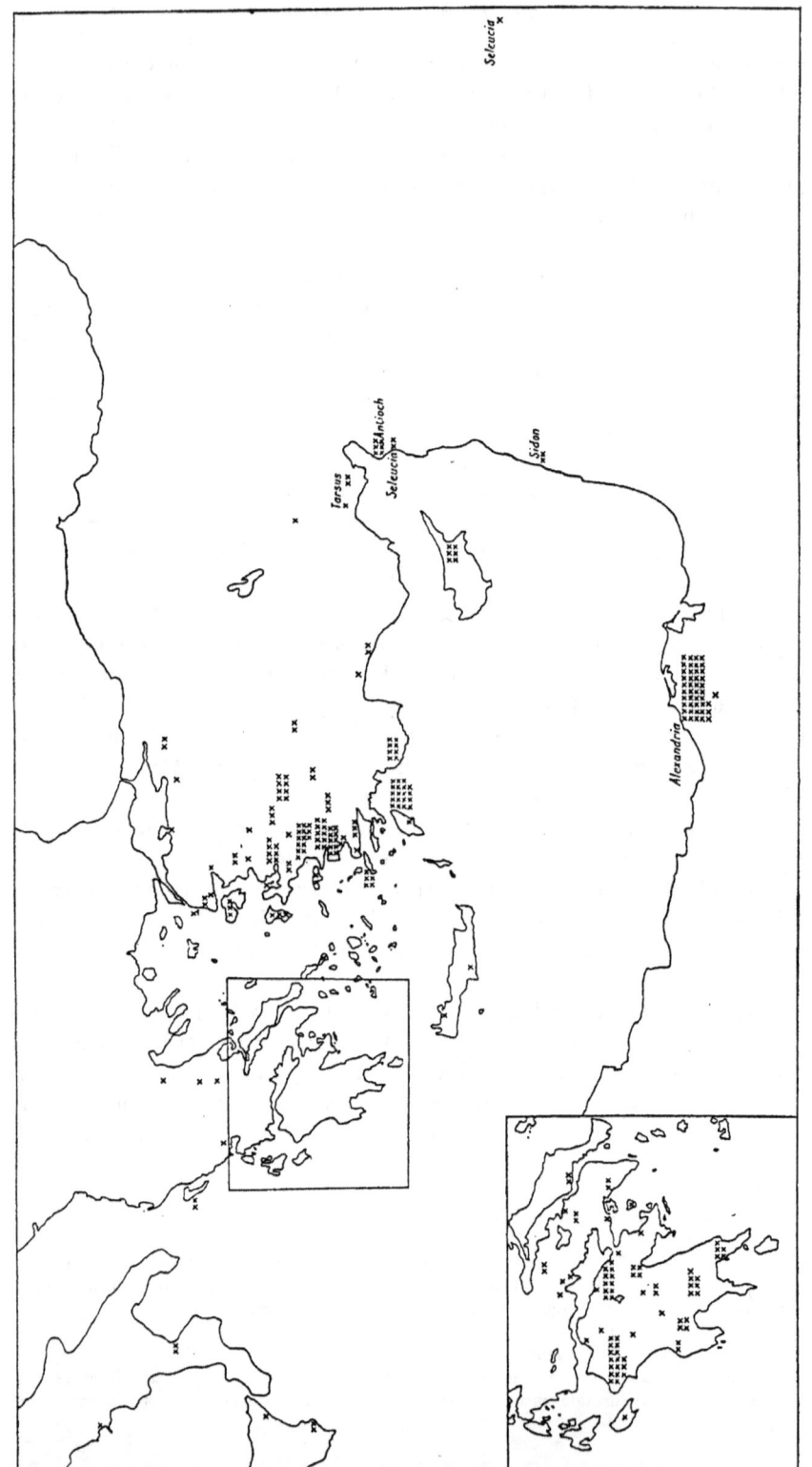

Fig. 8.2 The origins of Olympic victors 300 BCE–400 CE.

themides, agônes themateitai, or prize games, most of which offered money or other valuable prizes.⁹ It would seem, however, that apart from the prize money, there was no substantial difference between these festivals and the more prestigious games. We find the same athletes and artists competing in the same disciplines, according to the same rules. All festivals shared in a kind of homogeneous common Greek festival structure, which appears to have changed very little over the centuries. Literary, archaeological, and above all epigraphical evidence suggests that by the Roman period this traditional Greek festival was popular as never before. In the entire Greek world, but above all in Roman Asia Minor, old festivals were revived or reorganised, and new ones were founded in large numbers. Louis Robert describes this phenomenon as an "agonistic explosion."¹⁰ There was hardly a town without at least one or two agonistic festivals on its calendar to boast about.

Festive life in the East developed its own dynamics. Small festivals, for locals only, were "upgraded": disciplines were added, and prizes increased, to attract competitors from further afield.¹¹ The more successful festivals attracted the top performers of their time: (professional) athletes and artists from all over the Greek world, who could command a hefty appearance fee (just as modern tennis-stars do). There was strong competition between festivals, and the organisers vied with each other to attract the best performers, or the largest crowds. They competed by offering larger cash prizes, or by adorning their festivals with resounding titles. Many cities longed for festivals with the more prestigious stephanitic (or crowned) status, and they declared their festival Isolympic, or Isopythian (that is "equal to the Olympic or Pythian Games"). This need not mean more than that they copied the programme of the games at Olympia or Delphi in detail.¹² It has been suggested, however, that local festival organisers were ready to fork out large sums of money to have the right to organise their own version of the Olympic games: the late writer Malalas records that the people of Antioch paid the Eleians for the right to organise Olympic games in Syria.¹³ If true, the Salt Lake City Olympic Committee can claim to stand in a long tradition! Only there was at that time no scandal: no member of the Eleian Olympic Committee was asked to resign.

Cities sent out envoys to the entire *oikoumenê* – that is, the entire Greek world – inviting everybody to their games. Formal observers *(theoroi)* received seats of honour in the theatres and stadia, and special envoys were sent to share in the sacrifices *(synthytai)*.¹⁴ In the Roman period, when the emperor became the obvious arbiter of all things Greek, granting of stephanitic status was in his gift (such festivals were technically known as a *dorea* of the emperor).¹⁵ Cities aiming to outdo each other accumulated imperial games. The city of Tarsus organised

⁹ The distinction is explained in e.g. Robert: 1982, Pleket: 1975 and Spawforth: 1989.
¹⁰ Robert: 1982, 38.
¹¹ See below for the "upgrading", and the addition of prizes to the festivals in Oinoanda.
¹² Robert: 1974 for Olympic Games in Ephesus, and other local imitations.
¹³ Pleket: 1978, 15–18.
¹⁴ Rouché: 1993, 182–9, nos 58–64 discusses a number of texts that record the celebration by various cities of a grant to Aphrodisias of a stephanitic festival in which they appeared as "joint sacrificers". There were reserved seats in the stadium for envoys of the cities of Mastaura and Antiocheia: 87. no. 45.4 and 96, no. 45.34.
¹⁵ Mitchell: 1993, 224.

Hadriania Olympia, Kommodeia Olympia (later renamed the Severeia Olympia, which under Caracalla were known as the Severeia Antoneia Olympia), as well as Augustia Aktia.[16]

Cities were rightly proud of such festivals. Even if each festival took up no more than a few days a year, together they must have made a tremendous and lasting impact on the city and its institutions, on built-up space, and on the very rhythm of urban life. Large sums of money were invested in order to build proper facilities (stadia, theatres, gymnasia), while political time was dedicated to proposals for setting up new foundations, special magistrates appointed to oversee the events, and coinage issued to commemorate and advertise new contests.[17] The ritual calendar had to be adapted to accommodate new or expanded celebrations. And of course, hundreds if not thousands of inscriptions were set up in public spaces too in permanent commemoration of victors, festival organisers, and other benefactors, or to mark the successful completion of yet another contest. The festival was a defining characteristic of Greek civic life under Roman rule.[18] What I want to do in the rest of this paper is to consider in more detail the impact of such festivals, of this dense festive culture, on life in some Greek cities of the Roman period. What meanings did these festivals generate for the inhabitants? What did these festivals do for them?

CIVIC FESTIVALS

When we talk about festivals in the Roman period, we must remember that most of them were not financed from public funds, from taxpayers' money. As with most amenities of public life, the costs were met from private purses: they were paid for by upper-class benefactors such as Vibius Salutaris from Ephesus, Caius Iulius Demosthenes a second century CE benefactor of the Lycian city of Oinoanda and many, many others.[19] To them festivals were on a par with the other acts of euergetism, such as the construction of buildings, or contributions to the food supply. C. Iulius Demosthenes sums it all up in the inscription that commemorates his festival:[20]

> When Claudius Capito Rubrianus was high priest of the emperors, on 24 Artemeisios [25 July], I, C. Iulius Demosthenes, son of Apollonius, of the Fabian tribe, *prytanis* and secretary of the council of the Oinoandians, as I have loved my dearest homeland since my earliest youth, and have not only maintained, but surpassed the generosity of my ancestors towards it in the annual subsidies which I made to ensure fair prices in the market and in providing a boundless supply of [...] to the magistrates, and as I have constructed a food market with three stoas facing it, two with one and one with two storeys, and have spent more than 15,000 *denarii* on this and the purchase of the houses which were removed to make way for this building, and as I wish to leave behind for

---

[16] Ziegler: 1985, 32.
[17] Wörrle:1988 on the impact of the Demostheneia in Oinoanda. For coinage see e.g. Harl: 1987, 64 ff.; Ziegler: 1985, and Mitchell: 1993, 223.
[18] Mitchell: 1993, 217.
[19] The classic account of euergetism is Veyne: 1976, cf. Andreau et al.: 1978; Garnsey: 1991. Vibius Salutaris is discussed in Rogers: 1991b.
[20] *SEG* xxviii, 1462, ll. 6–12. The text was published with extensive comments in Wörrle: 1988. The English translations used here are those of Mitchell: 1990.

my homeland, in like manner with these buildings, a permanent capital fund, publicly promise (the foundation of) a thymelic [a theatrical] festival to be called the *Demostheneia*, which will be celebrated after three-year intervals just as the other penteteric festivals are celebrated ...

Festivals were apparently deemed to be as essential to the citizens as the provision of their daily bread. Now, when such benefactors paid for public festivals, when they revived old festivals, or invented new ones, they were not trying simply to please the crowds with free entertainment. These festivals were used to make serious political statements about the kind of community in which they, the benefactors, thought they lived, or would wish to live. Among the issues that such festivals addressed were the importance of being Greek in a modern world, the realities of Roman power, and the principles underlying the social hierarchy.

GREEK CULTURE AND IDENTITY

The first issue we may want to discuss is the importance of Greek culture and identity. What was the point of all these Greek-style festivals? I take as my starting-point the foundation of Demosthenes which offers a detailed blueprint of how such festivals were run.[21]

On the Augustus day of Artemeisios [1 July], a competition for trumpeters and heralds, in which the victors will be given a prize of 50 *denarii*; then, after the meetings of the council and the assembly on the 5th, a competition for writers of encomia in prose, in which the victors will be given 75 *denarii*; the 6th day to be left clear because of the market which takes place then; the 7th, a competition for poets, in which the victors will be given 75 *denarii*; the 8th and 9th, a competition for playing the shawm with a chorus *(chorauleia)*, the first prizewinner will be given 125 *denarii*, and the second 75 *denarii*; the 10th and 11th, a competition for comic actors, the first prizewinner will be given 200 and the second 100 *denarii*; the 12th, a sacrifice for ancestral Apollo; the 13th and 14th, a competition for tragic actors, the first prizewinner will be given 250, and the second prizewinner 125 *denarii*; the 15th the second sacrifice for ancestral Apollo; and the 16th and 17th, a competition for *kitharôdoi* [singers accompanied with the lyre], who shall receive as first prize 300 *denarii* and as second prize 150 *denarii*; the 18th an open competition for all, for which will be given a first prize of 150 *denarii*, and a second of 100 *denarii*, and a third prize of 50 *denarii*; and 25 *denarii* will also be given to the person who provides the scenery; the 19th, 20th and 21st, hired performances among which will be mime artists, acts and displays, for which prizes are not provided; and the other acts which are for the benefit of the city are hired for these days, for which 600 *denarii* will be paid; the 22nd, gymnastic competitions for citizens, on which 150 *denarii* will be spent ...

Demosthenes makes a maximal use of familiar Greek categories: for all the events, for the order in which they were performed, and for their relative importance in his scheme of things (expressed by the value of the prizes) we can find parallels in other Greek cities of the Hellenistic and Roman period.[22] Demosthenes does not present this experience as something new, or so it would seem at least. Other festival

---

[21] *SEG* xxviii, 1462, ll. 37–46.
[22] Wörrle: 1988, 227–58; cf. Jones: 1990.

competitions in Oinoanda were cast in a similar traditional mould. Apart from the Demostheneia we know of five other festivals, most of which were athletic.[23] Statue bases in honour of the victors give us the names of wrestlers, pankratiasts, and boxers, all familiar figures of Greek athletics.

A third-century festival that was funded by a Lucius Pilius Euarestos is of particular interest here, as it seems to take a dual approach: initially set up as an athletic contest, it was later upgraded so as to include artistic competitions as well.[24] The reason may be obvious: the donor is described as *grammatikos:* he was the local orator, who taught (Greek) literature to the young men of the city, possibly in the colonnades of the *gymnasion.* An inscription in the *agora* allowed him to present himself as the guardian of Greek culture, which he defined in artistic as well as in athletic terms:

> *Agonothetês* for life, I have put up prizes for the strong in the famous stadia of athletic Heracles. But one who has earned his living from the Muses ought to have provided gifts for his own Muses; therefore having celebrated myself this fifth *themis*, I have put up prizes welcome to the Muses for artistic performances and, obedient to the holy command of Phoebus, son of Leto, I have adorned strong Alcides with the Muse. And I pray the immortals that my children, my city and my country will always celebrate these festivals, unharmed. Your wife's famous brother wrote this, Fronto, having trained his mind in composition.

It is significant that his "famous brother-in-law, Fronto" who seems to have composed part of the inscription, was himself a prominent wrestler who prided himself here on his literary skills as well.[25] Sport and literature are more or less equivalent and combinable signs of true *paideia,* Greek culture.

At first sight it looks as though the inhabitants of Oinoanda, and no doubt of countless other cities, were presented by such men with solid Greek Heritage stuff; that they were offered an image of themselves, of their own community, as standing in a long unchanging Greek tradition. But matters were more complicated than that. Oinoanda itself had a history that went no further back than the third century BCE, when it had been founded as a colony of Termessos.[26] More generally, the Greek character of Lycia was not unproblematic.[27] The Lycians had long lived at the fringes of the Greek world, but until the fourth century BCE they had not been part of it. They had sided with the Persians in the 480s (as they had done with the Trojans in an earlier conflict between Asians and Greeks), and they were finally drawn into the Greek world by Alexander.[28] For much of the Hellenistic period the Ptolemies were their formal overlords, but the Lycians maintained a high degree of independence, although their cities developed Greek-style political institutions. The arrival

---

[23] Hall and Milner: 1994 conveniently collects all the evidence for agonistic life in Oinoanda. The texts are reproduced in *SEG* xliv, 1165–1201.

[24] Hall and Milner: 1994, 8–30.

[25] See *SEG* xliv, 1165 for Fronto's victory. Strictly speaking there are two possibilities: Either Φρόντων is a nominative, in which case he is the author of at least part of the inscription, or it is a vocative, in which case the inscription is addressed to Fronto, whose statue was standing alongside that of his brother-in-law. Milner ad loc. discusses both options, but prefers to read Fronto as a nominative.

[26] Bean: 1978, 170.

[27] Bean: 1978, 19-31 and Farrington: 1995, 120–32 have brief historical surveys.

[28] Bean: 1978, 24.

of the Romans in the second century BCE had brought them freedom (in 167); the Lycian *koinon* became in this period their most important political body. They were formally incorporated as a province in the Roman Empire in combination with already provincialised Pamphylia by Claudius, but even then the *koinon* continued to function. They had set up inscriptions in their own language until the third century, and they retained a distinctive funerary culture until well into the Roman period. In material terms Greek-style public building had come only with Roman rule. It was only under the Roman emperors, and with their active support, that Lycians were inventing themselves as full-blown Greek communities. Seen in this light, agonistic festivals were an invented tradition that really flourished as part and parcel of this political-cultural package. So, Demosthenes' curiously old-fashioned programme was perhaps more of a novelty than it might have seemed.[29]

To pursue this point a little further: it remains to be seen how popular this brand of games was with the Oinoandians themselves. It is perhaps a sobering thought that there are no records in Oinoanda of any local victors in the artistic contests set up by Demosthenes. None of Euarestos' pupils seems to have been able to lay his hands on an artistic prize. The only seeming exceptions are consolation decrees set up for young boys who had showed enormous literary promise, but who unfortunately had died before they had been able to win anything.[30] Such documents are, of course, revealing of the self-image of the local élite, but they may mask a considerable degree of cultural inadequacy!

This phenomenon was not limited to Oinoanda: the festival of the Meleagreia in Balboura, which was explicitly modelled on the cultural programme of the Demostheneia did not yield any local cultural champions either.[31] The only local victors that we know of are boys and men who had won in the purely athletic competitions – mainly wrestling – that were appended to these cultural festivals. More than 130 years after Demosthenes set up his festival, one of his descendants decided to yield to the inevitable by making funds available also for prizes and statues in the athletics competitions that were open only to the citizens.[32]

Unless we assume either that victory in the artistic competitions was not valued enough by the local élites to warrant commemoration, or that it is a matter of chance that no artistic inscription has survived, we must conclude that local victories in these contests were scarce. The artistic competitions were probably dominated by travelling professional artists (*technitai*), who did not bother to record their victories in these rather modest local affairs.[33] It would seem, therefore, that just as the famous philosophical inscription of Diogenes appears to have failed to turn one single Oinoandian towards a more Epicurean lifestyle, the civilising offensive of Demosthenes and his peers similarly failed to generate much artistic activity among the locals. To them Greek culture apparently equalled Greek-style wrestling.

---

[29] Jones: 1990 emphasises that the purely cultural contest was a rarity not only in Oinoanda, but more widely in the Roman East.
[30] *SEG* xliv, 1191 and 1198.
[31] Milner: 1991.
[32] *SEG* xliv, 1183, 1184.
[33] They are discussed by Forbes: 1955; Pleket: 1973; Roueché: 1993. See Stefanis: 1988 for a prosopography.

It is important to adopt a proper perspective here. Wrestling was a highly respectable, and symbolically powerful aspect of ancient cultures. Its cultural significance may have been particularly high in these areas of Anatolia, where wrestling had been an important ritual activity long before the arrival of Greeks and Romans.[34] It should not surprise us that a process of acculturation took shape through a selective borrowing of cultural traits, particularly of those that harmonise most with earlier practices. Greek athletics were apparently adapted to suit the needs and potential of the locals.

Appropriation and adaptation of a past for purposes of the present are of course common features of invented traditions all over the world. The ideals behind cultural Hellenism were not politically innocent: these festivals were not just the antiquarian fads of schoolmasters. All over the eastern provinces, Hellenism was a major ideological force in the hands of local élites, used to provide a common identity to dominant groups in widely divergent cities and provinces.[35] Demosthenes, Euarestos, and others may well have expected that their attempts to present themselves as the servants of the Muses, as the protagonists of a Greek cultural revival, justified and legitimised their economic and political hold over their community. *Paideia* ("learning"), athletics included, was without a doubt a crucial element of the self-image of the urban élites in the Roman East, even in areas where the local population was not fully ethnically Greek.[36] Mastery of Greek culture might even have been of greater significance where the élites themselves were heavily implicated in the Roman administration, or especially when their own claim to Greekness was tenuous. Demosthenes was a member of the equestrian class (*equites*) and he had served the Roman administration as procurator in Sicily, before settling down in his hometown Oinoanda.[37] It should perhaps also be noted that the Pilii, the family of Euarestos, were the descendants of Roman traders– or perhaps of one of their freedmen.[38] The Greek festivals of the Roman Empire and their organisers were clearly implicated in the wider political developments of the time.

FESTIVALS AND THE EMPEROR

It is worthwhile pursuing this Roman connection a little further. It is important to note that Demosthenes' festival "was framed by its references to Roman power."[39] Care was taken to enlist the support of the "most cultured of emperors" (μουσικώτατος βασιλεύς in the words of Athenaeus).[40] Demosthenes was on his own account a personal acquaintance of Hadrian,[41] and the dossier opens with a letter from the emperor warmly recommending Demosthenes' project to the Oinoandians.

---

[34] See e.g. Poliakoff: 1987; for Anatolian predecessors, Carter: 1988; Puhvel: 1988.
[35] The importance of *paideia* is well explained in Brown: 1992, esp. ch. 2 "*Paideia* and power".
[36] Brown: 1992, 37.
[37] Wörrle: 1988, 55–69.
[38] Hall and Milner: 1994, 26.
[39] Jones: 1990, 487.
[40] Athenaeus 3.115B.
[41] *SEG* xxviii. 1462. ll. 103–4: τοῖς Σεβαστοῖς ἐ[πὶ τοῖς κ]αλλίστοις ἐγνωσμένος.

The emperor Caesar Trajan Hadrian Augustus, son of the god Trajan Parthicus and grandson of the god Nerva Germanicus, Pontifex Maximus, with tribunician power for the 8th time, consul for the 3rd time, greets the magistrates, council and people of the Termessians of Oinoanda. I praise Iulius Demosthenes for the patriotic zeal he has shown to you, and I confirm the musical competition which he has promised to you. He himself will contribute the cost from his own treasuries ...[42]

Who could resist a request like this? Once you begin to look for them, you will find imperial fingerprints all over the Demostheneia. The emperor and his cult pervaded every aspect of the foundation and the *panegyris*. The festival was supposed to start on the "Augustus day", i.e. the first day of the month (l. 14), the agonothete wears a crown with the image of the emperor (l. 55), imperial sacrifices were performed (ll. 57–8), and ten *sebastophoroi* ("imperial carriers") "dressed in white with crowns of wild celery" carried images of the emperor in the procession (ll. 62–3). It has been suggested, therefore, that the festival was especially designed to please Hadrian, whose cultural tastes were well known, and whose presence in the region may have prompted this remarkable display of loyalty.[43]

Not all emperors may have been as enthusiastic as Hadrian – of whom Aelius Aristides said that he had turned the whole empire into one gigantic festival procession – but they all were pleased to see these festivals as welcome expressions of loyalty. Local benefactors were ready to comply.[44] Most emperors at least allowed the cultivation of an image of themselves as the protectors of traditional Greek culture. Throughout the Roman East we can witness how Greek festivals were closely linked with emperors, in particular with the imperial cult. A good example is the festival of the Aktia, which Augustus instituted in 27 BCE at Nikopolis to celebrate his victory over Antony and Cleopatra.[45] The emperor declared that the Aktian Games were to have equal prestige with the traditional panhellenic games, and they were duly added to the circuit or *periodos*. He also founded similar games in Naples, the Sebasta in CE 2. Tiberius and Germanicus registered their interest in the Olympic Games by taking part, and – not surprisingly – they won.[46] Nero did the same, but the sources represent this as a PR débâcle.[47] Domitian set up a festival in Rome itself, the Capitolian Games (CE 86) which also acquired panhellenic status.[48] Later emperors also promoted Greek athletic festivals in Italy and in the provinces in various ways. Roman observers may have seen this as a deplorable new departure, but from a Greek perspective it was the logical outcome of a development that had already started under the Hellenistic kings.

At a more modest – local – level, traditional festivals also recognised the inevitability of Roman power; titles such as Augusteia and Sebasteia or other imperial titles

[42] *SEG* xxviii, 1462, ll. 1–3.
[43] Jones: 1990, 487–8.
[44] Mitchell: 1993, 219. Hadrian's successor may have been a little less keen on promoting festivals: his famous letter to the Ephesians commends a benefactor for offering the city buildings instead. The Ephesians had wanted the festival (*IK* 15 1493). Demosthenes could not be faulted on this: he also had paid for buildings, as we saw above.
[45] Herz: 1988.
[46] *IvO*, 220 (Tiberius) and 221 (Germanicus).
[47] Cf. Alcock: 1994.
[48] Cf. Caldelli: 1993.

were added to ancient names, and others were newly founded to honour specific emperors.[49] We may note that the festivals organised by Demosthenes' successors in Oinoanda all honoured Roman emperors through the addition of (temporary) imperial epithets,[50] and we know that he himself also organised a league-festival in honour of that most unlikely recipient of imperial cult, Vespasian.[51]

It should perhaps be noted here that Lycia was not unique in this respect: even in mainland Greece agonistic festivals were often the product of the imperial system. The rich agonistic life of Roman Sparta was mainly a creation of the imperial period, with at least two festivals, the Kaisareia and the Olympia Kommodeia explicitly set up in honour of Roman emperors.[52] Nor should we forget that the Athenian ritual calendar was fully reorganised under Hadrian, who not only introduced new games such as the Panhellenia, the Hadriania, the Olympia, and the Antinoeia in Eleusis, but who also restored the Panathenaic Games to something of their former splendour.[53] Even the Athenians sometimes had to be told how to be Greek.

Everywhere Greek agonistic festivals were used to accommodate the realities of Roman power, and to negotiate the relations between the local communities and the centre in Rome. Throughout the East the Roman imperial cult was probably the most important vehicle for the establishment of Greek agonistic festivals,[54] but even festivals that were not formally in honour of the emperors were suffused with references to Rome.

It is relevant to note that this development had been prefigured in the Republican period. The oldest Greek-style festival in Lycia (in Xanthos in 188 BCE) was called the *Romaia*, the Roman Games, thus raising the question of what it was that Lycians thought that they were doing: were they Hellenising or Romanising when they staged Greek-style contests?[55] Whatever else these festivals did, they certainly complicated any easy distinction between what was Greek and what was Roman.

THE STATUS OF THE PERFORMERS

So far I have looked at these festivals from the vantage-point of the organisers and imperial centre, but I should also like to investigate what these festivals meant to the competitors. Who were the athletes? And what was the place of athletics in civic life?

This is a complex story, and I cannot go into detail here, but some points need to be made. Modern histories of Greek athletics tend to repeat the old-fashioned prejudice that Greek athletics of the Roman period was increasingly a professional affair, with all the moral problems that came with that. Professionalism in sport – it is said – had driven the true amateurs out, and replaced them with uncultured

---

[49] Mitchell: 1993 has a convenient survey of emperors and festivals in Roman Asia Minor.
[50] Hall and Milner: 1994, 29.–30.
[51] *SEG* xliv, 1185.
[52] Cartledge and Spawforth: 1989, ch. 13.
[53] Follet: 1976, 317–50, Spawforth and Walker: 1985, 90–1, and Jones: 1996.
[54] Mitchell: 1993, 219.
[55] Robert: 1978.

musclemen. Lofty ideals and love of the sport had been replaced with greed and vulgarity. Yet, this simplistic picture cannot be maintained.[56]

We cannot deny that many competitors in the Roman period received considerable money prizes, and that in this sense they were professionals. It is also clear that the existence of cash prizes would have allowed talented individuals – without an independent source of income – to pursue an athletic career and earn large sums of money. Some of the most famous athletes of the Roman world may have followed this path. However, it is fair to say that by and large athletic competitions were not lower-class affairs. It is actually pretty difficult to put one's finger on athletes of demonstrably lower-class background. The international stars who toured the festivals of the Roman world are more often than not connected with the élites in the Greek cities.[57] If we were to look for modern parallels, I would rather compare them with international tennis players, than with football heroes such as Paul Gascoigne.

I shall provide one example from Oinoanda. Among the most celebrated of the Oinoandian athletes was the wrestler L. Septimius Flavianus Flavillianus. He is known from four inscriptions in Oinoanda that record his progress. The first text that mentions him is an honorific inscription of about CE 212 set up by the proud home-city (*patris*) when he had won the boys' wrestling in the Meleagreia. He was apparently already so promising that he was styled *paradoxos*.[58] In the 230s he appears to have won the men's wrestling and *pankration* in the same contest. One of the two inscriptions commemorating this achievement shows that in the meantime he had embarked on an international athletic career, listing his victories at Athens, Argos, Ephesos, and even at the Sebasta in Neapolis.[59] Finally, an inscription from 231–2 shows him again victorious in the *pankration* in the games organised by Euarestos. The inscription lists some of his other victories, and as a mark of status informs the reader that he had citizenship in no fewer than three Lycian cities.[60] To achieve such distinction, Flavillianus must have lived the life of a top sportsstar, dedicating time, money and effort to his considerable talents, of which he was clearly proud. He was, however, also a member of the aristocratic family of the Licinnii, well-known purveyors of Roman administrators and imperial priests. His father Flavianus Diogenes, was a Lyciarch – an official in the Lycian *koinon* – a position that was reserved only for the wealthiest and most respectable notables in the League.[61] Flavillianus' triple citizenship reflected his background as much as it did his athletic success.

---

[56] Gardiner: 1930; Harris: 1964; Harris: 1972. This whole debate is bound up with nineteenth-century prejudices about professionalism in sport, and an idealisation of the classical Greek past. Cf. Young: 1988. The excellent new account of Greek sport by Golden does not fall into this trap, but unfortunately does not concern itself with later Greek history (Golden: 1998).
[57] The same can of course be said about the athletes of the classical Greek world. For the argument that the upper classes were never absent from Graeco-Roman athletics see Pleket: 1974; Pleket: 1975; Pleket: 1992.
[58] *SEG* xliv, 1194.
[59] *SEG* xliv, 1195 and 1196.
[60] *SEC* xliv, 1169.
[61] He appears in the famous genealogical inscription of Licinnia: *IGR* III, 500 (V). Cf. Hall and Milner: 1994, 15, and Hall et al.: 1996, 122–3.

Yet, this distinguished aristocrat would happily have collected the cash prizes that were on offer at the games, or received the *opsônion* (pension) that some cities offered to successful performers.[62] But he would probably not have described himself as a "professional": his sport was not an *epitêdeuma*. There was a fine line between receiving money as a prize for an athletic achievement, and receiving money as a wage.

People like Flavillianus were dominating the international athletic scene.[63] There is no reason to assume that they insisted on a special identity by participating only in the more prestigious "stephanitic games" or that they shunned the more extreme (violent) sports: upper-class boxers, pankratiasts and wrestlers are as common as upper-class runners, pentathletes or musicians.

The main reason for this – perhaps surprising – state of affairs is that the essential training in athletics, just as that in literature and music, was closely bound up with the culture of the *gymnasion*, and this remained at all times the realm of a self-selecting crowd.[64] *Gymnasion* education may not have been limited to the bouleutic classes – we know of urban craftsmen and traders who registered an interest – but it will not have extended much beyond a broad middle class. Any long-term commitment to the *gymnasion*, however, must have been an option open only to the happy few. Despite occasional subsidies for talented youngsters from outside the élite, or individual sponsorships, athletes tended to come from well-to-do families, who could afford to spend the time and money needed for a lasting career in the *gymnasion*.[65]

The age-class most frequently associated with the *gymnasion* was that of the ephebes (roughly the 16 or 18 to 20 year-olds). Specialist teachers, hired by the city or paid for by benefactors, instructed them in the range of athletic, artistic and intellectual activities that were essential to the self-image of the local élites, as cultivated as well as cultural Greeks. Other age-groups, particularly the *paides* and the *geraioi* ("elders") were known to frequent the place as well.[66] Although the ephebes had to learn their Homer, of course, much of their time must have been dedicated to preparing for the athletic contests that were such a common feature of *gymnasion* life. *Gymnasion* regulations tell us that the boys and ephebes competed internally, inside the *gymnasion* in exactly the same disciplines as the adults in the official festivals.[67] Some cities went so far as to inscribe long lists of names of victors in these school games on the walls of public buildings, as happened for example at Termessos.[68]

From among this crowd *some* talented youngsters opted for a life as a full-time athlete and toured the international circuit, but most would compete only in the – often numerous – festivals of their own home town. The cities were keen

---

[62] Pliny, *Ep.* 10.118–19.
[63] For the parallel case of the Milesian *periodoneikês* and councillor Thelymitres, see Günther: 1986.
[64] Cartledge and Spawforth: 1989, 188–9. Kleijwegt: 1991, 75–88.
[65] *P.Zenon* 59060 for a case of sponsorship in Hellenistic Egypt. See also *IK* 16, 2005 with Robert: 1967, 8–32 for a case from Ephesus.
[66] van Rossum: 1988, 178–88.
[67] Gauthier and Hatzopoulos; 1993, 95.
[68] *TAM* III. 1, nos 199–206.

to immortalise the athletic successes of their sons, by statues and inscriptions. Victory in a foreign contest, especially in prestigious ones such as the Olympic Games, was highly prized, but victory in a local contest was also reason for celebration.[69] Hundreds of victory inscriptions were set up, often at prestigious, and symbolically important locations in the city: in the *agora*, in the *gymnasion*, alongside major roads. In Oinoanda, victors were commemorated alongside major benefactors and top magistrates in the *agora* and in the "Esplanade" (the old *agora*), where the inscription of Diogenes the Epicurean was found, and in many other prominent locations as well.[70] If we turn our attention to neighbouring Termessus, it becomes obvious to what extent the image of athletic victory could totally dominate an urban landscape. There were several spaces in this Pisidian city that were used for the public display of inscriptions: the *agora*, stoas around the *agora*, the *bouleuterion*, the main temple, the two *gymnasia* and a colonnaded avenue just north of the city centre. At all these places we find agonistic inscriptions, mainly honorific monuments for successful athletes. There was no escape: wherever you went in Termessus, you were confronted with the powerful image of the victorious youth.[71]

The situation in Termessus may have been exceptional, but the large numbers of agonistic inscriptions throughout Asia Minor suggests that athletic victory was one of the most powerful and widespread images around. Now, because we know the names of hundreds of successful athletes and performers, it can easily be demonstrated that the glittering prizes for artistic and athletic achievement – at least public commemoration of such successes – tended to go to those best fitted to receive them: the members of the leading families of the cities. Known local victors can routinely be linked to the prominent land-owning families (the same ones who provided also the magistrates and benefactors of the cities). The epigraphic record of Termessus illustrates the trend: the rich display of agonistic inscriptions served primarily to honour members of a few élite families.[72] What was at stake was not just the celebration of athletic success, but its social localisation in the hands of a few élite families. Victors are being praised for being wrestlers *and* priests, for being pankratiasts *and* benefactors; for being boxers *and* the scions of prominent families. Inscriptions seem to present athletic success as something of a birthright, a class-attribute among others like wealth, or benevolence, or indeed other aspects of *paideia*.

It is interesting to consider how this was achieved. The élites had a natural advantage, of course, when it came to securing epigraphical commemoration, as many inscriptions went back to private initiatives. Sometimes, however, more drastic steps were taken; in the Meleagreia in Balboura, for example. Most of its victory inscriptions run like this:

---

[69] The commemorative inscriptions often emphasised any victories in the traditional Panhellenic contests by mentioning these first. A boxer from Miletus stated that he had been *Olympioneikês Peisaios*, i.e. that he had won in the original Olympic Games, not in some local imitation! (*I Milet* II, 500).

[70] Hall and Milner: 1994 with maps on pp. 10, 12, 14, and 16.

[71] The inscriptions can be found in *TAM* III.1, nos 141–213. There is a map on p 365. Appendix I gives precise information of the location of individual inscriptions. I discuss the organisation of the epigraphic display in Termessos in: van Nijf: forthcoming.

[72] Cf. *TAM* III.1. Appendix V: "Stemmata gentium" for the most prominent families.

In the first agonotheteship for life of Thoantianos, son of Thoantianos, son of Meleager, son of Castor, the festival celebrated now also for the 4th time from the gift of Meleager son of Castor, his grandfather: Mousaios (son of Mousaios, son of Mousalos, son of Troilos, son of Mousaios, son of Polydeukes) alias Kalandion, a man of first rank in the city, kinsman of League officials of the Nation, his father a League Official, having won the men's wrestling.[73]

The inscription celebrates the victor as well as the organiser of the games; there is a lot of attention given to the (prominent) families of the two men, who bask in the reflected glory. But accidents did happen. One victor mentions only an ethnic, where others listed their entire pedigree: was this because he had no pedigree worth mentioning?[74] Such an outcome was embarrassing, and may have been avoided where possible. A small number of inscriptions honour joint winners of the wrestling-contests: it is interesting to note that in nearly all these cases, one of the joint winners is well connected, and clearly identifiable as a member of the élite, whereas the other one seems much less distinguished (short or no pedigree, no officials to boast about and so on).[75] It is just conceivable that the (élite) judges in these wrestling-matches would step in and declare a draw, at the moment that a less well-connected wrestler was about to win. No doubt, such a decision was justified – against a popular outcry? – with reference to historic precedent: had Achilles not likewise intervened in the wrestling-contest between Odysseus and Aias? "You have both won", they may have said, "take equal prizes and withdraw."[76]

Finally, we should perhaps get really suspicious, when we find honorific inscriptions set up for athletes who had competed honourably, but who somehow had not managed to win anything. Valerius Hermaios is an example from Oinoanda. He had taken part "with distinction" in the boys' wrestling in CE 207. He had not won, but his father was the agonothete, so he got a statue anyway.[77] There are apparently people who did not need to win to acquire an honorific statue.[78]

If nothing else, these texts make clear that physical excellence was still a major criterion of masculinity, and of élite status. Maud Gleason, I suggest, makes a wrong assumption when she writes:

> Perhaps physical strength once had been the definitive criterion of masculine excellence on the semi-legendary playing fields of Ilion and Latium, but by Hellenistic and Roman times the sedentary elite of the ancient city had turned away from warfare and gymnastics as definitive agonistic activities, firmly redrawing the defining lines of competitive space so as to exclude those without wealth, education or leisure.[79]

Quite the contrary: men were still being made in the *gymnasion*, and athletic success was no less a prerequisite for élite status and for claiming a Greek identity than were rhetorical or literary skills.

---

[73] *SEG* xli, 1345.
[74] Milner: 1991, 39, no. 11 (= *CIG* 4380h): cf. *SEG* xli, 1353.
[75] Milner: 1991, 34, no. 7 (= *CIG* 4380g): cf. *SEG* xli, 1349; *SEG* xli, 1352.
[76] *Illiad* 23.735; "Do not contend any longer or wear yourselves out with these evils. You have both won; take equal prizes and withdraw" (Μηκέτ' ἐρείδεσθον, μηδὲ τρίβεσθε κακοῖσι | νίκῃ δ'ἀμφοτέροισιν | ἀέθλια δ'ἶσ' ἀνελόντες).
[77] *SEG* xliv, 1191: another example: *SEG* xli, 1351.
[78] Robert: 1960, 356–8 for more examples.
[79] Gleason: 1995, 159.

FESTIVALS AND THE SOCIAL ORDER

So far, I have demonstrated that agonistic festivals were a major ingredient of Greek culture under Roman rule. I have argued that festivals were heavily implicated in the symbolic structures that upheld Roman rule, and I have suggested that they served the class interests of an élite which was eager to establish its Greek credentials. One might then justifiably ask, what role there was in all this for the common man, the ordinary citizen of Oinoanda and other cities of the Roman East? What did such festivals do for them?

It is always possible of course that the citizens actually enjoyed the rhetorical and poetical contests that Demosthenes had set up. Maud Gleason even thinks that "the form of competitive masculine activity that proved most electrifying as a spectator sport was rhetoric".[80] I rather suspect that this popularity was a mirage fabricated by the sophists themselves. Demosthenes drops some hints as to what constituted real popular entertainment: towards the end of the festival (on days 19 to 21) he provides for: "hired performances among which will be mime artists, acts and displays ... and other acts which are for the benefit of the city."[81]

If these entertainments featured performers such as the Carthaginian *ischyropaiktês* (strong man), of whom we know from Delphi, or the *kinaidologos* (reciter of obscene songs) whose tombstone was found in Apollonia, or some other type of juggler or entertainer, we might conclude that a rift sometimes existed between the tastes of the masses, and those of the happy few around Demosthenes.[82] But it is significant that he made this concession to popular taste. Moreover this was a practice common enough to lead some moralists to issue a stern warning to would-be politicians and benefactors, that they ran the risk of "enslaving" themselves to the masses by putting on these displays.[83] It is conceivable, too, that the ordinary citizens would enjoy the tax-free festival market that was appended to the main celebration, which would offer an opportunity to buy the odd luxury import, and perhaps to eat some special delicacies.[84] Finally, like many other benefactors, Demosthenes arranged also for money-distributions and sacrificial banquets which to the recipients may well have represented the *pièce de résistance* of the whole show.[85]

It is important, however to consider what Demosthenes is doing with these standard ingredients of Greek festivals. It is often assumed that civic euergetism was undifferentiated, and that its benefits were showered upon the cities as a whole.[86] Recent studies have demonstrated, however, that civic benefactions often displayed a tremendous concern with the corporate order of society. This was particularly so in the case of civic banquets and public distributions of food or money, which were

---

[80] Gleason: 1995, 159.
[81] *SEG* xxxviii, 1462, ll. 44–5.
[82] The *kinaidologos* in Cabanes: 1997, no. 226; the others are mentioned in Robert: 1928, 422–5.
[83] Quet: 1981 on Dio Chrysostom and Plutarch.
[84] The *panegyris* is discussed by Wörrle: 1988, 209–15. For a general discussion see de Ligt: 1993; de Ligt and de Neeve: 1988. For the special foodstuffs consumed at festivals, cf. van Nijf: 1998, 332–3.
[85] See Schmitt-Pantel: 1992 for an excellent study of the role of public banquets and distributions in Greek society.
[86] Veyne: 1976; for a critique of this position, see Rogers: 1991a, esp. 97. and my discussion in van Nijf: 1997, 156–88.

well suited for expressing status differentials, as has been amply demonstrated in the case of the *sportulae* ("handouts") in the towns of Roman Italy.[87] I have argued elsewhere that benefactors in the Roman East also adopted this practice.[88]

So, what happened in Oinoanda? Early on in the inscription Demosthenes arranges for *dianomai* (hand-outs) to sub-sections of Oinoandian society:

> anything else that is remaining from the prizes of competitors who by chance do not appear, will be given as a judges' fee to the members of the *boule* and to the *sitometroumenoi* ("recipients of the distribution") since the *bouleutai* should serve as judges and *sitometroumenoi* who are not members of the *boule* should be picked by lot until a total of 500 is reached, so that each receives three *denarii*; and the remaining 300 *denarii* and anything left over from the prizes shall be divided between the citizens who are not among the *sitometroumenoi* and the freedmen and the country dwellers (*paroikoi*) ...[89]

Other benefactors in Oinoanda envisaged a similar line-up for their hand-outs, thereby giving a monetary expression to social hierarchy.[90] There are other instances in the Demostheneia where an image of the social order in Oinoanda was presented. Demosthenes gave instructions for a civic procession, consisting of the main magistrates and officials of the city (most of whom belonged to the same social class as Demosthenes himself):

> The following will process through the theatre and will sacrifice together during the days of the festival, according to the way the agonothete gives written instructions for each communal sacrifice: the agonothete himself, one bull; the civic priest of the emperors and the priestess of the emperors, one bull; the priest of Zeus, one bull; the 3 panegyriarchs, one bull; the secretary of the council and the 5 *prytaneis*, 2 bulls; the 2 *agoranomoi* ("market officials") of the city, one bull; the 2 gymnasiarchs, one bull; the 4 treasurers, one bull; the 2 *paraphylakes* ("officials in charge of defence"), one bull; the ephebarch, one bull; the *paidonomos*, one bull; the supervisor of public buildings, one bull; of the villages with their associated farmsteads, one bull [here follows a list of names of villages on the territory of Oinoanda ...[91]

The procession produces a kind of image of society. It is not a perfect image, but at best an approximation: it exaggerates the importance of some groups, and neglects others.[92] Civic rituals like these do not list every social category, only those that are deemed worthy to express social values. They thus provide an idealised representation of society which corresponds structurally rather than formally to the "social reality".

[87] Duncan-Jones: 1982, 138–44: cf. van Nijf: 1997, 152–6.
[88] I discuss the cases of Aba of Histria and Epaminondas of Akraiphia and several others in van Nijf: 1997, 149–88.
[89] Wörrle: 1988, SEG xxxviii, 25 ff. The *sitometroumenoi* (grain recipients) were a privileged group of citizens in several Lycian cities. They appear most often as a separate category in hand-outs of money or grain. See: Wörrle: 1988, 123–34.
[90] SEG xliv, 1187: Marcia Aurelia Polykleia directs her *dianomai* to the "500" (10 *denarii* each), to the *demotai* (2 *denarii* each), to the perpetual *sebastophoroi*, the *sebastophoroi* for the day and the *mastigophoroi* (1 *denarius* per day).
[91] SEG xxxviii, 1462, 67–74.
[92] This type of analysis of ritual has been very fruitful in the case of early modern Europe: classic examples are Muir: 1981, and Darnton: 1984; see also Muir: 1997. These methods were successfully applied to the ancient world by Rogers: 1991b and Price: 1985, esp, ch. 5. I have myself used the concept of civic rituals in the context of ritual representation of professional associations in van Nijf: 1997.

Such ritual occasions are not only a model *of* society, they are also set up as a model *for* society. The details of the idealised image are dictated by the interests of the ruling classes. They set themselves apart from the others and define, through ritual, the relationships among the groups that made up society. These distributions, banquets and processions are, to use Robert Darnton's phrase, a way in which people "put their world in order".[93]

Demosthenes' view of the local hierarchy may not have been the only one available; his colleagues may have wanted to fill in the details rather differently. Indeed such a ritual order may have been used to gloss over deeper divisions in society. The image projected by Demosthenes may have been contested by some of his compatriots. Guy Rogers has argued that the inscription shows signs of protracted negotiations in the background, exactly centring on issues such as ritual representation.[94] Indeed no society exists in which there are not conflicting ideas of how the world should be ordered. "Political rituals tend to camouflage such tensions, especially by representing more political harmony than might actually exist."[95] At any rate, Demosthenes himself clearly reckoned with the possibility that the festival would occasion ritual violence. The agonothete had to appoint a "police force" of "twenty μαστιγοφόροι (whip carriers) dressed in white clothing without underwear, also carrying shields and whips, who will be in charge of good order in the theatre (ἐν τοῖς θεάτροις εὐκοσμία)".[96]

We may also point to the two agelarchai ("supervisors") who were to be chosen from boys of the noblest families (εὐγενέστατοι παῖδες) in order to supervise the activities of another potential source of trouble: young children. With these precautions in place, the scene was set for an orderly display of civic unity.

The fact that Demosthenes and his colleagues were able to persuade the population to act out their versions of the local hierarchy in huge mass-participation rituals, and could have the detailed arrangements for these set in stone, suggests that they were able to impose their own sense of order on their fellow Oinoandians. Through the ritual they persuaded their fellow citizens, their Roman overlords, and no doubt themselves, that they had succeeded in their mission to keep the population under control, to maintain a *"quietissimus populus"*.[97]

The cumulative effect of the many festivals that the Lycian benefactors organised was to establish these benefactors, and the members of their families, not only as the guardians of Greek culture, but also as a separate, superior stratum in society. Festive euergetism thus helped to legitimise an increasingly oligarchic political system, which was securely locked into an all-embracing imperial system. It can be seen that the preservation – or invention – of such traditional elements of Greek culture as artistic and athletic festivals was not simply a matter of love of sport, of dry antiquarianism, or even of a romantic harking back to a Greek past: these games were used to project an image of a well-ordered society to the outside world

---

[93] Darnton: 1984.
[94] Rogers: 1991a.
[95] Muir: 1997, 230.
[96] *SEG* xxxviii, 1462, ll. 63–4.
[97] Brown: 1992.

by presenting a local hierarchy with the members of pro-Roman élites firmly in control. The emperor must have loved it.

CONCLUSION

To sum it all up then: there have been three related arguments running through my paper.

1. I have used mainly epigraphic evidence to show the vital importance of traditional Greek festivals for civic life in the Greek East. I have focused on a few cities, but thousands of agonistic inscriptions, honouring athletes and performers, commemorating benefactors and thanking emperors, not to mention the archaeological remains of *gymnasia*, *stadia*, theatres, testify to the popularity of festivals throughout the Greek East. From the vantage-point of the ordinary provincial, Greek civic culture under Roman rule was a markedly festive culture.

2. I have also argued that the Greek festive culture of the Roman period was appropriated to serve the needs both of the local élites, and of the central authorities in Rome. It mobilised the resources of a glorious Greek past enabling urban élites to display their social superiority in several ways. But at the same time it was clearly focused on Rome and the emperor, who ultimately underwrote the hierarchical world-view of which it was an expression. Festivals were in many important respects an invented tradition that effectively blurred the boundaries between Greek and Roman.

3. Finally, I have made a case for athletics as an alternative passport to Greek identity. There can be no doubt that a small and hyper-literate élite continued to define Greek *paideia* exclusively in terms of access to a formal literary and rhetorical culture, and they may well have been the dominant voice. I suspect, however, that many people – members of local elites as well as upwardly mobile individuals – would have found athletic competition a more attractive way of staking out a claim to Greek identity and social status.

Agonistic festivals, then, were used to promote interpretations of the past that were highly coloured by contemporary political events; they set out the rules for a social hierarchy, and located these firmly within an imperial context. The main beneficiaries of these rituals were of course the members of the élite classes: the councillors, and their families who funded the festivals. Their social importance was underlined by the hierarchical set-up of the processions and sacrificial banquets, and they often had the front seats in the *stadia* from where they could watch their sons as the intended star-performers of the shows. Agonistic festivals were not least an occasion for the local elites to put *their* world in order. Greek festivals had always had "political" functions, but it would seem that with the passing of time these became more important. Greek athletic festivals of the Roman period made clear what a city was about, what everybody's place was, and what principles were underlying the social order. Games and festivals were serious play.

WORKS CITED

Alcock, S. E. (1994) "Nero at play? The emperor's Grecian Odyssey" in J. Elsner and J. Masters (eds) *Reflections of Nero: culture, history and representation* (London) 98–111.

Andreau, J., Schmitt, P. and Schnapp, A. (1978) "Paul Veyne et l'évergétisme" *Annales ESC* 33(2): 307–25.

Bean, G. E. (1978) *Lycian Turkey* (London).

Brown, P. (1992) *Power and persuasion in late antiquity: towards a Christian empire* (Madison).

Burkert, W. (1987) "Die antike Stadt als Festgemeinschaft" in P. Hugger, W. Burkert and E. Lichtenhahn (eds) *Stadt und Fest. Zur Geschichte und Gegenwart europäischer Festkultur* (Stuttgart) 25–44.

Cabanes, P. (ed.) (1997) *Études épigraphiques grecques 2. Corpus des inscriptions grecques d'"Illyrie méridionale et d'Épire 1.2* (Paris).

Caldelli, M. L (1993) *L'agon Capitolinus. Storia e protagonisti dall'istituzione domiziana al IV secolo* (Rome).

Carter, C. (1988) "Athletic contests in Hittite festivals", *Journal of Near Eastern Studies* 47: 185–7.

Cartledge, P. A. (1985) "Greek religious festivals" in P. E. Easterling. and J. V. Muir, (eds) *Greek religion and society* (Cambridge), 98–127.

Cartledge, P. and Spawforth, A. (1989) *Hellenistic and Roman Sparta* (London).

Darnton, R. (1984) "A bourgeois puts his world in order: the city as a text" in *The great cat massacre and other episodes in French cultural history* (Harmondsworth), 105–40.

de Ligt, L. and de Neeve. P. W. (1988) "Ancient periodic markets: festivals and fairs", *Athenaeum* 66: 391–416.

de Ligt, L. (1993) *Fairs and markets in the Roman empire. Economic and social aspects of periodic trade in a pre-industrial society* (Amsterdam).

Decker, W. (1995) *Sport in der griechischen Antike. Vom minoischen Wettkampf bis zu den Olympischen Spielen* (Munich).

Duncan-Jones, R. P. (1982) *The economy of the Roman empire. Quantitative studies* (Cambridge; ed. 2; 1st ed. 1974).

Ebert, J. (1997) "Zur neuen Bronzeplatte mit Siegerinschriften aus Olympia (Inv. 1148)", *Nikephoros* 10: 217–33 (reprinted in J. Ebert, *Agonismata* (Stuttgart and Leipzig 1997), 317–35).

Farrington, A, (1995) *The Roman baths of Lycia. An architectural study* (Ankara/London).
(1997) "Olympic victors, and the popularity of the Olympic Games in the imperial period" *Tyche* 12: 15–46.

Finley, M. I. and Pleket, H. W. (1976) *The Olympic Games, the first thousand years* (London).

Follet, S. (1976) *Athènes au IIe et au III siècle. Études chronologiques et prosopographiques* (Paris).

Forbes, C. A. (1955) "Ancient athletic guilds", *Classical Philology* 50: 238–52.

Gardiner, E. N. (1930) *Athletics of the ancient world* (Oxford).

Garnsey, P. (1991) The generosity of Veyne", *Journal of Roman Studies* 81: 164–8.

Gauthier, P. and Hatzopoulos, M. B. (1993) *La Loi gymnasiarchique de Beroia* (Athens).

Gleason, M. W. (1995) *Making men: sophists and self-representation in ancient Rome* (Princeton).

Golden, M. (1998) *Sport and society in ancient Greece* (Cambridge).

Günther, W. (1986) "Ehrungen für einen Milesischen Periodoniken" in H. Kalcyk, B. Gulath and A. Graeber (eds) *Studien zur alten Geschichte S. Lauffer zum 70. Geburtstag dargebracht* (Rome) 316 ff.

Hall, A. and Milner, N. (1994) "Education and athletics. Documents illustrating the festivals of Oenoanda" in D. French (ed.) *Studies in the history and topography of Lycia and Pisidia in memoriam A. S. Hall* (Oxford), 7–47.

Hall, A., Milner, N. P. and Coulton, J. J. (1996) "The mausoleum of Licinnia Flavilla and Flavianus Diogenes of Oenoanda: epigraphy and architecture", *Anatolian Studies* 46: 111–44.

Harl, K. W. (1987) *Civic coins and civic politics in the Roman East AD 180–275* (Berkeley).

Harris, H. A. (1964) *Greek athletes and athletics* (London).

(1972) *Sport in Greece and Rome* (London).

Herz, P. (1988) "Die Entwicklung der griechischen Agonistik in der Kaiserzeit" in N. Müller and M. Messing (eds) *Olympische Studien* (Niedernhausen) 111–31.

Jones, C. P. (1990) "A new Lycian dossier establishing an artistic contest and festival in the reign of Hadrian", *Journal of Roman Archaeology* 3: 484–8.

(1996) "The Panhellenion", *Chiron* 11: 29–56.

Kleijwegt, M. (1991) *Ancient youth. The ambiguity of youth and the absence of adolescence in Greco-Roman society* (Amsterdam).

Milner, N. P. (1991). "Victors in the Meleagria and the Balbouran élite", *Anatolian Studies* 41: 23–62.

Mitchell, S. (1990). "Festivals, games, and civic life in Roman Asia Minor", *Journal of Roman Studies* 80: 183–93.

(1993) *Anatolia. Land, men and gods in Asia Minor, i. The Celts in Anatolia and the impact of Roman rule* (Oxford).

Moretti, L. (1957) "Olympionikai, i vincitori negli antichi agoni olimpici", *Memorie della classe di scienze morali e storiche dell'accademia dei Lincei, Rome* 8 (Ser. 8a): 59–198.

(1970) "Supplemento al catalogo degli Olympionikai", *Klio* 52: 295–303.

(1992) "Nuovo supplemento al catalogo degli Olympionikai" in W. Coulson and H. Kyrieleis (eds) *Proceedings of an international symposium on the Olympic Games, 5–9 September 1988* (Athens) 119–28.

Muir, E. (1981) *Civic ritual in Renaissance Venice* (Princeton).

(1997) *Ritual in early modern Europe* (Cambridge).

Pleket, H. W. (1973) "Some aspects of the history of athletic guilds", *Zeitschrift für Papyrologie und Epigraphik* 10: 197–227.

(1974) "Zur Soziologie des antiken Sports", *Mededelingen van het Nederlands Historisch Instituut te Rome* 36: 57–87.

(1975) "Games, prizes, athletes and ideology: some aspects of the history of sport in the Graeco-Roman world", *Stadion* I: 49–89.

(1978) "Olympic benefactors", *Zeitschrift für Papyrologie und Epigraphik* 20: 1–18.

(1992) "The participants in the ancient Olympic games: social background and mentality" in W. Coulson and H. Kyrieleis (eds) *Proceedings of an international symposium on the Olympic Games, 5–9 September 1988* (Athens), 147–52.

Poliakoff, M. B. (1987) *Combat sports in the ancient world. Competition, violence, and culture* (New Haven and London).

Price, S. (1985) *Rituals and power: the Roman imperial cult in Asia Minor* (Cambridge).

Puhvel, J. (1988) "Hittite athletics as prefigurations of ancient Greek games" in W. J. Raschke (ed.) *The archaeology of the Olympics. The Olympics and other festivals in antiquity* (Madison) 26–31.

Quet, M.-H. (1981) "Remarques sur la place de la fête dans les discours de moralistes grecs et dans l'éloge des cités et des évergètes aux premières siècles de l'Empire" in *La fête, pratique et discours, d'Alexandrie hellénistique à la mission de Besançon* (Paris/Besançon)

41–84. (Centre de recherches d'histoire ancienne. Annales littéraire de l'Université de Besançon, volume 42).
Rigsby, K. J. (1996) *Asylia. Territorial inviolability in the Hellenistic world* (Berkeley and Los Angeles).
Robert, L. (1928) "Études épigraphiques. Première serie", *Bulletin des correspondances Helleniques* 52: 407–25 [= OMS II 878–96].
—— (1960) *Hellenica* 11–12 (Paris).
—— (1967) "Sur des inscriptions d'Éphèse", *Revue de Philologie*: 7–84 [= OMS VI 347–424].
—— (1974) "Les femmes théores à Éphèse", *Comptes Rendues de l'Académie des Inscriptions et Belles Lettres*: 176–81 [= OMS V 669–74].
—— (1978) "Catalogue agonistique des Rômaia de Xanthos", *Revue Archéologique*: 277–90 [= OMS VII, 681–95].
—— (1982) "Discours d'"ouverture" in Πρακτικά του Η' διεθνούς συνεδρίου Ελληνικής και Λατινικής επιγραφικής, Αθήνα, 3–9 Οκτωβρίου 1982, τόμος Α (Athens) 35–45. [= OMS VI 709-19].
Rogers, G. M. (1991a), "Demosthenes of Oenoanda and models of euergetism", *Journal of Roman Studies* 81: 91–100.
—— (1991b) *The sacred identity of Ephesos* (London).
Roueché, C. (1993) *Performers and partisans at Aphrodisias in the Roman and late Roman periods: a study based on inscriptions from the current excavations at Aphrodisias in Caria* (London).
Schmitt-Pantel, P. (1992) *La Cité au banquet. Histoire des repas publics dans les cités grecques* (Rome).
Spawforth, A. (1989) "Agonistic festivals in Roman Greece" in S. Walker and A. Cameron (eds) *The Greek Renaissance in the Roman Empire. Papers from the 10th British Museum classical colloquium*: 193–7
Spawforth, A. and Walker, S. (1985) "The world of the Panhellenion, i: Athens and Eleusis", *Journal of Roman Studies* 75: 78–104.
Stefanis, I. E. (1988) Διονυσιακοί τεχνίται. Σύμβολες στην προσωπογραφία του θεάτρου και της μουσικής των αρχαίων Ελλήνων (Iraklio).
van Nijf, O. M. (1997) *The civic world of professional associations in the Roman East* (Amsterdam).
—— (1998) "Het dagelijks brood: de prijsinscripties in Ephese", *Lampas* 31(4): 321–35.
—— (forthcoming) "Inscriptions and civic memory in the Roman East" in A. Cooley (ed.) *The afterlife of inscriptions* (Oxford).
van Rossum, J. A. (1988) *De gerousia in de Griekse steden van het Romeinse Rijk* (Diss. Leiden).
Veyne, P. (1976) *Le Pain el le cirque. Sociologie historique d'un pluralisme politique* (Paris).
Wörrle, M. (1988) *Stadt und Fest in kaiserzeitlichen Kleinasien. Studien zu einer agonistischen Stiftung aus Oenoanda* (München).
Young, D. C. (1988) "How amateurs won the Olympics?" in W. J. Raschke (ed.) *The archaeology of the Olympics. The Olympics and other festivals in antiquity* (Madison), 55–75.
Ziegler, R. (1985) *Städtisches Prestige und kaiserliche Politik. Studien zum Festwesen in Ostkilikien im 2. und 3. Jahrhundert n. Chr.* (Düsseldorf).

PART V

Athletic Representations

Introduction to Part V

The problems of representation are of course everywhere in the material we have looked at already, but here I want to turn to two articles which come to grips in more depth with particular bodies of literary or artistic material. Both, in particular, deal, albeit in very different ways, with the function of athletic images, which were such a familiar sight in the ancient world.[1]

Leslie Kurke's focus is on the prestige of athletic victory. She stresses that at least for the period of the sixth and fifth centuries BCE, we need to understand that athletic victory was not simply the object of idealisation, but was felt to have an almost talismanic power. That power – *kudos* in Greek – was embodied in the athlete's crown, and as such could be passed on to the athlete's home city when the crown was dedicated there. One of the functions of athletic victory statues was to compensate the victorious athlete for this donation of his *kudos*, as part of a wider process of reintegrating him into the community. She also suggests that the statues invited the viewer to relive and so perpetuate the moment of the athlete's original crowning. Finally, she discusses the phenomenon of athletes who were worshipped as heroes, and suggests that this happened in particular when there is an imbalance in the "economy of *kudos*", for example when an athlete has excessive *kudos*, or alternatively when an athlete's statue is damaged, or an athlete is not honoured with a statue in the proper way.[2] Others more recently have followed Kurke's New-Historicist approach to Pindar.[3] Particularly important here is the work of Nigel Nicholson, who picks up on Kurke's discussion of the talismanic prestige of victory, and draws attention to some of the silences which help to reinforce that ideology.[4] He shows how the ideal of athletic victory as a demonstration of inborn aristocratic virtue is maintained by consistent suppression of the involvement of the lower-class figures, such as athletic trainers and charioteers and jockeys, on whom that victory often depended.

In the second article for the section we jump ahead by half a millennium to Greek athletics under Rome. Zahra Newby's article carries forward many of

---

[1] On athletic victory statues Hyde (1921) is still a useful account; see also Rausa (1994) (in Italian).
[2] On heroisation of athletes, see also Bohringer (1979) (in French).
[3] See Kurke (1991) for further discussion of Pindar. Other good introductions to Pindar's representations of athletic victory include Lee (1983) and Spivey (2004) 135–47.
[4] Nicholson (2005); see also (amongst others) Burnett (2005).

the themes raised by the second of the Robert articles, in chapter 6. As we have seen, one of the consequences of Robert's work is the breaking down of any clear dichotomy between Greek and Roman attitudes to spectacle. Rome was itself, by the second century CE, an important city in the Greek festival calendar. In the past, as I suggested briefly in the introduction to this volume, it has been thought that Roman interest in Greek athletic images did nothing to prove any wider interest in athletic practice. One of Newby's achievements in this piece and elsewhere is to complicate that picture, through careful examination of images of athletes, particularly mosaic images, in their original contexts. She sketches evidence for Roman suspicion of Greek sport in the Republican period, but then goes on to suggest that much of the mosaic evidence, most of it dating from the first to third centuries CE, points to Roman interest not only in athletic festival contests, which would have been familiar in particular because of the festival of the Capitolia celebrated at Rome from the reign of Domitian onwards, but also a related interest in gymnastic training. In the latter case, the placement of athletic images in areas of bath buildings used for gymnastic exercise encourages an identification between the exercisers and the Greek-style mosaic figures. More generally speaking, she makes an important contribution – as also in her other publications on the subject[5] – to expanding our view of the richness and variety of the ancient world's athletic imagery.

This section might well have spent more time reviewing the complexities of literary representation of athletic activity; in fact, a differently organised volume might have found a separate section for that topic on its own. There are relevant publications on a great range of different texts: the athletic contests of ancient epic, ranging from Homer to Virgil and beyond;[6] athletic subjects in the literature – especially tragedy and comedy – of fifth- and fourth-century Athens;[7] or in the Greek novelistic or rhetorical literature of the Roman Empire.[8] Nevertheless, it seems to me that there is a certain appropriateness in dealing with literary and artistic representation together simply because, as Kurke's article shows so vividly, and as we saw also in the text from Philostratus' *Imagines* discussed in the introduction, quasi-visual description of the athletic body was a key feature of literary engagement with ancient athletics.[9] Both satirical and idealising writings on the subject rely on the ubiquity and familiarity of images of the athletic body, revelling in their own capacity to conjure up images of athletic physicality before the mind's eye of their readers. In much the same way we see literary descriptions of athletics regularly drawing on the language of inscriptions.[10] That cross-fertilisation illustrates vividly why an understanding of ancient athletic culture requires command

---

[5] See esp. Newby (2002) and (2005).
[6] E.g., see Kitchell (1998) and Kyle (1984) and (2007) 54–71 on athletics in Homer, with special reference to the funeral games of Patroklos in *Iliad* 23; Willis (1941), Briggs (1975), Lovatt (2005) and König (2005) 205–53 on athletics in Latin epic.
[7] For critical accounts of athletics in classical Athens, see Kyle (1987) 124–54.
[8] See König (2005), with reference in particular to Lucian, Dio Chrysostom, Pausanias, Galen and Philostratus.
[9] See also König (2005) 97–157 on Dio Chrysostom's orations in honour of the deceased athlete Melankomas, described in statuesque and idealising terms.
[10] See König (2005).

over such a wide variety of different sources. If we compartmentalise these different spheres of athletic representation, assuming they should be studied separately, we cut ourselves off from the full richness and multifacetedness of ancient reimaginings of sporting achievement.

9 *The Economy of* Kudos*

LESLIE KURKE

This volume was organised (at least partly) to see if the method and interests of the New Historicism could fruitfully be applied to the study of archaic Greece. "CULTURAL POETICS", the term Stephen Greenblatt coined to characterise his approach, aims to break down the barriers between literary text and cultural/historical context. It encourages us to "read" texts as context, and history itself as text, both informed by multiple, competing symbolic strategies and symbolic economies.[1] My aim in this essay is to develop a cultural poetics of athletic victory in the sixth and fifth centuries BCE, drawing on the "high art" of *epinikion* but not depending on it exclusively to establish the circulation of powers and honors that subtended athletic success.

I begin with an observation and a question. The observation is the persistent connection between *kudos* and crowns in the diction of *epinikion*. For example, in *Olympian* 4 Pindar prays to Zeus:

> Receive this Olympic-victory *kômos* by the grace of the Charites, the longest-lasting light of achievements broad in strength. For it comes from the chariots of Psaumis who, crowned with olive from Pisa, hastes to rouse *kudos* for Kamarina. (*Ol.* 4.8–12)[1a]

---

* A shorter version of this essay was delivered at the 1990 American Philological Association Annual Meeting in San Francisco, and the section on victor statues was presented as a talk at Dartmouth College in October 1992. I owe thanks to Martin Bloomer, Tom Cole, W. R. Connor, Joseph Day, Crawford Greenewalt Jr, Tom Habinek, Paula Perlman, Seth Schwartz, Deborah Steiner, Kate Toll, and Emily Vermeule for reading and commenting on various versions. The contributions of Carol Dougherty to the essay's substance and organization require special thanks: even when the work has not been "officially" collaborative, she has made a tremendous difference. Originally published in Dougherty, C. and Kurke, L. (eds) *Cultural Poetics in Archaic Greece: Cult, Performance, Politics* (Cambridge: Cambridge University Press, 1993), pp. 131–63.

[1] See Greenblatt 1980, 1988; Veeser 1989.

[1a] Οὐλυμπιονίκαν
δέξαι Χαρίτων θ'ἕκατι τόνδε κῶμον,
χρονιώτατον φάος εὐρυσθενέων ἀρετᾶν
   Ψαύμιος γὰρ ἵκει
ὀχέων, ὃς ἐλαίᾳ στεφανωθεὶς Πισάτιδι κῦδος ὄρσαι
σπεύδει Καμαρίνᾳ.
[1b]   ἐπεὶ στεφάνους
ἐξ ὤπασεν Κάδμου στρατῷ ἐξ ἀέθλων,
καλλίνικον πατρίδι κῦδος.

And in *Isthmian* I, the poet intends to celebrate the Isthmus:

since it bestowed six crowns from contests on the people of Kadmos, victorious *kudos* for the fatherland. (*Isthm.* 1.10–12)[1b]

Nor is this association of *kudos* with the victor's crown limited to Pindar. Thus we find in an address to the victory in Bacchylides:

however many times by the grace of Victory having bound your blond head with flowers you established *kudos* for broad Athens and glory for the Oineidai. (Bacchyl. 10.15–18)[2]

The question is very simple – what does *kudos* mean in *epinikion* and why its persistent connection with the victor's crown? Emile Benveniste once argued compellingly from the Homeric evidence that *kudos* is not merely a synonym for *kleos* (as it is often taken), but rather signifies special power bestowed by a god that makes a hero invincible:

The gift of *kudos* ensures the triumph of the man who receives it: in combat the holder of *kudos* is invariably victorious. Here we see the fundamental character of *kudos*: it acts as *a talisman of supremacy*. We use the term talisman advisedly, for the bestowal of *kudos* by the god procures an instantaneous and irresistible advantage, rather like a magic power, and the god grants it now to one and now to another at his good will and always in order to give the advantage at a decisive moment of a combat or some competitive activity.[3]

Hermann Fränkel came independently to very similar conclusions. He observes in a footnote to *Early Greek Poetry and Philosophy*:

Anthropologists have failed to notice that no Homeric word comes as close to the widely discussed *mana* and *orenda* as *kudos* does. The traditional rendering "Fame" is false. *Kudos* never signifies the fame which spreads itself abroad. Fame (*kleos*) is applicable even to the dead, but *kudos* belongs only to the living (*Il.* 22, 435ff.). From Homer to late antiquity derivations of *kudos* serve to designate the feeling of a man sure of himself and confident of the future.[4]

Benveniste also notes that in Homer the formula *kudos aresthai*, "to win *kudos*" is "often accompanied by a dative indicating the beneficiary": the Homeric warrior wins *kudos* for his king or his people.[5] We might add that, in Homeric epic, only two words take the epithet *kudianeira* "bestowing *kudos* on men" – *machê*, "battle," and *agorê*, the "gathering place for assemblies and athletic contests." To judge from the distribution of *kudos* in later texts and inscriptions, battle and contests remain the arenas for the winning of *kudos*. Thus the term figures most prominently in

---

[2] ὁσσά(κις) Νίκας ἕκατι
ἄνθεσιν ξανθὰν ἀναδησάμενος κεφαλάν
κῦδος εὐρείαις Ἀθάναις
θῆκας Οἰνείδαις τε δόξαν.

For other examples, see Pind. *Ol.* 5.1–8; Bacchyl. 1.155–65, 13.58–60. All quotations of Pindar are cited from Snell and Maehler 1980; those of Bacchylides from Snell and Maehler 1970.

[3] Benveniste 1973: 348.

[4] Fränkel 1973: 80 n. 14. For anthropological discussions of *mana* and *orenda*, see Lehmann 1915; Mauss 1972: 108–21.

[5] Benveniste 1973: 351.

two classes of inscriptions: those commemorating war dead and those celebrating athletic victory.[6]

I

Given the continuity in the two spheres of *kudos*, does it retain any of its Homeric force (of talismanic power, or *mana*) in the fifth century? But before I can address the observation and the question, it is necessary to rehearse the evidence for the talismanic power of athletic victors in antiquity. This evidence is well known: the *mana* of athletes used to be a commonplace. It has now fallen into disrepute, however, because of its associations with the Cambridge anthropologists – James Frazer, Francis Cornford, and Jane Harrison.[7] But it should be possible to disengage "talismanic power" from the accoutrements of the Cambridge school – divine kingship, succession myths, and weather magic – defining it narrowly, with Benveniste, as magical potency in battle.

Consider the evidence. On a couple of occasions, Plutarch tells us that victors at the crown games were traditionally stationed beside the Spartan king when he went into battle:

> In Lakedaimon, there was a special place in the ranks for victors at the crown games, stationed to fight around the king himself. (*Quaest. conv.* 2.5.2)[7a]

And in the *Life of Lykourgos* (22.4):

> The king used to go against the enemy having with him one who had won a crown contest.[7b]

Modern scholars have tended to follow Plutarch in giving this phenomenon a rationalistic explanation – it is because, they claim, athletics is such good training for war.[8] But two thing should make us suspicious of such a rationalistic account. In the *Quaestiones convivales*, Plutarch uses the plural "victors at the crown games" (τοῖς νενικηκόσι στεφανίτας ἀγῶνας), which might suggest an élite corps of athletes as crack troops. But in the *Life of Lykourgos* the biographer uses a singular, – "one who had won a crown contest" (στεφανίτην ἀγῶνα νενικηκότα). A single athletic victor hardly makes a swat team and suggests that he is not a fighting force so much as a talisman of victory (as the Spartan king himself was).[9]

---

[6] For the epithet *kudianeira*, see *Il.* 4.225, 6.124, 7.113, 8.448, 12.325, 13.270, 14.155, 24.391 (with *machê*) and *ll.* 1.490 (with *agorê*). *Agorê* in Homer normally designates the assembly (as at *Il.* 2.144, 2.149; *Od.* 9.112), but on occasion it also functions as a substitute for *agôn*, the gathering place for contests (as at *Od.* 8.109). For *kudos* in athletic and military inscriptions, see *CEG* 4, 519, 657, 785, 790, 879, Ebert nos. 64, 69, 74, 75, 76, 78, 79, Peek no. 40. Notice also Pindar's formulation "whoever in contests or war wins luxurious *kudos*" (*Isthm.* 1.50).

[7] See Frazer 1935: 89–105 and Cornford in Harrison 1912: 212–59. More recently, Versnel 1970: 155–63 has revived the theory using the *mana* of iselastic victors as a parallel for the Roman triumph.

[7a] ἐν δὲ Λακεδαίμονι τοῖς νενικηκόσι στεφανίτας ἀγῶνας ἐξαίρετος ἦν ἐν ταῖς παρατάξεσι χώρα, περὶ αὐτὸν τὸν βασιλέα τεταγμένους μάχεσθαι.

[7b] ἐχώρει δὲ ὁ βασιλεὺς ἐπὶ τοὺς πολεμίους ἔχων μεθ' ἑαυτοῦ στεφανίτην ἀγῶνα νενικηκότα.

[8] E.g., Lonis 1979: 27–35.

[9] Cartledge 1987: 109–10, citing Weber 1978: 1285 and Taeger 1957: 33; cf. Versnel 1970: 158.

The other thing that should make us suspicious is that, in both passages, Plutarch specifies a victor at the *crown* games. If it were just a question of physical conditioning, surely any athletic victor would do, but instead we find a limitation that is inexplicable on purely rationalistic grounds.

In the same section of the *Quaestiones convivales,* Plutarch also reports that it is customary to tear down a part of the city wall for the entrance of athletic victors:

> And the fact that, for the reentry of athletic victors, they bid them cast down a part of the city wall has such an intent: that there is no great benefit of walls for a city which has men able to fight and to win. (*Quaest. conv.* 2.5.2)[9a]

Plutarch's account (if not his rationale) is confirmed by the description of Nero's triumphal return from Greece in Suetonius:

> Returning from Greece to Naples (because he had exhibited his skill there first), he entered with white horses where a part of the wall had been cast down, as is the custom for victors at the holy games; in a similar way [he entered] Antium, thence Albanum, thence Rome. But [he entered] Rome also in that chariot in which Augustus had once celebrated a triumph, and in a purple garment and a cloak decorated with gold stars, wearing on his head his Olympic crown, carrying his Pythian crown in his right hand, with a parade proceeding with the titles of all the rest [of the contests], where and whom he had beaten, by what song or plot of stories. (*Ner.* 25)[9b]

Suetonius adds an important detail when he notes, "ut mos hieronicarum est" – "as is the custom for victors at the holy games."[10] The "holy games," as they are defined from Pindar through agonistic inscriptions of the Hellenistic and Roman periods, are the *crown* games – the games of the *periodos.*[11] Precisely the same limitation seems to apply here as in the first case, the attendance on the Spartan king. In this case, at least, a historian of Roman religion, H. S. Versnel, is willing to countenance the possibility of talismanic power. He explains this strange practice, which breaches the walls and then, immediately after the victor's entry, seals up the gap, as a rite that symbolically seals the victor's power, his magical supremacy, within the city.[12]

[9a] καὶ τὸ τοῖς νικηφόροις εἰσελαύνουσιν τῶν τειχῶν ἐφίεσθαι μέρος διελεῖν καὶ καταβαλεῖν τοιαύτην ἔχει διάνοιαν, ὡς οὐ μέγα πόλει τειχῶν ὄφελος ἄνδρας ἐχούσῃ μάχεσθαι δυναμένους καὶ νικᾶν.

[9b] Reversus e Graecia Neapolim, quod in ea primum artem protulerat, albis equis introiit disiecta parte muri, ut mos hieronicarum est; simili modo Antium, inde Albanum, inde Romam; sed et Romam eo curru, quo Augustus olim triumphaverat, et in veste purpurea distinctaque stellis aureis chlamyde coronamque capite gerens Olympiacam, dextra manu Pythiam, praeeunte pompa ceterarum cum titulis, ubi et quos quo cantionum quove fabularum argumento vicisset.

[10] We should keep in mind that Suetonius was a serious scholar of things Greek (who wrote an antiquarian treatise *On Greek Games)* and Nero an obsessive Hellenizer (on Suetonius, see Wallace-Hadrill 1983: 44–8; on Nero, see Griffin 1984: 43–4, 85, 208–20). For the custom of breaking down a part of the wall, cf. the more skeptical report of Dio Cass. 62.20, and Vitr. 9, pref. I; see also Sherwin-White 1966: 729 and P. Herrmann 1975: 156.

[11] Cf. Pindar *Ol.* 8.64, *Ol.* 13.15, *Nem.* 6.59; Robert 1967: 16–18. Pleket 1975: 56–65 diverges somewhat from the traditional interpretation, defining the holy games as a larger category that includes but is not limited to "crown games". For a thorough discussion of the categories holy games, crown games, iselastic games, and thematic games, see Pleket 1975: 54–71.

[12] Versnel 1970: 155–62. Gagé 1953: 177–9 aptly cites the Trojan horse as a parallel: recall that, in Vergil, the walls of Troy are breached to bring in the horse because it is believed by the Trojans to be a talisman of supremacy that will ensure their conquest of Greece *(Aen.* 2.189–94, 234–40). Martin

Finally, there is Diodorus Siculus' account of a battle between the Krotoniates and the Sybarites in the sixth century BCE. According to Diodorus, the Sybarites forced the Krotoniates into a war over suppliants to whom the Krotoniates had given sanctuary. The Krotoniates engaged the Sybarites in battle, outnumbered three to one:

> With Milo the athlete commanding and, on account of the superabundance of his bodily force, first having turned those stationed against him. For this man, a six time Olympic victor and having the courage to go with his bodily nature, is said to have entered into battle crowned with his six Olympic crowns and wearing the garb of Herakles with lion skin and club. And [it is said] that he was marvelled at by his fellow citizens as being the cause of victory. (Diod. Sic. 12.9.5–6)[12a]

No rationalistic explanation can do justice to this passage – Milo goes into battle wearing his six Olympic crowns and single-handedly turns the enemy.[13] This account is intended to be *thauma* (a marvel), as Diodorus' last sentence signals. We must conclude that the Olympic victor in his Olympic crown was believed to have magical potency on the battlefield.

But, it may be objected, all this evidence derives from very late sources – do we have any suggestion of a belief in the talismanic power of athletic victors in the sixth or fifth century BCE? In light of these passages, it is worth looking carefully at Herodotus' account of the Elean seer Teisamenos (Hdt. 9.33–5). Consulting the Delphic oracle about offspring, Teisamenos is informed that he will "win five of the greatest contests" (ἀγῶνας τοὺς μεγίστους ἀναιρήσεσθαι πέντε). As a result, he goes into training and enters the Olympic pentathlon, missing the victory by a single fall. Thereupon, the Spartans realise that the oracle "refers not to athletic contests but to the contests of war" and attempt to recruit Teisamenos for the Spartan army:

> But the Lakedaimonians, having come to understand that the oracle referred not to athletic contests but to the contests of war, were attempting, having persuaded Teisamenos with a wage, to make him leader of wars together with their Heraklid kings. (Hdt. 9.33)[13a]

But Teisamenos will join the Lakedaimonian forces only on terms of becoming a Spartan citizen. When the Spartans finally agree to his terms in fear of the Persian expedition, Herodotus concludes his story triumphantly:

Bloomer suggests to me that we should read the victor's crown as itself a metonymy for the circuit of the city walls, which can be brought into the city only through a break in this larger circuit.

[12a] Μίλωνος τοῦ ἀθλητοῦ ἡγουμένου καὶ διὰ τὴν ὑπερβολὴν τῆς τοῦ σώματος ῥώμης πρῶτου τρεψαμένου τοὺς καθ' αὑτὸν τεταγμένους. ὁ γὰρ ἀνὴρ οὗτος, ἑξάκις Ὀλύμπια νενικηκὼς καὶ τὴν ἀλκὴν ἀκόλουθον ἔχων τῇ κατὰ τὸ σῶμα φύσει, λέγεται πρὸς τὴν μάχην ἀπαντῆσαι κατεστεφανωμένος μὲν τοῖς Ὀλυμπικοῖς στεφάνοις διεσκευασμένος δὲ εἰς Ἡρακλέους σκευὴν λεοντῇ καὶ ῥοπάλῳ· αἴτιον δὲ γενόμενον τῆς νίκης θαυμασθῆναι παρὰ τοῖς πολίταις.

[13] The garb of Herakles is also significant in this context. In a sense, Herakles is the talismanic hero par excellence, and as such he provides a model both for athletics (in Pindar [cf. Slater 1984: 249–64] and on the metopes of Zeus's temple at Olympia [cf. Raschke 1988: 43–8]) and for war. For evidence of Herakles as a talismanic hero in war, we should note that, according to Herodotus, two major battles of the Persian Wars were fought near precincts of Herakles (Marathon, Hdt. 6.108; Thermopylae, Hdt. 7.176; cf. Boedeker 1988: 46). As a parallel for Milo's assumption of the garb of Herakles for battle, cf. Diod. Sic. 16.44.3.

[13a] Λακεδαιμόνιοι δὲ μαθόντες οὐκ ἐς γυμνικοὺς ἀλλ' ἐς ἀρηίους ἀγῶνας φέρον τὸ Τεισαμενοῦ μαντήιον, μισθῷ ἐπειρῶντο πείσαντες Τεισαμενὸν ποιέεσθαι ἅμα Ἡρακλειδέων τοῖσι βασιλεῦσι ἡγεμόνα τῶν πολέμων.

But when the Spartiates agreed also to these terms, thus indeed did Teisamenos the Elean, having become Spartan, take five of the greatest contests with them, serving as seer. (Hdt. 9.35)[13b]

Herodotus' diction in this context bears striking similarities to the official victory announcement at the games. As R. W. Macan observes, "It marks the solemnity of the occasion with a quasi-heraldic flourish."[14] Herodotus' narrative confirms (even as it collapses) contests and war as two parallel spheres for the winning of *kudos*. It is as if Teisamenos, with the oracle's sanction, simply vaults over the intermediate step of athletic victory, moving straight to talismanic potency in battle. Indeed, the phrase Herodotus uses for his participation in battle "to make Teisamenos leader of wars together with their Heraklid kings" (Τεισαμενὸν ποιέεσθαι ἅμα Ἡρακλειδέων τοῖσι βασιλεῦσι ἡγεμόνα τῶν πολέμων), suggests much more than the service of a seer. Commentators have expended a great deal of ingenuity to avoid the obvious meaning of the phrase,[15] but Teisamenos' close association with the Heraklid kings as "leader of wars" is explicable within the framework of talismanic power. Teisamenos, like the Spartan kings themselves, would be a leader by virtue of his charismatic authority, so that we need not assume that Herodotus said *hêgemôn* when he meant *mantis*.

The anecdotes of Plutarch and Diodorus Siculus are also very suggestive in general for the Greeks' predilection for crown victors as commanders in war and in the foundation of cities.[16] There are, in fact, a fair number of Olympic victors who act as oikists between the seventh century and the fifth.[17] The earliest is Chionis of Sparta, three-time Olympic victor, who, according to Pausanias, "had a share in the expedition with the Theraean Battos and founded Kyrene with that one" (Paus. 3.14.3).[18] Next is Phrynon, Olympic victor and leader of the Athenian expedition to Sigeum around 600 BCE.[19] Herodotus tells us of two Olympic victors who became oikists in the late sixth century: Philippos of Kroton, who accompanied the expedition of Dorieus in the 520s (Hdt. 5.47), and Miltiades, the son of Kypselos, whom the Dolonkoi took as their oikist to the Thracian Chersonese (Hdt. 6.36). The way in which Herodotus narrates the latter story suggests that there is an association in the mind of the historian between Miltiades' Olympic

---

[13b] συγχωρησάντων δὲ καὶ ταῦτα τῶν Σπαρτιητέων, οὕτω δὴ πέντε σφι μαντευόμενος ἀγῶνας τοὺς μεγίστους Τεισαμενὸς ὁ Ἠλεῖος, γενόμενος Σπαρτιήτης, συγκαταιρέει.

[14] Macan 1908: 1.670. On the form of the victory announcement, see later.

[15] Thus How and Wells 1928: 2.302: "This cannot mean that the seer was to share the actual command in war, for in comparison with this the grant of citizenship would be nothing. It seems to refer to the position of the kings as priests, since they offered sacrifice before all important undertakings ... Tisamenus was to act with them in this". Similarly Macan 1908: 1.667 (ad 9.33, l. 13); see also Fontenrose 1989: 94: "As *mantis*, and therefore as *hegemon*, he would be victorious in five great battles."

[16] For the close connection between military expeditions and colonial ventures in this period, see Dougherty (1993).

[17] See Hönle 1972: 47–8, 157–8.

[18] Chamoux 1953: 123–4 takes Chionis as an official representative of Sparta, which, as the mother city of Thera, appropriately joined the colonial expedition to found Kyrene.

[19] See Diog. Laert. I. 74; Strab. 599–600. Berve 1937: 28–9 argued quite plausibly that Phrynon's expedition only makes sense as a colonial venture. See also Hönle 1972: 47–8. The tradition of Phrynon's duel, one-on-one, with Pittakos (Diog. Laert. 1.74; Strab. 600; Suda s. v. Πιττακός; Plut. *malign. Herod.* 15; schol. ap. Aesch. *Eum.* 398) may also reflect a belief in the athlete's talismanic power.

victory and his role as oikist: uncharacteristically for Herodotus, he does not mention that Miltiades was an Olympic victor when he is first introduced to the narrative; the Athenian aristocrat is characterised simply as "of a household which kept four-horse-chariots" (ἐὼν οἰκίης τεθριπποτρόφου) (Hdt. 6.35).[20] Instead, the fact of his Olympic victory is reserved for the quasi-heraldic announcement of his role as founder:

> Thus indeed Miltiades, the son of Kypselos, who was before this an Olympic chariot victor at that time took every one of the Athenians who wanted to participate in the expedition and sailed together with the Dolonkoi and took the territory. (Hdt. 6.36)[21]

The last instance of a victor-oikist known to us from literary sources is Leon of Sparta, who won an Olympic chariot victory in 428 BCE.[22] This same Leon was probably one of the three commanders dispatched from Sparta to found Herakleia Trachinia in 426 BCE, as Thucydides tells us (Thuc. 3.92: "the expedition was led by three Spartans, as founders of the colony: Leon and Alkidas and Damagon"– οἰκισταὶ δὲ τρεῖς Λακεδαιμονίων ἡγήσαντο, Λέων καὶ Ἀλκίδας καὶ Δαμάγων).[23] If it is characteristic of Herodotus to mention that an oikist is an Olympic victor, it may well be characteristic of Thucydides to suppress the fact. Simon Hornblower has argued that there may have been a religious element involved in the choice of Alkides as one commander of this expedition, for his name makes him an ideal candidate to found a colony named Herakleia in the neighborhood of Trachis. Yet, according to Hornblower, Thucydides consistently suppresses the religious element.[24] The same argument might be extended to Thucydides' failure to mention Leon's Olympic victory. If this is the case, Thucydides' silence tends to corroborate the claim that crown victors were believed to have special, talismanic power that contributed to the success of such colonial ventures.

Similarly, we know of several cases of victors at the great games serving as military commanders. Pausanias reports that Phanas of Messenia was an Olympic victor in the long race who commanded beside Aristomenes in the Second Messenian War (Paus. 4.17.9). Herodotus mentions Eualkides, crown victor and commander of the Eretrians during the Ionian Revolt (Hdt. 5.102).[25] In this light, it is worth considering Herodotus' account of another crown victor, Phayllos of Kroton. Right before the Battle of Salamis, the historian reports, "Of those living outside [Greece], the Krotoniates were the only ones who came to aid Greece when she

---

[20] For Herodotus' normal practice, see 1.31, 5–47.1, 5.71.1, 5.102.3, 6.103.2, 8.47.

[21] οὕτω δὴ Μιλτιάδης ὁ Κυψέλου, Ὀλύμπια ἀναραιρηκὼς πρότερον τούτων τεθρίππῳ, τότε παραλαβὼν Ἀθηναίων πάντα τὸν βουλόμενον μετέχειν τοῦ στόλου ἔπλεε ἅμα τοῖσι Δολόγκοισι καὶ ἔσχε τὴν χώρην. Macan 1895: 1.296 (ad 6.36, l. 2) speculates that Herodotus is here reproducing the formulae of an inscription. If this is so, it suggests that a significant connection between Miltiades' athletic victory and his status as oikist was felt by the erectors of the monument that was Herodotus' source.

[22] Moretti 1957: no. 332; date proposed by Hönle 1972: 157–8.

[23] Thus Hönle 1972: 157–8.

[24] Hornblower 1991: 506–7.

[25] Other possible military commanders who were crown victors are Alkmeon of Athens (Moretti 1957: no. 81), Promachos of Pellene (Moretti 1957: no. 355), and Stomios of Elis (Moretti 1957: no. 404). There is, of course, a class issue here as well: in this period, victors at the panhellenic games tended to be aristocrats (*pace* D. C. Young 1984), who also tended to be chosen military commanders. I will consider the overlap between these categories later.

was in danger with one ship, whose commander was Phayllos, three-time Pythian victor" (ἀνὴρ τρὶς πυθιονίκης Φάϋλλος, Hdt. 8.47). We might think one ship is very paltry aid, but the parallel of a *single* crown victor fighting beside the Spartan king should give us pause.[26] Perhaps the substantive aid was not the ship, but the man it carried, a talisman potent with three Pythian victories. Indeed, Herodotus himself offers an intriguing parallel for this one ship a few chapters later when he mentions that, after an earthquake, the Greeks at Salamis sent a ship to Aigina to fetch the Aiakidai (8.64, 8.83). According to Aiginetan tradition, it was this ship that initiated the battle (8.84). I suggest that there is a precise analogy between the one ship bearing the Aiginetan heroes and that which carried the crown victor – both contribute their talismanic power, their *mana*, to the fighting force.

II

Thus, there seems to be good evidence stretching back to the fifth century BCE for the *mana* of crown victors. But as Benveniste and Fränkel have suggested. the Greek word for *mana* is *kudos*. To answer the question with which I began, I propose that we understand epinikian *kudos* as the civic adaptation of its Homeric precursor, with the city replacing the Homeric king as beneficiary of the victor's *kudos*. Consider in this light the first triad of *Olympian* 5:

> Daughter of Ocean, receive with laughing heart the sweet peak of highest achievements and crowns from Olympia, the gifts of the untiring-footed chariot and of Psaumis. Exalting your city which nurtures the people, O Kamarina, he honored the six double altars at the greatest festivals of the gods with sacrifices and the five-day competition of contests, with horses and mules and single-horse racing. And having won he dedicated to you luxurious *kudos*, and he heralded his father Akron and his new-founded seat. (*Ol*. 5.1–8)[26a]

The poet begins by invoking the victor's city, Kamarina, and asking her to receive "the sweet peak of achievements and Olympic crowns" (a typically Pindaric zeugma of concrete and abstract; cf. *Pyth*. 8.19–20). He proceeds to assert that the victor has dedicated *kudos* for his city (τὶν δὲ κῦδος ἁβρὸν νικάσας ἀνέθηκε). Notice especially *anethêke* (ἀνέθηκε) here, which is the technical term for making a dedication.[27] What the victor offers and what the city receives frame the triad, equating his *kudos* with the proffered crown.

---

[26] In explaining the peculiarity of one ship, some modern scholars have tended to follow Pausanias, who claimed that Phayllos happened to be in mainland Greece when the Persian invasion occurred and that he responded by manning his own ship (Paus. 10.9.2; thus Macan 1908: 1.2.431–2). We should note, however, that there is no hint of this explanation in Herodotus, so that it may be a later conjecture, invented to rationalize the oddness of one ship.

[26a] Ὑψηλᾶν ἀρετᾶν καὶ στεφάνων ἄωτον γλυκὺν
τῶν Οὐλυμπίᾳ, Ὠκεανοῦ θύγατερ, καρδίᾳ γελανεῖ
ἀκαμαντόποδός τ' ἀπήνας δέκευ Ψαύμιός τε δῶρα·
ὅς τὰν σὰν πόλιν αὔξων, Καμάρινα, λαοτρόφον,
βωμοὺς ἓξ διδύμους ἐγέραρεν ἑορταῖς θεῶν μεγίσταις
ὑπὸ βουθυσίαις ἀέθλων τε πεμπαμέροις ἁμίλλαις
ἵπποις ἡμιόνοις τε μοναμπυκίᾳ τε. τὶν δὲ κῦδος ἁβρὸν
νικάσας ἀνέθηκε, καὶ ὃν πατέρ' Ἄ-
κρων' ἐκάρυξε καὶ τὰν νέοικον ἕδραν.

[27] See LSJ, s.v. ἀνατίθημι II.

The same equation of *kudos* and crowns figures in agonistic inscriptions.[28] In the inscriptions and elsewhere, "crowning the city" is a common formula for victory. Thus in an epigram that Joachim Ebert dates to the first half of the fifth century (Ebert 12 = *Anth. Pal.* 16.2):

> Come to know Theognetos looking upon him, the boy Olympic victor, skilled charioteer of the wrestling, most beautiful to see, but in competing no worse than his form, who crowned the city of good fathers.[28a]

Admittedly, this is a very ornate example, attributed in the *Palatine Anthology* to Simonides. Ebert 35 (= *Anth. Pal.* 13.15) offers a somewhat less showy version from the fourth century BCE:

> I am Dikon son of Kallimbrotos, and I was victorious four times at Nemea, twice at Olympia, five times at Pytho, and three times at the Isthmus. And I crown the city of the Syracusans.[29]

'To crown the city" as a formula for victory points to a significant ritual event (a point to which I shall return). But it is worth noting that, on occasion, the verb κυδαίνω ("I bestow *kudos*") replaces στεφανόω ("I crown"). Thus in a late inscription from Ephesus (the last two lines after a long victory catalog):

> Accordingly, I bestow *kudos* upon my father Eirenaios and my homeland Ephesus by means of immortal crowns. (Ebert 76B.9–10 = *I Olympia* 225, 49 CE)[29a]

Notice the instrumental dative στέμμασιν ἀθανάτοις ("by means of immortal crowns"): the inscription tells us explicitly that the victor's crowns are the means by which he bestows *kudos* on his city.[30] Furthermore, the functional equivalence of στεφανόω ("I crown") and κυδαίνω ("I bestow *kudos*") with the city as object bespeaks the same association that we find in Pindar and Bacchylides.

---

[28] Unfortunately, many of the early inscriptions are badly mutilated: the association of *kudos* and crowns may occur in *CEG* 834 (= Ebert 58) and Ebert 64.4.

[28a] Γνῶθι Θεόγνητον προσιδών, τὸν ὀλυμπιονίκαν
παῖδα, παλαισμοσύνας δεξιὸν ἡνίοχον,
κάλλιστον μὲν ἰδεῖν, ἀθλεῖν δ᾽οὐ χείρονα μορφῆς,
ὃς πατέρων ἀγαθῶν ἐστεφάνωσε πόλιν.

[29] Εἰμὶ Δίκων υἱὸς Καλλιμβρότου, αὐτὰρ ἐνίκων
τετράκις ἐν Νεμέᾳ, δὶς Ὀλύμπια, πεντάκι Πυθοῖ,
τρὶς δ᾽Ἰσθμῷ. στεφανῶ δ᾽ἄστυ Συρακοσίων.

Cf. Ebert 67 (*Anth. Pal.* 9.588); 71 (*SEG* iii 398); Moretti 1957: no. 38 (*IG* vii 530); *IG* xii suppl., 257; *Fouilles de Delphes* iii.2.67; *IG* ii² 3138.3–4; and "Demosthenes" 58.66; "Epichares, my grandfather, having won the boys' stade race at the Olympics, crowned the city" (ἐστεφάνωσε τὴν πόλιν). See also Theotimos ap. schol. ap. Pind. *Pyth.* 5.34 (Drachmann 1964: 2.176) and Pliny *HN* 7.26, "more sacris certaminibus vincentium: neque enim ipsi coronantur, sed patrias suas coronant" (in the manner of those who win at the holy games: for they are not themselves crowned, but they crown their homelands); for more examples, Robert 1967: 19–23.

[29a] τοιγὰρ κυδαίνω γενέτην ἐμὸν Εἰρηναῖον
καὶ πάτρην Ἔφεσον στέμμασιν ἀθανάτοις.

[30] Although this inscription is very late, we find a close parallel for its diction in Pindar *Ol.* 10.66: "Echemos bestowing *kudos* on Tegea in the wrestling" (ὁ δὲ πάλᾳ κυδαίνων Ἔχεμος Τεγέαν), which answers the question "Who then was allotted a brand new crown?" (τίς δὴ ποταίνιον ἔλαχε στέφανον) at 60–1. See also Pind. *Pyth.* 1.31 (of Hieron's announcement of the newly founded city of Aitna at the Pythian Games): κλεινὸς οἰκιστὴρ ἐκύδανεν πόλιν. This continuity, spanning five centuries, supports the contention of Pleket 1974: 79, 1975: 71–89 that the aristocratic *ideology* of the games endured (in spite of changes in the social status of competitors) well into the Roman period.

Other inscriptions clearly equate the victor's crown with *kudos* for his city. In a late inscription from Miletus, we read:

> The Telephidai crowned you from the contests of Herakles, and Miletus received the *kudos* of your wrestling. (Ebert 74.1–2 = *Milet* III 164, after 129 BCE)[30a]

And in an elegant dedicatory inscription preserved by Herodotus:

> Having bridged the Bosphorus, full of fish, Mandrokles dedicated to Hera a memorial of the bridge, having put a crown about himself and *kudos* about the Samians, when he accomplished it according to the intent of King Darius. (Hdt. 4.88)[30b]

This is not an athletic inscription, but a dedication to commemorate a different kind of remarkable achievement – the bridging of the Bosphorus for Darius' Scythian campaign. Still, the link between the individual's crown and *kudos* for his city is so compelling that it surfaces even here, where the crown is purely metaphorical.[31]

I suggest we read all these passages against the background of the rites that we know accompanied the victor's re-entry to his city. The re-entry itself was a very significant moment – we have one description in Diodorus Siculus of a fifth-century Akragantine victor escorted into the city by three hundred chariots drawn by white horses (Diod. Sic. 13.82.7–8). The crowds invoked blessings, pelted the victor with crowns, and bound *tainiai*, or fillets, about his head.[32] The procession went conspicuously through the main streets to the center of the city, where the victor was announced (just as he had been at the games).[33] The victor's crown was an important part of the ritual – indeed, as Louis Robert informs us, the technical term for the ceremony was *eisagein ton stephanon* to "bear in the crown".[34] After the announcement of the victor, the crown was often dedicated at the shrine of a local god or hero.[35]

This ritual practice, I believe, lies behind Pindar's request to Kamarina to receive the victor's crown in *Olympian* 5. We find the same request in other poems, addressed either to the city personified or to a local deity. Thus in *Pythian* 12:

[30a] Τηλεφίδαι σε ἔστεψαν ἀφ' Ἡρακλείος ἀγ[ώνων],
Μίλητος δὲ τεᾶς κῦδος ἔδεκτο πάλα[ς].

[30b] Βόσπορον ἰχθυόεντα γεφυρώσας ἀνέθηκε
Μανδροκλέης Ἥρῃ μνημόσυνον σχεδίης,
αὑτῷ μὲν στέφανον περιθείς, Σαμίοισι δὲ κῦδος,
Δαρείου βασιλέος ἐκτελέσας κατὰ νοῦν.

[31] For a parallel instance of a metaphorical crown linked to *kudos*, see *Anth. Pal.* 7.251 (= Simonides 121 D), Here the terms are reversed: those dead in battle "crown their homeland with unquenchable *kleos*" and thereby win *kudos* for themselves.

[32] Cf. Thuc. 4.121.4, and the vase representations collected in Jüthner 1898. See also Gardiner 1910: 206; Slater 1984: 245–7.

[33] As in the Ephesian inscription, Keil and Maresch 1960: no: 5 coll. 78–80, ll. 7–12 (ca. 300 BCE): "The Boule and the demos resolved to announce him in the Agora, just as the other victors are announced" ([ἔδοξε]ν τῆι βουλῆ(ι) καὶ τῶι δήμωι ... ἀναγγεῖλαι αὐτὸν ἐν τῆι ἀγοραῖ καθ[ά]περ οἱ ἄλλοι νικῶντες ἀναγγέλλονται). See the discussion of Robert 1967: 14–17.

[34] Or εἰσελαύνειν τὸν στέφανον, "to drive in the crown," from which the term "iselastic" derives: the iselastic games were those from which the victor had the privilege of re-entering his city in a chariot. See Robert 1967: 17–18; Pleket 1975: 62–4.

[35] See J. H. Krause 1838: 197–201; Stengel 1920: 210–11; Blech 1982: 114; Slater 1984: 245 with n. 24. For evidence for the dedication of the crown in Pindar, see *Ol.* 9.110–12; *Nem.* 5.50–4; *Nem.* 8.13–16 (*mitra*).

I ask you, shining one, most beautiful of mortal cities ... receive this crown from Pytho for glorious Midas, and receive [the man] himself, who has beaten Greece in his craft. (*Pyth.* 12.1.5–6)[35a]

And again, in *Olympian* 13, the poet prays to Zeus:

Receive for him the ordinance of crowns accompanied by the *kômos*, which he leads from the plains of Pisa, winning the stadion race together with the pentathlon.[35b]

Notice especially "the ordinance of crowns accompanied by *kômos*, which he leads from the plains of Pisa" (στεφάνων ἐγκώμιον τεθμόν, τὸν ἄγει πεδίων ἐκ Πίσας). In this phrase, Pindar comes as close as he ever does to the technical term εἰσάγειν τὸν στέφανον. Some critics have preferred to understand the crown in these passages as a metaphor for the poet's song,[36] but there is much to be said for taking these injunctions literally, as references in *epinikion* to the victor's public dedication of his crown on his return home. *Olympian* 5 then adds the final term: by its equation of crowns received with the dedication of *kudos* for the city it suggests that the victor shares his talismanic power with his community by dedicating his victory crown. It is worth noting also that in all three of the passages with which I began, the poet's language transfers the victor's crown to the public sphere, identifying it with *kudos* for the city.[37]

Thus I would modify the thesis of Frank J. Nisetich, who argued that the moment of crowning at the games was so important that Pindar evokes it again and again in his verse. I would add that rituals involving the victor's crown punctuate *both* ends of his journey – first at the games and then on his return home.[38] Both moments are laden with *kudos* and the civic community participates in both – at the games, because the city also figures in the victory announcement; at home, because the ritual of re-entry culminates in the *public* display and dedication of the crown. Both rituals are necessary to acknowledge the victory and to share the victor's talismanic power with his community.

Accordingly, we might describe all the rites involving the victor as an "economy of *kudos*" – a circulation of powers and honours whose goal is to achieve a harmonious sharing of this special commodity within the city. The victor invests the money and effort needed to train and to win, and then heralds his city at the moment of crowning (and, of course, he is not obliged to do so – he can announce

---

[35a] Αἰτέω σε, φιλάγλαε, καλλίστα βροτεᾶν πολίων
[...]
δέξαι στεφάνωμα τόδ' ἐκ Πυθῶνος εὐδόξῳ Μίδᾳ
αὐτόν τε νιν Ἑλλάδα νικάσαντα τέχνᾳ

[35b] δέξαι τέ οἱ στεφάνων ἐγκώμιον τεθμόν, τὸν ἄγει πεδίων ἐκ Πίσας, πενταέθλῳ ἅμα σταδίου νικῶν δρόμον.

[36] See esp. Nisetich 1975: 61–4.

[37] For more extended discussion of these passages, see Kurke 1991: 203–9, Cf. *Pyth.* 8.5 (and as a parallel for *Pythionikon timan* as a periphrasis for the victor's crown, see *Pyth.* 5.30, "the prize of the best chariot" ἀριοθάρματον ... γέρας). This interpretation may also apply to injunctions to "receive the *kômos*" at *Ol.* 6.98, *Pyth.* 5.22, *Pyth.* 9.73, and *Nem.* 4.11, since, at *Ol.* 8.9–10, Pindar links the *kômos* with the *stephanêphoria*. Thus *kômos* and *stephanêphoria* may represent two parts of the ritual re-entry, either one of which the poet can evoke as metonymy for the whole process. Cf. Heath 1988: 189–92.

[38] Nisetich 1975. For the importance of both ends of the victor's journey, see Gage 1953: 172–3.

a different city).³⁹ At home, he tenders the city his victory crown. The city, in response, rewards him for his victory with a lavish re-entry rite, crowns and fillets, the lifelong privilege of eating in the prytaneion, large monetary awards, special front-row seats in the theater, and sometimes a statue set up at public expense in the city or at the site of the games.⁴⁰

This symbolic economy of *kudos* is concretized as a circulation of crowns, whereby the crown itself becomes the bearer of *kudos* and its dedication the means of sharing that power with the city, For this reason, the link between the dictional evidence I have just reviewed and the anecdotal evidence considered earlier is the victor's *crown*. The association between *kudos* and crowns in *epinikion* and in the inscriptions explicates the strange limiting condition we observed in the later anecdotes: it is *only* crown victors who enter through a breach in the wall and crown victors who fight beside the Spartan king. Finally, remember Milo of Kroton marching out to battle wearing his six Olympic crowns.⁴¹

III

Within this economy of *kudos*, one particular form of honoring the victor deserves our closer attention: the victory statue. For on occasion, the epigrams that accompany such statues use the formula "the city crowned me winning with this image" (με ... νικῶντα ἐστεφάνωσε εἰκόνι τῇδε πόλις) (*CEG* 855.1–2, cf. *CEG* 799 [both ca. 300 BCE]). The language suggests that the victor's statue participates in the circulation of crowns that emblematizes the economy of *kudos*. How does the victor statue function within this symbolic economy? At the most obvious level, we can read the statue as recompense bestowed by the city for the victor's crown: a figurative exchange of crowns then motivates the diction of the inscriptions. Yet this reading hardly exhausts the statue's participation in an elaborate ritual economy. Just as the rites accompanying the victor's re-entry to his city reenact his original coronation at the games, we might say that the statue group makes eternal the possibility of such re-enactment. The inscriptions repeatedly emphasize the exact likeness of the statue to the victor, thereby confirming the tradition that victors

---

³⁹ Recall Astylos of Kroton, who, according to Pausanias (6.13.1), twice had himself "announced as Syracusan to gratify Hieron" (ἐς χάριν τὴν Ἱέρωνος ... ἀνηγόρευσεν αὐτὸν Συρακούσιον). The people of Kroton responded by turning his house into a prison and tearing down his statue in the temple of Hera Lakinia. I will consider later the importance of victor statues and the rituals that surround them; for now, I simply note that the severity of this punishment suggests there is a great deal at stake in the announcement of the victor's city. On punishments of athletes in general, see Forbes 1952.

⁴⁰ For the privilege of eating in the prytaneion, see Xenoph. fr. 2 DK; Pl. *Ap.* 36d; *IG* i² 77; *IG* xii, fasc. 5, 274, 28 1, 289 (Paros), and 1060 (Keos); for large monetary awards, see Plut. *Sol.* 23.5; Ath. 12.522a-d; Diog. Laert. 1.55, and Inscription from Ephesus (Keil and Maresch 1960: no. 5 coll. 78–80, where the monetary reward is specifically designated "money for the crown" – ἀργύριον εἰς τὸν στέφανον). Modern discussions of rewards for crown victors include J. H. Krause 1838: 199–201; Pleket 1974: 67, 1975: 59; D. C. Young 1984: 128–33; Serwint 1987: 10–19.

⁴¹ This association of *kudos* and crowns may also explain why, for the Greeks, the crown games were the "holy games". Again, we may engage in the exercise of reading literally: the reason the holy games are holy is that winning marks the athlete out by bestowing on him special power. The crown of the crown games is the emblem of *kudos*.

had the privilege of erecting statues that were life-size but no larger.[42] For example, the earliest preserved inscription from an Olympic victor monument (*CEG* 394, first half of the sixth century BCE) insists that the image is "equal in height and thickness" (Ϝίσο(μ) μᾶκός τε πάχος τε) to the victor.[43] Other inscriptions make it clear that the statue was not just like the victor, but like him at the moment of victory or return. In an Olympic inscription from around 300 BCE, for example,

> Standing thus upon the Alpheios, the Pelasgian boxer once showed forth the ordinance of Polydeukes with his hands, when he was heralded victor. But, Father Zeus, also again bestow noble glory on Arcadia, and honor Philippos, who here leaned on four boys from the islands with straight battle. (*CEG* 827 = Ebert 55)[43a]

Here the inscription tells us explicitly that the statue re-creates the stance of the victor at the moment he won and was heralded.[44] And just as the statue replicates the victor as he was at the moment of victory, the words of the epigram reproduce the original victory announcement.

Several sources give us information about the form of the victory announcement. The oldest is a black-figure amphora of Panathenaic shape dated to the third quarter of the sixth century BCE, which depicts a herald before a victorious horseman, proclaiming ΔΥΝΕΙΚΕΤΥ:ΗΙΠΟΣ:ΝΙΚΑΙ (Δυνεικέτυ ἵππος νικᾷ – the horse of Duneiketos wins; Fig. 9.1).[45] There is also a fragment of Timotheos, which according to Plutarch celebrates his victory over Phrynis:

> Blessed were you, Timotheos, when the herald said, "Timotheos the Milesian beats the soft Ionian-singing son of Kamon. (Timotheos fr. 26/802 *PMG*)[45a]

From much later sources we get somewhat more elaborate versions of the victory announcement. Thus Diogenes Laertius preserves an anecdote about Diogenes the Cynic that depends on the formula uttered by the Olympic herald, "Dioxippos beats the men" (νικᾷ Διώξιππος ἄνδρας; Diog. Laert. 6.43). Dio Cassius offers the most elaborate version of all in his account of Nero's victory announcement at all the chief games of Greece: And the victory announcement was, "Nero Caesar wins this contest and crowns the Roman people and the inhabited world which is his own" (τὸ δὲ δὴ κήρυγμα ἦν· Νέρων Καῖσαρ νικᾷ τόνδε τὸν ἀγῶνα καὶ στεφανοῖ τόν τε Ῥωμαίων δῆμον καὶ τὴν ἰδίαν οἰκουμένην) (Dio. Cass. 62.14).

---

[42] Lucian *pro imag.* 11.
[43] I follow Ebert's interpretation of this phrase; for discussion (with earlier bibliography), see Ebert 1972: 251–4.
[43a] Ὅδε στὰς ὁ Πελασγὸς ἐπ' Ἀλφειῶι ποκα πύκτας
  τὸμ Πολυδεύκειογ χερσὶν ἔφανε νόμον,
  ἁμος ἐκαρύχθη νικαφόρος. ἀλλά, πάτερ Ζεῦ,
  καὶ πάλιν Ἀρκαδίαι καλὸν ἄμειβε κλέος,
  τίμασον δὲ Φίλιππον, ὃς ἐνθάδε τοὺς ἀπὸ νάσων
  τέσσαρας εὐθείαι παῖδας ἔκλινε μάχαι.
[44] Cf. *CEG* 862 (where the moment of return rather than that of crowning is highlighted), Ebert 56, 61 (*Anth. Pal.* 16.24), 67 (*Anth. Pal.* 9.588).
[45] British Museum B144 (*ABV* 307, 59).
[45a] μακάριος ἦσθα, Τιμόθε', ὅτε κᾶρυξ
  εἶπε· νικᾷ Τιμόθεος
  Μιλήσιος τὸν Κάμωνος τὸν ἰωνοκάμπταν.

The Economy of Kudos

Fig. 9.1 Herald announcing the victor in the horse race, as a youth approaches with tripod and crown. Black-figure amphora of Panathenaic shape, ca 570 BCE. London, British Museum B144. (Photo courtesy of the Trustees of the British Museum)

With these announcements we might compare early inscriptions, both prose and verse. In a prose inscription from Olympia dated to the first third of the fifth century we find the elements of the victory announcement pared down to the barest possible form: "Kallias son of Didymos won (the) *pankration*; Mikon the Athenian made (this statue)" (Καλλίας Διδυμίο Ἀθηναῖος παγκράτιον· / Μίκων ἐποίησεν Ἀθηναῖος) (Dittenberger and Purgold no. 146).[46] Some of the early verse inscriptions come close to the simplicity of their prose relatives – for example, a sixth-century inscription on a statue group of chariot, victor, and charioteer, as preserved for us by Pausanias:[47]

> Kleosthenes the son of Pontis from Epidamnos dedicated me when he won with the horses the noble contest of Zeus. (Paus. 6.10.6)[47a]

The only thing this couplet adds to the formula of the victory announcement (name of victor, patronymic, homeland, event, and site of games) is the fact of dedication, "dedicated me" (μ'ἀνέθηκεν).

Still other early inscriptions prefigure the more elaborate victory formula preserved by Dio Cassius. A late-sixth-century inscription recorded by Pausanias commemorates the victory of the racehorse Lykos:

> Swift-running Lykos, with victories once at the Isthmian Games, and two here, crowned the houses of the sons of Pheidolas. (Paus. 6.13.9)[47b]

As in the inscription on the pseudo-Panathenaic amphora, the horse itself figures in the nominative, and as in the proclamation of Nero, by his victories he "crowns" the house of his masters. We have seen this same formula of crowning for the fifth-century victor Theognetos; we can now appreciate how this inscription recreates the victory announcement in highly stylized form:

> Come to know Theognetos looking upon him, the boy Olympic victor, skilled charioteer of the wrestling, most beautiful to see, but in competing no worse than his form, who crowned the city of good fathers. (*Anth Pal.* 16.2)[47c]

The inscription captures the moment when Theognetos was the object of all eyes – the moment he stood before the Olympic herald.[48] With elaborate poetic periphrases, it informs us of his victory, of the site of the games, of his age class ("the boy victor", τὸν ὀλυμπιονίκαν παῖδα), of his event ("skilled charioteer of

---

[46] Cf. Dittenberger and Purgold 1896, nos. 143, 151, 152, 155, 158, 159, 162, 165, 167, 168, 173. It is worth noting that the prose inscriptions become more detailed with time, just as the announcements preserved in literary sources do: cf. Dittenberger and Purgold 1896, nos. 175, 177, 182.

[47] Cf. Paus. 6.9.9 and *CEG* 399. I ignore here as anachronistic Pausanias' distinction between hippic dedications and gymnastic memorials (Paus. 5.21.1): see Gardiner 1922: 123 and H.-V. Herrmann 1972: 243 n. 436.

[47a] Κλεοσθένης μ'ἀνέθηκεν ὁ Πόντιος ἐξ'Ἐπιδάμνου
νικήσας ἵπποις καλὸν ἀγῶνα Διός.

[47b] Ὠκυδρόμας Λύκος Ἰσθμι' ἅπαξ, δύο δ'ἐνθάδε νίκαις Φειδόλα παίδων ἐστεφάνωσε δόμους.

[47c] Γνῶθι Θεόγνητον προσιδών, τὸν ὀλυμπιονίκαν
παῖδα, παλαισμοσύνας δεξιὸν ἡνίοχον,
κάλλιστον μὲν ἰδεῖν, ἀθλεῖν δ'οὐ χείρονα μορφῆς,
ὃς πατέρων ἀγαθῶν ἐστεφάνωσε πόλιν.

[48] Cf. Pind. *Ol.* 8.17–20, *Ol.* 9.90–4, where the poet uses similar formulae to describe the beauty of a boy victor at the moment of crowning.

the wrestling", παλαισμοσύνας δεξιὸν ἡνίοχον), and of his crown as a communal honor.[49]

To say that the monument makes possible the eternal renewal of the moment of victory is not merely to repeat the claim that it memorializes the athlete forever in an idealized form. Indeed, it is a truism that the victor statue immortalizes its model, preserving him precisely as he was in his moment of glory and even assimilating him to the divine.[50] What I have in mind is at once more concrete and more firmly rooted in ritual practices than that modern aestheticizing formulation allows. I would like to follow the lead of Joseph Day, who has recently proposed that, in the archaic period, funerary and dedicatory inscriptions functioned together with their monuments as substitutes for the original ritual event or "scripts" for its re-enactment.[51] He has noted that such a model is also appropriate for epinikian inscriptions,[52] for the inscription traditionally contained some or all of the elements of the original victory announcement – the victor's name, his patronymic, his homeland, his event, and his age class. Therefore, when a passerby read the inscription aloud (and Jesper Svenbro has recently reminded us that reading in antiquity was almost exclusively reading aloud),[53] his voice was appropriated for the re-enactment of the original herald's announcement of the victor.

We can take the argument for the monument's ritual re-enactment yet a step further and suggest that the figurative references to crowning in the agonistic inscriptions evoke the original coronation of the victor. For we have evidence that the herald's public announcement of the victor's name, patronymic, and city took place *simultaneously* with his coronation by the Hellanodikas.[54] In this context, it is worth mentioning one of the more common types of victor statue, in which the victor stands at rest, wearing only a fillet.[55] Already by the Roman imperial period, it seems, this statue type was a source of puzzlement to viewers. Thus both Pausanias (6.14.6–7) and Philostratus *(Life of Apollonius* 4.28) offer somewhat fanciful explanations for the fillet depicted on an archaic statue of Milo of Kroton.[56] But in the archaic and classical periods, the fillet was the first token of

---

[49] Noteworthy is the omission of the victor's homeland, for which Ebert 1972: 58 offers two possible explanations: (1) his homeland Aigina may have been recorded in a prose inscription added to the epigram, or (2) this epigram may have come originally from a statue of Theognetos set up in Aigina itself (in which case we cannot connect this epigram with the Olympic statue of Theognetos described by Pausanias at 6.9.1).

[50] Thus, in different ways and to varying degrees, Hyde 1921: 71–99; Lattimore 1987; Serwint 1987: 18–24; Raschke 1988: 39–48; Vernant 1991: 159–63.

[51] Day 1989a, 1989b.

[52] Day 1989a.

[53] Svenbro 1988: 9, 23–4, 43–4, 53–73, following Knox 1968. So also Ebert 1972: 22; Day 1989a.

[54] See Gardiner 1910: 200–1, 205, 1955: 227–8; Nisetich 1975: 59, 64 with note 27. Nisetich adduces Eur. *Tro.* 220–3 and Paus. 8–40.2; he might have added a reference to the pseudo-Panathenaic amphora that we have already mentioned (Figure 9.1), for there a man approaches the victorious horseman bearing a tripod and a wreath as the herald announces the victory.

[55] See Hyde 1921: 148–55. Hyde (155) notes that the fillet is a much more common feature than an actual sculpted crown. See also Serwint 1987: 112–16.

[56] In Philostratus, Apollonius explains that Milo wears a fillet because he is represented as a priest of Hera. Pausanias' explanation of the fillet is much more far-fetched. He sees in it a representation of one of Milo's legendary feats of strength: "He would tie a cord round his forehead as though it were a ribbon or a crown. Holding his breath and filling with blood the veins on his head, he would break

Fig. 9.2 Crowning of athletic victor wreathed in fillets.
Black-figure amphora of Panathenaic shape.
London, British Museum B138. (Photo courtesy of the Trustees of the British Museum)

The Economy of Kudos 221

victory, whether bound on by the victor himself (as in Polykleitos' famous statue)[57] or by others immediately after the contest (as in the case of the Spartan Lichas binding a fillet on his victorious charioteer; Paus. 6.2.2). The public announcement and coronation of the victor took place afterward,[58] so presumably the athlete came forward to receive his crown still wearing his victory fillet (Fig. 9.2). If this was the case, the common type of the filleted athlete reproduced the victor just as he looked when he stood before the Hellanodikas to receive his crown. Thus the combination of epigram and victor statue elicited from its beholder a perfect re-creation of the original announcement and coronation. As the viewer lent his voice to the epigram that reconstructed the victory announcement, he stood in the position of the Hellanodikas and crowned the victor with his gaze.[59] Indeed, we know of at least one case in which the ritual re-enactment seems to have gone even further: Pausanias tells us that even in his time, the victor statue of Oibotas at Olympia was periodically crowned with real wreaths (Paus. 7.17.4).[60]

It is perhaps in the context of this elaborate ritual re-enactment that we should understand a formula preserved in two fourth-century BCE inscriptions. In an inscription from Olympia whose first line is completely lost we read:

> Stand and bestow *kudos* upon the achievement of the feet of this one. For twice he won the contest in the grove of Olympian Zeus, leaning his arm under a bronze shield, and first of the Cretans he beat all at Nemea and in [the festival] of Pallas Athena he was crowned. And twice he bears glory from under Parnassos, taking first place both in the diaulos and in the hoplitodromos. And not in vain did he wash the dust from his feet in the divine water of Kastalia. (*CEG* 849 = Ebert 48)[60a]

And in a badly damaged inscription from Thebes that Ebert dates to the fourth or third century BCE, on the basis of the letter forms:

> Stand and bestow *kudos* upon Lusixenos, [who in the Nemean grove won] victory from

---

the cord by the strength of these veins" (Paus. 6.14.7, trans. W. H. S. Jones). As Scherer 1885: 23–4, Gurlitt 1890: 413, and Hyde 1921: 106–7 saw long ago, Pausanias' entire fanciful narrative derives from a misunderstanding of traditional archaic sculptural forms. For more recent discussions, see Lattimore 1987: 255; Serwint 1987: 103–4.

[57] Cf. Paus. 6.4.5 and see Hyde 1921: 150–5 and Serwint 1987: 107–9 for discussion of the type.

[58] It is not certain whether the coronation occurred immediately after the contest or on the last day of the festival at Olympia; for discussion, see Gardiner 1910: 200–1.

[59] This reconstruction must remain largely speculative since we have very little solid evidence about which images went with which inscriptions. This aspect of ritual sheds new light on the observation of Nisetich 1975 that Pindar obsessively links crowns (real and metaphorical) with the naming of the victor in the odes. We can now link this practice with the victor monuments as ritual re-enactments in different media; that is, both monuments and *epinikion* function to reanimate the victor's *kudos* by restaging the victory announcement and coronation.

[60] See discussion on p. 230.

[60a] ἔσταθι κυ[δαίνων τοῦδε π]οδῶν ἀρε[τάν]·
δὶς γὰρ ἄε[θλον ἐνεί]κα[το] Ὀλυμπίου ἐν Διὸς [ἄ]λ[σ]ε[ι]
πᾶχυν ὑπ[αὶ] χ[αλκέ]αν ἀσ[π]ί[δ]α ἐρεισ[άμενος]·
πρᾶτος δ[ὲ Κρ]ητῶν [πά]ντας [νίκασε Νέμεια]
καὶ δ᾽ἐπ᾽Ἀθαν[α]ί[α]ς [Π]αλλ[άδο]ς ἐσ[τέφετο]·
δὶς δὲ ὑπὸ Παρνασσοῖο φέρει κλέος, [ἔν τε] δι[αύλωι]
τέρμα καὶ ὁπλοφόρ[ο]υ πρῶτος ἑλὼν ἀ[έ]θ[λου]·
οὐδὲ μάταν ἐλαφροῖσι κ[ό]νιμ περι[...]επει[...]αν
[π]ο[σ]σὶν Κασταλία[ς] θεῖον ἔνι[ψ]εν ὕ[δωρ]

the swift long-race when he outstripped the throng of boys. [Know that the youth of Thebes is] not without a share of divine crowns. (*CEG* 790 = Ebert 57)[61]

In the first inscription, the formula "stand and bestow *kudos*" (ἔσταθι κυδαίνων) prefaces an elaborate rendition of multiple victories at different contests and in different events, while the later inscription uses the same formula to commemorate a Nemean victor for a hometown audience. In spite of the fragmentary condition of the two epigrams, they seem to repeat the elements of the original victory announcements,[62] and in each case, they mention the victor's crowns ("he was crowned", ἐσ[τέφετο] *CEG* 849.6; "not without a share of divine crowns", θείων οὐκ ἄμορος στεφ[άνων] *CEG* 790.4). Insofar as the passerby's reading aloud and gaze re-create the original announcement and crowning of the victor, he can be said to "stand and bestow *kudos* upon" the image, even as the original act endowed the victor with talismanic power.[63] Thus the victory monument is doubly implicated in the economy of *kudos*, for it looks backward, as an honor that recompenses the victor's *kudos*, and forward, as the victor's talismanic double, perpetually regenerating his *kudos* in his absence.

For indeed, the absence of the victor – his eventual disappearance – is what the erection of the victory monument is predicated on. Because the victor will not always be available as bearer of *kudos*, the monument is fashioned to take his place. On a few occasions, the inscriptions themselves register the gap between the presence of the statue and the absence of the original victor.[64] Thus in a fifth-century distich from Olympia:

> Euthymos of Lokris, son of Astykles, I won the Olympic Games three times. And he set up this image for mortals to look upon. (*CEG* 399 = Ebert 16)[64a]

The verb "I won" (ἐνίκων) in the first line makes the statue speak as the victor, Euthymos of Lokris, but the abrupt third-person verb "he set up" (ἔστησεν) in the second line opens up a gap between the single past action of the now-absent victor and the eternal monument he set up.[65] In a more complex example from the early

---

[61] [Ἴστα]σο κυδαίνων Λυσίξεν[ον, ὃς Νεμεαίωι]
[εἰν ἄλ]σει νίκαν ὠκέος ἐγ δολί[χου]
[ἄρατ'], ἐπεὶ παίδων τέλος ἔδραμ[εν· ἴσθ' ὅτι Θήβας]
[ἁλικία] θείων οὐκ ἄμορος στεφ[άνων]
I accept Ebert's supplements; for a careful discussion of the merits and problems of other proposed supplements, see Ebert 1972: 173.
[62] We must assume that the first line of Ebert 48 contained the victor's name, patronymic, and ethnic. See Ebert 1972: 152.
[63] Cf. Ebert 1972: 152: "The passerby is supposed to announce the athletic fame of the one celebrated, which he does on the spot by reading aloud the epigram" (my translation).
[64] Svenbro 1988: 49–52 identifies this gap as the enabling condition of the earliest Greek inscriptions and suggests that it accounts for the "I" (ἐγώ) of the "oggetti parlanti" cataloged by Burzachechi 1962 and Häusle 1979. Cf. the discussion of D. C. Young 1983 on inscriptional ποτέ ("when").
[64a] Εὔθυμος Λοκρὸς Ἀστυκλέος τρὶς Ὀλύμπ' ἐνίκων·
εἰκόνα δ'ἔστησεν τήνδε βροτοῖς ἐσορᾶν.
[65] In this case, the oddness of the abrupt change from first to third person is palliated by the fact that the second half of the pentameter, "This ... for mortals to look at" (τήνδε βροτοῖς ἐσορᾶν) is a revision that appears to postdate the original inscription: it stands in an erasure and is slightly longer than the original half-line would have been. Roehl 1882: 108–9, followed by Dittenberger and Purgold 1896; Hyde 1921: 38; Moretti 1953: 30–2, 1957: 86; Ebert 1972: 70–1; and Lattimore 1987: 250–1

fourth century, the Spartan princess Kyniska shimmers in the play of presence and absence:

> My fathers and brothers [are] the kings of Sparta, and winning with the chariot of swift-footed horses, Kyniska set up this image. And I affirm that I alone of women from all Greece took this crown. (*CEG* 820 = Ebert 33; *Anth. Pal.* 13.16)[65a]

Here the notice of the actual victory and erection of the monument – "Kyniska, winning with the chariot, set up this image" – interrupts a first-person discourse of eternal presence: "*My* fathers and brothers [are] the kings of Sparta ... *I* affirm that *I* alone of women took this crown." As in the Euthymos inscription, the aorist third person verb ἔστασε shatters the perfect identification of victor and image, calling our attention to the erecting hand, now absent, of the victor.[66]

This rift is felt even more profoundly in the few inscriptions that collapse the commemoration of victory and burial. One such inscription preserved by Pausanias (probably from the second half of the fourth century) reads:

> Twice I win the men's single wrestling at Olympia and Pythia, three times at Nemea, and four times at the sea-girt Isthmus, Cheilon the son of Cheilon from Patrai, whom the Achaian people buried for the sake of his achievement when he perished in war. (Paus. 6.4.6)[66a]

---

conjecture that originally the city of Lokris or Euthymos' father had erected the statue, but that the Elean authorities "required the substitution of Euthymos as dedicant" (Lattimore 1987: 251; Roehl 1882: 108–9 suggested, *exempli gratia*, the supplement "his glorious fatherland" (πατρὶς ἀγαλλομένη) or "his father for his dear child" (παιδὶ φίλῳ γενέτωρ). In spite of these extenuating circumstances, I believe, the point stands: at least at the time when the inscription was altered, the shift from first to third person must have been received as acceptable. For a parallel (with no such curious history), see the Kyniska inscription (discussed below).

[65a] Σπάρτας μὲν βασιλῆες ἐμοὶ | πατέρες καὶ ἀδελφοί,
ἅρματι δ' ὠκυπόδων ἵππων | νικῶσα Κυνίσκα
εἰκόνα τάνδ' ἔστασε μόναν | δ' ἐμέ φαμι γυναικῶν
Ἑλλάδος ἐκ πάσας τόν|δε λαβεῖν στέφανον.

[66] I follow the reading of Ebert, who acknowledges the awkwardness of the shift from first to third person and back again, but is at a loss to explain it, except as the avoidance of an excessive frequency of *a-sounds* (1972: 112). Hansen (apud *CEG* 820) simply emends the stone's "he set up" (ἔστασε) to "I set up" (ἔστασα), claiming that there are no good parallels for such a shift from first to third person within an epigram before 300 BCE. But as Hansen himself notes (1989: 229) aside from the anomalous *CEG* 399 (see note 65), *CEG* 493 and *CEG* 595 exhibit the same shift between first and third person. For the reasons stated in the text, I believe the third-person (ἔστασε) should be retained rather than normalized as Hansen does. We find a similar effect, without the change of person in *CEG* 828 (= Ebert 38; 368 BCE):

> I was Hellanodikas then when Zeus granted to me to win the Olympics for the first time with prize-winning horses, but the second time again in succession with horses; and I was Troilos the son of Alkinoos.

Ἑλλήνων ἦρχον τότε Ὀλυμπίαι ἡνίκα μοι Ζεύς
δῶκεν νικῆσαι πρῶτον Ὀλυμπιάδα
ἵπποις ἀθλοφόροις, τὸ δὲ δεύτερον αὖτις ἐφεξῆς
ἵπποις· υἱὸς δ' ἦν Τρωίλος Ἀλκινόο.

As Ebert notes (1972: 129), the use of the imperfect ἦν in the last line of the inscription need not indicate that the victor was already dead at the time the monument was erected; it simply imagines the monument from the perspective of a future audience. Thus ἦν too registers the absence of the victor and the presence of the image.

[66a] Μουνοπάλην νικῶ δὶς Ὀλύμπια Πύθιά τ' ἄνδρας
τρὶς Νεμέᾳ, τετράκις δ' Ἰσθμῷ ἐν ἀγχιάλῳ,
Χείλων Χείλωνος Πατρεύς, ὃν λαὸς Ἀχαιῶν
ἐν πολέμῳ φθίμενον θάψ' ἀρετῆς ἕνεκεν.

The two distiches of the poem construct an elaborate opposition, juxtaposing e parallel realms of contests and wars, the eternal present "I win" (νικῶ) to the past event "buried" (θάψ(ε)), and the first person to the third. In the first two lines the statue speaks as the victor, but the relative clause in the third line modulates from identification to differentiation. The effect of this shift from first person to third and from present to past is to disengage the historic Cheilon, the man buried by the Achaians, from the eternal renewal of victory that the first distich enacts. It is the existence of the monument itself that enables the affirmation νικῶ.

A third-century funerary inscription from Miletus achieves a similar effect, while inverting the relation of first to third person:

> Those who guide straight with their ordinances the Olympic Festival, glorious to all the Greeks, crowned – and the immortals who reverence the memorials of victory [are] witnesses – Kleonikos winning the boys' wrestling without a fall. But I ... eidas, set up this memorial for my brother, and the polished column is fixed upon his tomb announcing his skill. But all Greece holds remembrance. (Ebert 65 = *Milet* 1238)[66b]

As Ebert notes, the first four lines do not look like a funerary epigram – instead, they echo and elaborate traditional formulae of agonistic inscriptions. Only with lines 5–7, with the appearance of the victor's brother as "I," does the occasion of the epigram become clear. The brother's "I" (ἐγώ) and his single past act of erecting the monument ("I set up": (ἔτεοξα) register with finality the victor's absence.

But again, this inscription reveals with particular clarity the function of the erected monument. The inscribed stone does not just mark the gap – the absence of the victor – it serves to replace him and renew his memory in a restored eternal present (notice the present participle "announcing" (ἀγγέλλων), and the present verb "holds" (ἔχει) in the last line). Given what we have seen of the agonistic epigrams' re-creation of the original victory announcement, it is tempting to read "announcing" here in its technical sense. The monument appropriates the voice of the herald, to repeat in perpetuity Kleonikos' victory. Although this inscription is late and part of a funerary monument rather than a victor group, I suggest that its strategies are comparable to those of earlier victor statues and epigrams. We might say that the victor monument inserts itself into the gap between presence and absence as a *kudos*-producing machine.

All this suggests that the emphasis on the exact likeness of the statue to the victor (both in the inscriptions and in the construction of a life-size image) is more than aesthetic: the statue is fashioned as an exact replica of the victor, as his talismanic double. In this sense, we might extend the argument of Jean-Pierre Vernant from early Greek images of the gods and of the dead to victor statues, and see in them the "presentification of the invisible" rather than the secular "imitation of appearance":

[66b] ['Εστεφο]ν εὐθὺ νόμοισι πανήγυριν ἡνιοχοῦντε[ς]
[Ἑλλησ]ι κλεινὴν πᾶσιν Ὀλυμπιάδα –
[μάρτ]υρες ἀθάνατοι νίκης μνημεῖα σέβοντες –
[ἀπτω]τεὶ νικῶντα πάλην παῖδας Κλεόνικο(ν)·
[αὐτὰ]ρ ἐγὼ τόδε ἔτεοξα κασιγνήτωι μνημεῖον
[...]ειδας, ξεστὸς δὲ κίων (ἐ)πὶ σήματι ἄραρε
[τέχν]ην ἀγγέλλων· μνήμην δ'ἔχει Ἑλλὰς ἅπασα.

Figure of the gods, figure of the dead. In each case, the problem is the same: by means of localization in an exact form and a well-determined place, how is it possible to give visual presence to those powers that come from the invisible and do not belong to the space here below on earth? The task is to make the invisible visible, to assign a place in our world to entities from the other world. In the representational enterprise, it can be said that at the outset, this paradoxical aspiration exists in order to inscribe absence in presence, to insert the other, the elsewhere, in our familiar universe. ... However the sacred power is represented, the aim is to establish a true communication, an authentic contact, with it. The ambition is to make this power present *hic et nunc*, to make it available to human beings in the ritually required forms.[67]

The ritual forms that surround the victor statue – the re-enactment of the crowning and victory announcement it enables – confirm its participation in the symbolic economy of *kudos*. Indeed, the talismanic quality of the image as the victor's double figures most prominently in stories where the ritual norms are transgressed, and it is to these that we now turn.

IV

By scenes of transgression I refer to those cases in which victors are "canonized" as cult heroes, for the economy of *kudos* outlined here will help, in turn, to explain that phenomenon. The class of heroized victors, which has been the subject of a great deal of discussion recently, includes Philippos of Kroton, Hipposthenes of Sparta, Polydamas of Skotusa, Diognetos of Crete, Euthykles of Lokris, Oibotas of Dyme, Kleomedes of Astypalaia, Euthymos of Epizephyrian Lokris, and Theagenes of Thasos.[68] Fontenrose, who produced the most detailed collection of the victor-hero stories, explicates the phenomenon as the superimposition of a legendary hero type onto a historical (or quasi-historical) figure: "The hero-athlete tale, therefore, belongs to a wider type of hero legend, and the athlete is a special case of the legendary hero who was warrior, hunter, and athlete in one. The legend type

---

[67] Vernant 1991: 153. Vernant himself acknowledges the applicability of this analysis to victor statues: If the archaic statue uses the human figure to convey this set of "values" that in their plenitude only belong to divinity and appear like a fragile reflection when they gleam on the body of mortals, we can then understand how the same image, the votive Kouros, can sometimes represent the god himself or sometimes a human person who, *by virtue of his victory in the Games or through some other consecration*, is revealed as "equal to the gods". (Vernant 1991: 161; my emphasis)
Yet he also traces a development whereby the image as a "copy that imitates a model" represents a new state: "The human figure must have ceased to incarnate religious values; in its appearance, it must have become in and for itself the model to be reproduced" (Vernant 1991: 163). I am not so sure a clear evolutionary model is appropriate: it may be that the two conceptions of figural art co-existed for a long time. As a parallel, see Mango 1963, who discusses the reception of ancient statuary in the Byzantine era and notes the co-existence in the sources of a belief in the magical power of statues and an interest in their artistic, mimetic qualities (which he analyzes in terms of "popular" and "intellectual" responses respectively).

[68] For discussions, see Gardiner 1916–17; Mylonas 1943–4; Pouilloux 1954; Fontenrose 1968; Hönle 1972: 98–106; Bohringer 1979; Crotty 1982: 122–31; Lattimore 1987; Serwint 1987: 19–24. I follow Serwint's list rather than that of Fontenrose, who includes many figures who fit his hero type, though they are not necessarily athletic victors. For summaries of the stories attached to these victors, see Fontenrose, Crotty, and Serwint.

tended to attach itself to famous athletes and shape them into legendary heroes."[69] Fontenrose's analysis offers us a descriptive paradigm for the assimilation of certain athletic victors to an ancient combat myth. What it does not provide is any motivation for this process – why should athletic victors in particular be available for such assimilation? That is to say, in what way were victors perceived by the Greeks as particularly like cult heroes? Nor does Fontenrose's model explain why only certain athletic victors achieved cult status. As E.N. Gardiner pointed out long ago, only a handful of the approximately eight hundred Olympic victors known to us from antiquity were worshiped as heroes.[70] Thus any explanatory model must account not only for what made certain athletes like cult heroes, but also for what made most unlike them.[71]

Furthermore, Fontenrose observes without being able to explain the prominence of victor statues in many of the athlete-hero legends he catalogs.[72] Thus in the stories of Theagenes, Euthykles, and Euthymos, it is something done to the victor's *statue* that precipitates heroization, while the statues of Theagenes and Polydamas were reputed to have healing powers, long after their deaths (Lucian *Deor. conc.* 12). Finally, in the case of Oibotas (and perhaps Kleomedes), it is the lack of a statue and the honor it represents that provokes the anger of the athlete-turned-*daimôn*. All these story patterns become comprehensible once we situate the victor statue within the economy of *kudos*. As the victor's magical double, the statue continues to embody his talismanic power even after his disappearance and/or eventual death. In the case of athlete-heroes, where, as we shall see, there is a transgression or violation of the proper circulation of *kudos*, the statue functions as a kind of lightning rod, focusing and drawing off this imbalance of dangerous energy.[73]

Let us begin with the observation of François Bohringer that we can pinpoint the phenomenon of athletic heroization to a precise historical context: most of these athletes either belong to the first half of the fifth century or are eighth century winners who seem to receive cult honors starting in the fifth century.[74] It is Bohringer's contention that what makes these athletes different from all the others is that their *cities* confront a period of crisis – either from internal stasis or from the threat of an

---

[69] Fontenrose 1968: 87.
[70] Gardiner 1916–17: 96, followed by Mylonas 1943–4: 289 and Serwint 1987: 19.
[71] Nor does it solve the problem to claim, as Gardiner 1916–17: 96–7, Mylonas 1943–4: 284–9, and Serwint 1987: 19–24 do, that these athletes' "special recognition … had nothing to do with their athletic victories" (Serwint 1987: 19). Such a claim smacks of special pleading: it can hardly be a coincidence that all nine had some connection with the great games. What these scholars' elaborate counterarguments do suggest is that there was a complex interplay of factors involved in heroization, only one of which was athletic victory.
[72] Fontenrose 1968: 78. Note Fontenrose's characteristics (K), "The athlete had something to do with rock and stone," and (M), "His statue was powerful or extraordinary."
[73] I am indebted here to Vernant's discussion of the colossus as magical double:
> [The colossus] served to attract and pin down a double which found itself in abnormal circumstances. It made it possible to reestablish correct relations between the world of the dead and the world of the living … The colossos fulfils several complementary functions: it is a visible representation of the power of the dead man, it embodies the active manifestations of it, and it regulates the relationship between it and the living. (Vernant 1983: 314)

[74] Bohringer 1979. Gardiner 1916–17: 97, Moretti 1957: 84, and Hönle 1972: 99 also note that this is predominantly a late-sixth- and early-fifth-century phenomenon.

external enemy.⁷⁵ As an example of the former he cites Theagenes of Thasos, whom Pouilloux argued was an active part of the pro-Athenian government of the city in the 450s and 440s.⁷⁶ The saga of his statue – that it was whipped nightly after his death by an enemy, until one night it fell on the enemy and killed him, then was cast into the sea, and miraculously recovered and restored by command of the Delphic oracle (Paus. 6.11.6–9) – maps in symbolic form the struggles for supremacy of the pro-Athenian faction against the opposition. As a parallel, we might think of the story recounted by Thucydides in which the Amphipolitans rejected Hagnon the Athenian as their oikist in the 420s, installing in his stead a cult of Brasidas, the victorious Spartan commander killed in the Battle of Amphipolis (Thuc. 5.11).

As an example of the second possibility – the threat of an external enemy – Bohringer cites the case of Euthymos of Lokris, reputed to be the son of the river Kaikinos, which marked the boundary between Lokris and Rhegion. We know that in the 470s, Rhegion was a very belligerent neighbour, threatening to expand into the territory of Lokris.⁷⁷ Under the circumstances, it was clearly advantageous for Lokris to claim a local hero whose river-god father circumscribed the limit of Rhegian territory. Or again, Bohringer suggests that the heroization of Oibotas sometime before 460 BCE was the result of the annexation of his city, Paleia, by neighboring Dyme. Along with the city, the eighth-century athletic victor was also annexed, grafted onto a pre-existing hero cult to legitimate the takeover.⁷⁸ This is not to suggest that these instances represent the cynical manipulation of cult for political ends: it seems rather that the political was still firmly embedded in a set of symbolic forms that included *kudos* and hero cult.

These, then, are the political conditions that can precipitate heroization. And we can say that athletes are available for heroization because they already participate in the realm of talismanic power. But if we ask how the Greeks themselves seem to have conceptualized and represented the process, it is as an imbalance in the economy of *kudos*. That is, those athletes become heroes who possess a superabundance of *kudos* or who suffered in life from a dearth of proper honors in response to their *kudos*.⁷⁹ In the first category, consider Philippos of Kroton, who died in the battle against Egesta in 520 BCE. Herodotus tells us, "And there died together

---

⁷⁵ Bohringer's model of crisis in fifth-century Greece corresponds well to Weber's general analysis of the origins of charismatic authority. As Weber observes:
> All extraordinary needs, i.e., those which transcend the sphere of everyday economic routines, have always been satisfied in an entirely heterogeneous manner: on a *charismatic* basis ... the "natural" leaders in moments of distress – whether psychic, physical, economic, ethical, religious, or political – were neither appointed officeholders nor "professionals" in the present-day sense ... but rather the bearers of specific gifts of body and mind that were considered "supernatural" (in the sense that not everybody could have access to them). (Weber 1978: 1111–12; see also 1148)

⁷⁶ Pouilloux 1954: 72–7.
⁷⁷ Cf. Pind. *Pyth.* 2.18–20 with scholia (Drachmann 1964: 2.37–8).
⁷⁸ Bohringer 1979: 10–13. Pausanias notes and tries to rationalize the discrepancy between Oibotas' athletic inscription at Olympia (which designates Paleia as his hometown) and the tradition of his cult in Dyme (Paus. 7.17.6–7). For a different explanation of the discrepancy, see Ebert 1972: 85–6.
⁷⁹ The analysis of Crotty 1982: 122–31 accounts for the second category as those who fail to achieve reintegration in their communities. The weakness of Crotty's model, however, is that it does not account for the first category of victors – those who do not seem to be alienated from their communities in any way.

with him Philippos the son of Boutakides, the Krotoniate, who was an Olympic victor and the most beautiful of the Greeks at his time (ἐών τε Ὀλυμπιονίκης καὶ κάλλιστος Ἑλλήνων τῶν κατ' ἑωυτόν). And because of his beauty, he received from the Egestans what no other [ever had]: over his tomb having established a heroön, they propitiate him with sacrifices" (Hdt 5.47). It appears that, in this narrative, his beauty *on top of* his Olympic victory stands as a sign of extraordinary divine favor and power.[80] A similar case is that of Polydamas of Skotusa. An Olympic pankration victor (408 BCE), he is described by Pausanias as "the tallest of all men except those called heroes". Pausanias goes on to tell us that Polydamas (emulating Herakles) killed a lion with his bare hands, defeated three of the Persian immortals in single combat, and accomplished many other "marvels" (*thaumata*) of strength (Paus. 6.5.4–8). Again, consider the stories that cluster around Euthymos of Epizephyrian Lokris. A boxer who won Olympic victories in 484, 476, and 472, he is said to have exorcised the Hero of Temessa, who haunted the city and exacted tribute of one local maiden a year (Paus. 6.6.4–11). According to Callimachus and Pliny the Elder, his two victory statues, one at Olympia and the other in Lokris, were struck by lightning on the very same day. The Delphic oracle, consulted about this marvel, bid the Lokrians sacrifice to Euthymos as a hero while he lived and as a god after his death.[81] We might describe lightning in this narrative as *kudos* made visible, a tangible sign from heaven singling out Euthymos for extraordinary, divine honors.[82]

The second category of victors comprises those who do not receive adequate acknowledgment and recompense for their *kudos* during their lifetimes. This failure of acknowledgment can take place either at the games or on their return home – the two nodes of significant ritual activity we identified earlier. For the individual, this breakdown in the economy of *kudos* means that the honor that is ultimately paid must be all the more extreme. For the victor's city, the circulation of *kudos* does not operate as it should, so that we might say that the only way the city can participate in the victor's power is by instituting cult. Consider first Kleomedes of Astypalaia, who killed his opponent in a boxing match at Olympia in 496 BCE. He was denied the victor's crown, returned home, and in a fit of insanity killed sixty local schoolboys by knocking down the pillar supporting the schoolhouse roof. When the Astypalaians pursued him to stone him, Kleomedes hid in a box in the temple of Athena.[83] Opening the container, his baffled fellow citizens found nothing and, consulting the Delphic oracle, were informed, "Kleomedes is the last of the heroes: honor him with sacrifices, since he is no longer mortal" (Paus. 6.9.6–8). Here it seems that, having been deprived of the normal victory and re-entry rites, Kleomedes carries his *kudos* with him as a dangerous potency. A more extreme recompense is required to defuse that power and achieve the proper "circulation"

---

[80] For the pattern of heroizing a potent military enemy, see Visser 1982.

[81] Callim. frs. 98–9 Pfeiffer; Pliny *HN* 7.152.

[82] According to Plutarch, the bodies of those struck by lightning do not decay (*Quaest. conv.* 4.665c–d), while according to Artemidorus, to dream of lightning is fortunate for athletes, since it signifies victory (*Oneir.* 2.9). I owe both references to Serwint 1987: 51–2. Cf. Rohde 1920: 581–2: app. I; A. B. Cook 1925: 2.1.9, 22–36.

[83] Where perhaps, in the "normal" course of things, he might have dedicated his crown or set up a victory statue.

of *kudos*.⁸⁴

The story of Euthykles of Lokris provides another instance of a failure of honor that leads to a breakdown in the economy of *kudos*. According to Callimachus (frs. 84 and 85 Pfeiffer), Euthykles of Lokris won the Olympic pentathlon and some time thereafter was sent as ambassador to another city. He returned to Lokris with a set of mules (ἀπηναίους ... ὀρῆ[ας]) presented to him by a guest-friend. The demos of Lokris, "ever choked over the wealthy," interpreted the gift as a bribe and condemned Euthykles.⁸⁵ In addition, the Lokrians proceeded to mutilate his victory statue, which the city itself had erected. Thereupon, they suffered famine and consulted the Delphic oracle, who told them, "When you hold in honor the one without honor, then you will plow your land" (ἐν τιμῇ τὸν ἄτιμον ἔχων τότε γαῖαν ἀρόσσεις; Oinomaos of Gadara apud Euseb. *Praep. Evang* 5.34.15–16). When they understood the oracle, the Lokrians built an altar to Euthykles and honored his statue "like that of Zeus" (Callimachus fr. 85 [dieg. II 5] Pfeiffer).

The nearest parallel for the elements in this account is the story of Astylos of Kroton (see note 39), which also reveals what is at stake for the citizens of the victor's city. Recall that Astylos had himself "announced as Syracusan to gratify Hieron" (Paus. 6.13.1), whereupon the citizens of Kroton turned his house into a prison and tore down his local victor statue. In this instance, Astylos' use of the ethnic Syracusan in the victory announcement transfers his talismanic power to Hieron's city: under the circumstances, it is quite understandable that his fellow citizens should dismantle his victor statue, that *kudos*-producing machine. The parallel suggests that for the Lokrians also the issue of Euthykles' loyalty is an issue of who enjoys his special power: in the gift of mules, we might say, the Lokrians read a competing economy of powers and honors. Indeed, the gift of mules and a car may itself be significant, since it allows Euthykles to re-enact the *eiselasis* awarded to crown victors, but now under the auspices of another city. It turns out, however, that the Lokrians' suspicion is unjustified, and greater honor must be paid Euthykles as a result (notice the emphasis on τιμή and the pun on ἄτιμος in the oracle).

Finally, there is the example of Oibotas, eighth-century Olympic stadion victor. According to Pausanias, he was the first Achaian to win at Olympia, and yet he received "no special honor" (γέρας οὐδὲν ἐξαίρετον; 7.17.13) from the Achaians on his return home. Angered at this lack of proper acknowledgment, Oibotas cursed the Achaians, praying that they might never have another Olympic victor. Three centuries later, the Achaians finally consulted the Delphic oracle about "why they were always missing the mark of the crown at the Olympics" (στεφάνου τοῦ Ὀλυμπίασιν ἡμάρτανον; 7.17.13). The oracle informed them and they honored Oibotas with a statue at Olympia, whereupon an Achaian immediately won the stade race (in 460 BCE).⁸⁶ After that, says Pausanias,

---

⁸⁴ For another example of this pattern, we might cite Diognetos of Crete, a shadowy figure of whom we know only that he killed his boxing opponent Herakles (!) and so was denied the Olympic crown by the Elean authorities. Our only source, Ptolemy Hephaestion (ap. Phot. *Bibl.* 190. 151b) records that "the Cretans honor this Diognetos as a hero".

⁸⁵ Euseb. *Praep. Evang.* 5.34.15–16 preserves the tradition that Euthykles was imprisoned and subsequently died. Callimachus appears to make no mention of the athlete, concentrating his attention entirely on the fate of Euthykles' statue.

⁸⁶ In fact, this account ignores the fact that Achaians won at the Olympics in 688, 512, and 496 BCE.

Even to my time, those of the Achaians who are going to compete at the Olympic Games still make offerings to Oibotas, and, if they win, they crown the statue of Oibotas at Olympia. (Paus. 7.17.14)[86a]

It is as if Oibotas has simply been inserted as an extra station in the Achaians' circulation of *kudos*. With each new Achaian victory, his statue is recrowned and his original talismanic power reactivated. And in this light, one other story Pausanias tells about Oibotas is worth mentioning. He reports with disbelief what some of the Greeks say: that although he won the Olympics in the eighth century, Oibotas "fought together with the Greeks at the Battle of Plataea" (Paus. 6.3.8). This anecdote (which Pausanias transmits without crediting) suggests the benefits thought at an earlier time to accrue for the city that tapped into the *kudos* of a victor by transforming him into a cult hero.

V

We have located the conceptual origin of athletic heroization in an imbalance in the symbolic economy of *kudos*. But our analysis must still account for the temporal localization of this phenomenon. Clearly, the first half of the fifth century was not the only period of crisis or major danger for the Greek cities, so why was the heroization of athletic victors generally restricted to this era? It is perhaps that the late sixth and early fifth centuries saw a crucial conjunction of factors: on the one hand, a period of great external threat and internal upheaval; on the other hand, a serious bid for talismanic power by a beleaguered aristocracy. That is to say, perhaps we must ground our cultural poetics in a politics and see the phenomenon of *kudos* as an attempt by the aristocracy to lay claim to special power within the polis. J. K. Davies has observed that aristocratic participation in chariot racing at the great games increased dramatically in the sixth and fifth centuries BCE, and then dropped off again in the fourth. He explains this phenomenon as the deployment of property power as a substitute for the aristocracy's waning cult power within the city, to be replaced, toward the end of the fifth century, by rhetorical skill. All we need add to Davies' model is that charismatic authority is involved at least in the first two forms of power.[87] Thus Max Weber himself mentions the hereditary priesthoods of ancient Greece as a form of "charismatic blood relationship". As this institutionalized form of charisma recedes in the face of the rational order of the

---

[86a] διαμένει δὲ ἐς ἐμὲ ἔτι Ἀχαιῶν τοῖς ἀγωνίζεσθαι μέλλουσι τὰ Ὀλύμπια ἐναγίζειν τῷ Οἰβώτᾳ, καὶ ἢν κρατήσωσιν, ἐν Ὀλυμπίᾳ στεφανοῦν τοῦ Οἰβώτα τὴν εἰκόνα.

[87] Davies 1981: 88–131. Davies' model applies specifically to Athens, but we might extend it mutatis mutandis to aristocrats and others throughout the Greek world. Indeed, we can observe several different constituencies in different places seeking legitimacy or renewed talismanic authority through athletic victory. In western Greece, this is the period of intensive participation in the great games by tyrants; in Sparta, the kings and certain aristocrats who opposed the ephors were very active in chariot-racing competitions (on chariot racing as a significant political gesture by the Spartan aristocracy, see Hönle 1972: 146–59). In this context, it is worth noting that one of the latest-known victor-heroes is Kyniska of Sparta, daughter and sister of Spartan kings, who, according to Plutarch (*Ages.* 20), was encouraged in her horse-racing proclivities by her brother, King Agesilaos. Do her competition and heroization reflect a final bid for renewed talismanic authority by the Spartan kingship in the face of the encroaching power of the Ephorate?

polis, aristocrats seek to renew their power and prestige within the city by personal charisma won at the great games.[88]

Indeed, we can see this contested form of power, its lines of conflict, inscribed in two of the most familiar texts of the fifth century– Herodotus' account of the meeting of Solon and Croesus (Hdt. 1.30–3) and Xenophanes fr. 2 DK. In Herodotus, the encounter of the fabulously wealthy Lydian king and the Athenian sage occupies a prominent place. In the famous anecdote, Solon answers Croesus' question, "Who is the most blessed (ὀλβιώτατος) of mortals?" by naming three Greek private citizens. To the relentless materialism of Croesus Solon opposes a symbolic economy of *kudos* in the two complementary realms of war and contests.[89] Though it is not often remarked (because Solon's paradigms are most often misread as a valorization of the simple life of the ordinary citizen), Tellos, as well as Kleobis and Biton, achieve extraordinary feats and enjoy extraordinary honor. Tellos the Athenian, whom Solon "considers the most blessed of men, died a glorious death in battle after routing the enemy" (τροπὴν ποιήσας τῶν πολεμίων ἀπέθανε κάλλιστα; 1.30.5). The Athenians buried him "at public expense in the very spot where he fell and honored him greatly." Both his burial on the battlefield and Herodotus' expression ἐτίμησαν μεγάλως ("honoured him greatly") suggest that Tellos received cult honor after death (like those fallen and buried at Marathon and Plataea).[90]

As the complement to Tellos, Kleobis and Biton achieve an extraordinary feat in peacetime. Yet when we look closely at Herodotus' narrative, we discover that the shape of their story is the shape of athletic victory. We are told at the outset that the two had remarkable strength of body, and the proof is that both were "prizewinners" (ἀεθλοφόροι). Herodotus continues "and especially this story is told" (καὶ δὴ καὶ λέγεται ὅδε λόγος). Καὶ δὴ καὶ in Herodotus conventionally adds the emphatic term to a series to which it belongs, so that here it situates the entire ensuing narrative under the sign of athletic victory.[91] And indeed, Kleobis and Biton are represented as engaged in a race, competing against the clock to bring their mother to the festival on time. When they reach the temple, the Argives surround them, "calling blessed the strength of the young men, and the Argive women blessing the mother for such children". Herodotus' narrative here evokes the *makarismos*, "the calling blessed," that traditionally accompanied the binding-on of fillets or the *phyllobolia* of the athlete immediately after the victory.[92] Finally, after their magical death, the Argives dedicate images of them at Delphi "on the grounds that they proved themselves to be the best men" (ὡς ἀνδρῶν ἀρίστων γενομένων). Here again, Herodotus' narrative replicates the conventions of athletic victory and its commemoration.

---

[88] Quote from Weber 1978: 1137. According to the model of Weber (1978: 1111–1300), charisma always starts as personal and discontinuous (in contrast to patriarchal or bureaucratic authority). It can be institutionalized to support the claims of royal or aristocratic power, but eventually the institutionalized form gives way before the rational order of discipline and/or the worldly concerns of economics.

[89] For a similar interpretation of Solon and Croesus, see Konstan 1983: 15–19; cf. Konstan 1987 (on the contrast Herodotus constructs between Greek and Persian notions of value in the *Histories*).

[90] Cf. How and Wells 1928: I. 68; Loraux 1986: 38–42.

[91] On Herodotus' use of καὶ δὴ καί, see Denniston 1954: 255–6; Erbse 1956: 215–16.

[92] Cf. Bacchyl. 3.10; Pindar *Nem.* 11.11–12; Eur. *Bacch.* 1180,1242–3; Timoth. fr. 26 *PMG*.

But Tellos and Kleobis and Biton are not only the embodiments of *kudos* in war and contests, respectively; they are also represented in Solon's discourse as aristocrats perfectly integrated into their civic communities. Again, because scholars tend to see the narrative as a valorization of the ordinary citizen, the aristocratic milieu of the story is rarely noted. But we are told that Tellos' children were "*kaloi t' kagathoi*" (gentlemen) and that his death was "*lamprotatê*" (most glorious) (practically a buzzword in Herodotus and Thucydides for aristocratic display).[93] Kleobis and Biton, too, given that they were athletic victors, were likely to be aristocrats.[94] Yet these narratives strike a careful balance between the exceptional achievement of individual aristocrats and their participation in their civic communities. In the case of Tellos, it is easy to see how his death in battle functions as both a personal triumph and a civic good, but the treatment of Kleobis and Biton suggests that the civic advantages of athletic victory are somewhat more ambiguous. It is perhaps for this reason that all the elements of athletic victory are displaced in their story from agonistic competition itself to the transportation of their mother to a civic festival of Hera, for the latter stands unambiguously as the service of the common good.[95]

Once we discern in Tellos and Kleobis and Biton aristocratic embodiments of the economy of *kudos*, we can recognize that Herodotus' narrative participates in the "contest of paradigms" so characteristic of the late archaic period.[96] In setting these figures up as *paradeigmata* of human blessedness, the narrative attempts to make the values they represent into the only possible civic values. That these values are contested we can see from Xenophanes fr. 2 DK, a text that we must set in dialogue with Herodotus' account. In Herodotus, Solon opposes the purely material economy of Croesus with a symbolic economy of *kudos*. In the fragment of Xenophanes, the poet's voice espouses just the opposite: he rejects the symbolic economy that subtends athletic victory in favor of a material economy of civic acquisition. Xenophanes does not deny that athletic victors are possessors of *kudos*, for he begins his denunciation of athletics, "But if someone should win victory by the swiftness of his feet, or in the pentathlon, where the precinct of Zeus [is] beside the streams of Pisa in Olympia, or wrestling, or even having the grievous boxing, or the terrible contest which they call the pankration, then he would be more prestigious for his fellow citizens to look upon" (ἀστοῖσίν κ'εἴη κυδρότερος προσορᾶν; fr. 2.1–6).[97] Yet the poet resolutely refuses to engage the issue of athletics

---

[93] Also, according to the model of Loraux 1986: 42–56, the very fact that Tellos is remembered by name, rather than in an anonymous *dêmosion sêma*, harks back to an aristocratic paradigm of the "fine death".

[94] Though D. C. Young 1984 has challenged the assumption that athletic victors of the archaic and classical periods were inevitably aristocratic, it is likely that panhellenic victors at such an early date would have been upper class, since they alone had the necessary funds and leisure time for arduous training and competition. See Kyle 1985, Instone 1986, and Poliakoff 1989 for critiques of Young's argument.

[95] For an expression of similar ambivalence about the communal value of athletic victory, cf. Tyrtaios fr. 12 W, lines 1–16.

[96] I borrow the phrase "contest of paradigms" from V. Turner 1974: 14. For more discussion of this phenomenon in the late archaic period, see Kurke 1991.

[97] With this acknowledgment and subsequent rejection of talismanic power, we might compare Euripides' denunciation of athletic victors (from a fragment of the *Autolykos* preserved in Athenaeus). There, the unknown speaker insists that men who are "wise and good," "restrained and just" are more

on the level of this symbolic economy. Instead, he shifts the terms in the last lines of the fragment, focusing on the city's "good government" and material prosperity: "For not even if a good boxer should be among the people, or one who is good at the pentathlon or wrestling or in the swiftness of his feet, the very thing which is most honored of all the works of strength of men in the contest, would the city on that account be more orderly. But there would be small joy for the city in this - if someone competing win beside the banks of Pisa – for these things do not fatten the city's coffers" (οὐ γὰρ πιαίνει ταῦτα μυχοὺς πόλιος; fr. 2.15–22). Certain modern scholars have read Xenophanes' poetry as an attack on aristocratic values, and we may apply that interpretation to fr. 2 as well.[98] In response to a serious aristocratic bid for renewed talismanic authority within the community, Xenophanes counters with a very different model of civic good, consciously rejecting charismatic power in favor of material well-being.

It is within this contest of paradigms that we must situate the victory odes of Pindar and Bacchylides. I began this essay by asking about the meaning of *kudos* within *epinikion*. If the economy of *kudos* does indeed have the political component I am suggesting, we should perhaps invert the priority of the terms: it is not *kudos* that resides within *epinikion*, but rather *epinikion* that functions within the economy of *kudos*. It is then no accident that *epinikion* as a genre appeared in the late sixth century and enjoyed its heyday in the first half of the fifth. *Epinikion*, victor statues, *and* the heroization of athletic victors proliferated in this period, all symptoms of an active negotiation between the aristocracy and the community at large over the forms of charismatic power. For all three – *epinikion*, victor statues, and athlete-hero cult – publicly restaged the original circulation of the crown in order to renew in perpetuity the victor's special power for his city.

WORKS CITED

Benveniste, E. 1973. *Indo-European Language and Society*. Trans. E. Palmer. London: Faber & Faber.
Berve, H. 1937. *Miltiades: Studien zur Geschichte des Mannes und seiner Zeit*. Hermes Einzelschriften, vol. 2. Berlin: Weidmann.
Blech, M. 1982. *Studien zum Kranz bei den Griechen*. Berlin: Weidman.
Boedeker, D. 1987. "Protesilaos and the End of Herodotus' Histories". *CA* 7.30–48.
Bohringer, F. 1979. "Cultes d'athlètes en Grèce classique: Propos politique, discours mythique". *REA* 81.5–18.
Bowra, C. M. 1971. "Xenophanes on the Luxury of Colophon". In *On Greek Margins*. Oxford: Oxford University Press.
Burzachechi, M. 1962. "Oggetti parlanti nelle epigrafi greche". *Epigraphica* 25.3–54.
Cartledge, P. 1987. *Agesilaos and the Crisis of Sparta*. Baltimore, Md.: Johns Hopkins University Press.

---

advantageous to the city than victorious athletes (Eur. fr. 282 Nauck²). Nonetheless, the speaker acknowledges that athletic victors go "splendid in their youth and objects of admiration for the city" (λαμπροὶ δ' ἐν ἥβῃ καὶ πόλεως ἀγάλματα). The designation of victors as "objects of admiration" (ἀγάλματα), is especially interesting in this context – we can understand the term etymologically as "objects of admiration", but its conventional meaning at this time is "a statue", especially "an image of a god".

[98] See Mazzarino 1947; Bowra 1971: 115–21; Fränkel 1973: 328–33.

Chamoux, F. 1953. *Cyrène sous la monarchie des Battiades*. Paris: Bibliothèque des Écoles françaises d'Athènes et de Rome. Fasc. 77.
Cook, A. B. 1925. *Zeus: A Study in Ancient Religion*, vol. 2: *Zeus God of the Dark Sky (Thunder and Lightning)*. Cambridge: Cambride University Press.
Cornford, F. M. 1927. "The Origin of the Olympic Games". In J. Harrison, *Themis: A Study of the Social Origins of Greek Religion*, 2d ed. Cambridge: Cambridge University Press.
Crotty, K. 1982. *Song and Action: The Victory Odes of Pindar*. Baltimore, Md: Johns Hopkins University Press.
Davies, J. K. 1981. *Wealth and the Power of Wealth in Classical Athens*. Salem, N.H.: Ayer.
Day, J. W. 1989a. "Early Greek Dedicatory Epigrams as Substitutes for Ritual". Paper presented at the annual meeting of the American Philological Association, Boston, December 30, 1989.
Day, J. W. 1989b. "Rituals in Stone: Early Greek Grave Epigrams and Monuments". *JHS* 109. 16–28.
Denniston, J. D. 1954. *The Greek Particles*, 2nd ed. Oxford: Oxford University Press.
Dittenberger, W., and J. Purgold, eds 1896. *Ausgrabungen von Olympia*, vol. 5. Berlin, Asher.
Dougherty, C. 1993. "It's murder to found a colony". In *Cultural Poetics in Archaic Greece: Cult, performance, politics*. Ed. C. Dougherty and L. Kurke. Cambridge: Cambridge University Press. 178–98.
Drachmann, A. B., ed. 1964. *Scholia Vetera in Pindari Carmina*. 3 vols. Amsterdam: A. M. Hakkert.
Ebert, J., ed. 1972. *Griechische Epigramme auf Sieger an gymnischen und hippischen Agonen*. Abhandlungen der sächsischen Akademie der Wissenschaften zu Leipzig, Phil.-hist Kl. vol. 63, pt. 2.
Erbse, H. 1956. "Der erste Satz im Werke Herodots". In *Festschrift Bruno Snell*. Ed. H. Erbse. Munich: Beck. 209–22.
Fontenrose, J. 1968. "The Hero as Athlete". *CSCA* 1.73–104.
Forbes, C. A. 1952. "Crime and Punishment in Greek Athletics". *CJ* 47.169–73.
Fränkel, H. 1973. *Early Greek Poetry and Philosophy*. Trans. M. Hadas and J. Willis. New York: Harcourt.
Frazer, J. G. 1935. *The Golden Bough*, part 3: *The Dying God*, vol. 4. New York: Macmillan.
Gagé, J. 1953. ""Fornix Ratumenus": L'entrée "iselastique" etrusque et la "porta Triumphalis" de Rome". *Bulletin de la Faculté des Lettres de Strasbourg* 31.163–80.
Gardiner, E. N. 1910. *Greek Athletic Sports and Festivals*. London: Macmillan Press.
Gardiner, E. N. 1916–17. "The Alleged Kingship of the Olympic Victor". *BSA* 22.85–106.
Gardiner, E. N. 1922. Review of W. W. Hyde, *Olympic Victor Monuments and Greek Athletic Art*. *JHS* 42.123–4.
Gardiner, E. N. 1955. *Athletics of the Ancient World*, 2d ed. Oxford: Oxford University Press.
Greenblatt, S. 1980. *Renaissance Self-fashioning from Moore to Shakespeare*. Chicago: University of Chicago Press.
Greenblatt, S. 1988. *Shakespearean Negotiations: The Circulation of Social Energy in Renaissance England*. Berkeley and Los Angeles: University of California Press.
Griffin, M. 1984. *Nero: The End of a Dynasty*. New Haven, Conn.: Yale University Press.
Gurlitt, W. 1890. *Über Pausanias*. Graz: Leuschner & Lubensky.
Hansen, P. A. 1983. *Carmina Epigraphica Graeca (Saec. VIII–V)*. Berlin: de Gruyter.
Hansen, P. A. 1989. *Carmina Epigraphica Graeca (Saec. IV. A. Chr. N.)*. Berlin: de Gruyter.
Harrison, J. E. 1912. *Themis: A Study of the Social Origins of Greek Religion*. Repr. 1927. Cambridge: Cambridge University Press.
Häusle, H. 1979. "ΖΩΟΠΟΙΕΙΝ – ΥΦΙΣΤΑΝΑΙ": Eine Studie der frühgriechischen inschriftlichen Ich-Rede der Gegenstände." In *Serta Philologica Aenipontana*, vol. 3.

Ed. R. Muth and G. Pfohl. Innsbruck: Sprachwissenschaftliche Institut der Leopold-Franzens-Universität. 23–139.
Heath, M. 1988. "Receiving the κῶμος: The Context and Performance of Epinician." *AJP* 109.180–95.
Herrmann, H.-V. 1972. *Olympia: Heiligtum and Wettkampfstätte*. Munich: Hirmer.
Herrmann, P. 1975. "Eine Kaiserkunde der Zeit Marc Aurels aus Milet". *Istanbuler Mitteilungen* 25.149–66.
Hönle, A. 1972. *Olympia in der Politik der griechischen Staatenwelt von 776 bis zum Ende des 5. Jahrhunderts*. Bebenhausen: Lothar Rosch.
Hornblower, S. 1991. *A Commentary on Thucydides*, vol. 1: *Books I–III*. Oxford: Oxford University Press.
How, W. W., and J. Wells. 1928. *A Commentary on Herodotus*, 2 vols. Oxford: Oxford University Press.
Hyde, W. W. 1921. *Olympic Victor Monuments and Greek Athletic Art*. Washington, D.C.: Carnegie Institution of Washington.
Instone, S. 1986. Review of D. C. Young, *The Olympic Myth of Greek Amateur Athletics*. *JHS* 106.238–9.
Jüthner, J. 1898. "Seigerkranz and Siegerbinde". *Jahreshefte des Österreichischen Archäologischen Instituts in Wein* 1.42–8.
Keil, J., and G. Maresch. 1960. "Epigraphische Nachlese zu Miltners Ausgrabungsberichten aus Ephesus". *Jahreshefte des Österreichischen Archäologischen Instituts* 45, Beiblatt, coll. 75–100.
Knox, B. M. W. 1968. "Silent Reading in Antiquity". *GRBS* 9. 421–35.
Konstan, D. 1983. "The Stories in Herodotus' Histories: Book 1". *Helios* 10.1–22.
Konstan, D. 1987. "Persians, Greek and Empire". *Arethusa* 20.59–73.
Krause, J. H. 1838. *Olympia*. Vienna: F. Beck.
Kurke, L. 1991. *The Traffic in Praise: Pindar and the Poetics of Social Economy*. Ithaca, N.Y.: Cornell University Press.
Kyle, D. G. 1985. Review of D. C. Young, *The Olympic Myth of Greek Amateur Athletics: Echos due Monde classique/Classical Views* 29 (n.s. 4).134–44.
Lattimore, S. 1987. "The Nature of Early Greek Victor Statues". In *Coroebus Triumphs: The Alliance of Sport and the Arts*. Ed. S. J. Bandy. San Diego, Calif.: San Diego State University Press. 245–56.
Lehmann, F. R. 1915. "Mana: Eine begriffgeschichtliche Untersuchung auf ethnologischer Grundlage". Ph.D. diss., University of Leipzig.
Lonis, R. 1979. *Guerre et religion en Grèce à l'époque classique: Recherches sur les rites, les dieux, l'idéologie de la victoire*. Centre de recherches d'histoire ancienne, vol. 33. Paris: Les belles lettres.
Loraux, N. 1986. *The Invention of Athens: The Funeral Oration in the Classical City*. Trans. A. Sheridan. Cambridge, Mass.: Harvard University Press.
Macan, R. W. ed. 1895. *Herodotus: The Fourth, Fifth, and Sixth Books*, 2 vols. London: Macmillan Press.
Macan, R. W. 1908. *Herodotus: The Seventh, Eighth, and Ninth Books*, 2 vols. London: Macmillan Press.
Mango, C. 1963. "Antique Statuary and the Byzantine Beholder". *Dumbarton Oaks Papers* 17.53–75.
Mauss, M. 1972. *A General Theory of Magic*. Trans. R. Brain. New York: Norton.
Mazzarino, S. 1947. *Fra oriente e occidente: Ricerche di storia greca archaica*. Florence: Le Nuove Italia.

Moretti, L. 1953. *Iscrizioni agonistiche greche*. Rome: A. Signorelli.
Moretti, L. 1957. *Olympionikai, i vincitori negli antichi agoni olimpici*, ser. 8, vol. 8, fasc. 2. Rome: Accademia nazionale dei Lincei.
Mylonas, G. 1943–4. "Athletic Honors in the Fifth Century". *CJ* 39.278–89.
Nisetich, F. J. 1975. "Olympian 1.8–11: An Epinician Metaphor". *HSCP* 79.55–68.
Peek, W. 1955. *Griechische Versinschriften*, vol. 1: *Grabepigramme*. Berlin: Akademie.
Pleket, H. W. 1974. "Zur Soziologie des antiken Sports". *Medelingen van het Nederlands Institut te Rome* 36 (n.s. 1). 57–87.
Pleket, H. W. 1975. "Games, Prizes, Athletes and Ideology: Some Aspects of the History of Sport in the Greco-Roman World". *Stadion* 1.49–89.
Poliakoff, M. 1989. Review of D. C. Young, *The Olympic Myth of Greek Amateur Athletics*. *AJP* 110.166–71.
Pouilloux, J. 1954. "Recherches sur l'histoire et les cultes de Thasos de la fondation de la cité à 196 avant J.-C.". Ph.D. diss., University of Paris.
Raschke, W. J. 1988. "Images of Victory: Some New Considerations of Athletic Monuments". In *The Archaeology of the Olympics: The Olympics and Other Festivals in Antiquity*. Ed. W. J. Raschke. Madison: University of Wisconsin Press. 38–54.
Robert, L. 1967. "Sur des inscriptions d'Ephèse". *Revue de Philologie* 3d ser. 41.7–84.
Roehl, H. ed. 1882. *Inscriptiones Graecae antiquissimae praeter Atticas in Attica repertas*. Berlin: G. Reimer.
Rohde, E. 1920. *Psyche: The Cult of Souls and Belief in Immortality among the Ancient Greeks*, 8th ed. Trans. W. B. Hills. New York: Harcourt, Brace, Jovanovich.
Sherer, C. 1885. "De olympionicarum Statuis". Inaug. diss., University of Göttingen.
Serwint, N. J. 1987. "Greek Athletic Sculpture from the Fifth and Fourth Centuries BC: An Iconographic Study". Ph.D. diss., Princeton University (DA order no. 8724798).
Sherwin-White, A. N., ed. 1966. *The Letters of Pliny*. Oxford: Oxford University Press.
Slater, W. J. 1984. "Nemean One: The Victor's Return in Poetry and Politics". In *Greek Poetry and Philosophy: Studies in Honour of Leonard Woodbury*. Ed. D. E. Gerber. Chico, Calif.: Scholar's Press. 241–64.
Snell, B., and H. Maehler, eds 1970. *Bacchylidis Carmina cum Fragmentis*. 10th ed. Leipzig: Teubner.
Snell, B., and H. Maehler, eds 1980. *Pindarus*, part 1: *Epinicia*. 6th ed. Leipzig: Teubner.
Stengel, P. 1920. *Die griechischen Kultusaltertümer*, 3d ed. Munich: C. H. Beck.
Svenbro, J. 1988. *Phrasikleia: Anthropologie de la lecture en Grèce ancienne*. Paris: Decouverte.
Taeger, F. 1957. *Charisma: Studien zur Geschichte des antiken Herrsherkultes*, 2 vols. Stuttgart: W. Wohlkammer.
Turner, V. 1974. *Dramas, Fields, and Metaphors: Symbolic Action in Human Society*. Ithaca, N.Y.: Cornell University Press.
Veeser, H. A. ed. 1989. *The New Historicism*. New York: Routledge & Kegan Paul.
Vernant, J.-P. 1983. *Myth and Thought Among the Greeks*. London: Routledge & Kegan Paul.
Vernant, J.-P. 1991. *Mortals and Immortals*. Ed. F. Zeitlin. Princeton, N.J.: Princeton University Press.
Versnel, H. S. 1970. *Triumphus: An Inquiry into the Origin, Development, and Meaning of the Roman Triumph*. Leiden: E. J. Brill.
Visser, M. 1982. "Worship Your Enemy: Aspect of the Cult of Heroes in Ancient Greece". *HTR* 75.403-28.
Wallace-Hadrill, A. 1983. *Suetonius: The Scholar and His Caesars*. London: Duckworth.
Weber, M. 1978. *Economy and Society: An Outline of Interpretative Sociology*. Ed. G. Roth and C. Wittich. Berkeley and Los Angeles: University of California Press.

Young, D. C. 1983. "Pindar Pythians 2 and 3: Inscriptional ποτέ and the "Poetic Epistle"". *HSCP* 87.31–48.

Young, D. C. 1984. *The Olympic Myth of Greek Amateur Athletics*. Chicago: University of Chicago Press.

10 Greek Athletics as Roman Spectacle: The Mosaics from Ostia and Rome*

ZAHRA NEWBY

With the release in the year 2000 of the film *Gladiator*, and the exhibition "Gladiators and Caesars" in Hamburg and London, Roman spectacular entertainments, never out of the public eye for long, have returned once again to the limelight. Chief among these entertainments are gladiatorial games and chariot races, exerting a pull on the modern imagination through the famous re-enactments of them in popular films – such as *Spartacus* or the famous chariot race in *Ben-Hur* – as much as through our knowledge of their popularity in antiquity, often summed up in Juvenal's comment that the Roman *plebs* wanted only "panem et circenses" ("bread and circuses").[1] Yet there was more to Roman spectacle than gladiators and chariots, popular as these were. The aim of this paper is to use the visual evidence from mosaics in Ostia and Rome to investigate the Roman reactions to another type of public spectacle, Greek athletic contests. These were held in Rome periodically from 186 BC, and gained a new momentum in AD 86 with Emperor Domitian's institution of a permanent four-yearly festival on Greek lines in honour of the Capitoline triad (Suetonius, *Domitian* 4).

A series of mosaics with athletic themes has been found in Ostia and Rome, mostly dating to the second and third centuries AD. This visual evidence provides a useful complement to the literary evidence traditionally called upon to illuminate Roman attitudes to Greek athletics. Much of the literary evidence seems hostile to Greek-style athletics, whether as a spectacle or as an activity for Roman citizens themselves to partake in. Thus Cicero declared that Pompey himself recognized that he had wasted "oil and effort" on the athletes involved in the opening ceremonies for his theatre, and elsewhere criticized the Greek gymnasium, quoting

---

* Originally published in *Papers of the British School at Rome* 70 (2002), pp. 177–203. The research for this paper was carried out whilst I held a Rome Award at the British School at Rome, April to June 2000. I would like to thank Maria Pia Malvezzi of the School for her help in obtaining *permessi* and Anna Gallina Zevi of the Soprintendenza Archeologica di Ostia for access to their archives. The Soprintendenza Archeologica di Ostia, the Soprintendenza Archeologica di Roma and the Fototeca Unione have all kindly supplied photographs. I am also grateful to all those who commented on the versions of this paper that I gave in Rome, Warwick and Leicester or have read drafts of it.

[1] Juvenal, *Satire* 10.81, a sentiment repeated by Fronto, *Principia Historiae* 18.24–5. On the representation of spectacles in film, see Eloy, 1990; Wyke, 1997. For the exhibition, see the catalogue by Köhne and Ewigleben, 2000. Papers on Roman spectacles and their representation in art can be found in: Domergue, Landes and Pailler, 1990; Bergmann and Kondoleon, 1999.

approvingly Ennius's line that "to strip the body naked among citizens is the start of vice" (Cicero, *ad Fam.* 7.1; *Tusc.* 4.70).[2]

The different attitudes of Greece and Rome towards participation in public festivals are also summed up by Nepos: whereas in Greece it was the highest honour to be declared a victor at the Olympic Games, in Rome to appear as an athlete or actor in public brought down *infamia* (Nepos, *pr.* 5).[3] Yet this analysis of the literary evidence is, at best, a partial one. Similar ideas do indeed occur in later writers too, as, for example, in the views expressed by those hostile to Nero's introduction of the Greek-style *Neronia* in AD 60, or in Pliny's disparaging reference to the Capitoline games in a letter discussing the dissolution of a festival at Vienne (Tacitus, *Annales* 14.20; Pliny the Younger, *Letters* 4.22.7). Yet there are also increasing signs that Greek athletics were in fact becoming more popular, both as a spectacle and an activity. So, at the end of the first century AD, the *Epigrams* of Martial show Romans exercising in the baths, in wrestling, weightlifting and ball games, while Juvenal and the Younger Pliny both attest to the craze for training in the Greek manner (for example, Martial 14.49).[4] Indeed it seems likely that it is precisely because of this background of enthusiasm that Tacitus and Pliny made the comments they did.

This new interest in training "à la Greque" may well have been encouraged by the new prominence of Greek athletics in the Roman festival calendar. After a series of ad hoc athletic performances in previous Roman games and the abortive introduction of Nero's five-yearly *Neronia* in AD 60, a permanent Greek-style festival incorporating athletic, dramatic and equestrian events was finally instituted at Rome by Domitian in AD 96.[5] While some athletic events such as boxing and wrestling had long been part of native Italian *ludi,* this festival was run on Greek lines and attracted athletes and performers from across the mediterranean world, many of high status.[6] Indeed, by the 140s, Rome had become the festival capital of the empire and housed the headquarters of the international guilds for both athletes and actors.[7] While most citizens of Rome seem to have stopped short of competing publicly in the athletic events of this festival (though some certainly competed in the poetic contests) (Caldelli, 1993: 90–1), it seems likely that the new prominence of athletics in these public spectacles may have encouraged its adoption in private.

It is here that the mosaic evidence becomes important. Whereas the majority of our literary references to athletics belongs to the period from the first century BC to the early second AD, the visual evidence provided by the mosaics is generally later, starting in the Hadrianic period and continuing until well into the third century AD. It thus provides us with the opportunity to examine the reception of Greek athletics in this later period, when the Capitoline games at Rome were fully established. The placement of these mosaics in a variety of spaces, especially public bathing

---

[2] On Roman attitudes to athletic nakedness, see Crowther, 1980–1.
[3] See discussion of Edwards, 1993: 98–9.
[4] See Juvenal, *Satire* 3.68 on the rustic Roman wearing Greek medals and Pliny, *Panegyric* 13.5. on men training under the supervision of a "Graeculus magister". Later, too, Lucian included personal trainers among the entourage of rich Romans: *On Salaried Posts in Great Houses,* 4.
[5] For a full discussion of this festival, its predecessors and its popularity, see Caldelli, 1993.
[6] On *ludi*, see Thuillier, 1996: 39. On the status of Greek athletes, see van Nijf, 1999; 2001.
[7] On the athletic guild, see: Glotz, 1912; Forbes, 1955; Pleket, 1973; Caldelli, 1993.

complexes, also suggests their reception by a wider audience than that of the élite literary texts. In my analysis of these mosaics, then, I wish to consider how they represent athletics, both as a spectacle and as an activity in which the viewers themselves might have been engaged. Through this examination of the ways in which Greek athletics were experienced in the area of Rome and its suburbs, I hope to shed light on the wider question of the integration and recreation of Greek culture in Roman life during the course of the Roman empire.[8]

THE MOSAICS FROM OSTIA

Among the wealth of floor mosaics, mostly black and white, that paved the buildings of ancient Ostia we know of at least ten featuring athletic scenes.[9] Most of these come from bathing establishments, though three come from other types of building.[10] While a range of dates has been suggested for them, all belong to the period between the reigns of Hadrian and the Severan emperors, like similar mosaics from Rome and its environs, with perhaps one polychrome mosaic belonging later in the fourth century.[11]

The scenes represented on the mosaics vary from simple groupings of pairs of athletes, to larger and more complex compositions that contain indications of the prizes for victory and the setting in which the contests are to be understood as taking place. It is possible that the latter may have evoked particular historical athletic contests that took place either in Ostia or, more likely, in nearby Rome. A historical context is definitely implied for certain of the mosaics by the labelling of individual figures with names, as on the mosaic from the Inn of Alexander Helix. In other cases, however, even though prizes are shown, the location of the scenes can be ambivalent and evocative of a general world of Greek athletic competition rather than of particular Roman spectacles or contests. In other mosaics there may be a particular connection to the activities that took place in the room, indicating that mosaics, like sculpture, could be chosen because of the appropriateness of their theme to particular locations.[12]

---

[8] On the introduction of athletic festivals as part of Roman philhellenism, see Ferrary, 1996: 192–203.
[9] See the discussions of Becatti, 1961: 320–1, 350–1 and Floriani Squarciapino, 1985–6: 87–144; 1986–7: 170, n. 12.
[10] Large baths – Baths of Neptune and Porta Marina; smaller establishments – Baths of Trinacria, Via Severiana, the Terme Marittime and the private baths within the "Palazzo Imperiale". Other establishments: the House of Apuleius, the Inn of Alexander Helix and the so-called "Caseggiato del Lottatore".
[11] On the popularity of athletic scenes at this period, see Becatti, 1961: 320–1, 350–1; Blake, 1936: esp. pp. 162–6. The latest mosaic is that from the baths on the Via Severiana, which is dated either to the Severan period or to the fourth century.
[12] This has been argued most cogently in relation to sculpture by Neudecker (1988). On the sculptural decoration of baths, see also Manderscheid, 1981. For similar ideas in relation to mosaics, see: Clarke, 1979; Kondoleon, 1995; Dunbabin 1999: 304–16.

SIMPLE PAIRS OF ATHLETES: THE BATHS OF NEPTUNE AND THE HOUSE OF APULEIUS

One of the simplest examples of athletic mosaics in Ostia is also probably amongst the earliest. The Baths of Neptune, along the Decumanus, seem to be a Hadrianic remodelling of an earlier Domitianic set of baths, and are usually identified with a bath complex named on an inscription as begun under Hadrian and completed by Antoninus Pius (Zevi and Granelli, 1999).[13] The mosaic paves a room that in the original plan of the baths had an opening on its western side to the palaestra area, later closed off. Becatti dated it to AD 139 (1961: 52, no. 72).[14] It appears to have shown four pairs of athletes, oriented to be viewed from the edges of the room, suggesting a space where viewers moved around rather than viewing the scenes from a static position (Fig. 10.1). On the north side stands a pair of boxers wearing spiked gloves. Next to them is another pair of athletes, probably pancratiasts, one of whom is already defeated and sits on the ground. Much of the mosaic on the south side is destroyed, with only the top of the head of a figure surviving at the far right and a lunging athlete about to start wrestling shown to the left.

There are no indications of a specific context for the activities shown on the mosaic, such as prizes for the victors, and so we might be tempted to compare these pairs of wrestlers and boxers with the human inhabitants of this palaestra space, working up a sweat before their bath. We know from authors like Martial, Juvenal and Seneca that exercises such as weightlifting, ball-play and wrestling took place in the baths as a prelude to cleansing (Nielsen, 1990: 144).[15] The location of the mosaic in a room on the edge of the palaestra and the lack of a black border to the scene on the side of the door encourage this sort of blurring between the scenes represented on the floor and those taking place in reality. A similar blurring of the line between image and reality occurs elsewhere in Ostia. In the Baths of Buticosus, an image of a man holding a bucket and labelled as Buticosus seems likely to represent the slave in charge of the baths, while in the Baths of the Seven Sages another similar figure may represent either a slave or a bather.[16]

Yet, while the viewer seems encouraged by the placement and imagery of the mosaic to make such an identification with the bathers themselves, in other details the mosaic image is also distanced from them. Although the nudity of the figures probably helped to encourage an identification with the bathers, most of whom seem to have gone naked, the gloves and *cirrus* (a top-knot worn in the hair) worn by some of the figures would also have distanced them.[17] These two attributes seem instead to

---

[13] Earlier accounts were provided by Bloch, 1938: 246, 276–9 and Meiggs, 1973: 409–10. The inscription is *CIL* XIV 98. They were later repaired by P. Lucilius Gamala (*CIL* XIV 376), referred to as "thermas quas divus Pius aedificaverat", and are probably those mentioned in the *Historia Augusta, Antoninus Pius* 8.3 as "lavacrum Ostiense".

[14] It paves room D on his map (p. 48, fig. 15). It is of a noticeably different style to the more famous Neptune and Amphitrite mosaics in the baths, and was probably executed by a different workshop.

[15] The majority of the sources dates from the mid-first century onwards, perhaps reflecting an increasing interest in sport as recreation at this time.

[16] Buticosus: Becatti, 1961: 29–30; no. 51, dated to AD 115. Baths of the Seven Sages (holding a strigil?): Becatti 1961: 137. For similar figures in the baths of the fourth-century villa at Piazza Armerina, see Carandini, Ricci and de Vos, 1982: 359–62, room 5, pl. 61.

[17] On apparel in the baths, see Nielsen, 1990: 140–2.

Fig. 10.1 Room D (off palaestra), Baths of Neptune, Ostia.
(Archivio Fotografico della Soprintendenza Archeologica di Ostia neg. no. C787)
(Reproduced courtesy of the Soprintendenza Archeologica di Ostia)

suggest that we are looking at professional athletes engaged in public competition.

Indeed, the *cirrus* is generally regarded as a sign that the athletes depicted are professionals, though there is in fact a great variety in the way it is represented and some athletes do not wear it at all.[18] If the presence of the *cirrus* did connote the idea of professional athletics, its absence may suggest amateur activity. It seems difficult, however, to draw hard rules about what exactly the *cirrus* meant to contemporary viewers, and it may be simply that some athletes chose to wear it while others did not.

Here, the interpretation of the *cirrus* as a sign of professionalism is reinforced by the presence of spiked gloves on the hands of the boxers, surely a sign of official competition and inappropriate for use in everyday training, but is simultaneously undermined by the absence of prizes or officials and the placement of the mosaic.[19] This mosaic, then, straddles the line between two types of reality – that of physical exercise in the baths and of athletic competition between professionals in a public spectacle.

A similar representation of a pair of athletes appears in a fragmentary mosaic from the nearby House of Apuleius, named by Lanciani after an inscribed water-

[18] *Cirrus* and professionalism: for example, Gardiner, 1930: caption to fig. 74; Gassowska, 1966. Suetonius, *Nero* 45.1. Most recently, see Thuillier, 1998 (suggesting that it may instead distinguish young athletes from the older, bearded, contestants).

[19] On boxing gloves, see Poliakoff, 1987: 68–79. Lee, 1997 has suggested that they were made of leather rather than metal, the spikes representing gloved fingers.

pipe found directed towards the house (Lanciani, 1886: 163).[20] The mosaic paves a room in the western section of the house and shows the upper part of two figures. Both wear their hair tied back in a low *cirrus*, like the wrestler in the previous mosaic, and have one arm raised and the other lowered. They are perhaps in the midst of a wrestling match, though the fragmentary state of the mosaic makes it difficult to tell whether any other objects or figures were present originally (Becatti, 1961: 88, no. 148).[21]

SCENES OF ATHLETIC VICTORY

Other mosaics move on from these simple depictions of athletic activity, and provide indications of a competition for prizes without, however, indicating any one historical event in particular. In a fragmentary mosaic paving a heated room in the Baths of the Trinacria, dated by Becatti to the end of the second century, we see the upper parts of four figures (Fig. 10.2) (Becatti, 1961: 141–2, no. 278).[22] The one in the centre appears to be naked and raises his right arm to a figure who approaches from the left. This figure touches the athlete's head with his left hand. From the diagonal white lines shown running across his body we can tell that he is clothed. He should probably be understood as crowning the central figure rather than as his sparring partner in a wrestling match, though the apparent absence of a crown and the gesture of the central figure's right arm make it difficult to tell. Another draped figure stands to the far left. To the right of the group a third figure approaches, holding a short palm branch aloft in his right hand. He too is clothed and appears to be the umpire of the games, awarding victory to the central figure. The presence of this figure and the palm branch thus clearly set this scene within a competitive context, where prizes are awarded for athletic success. While the images discussed above might have alluded to the athletic exercises practised in the baths as a prelude to bathing, here we seem to be in an agonistic context.

The stress on athletics within an agonistic context, with prizes for the victors, reappears in the other mosaics from Ostia. In Visconti's excavation of the so-called "Palazzo Imperiale", an ornately decorated establishment lying towards the west of the city in Region III, he discovered a series of rooms belonging to a set of baths, probably part of a private establishment.[23] More recent excavations in the 1980s showed that these baths also extended to the south of those initially discovered (Scrinari, 1988). The area discovered by Visconti consisted of a large courtyard surrounded by a number of baths and rooms leading off. A room to the side of one of the baths was paved with a black and white mosaic, of which Visconti recorded that it showed "a representation of athletes shown in various gymnastic poses with in the middle a victor who places a crown upon his head" (1857: 336). Unfortunately, the mosaic no longer survives and Visconti did not elaborate about the type of crown shown. However, the mosaic seems to have shown scenes both of athletes

[20] See also Becatti, 1961: 86–90; Meiggs, 1973: 351.
[21] It paves room G on his map and is dated by him to the early third century AD.
[22] Only two figures are visible today.
[23] On this complex, see, most recently, Spurza, 1990. Bloch (1938: 178–9) suggests an initial construction date shortly after AD 139.

Fig. 10.2 Room D (heated). Baths of the Trinacria, Ostia.
(Archivio Fotografico della Soprintendenza Archeologica di Ostia neg. no. B3229)
(Reproduced courtesy of the Soprintendenza Archeologica di Ostia)

partaking in athletic activity and of at least one being rewarded for his success.

In part these images can be compared with the simple scenes of victorious charioteers that appear on the wall-paintings of a corridor in the Insula of the Charioteers, also in Ostia (Mols, 1999: 354–8, fig. 99). Here we find two representations of victorious charioteers, each on a two-horse chariot and holding a crown in the right hand and a long palm on the left. These attributes of victory are exactly the same as those that we find in the depictions of athletes on mosaics. Painted representations of athletes also come from a context nearby. A wall of a room in the Baths of the Seven Sages, adjoining the Insula of the Gladiators, shows the remains of two figures (Mols, 1999: 293–5, figs 52–3). Both are naked and tanned, and a metal vase is shown lying by the feet of one of them, probably representing a victory prize. While no palms or crowns remain, it is possible that at least one was shown crowning himself since he has his right arm raised towards his head. A later mosaic found in the 1980s in the southern part of the "Palazzo Imperiale" baths also shows images of charioteers appearing in a similar context to the lost mosaic of a victorious athlete (Scrinari, 1988). Here six figures are represented, carrying long palms and wearing spiked crowns on their heads. Like certain of the athletic mosaics that I shall discuss below, they are also inscribed with their names and those of their victorious horses. Athletic and circus victories thus seem to be represented by a similar iconography. Images of successful charioteers are usually interpreted as showing the popularity of this form of entertainment. The appearance of athletes depicted in a similar way should, then, likewise be seen as a sign of popular delight in this form of spectacle. However, their appearance in bathing complexes also suggests another level of significance, linking athletic performances in public spectacles with activities within the baths.

It is unclear whether we should see these images as generic representations of athletic or equestrian competitive activity, or as alluding to particular events that took place in the locality. We have no firm evidence about whether chariot races took place in Ostia and, if so, where they were held. The archaeological evidence has revealed no signs of a circus or amphitheatre, though it is certain that gladiatorial games, at least, were performed here.[24] It seems likely, however, that the Ludi Castorum, held in honour of the Dioscuri, would have included chariot races, possibly held simply on the nearby seashore.[25] The visual images, however, could also refer to the chariot races of nearby Rome, as seems to have been the case in the famous Circus relief, probably from Ostia, that is now conserved in the Vatican.[26]

When considering the mosaics and paintings representing athletic scenes it is also uncertain whether we should see them as reflecting local events. We do not have any firm references to athletic displays at Ostia in the inscriptional record, though Roman *ludi* could include boxing and wrestling matches, and such displays may well have been shown in the theatre, as during the celebrations of the dedication of the theatre of Pompey at Rome in 55 BC. As with the equestrian events, it is also possible that they reflect the entertainments of nearby Rome.[27] Yet for the athletic images there is also a third alternative: that they reflect informal athletic activities and contests within the baths of Ostia. As mentioned above, we have plenty of evidence that athletic pursuits took place in the baths, many of which were equipped with palaestrae.[28] It is quite likely that these often included informal competitions, perhaps with some form of prizes given to the victors. Juvenal, in his satire upon the adoption of Greek culture by native Romans (*Satire* 3.68), referred to the rustic Roman as wearing "niceteria", "prizes of victory", on his oiled neck, though he did not tell us the sort of contests he had been involved in. This whole passage seems to refer to an amateurish adoption of Greek pursuits rather than actual involvement in public agonistic contests and so the prizes may well be those won in informal competitions amongst peers, though as prizes "worn on the neck" they sound more like modern-day medals than the crowns and palms that we see in the visual record.

Some types of competitions certainly did take place in the baths. The funerary inscription of Ursus boasts of his success in playing ball games in the Baths of Trajan, Agrippa, Titus and Nero in Rome and the applause that he won from all those watching (*CIL* VI 9797). Whether these were staged contests, or simply

---

[24] Meiggs (1973: 425–8) and Pavolini (1986: 239–45) have discussed spectacles at Ostia. The *Fasti Ostiensis* (Qa) include reference to a *munus gladiatorum* and *venatio* in AD 152: Bargagli and Grosso, 1997: 50–1.

[25] *CIL* XIV 1. See also Zevi, 1996: 77.

[26] Ex-Lateran collection. See Kleiner, 1992: 236–7.

[27] Caldelli (1998) concluded that Ostia probably did not have an agonistic life of its own, but was instead dominated by that of Rome.

[28] In Ostia only the larger baths include such premises: the Baths of Neptune, the Forum Baths and the Baths at Porta Marina.

games that attracted a large audience, is unclear. Yet it does seem likely that semi-public athletic competitions were staged within the baths at Rome, as is suggested by the presence of a stadium built into the back wall of the Baths of Caracalla at Rome (Nielsen, 1990: 53). It is also likely that members of the synod of athletes at Rome would have exercised in the Baths of Trajan, next to their guild headquarters, for which the chief priest of the synod as *epi balaneion* (official in charge of the baths) was responsible (Caldelli, 1992). Such training could attract considerable audiences, as we see in Dio's account of the boxer Melancomas that starts with the description of a large crowd watching the athlete Iatrocles shadow boxing in the gymnasium at Naples (Dio Chrys. *Oration* 28.1–3).[29] Such professional athletes would also have been visible in the baths at Rome, either in training or engaged in public competition.

Some of these athletes may also have passed through Ostia. Indeed, fragmentary inscriptions from Ostia recall honours granted to victorious performers. One decree seems to honour the pantomime actor M. Aurelius Pylades and may well have been prompted by his successes at Rome (*CIL* XIV 4624). The other two, which Caldelli suggested could both belong to the same decree, seem to honour a local man for victories in festivals around the empire, though his speciality is not recorded (*CIL* XIV 474, 470a and b; Caldelli, 1998). The inscriptions date to the third century and suggest that by now, at least, the successes of a local man in Greek agonistic festivals were as highly regarded in Ostia as they were in the Greek east. The athletic mosaics too should be seen as part of this changing culture, where participation in public festivals was beginning to lose its stigma and some performers could even receive public honours.

ALLUSIONS TO PARTICULAR GAMES?
THE TERME MARITTIME AND BATHS AT PORTA MARINA

Most of the mosaics discussed so far have presented only general allusions to victory and public competitions. In two other complexes, however, the prizes shown are more highly individualized and may allude to a particular set of games. Two athletic mosaics come from a small, highly decorated set of baths situated on the line of the Sullan Walls to the west of the town and known as the Terme Marittime. The baths as they survive today appear to be a Severan remodelling and expansion of a previous set dating to the Hadrianic period (Bloch, 1938: 277–8; Calza and Becatti, 1974: 44–5). The black and white mosaics decorating them are part of this Severan expansion. Of the four rooms where mosaics were found, two are decorated with marine scenes, whilst the third, a heated apsidal room, only preserves about a third of the mosaic, as it was excavated in the mid-nineteenth century (Becatti, 1961: 110–13, no 210 with fig. 45).[30] The excavation drawing and an old photo-

---

[29] See also Suetonius, *Nero* 40.2, on Nero watching the athletes at Naples.

[30] See also Paschetto, 1912: 302–7. Note, however, that he, like Bloch (1938: 278), erroneously identified this set of baths with those excavated and named as "Thermae Maritimae" by Gavin Hamilton, whereas the legend to P. Hol's 1804 map (conserved in the Archives of the Soprintendenza at Ostia Antica) shows that these took place at the site of those now called the "Porta Marina" baths, as was recognised rightly by Pavolini (1983: 171–2).

Fig. 10.3 Room B (heated), Terme Marittime, Ostia.
(Fototeca Unione neg. no. F7260)
(Reproduced courtesy of the Fototeca Unione, at the American Academy in Rome)

graph (Fig. 10.3) show that this mosaic originally featured two figures in the apse, surrounded by winged Cupids, probably to be identified with Neptune and his consort (Becatti, 1961: fig. 43, tav. 110).[31] In the main body of the floor the centre was occupied by the figure of a trumpeter, dressed in a cloak and holding a large tuba in front of him. Similar figures appear on a number of athletic representations, often in scenes of the crowning of victorious athletes (Castagnoli, 1943–5: fig. 27). Above the trumpeter hung a circular object with protrusions around its edge – identified by Becatti and the original excavators as a lamp but actually, I would argue, a representation of the crown worn by a victorious athlete. To either side, the trumpeter was flanked by scenes oriented towards the sides of the room. These showed wide-bodied vases placed on tables, next to athletic Cupids, boxing on one side, and with the contest already over and one Cupid holding a palm of victory on the other. At the base of the mosaic is the only section that survives today. This shows two rather stocky athletes, shown without wings and therefore presumably not Cupids, standing either side of a table. On the table lie two cylindrical objects with protruding strings, perhaps boxing gloves, and a pot or jug. A long palm leans against the table. The athlete standing to the left is clearly the victor, shown holding a palm and with his right hand raised towards the crown on his head. The other holds a smaller palm, perhaps the prize for second place. This mosaic differs from those discussed so far in that it seems to merge the human practice of athletics,

---

[31] Becatti only identified one reclining figure in the apse, but the photograph clearly shows the remains of another seated figure too.

represented by the figures at the bottom, with the mythical realm, as embodied by the Cupids. A similar mythological representation of athletics occurs in the House of Bacchus and Ariadne, where the divine couple are shown watching a wrestling match between Pan and Cupid (Becatti, 1961: 155–8, no. 293, tav. 80).

Yet it also includes details that seem to relate to real-life competitions. The victorious athlete wears a distinctive crown with five protrusions. The schematic style of the mosaic makes it hard to distinguish the details of this crown, but it does have a certain similarity to the crowns that appear carried and worn by successful athletes on the mosaics from the Baths of Caracalla in Rome (Werner, 1998: 217–51).[32] In these mosaics we see athletes wearing or carrying a crown with five protrusions. Similar crowns appear on a mosaic discovered near Gafsa in North Africa, where they are shown worn both by successful athletes and by the *agonothetês* of the games (Khanoussi, 1988).[33] These protrusions seem to represent flowers, as on the mosaic showing a victorious charioteer in the baths at Piazza Armerina, where a similar crown is worn by the trumpeter (Gentili, 1956: fig. 5).[34] In the Baths of Caracalla, one of the side panels of the mosaics shows another type of crown, this time with three protrusions rather than five. Here the protrusions are carefully shown to be busts, as they are on another similar crown worn by a bearded and draped figure on the mosaic of the great baths at Aquileia, identified by his dress as an *agonothetês* or umpire at the games (Lopreato, 1994: pl. 47.1). It may be that these crowns with busts relate to specific sets of games, since we know that at the *Capitolia* Domitian is said to have presided wearing a crown decorated with the busts of the Capitoline triad (Suetonius, *Domitian* 4.4).[35] The crowns of flowers, then, could represent the prize given to the victorious athletes in these sacred games, in line with the practice in Greece where the prize for winning in the Olympic Games was a crown of wild olive.[36] On the Terme Marittime mosaic, I would suggest that the central object is supposed to represent a suspended larger-scale version of the victor's crown shown below: a crown made up of flowers and tied at the back with ribbons, the ends of which can be seen hanging down. This, along with the display table below and the trumpeter in the centre, evokes a scene of public competition for prizes, similar to that which we find in the Porta Marina mosaic discussed below, but here set in a semi-mythical world where Cupids too compete in the sight of Neptune.

Another crown with protrusions is just visible in another mosaic from the Terme Marittime, found in a nearby room that Paschetto identified as an apodyterium (changing room) (Paschetto, 1912: 305; Becatti 1961: 110, no. 209) (Fig. 10.4). Unfortunately it is badly damaged and only the remains of two boxers, a man

---

[32] Unfortunately, the mosaics are heavily restored.
[33] For other athletic mosaics in North Africa, see Khanoussi, 1991.
[34] Elsewhere in the villa girls are shown making the crowns out of roses.
[35] See, on crowns with busts, Inan and Alföldi-Rosenbaum. 1979: 38–44; Alföldi-Rosenbaum, 1994: 104, pl. 51. Floriani Squarciapino (1986–7: 169, n. 11) has discussed the possible link between crowns and particular festivals.
[36] Guarducci, 1982 suggested that crowns of roses were given as prizes at the *Neronia*. Caldelli (1993: 54) suggested that crowns of oak were given in the Capitoline games, though more recently (1998) she has suggested that the lamps with rose crowns studied by Guarducci (some of them from Ostia) could also refer to the Capitoline games.

Fig. 10.4 Room A, Terme Marittime, Ostia.
(Archivio Fotografico della Soprintendenza Archeologica di Ostia neg. no. A1558)
(Reproduced courtesy of the Soprintendenza Archeologica di Ostia)

carrying a sack and part of another man can be seen on the photograph. Both boxers wear long gloves that are laced up their arms, and the one to the left raises his hand to a crown of victory on his head that, according to Becatti, was decorated with studs in relief, just visible here. Both these mosaics appear within the bathing rooms of the complex, from the apodyterium ("changing-room") and caldarium ("hot-room") respectively. There is thus less of a direct allusion to the exercises that bathers might themselves have been engaged in. Here, instead, the concentration is perhaps on particular sets of games, as indicated by the crowns, merged with the playful atmosphere provided by the figures of Cupids.

It is time now to consider the most complex of the Ostian mosaics, that from the Baths of Porta Marina, also known as the Baths of Marciana from a portrait bust found there (Fig. 10.5) (Manderscheid, 1981: 79).[37] This mosaic paves a room opening onto the frigidarium ("cold room") and placed close to the palaestra, identified by Floriani Squarciapino (1986–7: 164) as an apodyterium. In the centre of the mosaic the scene is oriented towards the entrance to the room. It shows a table with an ornate spiked crown and a palm. A bearded and balding herm stands next to the table, with a hoop and palm resting against it, and beneath it a bucket, a hoop with three strigils and a leather ball. A metal bowl stands nearby. In front of these objects is a scene of two naked boxers standing in front of a dressed umpire. One of these, a bearded man, appears to be remonstrating with the umpire while the other

[37] Portraits of Trajan and Sabina were also found, corresponding to the Trajanic–Hadrianic date suggested for these baths.

Fig. 10.5 Apodyterium near the palaestra, Baths of Porta Marina, Ostia. (Image oriented to show the view from the entrance to the room) (Author's photograph)

raises his hands in victory. Both wear spiked gloves. Behind the umpire is another herm, with a youthful beardless face.

The scenes on the other three sides are all oriented towards the walls, encouraging the viewer to move around the room to see them. On the opposite long side we see at the left two athletes apparently at rest. One holds a hoop with strigils and an oil flask in his left hand and something, now lost, in his right.[38] The other holds a strigil in his right hand. Both wear their hair in a low *cirrus* on the nape of the neck. Next to them another pair of athletes are shown embarking on a wrestling match. On one short side is a single athlete holding cylindrical objects in his hands. These may be *halteres* or jumping weights, indicating that he is a long jumper, though the way he is holding them, with one raised high and the other lowered, suggests that they could be weights used for training.[39] On the other short side we see in the centre an athlete holding a discus that he is preparing to throw, and, to the right, the figure of a trumpeter, blowing into his trumpet with his left hand raised towards the spiked crown on his head. Floriani Squarciapino has suggested that this crown should be understood as equivalent to that shown on the table, which is however shown in greater detail, and that both suggest the prizes for victory in the games represented (Floriani Squarciapino, 1986–7: 164, 173–9).

Through the depiction of this individualised spiked crown, the mosaic seems to make a reference to the world of public athletic competition, though we cannot identify which particular games are being alluded to. Moreover, the location of

---

[38] Floriani Squarciapino (1986–7: 167) suggested that it is a palm, though it appears to be bent over his hand.

[39] As described by Martial, *Epigrams* 14.49.

these games is itself indicated by the presence of herms that suggest a gymnasium setting for the scenes. Thus this mosaic, like those elsewhere, may allude to a specific historical event. Yet certain details in the mosaic also suggest that it could have been read as having more general significance. It is noticeable that not all the athletes shown in the mosaic wear the *cirrus*. In particular, the two boxers standing before the umpire are distinguished from one another by their different facial characteristics, one bearded, the other not. Does the lack of *cirrus* in the depiction of these two alter our interpretation of them? If we were to see this part of the mosaic alone without the rest, the representation of two athletes, one older, one younger, in front of an umpire and a herm might instead conjure up the ideal of athletics in the Greek gymnasium rather than a professional competition. The fact that the herm in the middle of the mosaic appears to show a balding figure with a long beard, similar to a philosopher portrait, again encourages us to set these activities within the wider world of the Greek gymnasium, which included intellectual as well as athletic activity.[40] Yet the spiked gloves worn by the boxers suggest public competition, rather than an amateur boxing match in the gymnasium.

Thus the mosaic seems to point in several different directions simultaneously, both towards athletic competitions as they might have appeared during a particular set of games, perhaps at Rome, and towards athletics as part of the broader world of Greek culture. The figures of athletes holding strigils on the other side of the mosaic also invite this duality of viewing. While they wear the *cirrus* and thus appear as "professional" athletes, they are not involved in any athletic activity but rather appear to be, like the bathers who would be viewing this mosaic, engaged in the task of cleaning themselves with oil and strigils. As in the mosaic from the Baths of Neptune, the image simultaneously invites the bathers viewing it to identify themselves with the figures represented there, and also distances them by the presence of attributes such as the *cirrus* and brutal gloves. The fact that in both these sets of baths the mosaic is placed close to the area of the palaestra, where bathers could themselves exercise, reinforces this blurring of the line between the bathers and the mosaic figures. The reference to the gymnasium achieved through the presence of the herms also adds to the picture evoked: these athletes are not just those that can be seen in competitions in Italy, but they also carry the intellectual cachet of Greek gymnasium life.[41] This mosaic, then, suggests that athletics could have a wider cultural significance for its ancient viewers and practitioners.

INDIVIDUAL ATHLETES ON MOSAICS

In the mosaics I have considered so far allusions to the world of athletic competition and individual athletic spectacles have been achieved mostly through the representation of particular types of prizes, perhaps to be associated with those that were given to victorious contestants. In a number of other mosaics from Ostia and

---

[40] Circuses could also be decorated with herms, but these are usually represented as showing youthful figures: Humphrey, 1986: 52–3 and figs 59–65.
[41] The fact that a philosopher portrait is chosen for the central herm, rather than one of Hermes or Hercules, suggests that the intellectual side of gymnasium life is being clearly signalled here.

Fig. 10.6 Inn of Alexander Helix, Ostia.
(Archivio Fotografico della Soprintendenza Archeologica di Ostia neg. no. B888)
(Reproduced courtesy of the Soprintendenza Archeologica di Ostia)

nearby Rome, however, we find another way of evoking the contemporary athletic spectacles – through the representation of individually named athletes.

In Ostia, the most important example is the mosaic pavement in the Inn of Alexander Helix (Fig. 10.6). In addition to two other scenes, of Venus admiring herself in a mirror and of a pair of grotesquely phallic fighting dwarves, this shows two athletes named above as Alexander and Helix (Becatti, 1961: 205–7, no. 391). They both hold their fists clenched, but do not appear to be wearing gloves and are probably engaged in the pancration contest, a combination of boxing and wrestling. Between them stands a short palm, similar to that on the Baths of the Trinacria mosaic, and to the side is an over-life-sized representation of a metal bowl or cup, probably the prize for victory in this context and similar to that shown on the wall-painting in the Baths of the Seven Sages. Jones (1998) has identified the figures as the athletes Aurelius Alexander and Aurelius Helix, both attested in the epigraphic record as being prominent at Rome in the early third century: Alexander as high priest of the athletic synod and Helix as a victor in the Capitoline games of AD 218. Helix here wears a *cirrus* of a rather different type to that seen before, shown as a tuft of several strands of hair high up on the back of the head and similar to that worn by a number of the athletes on the polychrome mosaics from the palaestrae of the Baths of Caracalla in Rome, which can also be dated to the early third century.[42]

---

[42] The dating of the mosaics is controversial, with some scholars putting them in the early third century (that is, the Severan period), at the time of the initial dedication of the baths or shortly afterwards (Insalaco, 1989; DeLaine, 1997: 239–40; Dunbabin, 1999: 68), while others argue for a later date, in the fourth century (Floriani Squarciapino, 1985–6: 113; Darmon and Rebourg, 1994: 99).

Fig. 10.7 Cassegiato del Lottatore, Ostia. (Author's photograph)

Their presence here in an inn seems less to suggest a parallel between the viewers and the athletes, and rather can be compared with graffiti celebrating individual charioteers or gladiators. It is a sign of the fame of certain prominent athletes, and the fan-clubs they could attract. The concentration here certainly appears to be on athletics as a spectacle, like gladiatorial shows or chariot races, rather than as an activity the clients themselves engage in.

Named athletes also occur on the mosaic from the Caseggiato del Lottatore in Region V in Ostia, though the oddities in their names make them harder to associate with otherwise attested individuals (Pavolini, 1986: fig. 104) (Fig. 10.7). This mosaic paves the threshold to the building. It shows two athletes, framed within a guilloche border and set on a ground line formed by a single black line. The left athlete is sunk down in an attitude of defeat, whereas the other has both hands raised, perhaps in triumph. Neither wears gloves, and it seems likely that the competition was a wrestling match. Both figures are named, the defeated as SACAL and the victor as ARTEMI, possibly short for Artemidorus. The mosaic is not included in Becatti's catalogue, but a date in the early third century was suggested by Floriani Squarciapino (1986–7: 171, n. 12). If Pavolini was right to identify this building as the headquarters of a local guild of athletes, the mosaic acts like an advertisement, showing both the activities associated with the building and, possibly, a famous son (Pavolini, 1983: 212–13).[43]

These two mosaics show us examples of Greek athletes within non-bathing contexts. In both the stress seems to be on particular famous athletes and their victories, though the contest between Alexander and Helix is still unresolved.

---

[43] Hermansen (1981: 76–7, 113–15) also saw the layout of the building as suitable for a guild headquarters, though he was unaware of the mosaic.

Fig. 10.8 Heated room, baths on the Via Severiana, Ostia.
(Archivio Fotografico della Soprintendenza Archeologica di Ostia neg. no. R3269, 16)
(Reproduced courtesy of the Soprintendenza Archeologica di Ostia)

Here athletic competitions are spectacles, regulated by guilds and discussed in bars, just as other forms of public spectacles were. A parallel scene to these mosaics can be found in the mosaic discovered in the 1980s in the Palazzo Imperiale in Rome, discussed briefly above. Here the victorious charioteers and their horses are named, suggesting the depiction of individual sporting heroes, perhaps of local fame (Scrinari, 1988). While this mosaic seems to be later than the athletic images, probably dating to the fourth century, the iconography of victory – the palms and distinctive crowns – is similar, suggesting that it belongs to the same general category, again reinforcing the idea that for the viewers of these mosaics the sporting heroes of the circus and the stadium were seen as the same sorts of people, despite probable differences in status.[44]

Portraits of particular sporting heroes could also be found in baths, as in the most recent find from Ostia, a mosaic from the bath complex along the Via Severiana, close to the synagogue, which was unfortunately stolen shortly after discovery (Fig. 10.8) (Floriani Squarciapino, 1985–6).[45] This mosaic differs from the rest in being polychrome, and has a number of similarities with the mosaics from the Baths of Caracalla and those found at Aquileia, both mentioned above. Like them, it shows a number of separate panels containing busts, five in number. Four of the figures are marked as athletes by their nudity and the presence in one of a short

---

[44] It is also worth noting that charioteers from the various factions also took part in the Capitoline games; Thuillier, 1996: 102.

[45] The photograph included here does not show the figure of Musiciolus.

Fig. 10.9 Mosaic from the baths on the Via Portuense, Rome.
(Servizio di Fotoriproduzione, Soprintendenza Archeologica di Roma inv. 125523)
(Reproduced courtesy of the Soprintendenza Archeologica di Roma)

palm. The fifth is shown as greying and bearded and is dressed in a cloak. He is clearly a trainer or umpire. All five are named with what appear to be nicknames – Musiciolus, Ursus, Faustus, Luxsurius and Pascentius. Similar names often appear as given to gladiators or even animals on mosaics elsewhere, and we know that athletes were also given such nicknames, like the athlete Herminus of Hermopolis, who was also known as Moros (*B.M. Papyri* III, 1178). Like the mosaics from the Baths of Caracalla at Rome and the baths at Aquileia that it resembles, the dating of this mosaic is uncertain. While Floriani Squarciapino dated it to the fourth century on the basis of the date she favoured for the Baths of Caracalla mosaics (Floriani Squarciapino, 1985–6: 113), an earlier dating for these could suggest a date in the third century. Whichever date is favoured, it seems to be among the latest of the athletic mosaics from Ostia and differs substantially from the others in its presentation of portraits busts rather than of athletes, albeit individualised, shown in a narrative account of athletic activity.

When we look at the mosaics from Rome, we find a number of named athletes appearing in bathing contexts. Thus the mosaics found in the ruins of a Hadrianic bath building on the Via Portuense at Rome include names among their representation of athletes.[46] One of these mosaics represents a frieze in which the figures of two boxers at the right of the panel were included with five other figures (Fig. 10.9) (Fornari, 1916: 314, fig. 1). Unfortunately, part of the mosaic is missing, making it impossible to identify the three figures represented there, though from the remains of the top of their heads it seems clear that they were either not as tall as the other figures or were shown sitting or crouching. A figure to the right of this group seems

---

[46] Fornari (1916) suggested that the mosaics too should be dated to the Hadrianic period. See also Blake, 1936: 163.

Fig. 10.10 Mosaic from the baths on the Via Portuense, Rome.
(Servizio di Fotoriproduzione, Soprintendenza Archeologica di Roma inv. 125521)
(Reproduced courtesy of the Soprintendenza Archeologica di Roma)

to be directing his flute playing to them, and thus they may have been shown as dancing. Another naked figure wearing a high *cirrus* stands watching at the left, with his right hand raised to his chin. The presence of the flute player in this scene suggests that this is not solely a scene of athletic competition but may instead have been a composite image including references to a number of the spectacles or competitions that took place in a particular show.[47] We are perhaps here in the world of Roman *ludi*, rather than Greek athletic festivals, during which boxing matches and theatrical displays took place. The allusion to a specific festival is heightened by the presence of names above all the figures, identifying them respectively as Cepalas, Glycon, Capreatio, Collibas, Anticorchis, Moscas and Spintharos.

On the second mosaic the contests are closer to those that we find at Ostia (Fig. 10.10). Again the scene is arranged in a frieze-like manner. To the left of the panel a pair of wrestlers compete in front of a draped umpire. Neither wears the *cirrus*, though one appears to be bearded, the other unbearded. To the right of this group we see the remains of another naked figure moving to the right, perhaps in the act of boxing. Another fragment of mosaic may belong to the right end of this panel (Floriani Squarciapino, 1986–7: 175, fig. 6). It shows the lower part of two figures. At the far right is the draped figure of a trumpeter, his instrument just visible on the left. He is turned to the left, towards another figure who seems to be standing frontally, with bare legs. While most of this figure is lost, comparison with other images suggests that he was probably portrayed as a victorious athlete, being hailed by the trumpeter and possibly crowning himself.

---

[47] The Greek Capitoline games included musical as well as athletic contests, but so too did a number of the Roman *ludi*. The flautist appears to be shown as macrophallic, perhaps suggesting a comic show, but this may be an unintended effect due to the use of white lines to delineate the muscles of the thigh.

Between the two figures is the inscription [D]OMESTICVS. This may be the name of the victorious athlete. Indeed, we know of one Domesticus who was certainly present in Rome between AD 134 and 143. This is the pancratiast M. Ulpius Domesticus of Ephesus, who acted as ambassador for the Guild of Athletes to procure from Emperors Hadrian and Antoninus the right to build a guild headquarters in Rome in the area next to the Baths of Trajan.[48] We know that he served as chief priest of the synod, a role that usually went to successful athletes, and indeed he is labelled in inscriptions as "pancratiast *periodonikês*" – holding victories in all four of the great panhellenic games (*IG* XIV 1110). Moretti suggested that these victories should be put before his embassy to Hadrian in AD 134 and suggested an Olympic victory in 129 (Moretti, 1957: 162–3, no. 844). We do not know whether he was also victorious in the Capitoline games, but his later presence in Rome makes it likely that he competed in these too.[49]

The brick stamps of the bath building suggest a construction date after AD 123–6. It is possible, then, that Domesticus was indeed present as a competitor in Rome at the Capitolia of 128 or 132, at the same time that the mosaics were being executed, and that this inscription should be seen as referring to him. The fact that one of the mosaics seems to refer to Roman spectacles, during which boxing matches also took place, whereas the other shows Greek-style athletics and includes a name that can be associated with a high-status Greek athlete, suggests that Greek athletics could be seen as part of the whole range of public spectacles. It is possible that the figures named on the one mosaic were of a much lower status than Domesticus, yet the mosaics themselves obscure this. If this is a valid interpretation of the mosaics, and the lacunae make it impossible to be certain, then the differences in hair style may also be significant. It is interesting that on the mosaic with the flute player, all the figures wear the *cirrus* in their hair. On the other mosaic, however, the two wrestlers to the left are shown with their hair loose, though, like the boxers on the Porta Marina mosaic, one is clean-shaven and the other bearded. It may be, then, that the mosaic differentiates between professional, low-status entertainers on the one mosaic, and free-born citizens on the other.

Another mosaic inscription that may refer to an Olympic victor is found on a mosaic from a private bath suite on the Via Nomentana, probably part of an élite villa (Gatti, 1888a: 459; 1888b: 333; Blake, 1936: 166). This black and white mosaic showed a life-size figure of an athlete with his right hand to his head, perhaps in the act of crowning himself, and holding a palm branch in his left hand. To the right of the figure was written "Eutyches qui et Nynnys", "Eutyches who is also known as Ninnus". As mentioned above, we know of other athletes given nicknames, and indeed an athlete P. Pompeius Eutyches also known as Ninnaros is attested as twice *periodonikês* on an inscription from Philadelphia in Asia (Moretti, 1957: 157, nos. 785 and 757). While the name differs slightly, it seems quite possible that this mosaic is referring to this very Olympic victor. If Moretti was right to date these victories to the first century, we would seem to have here a reference to a famous

---

[48] See above, p. 239, n. 7.
[49] A later chief priest of the synod, M. Aurelius Demostratus Damas, was certainly also a victor in the Capitoline games: Caldelli, 1993: cat. 40.

Greek athlete of the past, just as an early third-century mosaic in the House of the Porticoes at Seleucia near Antioch contains a portrait of the athlete Nicostratus of Aegeae, who was victorious in the mid-first century AD.[50] More inscribed names appear on a similar mosaic found in the remains of villa baths on the Caelian Hill in Rome (Visconti, 1886).[51] All these mosaics belong in the second century AD and, where the names can be identified with known athletes, appear to evoke victorious athletes from the Greek world who competed in the panhellenic games at Olympia as well, possibly, as in those at Rome.

We are encouraged to recognise these famous victors and the events in which they are engaged. The mosaics from the Via Nomentana and the Caelian suggest that such fondness for the heroes of sporting events was not just the preserve of the lower classes, as the snooty references to similar attachments to actors or pantomimes in the literary sources might suggest, but could rather characterise all members of the social scale. The wide range of people interested in athletic pursuits also seems to be suggested by the mosaics at Ostia, found both in contexts with a wide public exposure, such as the Inn or the Baths of Neptune, as well as in more exclusive establishments such as the Palazzo Imperiale or the richly-decorated Terme Marittime.

CONCLUSIONS

I have suggested, then, that these athletic mosaics could have had a range of associations. On the one hand, those with named athletes conjure up particular athletic victors, possibly those victorious in the Capitoline games at Rome, or other festivals along Greek lines. They suggest that famous sporting heroes, like famous gladiators or actors, could also attain popular renown. By stressing the entertainment value of such activities, the mosaics would seem to objectify their subjects, putting Greek athletes into the same class as the lower-class, but equally famous, heroes of the circus or stage. The "Greekness" of the games, and the fact that in the Greek world an athletic victory brought honour on both the athlete and his home city, seem to be overshadowed by their role as spectacle. Yet the placement of many of these mosaics in areas of the baths associated with athletic exercises also undermines this objectification. It encourages, instead, an identification between the bathers and the figures shown beneath them, who could serve as a model to which to aspire. Here the Greekness of the athletes may well be important, indicating that the identification was with individuals of free birth, and sometimes high status, thus absolving the bather from the charge of deplorable behaviour. Indeed, rather than an allusion to particular contemporary individuals, some of the mosaics could instead be alluding to the wider world of Greek culture, in which exercise in the gymnasium was a crucial part of an élite education, as is suggested by the presence of herms in the Porta Marina mosaic.

Thus the mosaics suggest a picture of changing attitudes to Greek athletics among the Roman public. The identification made in some of them between

---

[50] Levi, 1947: 115–16 and Baity, 1981: 376 dated it to the Severan period.
[51] See also Blake, 1936: 166.

athletics in the baths and the prizes won at public festivals suggests that the new craze for Greek-style physical training, attested by Pliny the Younger and Juvenal, may have been influenced directly by the introduction of Greek-style festivals to Rome. Yet the very introduction of these festivals shows the status of Greek culture at this time. The fact that Roman emperors were keen to put Rome at the heart of the Greek festival circuit shows their desire to integrate Greek culture into Roman life as well as to control it.[52] While élite writers of the Republic and early Empire expressed their disapproval of the corrupting influence of Greek athletics on Roman morals, these mosaics show its steady progression into Roman life during the course of the second and third centuries. By the middle of the third century, we find Ostia publicly honouring one of its citizens as a victor in festivals across the Mediterranean world and Emperor Alexander Severus renowned as an exceptional wrestler.[53] While public athletic victories may never have had the status they did in the Greek east, these mosaics suggest that Greek athletics did become firmly integrated into Roman culture – both as public spectacle and as part of the social world of the Roman baths.

WORKS CITED

Alcock, S. E. (1994) Nero at play? The emperor's Grecian Odyssey. In J. Elsner and J. Masters (eds), *Reflections of Nero. Culture, History and Representation:* 98–111. London, Duckworth.

Alföldi-Rosenbaum, E. (1994) A *Flamen Augustalis* on a mosaic pavement in the "Grandi Terme" of Aquileia. In J. P. Darmon and A. Rebourg (eds), *La mosaïque greco-romaine* IV: 101–5 with pl. 51. Paris; Association Internationale pour l'Étude de la Mosaïque Antique.

Balty, J. (1981) La mosaïque antique au Proche-Orient I. Des origines à la Tétrarchie. *Aufstieg und Niedergang der Römischen Welt* II.12.2: 347–429. Berlin, De Gruyter.

Bargagli, B. and Grosso, C. (1997) (eds) *I Fasti Ostienses. Documento della storia di Ostia.* Ostia, Soprintendenza Archeologica.

Becatti, G. (1961) *Mosaici e pavimenti marmorei. Scavi di Ostia* IV. Rome, Libreria dello Stato.

Bergmann, B. and Kondoleon, C. (1999) (eds) *The Art of Ancient Spectacle.* Washington, National Gallery of Art/Yale University Press.

Blake, M. E. (1936) Roman mosaics of the second century in Italy. *Memoirs of the American Academy in Rome* 13: 69–214.

Bloch, H. (1938) *I bolli laterizi e la storia edilizia.* Rome, C. Colombo.

Caldelli, M. L. (1992) Curia athletarum, iera xystike synodos e organizzazione delle terme a Roma. *Zeitschrift für Papyrologie und Epigraphik* 93: 75–87.

Caldelli, M. L. (1993) *L'agon capitolinus.* Rome, Istituto Italiano per la Storia Antica.

Caldelli, M. L. (1998) Varia agonistica ostensia. In G. Paci (ed.), *Epigrafia romana in area adriatica:* 225–47. Macerata, Istituti Editoriali e Poligrafici Internazionali.

Calza, G. and Becatti, G. (1974) *Ostia* (ninth edition, revised by M. Floriani Squarciapino). Rome, Istituto Poligrafico e Zecca dello Stato.

---

[52] For a discussion of Nero's attitude to Greek culture, see Alcock, 1994. Caldelli, 1993: 7–52 and Ferrary, 1996: 192–203 have discussed the significance of the introduction of Greek-style festivals to Rome.

[53] *CIL* XIV 474, discussed above; SHA, *Severus Alexander* 27 "palaestes primus fuit", see Castagnoli, 1943–5: 14.

Carandini, A., Ricci, A. and de Vos, M. (1982) *Filosofiana. The Villa of Piazza Armerina*. Palermo, S. F. Flaccovio.
Castagnoli, F. (1943–5) Il capitello della Pigna Vaticana. *Bullettino della Commissione Archeologica Comunale di Roma* 71: 1–30.
Clarke, J. R. (1979) *Roman Black-and-White Figural Mosaics*. New York, New York University Press.
Crowther, N. B. (1980–1) Nudity and morality: athletics in Italy. *Classical Journal* 76: 119–23.
Darmon, J. P. and Rebourg, A. (1994) (eds) *La mosaïque gréco-romaine* IV. Paris, Association Internationale pour l'Étude de la Mosaïque Antique.
DeLaine, J. (1997) *The Baths of Caracalla (Journal of Roman Archaeology Supplement 25)*. Portsmouth (RI), Journal of Roman Archaeology.
Domergue, C., Landes, C. and Pailler, J.-M. (1990) (eds) *Spectacula* I. *Gladiateurs et amphithéatre. Actes du colloque tenu à Toulouse et à Lattes les 26, 27, 28 et 29 mai 1987*. Lattes, Editions Image.
Dunbabin, K. M. D. (1999) *The Mosaics of the Greek and Roman World*. Cambridge, Cambridge University Press.
Edwards, C. (1993) *The Politics of Immorality*. Princeton, Princeton University Press.
Eloy, M. (1990) Les gladiateurs au cinéma. In C. Domergue, C. Landes and J.-M. Pailler (eds), *Spectacula* I. *Gladiateurs et amphithéatre. Actes du colloque tenu à Toulouse et à Lattes les 26, 27, 28 et 29 mai 1987*: 277–94. Lattes, Editions Image.
Ferrary, J. L. (1996) Rome, Athènes et le philhellénisme dans l'empire romain, d'Auguste aux Antonins. In *Filellenismo e tradizionalismo a Roma nei primi due secoli dell'Impero. Atti dei convegni lincei* 125: 183–210. Rome, Accademia Nazionale dei Lincei.
Floriani Squarciapino, M. (1985–6) Nuovi mosaici ostiensi. *Atti della Pontificia Accademia Romana di Archeologia. Rendiconti* 58: 87–144.
Floriani Squarciapino, M. (1986–7) Un altro mosaico ostiense con atleti. *Atti della Pontificia Accademia Romana di Archeologia. Rendiconti* 59: 161–79.
Forbes, C. A. (1955) Ancient athletic guilds. *Classical Philology* 50: 238–52.
Fornari, F. (1916) Scoperte di antichità nel suburbio. *Notizie degli Scavi di Antichità*: 311–18.
Gardiner, E. N. (1930) *Athletics of the Ancient World*. Oxford, Clarendon Press.
Gassowska, B. (1966) *Cirrus* in vertice. In *Mélanges offerts à Kazimierz Michalowski*: 421–7. Warsaw, Panstwowe Wydawn Namkowe.
Gatti, G. (1888a) Scoperte di antichità in Roma e nel suburbio. *Notizie degli Scavi di Antichità*: 434–59.
Gatti, G. (1888b) Scoperte recentissime. *Bullettino della Commissione Archeologica Communale di Roma* 16: 327–34.
Gentili, G. V. (1956) *The Imperial Villa of Piazza Armerina* (English translation). Rome, Istituto Poligrafico dello Stato.
Glotz, G. (1912) Xystos (2). In C. Daremberg and M. E. Saglio (eds), *Dictionnaire des antiquités grecques et romains* V: 1027–31. Paris, Hachette et Cie.
Guarducci, M. (1982) Una nuova officina di lucernette romane: gli *Aeoli*. *Römische Mitteilungen* 89: 103–31.
Hermansen, G. (1981) *Ostia. Aspects of Roman City Life*. Alberta, University of Alberta Press.
Humphrey, J. H. (1986) *Roman Circuses. Arenas for Chariot Racing*. London, B. T. Batsford Ltd.
Inan, J. and Alföldi-Rosenbaum, E. (1979) *Römische und Frühbyzantinische Porträtplastik aus der Türkei. Neue Funde*. Mainz am Rhein, von Zabern.
Insalaco, A. (1989) I mosaici degli atleti dalle terme di Caracalla. *Archeologia Classica* 41: 293–327.

Jones, C. P. (1998) The pancratiasts Helix and Alexander on an Ostian mosaic. *Journal of Roman Archaeology* 11: 293–8.
Khanoussi, M. (1988) Spectaculum pugilum et Gymnasium. *Comptes Rendus de l'Académie des Inscriptions*: 543–61.
Khanoussi, M. (1991) Les spectacles des jeux athlétiques et de pugilat dans l'Afrique Romaine. *Mitteilungen des Deutschen Archäologischen Instituts, Römische Abteilung* 98: 315–22.
Kleiner, D. E. E. (1992) *Roman Sculpture*. New Haven/London, Yale University Press.
Köhne, E. and Ewigleben, C. (2000) (eds) *Gladiators and Caesars. The Power of Spectacle in Ancient Rome* (English version edited by R. Jackson). London, British Museum Press.
Kondoleon, C. (1995) *Domestic and Divine: Roman Mosaics in the House of Dionysos*. Ithaca/London, Cornell University Press.
Lanciani, R. (1886) XII Ostia. *Notizie degli Scavi di Antichità*: 162–5.
Lee, H. M. (1997) The later Greek boxing glove and the "Roman" Caestus: a centennial reevaluation of Jüthner's "Éber Antike Turngeräthe". *Nikephoros* 10: 161–78 with pls 2–7.
Levi, D. (1947) *Antioch Mosaic Pavements*. Princeton, Princeton University Press.
Lopreato, P. (1994) Le grandi terme di Aquileia. I mosaici del frigidarium. In J.-P. Darmon and A. Rebourg (eds), *La mosaïque gréco-romaine* IV: 87–99 with pls 39–50. Paris, Association Internationale pour l'Étude de la Mosaïque Antique.
Manderscheid, H. (1981) *Die Skulpturenausstattung des Kaiserzeitliche Thermenanlagen*. Berlin, Mann.
Meiggs, R. (1973) *Roman Ostia* (second edition). Oxford, Clarendon Press.
Mols, S. T. A. M. (1999) Decorazione e uso dello spazio a Ostia. Il caso dell'*Insula* III.X. *Mededelingen van het Nederlands Instituut te Rome* 58: 247–386.
Moretti, L. (1957) *Olympionikai. I vincitori negli antichi agoni Olimpici*. Rome, Accademia Nazionale dei Lincei.
Neudecker, R. (1988) *Die Skulpturenausstattung Römischer Villen in Italien*. Mainz am Rhein, P. von Zabern.
Nielsen, I. (1990) *Thermae et Balnea. The Architecture and Cultural History of Roman Public Baths*. Aarhus, University Press.
Paschetto, L. (1912) *Ostia Colonia Romana. Storia e monumenti*. Rome, Poliglotta Vaticana.
Pavolini, C. (1983) *Ostia (Guida Archeologica Laterza)*. Bari, G. Laterza.
Pavolini, C. (1986) *La vita quotidiana a Ostia*. Bari, G. Laterza.
Pleket, H. W. (1973) Some aspects of the history of the athletic guilds. *Zeitschrift für Papyrologie und Epigraphik* 10: 197–227.
Poliakoff, M. B. (1987) *Combat Sports in the Ancient World*. New Haven/London, Yale University Press.
Scrinari, V. (1988) Ostia antica. Il cosiddetto Palazzo imperiale. Decorazioni musive. *Archeologia Laziale* 9: 185–90.
Spurza, J. M. (1990) Il cortile centrale del cosiddetto palazzo imperiale ad Ostia antica. *Archeologia Laziale* 10: 157–63.
Thuillier, J.-P. (1996) *Le sport dans la Rome antique*. Paris, Editions France.
Thuillier, J.-P. (1998) Le *cirrus* et la barbe. Questions d'iconographie athlétique romaine. *Mélanges de l'École Française de Rome. Antiquité* 110: 351–80.
Van Nijf, O. (1999) Athletics, festivals and Greek identity in the Roman East. *Proceedings of the Cambridge Philological Society* 45: 176–200.
Van Nijf, O. (2001) Local heroes: athletics, festivals and élite self-fashioning in the Roman East. In S. Goldhill (ed.), *Being Greek under Rome*: 306–34. Cambridge, Cambridge University Press.

Visconti, C. L. (1857) Escavazioni di Ostia dall'anno 1855 al 1858. *Annali dell'Istituto di Corrispondenza Archeologica* 29: 281–340.
Visconti, C. L. (1886) Trovamenti di oggetti d'arte e di antichità figurata. *Bullettino della commissione Archeologica Comunale di Roma* 14: 49–53.
Werner, H. (1998) *Die Sammlung Antiker Mosaiker in den Vatikanischen Museen.* Vatican, Monumenti Museo e Gallerie Pontificie.
Wyke, M. (1997) *Projecting the Past: Ancient Rome, Cinema and History.* New York/London, Routledge.
Zevi, F. (1996) Sulie fasi più antiche di Ostia. In A. Gallina Zevi and A. Claridge (eds), *"Roman Ostia" Revisited. Archaeological and Historical Papers in Memory of Russell Meiggs*: 69–89. London, British School at Rome.
Zevi, F. and Granelli, A. (1999) Le terme di Nettuno: stratigrafia e fase edilizie pre-adrianee. *Mededelingen van het Nederlands Instituut te Rome* 58: 80–2.

PART VI

Greek Athletics and the Modern World

Introduction to Part VI

This final section comprises two pieces which between them shed light on the processes by which the athletics of the Greek world is reshaped, manipulated, reimagined and paralleled within modern sport and modern athletic scholarship.

David Young's article, first of all, might equally well have been placed in section 4, with Pleket and van Nijf, as an exploration of the ideals and commemoration of competition and victory. I include it here, however, because it also makes a decisive contribution to debate about the similarities and differences between ancient and modern sport. The sports historian Allen Guttmann has isolated seven characteristics which he feels distinguish modern sport (or at any rate modern American sport), and compares them systematically with more "primitive' traditions, to see how well his characterisation holds up.[1] His seven principles are secularism, equality of opportunity, rationalisation, quantification, the quest for records, bureaucratic organisation, specialisation. At least some of those principles, despite Guttmann's beliefs to the contrary, are in fact obvious features of Greek athletic tradition in the ancient world. Young makes that clear in this article for the "quest for records", showing that ancient practices of recording athletic records are very much closer to modern practice than has often been imagined. On that account, for all the enormous cultural differences between ancient and modern sporting experience, which Young's own work on amateurism has helped to expose,[2] confidence in the *uniqueness* of modern sport comes to look rather misguided. Young also suggests that the desire to set new records via unprecedented combinations of victories may have led to increasing diversification, as athletes strove for uniqueness by winning in a number of different events. That claim challenges the standard view from the first half of the twentieth century that Greek athletics became increasingly specialised and professionalised from the late classical period onwards.

The processes by which the modern Olympic tradition came into being are discussed at more length in the introduction to this volume. One problem of recent scholarship has been a tendency to oversimplify those developments, in a way which fails to do justice to the complexity of the ideological and political pressures and motivations which guided the many different actors who were involved. For example,

---

[1] Guttmann (1978), esp. 15–55; restated with no account of intervening criticisms in Guttman (1994) 2–4.
[2] See esp. Young (1984).

as I suggested in the introduction, there has been a tendency to underestimate the degree to which other players, in addition to Coubertin, took a key role in the refoundation of the modern Olympics.[3] Donald Kyle's discussion of the work of E. Norman Gardiner, one of the pioneers of athletic scholarship in twentieth-century Classics (whose work is still widely available in university libraries), stands out from that tendency towards oversimplified story-telling, delving in depth into some of the cultural influences which helped to form Gardiner's by now notorious views on the decline of ancient athletics due to the onset of professionalism. Kyle's account is a masterful and vivid dissection of the life and career of one individual. It also sheds light on the athletic culture of the first half of the twentieth century more broadly. To take just one example, his account makes clear the danger of seeing the many individuals with links to the early Olympics and the amateur movement as an undifferentiated body: Gardiner, he explains, was himself highly suspicious of Coubertin and his Olympic refoundation. Finally, Kyle's article in particular seems an appropriate place to finish this volume, with its concluding call for self-consciousness about the way in which our own vision of and interest in ancient athletics is necessarily formed by factors within our present-day culture which may not always be obvious to us at first sight.

---

[3] For correctives, see Young (1987) and (1996); Llewelyn Smith (2004).

11 *First with the Most: Greek Athletic Records and 'Specialisation'**

DAVID YOUNG

"I claim that the sports record is a recent invention and a talisman for the idea of progress in a disciplined, industrialized meritocratic mass society."[1]

So, in 1992, Richard Mandell restated a thesis that he first presented in 1976. In 1978 Allen Guttmann developed much the same idea in his important theoretical study, *From Ritual to Record*. Guttmann's book, powerfully influencing some new thinking in the field of sports studies, led to much discussion and some controversy. In 1990 there appeared a special volume of essays, edited by Carter and Krüger, which questioned Guttmann's thesis especially with respect to the recent origin of the sports record, the belief that pre-modern societies had no real notion of keeping and breaking records in sports. Invited to write the final chapter in that volume, to assess the previous essays, Guttmann modified his views in some respects where he had spoken categorically before. But he was able to maintain his overall thesis rather strongly, observing that the other essays offered little to contradict his point, and that some cases of disagreement misconstrued what his original positions had been.[2]

Ancient Greek athletics have more to contribute to this controversy about the modernity of record-keeping than has so far appeared. I do not wish here to question the overall validity of Mandell's and Guttmann's thesis and their assertion that quantification of records is a special feature of modern, industrialized society, especially if by "quantification" we mean "expressed by numbers that measure time or distance". In most respects that thesis seems to me rather sound. I focus rather on one feature of the controversy, which Guttmann well explains in his closing essay in Carter and Krüger's collection; namely, the concepts of keeping, setting, and breaking records. Seeking to distinguish the recording of data in mediaeval societies from the modern record and from "setting and breaking records", Guttmann writes:

---

* Originally published in *Nikephoros* 9 (1996), pp. 175–97.

[1] R. Mandell, review of W. Decker, *Sports and Games in Ancient Egypt*, transl. by A. Guttmann, New Haven 1992, in: *Natural History*, July 1992, 58–61 (60–61). For the abbreviations used in the following article see the Bibliography.

[2] Mandell's earlier statements appeared several places, most notably in: *Stadion* 2, 1976, 250–64. A. Guttmann, *From Ritual to Record*, New York 1978; J. M. Carter/A. Krüger (eds), *Ritual and Record*, New York/London 1990. The bibliography and a historical survey of the theory and its resulting controversy appeared in Carter/Krüger 1–11 (with further comments throughout the volume). Guttmann's concluding essay there: 153–60. As Guttmann succeeded Mandell in developing the basic thesis of the modernity of records, H. Eichberg had preceded him. Carter and Krüger's survey explains how the positions of those three authors of the theory differ in details.

As I have repeatedly tried to explain, the modern sports record is an unsurpassed but presumably surpassable quantified achievement. This use of the term *record*, derived from the phrase "the best recorded achievement", first appeared in English in the mid-nineteenth century.[3]

It is in these elements that I believe the Greeks clearly anticipated the modern sports record: "an unsurpassed but presumably surpassable quantified achievement", and "the best recorded" (though the words "quantified" and "best" are not terms that the Greeks used in their record-keeping system).[4] Since my study of "specialization" in Greek athletics presented below so strongly relates to this general controversy over the modernity of the sports record, I translate all the Greek, to make the argument accessible to sports historians outside the field of Classics.[5]

In the Olympic Games of AD 69, there competed a Greek runner named Polites from Caria, near what is now Bodrum on the west coast of Turkey. Polites won the *stade* (200 meters), the *diaulos* (400 meters), and the *dolichos* (5000? meters), all in one Olympiad – in the same day, in fact.[6] Anyone attentive to sport knows that to win both the short sprint and the distance race at the Olympics is a nearly incredible achievement. We have seen no runner so versatile in modern times. Our athletes specialize either in the sprints, middle distance, or long distances, and our sporting culture assumes that the same athlete could not excel at all three. The various distances require, our coaches would say, different types of muscles, different kinds of breathing, training and technique. Polites' diversity at running seemed exceptional in antiquity, too, and draws Pausanias' praise. He calls it a μέγα θαῦμα, "a great marvel," and adds that Polites could switch from the distance style to the sprint in a very brief time. His finishing "kick" in the distance race must have been something special to see.

I return to Polites much later, when it will be clearer why and how so unusual an

---

[3] Guttmann in: Carter/Krüger 157.

[4] Guttmann himself once made a passing reference to the kind of Greek record that I study here, but suggested that it did not qualify. *From Ritual to Record*, 50:
> There was a second kind of quantification that began under the Greeks ... professional athletes frequently boasted that they were the first to have won seven victories at seven different festivals or three times in a row at this or that famous site. It is still a long way from this type of scoring to the lengthy statistical appendices with which modern biographies terminate, but the first steps were taken.

But statistical appendices are not really what Guttmann himself means by a "record". Further, it was not just the "professional athletes" themselves who "boasted" these ancient records; the material below shows that chroniclers and historians dutifully kept track of the athletes' record achievements for centuries after their deaths.

[5] For the same reason, I seldom elaborate on such technical questions as the readings and supplements in the Greek inscriptions, and other difficulties in the ancient sources. Most classical sports historians know rather well the sources with which I deal here, and the difficulties in their precise interpretation. Unless such questions directly affect the points I wish to make, I leave them aside lest they encumber and obscure my main theses.

[6] Pausanias 6.13.3. I have recast the distances to their closest modern equivalents. The *stade* (one length of the stadium track) at Olympia was actually just over 192 meters; the *diaulos* was two *stades* long. The actual length of the *dolichos* is still disputed. I have reluctantly followed the usual conclusion, twenty-four laps (E. N. Gardiner, *Greek Athletic Sports and Festivals*, London 1910, 270; M. I. Finley/H. W. Pleket, *Olympic Games: The First Thousand Years*, New York 1976, 35) despite *Anth.Pal.* 9.319 (which suggests twenty laps), and other sources which suggest far fewer.

athlete came about in ancient Greece. I first focus on the much-discussed concepts "records" and "specialization". E. N. Gardiner wrote the two most influential books on ancient athletics. In his 1930 book he said, "The Greek did not care for records, and he kept no records." This belief spread from Gardiner to others, even to distinguished historians of modern sport, such as Mandell and Guttmann.[7] Gardiner's assertion proves quite false, founded on a mistakenly narrow view of what constitutes a record. The Greeks kept athletic records, kept them meticulously, and they cared. How fervently they cared emerges as we proceed.

First I must question another of Gardiner's notions that has spread unchallenged until it permeates almost all writing on Greek athletics; namely, the idea of "increasing specialization", to use Harris' term.[8] Gardiner coined this idea and related phrases as he condemned the "Rise of Professionalism", which he placed in the fifth century BC. Before its end, he writes,

> [T]he excessive prominence given to bodily excellence had produce specialization and professionalism. From this time sport, overdeveloped and over-specialized, became more the monopoly of a class ... specialization, professionalism, corruption – Unfortunately the signs of excess are no less manifest today ... History repeats itself strangely ... the same tendency to specialization and professionalism ...[9]

Nowadays many might pause at Gardiner's words "excessive prominence'; for we no longer rank athletic ability so low on the scale of human excellences as the Victorians did. But the point of Gardiner's critique should be clear: he is writing about his own world, where the Victorian Gentleman athlete sought to suppress the hated "professional", the working class man who took the time to develop special skill in the event where he wished to compete. "Specialization and professionalism" are for Gardiner so intertwined that they become a single phrase, much like *kaloskagathos* in Plato. And the "increasing professionalism" of the fourth and later centuries, Gardiner claims, saw a corresponding decrease in athletes' versatility. As "professionalism" progressed, more and more athletes who would have, in former days, practiced and competed in several events, began to concentrate on a single event. "[T]he would-be champion had from boyhood to devote himself to training. He soon found that it was necessary to concentrate on some particular event, to specialize.'[10] That excessive specialization led, the theory goes, to a new breed of athlete who had little or no skill, mental or physical, outside his one event; and it led to a very narrow kind of physical training, so highly focused on a single type of athletic performance that it was unhealthy for the athlete's general well-being.

---

[7] E. N. Gardiner, *Athletics of the Ancient World*, Oxford 1930, 2; besides Mandell (above) cf. Guttmann, *From Ritual to Record*, esp. 51 (citing Finley/Pleket 22 – who, however, go on to note that the Greeks "kept other kinds of records" and then cite poor examples of the "other kinds" [their comment on the same page on the "walkover" is, incidentally, disproved by the "walkover", ἀκονιτί, records of Dromeus and Theogenes noted below]).

[8] H. A. Harris, *Greek Athletes and Athletics*, Bloomington/London 1964, 75: "there was a constantly increasing degree of specialization"; Finley/Pleket 70: "athletic professionalism and specialization that had set in ... increasingly specialized athletes". From our technical literature, the notion spread to popular books: "By the beginning of the fourth century, professional athletes, proficient in one sport only, were firmly entrenched" (L. and G. Poole, *History of the Ancient Olympic Games*, New York 1963, 11).

[9] Gardiner, 1910, 4–5.

[10] Gardiner, 1930, 101.

In my *Olympic Myth* I argued that there never was any "rise of professionalism" in the fifth century, nor "increasing professionalism" in the late classical and Hellenistic periods – because, in modern terms, all Greek athletes were professionals from the start. "Amateur athlete" was the one thing the Greeks had no word for. The evidence suggests that the wrestler Milo, in the sixth century, was just as professional as Theogenes, in the early fifth, Dikon in the fourth, or, for that matter, Philinos of Kos in the third. There is no evidence that amateurism of any kind was ever known in Greece. I here stand by the evidence in my book, and argue no more about professionals and non-professionals.[11] I examine the concomitant "baggage" of "increased professionalism", namely, the theory of "increased specialization". If the theory of increased professionalism is false, can its offspring – part and parcel of its parent – be valid? No. I know of only one ancient text that Gardiner could have cited as evidence (he did not); namely, the good doctor, but reckless sports historian, Galen. "In the old days ... a single man ... competed not only in wrestling, but also in foot-racing, and one person often won both these events and the javelin, *diskos*, and chariot races as well. But later things changed ..."[12] Neither Galen nor Gardiner cites an ancient text nor the case of even one ancient athlete to support their assertions. Harris realizes that Polites' case noted above contradicts the theory, and he must call it an "exception'; but neither he nor anyone else specifies an athlete to prove the rule.[13] The genuine evidence for the so-called period of "increased specialization" in Greece actually demonstrates the exact opposite; namely, an increase in versatility. Later athletes seem to develop champion-level skills in a greater number of events than their predecessors. But the cause for this chronologically decreasing specialization has nothing to do with amateurism, professionalism, or any gradation between. It results from the nature of Greek athletic record-keeping and record-breaking, which compelled many an athlete to become less specialized if he was ever to set a new record.

Perhaps because Gardiner roundly declared that the Greeks kept no records, no comprehensive study of Greek athletic record-keeping has appeared since M. N. Tod's pioneering *Greek Record-Keeping and Record-Breaking*, which pointedly questioned Gardiner's assertion.[14] Tod indeed notes that the absolute marks of individual Greek athletic performances were not recorded. Obviously there were no stop watches for the running events. But even in events where measurement was easy, such as the discus throw, the marks were not kept for future reference (reported long jumps of more than 50 feet are surely false).[15] So Greeks kept no records like

---

[11] D. C. Young, *Olympic Myth of Greek Amateur Athletics*, Chicago 1984.

[12] 5.870–1 (Kühn).

[13] Harris, 1964, 75.

[14] In: *Classical Quarterly* 43, 1949, 105–12. Dietrich Ramba's *Recordmania in Sports in Ancient Greece and Rome* (in: Carter/Krüger 31-9) unfortunately fails to improve much on Tod's work itself, and is understandably dismissed by Guttmann (in: Carter/Krüger 156–7).

[15] Reports of jumps by Chionis and Phayllos beyond 50 feet are first found in questionable circumstances in doubtful, late sources. There is no report of either jump for hundreds of years after each man's death, and these centuries-later reports are quite unreliable; for good arguments against them see E. N. Gardiner, *Phayllos and his Record Jump*, and *The Ancient Long Jump*, in: *Journal of Hellenic Studies* 24, 1904, 70–80; 179–94.

our own measured in minutes and meters. But there are other kinds of records, as in our baseball, tennis, or golf; or in the Guinness Book of World Records.

These records are founded, in simple terms, on who was the first to do the most: to win, to put it in modern terms, something like the US, British, and French Open tennis championships all twice in a row; or Wimbledon eleven times. The Greeks indeed kept and coveted such records, employing a highly developed system that recorded which athlete was the first to win each event; or who was the first to win a particular combination or number of victories. Aristotle commends this concept in general terms. When he discusses how a speaker should praise someone, he says, "one should use much amplification, such as "he was the first (*prôtos*) to do such and such" or "he was the only one (*monos*) to do it".[16]

Pausanias and Greek inscriptions bear witness to the system in athletics. And Tod explains how it works: "The idea was usually expressed in very simple and almost stereotyped formulae, whose key words are *heis monos kai prôtos* [the one, the only, and the first], varied by combination and by the addition of phrases lending emphasis and expressiveness."[17] These are the phrases that concern us here, the "first to do such and such", or the "only one", or, "no one else on earth has done it so many times".

I turn first to the simplest of records, a national record, from the base of one statue in a three-statue group at Delphi. "You are the first man (*prôtos*) from Thessalian land, Hagias, of Pharsalas, son of Aknonios, to win the Olympic *pancration* (no-holds-barred)."[18] The word *prôtos*, "first," formally announces the record, but it applies only to Thessalians. It is no world record. But a world record could be set even in a limited category, such as family victories at a single celebration of the Pythian Games, second only to the Olympics in prestige. This Delphi statue group had the statues of three brothers, all three victors at some early fifth-century Pythiad. They are, besides the no-holds-barred victor, Hagias, the wrestling victor, Telemachos, and Agelaos, winner of the boys' *stade*. The inscription on Agelaos' statue base reads:

> These men had the same strength for winning
> victory, and I, Agelaos, am the brother of
> them both. At the same time as these men
> I was victorious at the Pythian games, in
> the boys' stade. Of all mortals we are
> the only ones to win these crowns.
> (μοῦνοι δὲ θνατῶν τούσδε ἔχομεν στεφάνους)[19]

Another inscription states a gender record: the only woman to win the Olympic chariot contest.

---

[16] Aristotle, *Rhetoric* 1.1368a.
[17] Tod 110–11.
[18] Ebert 43 (early fifth cent. BC): Ὀλύμπια παγκράτιον, Φαρσάλιε νικᾷς, Ἁγία Ἀκνονίου, γῆς ἀπὸ Θεσσαλίας (Moretti 192 and others give the name as Agias), Since the *pancration* combined boxing, wrestling and other forms of fighting, "no-holds-barred" seems the best English translation (though biting and eye-gouging were forbidden).
[19] Ebert 46. On 7 April 1979, the American professional baseball pitchers, Bob and Ken Forsch, became "the first set of brothers to hurl no-hitters in the major leagues" (*Santa Barbara News Press*, 8 April 1979, C-1).

> The kings of Sparta are my fathers and brothers.
> I, Kyniska, winning with my chariot and swift horses
> set up this statue. I declare that I am the only woman
> ever from all of Greece to take this crown.[20]

These athletes somehow set a record with no more than one victory each. Most records required some kind of multiple victory. A frequent type of record consists of victories in successive Olympiads. Here the great sixth-century wrestler Milo established a record that was never broken or tied, Olympic wrestling champion for five or six Olympiads.[21] But such records required a very long career, Milo's spanning two decades. There was another, quicker way to set a record, to win a unique set of victories; namely, to combine victories in different events for the first time. That meant to diversify, and here the question of specialization is clearly raised.

Most known records come from inscriptions, either actual stones or those quoted by Pausanias. But a few are preserved in the athletic poems of Pindar and Bacchylides.[22] At *Olympian* 13.29-31 Pindar asks Zeus to accept the victory celebration of the Corinthian athlete, Xenophon, who has been declared, at Olympia, "victor at the same time in both the pentathlon and the *stade* [200 meters]" (πενταέθλῳ ἅμα σταδίου νικῶν δρόμον). Then Pindar formally proclaims that Xenophon's winning combination, the pentathlon and the *stade*, is a "world record" at the Olympics: "No mortal man ever before has met with this combination": ἀντεβόλησεν τῶν ἀνὴρ θνατὸς οὔπω τις πρότερον.

Xenophon's achievement was remarkable. He could claim both our titles, "world's best all-around athlete", and "world's fastest human", as we call our all-around and our sprinting champions. So far as I can determine, Xenophon's record stood unmatched throughout the rest of antiquity;[23] nor in modern Olympic history has anyone ever won a double victory in our equivalents, the 100 meters and the decathlon. Xenophon's victories occurred in 464, after, Gardiner would say, the age of increased specialization had already begun. But the evidence suggests that the fifth century marks the beginning of increased diversity, when athletes began to train to Olympic champion form in various types of events.

One of the most fabled ancient athletes was Theogenes (Theagenes[24]) of

---

[20] Ebert 33: ... ἅρματι ... νικῶσα Κυνίσκα ... μόναν δ' ἐμέ φαμι γυναικῶν Ἑλλάδος ἐκ πάσας τόνδε λαβεῖν στέφανον (Moretti A421). Since the owners of racing stables need not attend the games to be declared victors, women could win Olympic equestrian events. Kyniska won two Olympic crowns; several other women followed her as Olympic equestrian victors (listed in H. A. Harris, *Sport in Greece and Rome*, New York 1972, 178).

[21] Uncertainty whether Milo (Moretti A479) was adult Olympic wrestling victor five or six times results from his victory as a boy in 540 (Moretti 115), conflicting ancient sources, and differing interpretations of those that say he won six times. Most scholars follow the text of Pausanias 6.14.5, which says that Milo's six victories included one in the boys' division. They then merely reject (or emend "seven" to "six") the Simonidean epigram which says he won "seven" Olympic victories (Ebert 61, Simonides 25 Page, *Epigrammata Graeca*). See the discussion at Moretti 122.

[22] Bacchylides 3.15 expresses Hieron's equestrian record: μόνον ἐπιχθονίων, "the only man on earth", the very same phrase used in Theogenes' Isthmian record (Ebert 37, below).

[23] Gorgos of Elis (see n.38, below) joined one of his four pentathlon victories with a victory in the *diaulos*, but not in the *stade* (Pausanias 6.15.9).

[24] Ancient sources vary in the spelling of his name; I follow Moretti (A659) and most others in making it Theogenes.

Thasos, an island in the northern Aegean. In the 480 BC Olympics, Theogenes entered both the boxing and the no-holds-barred. He dethroned the defending champion in boxing, Euthymos of Greek Italy. But exhausted or injured from this boxing final, Theogenes was unable to compete in the no-holds-barred final. He thus gave Dromeus of Arcadia an easy record, duly recorded by Pausanias: "First man of whom we know to win the Olympic no-holds-barred by a forfeit (walkover)": πρῶτος ὧν ἴσμεν ἀκονιτὶ λαβεῖν.²⁵ The Olympic officials, apparently embarrassed by Theogenes' failure to compete in the no-holds-barred finals, fined Theogenes an immense amount of money, equal to several hundreds of thousands of dollars. He easily paid. Although Pausanias says the Olympic officials accused Theogenes of entering the boxing just to spite Euthymos, Pausanias himself says that Theogenes entered both the boxing and the no-holds-barred because "he wished to win both events at the same Olympiad". Theogenes was a seeker of records, and hoped for a "same day" double. He settled for a little less. In the next Olympiad he was not entered in the boxing, but he won the no-holds-barred. That victory, coupled to his earlier boxing crown, made him the first man ever to combine victories in both those Olympic combative events. He thus set a new record.²⁶ Theogenes' inscription provides, in fact, a model for the vocabulary of Greek record-breaking.²⁷

> Never did Thasos bear one such as you, son of Timosthenos, and you have by far the most praise for strength among the Greeks. For never before was the same man crowned at Olympia winning in both boxing and pankration (οὐ γάρ τις Ὀλυμπίᾳ ἐστεφανώθη ὡύτος ἀνὴρ πυγμῇ παγκρατίῳ τε κρατῶν)

That Olympic record naturally comes first. Next comes Theogenes' record at the Pythians at Delphi, line 5: "of three crowns, one was uncontested (*akoniti*)." World record: "No man had done it before": τὸ δὲ θνητὸς ἀνὴρ οὔτις ἔρεξε ἕτερος. Some phraseology here is remarkably like Pindar's announcement of Xenophon's record at *Ol.* 13 .31 (above): "no mortal man ever before" (ἀνὴρ θνητὸς οὔπω τις πρότερον). Then comes Theogenes' Isthmian record (7–9): in nine Isthmiads, ten victories. For twice the herald proclaimed him world record holder, the "only man on earth to win both boxing and no-holds-barred in a single day", μοῦνον ἐπιχθονίων πυγμῆς παγκρατίου τ' ἐπινίκιον ἤματι τωὐτῷ. Theogenes had nine victories at the Nemean Games, and a grand total of 1,300 victories in all the festivals he entered. In twenty-two years, he was never beaten in boxing.²⁸

---

²⁵ Pausanias 6.6.5–6 and 6.11.4; Moretti 202.
²⁶ Pausanias 6.6.5–6; 6.11.2–9; Moretti 201, 215.
²⁷ Ebert 37.
²⁸ Some scholars doubt the accuracy of Theogenes' inscription; Finley/Pleket 68 call the 1,300 victories "mathematically impossible". That figure indeed seems unlikely; but Theogenes entered many events in many minor meets, and his career in minor meets might have been longer than twenty-two years. There is no reason to doubt his records at the major games of the circuit, with which I am concerned here. Pausanias tells several fabulous tales about Theogenes' birth and powers after death. There was later a hero cult of Theogenes at Thasos. Most of what is known – and far more that is not known – about Theogenes, the tales about him, and his hero-cult is in J. Pouilloux, *Recherches sur l'histoire et les cultes de Thasos*, Paris 1954. I agree with P. M. Fraser's judgment (review of Pouilloux in *AJA* 61, 1957, 98-103) that much in Pouilloux's account of Theogenes is "fancy" and outright "mythology" (see my *Olympic Myth*, 150–2).

Theogenes was clearly more versatile than the Olympic boxers and pancratiasts of the archaic period who had come before him. Otherwise he could not have been the first to win in both events. Yet another athlete, Kleitomachos of Thebes, developed even more versatility in the combative events. Kleitomachos dates from the Hellenistic period, precisely when Gardiner and the others claim this deplorable "professionalism and specialization" was complete.[29]

Pausanias tells us about Kleitomachos and the Olympics of 212 BC. Kleitomachos was the defending no-holds-barred champion, having won that event an Olympiad before, in 216. In 212 he entered both the no-holds-barred and the boxing, thereby following the path of Theogenes in 480. Another athlete, too, wished to double: Kapros of Elis. But Kapros entered the no-holds-barred and the wrestling. He won the latter, wrestling, which took place first of the three events. Kleitomachos had not yet competed. Kleitomachos then proposed that the no-holds-barred be moved ahead of the boxing, apparently regarding the boxing as the more likely to produce an injury. He probably remembered Theogenes' case. The officials agreed to accommodate him, and to change the order of events. But Kleitomachos then lost his no-holds-barred crown to Kapros, and Kapros thus achieved his own double victory, wrestling and no-holds-barred. Kleitomachos went on to win the boxing, which coupled with his no-holds-barred crown in the previous Olympiad, made him, as Pausanias duly notes, the "second man, after Theogenes" (δεύτερος μετὰ Θεαγένην), more than 250 years before, to win that difficult Olympic double.[30]

Kleitomachos thus merely tied, but did not break, Theogenes' Olympic record. He had tried to break it, it seems. That is why he entered the no-holds-barred again in 212, even though he already had a no-holds-barred crown from 216. For Theogenes' double came in two parts, two separate Olympiads. Had Kleitomachos won both events on that one day in 212, he would have broken the record, which would then have read: "Kleitomachos was the first man on earth to win both boxing and no-holds-barred at Olympia on the same day." But instead the new record fell that particular day to his pancratiast foe, the double victor Kapros. Pausanias carefully phrases Kapros' new record (*prôtos anthrôpôn*), as does Africanus, who adds that a new title was entered in the official recordbook: "Kapros was the first man to win both no-holds-barred and wrestling since Herakles, and is recorded (*anagraphetai*) 'Second, after Herakles'."[31]

Herakles, of course, is a mythical athletic figure; the title was probably political, designed to match Kleitomachos' title, "second, after Theogenes". That title, "so many after Herakles" was then applied, *seriatim*, to any athlete who tied Kapros' double in wrestling and no-holds-barred. Thus Nikostratos in 37 AD was the "eighth after Herakles" to win this same double. There was no "ninth after Herakles" – not because there were no athletes so versatile. There were more athletes capable of the double win, Julius Africanus assures us. But, he says, the Olympic officials retired the "so many after Herakles" title by refusing to accept any more such double

---

[29] Moretti A391.
[30] Pausanias 6.15.3–5.
[31] Pausanias 6.15.10; Africanus *ad* Olympiad 142. We would probably say "the first since Herakles", but the Greeks counted inclusively, counting Herakles as the first.

entries.³² How does all this affect the case for increased specialization in the Hellenistic and Roman periods? Before 212, there was no athlete who won both wrestling and no-holds-barred. From 212 BC to 37 AD there were seven such athletes. After 37 AD there were even more "capable" (δυνάμενοι is Africanus' word) of it, but they were barred from doing it. This evidence runs directly counter to the theory of total specialization.

I return to Kleitomachos of Thebes, who lost the 212 BC no-holds-barred to Kapros and managed to tie (but not break) Theogenes' Olympic record. He had a far better day at the Isthmian Games soon thereafter. He finally broke one of Theogenes' old records. I translate the inscription.³³

> Just as you see, friend, the bronze strength of this statue of Kleitomachos, so Greece saw the might of the man. No sooner did he undo from his hands the bloody boxing gloves but he was doing battle in the fierce no-holds-barred. In the third event, he did not sand his shoulders; but wrestled without being thrown, to win his third trial at the Isthmus. He is the only man of all the Greeks to achieve this prize (μοῦνος δ' Ἑλλάνων τόδ' ἔχει γέρας). Thebes, seven-gated city, and his father, Hermokrates, have crowned him, too.

Theogenes' Isthmian record was especially difficult to surpass. Not only did he win the boxing and no-holds-barred there "on the same day" (ἤματι τωὐτῷ), but he did it twice. Studying Theogenes' Isthmian record, Kleitomachos would immediately see that the approach which he used wisely enough, but without success at Olympia, would not succeed at the Isthmia. At the Isthmia, mere victories in boxing and no-holds-barred, even on the same day, would not even tie the record. There was only one solution: to diversify even further. And so this athlete in the supposed heyday of specialization becomes amazingly unspecialized. He won the boxing, wrestling, and no-holds-barred. Whatever we may think of the combative events and their participants, any man who became a master of all three combative events at one of the Big Four Crown Games is impressive – well-deserving his title, "The only one of all the Greeks – *mounos Hellenôn* – achieve this prize".

H. W. Pleket, agreeing with Louis Robert, has objected to the tendency of some scholars to write off all such record-breaking formulas as the lies or exaggerations of bragging athletes. Robert's words are: "There is no reason to take as lies or exaggerations the mention of victories won as first of the Milesians (*prôtos Milêsiôn*), first of the Ionians (*prôtos Ionôn*), first of all (*prôtos pantôn*) etc., and to treat them with a tone of sarcastic and suspicious humour".³⁴ Robert and Pleket are correct. The details of the record cannot be full of lies or exaggerations; for the entire Greek world was watching, so to speak. A Greek athlete could no more claim that he won two Olympic victories on the same day – if he had not – than Carl Lewis could claim that he had jumped "over 30 feet, almost a foot beyond Beamon and Powell", when he has not.³⁵

---

³² Africanus *ad* Olympiad 204.
³³ Ebert 67.
³⁴ L. Robert, *Les épigrammes satiriques de Lucillius sur les athlètes*, in: *L'épigramme grecque, Entretiens sur l'Antiquité classique* 14, 1968, 181–295 (183), partially quoted in H. W. Pleket, *Games, Prizes, Athletes and Ideology*, in: *Stadion* 1, 1975, 49–89 (79).
³⁵ I also stress that it does not always seem to be the athletes themselves who dictate the text of their epigrams – and that when Pausanias or Africanus records a "first" or "first on the same day" feat for

Although Pleket rightly rejects the notion that the record-breaking phrases are the products of lying, boasting athletes, he does not see their essential nature. He views them as monotonous expressions of "surplus values". "The epigraphic documents reflect the monotony of the literary sources in this respect. Victory in itself was not enough. There is a tendency to add, so to speak, a "surplus value" to that of the victory in itself." As examples of these "surplus values", he lists the very phrases of Greek record-keeping that we have seen above, including "on one day" and "first of all human beings".[36]

Similarly Tod, who defined the Greek method of record setting, did not fully understand it. In the midst of his discussion he draws back and says, "What is the Greek word for "record"? I do not know, but I suggest ὑπερβολή – though I know no example of its use in precisely this sense, and the word does not occur ..." Yet he goes on to say, "Usually, however, keywords are *heis*, *prôtos* and *monos* [the one, the first, and the only], varied by combination and by the addition of phrases lending emphasis and expressiveness."[37] It is clear now that the end of Tod's statement is wrong. Such phrases as "in the same day" are not superfluous; nor do they aim at mere expressiveness or emphasis. They aim at essential accuracy. They are the actual records themselves, just as surely as Mike Powell's astounding long jump record is precisely 29'4½", not "over 29 feet" or "a very long way".

My point is this: these phrases are no kind of "emphasis" or embellishment. They express more than "surplus-value". They are precision documents and the stuff that athletes' careers were made of. To judge from what we know of Kleitomachos, these details, surplus-values, these records actually determined which events an athlete would enter in a particular festival, even which events he would train for, or become especially proficient – "specialized" – in. In Kleitomachos' case, this meant a less "specialized" training program that would make him of championship class in all three combative events. Furthermore, surely it was his attempt to break Theogenes' record that induced him to ask the Olympic officials to alter the sequence of events on the program. This request is an intriguing antecedent to Michael Johnson's request that the Atlanta 1996 officials change the program to accommodate his hopes to achieve a similar, unprecedented double.

We may better understand the Greek system of setting records, if we examine the strategy of the contemporary athlete, Carl Lewis at the 1984 Olympics, where many people expected Lewis to try to break Bob Beamon's long jump record of 29' 2½". Yet Lewis did not even take all his allotted jumps. When it was clear that he would win, he retired, leaving attempts at what Gardiner and Guttmann would call a "record", a distance in meters, unspent. The spectators, not understanding,

---

an archaic athlete, he is not a bragging athlete but an author centuries later, with access to documents that preserve an ancient feat, often recorded not by the athlete himself but others. Thus Guttmann's comment, "Professional athletes frequently boasted that ..." (above, note 4) somewhat misses the mark. See also the discussion of the inscription on Chionis' stele at Olympia (below).

[36] Pleket, 1975, 79.

[37] Tod 110–11. His specific examples begin with phrases that might be redundant, such as *prôtos kai monos* (first and only) or *prôtos tôn ap' aiônos*. But he further lists national and gender records among those just "lending emphasis", and Tod 111, note 5 ("For other examples see p.109, n.3") shows that he would also include such phrases as "on the same day", as emphatic but not essential.

expressed their disapproval by booing. They mistook Lewis' strategy for either diffidence or arrogance. But it was strategy. Lewis was not likely to break Beamon's record, no matter how many tries he took. By conserving his strength in the jump, he succeeded in his calculated plan to match, at least, a record even more venerable than Beamon's. That was Jessie Owens' 1936 record for most victories in track and field in a single Olympiad. Lewis thus became "the second man, after Jesse Owens, to win an Olympic track and field quadruple". He tied Owen's record, and earned a title much like that which Kleitomachos acquired at Olympia, "second, after Theogenes". World records in the pole vault fall often each year (and excellent world record feats there by such vaulters as Kozakiewicz and Vigneron are long forgotten); even Beamon's seemingly unbreakable record is now broken. But the record which Owens and Lewis share remains.

I now turn to the ancient Greek running records. The first known runner with multiple victories is Pantakles of Athens (Moretti A520), who won the Olympic *stade* in both 696 and 692. In 692 he probably won the *diaulos* as well. The next known multiple victor in running is Chionis of Sparta (Moretti A169) soon thereafter, who won both *stade* and *diaulos* three Olympiads in a row, from 664–656.[38] Since it required a long sprinting career, and success in each of six starts, Chionis' record seems impressive, even for those early years of the games. To surpass it would imply a career spanning four Olympiads. As we see soon, a later inscription suggests that in the fifth century, at least, Chionis' seventh-century performance was indeed viewed as a "record".

Yet in 512, a century and a half later, Phanas of Pellene managed to set a new Olympic running record (Moretti A539). For in the meantime a new event, the armed race, run in armor for a *diaulos* length, had been added to the program. Phanas managed to win *stade*, *diaulos* and armed race at the 512 Olympics. Africanus lists this as a record: "Phanas of Pellene. He was the first (*prôtos*) to achieve a triple victory – *stade*, *diaulos* and armed race.'[39] Phanas capitalized on diversity more than quantity to post his new record.

In the 480s BC the best runner in the Greek world was Astylos, who competed for Croton, Italy, before transferring to Syracuse, Sicily (Moretti A128). We cannot enter a dead person's mind, but we may assume that he was a person as thoughtful as Carl Lewis. Let us assume that he, like Lewis, consciously sought a strategy; then let us look at the running record from Astylos' point of view. There was no

---

[38] I follow Moretti in assigning Chionis only three victories in the *stade*. But there is a significant problem; namely, Pausanias 3.14.3 reports that an inscription in Sparta assigned Chionis four victories in the *stade*, three in the *diaulos*, for a total of seven. Africanus is equally clear in stating that Chionis won precisely three *stade* races, Olympiads 29, 30 and 31; his list of *stade* victors assigns the victories in Olympiads 28 and 32 to other athletes. Pausanias' and Africanus' versions are irreconcilable. Modern scholars generally follow Rutgers' arguments and solution (notes *ad* Olympiads 28–29 in: I. Rutgers [ed.], *Sextus Julius Africanus: Olympionicarum Fasti*, Leiden 1862; reprint Chicago 1980); namely, to conclude that Pausanias' version is somehow in error.

Shortly before Chionis, Philombrotos of Sparta had won the pentathlon at three successive Olympiads (Moretti A553, Africanus *ad* Olympiad 26). That record was surpassed (at an uncertain date) by Gorgos of Elis who won four Olympic pentathlons in a row (Moretti 961–6). Pausanias 6.15.9 gives his achievement record status ("the only one of men up to my time").

[39] Africanus *ad* Olympiad 67.

way for a runner to beat Phanas' record of three running victories in one Olympiad unless a sprinter could become a distance runner as well and win all four footraces. There was no way to beat Chionis' record other than to endure four Olympiads (more than twelve years in peak condition), and be successful every time. But by matching Phanas' and Chionis' records, combining versatility with quantity, he could set a new one.

That he did, winning the *stade* and *diaulos* in three successive Olympiads, 488–480, and at least one armed race, as well, along the way. Astylos may have won anywhere from one to four armed races. Our sources are not clear.[40] But that Astylos set a new record is clear – and it was painfully clear to Chionis' countrymen, the Spartans, who, below the list of victories on Chionis' commemorative stele at Olympia, carefully added, "There was no armed race yet" in Chionis' time.[41] Humorous perhaps to us, that phrase, for the Spartans, set the record straight. For they clearly implied that Chionis, their compatriot, would have kept his running record, if the armed race had not been added; or, had there been an armed race in Chionis' day, the Spartan would have won it. In either case, this defensive comment on Chionis' *stele* is an important witness to the rigor with which ancient athletic records were kept, and to their international acceptance. No one could pass a false record for a true one.

Astylos' record, not surprisingly, stood for more than three centuries. What other runner could be so versatile, and yet maintain an even longer career at the very top? None, it must have seemed. There passed three centuries. But finally such a runner appeared. He was a Rhodian athlete named Leonidas. Leonidas set an almost incredible record by winning all three races for four Olympiads in a row, 164–152 BC.[42] It is difficult to reconstruct this man's training regimen, here in the heart of the Hellenistic period, the supposed era of decadent professionalism and the "age of specialization". How did he maintain the conditioning and form – and success, fragile at every point – in three different events for so long? He proved to be the best *stade* runner in the Greek world, the best in the *diaulos*, and the best in the armed race for twelve years, four Olympiads – twelve separate Olympic races without a loss. In the shorter races, such as these, even our best runners are not nearly so consistent. Many unexpected difficulties may cause a failure: an uncharacteristic slow start, a bump from a fellow competitor, a brief minor illness, or what many athletes call "just a bad day". But Leonidas had no such failure in twelve Olympic races. It is no wonder that his Olympic record was never broken, and it stands today as a monument to that athlete's talent, determination, training, strategy and – in view of the fragile character of each race – good fortune.

What could subsequent runners do to surpass Leonidas? That question surely posed itself to coaches and athletes in antiquity, which, we have seen, was rigorously

---

[40] See Moretti, comments on 178–9, 196–8, 219. Moretti tentatively dates the one certain armed race crown to 480.

[41] Pausanias 6.13.2. Pausanias 3.14.3, which reports Chionis' inscription at Sparta (above, n.38), also comments that the armed race did not exist in Chionis' time; but Pausanias does not state directly that those words themselves were in the text of the inscription at Sparta. Perhaps Pausanias added that information there from his knowledge of the inscription at Olympia.

[42] Moretti A440, Victories 618–20, 622–4, 626–8, 633–5.

cognizant and covetous of such records. I believe it posed itself to an excellent runner named Polites, born in Caria about the middle of the first century AD. The obvious course would be to plan and train for an Olympic sprinting career that would span yet one more Olympiad, five Olympiads, at least sixteen years as the best runner in the world, in which any loss in any of the fifteen races (or first thirteen, at least) would mean failure to the overall plan to set a new Olympic record. It is virtually unthinkable. Polites chose another route, namely, to diversify. There was one Olympic running combination that had never been achieved. It too must have been virtually unthinkable; namely, the best sprinter in the Greek world must be the best distance runner, as well – a *stade, diaulos* and a *dolichos* combination victory. In the history of modern athletics, no one has excelled at both distance running and sprinting at the top level of international competition. In the ancient world, eight centuries had passed with no runner of such versatility. We are quite ignorant of what Polites' training methods might have been, what the requisites were, what muscle development, what conditioning of breath control might enable a man to excel at two such divergent types of running. I leave the physiological and training questions to others. But Polites' record speaks for itself. At the Olympic Games of AD 69, Polites succeeded in his goal: new record. Polites was the first and only man ever to win the *stade, diaulos* and distance race at the Olympic Games. His versatility, we recall, was a "great marvel".[43] And it perhaps remains a lesson in the ability of the human body to diversify through training – a lesson which modern coaches and students of physiology might well study.

I summarize my argument. Although all scholarly and popular studies tell us that antiquity saw increasing athletic specialization as the centuries moved on, Gardiner and the other proponents of that theory cite no ancient evidence for it. They may refer to a few verbal attacks on athletes in general, such as the often-cited passages from Euripides and Dio Chrysostom, none of which concerns specialization within the field of athletics. But Gardiner's main source for ancient specialization was his strange procedure that made his own England the prototype of ancient Greece. Even Galen's assertion of the same theory in antiquity proved groundless. The evidence reviewed here suggests the very opposite of this standard thesis.

The athletes studied above are exceptional, but they cannot be exceptions to a general rule of increasing specialization that supplanted an earlier period where athletes were more versatile. The proof is in the very nature of Greek record-keeping: "first man ever", "no one else ever before". Such phrases will not allow for an earlier period of athletes with greater versatility. Yet if the evidence suggests that ancient Greek athletes became progressively less specialized, they did not do so for any reason related to the rise or fall of professionalism. They diversified

---

[43] Moretti A570, Victories 796–8; Pausanias 6.13.3 (above). Moretti's comment on 796–8 notes that victories by the same athlete in both *stade* and *dolichos* are rare, but cites a few cases, none of which matches Polites' achievement. In the classical period a Spartan won *stade, diaulos* and *dolichos* "all in one day" at some lesser, local festivals, where his competitors would not have been of Olympic quality (*IG* V.1, 213). *IG* V.2, 142 records that the Tegean runner Damatrios (Moretti A195), in Hellenistic times (Moretti 593 suggests 208 BC), won the boys' *stade* at Olympia. In his later, adult career all his victories are in the *dolichos*, an impressive list with many victories in all the important games of the circuit including one Olympic *dolichos* victory. But if he ever entered a major *stade* race as an adult, he lost.

because it was a good way – perhaps the only way – for ancient Greeks to break the records set by the athletes of old.

That conclusion directly concerns the current controversy over whether or not "the record" is a "recent phenomenon". I think the ancient evidence gives the decisive answer: No, the keeping and setting of records was part and parcel of ancient Greek athletics for centuries – so treasured a feature of Greek athletics that it even determined, in some cases, which events an athlete would train himself to master at the championship level. And the system well suits Guttmann's major criteria. "No man has ever done it before" clearly qualifies as "unsurpassed". Although the presumptions of ancients are long lost to us, Guttmann's other requirement, "presumably surpassable", seems well met by the mere fact that some records were indeed surpassed. And, in the cases of athletes such as Polites and Kleitomachos, I think we see proof of "presumably surpassable" in the very choice of events which they sought to master and win. Guttmann put especial weight on the word "record" itself. He noted that the English word's earliest appearance relative to sports dated from the nineteenth century, implying that no one had yet identified a pre-modern equivalent.[44] But Africanus uses the equivalent Greek technical term "is recorded" (*anagraphetai*) with respect to Kapros' record.[45] And in reporting the record of Dromeus, victor over Theogenes in 480, Pausanias said, "The first of whom we know".[46] If not absolutely equivalent to "on record", the phrase "of whom we know" is so close, for an ancient Greek, that it, too, should meet even that criterion, as well.

I do not claim that ancient Greece wholly anticipated our modern records and our system for keeping and breaking them. But the ancient records and the Greek system have enough points of strong contact with our own that they should play a stronger role in the debate over the newness of records than they have so far played. If we compare the Greek system with modern records in such sports as golf, tennis and baseball, there is little intrinsic difference. For all the similarities, however, there are important differences between ancient and modern records. Besides our interest in who was "first with the most", we, unlike the ancient Greeks, also care intensely about the abstractions of time and distance. We have many more sports, athletes and occasions for competition than the Greeks did. Our records therefore are indeed more quantified, far more in number – and more frequently broken. An ancient record often outlasted the record-breaking athlete's lifetime, sometimes remaining for centuries an unsurpassed but theoretically surpassable goal for later athletes. Except for our own "first with the most" category, our records are usually short-lived; that is one reason Beamon's long jump record so impressed us. In track and field athletics, most records last just a few years at best; in the pole vault, it seems, a few months, or even days, or at worst – a few minutes.

---

[44] I recall here Tod's inability to find an exact, one word to one word equivalent in Greek (above).

[45] Africanus *ad* Olympiad 142 (above). For its technical value, "record, register", see LSJ, *A Greek-English Lexicon*, s.v. ἀναγράφω; cf. the entries for the noun, ἀναγραφεύς, one with the office of "recorder" or "registrar".

[46] ὧν ἴσμεν (Pausanias 6.11.4 [above]). Cf. "the only one of men up to my time" in Pausanias 6.15.9 (n.38, above).

WORKS CITED

If a work is cited more than once, the bibliograpical citation is omitted after the first citation, and, unless ambiguity might result, I merely give the author's name in subsequent citations. For the abbreviations Moretti and Ebert, see those authors' entries below. For "Africanus" see below under Rutgers. There are manytranslations of Pausanias for those who do not read Greek; I know of no translation of Africanus.

J. M. Carter/A. Krüger (eds), *Ritual and Record*, New York/London 1990.
J. Ebert, *Griechische Epigramme auf Sieger an gymnischen und hippischen Agonen*, Berlin 1972.
   Citations are by inscription number; thus Ebert 43 means "inscription 43" (not page 43).
M. I. Finley/H. W. Pleket, *Olympic Games: The First Thousand Years*, New York 1976.
E. N. Gardiner, *Greek Athletic Sports and Festivals*, London 1910.
E. N. Gardiner, *Athletics of the Ancient World*, Oxford 1930.
A. Guttmann, *From Ritual to Record*, New York 1978.
H. A. Harris, *Greek Athletes and Athletics*, Bloomington/London 1964.
L. Moretti, *Olympionikai. I vincitori negli antichi agoni Olimpici*, Rome 1957. Abbreviated citations preceded by "A" refer to the athlete numbers in Index I (186–95); those not preceded by "A" refer to the victory numbers themselves (not pages). Thus Moretti A520 means "athlete no. 520" but Moretti 265 means "victory no. 265".
H. W. Pleket, *Games, Prizes, Athletes and Ideology*, in: *Stadion* 1, 1975, 49–89.
I. Rutgers (ed.), *Sextus Julius Africanus: Olympionicarum Fasti*, Leiden 1862; reprint Chicago 1980 (citations are by Olympiad, not page number).
M. N. Tod, *Greek Record-Keeping and Record-Breaking*, in: *Classical Quarterly* 43, 1949, 105–112.

ADDENDUM (DECEMBER 1996)

The above article was written before the 1996 Atlanta Olympic Games, which offer much to clarify my arguments and the issues. The attention which 1996 athletes and news media gave to the "first with the most" type of record studied above has led me to reconsider the very basis of the controversy about the modernity of sports records. We have precisely the same mania for "first with the most" style records as the Greeks had. This is the standard type of record in such sports as tennis and golf, even, in the main, in such sports as baseball and football.[47] Thus our sports records are, in many cases, no different from those of ancient Greece.

As for those other cases, perhaps the current controversy about the modernity of athletic records should focus less on modern social theory and more on ancient history. The only sports that emphasize absolute records – the kind called records in this controversy – are sports such as track and field athletics, swimming and weight lifting, all individual sports where achievement is readily measured in absolute terms.[48] The principal reason why we have records in minutes and meters,

---

[47] What few absolute records there are in these sports are secondary to the other kind and measurable individual feats like the track and field records mentioned in the next paragraph: e.g., the longest recorded drive in golf or field goal in American football.

[48] Guttmann, *From Ritual to Record*, 51–2 suggests that the unquantifiable – but arbitrarily quantified (by arbiters) – performances of gymnasts and divers are essentially the same as the absolute records of time, weight and distance. But people and record books do not accord gymnastics and other

besides our Greek style records, may be wholly unrelated to our supposed meritocracy, and only secondarily related to our modern industrialized society. The main reason we have records measured in minutes, meters and kilograms may simply be that we have universally accepted weights and measures. Ancient Greece did not; each individual city-state had its own standards for weights and measures. A foot at Delphi was not the same as a foot at Olympia, nor a foot at Isthmia or Athens. We have no assurance that the weight of a Pythian discus or javelin was the same as anywhere else, nor even the same from year to year.

The ancient Greeks were fascinated with the question of the limits of human achievement. If they had had universally accepted measurements, I strongly suspect they would have formulated the same kind of absolute records that we have. But to speculate this way is futile. The important point is this: since it was quite impossible to conceive or maintain such athletic records in antiquity, we cannot find the ancients' inattention to them of much significance. We are indeed different from the Greeks. But that difference probably results more from our ever-shrinking world of communication and commerce than from differing attitudes toward athletic achievement.

I now turn to the 1996 Olympic Games themselves. I noted above an ancient parallel for Michael Johnson's request that the order of events be changed to enable him to seek an unprecedented double victory in both the 200 and the 400 meters. In 212 BC Kleitomachos asked the Olympic officials to alter the sequence of events so that he might achieve an unprecedented double, a new record. His request succeeded but Kleitomachos did not: he lost one of the two events. Thus Michael Johnson's double victory – his new record – seems all the more impressive. Johnson would surely grasp ancient Greek principles of record-keeping. About his unique double in Atlanta he said:

> I wanted to make history.[49] The world record is just a bonus. A lot of people can say they held a world record – I held the 200 record coming in here – but nobody else can say they made history by being the first man to win the Olympic 200 and 400.[50]

We can Hellenize all this by writing, "I, Michael Johnson, *prôtos enikêsa* the Olympic 200 *te kai* 400" and admire his humility for not adding *epichthoniôn* (i.e. "first of mortals").[51]

---

arbitrarily decided scores the same importance as track and field world records; the "first with the most" kinds of records eclipse all arbitrary scores even here. My copy of the Guinness Book of Olympic Records does not even include gymnastics and diving in its table of "Oympic Records" (only sports such as swimming and weightlifting). Not even arbitrary records are kept in sports without arbiters, such as tennis and golf.

[49] In the May 1974 United States Volleyball Association Tournament in Knoxville, Tennessee, the University of California, Santa Barbara (UCSB) team won both the college division and the open division titles. The front page of the *Santa Barbara News Press*, 19 May, 1974 reported, "The UC Santa Barbara Gauchos became the first collegiate team in history to win two titles in the United States Volleyball Assoc. Tournament." And on B1, the newspaper quoted the UCSB coach, "We won two! We made history!'

[50] Quoted in *Runner's World*, November 1996, 75.

[51] Johnson's "nobody else" is the οὔτις ἕτερος of Theogenes' Pythian record (Ebert 37.6; cf. Pindar *Ol.* 13.31, etc.). Johnson could not add ἤματι τὠυτῷ ("on the same day"); but as others seek to tie (or surpass) his record in coming decades, it will be duly noted that Johnson's combination came in a single Olympiad – another runner's 200 victory in one Olympiad and a 400 victory in the next will not suffice.

Johnson leaves no doubt which record he values the more: he makes little of – nearly contemns – his new "world record", an almost incredible 19.32 (the only record modern sports historians would allow him, if we apply their criteria for ancient times to modern times). But he exults in – almost gloats over – his "first-ever" combination victory. If we were to deny that he set a "record" in that respect and tell him, "Such things do not count, that is no record", Johnson might well take the matter ill.

I also cited above the case of Carl Lewis in the 1984 Los Angeles Olympics when he offended many in the crowd by forgoing more attempts at Beamon's will-o'-the-wisp long jump record to concentrate on tying Jesse Owens' record of four Olympic gold medals in track and field. His strategy worked – ever since 1984 he has been the first man since Jesse Owens in 1936 to win four Olympic golds in track and field in one Olympiad. Now, in Atlanta, Lewis became – obviously – the first man ever to win the long jump four times in a row. But that is not all. With this victory, he became the first man since Al Oerter in 1968 to win any track and field event four times in a row – and the first man since Paavo Nurmi in 1928 to win nine gold medals in Olympic track and field in a single career. Lewis too would understand ancient Greek record-keeping; he confirms my interpretation of his 1984 strategy. In his own 1996 words:

> This ninth gold medal is the most special of my career ... In 1984, they booed me after the long jump, but I don't think there's an athlete on earth who hasn't been booed ... Now I think about Jesse Owens and the kinds of things he told me in person ... I think about Al Oerter, because he was so nice to me ...[52]

One can see why the "ninth gold medal is the most special of [his] career". For with that ninth gold – someone will surely point out – Lewis is the first and only, *prôtos kai monos* athlete to achieve all three coveted records for the most gold medals in Olympic track and field. Those three record categories are: most golds in one Olympiad; most golds in one event; and most golds in one career. Though he is not the only one in any of those categories, he is unsurpassed in all three. That itself is unsurpassed. He holds the record for holding the most gold medal records in Olympic track and field.[53] No other man is unsurpassed in all three. "[T]he sports record is an unsurpassed but presumably surpassable quantified achievement." As Olympic athletes over the next decades – perhaps even centuries – seek to tie or surpass Lewis' record, they might thank the 1996 USA coaches, who excluded Lewis from the 4 x 100 meter relay. For they thereby eliminated Lewis' chance to surpass Nurmi and win a tenth career gold medal. True, he might well have failed to get that tenth medal.[54] But we will never know. Who really expected Lewis to win that ninth gold in the long jump? He proved to be an unsurpassed champion.

---

[52] Quoted in *Runner's World*, November 1996, 77.
[53] Of the 1974 USVBA championship tournament and the 1974 UCSB volleyball team, one observer noted that this tournament "included more "firsts" than any previous Nationals in the history of the sport" (see n. 3, above).
[54] The Lewis-less USA relay team set a new record anyway: the first USA Olympic 4 x 100 relay team in history to lose without being disqualified (as in 1912, 1960 – and 1988, when the USA coaches also chose a Lewis-less team).

12 E. Norman Gardiner and the Decline of Greek Sport*

DONALD G. KYLE

If sport history is the historical study of the phenomenon of sport, sport mythology includes the beliefs, legends and folklore, preconceptions and misconceptions about sport in general or about specific sports, athletes, or sporting events. The nature of mythology is exceedingly complex, but "myths" tend to fall into two groups or levels – major and minor illusions. Micro-myths are minor, specific, or local myths: traditional tales and aetiologies perpetuated by oral traditions, literature, art and iconography. These are fictions and rationalizations generated to explain and also to entertain. They often have been expanded and embellished to the point that any historical kernel is little more than an early impetus. Macro-myths are broadly based views popularly held and transmitted: comforting stereotypes and fallacies that are largely historically inaccurate or unprovable, yet psychologically or ideologically durable and compelling. In corollary forms they transcend generations and local cultural boundaries. Theirs is the realm of universal symbols and motifs, such as the hero, the golden age, and creation. With various and varying "meanings" at different levels, these are simplifying conceptual frameworks for otherwise overwhelmingly complex and disparate realities. As historians we endeavor to refute, replace and above all understand why both types of myths emerge and persist; but as W. H. McNeill has demonstrated, in studying diachronic human experience from man-made evidence, we cannot tell it "exactly as it was."[1] We play a game within a game; and, ironically, realistically in history – as idealistically in sport – "participating is more important than winning."

As a subdiscipline of history or sport studies, sport history has come of age and entered an increasingly revisionistic and demythologizing stage. Many popular beliefs and traditional scholarly interpretations concerning sport in various ages and cultures are being re-evaluated and modified – nowhere more so than in ancient sport studies. Historically it is easiest to make "progress" demythologizing at the micro-myth level, where we often deal with specific and directly correctible myths.

---

* Originally published in Kyle, D. G. and Stark, G. D. (eds), *Essays on Sport History and Sport Mythology* (Texas University Press, College Station, TX: Texas A&M Press, 1990), pp. 7–44.

[1] See W. H. McNeill, *Mythistory and Other Essays* (Chicago: University of Chicago, 1986), including his "Mythistory, or Truth, Myth, History and Historians", *American Historical Review* 91 no. 1 (1986): 1–10, on how historians influence and are influenced by their culture. Similarly, but with reference to ancient history, M. I. Finley, *Ancient History: Evidence and Models* (New York: Viking Penguin, 1986), explains that all historians use conceptual schemes or simplifying assumptions to make sense of the complexities of human history.

By research, improved techniques, and new or re-examined evidence, we are finding new "facts" and rejecting old myths. For example, we can reject the micro-myth that there was an ancient Greek marathon race: no ancient Greek would run twenty-six miles without at least delivering a message."[2] Such micro-myths stem from the macro-myth that the modern Olympics were modelled accurately on the ancient games and ideals. Progress in sport history is, in part, our improving and empirically sounder body of fact – more studies and more reliable information.

Impeding our progress in sport studies is an irritating micro-myth that sport history is an undisciplined hobby – athletic antiquarianism. For too long historians have under-studied something integral to and distinctive of ancient and all societies.[3] Sport history is too often seen, especially by academics, as a hobby for amateurs, physical educationalists, and retired jocks. Since sport is related to play (unstructured diversion involving fun), supposedly the study of sport involves undisciplined play and fun as well. This misconception has to go. Modern sport itself may be autotelic, but, like all history, sport history is studied for the end of human understanding of our past, our condition and our nature. Sport history is especially valuable because as individuals and societies we often reveal our true selves when we engage in or watch competition. The recent explosion in both the quality and quantity of sport history proves the image of sport studies as nonscholarly diversion to be a myth, and it now leads to our increasing ability to confront sport at the macro-myth level.

It remains difficult, however, to work on the broader and deeper level of macro-myths – the level of the philosophy and not just the fact-finding of history. Here myths often relate to universal concerns – the nature of humanity, God and process and causality in history. Here we encounter deeply-rooted ideological biases, facile or comforting generalizations, cherished ideals, symbols, icons and "isms."[4] Such myths are even harder to deal with when there are parallel or related myths in both the culture of the historian and the culture being studied. Shared follies take on the aura of shared truths.

In general in the modern West, sport macro-myths include the idealization of sport through the ages as positive, humanistic, progressive, and "civilizing".[5]

---

[2] See F. J. Frost, "The Dubious Origins of the "Marathon"," *American Journal of Ancient History* 4 (1979): 159–63. Other examples: the ancient Olympic truce did not establish a "total and binding truce" throughout Greece: see M. Lämmer, "The Nature and Function of the Olympic Truce in Ancient Greece", in Y. Imamura et al., eds, *History of Physical Education and Sport*, vol. 3 (1975–6) (Tokyo: Kodancha, 1977), 37–52; and the five Olympic rings are not an ancient symbol: see David C. Young, "The Riddle of the Ring", in Susan J. Bandy, ed., *Coroebus Triumphs* (San Diego: San Diego State University, 1988), 257–76.

[3] The status of sport studies until recently has delayed major works on obvious topics like the Roman circus. Jean-Paul Thuillier, "Les Cirques Romains", *Échos du Monde Classique/Classical Views* 31 n.s. 6 (1987): 93–4, refers to "un certain blocage intellectuel" causing a preference for studies of religious over sporting architecture. It is ironic that two of the most provocative studies of the last decade have come from classicists who happened upon sport history. Cf. David C. Young, *The Olympic Myth of Greek Amateur Athletics* (Chicago: Ares, 1984), vii–viii; and David Sansone, *Greek Athletics and the Genesis of Sport* (Berkeley, Los Angeles and London: University of California, 1988), xiii–xiv.

[4] E.g. John M. Hoberman, *Sport and Political Ideology* (Austin: University of Texas Press, 1984), discusses major twentieth-century European sport ideologies as expressions of political doctrine.

[5] Cf. Norbert Elias and Eric Dunning, *Quest for Excitement: Sport and Leisure in the Civilizing Process* (Oxford: Basil Blackwell, 1986).

Sport is seen as socially, politically and internationally beneficial – as an activity promoting friendship, liberalizing of views and social mobility, and as a deterrent to actual warfare. Sport is seen as heroic and its stars as worthy of hero worship. Sport is morally didactic, teaching teamwork, initiative and self-reliance. Sport is healthy, building body and character as well as moral well-being. Sport is refreshing – a temporary reversion to noble savagery with cathartic and enduring benefits and lasting moral elevation. Sport is sexually benign or neutral – nonerotic despite its virile men and graceful women. Sport is natural, clean and unspoiled, uncorrupted and worthy of protection from evils. Sport is amateur, at least in origin and at the level of widespread participation, not commercial. Needless to say, many of these macro-myths have suffered severely in our age of steroids, mass media, gambling and demythologizmg scholarship. Nevertheless, such myths do not die easily.

In a seminal article in 1975, H. W. Pleket said that, in addition to antiquarianism, sport studies have suffered from a "classicist bias", a preference for amateurism, and a tendency to impose rise and fall patterns.[6] Such mythologizing misconceptions and preconceptions about Greek sport have had their most influential protagonist in E. Norman Gardiner (1864–1930). While not the originator of the idea, Gardiner has greatly contributed academically to the persistence over the decades of the notion that ancient Greek sport experienced a well-defined historical decline as a consequence of "excess" and the weakening of an ideal. Gardiner's mythology was influenced by his own experience as an athlete, classicist and schoolteacher, as well as by his Victorian cultural milieu, his mentors and his ancient sources.

Even at my first casual reading of Gardiner as a graduate student, I felt his schema of Greek sport was reductionistic and I did not care for the personality behind the pages. For Gardiner, sport reached its height and actualized its ideal in the organized but amateur panhellenic games. Soon, however, sport fell victim to its own popularity and started to deteriorate in the second half of the fifth century BC, with a dangerous expansion of athletic festivals and honors for victors leading to over-competition and professionalism. Gardiner presents decline and fall as the historical process, and professionalism as the historical proof of that process.

Gardiner's editorial comments showed him to be an idealist dreaming of a golden age, and a moralist condemning a fall from grace. He also seemed a social elitist and at times even a racist. Nevertheless, as my dissertation topic on ancient athletics emerged, I came to delight in Gardiner. At the time I did not care *why* he was biased – I was grateful that he was. Here was a monumental straw man and graduate school had just honed my incendiary skills. Fortunately, both I as a historian, and ancient sport studies as a discipline, have matured somewhat in recent years. The study of ancient sport is now moving past Gardiner to a point where, beyond simply rejecting many of his micro-myths, we need better to understand his macro-mythology. Demythologizing entails refutation but also explication.

In terms of his domination of the field, and his scholarship, style and sincerity, Gardiner is to the supposed decline of Greek sport what Gibbon has been to the "decline and fall" of the Roman Empire. Almost sixty years after his death

[6] H. W. Pleket, "Games, Prizes, Athletes and Ideology. Some Aspects of the History of Sport in the Greco-Roman World", *Stadion* 1 (1975): 51.

Gardiner's publications remain standard reference works.⁷ Most recent evaluations of Gardiner have been generally positive, despite reservations about his biases and outdated archaeology. In 1978 Stephen G. Miller wrote:

> The timelessness of Gardiner's work lies, then, partly in his enormous learning. It lies even more, however, in his ability to write intelligibly for both the interested layman and the specialized scholar ... His learning sits gracefully upon his lucid prose, and one recognizes that Gardiner knew his subject matter intimately, cared for it tremendously, and wanted to share it generously.⁸

For decades Gardiner was authoritative and his follower H. A. Harris continued in the same vein, but the tarnished modern Olympics and the increasingly professional and spectacular nature of modern sport eventually made Gardiner's ideals seem out of place. Since the mid-1970s Gardiner has been challenged more and more, by I. Weiler, H. W. Pleket, M. B. Poliakoff, and others on the sociology, origin and even the techniques of Greek sport. Scathing criticism of Gardiner came in 1984 from David C. Young, a major contributor to the demythologizing of Greek and Olympic sport history. Young sees Gardiner as an absolutely dedicated amateurist and as an influential popularizer of the Olympist mythology. In Young's eyes Gardiner is a poor and not a disinterested historian with "cavalier historical analogies" and weak interpretations of evidence. A "classical scholar of the second rank", Gardiner indulged in "chronological legerdemain" – misdating persons and events to champion a delusive conspiracy.⁹

Young has admirably exposed the mythological substructure of modern Olympism, but on Gardiner his tone is rather intolerant. There is a baby in the bathwater. Where Young sees conspiracy and class warfare, I also see mythology and problems endemic to sport history. Aspects of Gardiner's life and world made it virtually impossible for him to be objective about sport or Greece. We need to understand what Gardiner brought to, put in and found in the history of Greek sport. To that end this paper examines and attempts to explain Gardiner's remarkable approach to sport history by discussing his life, works and ideas on Greek sport, and by relating those ideas to Gardiner's cultural milieu and the ancient materials he used.

---

⁷ For Gardiner's bibliography and abbreviations used herein, see the appendix. The *Oxford Classical Dictionary.* 2nd ed., cites him on "Olympics", "Olympian Games", and "Athletics". *Der Kleine Pauly, Lexicon der Antike,* 1964–75, 5 vols., vol. 1 (1964): 140, recommends *GASF* and *AAW* on "agon(es)"; vol. 4 (1972): 283, recommends *OL* on "Olympia". *The Encyclopaedia Britannica Macropaedia.* vol. 25 (1986): 201, recommends *GASF* and *AAW* on "Olympic Games".

⁸ *AAW,* "Preface to the American Edition", v. In *Greek and Roman Athletics: A Bibliography* (Chicago: Ares, 1984), 17, Thomas F. Scanlon says Gardiner "remains the most distinguished and lucid English writer on Greek athletics ... [*GASF* is] still the single most useful English book on that topic." Grant L. Dunlop, in an introduction (no page numbers) for Brown Reprints to the 1970 reprint of *GASF,* says, "His treatment of the subject was so exhaustive, his scholarship so thorough, that other writers in the field could only stand back in awe."

⁹ See his *Myth,* especially chap. 6, "E. N. Gardiner, James Thorpe, and Avery Brundage", 76–88. Cf. my review in *Échos du Monde Classique/Classical Views* 29 n.s. 4 (1985): 134–42.

GARDINER'S LIFE, WORKS, AND IDEAS ON GREEK SPORT

E. Norman Gardiner was born on 16 January 1864, the only son of Reverend Edward Imber Gardiner of Buckingham, who was an Oxford MA graduate of Magdelan Hall in 1864 and became rector of Radwell in Hertsfordshire in 1882. The younger Gardiner won a scholarship, went away to public school at Marlborough, matriculated in 1883 and went to Corpus Christi College, Oxford, as an exhibitioner (a student maintained by a donated allowance). He received second honors in the classical schools and earned a BA and MA by 1890, and ultimately a DLitt. by 1925.[10] At Oxford Gardiner was a rower in several crews for Corpus Christi, and his obituary in *The Times* mentions that he played rugby football for Devonshire from "1887 to 1900" and for the Western Counties in 1888–9.[11] After three years as master at Newton College, Gardiner settled down in 1890 at Epsom College in Surrey to remain there, as a house master and then as assistant master (for some twenty-five years), until his retirement to Oxford in 1925.

Around 1900 Gardiner took up serious research on ancient sport. He joined the prestigious and influential Society for the Promotion of Hellenic Studies in 1902 and published his first of several articles in the *Journal of Hellenic Studies* (*JHS*) in 1903.[12] Lists of members and officers of the Hellenic Society published in *JHS* show that he became a member of its council in 1906 and that he died as a member of the council of 1930–1. Minutes from the proceedings of the society for 1930–1 note Gardiner's death as a loss to the society and its council.[13]

Widespread concern about challenges to classical education led the society in 1921–2 to establish the Committee on the Further Popularisation of the Classics, commonly known as the Popularisation Committee. Gardiner served on this ten-person committee with classisists such as J. D. Beazley, H. Last and P. N. Ure. In the 1920s the committee created a new policy for student associate memberships, arranged a course of popular lectures by distinguished scholars, and issued three advisory pamphlets. Gardiner also personally contributed a lecture text for a slide set on "Olympia and Greek Athletics".[14] Actively combating the decline of classical studies at all levels, Gardiner also joined the Roman Society and the Classical Association. In retirement at Oxford, he appears in the listings of the officers of

---

[10] I would like to acknowledge the assistance of Mrs Christine Butler, assistant archivist, Corpus Christi College, Oxford; Drs D. J. Geagan, Douglas M. Swallow and Gary D. Stark; and the library staffs of the University of Texas at Arlington and McMaster University. Normal biographical reference sources, such as the *Dictionary of National Biography*, simply ignore Gardiner, but see *The (London) Times* 21 Oct. 1930, p. 19, col. 3; *The Pelican Record* 20 no. 1 (1930) 16–17; *Classical Review* 44 no. 6 (Dec., 1930), 209–10, "Notes and News"; and Joseph Foster, *Alumni Oxonienses: Members of the University of Oxford, 1715–1888* (Oxford and London: Parker and Co., 1888), vol. 1–2, 507.

[11] The former dates seem to be in error: Gardiner probably played rugby for Devonshire while a master at Newton College for three years after Oxford (1887–90), with his play for the Western Counties (1888–9) as the highlight of his career.

[12] See appendix. George A. Macmillan, *A History of the Hellenic Society* (London: Society for the Promotion of Hellenic Studies, 1929), xxxiii, under "Publications" takes special notice of the significance of Gardiner's contributions to *JHS* along with those of W. W. Tarn and J. D. Beazley. Gardiner also attended and participated in annual general meetings of the Society: Macmillan, *Hellenic Society*, xliii, xlviii; "Victor," 85.

[13] *JHS* 51 (1931): xx, xxv.

[14] Macmillan, *Hellenic Society*, xxxiv–xxxvi, xxxix.

the Classical Association as one of the honourable secretaries in 1926, a position he held until his death.[15]

Gardiner died on 20 October 1930, at his beloved Oxford, leaving behind a considerable legacy for ancient sport studies.[16] As the journal of the Classical Association, the *Classical Review* of December, 1930 included an obituary notice, "From a correspondent", which comments that, "in a word, Dr Gardiner saved his theme from the Reallexicographers by making it a living and attractive subject". The notice depicts Gardiner as a quiet man, "a diligent and interesting specialist" with a "simple and detached manner": "His interesting but unassuming personality and his obvious dislike for polemics mark him out as an unusual man whom it was a privilege to have as a friend."[17] This is not quite the image of Gardiner that comes across in his works, but he clearly was a member of a circle of devoted friends and scholarly colleagues. His prefaces acknowledge eminent Hellenists including P. Gardner, B. Ashmole and J. D. Beazley. The notice adds, "As one of the Secretaries [of the Classical Association], he was both vigorous and sympathetic. In Roman archaeology, as in Greek, he was always ready to help and encourage all enterprise and research." Immediately following the notice is a comment by the association: "As Secretary of the Classical Association he found many ways of placing the *Classical Review*, and the interests of classical learning in the widest sense, in his debt."

As we shall see below, Gardiner was strongly influenced by his public school and university education, his cultural environment and his intellectual circle. Central to understanding Gardiner, I believe, is his probable self-perception first and foremost as a teacher, secondly as a scholar, and thirdly as a former athlete.[18] For good and ill, Gardiner, by virtue of his education and occupation, was a Victorian gentleman and a Hellenist. His comments on Greece, sport and education were not fully objective, nor were they so intended.

Understanding Gardiner entails examining all his publications concerning his historiography (aims and methods), his mythology (biases and ideology), and his sources (both modern and ancient). In all Gardiner produced three books, two edited schoolboy texts, fifteen articles and various book reviews (see appendix). Between 1903 and 1907 he published nine lengthy articles in the *Journal of Hellenic Studies* on various Greek athletic events and related technical problems.[19] Amounting to more than 170 pages, these articles represent a remarkable output. In them Gardiner emerges as an idealistic and sometimes arrogant scholar who could

---

[15] *Classical Review* 40 nos. 1–2 (Feb.–Mar. 1926) through 44 no. 5 (Nov., 1930).

[16] *The (London) Times* Jan. 15, 1931, p. 8, col. 6.

[17] *CR* 44 no. 6 (Dec. 1930): 209–10.

[18] *GASF*, Preface, viii: "The attempt [to write a full history of Greek athletics] is an ambitious one, perhaps too ambitious for one whose occupation has left him little time for continuous study."

[19] "Pentathlon" is an examination of various hypotheses concerning the method of deciding victory in the pentathlon. Gardiner returned to the issue in *JHS* in 1925 with a brief piece agreeing with Pihkala's suggestion on the pentathlon and supporting the idea of applying this newly discovered (but unprovable) ancient system of "comparative victories" to the modern Olympics. "Phayllus" rejects the Greek epigram about Phayllus' fifty-five-foot jump as an exaggerated tall tale. "Jump" argues that the Greeks used only a long jump and a standing jump. "Foot Race", "Wrestling I", "Wrestling II", "Pankration", "Diskos", and "Javelin" all discuss evidence, techniques, rules, terminology and any relevant equipment. Almost all of this material ended up in *GASF*.

be intolerant in dealing with the works of others. When discussing athletic techniques, he frequently asserts the value of practical experience, modern comparisons and re-creations. He does not explicitly mention his own athletic experience, but he finds lack of experience a flaw in others.[20] The myths of amateurism and decline appear early in these early articles; both wrestling and the *pankration* are said to decline from the use of skill and grace to use of mere strength and increasing brutality.[21] The theme of decline is far more overt when Gardiner discusses heavy events than when he treats track and field, but not as overt as it would be later in his books, for here Gardiner was still working on technical questions more than historical patterns.

Unfortunately overshadowed by his more popular *Athletics of the Ancient World* (*AAW*) of 1930, *Greek Athletic Sports and Festivals* (*GASF*) of 1910 is the work in which Gardiner made his greatest academic contributions and his most fully documented articulation of his mythology of rise and fall. His preface to *GASF* explains his intention of combining technical or archaeological matters with an historical overview of Greek athletics. He arranged his chapters in order "to bring out the historical aspect of the subject, an aspect which is completely obscured in most of our text-books". Gardiner says he writes because there is no existing work on the subject in English, because of recent archaeological discoveries, and because of the relevance for modern Britain of the Greek sporting experience.[22] Not the first or last historian to claim but to fall short of a very high level of historiographical integrity, Gardiner declares that he has formed his own judgements and that his work is accurate.[23] Gardiner espouses cautious and principled research, but he is certain about the causes, chronology and results of the decline of Greek sport.

In 1912 his article "Panathenaic Amphorae" presented a specialized discussion of Panathenaic amphorae as evidence for sport. Here he attacks the theories of von Brauchitsch as "the merest moonshine" and argues, in part from the vases, that Athenian athletics declined through the latter part of the fifth century.[24] In "The Alleged Kingship of the Olympic Victor" of 1916, as he would do later, he credits the origin of Greek athletics to the human love of play and fighting, a secular impulse characteristic of northerners (by this, Gardiner means Europeans) and

---

[20] E.g.: "Pentathlon", 54; 56: "To anyone who has the least acquaintance with athletics, this is so obvious as scarcely to need restating ..."; 59: "This ingenious theory smacks of the midnight oil but surely not of the oil of the palaestra." Gardiner also was skeptical of the value of the ancient Scholiasts for their bookishness and lack of practical experience: "Pentathlon", 64; "Jump", 73; "Diskos", 3–4.

[21] "Pankration", 5, 12, says this was a contest of skill not strength before it became brutal with professionalism and specialization – a notion rejected by M. B. Poliakoff, "Melankomas, EK KLIMAKOS and Greek Boxing", *American Journal of Philology* 108 no. 3 (1987): 511–18.

[22] *GASF* viii:
The place of physical training and games in education, the place of athletics in our daily life and in our national life, are questions of present importance to us all, and in considering these questions we cannot fail to learn something from the athletic history of a nation which for a time at least succeeded in reconciling the rival claims of body and mind, and immortalizing this result in its art.

[23] Own judgements: *GASF*, viii, *OL*, viii. *GASF*, ix: "Further, I have endeavoured clearly to distinguish between what is certain and what is conjectural". Gardiner could be appropriately incredulous about some information, e.g. "Phayllus", 79: "Now no records are so liable to exaggeration as athletic records, especially when based not on written evidence but on report and tradition."

[24] "Amphorae", 190. Cf. my *Athletics in Ancient Athens* (Leiden: Brill, 1987), 176–7.

early societies.[25] The idea that early sport was essentially military and practical was carried over from *GASF* and would recur in *AAW*. In 1920 Gardiner published a light but revealing encomium on the work of a modern Canadian artist, Dr R. Tait McKenzie. He applauds McKenzie's revival of athletic sculpture and suggests that modern artists can learn from these efforts to represent the ideal athlete in form and in action. Gardiner's enthusiasm for his "friend" spilled over into praiseful references and illustrations in *AAW*.[26]

Olympia. Its History and Remains of 1925 followed *GASF* in combining technical (archaeological/topographical) and historical chapters. It made the results of recent German archaeological work at Olympia available for English readers, and it traced the history of Olympia and the festival. The work lacked much originality, but through detailed archaeological reporting and good illustrations it performed a valuable and enduring service. The book is notable for Gardiner's idealization of Olympia (with the nationalistic theme of panhellenism), for the racial myth of innate athletic prowess among northern peoples, and for the continued myth of decline.[27]

As Gardiner entered his sixth decade, his productivity did not diminish. It is revealing that even though he was now an established authority on sport, he took time in 1927–8 to edit selections from Livy and Virgil – simple instructional texts for public schoolboys. In *Extracts from Livy*, a new edition of Lee-Warner's work, Gardiner's aim was to enable the young student "to read with fair rapidity" and "to appreciate Livy's wonderful power of storytelling";[28] but Livy's moralizing on the decline of Italian natural vigor was attractive too. Gardiner's *Selections from Virgil's Eclogues and Georgics* was a well-received anthology with illustrations, notes and vocabulary.[29] Virgil's bucolic works seem appropriate for someone who viewed himself as a country gentleman, and Gardiner clearly sympathizes with Virgil's love of nature and the countryside.[30] It is interesting that in *Virgil* Gardiner atypically mentions Christianity.[31] Gardiner was a clergyman's son but he went away to school and embraced Humanistic Hellenism (see below). He probably was a knowledgeable and practicing Christian, but religion was not a major factor in his work.

Athletics of the Ancient World of 1930 has found Gardiner's widest audience, including use as a textbook. In the preface he declares his aim of giving "a short

[25] "Victor", 85, 87; *OL*, chap. 5, "The Origin of the Olympic Festival", 58–76.
[26] *AAW*, xiv: "I have also included illustrations of the athletic bronzes of my friend, Dr. R. Tait McKenzie. They are the nearest modern parallel to the athletic art of Greece." Also see "Wright", 145–6.
[27] Reviewing *OL*, R. M. Dawkins, *JHS* 46 (1926): 134, declares it "eminently satisfactory". W. W. Hyde, *AJPhil.* 48 (1927): 186–91, calls it "an authoritative presentation of all that is known about ancient Olympia and its famous games". Decline: e.g.: *OL*, 66, says the development of hero worship in the sixth century produced "excesses": honors became extravagant with the "decline of sport and the growth of luxury".
[28] *Livy*, Preface, v.
[29] H. Lister's book notice in *CR* 42 (1928): 68, says: "This is in every way a delightful book ... If we must have selections, let us have them like this."
[30] In his "Life of Virgil", 20. Gardiner cannot resist elaborating on a minor sporting point: Virgil's health prevents him from joining Maecenas at ball games. Gardiner, 24, 106, 109, applauds Virgil as a "practical bee-keeper" with "personal experience".
[31] *Virgil* 25, 81. Gardiner, 113–15, cannot escape religion concerning the 4th "Messianic" Eclogue: he is open to the idea that Virgil got his Messianic ideas indirectly from the East and from Isaiah; he reveres both Virgil and Isaiah as "great seers".

and simple account of the history and practice of athletics in the ancient world which will appeal to all who are interested in athletics and be of use to students of the past".[32] This was to be a "shorter and simpler" work (still over 300 pages in reprint editions), but "no mere abridgement of my earlier book". However, *AWW* is largely an abridgement, with paraphrases and echoes. In retirement at Oxford, Gardiner took his myths as established truths and articulated their elements and sources less fully.

In 1929 Gardiner had published for the first time in the *Classical Review* with his "Regulations for a Local Sports Meeting", a discussion of an inscription from Asia Minor. He probably was especially attracted by one regulation evidently intended "to prevent some pot-hunting professional coming in and carrying off the prizes".[33] Shortly after Gardiner's death the *CR* published his "A School in Ptolemaic Egypt", a brief discussion of two papyri recording arrangements for the training of a young athlete.[34] Again the chance to discuss professionalism perhaps was the stimulus: "Athletics in the third century BC was a profitable profession. Parents sending a boy to school would exhort the teacher to turn him into an athlete just as they sometimes today exhort the schoolmaster to teach their boys cricket, though not for quite the same motive."[35] Even from the grave, Gardiner was offering parallels and lessons from antiquity. We should not be blind to Gardiner's faults, including arrogance and dogmatism, but his scholarly productivity remains impressive. On questions of athletic technique he was deservedly recognized as *the* English expert, but major problems occur when Gardiner deals with moral or diachronic issues.

Gardiner's ideas deserve examination in detail, especially those in *GASF*, which offers the fullest and best documented version of his schema of the rise and fall of Greek sport. The pattern is dramatic and tragic: from natural roots sport comes of age as a larger-than-life hero with the tragic flaw of its own popularity leading to excess and hero worship. Gibbon felt Rome fell due to its immoderate greatness, and Gardiner sees the decline of sport as triggered by its excess popularity. Despite tragic warnings for moderation, sport strays from the pure ideal, and the weakened spirit allows corruption and excess. Specialization and professionalism signal the start of a long and sorrowful decline.

GASF establishes Gardiner's ideas on the beginning and early stages of Greek sport as a phenomenon arising from natural, secular origins and the agonal spirit

---

[32] *AAW*, xiii. Reviewing *AAW* in *JHS* 51 (1931): 305, H. Mattingly says "[T]he special value of the book lies in its expert presentation and interpretation of the abundant evidence, literary and monumental. Gardiner was a classical scholar with much personal experience and wide interest in athletics."

[33] "Regulations", 211.

[34] Cf. *AAW*, 116, addendum. "Notes and News", *CR* 44 no. 6 (Dec., 1930): 210, comments on the article: "... [I]t [along with the article of 1929] illustrates the wide range of his reading, his alertness in the search for evidence, and the sobriety of his judgement."

[35] "School", 211–12. Gardiner's personality, sometimes but not always humble, came out in reviews. In 1925 he is rather condescending to Wright's "somewhat inaccurate little book": he criticizes both Wright and Schröder (in 1928) for supporting scientific physical culture. He charges Schröder with inaccuracy, misinterpretations of vases and "little practical knowledge of athletics". By contrast, his 1928 review of Jüthner praises him as "master of his subject". Finally, *JHS* 50 Part II of 1930 (issued Jan. 30, 1931), 350, contains two posthumous reviews by Gardiner, one critical of Forbes for incompleteness and "the artificial separation of athletics and gymnastics", and one praising Séchan's as "a truly fascinating book" on the details and spirit of Greek dance, with chapters on the reform of modern dance.

of the "tall fair-haired" northern races. Out of weak ethnology or contemporary racism, Gardiner simply rejects the notion of Minoan athletics: the Greeks were the only "truly athletic nation of antiquity".[36] In his laudatory treatment of Homeric sport in *GASF,* Gardiner sees the essentials of the Greek ideal as already present, and as a natural expression of martial spirit and the love of effort. "Aristocratic and spontaneous" with no organized training, Homeric sport was part of the education of boys and the recreation of men, with excellence belonging to the nobles. For Gardiner this was sport on the rise towards the ideal but still lacking organized competitions and facilities. He presents the development of sport after Homer as involving an association with festivals. At the start of the sixth century Olympia had "a unique position as the national festival of Hellas"; it was a force for unity and a model for other festivals. With Olympia leading and others following, sport circa 500 BC was still joyful recreation but it had become more organized, popular and "democratic".[37]

For Gardiner, the true Greek athletic ideal was briefly and partially realized in the fifth century; it was both promoted by and expressed in athletic art and poetry. The idea of *paideia* or education is central to Gardiner's ideology; for him Greek sport and education were harmonious, moral, and joyful. "In the Periclean age, we cannot distinguish between the athlete and the *ephebos*. Every educated youth is an athlete, and every athlete is an educated youth and a citizen of a free state.'[38] The idea recurs in *AAW:* "To cultivate mind and body alike, to keep the balance between music and gymnastic, was the ideal of Greek education, but like all ideals it is hard to realize." The use of the present tense – that the ideal is hard to realize – is deliberate: Gardiner's model expression of the athletic ideal was the young Greek athlete whom he analogized to the British schoolboy.[39]

When Gardiner applauds early sport and the athletic ideal he often uses the image of sport as a fresh air, outdoor recreation with positive benefits. Early *gymnasia* in towns were for exercising, not athletic training: "The bulk of the population living an open-air country life in which war, hunting, and games played a considerable part, had no need of training." Early Greek athletics and education are idealized as practical for military purposes: "The athletic ideal of Greece is largely due to the practical character of Greek athletics ... Every Greek was a soldier, physical fitness was a necessity to him, and his athletic exercises were admirably calculated

---

[36] See *GASF*, 8–11; *OL*, 17–18, 34: *AAW.* 1, 14. Such ideas of Greek exclusiveness, advanced by J. Burckhardt and others, have now been challenged. Agonism was not uniquely or aboriginally Greek, yet, as Michael B. Poliakoff, *Combat Sports in the Ancient World* (New Haven and London: Yale University Press, 1987), 104–15, notes, the Greeks were distinctive in the number and nature of their competitions and in their institutionalization of rewards and recognition for victors.

[37] See *GASF,* chap. 2, "Athletics in Homer," especially 11–26: chap. 3, "The Rise of the Athletic Festival", 27–61; chap. 4, "The Age of Athletic Festivals, Sixth Century BC", 62–85. *GASF,* 60–2; *AAW,* 42: "Athletics were in sympathy with the growing spirit of democracy ... At the close of the sixth century the Greeks were literally a nation of athletes."

[38] *GASF,* 101; see chap. 5, "The Age of the Athletic Ideal, 500–440 BC", 86–121; 2–4.

[39] *AAW,* 100. In *GASF,* 184, Gardiner agrees with K. J. Freeman that Spartan education was the prototype of the English schoolboy system. "Foot Race", 261 and "Pentathlon", n. 39 on p. 62 parallel Greek athletic meets with those of British schools.

to produce this fitness."[40] Sport brought fitness and military preparedness, which brought victory in the Persian wars, which fostered panhellenism, which fostered athletics. It was too good to last.

The early games had been spontaneous and recreational but the potential for "evils" existed early on; and as the "spirit" weakened, sport strayed from the moderate ideal, and corruption set in during the fifth century. Popularity led to excess honors and then over-competition, specialization and technical training:

> The result of specialization is professionalism. There is a point in any sport or game where it becomes over-developed, and competition too severe, for it to serve its true purpose of providing exercise or recreation for the many. It becomes the monopoly of the few who can afford the time or money to acquire excellence, while the rest, despairing of any measure of success, prefer the role of spectators. When the rewards of success are sufficient there arises a professional class, and when professionalism is once established the amateur can no longer compete with the professional.[41]

Over-competition was "fatal to the true amateur spirit". Instead of athletics remaining "a recreation and a training for war, they became an end in themselves".

> Thus, early in the fifth century there arose "the pothunter", who spent most of his time travelling from city to city, picking up prizes ... For such a man athletics were no longer a recreation, but an absorbing occupation which left little time for other duties. When the "Shamateur" makes his appearance, professionalism is not far off.[42]

Performances improved but specialization and professionalism, the signs of a mortally wounded spirit, heralded a long, sorrowful decline. Soon a class of professionals monopolized and degraded sport socially and morally. Gardiner claims that, although the athletic ideal continued to have some influence at Olympia, in the age of decline professionals obsessed with records competed for profit, and idle, ill-fit masses simply watched. Decline was rampant by 400 and fully entrenched after 338 BC. "Thus within a century the whole character of Greek athletics was completely changed. From this time there is little to record save that all the evils which we have described grew more and more pronounced."[43]

Openly moralistic and dogmatic, Gardiner's rhetoric combines a classicist's scenario of tragic rise and fall with a Victorian gentleman's value-laden vocabulary. Good things include: natural, amateur, aristocratic, healthy, moral, vigor, youth, harmony and peace. Bad items include: luxury, excess, strife, philistine, professional, pale and evil. Friendly sporting rivalry was pure, masculine, participatory and nationalistic; it was moderate, moral and graceful rather than brutal, commercial or

---

[40] *GASF,* 61, 1, 107–8; *AAW,* 93, 42: "The victory of Greeks over Persians was the victory of free states over oriental despotism; it was the victory of a handful of trained athletes over hordes of effeminate barbarians."

[41] *GASF.* 130. Signs of problems appeared in the sixth century with a change in athletic attitudes to a more one-sided ideal: *GASF,* 78–9, 122. See also chap. 6, "Professionalism and Specialization, 440–338 BC"; *AAW,* chap 8, "Professionalism", 99–116.

[42] *AAW,* 3, 101; *GASF,* 5–6.

[43] *AAW,* 104, 44. See also *GASF,* 82, 131–2, and chap. 7. "The Decline of Greek Athletics, 338–146 BC", 146–72.

corrupt.[44] Gardiner feels that "excess", in popularity or preparations, ruins sport; it necessarily brings "nemesis".

> Nowhere is excess more dangerous than in athletics, and the charm of poetry and art must not blind us to that element of exaggeration which existed in the hero-worship of the athlete. The nemesis of excess in athletics is specialization, specialization begets professionalism, and professionalism is the death of all true sport.[45]

Note that excess precedes and brings about professionalism: Gardiner has a dramatic concept of historical process as well as an abhorrence for professionalism.

Despite Gardiner's faith in his mythology of decline, historically the concept of decline is very problematic. By definition and etymology "decline" (*declinatio*) means a pattern of negative change over time, a deterioration or a leaning/sloping/bending away from an earlier state, posture or condition. Decline, or progress, must be argued relative to something and via some criteria, and the soundest way to measure decline is in value-free quantitative terms, such as measurements of resources or population, preferably in large samplings. We must first know the status of the subject before, during, and after a time period. Perspective and criteria are all-important: in the Late Roman Empire imperial strength diminished but Christianity grew. A particular focus or qualitative criteria may simply indicate value judgements or mythology (held by the historian or the culture under study – or both).

Gardiner's chronology of decline is clear but forced. After the long rise of Greek sport, the brief age of the ideal (ca. 500–440 BC) is followed by increasing specialization and professionalism (ca. 440–338). Decline is outright from 338 BC to AD 393. This bald rise and fall schema is contrary to current conceptualizations of major developments in ancient history. Even studies of the "decline and fall" of the Roman Empire now avoid strict periodisation: they speak of "transformation", "fusion", and even the "myth" of the fall of Rome.[46] Of course Greek sport experienced historical change, but we no longer buy Gardiner's simple schema of a fifth-century crisis leading to a long, consistent decline.[47]

Gardiner's criteria and termini for decline were not actual historical circumstances in sport – not revenues, records or numbers of participants. He admits that during decline, crowds, participation, performances, facilities and festivals

---

[44] Cf. *GASF,* 2, 135. David C. Young's assertion in "How the Amateurs Won the Olympics", in Wendy J. Raschke, ed., *The Archaeology of the Olympics* (Madison: University of Wisconsin Press, 1988), 71, that "evil" is "a word appearing on almost every other page in Gardiner's books" is an overstatement, but "evil" was a well-worn and favourite word in Gardiner's moralizing: e. g. inter alia: *GASF,* 79; *OL,* 97, 134, 149; *AAW,* 100, 104–5.

[45] *GASF,* 122. "Excess" is Gardiner's word for hubris or insolence, the opposite of *aidos* or modesty. Cf. inter alia *GASF,* 79, 82, 112; *OL,* 66, 106; *AAW,* 99. The nemesis line appeared early and persisted: Phayllus", 71, *AAW,* 99.

[46] Cf. Richard Haywood, *The Myth of Rome's Fall* (New York: Crowell, 1958). For cautions about notions of monolithic and monocausal decline, and for a treatment of the problem of quantifying decline, see Ramsay MacMullen, *Corruption and the Decline of Rome* (New Haven and London: Yale University Press, 1988), 1–15.

[47] Scanlon, *Bibliography,* 17: "It can no longer be assumed that there was a "rise and fall' of Greek athletics which accompanied fifth century cultural progress ...". Scanlon's "The Ecumenical Olympics: The Games in the Roman Era", in Jeffrey O. Segrave and Donald Chu, eds, *The Olympic Games in Transition* (Champaign, Ill.: Human Kinetics Books, 1988), 37–64, shows that the games became transformed in the wider Roman world.

persisted and expanded.[48] Gardiner dates and asserts decline on the basis of selected examples from art and literature, Greek military history and the supposed shift to professionalism. He paints the history of an ideal so pure that it never really existed. He feels its best actualization came under the panhellenic and "purifying influence of the enthusiasm evoked by the war with Persia". The "noblest tribute" to the ideal was the athletic art and poetry it inspired. The date 440 is the turning point for Gardiner largely because by that time Pindar and Myron had stopped writing victory odes and making athletic sculpture.[49] After 440 Gardiner sees increasing criticism of sport in literature, and the Peloponnesian War replaces panhellenism.[50] Hence, for Gardiner, the athletic ideal that had fostered earlier unity and greatness *must* have collapsed. This simply is poor history, but it is also understandable mythologizing when one considers the cultural context of Gardiner's life.

CULTURAL AND MYTHOLOGICAL INFLUENCES ON GARDINER

In the course of his education and career Gardiner espoused three mutually reinforcing ideologies about games and education, athletics and the relevance of ancient Greece for the modern world; athleticism, amateurism and Victorian Humanistic Hellenism. Understanding Gardiner's works, ideas, and influence entails examining each of these three mythologies and their combined influence on Gardiner.

ATHLETICISM

An early and continuous mythological stream flowing through Gardiner's life and works is the ideology of athleticism concerning education and sport, whereby games are seen to inspire virtue and manliness. J. A. Mangan shows that athleticism greatly influenced British public schools from about 1860 to the 1940s.

> Physical exercise was taken, considerably and compulsorily, in the sincere belief of many, however romantic, misplaced or myopic, that it was a highly effective means of inculcating valuable instrumental and impressive educational goals; physical and moral courage, loyalty and co-operation, the capacity to act fairly and take defeat well, the ability to both command and obey.[51]

The origins of athleticism lay with various headmasters, notably C. J. Vaughn at Harrow, who introduced games for various reasons, including discipline, and then developed a rationalizing ideology. The movement spread to and from the universities; they received it from the schools and disseminated it further, since many schoolmasters and most diplomats came from Oxford or Cambridge. As

---

[48] "Wrestling I", 14; *GASF,* 79, 136; *OL,* 148; *AAW,* 44, 99, 102.
[49] *GASF,* 2, 4, chap. 5, "The Age of the Athletic Ideal. 500–440 BC", 86–121; *OL,* 106; *AAW,* 42–3, 53, 64.
[50] *GASF,* 122, 131, 135: "The struggle between Athens and Sparta ... contributed in no small degree to the decay of athletics."
[51] J. A. Mangan, *Athleticism and the Victorian and Edwardian Public School. The Emergence and Consolidation of an Educational Ideology* (Cambridge: Cambridge University Press, 1981), 9. Mangan explains (p. 2) that public schools were "for the well-to-do, expensive, predominantly boarding, independent of the state, but neither privately owned nor profit-making."

Mangan explains, under the influence of imperialism, athleticism involved an ironic combination of Christian gentility and Social Darwinism. It combined antithetical values: "success, aggression, and ruthlessness, yet victory within the rules, courtesy in triumph, compassion for the defeated". Widely supported by parents, press and public, athleticism connected muscular Christianity with the success of the British Empire via physical and moral vigor.[52]

The ideology of athleticism was fortified by symbolism, rituals, vocabulary and rhetoric. Mangan sees four categories of verbal symbols: the rhetoric of cohesion, of sexual identity, of patriotism, and above all of morality. Unity meant solidarity and cohesion. Manliness meant "asexual manliness": boys were to be manly in physique but they were not to have sexual knowledge or experience. Patriotism involved martial duty with games as a metaphor for war. Morality meant games built moral fibre; games were a preparation for the game of life. The rhetoric of athleticism bolstered the belief in Anglo-Saxon moral superiority via games, and it drew on the playing field for inspiration. "Metaphor, manners and myth went hand in hand."[53]

Gardiner is tied to athleticism by his biography, ideology and rhetoric. His public school, Marlborough, was one of Mangan's case studies. Marlborough was an example of a proprietary school, which was one financed initially by shareholders who purchased the right to nominate students. Established in 1843 mainly for the sons of clergymen, Marlborough played an important role in the development of athleticism. G. E. L. Cotton, headmaster from 1852 to 1858, introduced games, appointed young games players as masters to draw students to the playing fields, and preached the moral and physical benefit of games. Nevertheless, several Marlborough headmasters favored balance and moderation. G. C. Bell (1876–1903), headmaster over Gardiner was critical of the games ethos. The curriculum remained primarily classical and there was less anti-intellectualism than elsewhere: "[I]n all probability Marlborough was the most intellectual, and contained the most academically able boys, of the schools under consideration, yet here the new passion for the games field was very evident".[54]

After Marlborough Gardiner went to an athleticized Oxford and then carried athleticism into his teaching career at Epsom, a new school on Thomas Arnold's model and catering to the sons of doctors. Gardiner was hired by headmaster Rev. T. N. H. Smith-Pearse (1889–1914), "a confirmed classicist" under whom Epsom became a major school as the number of boys more than doubled.[55] Smith-Pearse was attracted to Gardiner by his background in rugby as well as in classics. Gardiner thus typifies what Mangan calls the "process of causality":

---

[52] Ibid., 28–42, 135–8.
[53] Ibid., 182–6, 199, 205–6. Mangan comments (p. 6) that athleticism "embraced a complex of ideas and feelings deliberately and carefully created through ritual and symbol: that it was, on occasion, a form of "pseudo-reasoning", a deliberate rationalization for ambitions such as status and power; and that it constituted value-judgements masquerading as facts to reinforce commitment."
[54] Ibid., 22–8, 88, 208.
[55] Brian Gardner, *The Public Schools. An Historical Survey* (London: Hamish Hamilton Ltd., 1973), 177.

The successful games player at school flourished in the same capacity at the university and then returned to school as lauded assistant master to set another generation of devotees along the same route. Thus a cycle of "schoolboy sportsman, university sportsman and schoolmaster sportsman was created".[56]

Gardiner became a schoolmaster sportsman, and with the insularity of his career, his values remained filtered by athleticism.

That athleticism vitiated Gardiner's works is all too obvious. Cherishing its values and rhetoric, Gardiner applauds the "friendly rivalry", "effort" and asexual masculine virtue of uncorrupted sport in early Greece as in English schools. Gardiner felt sport was educative but he was against excessive preparations or trained expertise. He opposed separating athletics from physical education and he favorably contrasts athletic education and competition with scientific physical education, both ancient and modern.[57]

In the post-Boer War era, Gardiner and athleticists argued that games aid military preparedness.

> The defeat of Persia not only gave a fresh impulse to the Panhellenic festivals: it raised athletic training into a national duty. The consciousness of a great danger safely past arouses a nation to a sense of its military and physical needs. We can remember only a few years ago the growth of rifle clubs, the cry for military and physical training that followed the Boer war.[58]

Athleticists exhorted boys to "play the game" and to learn moral lessons through games as a preparation for the "game of life". In Gardiner's words:

> Physical training is a valuable part of education and necessary in artificial conditions of life. But physical training is not sport, nor can it ever take the place of sport. There is no joy in it. It may develop the body and impart habits of discipline, but it cannot impart those higher qualities – courage, endurance, self-control, courtesy – qualities which are developed by our own games and by such manly sports as boxing and wrestling when conducted in the true spirit of manly rivalry for the pure joy of the contest; it cannot train boys "to play the game" in the battle of life.[59]

Like the Masters of Trinity and Caius admonishing Abrahams in the 1981 film *Chariots of Fire,* Gardiner felt sport was a matter of spirit not science, games not greed.

Victorian athleticism explains much about Gardiner and his work. It reinforced his notions of virtuous, friendly rivalry, asexual masculinity and the practicality of games as preparation for war and citizenship. Nationalism and imperialism contributed to Gardiner's racial notion that northerners were better by nature and by games. Teaching the sons of doctors only increased Gardiner's concern for "health" and "education". As a teacher he attended to the bodies, minds, and morality of youths.

---

[56] Mangan, *Athleticism*, 126.

[57] *GASF,* 4, 124, 187: "Both health-culture and professionalism are poles removed from the true Greek ideal of athletics." Also see *AAW,* 1–2; "Wright", 145; "Schröder", 125 and "Forbes", 350.

[58] *GASF,* 107.

[59] *AAW,* 98. Cf. Mangan, *Athleticism*, 198–200.

AMATEURISM

The second macro-myth prominent in Gardiner's life and works is amateurism, the view that proper sport is free of money and professionalism. David C. Young has rejected Gardiner's soon traditional notions that early Greek athletes were all idealistic, noble amateurs and that athletics degenerated with professionalism in the fifth century BC. He exposes Greek amateurism as a myth based on modern and unsatisfactory rather than ancient and reliable works, a myth in the sense of a "universal belief" and also in the sense of a comforting falsehood held by Olympists. Ancient athletes regularly competed for valuable prizes, Olympic victory brought wealth, and no stigma or word existed for "professional": the Greeks lacked both the ideology and the vocabulary of amateurism. Young offers evidence to deny Gardiner's thesis: stories Gardiner used to illustrate the evils of later professionalism actually belong to the sixth-century age of supposed amateurism. "The methodology is ... preposterous ... It recurs repeatedly and consistently, misleading readers far worse than ordinary sloppy scholarship".[60]

Young presents our modern notion of Greek sport as a product of amateurist class bias and bad scholarship. Providing a history of the Olympist myth of Greek amateurism from nineteenth-century roots, Young finds the origin of the amateurist (and shortly the Olympist) myth specifically in J. P. Mahaffy; and Young sees Percy Gardner as the crucial link in the transmission of amateurism from Mahaffy and Casper Whitney to Gardiner, Paul Shorey, Coubertin, Brundage and others.[61] Gardiner undoubtedly was influenced by Gardner but he also had read Mahaffy directly. Gardiner and Mahaffy agree in seeing the early Greeks as amateurs, intensive training as harmful, and later professionals as despicable. Gardiner would later echo Mahaffy's fears that cricket and boating were being "vulgarized by the invasion of the professional spirit", which did not support "sport for its own sake".[62]

As Young shows, Percy Gardner, Gardiner's mentor, was a staunch amateurist for whom "decline" meant the participation of the working classes. "Gardner's history of Greece is really nothing other than the history of Anglo-American sports from the 1860's to the 1890's seen through the gentleman amateur's eye." As Young notes, Gardiner admits the influence of Gardner:

> It is a fitting circumstance that this book should have been produced under the auspices of Professor Percy Gardner, seeing that he was unconsciously the originator of it. My

---

[60] Young, *Myth*, 78, 80–2. Young sees three elements in Gardiner's amateur ideology: 1) social elitism was the main issue, 2) money in sport is always evil, and 3) being too good in sports by excessive training is bad. Also see his "Professionalism in Archaic, and Classical Greek Athletics", *Ancient World* 7 nos. 1–2 (1983): 45–51: and his "How the Amateurs Won the Olympics," in Raschke, *Archaeology,* 55–75.

[61] Young, *Myth*, 51–3: "Although Mahaffy founded the myth of ancient amateurism, he never idealized the Greeks ... it was Percy Gardner who inspired E. N. Gardiner, the source of all our gross misconceptions about our subject."

[62] Gardiner does not refer to Mahaffy's "Old Greek Athletics", *Macmillan's Magazine* 36 (1879): 61–9, the piece that influenced P. Gardner – cf. 272 of Garnelr's "Olympia and the Festival", chap. 9, 265–304, of his *New Chapters in Greek History* (London: John Murray, 1892). However, Gardiner in "Foot Race", 267 n.33 and 269 n.37, cites p. 310 of Mahaffy's *Rambles and Studies in Greece*, 3rd ed. (London: Macmillan and Co., 1887): 275–95, which, aside from an introductory paragraph, is a verbatim republication of "Old Greek Athletics".

interest in the subject was first aroused by the chapter on Olympia in his *New Chapters from Greek History* (sic), which I read on my return from a cruise on the "Argonaut", in the course of which I had visited Olympia. Professor Gardner has read the book both in manuscript and in proof, and many improvements are due to his suggestions.[63]

Obviously Gardiner and Gardner shared numerous value judgements and drew similar "lessons" from Greek sport.[64] For example, like Gardner, Gardiner condemns professionalism;

> The evil effects of professionalism are worst in those fighting events, boxing, wrestling and pankration, where the feeling of aidos or honour is most essential. Here again the history of modern sport tells the same tale. Wrestling which was once a national sport in England has been killed by professionalism ... when a boxer will not fight unless he is guaranteed a huge purse whether he wins or loses he forfeits all claim to be called sportsman.[65]

Young demonstrates clearly that Gardiner "borrowed" ideas from the amateurists, and he effectively debunks the amateurist elements of the myth of decline. However, amateurism was not the only operational myth about sport and Greece in Gardiner's England,[66] and Gardiner was no myopic myrmidon. He could and did disagree with his mentors, and he increasingly turned to better German and English sources.[67] Also it is understandable that he would emulate Gardner, who was a senior classicist, formerly with the British Museum, and who had been Lincoln and Merton Professor of Classical Archaeology and Art at Oxford, Late Disney Professor of Archaeology at Cambridge, editor of *JHS* (1880–7), and president of the Hellenic Society (1906–10). The nineteenth century laid less emphasis than we do on originality. Fleshing out the ideas of a master was seen as worthwhile. Gardiner filled in and bolstered the chronological schema, going into technical points and beyond Olympia. He amassed and discussed more evidence on sport than any other British scholar.

Gardiner was influenced by amateurist scholars, but he also had a personal involvement. Born two years before the establishment of the Amateur Athletic Club, he was an amateur school athlete and rugby player. His lifetime saw the rise and fall of the amateurist movement and the early decades of the fledgling modern Olympics.[68]

---

[63] Young, *Myth*, 53–6. *GASF*, xi; Young, *Myth*, n. 47 on p. 52. Fifteen years later Gardiner acknowledged Gardner again in the preface to *OL*, viii.

[64] Gardner contributed many Hellenist ideas to Gardiner about nudity, art, climate, decline and more; cf. Gardner's *New Chapters*, 269–70, 271, 274, 299, 301.

[65] *AAW*, 105. Gardner denounces the "evil" results of professionalism as "fatal to the true amateur spirit" and charges that "when money enters into sport, corruption is sure to follow". See *GASF*, 134; *AAW*, 3, 103.

[66] As Young notes, in Raschke, *Archaeology*, 70: "The true author of amateurism was the British public school."

[67] In *OL*, 67, and "Victor", 96, Gardiner rejects as a "hasty and inaccurate generalisation" Gardner's notion, "Olympia", 299, that part of the victor's city's wall was torn down for his triumphal return. Young, *Myth*, n. 49 on p. 54: "Even E. N. Gardiner would not be taken in with that error." *AAW*'s selected bibliography lacks Gardner and Mahaffy and has more references to J. Jüthner than to anyone else – except to Gardiner himself. Gardiner also expressed debts to superior British scholars, as to J. D. Beazley in *AAW*, xiv.

[68] Young, *Myth*, 15–27, shows that the age of amateurism (1866–1913) actually postdates professional sport. For an economic history of the emergence of British professional sport, see Wray Vamplew, *Pay Up and Play the Game. Professional Sport in Britain 1875–1914* (Cambridge: Cambridge University Press, 1988).

Gardiner was a participant and advocate of amateur sport, and the history of sports in contemporary England disturbed him deeply.

> Of the evils of professionalism this is no place to speak ... The history of football during the last two years is ominous. On the hand we see the leading amateur clubs revolting from the tyranny of a Football Association conducted in the interests of joint-stock companies masquerading as Football Clubs; on the other hand we see the professional players forming a trades-union to protect themselves against the tyranny of this same commercialism. The Rugby Union has struggled manfully to uphold the purity the game ... Under these circumstances the history of the decline of Greek athletics is an object lesson full of instruction.[69]

Gardiner was lamenting the modernization of British football. After the development of ball games under the influence of the public schools, and the bifurcation of rugby and soccer, "professional" soccer began with the recruitment and payment of (especially Scottish) players. Separate amateur and professional leagues were established within the Football Association in 1885; amateur clubs could no longer compete with professionals, and "football mania" and massive spectatorship became the norm. During Gardiner's playing years the Rugby Union rejected professionalism as unacceptable but by the turn of the century rugby was split between professionals in the industrial north and educated amateurs in the south. Given such developments, Gardiner's comments are pointed and topical. He was comparing and confusing ancient and modern developments.[70]

Interestingly enough, while an ardent amateurist, Gardiner was not a great admirer of Coubertin's revived Olympics. He applauded their professed ideals but he was critical of the authenticity of technical aspects of the events.[71] Above all, he was skeptical about the dangers of over-competition.

> The promoters of these games were inspired by the ideal of ancient Greece, and wished to establish a great international athletic meeting which would be for the nations of the world what Olympia was for Greece. We must all sympathize with their aspirations. Unfortunately they do not seem to have realized the full lesson of Greek athletics, nor did they realize the dangers of competition on so vast a scale ... The experience of recent years has taught us that international competitions do not always make for amity, and do not always promote amateur sport. The events of the last Olympic Games ... have gone far to justify the forebodings of those who feared that one of the chief results of such a competition would be an increase in professionalism.[72]

Perhaps Gardiner may be forgiven some reservations about the modern Olympics, especially those of 1908 in London, which historians have called "the battle of Shepherd's Bush" because of the numerous protests against the British officiating. The *New York Times* said of these games that "as a means of promoting international

---

[69] *GASF*, 10; noted by Young, *Myth*, 76.

[70] William J. Baker, *Sports in the Western World* (Totowa, NJ: Rowan and Littlefield, 1982), 119–37. Young, *Myth*, n. 72 on pp. 76–7, notes Gardiner's analogy (*GASF*, n. 2 on p. 131; *AAW*, 50) of later Greek athletics to the use of hired football professionals from the country districts of Scotland to represent English towns.

[71] E.g.: "Diskos", 7, 10–11.

[72] *GASF*, 6–7, 1, 5.

friendship it has been a deplorable failure".[73] More and more the games of the English schoolboy seemed to be the only bastion of pure sport left for Gardiner.

VICTORIAN HUMANISTIC HELLENISM

The third and most pervasive and inclusive cultural influence on Gardiner was "Victorian Humanistic Hellenism", a widespread nineteenth-century intellectual enthusiasm for ancient Greece. Aware of themselves in a world in transition with industrialism, and political and moral change, Victorian intellectuals had a fin de siècle preoccupation with decadence and they increasingly revered ancient Greece as a humane and humanizing civilization.[74] Frank M. Turner characterizes the Victorian approach to Greece as "prescriptive" and "selective": "The Victorian study of the Greek heritage occurred in an arena of thoroughly engaged scholarship and writing. Disinterested or dispassionate criticism was simply not the order of the day." Hellenists hoped that proper study of classical art, literature, poetry and politics could teach proper values and bring inner peace and social harmony to contemporary society. Mostly conservatives and elitists, Hellenists generally opposed excessive commercialism, individualism, moral relativism, political radicalism, materialism and aspects of pluralism in society. They imposed their concerns, ideology and traditional morality and gentility on the Greeks. Then in turn they used these Victorian Greeks as rationalisations or lessons for aspects of contemporary life. The Victorians were not the only culture to view the past through the present but they were remarkably intense and overt in doing so.[75]

A key figure in the Hellenist idealization of Greek culture as the embodiment of proper Victorian values is Matthew Arnold (1822–88). Turner shows how Arnold retrojected British humanistic values onto the Greeks, idealizing them, especially in the period 530-430 BC, as beautiful, rational, placid and unified – a culture of "sweetness and light" – as a means to denounce the individualism, liberalism and utilitarianism of contemporary "barbarians" and "philistines". In seeing fifth-century Greece as relevant and modern, Matthew Arnold was influenced by the theory of historical cycles of his father, Thomas Arnold (1795–1842), who felt that all nations developed through organic stages comparable to those of individual human growth, maturation and decay. Widely believing in patterns of rise and fall, growth and decay, Victorians tended to see Greek literature and history as rising and falling in a parabola with a brief blaze and rapid decline.[76] Gardiner was not

---

[73] John Kieran, Arthur Daley and Pat Jordan, *The Story of the Olympic Games: 776 BC to 1976* (Philadelphia and New York: J. B. Lippincott, 1977), 63. *New York Times*, 29 July 1908, p. 9; noted in George R. Matthews, "The Controversial Olympic Games of 1908 as Viewed by the New York Times and The Times of London", *Journal of Sport History* 7 no. 2 (1980): 50.

[74] See Frank M. Turner, *The Greek Heritage* in *Victorian Britain* (New Haven and London: Yale University Press, 1981); Richard Jenkyns, *The Victorians and Ancient Greece* (Oxford: Basil Blackwell, 1980); and David Lowenthal, *The Past is a Foreign Country* (Cambridge: Cambridge University Press, 1985), 96–105. Arnaldo Momigliano, "Declines and Fall", *American Scholar* 49 no. 1 (Winter 1979–80), 40, contrasts the relative optimism of Gibbon and the eighteenth century with the atmosphere of the 1880s, "when the problem of decadence in its general terms had developed out of the roots of the social crisis of contemporary Europe".

[75] Turner, *Greek Heritage*, 4–8, 16, 82, 447.

[76] Ibid., "The Hellenism of Matthew Arnold", 17–36. Jenkyns, *The Victorians*, 60–2, 69, 73–7. Cf.

exceptional in his myth of decline or in his idealism about Greek sport and art.

The Hellenists' approach to Greek art is shown in the careers of the brothers Percy and Ernest Gardner, who together condemned the harshness and excesses of contemporary art and urged the emulation of the perceived purity, strength and reserve of Greek sculpture. Indebted heavily to the ideas of J. J. Winckelmann, the father of German Hellenism, the Gardners interpreted Greek art idealistically and believed in the influence of physical climate and cultural environment on the Greek artistic achievement. The fine air, sunshine and exercises of the Greeks allowed artists to observe nude athletes in the *gymnasia*, select the best parts to embody an ideal of beauty, and so reinforce a communal appreciation of beauty. The Gardners also applied the rise-and-fall organic pattern to Greek art and felt that political independence was essential for ideal art and sport.[77]

Profoundly influenced by his education, mentors and scholarly asssociates, especially in the Hellenic Society, Gardiner applied Hellenist inclinations to ancient sport and saw a singular Greek athletic ideal, the decline of which offered lessons for England.[78] Like other classicists, even great ones like Jebb, Jowett and Grote, Gardiner used contemporary terms, categories and concerns in his studies. He openly pushed analogies and studied Greek sport not for its own sake but for contemporary relevance and value. Any reader of Gardiner will agree that his works abound in typical Hellenist themes of natural beauty and serenity, fresh air, youthfulness and the importance of independence. His rhetoric and the premises of his chronological schema, as discussed above, are typically Victorian. His parallel of English schoolboys to Greek youths and their statues was a Victorian commonplace.[79] The evils and excesses of athletics attacked by Gardiner were those of contemporary English society: professionalism was but one facet of a broad pattern of perceived decline or falling away from an ideal state.

Sport and decline have too often formed a playing field for biases and ideologies; and Gardiner's Hellenism is similar to what Patrick Brantlinger calls "negative classicism": an elitist modern mythology or view of history that sees extensions of mass or popular culture, as in spectator sports, as leading to the decline of empires or cultures. Brantlinger points out inconsistencies in the negative classicism of nineteenth-century liberals, like Thomas Arnold, who favored democratization through education but not egalitarianism or great social disruption. They felt that ideally the masses could be enculturated, but they doubted the compatibility of democracy with cultural greatness. "Instead of their elevation through a wholesome absorption of "high culture", the masses", it was often feared, would drag everything down to their own level, perhaps smashing the very machinery of

---

Warren D. Anderson, *Matthew Arnold and the Classical Tradition* (Ann Arbor: University of Michigan Press, 1965).

[77] Turner, *Greek Heritage*, 39–42. Jenkyns, *The Victorians*, 44–5, 133–4, 195, 225.

[78] His idealism began early: "Pentathlon", 54: "The sense of Fairness and Order were characteristic of the Greek mind ..."

[79] *AAW*, 57; Jenkyns, *The Victorians*, 219–25, 248. E.g. W. W. Capes, Reader in Ancient History at Oxford, *University Life in Ancient Athens*, an 1877 publication of four Oxford lectures, reprint ed., (New York: G. E. Stechert and Co., 1922), 4–28, turns the Greek *ephebeia* (the institutionalized military training of young men) into a British school by discussing academic dress and final exams.

civilization in the process."[80] Modern sport and mass culture might bring popular access and better skills but, by what Brantlinger calls "the paradox of progress as decadence", they were still seen as decline. The paradox of progress as decadence clarifies inconsistencies in Gardiner. He considered Olympia democratic and Greece a nation of athletes, but when commoners participated, Gardiner feared corruption and debasement to the commoner's unhealthy level of materialism and spectatorship.[81] Commoners should have the right to compete in the games, but they should not actually do so; excellence and victory properly were the preserve of the better classes. In Gardiner's mind, when commoners competed and nobles withdrew, Greek civilization began to degenerate.

Even though anthropology and historicism were taking ancient studies in other directions during his lifetime, Gardiner's historical model remained an Arnoldian idealistic and organic one: Greek sport had an ideal or spirit from early times, it grew to full but brief realization at the top of the parabola, and then when the spirit weakened, a falling away set in. Gardiner shared in the Victorian fin de siècle attitude concerning the empire, morality, sport and more, and his inclinations understandably hardened as he aged.

GARDINER'S ANCIENT SOURCES AND THE ANCIENT CONCEPT OF DECLINE

Despite historical inconsistencies, Gardiner made Greek sport fit his idealism and schema.[82] We should not excuse him for this but we should understand him fully as influenced by his cultural milieu and also by his classical research. Using ancient evidence selectively and prescriptively to bolster his myths, Gardiner misread his sources to find and date an ideal age of amateurism, but he did not misread his sources concerning the ancient perception of history as in decline. His predisposition to see decline was reinforced by his classicist's familiarity with that motif in ancient literature – especially in Aristophanes.

Gardiner's use of ancient literary sources is often predictable and derivative. He uses Homer, as many Hellenists did, to suggest the pure infancy of the ideal. Homer shows the early joy of effort in sport. "There was nothing artificial about his sports: they were the natural product of a warlike race, part of the daily life of

---

[80] Patrick Brantlinger, *Bread and Circuses: Theories of Mass Culture and Social Decay* (Ithaca and London: Cornell University, 1983), 9–12, 31–2, 45, 50. Negative classicism interprets mass culture as a symptom or cause of social decay, often comparing modern society with the Roman imperial decadence of "bread and circuses" – the classical form of mass culture. This is a catastrophic or cyclical view of history rather than a progressive one. Brantlinger focuses on modern mass culture and the cultural effects of democratization, industrialism and mass media, but he also notes classical roots for the myth; cf. 53–81.

[81] Ibid., 185. Brantlinger could well be describing Gardiner when he says that modern conservatives, such as Ortega, Eliot and Camus, fear mass culture as "commercial rather than free or unconditioned, plebian or bourgeois and vulgar rather than aristocratic and "noble", based on self-interest rather than on high ideals ... urban ... rather than close to nature."

[82] The individual nature of Greek athletic competition, the absence in the crown games of team events, might have been a problem for Gardiner, but he escaped by turning the ideal athlete into a citizen-soldier who conformed to the collectivity of his *polis*.

the family." Later Pindar verbalizes the ideal at its height. Gardiner especially likes Pindaric *aidos*, a combination of dignity and modesty, and he emphasizes Pindar as panhellenic and patriotic.[83] We have already seen that the demise of Pindar approximates the demise of the ideal.

On the negative side, from Gardiner and Mahaffy, Gardiner uses a conventional cast of critics including Xenophanes, Euripides, Plato and military figures such as Alexander. Gardiner feels sympathy with Xenophanes, and reveres him as a tragic warner against sixth-century signs of excess adulation and rewards for athletes. Gardiner quotes and fully agrees with the diatribe against athletes from a fragment of Euripides's *Autolycus* – the "severest indictment of professionalism" and Gardiner's most concentrated source of anti-professional ammunition. The fragment, which was influenced by Xenophanes and came to influence Galen and others, rejects the custom of honoring victors more than good and wise men; it presents the athlete as a (soon stereotypical) physical caricature.[84] Gardiner declares that Euripides and Plato regarded athletes as militarily deficient. Moderns agree that such sources must be used with caution and that they had little or no impact on ancient sport, but for Gardiner they were enlightened and relevant.[85]

Gardiner makes typical use of later authors such as Galen,[86] but his use of Philostratus is somewhat curious. He unavoidably uses Philostratus' *Gymnastikos* many times on specific points, but, ironically, he makes little schematic use of Philostratus' assertion of a decline of sport with the rise of specialized intense training. Apparently Gardiner preferred to use sources of classical fame and authority, especially those contemporary with the stage of sport discussed. Moreover, Gardiner, who taught doctors' sons, disliked Philostratus' disparagement of the medical profession, and criticized him for his lack of technical knowledge of gymnastics.[87]

Most significant here is Gardiner's distinctive use of Aristophanes, for this comic playwright was not a major Victorian source. For both the theme and the chronology of decline, Gardiner's emphasis on Aristophanes, which derives from K. J.

---

[83] *GASF*, 13. Turner, *Greek Heritage*, 135–7, 171–3, and Jenkyns, *The Victorians*, 210–26, note that Victorians felt Homer expressed Greek ideals of the classical age analogous to those of Britain. *GASF*, 102–6, 109–12, applauds Pindar's moralism and his concept of *kaloskagathos*, the combination of beauty and goodness: Pindar shows the Greek educational aim of harmonious development of mind and body. Earlier, "Pankration", n.36 on p. 13, gave features of Pindar's ideal: "strength, beauty, training, skill, courage, endurance".

[84] *GASF*, 122, 131; *AAW*, 103. *GASF*, 5, 79: while Xenophanes showed signs of excess, Euripides, for Gardiner, shows the results of corruption. (Cf. Gardner, *New Chapters*, 302, who is cautious about the fragment: "Perhaps in the strictures of this poet we may see too much of the sophist ...") Nevertheless, Gardiner embraces Euripides as a former victor appreciative of manly sports: *GASF*, 131–2. *AAW*, 103, extensively quotes the fragment.

[85] *GASF*, 127–9; cf. Gardner, *New Chapters*, 300–1. See Jenkyns, *The Victorians*, 227–61, on Victorian use of Plato as a moralist and social critic advocating social duty against the trend to a pluralistic society. On Euripides and other critics as unreliable and ineffectual, see Kyle, *Athens*, 124–41.

[86] E.g. "Pankration", 13: Galen and medical writers condemn the evil effects of "the utterly unscientific system of training introduced by professionalism, a life of over-feeding, over-sleeping, over-exercise ..." *GASF*, 186–7: Galen has "breadth of mind and fearless love of truth".

[87] Uses of Philostratus: e.g. *OL*, 166; *GASF*, 174, 186–9; *AAW*, 55, 115–17. Criticisms of Philostratus: *GASF* 189–92, 287 n. 1: "Pankration", 12. Poliakoff, *Combat Sports*, 4, urges caution about notions of a golden age of sport in authors of the Second Sophistic, such as Plutarch, Lucian and Philostratus, who "have a tendency to take a nostalgic trip down memory lane".

Freeman rather than Mahaffy or Gardner, is crucial and strategic.[88] Since one of Aristophanes' main topics is education, Gardner's view of sport as a combination of athletics and education allows him to cherish and use this source extensively.

Analysis of Gardiner's works shows that passages from Aristophanes's plays are used (cited, referred to, paraphrased or quoted, or discussed) more than seventy times. Uses are roughly of two types: "neutral' – objective philological or technical cases concerning terms or rules; and "schematic" or "substantive' – value-laden uses to substantiate the chronology and extent of decline (e.g. quotes or paraphrases of Aristophanic criticism of contemporary sport). Gardiner made early and continuing use of Aristophanes, and most of these instances (about fifty) are neutral.[89] In works from between 1903 and 1906 there are more than twenty;[90] *GASF* cites Aristophanes over thirty-five times; *AAW* still has more than ten references but by then Gardiner does it even without footnotes.[91] Apparently Gardiner became familiar with the Greek playwright in his early technical research and came to value his potential for timely social criticism.

When making neutral use of Aristophanes, Gardiner is fine for his era, but the schematic cases, where Aristophanes and decline overlap in the *Clouds*, reveal mythologizing. There are about twenty such uses, some with extended discussion.[92]

---

[88] Jenkyns, *The Victorians*, 79: "[O]f all the great Greek writers Aristophanes had the least influence in the last century. The Victorians did not greatly value the comic muse, and in any case teachers shrank from introducing their pupils to so rich a store house of obscenity." Neither Gardner nor Mahaffy used Aristophanes in their articles on Greek sport. Cf. K. J. Freeman, *Schools of Hellas: An Essay on the Practice and Theory of Ancient Greek Education from 600 to 300 BC*, ed. M. J. Rendall (London: Macmillan, orig. publ. 1907; reprint ed. Port Washington, NY: Kennikat Press, 1969), who made considerable use of Aristophanes, 123–36, including the *Clouds* and *Frogs* on the history of sport. As a Hellenist, Freeman speaks, 3–5, of the "spirit of Hellas" and the "ideals" of Hellenic education; he seeks the "lesson" of Hellenic schools for the modem world. P. 287: Greeks had "a reasonable horror of undue specialization at school". Gardiner used Freeman's book in "Javelin", 267, when it appeared in 1907, and it turns up in the *GASF* bibliography. *GASF* and Freeman had the same publisher and Gardiner even used some of Freeman's illustrations and line drawings.

[89] Neutral uses (several are repetitions as material moves from *JHS* to *GASF* to *AAW*): *Knights* ll. 261–3: "Wrestling II", n. 34 on 272, 291–2; *GASF*, 399–400; ll. 272–3: *GASF*, n. 1 on 446; *AAW*, n. 1 on 215; l. 387: "Wrestling II", n. 60 on 280; l. 454: *GASF*, n. 1 on 446; *AAW*, n. 1 on 215; l. 491: "Wrestling II", 272; *GASF*, 386; *AAW*, 189; l. 496: "Wrestling II", n. 34 on 272; l. 571: *GASF*, n. 4 on 377; ll. 1159–62: "Foot Race", 264; *GASF*, n. 5 on 273; n. 1 on 276; n. 6 on 277; *AAW*, n. 2 on 136; l. 1238: *GASF*, n. 2 on 503. *Birds* l. 141: *GASF*, n. 2 on 468; l. 291: "Foot Race", 281; *GASF*, n. 2 on 287, 291; l. 442ff.: "Pankration", 5–6; *GASF*, n. 2 on 374; *GASF*, 438; *AAW*, 212. *Acharnians* l. 213: "Phayllus", 77, 78; *GASF*, 309; *AAW*, 152; l. 481: "Foot Race", n. 22 on 264; l. 571: "Wrestling II", n. 60 on 280. *Peace* l. 880: *GASF*, 217; l. 895: *GASF*, n. 2 on 374, n. 2 on 448; l. 899: "Pankration", 5; *GASF*, n. 2 on 448; *AAW*, 212. *Lysistrata* l. 82: *GASF*, 296; l. 1000: "Foot Race", 263; *GASF*, 277; l. 1002: "Foot Race", 290; *GASF*, 292–3. *Clouds* l. 522: "Wrestling II", 293; l. 966: *AAW*, 90; l. 973: *GASF*, n. 2 on 503. *Wasps* l. 1203 (sic) should be 1206: "Phayllos", 77; l. 1203: "Foot Race", 290; *GASF*, 293. *Frogs* l. 710: *GASF*, n. 1 on 481; l. 904: *GASF*, n. 5 on 376. *Wealth* l. 1129: *GASF*, n. 4 on 296. *Ecclesiazusae* l. 1090: "Wrestling II", 280. Unspecified general references on oriental cults: *OL*, 124.

[90] "Foot Race", 290, has several citations of Aristophanes, including use of the *Frogs* on the deplorable runner in the Kerameikos and on the "degenerate youth of Aristophanes' day"; 262 refers to the later decline of running "with the growth of professionalism and luxury". "Phayllus", 77, takes Aristophanes' old days as ca. the Persian War. In "Wrestling I", "Wrestling II" and "Pankration", Aristophanes is mainly used neutrally, with Philostratus and Galen brought in to show decline in later centuries. "Pentathlon", "Jump", "Diskos" and "Javelin" all lack both Aristophanes and the theme of decline.

[91] E.g. *AAW*, 152: no footnote for an obvious use of *Acharnians* 213.

[92] Schematic use of Aristophanes begins in "Foot Race": see note 90 above. By *GASF* the schema is strong with a half-dozen schematic uses of the *Clouds* (esp. 961ff.): *GASF* adds diachronic to the

Aristophanes gives Gardiner more reinforcement for more of his motifs and chronology of decline than any other ancient source. Consider, for example, this passage from *GASF,* 131–2, and its clone in *AAW,* 102:

> *GASF*, 131: At the time of the Persian wars the Greeks had been a nation of athletes. At the time of the Peloponnesian wars the mass of the people were no longer athletic. Aristophanes bitterly deplores the change [citing *Clouds* 961–1023; *Frogs* 1086]. At Athens the young men had deserted the palaestra and gymnasium for the luxurious baths and the market-place; pale-faced and narrow-chested, they had not even sufficient training to run the torch race.

> *GASF*, 132: While athletics were passing into the hands of professionals and losing their hold upon the people, the richer classes devoted themselves more and more to chariot and horse races ... The horsiness of the fashionable young Athenian is ridiculed by Aristophanes [citing *Clouds* passim].

> *AAW*, 102: Aristophanes sadly contrasts the pale, narrow-chested youths of his day with the men who fought at Marathon [citing *Clouds* 961–1022; *Frogs* 1086]. The wrestling-schools and *gymnasia* were deserted for the marketplace and the baths. The gilded youth of Athens found their sport in quail-fighting and horse-racing. They preferred to be spectators of the deeds of others rather than doers.[93]

Most sport historians have overlooked the significance of Aristophanes as a temporal or diachronic critic of sport: he gives nostalgia for the past and lamentation for the present. Most early critics merely condemn adulation for athletes as a *nomos* or traditional social custom. Aristophanes gives Gardiner the historical process of decline – a change in *nomoi*.

Overall Gardiner makes most (twice as much as of any other play) and fullest use of passages from the *Clouds,* especially lines 961–1023 – the debate between representatives of the old and new education. Gardiner uses Aristophanes to set the "old days" of the ideal in the Persian War era of supposed panhellenism. The *Clouds* offers "before and after" pictures of the products of traditional and new education – the good old days of Marathon and the sad new days of the Peloponnesian War. Gardiner points out Aristophanes' use of *aidos* and the ideal *kaloskagathos* (a combination of beauty and goodness).[94] Positive motifs include friendly rivalry, open air education and fitness. Negative motifs applied to Aristophanes's own day of the Peloponnesian War include pale, unathletic youths, immorality, luxury and baths. The *Frogs* also reinforces the *Clouds* with the educational theme of the corruptive influence of Euripides and Socrates. Degenerate youths lack the musical and gymnastic training of old, says Aeschylus, who fought at Marathon; and Dionysus demonstrates this with the anecdote about the torch race: crowds laugh

---

earlier mainly technical use of Aristophanes. *GASF,* chap. 6, has five schematic uses, with three of these repeated in *AAW,* chap. 7. Schematic uses: *Clouds* passim: *GASF,* 132; l. 835: *GASF,* 479; ll. 961–1023: "Amphorae", 187; *GASF,* 106, 131; *AAW,* 102; l. 991: *GASF,* 479; ll. 995ff.: *GASF,* n. 1 on 103; l. 1005: *GASF,* 472; l. 1008: *AAW* 84; l. 1045: *GASF,* 479. *Frogs* ll. 1086–7: "Foot Race", 290; *GASF,* 131, 292–3; *AAW,* 102; l. 1089ff.: "Foot Race", 290; *AAW,* 143. *Wealth* l. 1161: *GASF,* 129; *AAW,* 102. *Knights* l. 571: "Wrestling I", 21; l. 1060: *GASF,* 479. *Peace* ll. 33-4: *GASF,* no. 1 on 127.

[93] Gardiner here also condemns the influence of money on sport and cites *Wealth*, 1161.
[94] *GASF,* 103, first use of *Clouds* 995ff on *aidos*.

at the spectacle of an ill-fit youth.⁹⁵ Gardiner accepts at face value as Aristophanes' own words the image that the spirit is weak, the golden youth have withdrawn into horse racing, and the *gymnasia* are empty.

Gardiner's use of Aristophanes is sometimes strained or selective. He finds Aristophanes readily available on education and morality but he has to stretch to find athletic over-training and the corruptive influence of money. One problem is that, although Anstophanes' characters assert athletic decline via educational decline, they do not condemn rewards for athletes. Aristophanes mentions moral and physical decline and Gardiner himself links these with professionalism and money as symptoms and influences.⁹⁶ Perhaps most telling of Gardiner's mythologizing of and from Aristophanes is his assertion that Aristophanes would agree with the diatribe of Euripides, "his inveterate foe".⁹⁷

An exception to Gardiner's use of comedy is Aristophanes' bawdiness. The *Clouds* uses coarse bodily metaphors that Gardiner omits even though he and Aristophanes share the use of the body as symbolic of the man. Gardiner notes *Clouds* 966 saying boys were taught to sit with crossed legs but he does not say why. He cannot deal with Aristophanes's association of *gymnasia* with pederasty and so he ignores it.⁹⁸ Gardiner was uncomfortable talking about what he called "tender parts" of the body.⁹⁹

Uncritically avoiding the point of it all, Gardiner felt that Aristophanes spoke to and for him as a teacher. As conservatives, Gardiner and his version of Aristophanes shared heroes at Marathon, idealized old education, and lamented the Peloponnesian War and newfangled education.¹⁰⁰ Ironically, Gardiner's tragic scenario for sport (with his tragic vocabulary of excess and nemesis) rests heavily on sources that were meant to be comic (with exaggeration and the rude vocabulary of burlesque). Comic stereotypes become tragic warnings. Nevertheless, there were ancient sources asserting decline, and we must acknowledge the notion of decline in Greece as well as England.

---

⁹⁵ Also "Wrestling I", 21–2, makes schematic use of *Knights* 571 on the "dogged tenacity of the men of the older generation who had made Athens great ... The point is that these old Athenians, however clearly they were thrown, would never admit a defeat, but would wipe off the dust and go on wrestling, as though they had not been thrown at all." Where we now would see immorality or "winning above all", Gardiner saw a military metaphor, probably for the triumph at Salamis after the sack of Athens.

⁹⁶ From *Peace* 33ff., the metaphor of falling on food "like a wrestler" is used by Gardiner to suggest the gluttony of overdeveloped athletes. It probably just analogizes a beetle's movements to wrestling holds. Gardiner uses *Wealth* 1161f. on the fondness of Plutus for games to assert the excessiveness of prizes, but this may simply refer to embezzlement. Cf. Aristophanes' criticisms of the number of Athenian festivals: *Knights* 528, 1037; *Peace* 1036. Followers of Gardiner continued to misuse Aristophanes: e.g. C. Manning, "Professionalism in Greek Athletics", *Classical World* 11 (1917): 76–7; Thomas Woody, "Professionalism and the Decay of Greek Athletics", *School and Society* 47 (1938): 521–4.

⁹⁷ *GASF*, 132.

⁹⁸ *AAW*, 90. Pederasty and *gymnasia*: *Knights* 1385, 1387; *Clouds* 417, 991; *Peace* 762–3; *Wasps* 1025. Cf. K. J. Dover. *Greek Homosexuality* (Cambridge, Mass.: Harvard University Press, 1978), 40, 54–5, 138. Victorians excused license in Aristophanes and others in various ways; as Jenkyns, *The Victorians*, 281, says: "Greek smut is clean smut."

⁹⁹ E.g. "Pankration", 5; "Meeting", 210.

¹⁰⁰ J. P. Mahaffy, *Old Greek Education* (London: Kegan Paul, Trench and Co., 1881), 40–1, uses the *Clouds* but cautions that Aristophanes is exaggerating a traditional theme of the "good old days" and contemporary degeneracy. K. J. Dover, *Aristophanic Comedy* (Berkeley and Los Angeles: University of California Press, 1972), 114, calls Aristophanes' remarks about degenerate youth "a vivid comic caricature of familiar constant".

Just as Gardiner was not the first or last Englishman to sound the theme of the decline of British sport, the idea that sport – that society – was in decline from better old days was not an Aristophanic comic innovation. The idea of nostalgia for past athletic glory, and the assertion that athletics had declined from the good old days, begin at the start of Greek literature in Homer, an author Gardiner loved. From an earlier generation of better men who had contended against legendary figures, Nestor recalls past sporting victories when he was conspicuous among heroes *(Iliad* 23.630ff.). In the *Odyssey* when Odysseus challenges the Phaeacians he adds the proviso that he would not compete with the "men of old" (8.223). It would be pointless to compete against the supermen of the old days. Aristophanes' Nestor is the old Acharnian who used to run, and his hero is Phayllus, a famous athlete but also a military leader in the glory days of the Persian War.

Clearly Aristophanes' good old days theme had literary precedents. Homer's near contemporary, Hesiod, in the Myth of the Four Ages, presents *all* life in decline from the golden age.[101] Recent scholarship seems more open to the idea of progress in Greek thought in terms of human betterment, but J. B. Bury is still correct about the prevalence of the idea that the best age was in the past: "They dreamed of a golden age, but they generally placed it behind them. They sought it in simpler, not more complex, conditions." E. R. Dodds argues that the idea of progress was not wholly foreign to antiquity, but progress was used mainly by scientific writers concerning material progress. Most philosophers were hostile to the idea and often there was a tension between a belief in scientific or technical progress and a belief in moral regress.[102]

Gardiner was well familiar with the ancient notion of decline from a golden age in authors including Homer, Hesiod, Livy, Virgil and the Second Sophistic; but he makes most use of the motif from Aristophanes. The themes are well-worn ones: the corruption of natural, traditional life; moral decline into luxury; and condemnations of softness, effeminacy, social disruption, the city and indolence.[103] Steeped in the ancient classics and in Victorian negative classicism, Gardiner embraced from both eras the paradox of progress as decadence – that, while performances and crowds may progress quantitatively, as he admits, nevertheless the overall pattern is a process of qualitative decline in spirit, harmony, natural excellence and a noble ideal. As an idealist Gardiner preferred his qualitative criteria of decline, which are subjective and related to his perspective and value system – the stuff of sport mythology more than sport history.[104]

---

[101] *Virgil,* 114: Gardiner was familiar with Hesiod's metaphorical presentation of widespread social decline, an idea probably deriving from the Near East and persisting in the Greek mind.

[102] J. B. Bury, *Ancient Historians* (New York: Dover Publications. 1958; orig. publ. 1908), 205. In his *The Idea of Progress* (New York: Dover Publications. 1960; orig. publ. 1930), he sees the notion of indefinite progress as a comparatively recent idea absent in antiquity. E. R. Dodds, "The Ancient Concept of Progress", 1–25, in his *The Ancient Concept of Progress and Other Essays on Greek Literature and Belief* (Oxford: Clarendon Press. 1973).

[103] Such motifs intrude even in Gardiner's *Livy,* introduction, 1: Samnites degenerate when they settle down in cities in Capua: 13: contrasts healthy northern Italy with "Rome with its luxury and vice".

[104] In a perhaps telling note, Gardiner may be doing some soul-searching late in his career: *Virgil,* 90: Compare the Gospel of Labour [Georgic 1.118–46] with the picture of the Golden Age in Eclogue 4, or the account of the Fall in Genesis. Poets of all ages have dreamt of a Golden

CONCLUSION

Gardiner's mythologies came from his life, his world and his sources. As an idealist and a moralist, Gardiner was sincere and resourceful in making his contribution to the study of antiquity. He was a selective, engaged scholar led to misrepresentations by his convictions and enthusiasm. The ages of athleticism (ca. 1860–1940), amateurism (ca. 1866–1913), and Victorian Hellenism all overlap, peak and weaken during his lifetime. Given his personal involvement in sport, teaching and classical studies, and given the athleticism, amateurism and Hellenism of the era, it was perhaps inevitable that Gardiner share and perpetuate myths about ancient sport.

Pushing positive classicism on the ideal and negative classicism on decline, Gardiner eloquently said what he believed, and what he felt ancient evidence indicated, to an audience wanting to believe the same thing. Victorian themes of naturalism and decline appear even in Gardiner's minor works and in his reviews. Beyond his works on sport, his involvement with societies promoting classics and Hellenism and his editing of schoolboy texts indicate his sincere defence of classical education as relevant and practical. Gardiner became set in his ways early on and then remained somewhat isolated in Surrey and in his scholarly circle. His perception of ancient decline correlated with the decline he saw around him on so many fronts: professional athletics and scientific physical education were displacing games and sport, classical education was decreasing, and the empire and British morals and society seemed to be losing strength.

We now live in a different world: educators are suspicious of athleticism, the modern Olympics are in crisis, and anthropology has all but killed idealistic Hellenism. The history of ancient sport is being rewritten, and we find Gardiner curious. Yet, whatever we say in demythologizing sport history, we must realize that we ourselves will be demythologized by a future generation of sport historians. We will always "learn from the past", but what, why and how we learn are influenced by our present.[105] That's how the game is played.

Age, of an ideal state of nature. Did it ever exist? Can it ever exist? Is there more happiness in an unprogressive Golden Age than in a progressive civilization? How did evil come into the world, was it a punishment for sin, or that man might learn to conquer it?

[105] Lowenthal, *The Past,* shows that in trying to understand or preserve the pasts we inevitably alter it via human attitudes such as nostalgia and modernism. Pp. xvi–xvii, xxv: "The past is a foreign country whose features are shaped by today's predilection ... And as we remake it, the past remakes us."

APPENDIX
BIBLIOGRAPHY OF E. NORMAN GARDINER (1864–1930)

1. "The Method of Deciding the Pentathlon". *Journal of Hellenic Studies* 23 (1903): 54–70 (cited as "Pentathlon").
2. "Notes on the Greek Foot Race". *JHS* 23 (1903): 261–91. ("Foot Race")
3. "Phayllus and his Record Jump". *JHS* 24 (1904): 70–80. ("Phayllus")
4. "Further Notes on the Greek Jump". *JHS* 24 (1904): 179–94. ("Jump")
5. "Wrestling I". *JHS* 25 (1905): 14–31 ("Wrestling I")
6. "Wrestling II". *JHS* 25 (1905): 263–93. ("Wrestling II")
7. "The Pankration and Wrestling III". *JHS* 26 (1906): 4–22. ("Pankration")
8. "Throwing the Diskos". *JHS* 27 (1907): 1–36. ("Diskos")
9. "Throwing the Javelin". *JHS* 27 (1907): 249–273. ("Javelin")
10. *Greek Athletic Sports and Festivals: Handbooks of Archaeology and Antiquities*. London: Macmillan, 1910. Reprint ed.: Dubuque, Iowa: Brown Reprint, 1970. (*GASF*).
11. "Panathenaic Amphorae". *JHS* 32 (1912): 179–93. ("Amphorae")
12. "The Alleged Kingship of the Olympic Victor". *Annual of the British School at Athens* 22 (1916): 85–105. ("Victor")
13. "The Revival of Athletic Sculpture: Dr R. Tait McKenzie's Work". *The International Studio* 72 (1920): 133–8. ("McKenzie")
14. With Lauri Pihkala, "The System of the Pentathlon". *JHS* 45 (1925): 132–4. ("Pihkala")
15. *Olympia. Its History and Remains*. Oxford: Clarendon Press. 1925. Reprint ed.: Washington, DC: McGrath Publishing Co., 1973. (*OL*)
16. H. Lee-Warner, *Extracts from Livy*. New Illustrated Edition. Revised by E. Norman Gardiner. Oxford: Clarendon Press, 1927. (*Livy*)
17. *Selections from Virgil's Eclogues and Georgics*. Edited by E. Norman Gardiner. Oxford: Clarendon Press, [1928] 1930. (*Virgil*)
18. "Regulations for a Local Sports Meeting". *Classical Review* 43 (1929): 210–12. ("Regulations")
19. *Athletics of the Ancient World*. Oxford: Clarendon Press, 1930. Reprint eds: Oxford: Clarendon Press, 1955; 1965; 1967; 1971; Chicago; Ares, 1979. (*AAW*)
20. "A School in Ptolemaic Egypt". *Classical Review* 44 (1930): 211–13. ("School")

REVIEWS BY GARDINER

"Greek Athletics". By F. A. Wright. *JHS* 45 (1925): 145–6. ("Wright")
"Der Sport im Altertum". By Bruno Schröder. *JHS* 48 (1928): 125–6. ("Schröder")
"Körperkultur im Altertum". By Julius J. Jüthner. *JHS* 48 (1928): 252. ("Jüthner")
"Greek Physical Culture". By Clarence Forbes. *JHS* 50 (1930): 350. ("Forbes")
"La Danse Grecque". By Louis Séchan. *JHS* 50 (1930): 350–1. ("Séchan")

Guide to Further Reading

The general introduction and six section introductions provide suggestions for further reading in key areas in the footnotes. For that reason no separate guide has been included here. See especially the general introduction, pp. 1–16, for introductory works and sourcebooks, and for a survey of some of the key landmarks of research in the field in recent decades. The editorial sections confine themselves mainly to referencing English-speaking scholarship, but with occasional mention of key works of non-English scholarship where they have made a very important contribution to the field.

Chronology

BCE

776	Traditional foundation date of the Olympic festival.
580s–570s	Foundation of the *periodos* (i.e. sacred status given to the Pythian, Isthmian and Nemean festivals).
566	Foundation of the Panathenaia in Athens.
490, 480–479	Persian invasions of Greece.
431–404	Peloponnesian war.
365	Battle between the Arcadians and the Eleans in the Altis at Olympia. (See chapter 2.)
335	Reform of the Athenian ephebeia.
323	Death of Alexander the Great.
c. 280	Foundation of the Ptolemaia in Alexandria by Ptolemy II. (See chapter 5.)
c. 210	Recognition of the festival of the Leukophryeneia in Magnesia-on-the-Meander.
80	Sulla moves the year's Olympic festival to Rome.
31	Battle of Actium; beginning of Augustus' power in Rome.

CE

2	Foundation of the Sebasta in Naples.
60	Establishment of the festival of the Neronia by the emperor Nero (the first recurring Greek-style agonistic festival in Rome).
67	Nero competes in the rearranged Olympic festival.
86	Foundation of the Capitolia by the emperor Domitian
early 2nd century CE	Foundation of the Demostheneia at Oinoanda. (See chapter 8.)
138	Foundation of the Eusebeia at Puteoli, in honour of Hadrian.
mid 2nd century CE	Pausanias' visit to Olympia.
c. 219	Foundation of the Antoninia Pythia in Rome by Elagabal. (See chapter 6.)
c. 243	Foundation of the *agôn* of Athena Promachos in Rome by Gordian III. (See chapter 6.)
394	Banning of pagan festivals by the emperor Theodosius

1766	'Rediscovery' of the Olympic site
1870s	First systematic excavations at Olympia
1896	First Athens Olympics
1936	Berlin Olympics

Glossary

agôn (pl. *agônes*)	contest
*eiselastikos (*or *eisaktios)*	a contest victory which brings the privilege of processional entry for the victor into his own city (cf. *eiselaunein* – "to drive in", *eiselasis* – "victory procession")
hieros	a sacred contest
stephanitês	a "crown" contest
isolympic, isopythian	"equal to the Olympic festival", "equal to the Pythian festival"
oikoumenikos	"for the whole world"
periporphyros	having a prize of purple
talantiaioi, hêmitalantiaioi	with a prize of one talent, with a prize of half a talent
thematikos	a contest with money prizes (cf. *themateitês, arguritês, chrêmatitês*)
thymelikos	musical
agonothetês (pl. *agonothetai*)	president of the festival (usually with responsibility for both funding and administration)
agora	market-place
Altis	sacred grove at Olympia around the temple of Zeus
aretê	virtue (often used to describe the qualities associated with athletic victory and athletic education)
asylia	inviolability
athlon (also *epathlon)* (pl. *athla, epathla)*	prize
aulêtês	flute-player
bouleutêrion	council-chamber
brabeion	prize
brabeutês	umpire
chorêgos	chorus-leader, i.e. benefactor responsible for paying the costs of producing a chorus (esp. in classical Athenian drama)
cirrus	top-knot made from tied back hair, signalling professional athlete status
dêmos	people
denarius	unit of currency (very roughly one day's wage for an unskilled labourer in the early Imperial period)

diaulos	foot-race, twice a *stadion* in length
dolichos	long-distance foot-race
dôrea	grant by the emperor of sacred status for a festival
eirênê	peace
ekecheiria (pl. *ekecheiriai*)	truce
ephêbeia	period of training in the *gymnasion* for young men ("ephebes", *ephêboi*, sing. *ephêbos*) in their late teens; cf. *ephêbarchos* ("overseer of the ephebes")
epideixis	display
epinikion	victory ode
epistatês	athletic trainer
epitêdeuma	profession
euandria	beautiful manliness, physical fitness (title of a contest in *gymnasion* festivals)
grammatikos	grammar teacher
gymnasiarchos	official in charge of the *gymnasion*, usually with responsibility for both funding and administration
gymnasion (pl. *gymnasia*)	educational institution primarily for physical and military training
hellanodikês (pl. *hellanodikai*)	judge at Olympia
hieromênia	truce at the time of a festival
hieronikês	victor in a "sacred" contest
hoplitês	heavy armed foot-soldier; race in armour
hoplomachia	fighting with weapons (for training)
hoplomachos	weapons instructor
kaloi kagathoi	lit. "beautiful and good", i.e. "gentlemen", members of the elite
kômos	revel (often referring to the disorderly procession following a *symposion*); or, an ode sung on such an occasion
kudos	glory, talismanic power
ludi	games (in Roman tradition)
mêtropolis	"mother-city" (i.e. the city from which settlers are sent out to found a new colony)
mina	unit of currency (100 drachmai)
misthos	wage
neoi	young men (age category above the ephebes in the *gymnasion*)
neôkoros	honorific title given to the centre of the imperial cult in a province
obsonia (Latin), *opsônia* (Gk)	pension
oikoumenê	the inhabited world
paides	boys
paidagôgos	slave with responsibility for accompanying boys to and from school

Glossary

paideia	learning
paidonomos (pl. *paidonomoi*)	official in charge of supervising education
paidotribês (pl. *paidotribai*)	athletic trainer
palaistra (pl. *palaistrai*)	"wrestling-school" (equivalent to a *gymnasion*, but usually privately owned)
panêgyris	festival
panêguriarchês	festival president
pankration	combat sport, combining boxing and wrestling
paradoxos	amazing, out-of-the-ordinary
periodonikês	victor in the contests of the *periodos*
periodos	"circuit", i.e. the category of the most prestigious games in the Greek festival calendar (originally just the Olympic, Pythian, Nemean and Isthmian festivals; others added later)
peripolistikos	"travelling", "wandering"
polis (pl. *poleis*)	city
prytaneion	magistrates' hall, town hall (where official guests would be invited for free meals)
prytanis	magistrate (precise meaning can vary between cities)
pyrrhichê	war-dance
quadrigae	teams of horses (for chariot racing)
rhêtor	teacher of rhetoric
spondophoros	herald who announces the truce for the Olympic and other festivals
stadion	stadium or sprint-race (one length of the track)
stephanos	crown
symposion	drinking party
synthusia; synthutês (pl. *synthutai*)	shared sacrifice; official with responsibility for participating in a shared sacrifice on behalf of a city
technê	skill, profession
themata	money prizes
themis (pl. *themides*)	local contest, with money prizes (=*agôn themateitês*)
theôros (pl. *theôroi*)	ambassador with responsibility for (a) advertising the holding of a festival and/or seeking permission for a grant of sacred status or (b) for attending a festival on behalf of his city
trierarchos	benefactor responsible for naval funding
xenia	relationship of friendship; cf. *xenoi* (in this context): those involved in such relationships
xystos	covered running track

Works Cited

Arieti, J. A. (1974-5) "Nudity in Greek athletics", *Classical World* 68: 431-6.
Bachrach, S. D. (2000) *The Nazi Olympics: Berlin 1936*, Boston.
Biddiss, M. (1999) "The invention of the modern Olympic tradition", in Biddiss, M. and Wyke, M. (eds) *The Uses and Abuses of Antiquity*, Bern: 125-43.
Bohringer, F. (1979) "Cultes d'athlètes en Grèce classique: propos, politiques, discours mythiques", *Revue des études anciennes* 81: 5-18.
Bonfante, L. (1989) "Nudity as costume in classical art", *American Journal of Archaeology* 93: 543-70.
Briggs, W. W. (1975) "Augustan athletics and the games of *Aeneid* 5", *Stadion* 1: 277-83.
Burnett, A.P. (2005) *Pindar's Songs for Young Athletes of Aigina*, Oxford.
Caldelli, M. L. (1993) *L'Agon Capitolinus: storia e protagonisti dall' istituzione domizianea al IV secolo*, Rome.
Christesen, P. (2002) "On the meaning of gymnazao", *Nikephoros* 15: 7-37.
Christesen, P. (2007) *Olympic Victor Lists and Ancient Greek History*, Cambridge.
Coulson, W. and Kyrielis, H. (eds) (1992) *Proceedings of an International Symposium on the Olympic Games*, Athens.
Crowther, N. B. (1982) "Athletic dress and nudity in Greek athletics", *Eranos* 80: 163-8 (reprinted in Crowther 2004).
Crowther, N. B. (1984-5) "Studies in Greek athletics" *Classical World* 78: 497-558.
Crowther, N. B. (1985-6) "Studies in Greek athletics" *Classical World* 79: 73-135.
Crowther, N. B. (1990) "Recent trends in the study of Greek athletics", *L'Antiquité classique* 59: 246-55.
Crowther, N. B. (1991) "The Olympic training period", *Nikephoros* 4: 161-6 (reprinted in Crowther 2004).
Crowther, N. B. (1993) "Numbers of contestants in Greek athletic contests", *Nikephoros* 6: 39-52 (reprinted in Crowther 2004).
Crowther, N. B. (1994a) "The role of heralds and trumpeters at Greek athletic festivals", *Nikephoros* 7: 135-55 (reprinted in Crowther 2004).
Crowther, N. B. (1994b) "Reflections on Greek equestrian events: violence and spectator attitudes", *Nikephoros* 7: 121-33 (reprinted in Crowther 2004).
Crowther, N. B. (2001) "Visiting the Olympic games: travel and conditions for athletes and spectators", *International Journal of the History of Sport* 18: 37-52 (reprinted in Crowther 2004).
Crowther, N. B. (2004) *Athletika: Studies on the Olympic Games and Greek Athletics*, Hildesheim.
de Coubertin, P. (2000) *Olympism: Selected Writings, 1863-1937* (editing director, Norbert Müller; translated by William H. Skinner), Lausanne.
Decker, W. (1995) *Sport in der griechischen Antike*, Munich.

Dickie, M. (1993) ""*Palaistrites/palaestrita*": callisthenics in the Greek and Roman gymnasion", *Nikephoros* 6: 105–51.
Downey, G. (1939) "The Olympic games of Antioch in the fourth century AD", *Transactions of the American Philological Association* 70: 428–38.
Drees, L. (1968) *Olympia. Gods, Artists and Athletes*, London (translated by G. Onn; first published in German in 1967).
Ebert, J. (1972) *Griechische Epigramme auf Sieger an gymnischen und hippischen Agonen*, Leipzig.
Ebert, J. (1997) *Agonismata. Kleine philologische Schriften zur Literatur, Geschichte und Kultur der Antike*, Stuttgart.
Farrington, A. (1997) "Olympic victors and the popularity of the Olympic games in the Imperial period", *Tyche* 12: 15–46.
Finley, M. I. and Pleket, H. W. (1976) *The Olympic Games. The First Thousand Years*, London.
Gardiner, E.N. (1910) *Greek Athletic Sports and Festivals*, London.
Gardiner, E.N. (1925) *Olympia. Its History and Remains*, Oxford.
Gardiner, E.N. (1930) *Athletics of the Ancient World*, Oxford.
Gauthier, P. and Hatzopoulos, M. B. (1993), *La loi gymnasiarque de Beroia*, Athens.
Gebhard, E.R. (1993) "The evolution of a pan-hellenic sanctuary: from archaeology towards history at Isthmia", in Marinatos, N. and Hägg, R. (eds) *Greek Sanctuaries: New Approaches*, London: 154–77.
Glass, S. L. (1988) "The Greek gymnasium. Some problems", in Raschke (ed.): 155–73.
Golden, M. (1998) *Sport and Society in Ancient Greece*, Cambridge.
Golden, M. (2004) *Sport in the Ancient World from A to Z*, New York.
Golden, M. (2008) *Greek Sport and Social Status*, Austin.
Graham, C.C. (2001) *Leni Riefenstahl and Olympia*, Lanham.
Guttmann, A. (1978) *From Ritual to Record. The Nature of Modern Sports*, New York.
Guttmann, A. (1994) *Games and Empires. Modern Sports and Cultural Imperialism*, New York.
Hargreaves, J. (1986) *Sport, Power and Culture*, Cambridge.
Harris, H. A. (1964) *Greek Athletes and Athletics*, London.
Hargreaves, J. (1972) *Sport in Greece and Rome*, London.
Hargreaves, J. (1976) *Greek Athletics and the Jews*, Cardiff.
Hart-Davis, D. (1986) *Hitler's Games: The 1936 Olympics*, New York.
Hilton, C. (2006) *Hitler's Olympics: The 1936 Berlin Games*, Stroud.
Hodkinson, S. (1999) "An agonistic culture?", in Hodkinson, S. and Powell, A. (eds) *Sparta: New Perspectives*, Swansea: 147–87.
Hyde, W. W. (1921) *Olympic Victor Monuments and Greek Athletic Art*, Washington (reprinted in 2003: University Press of Pacific).
Kah, D. and Scholz, P. (eds) (2004) *Das hellenistische Gymnasion*, Berlin.
Kennell, N. M. (1995) *The Gymnasium of Virtue. Education and Culture in Ancient Sparta*, Chapel Hill.
Kitchell, K. (1998) "'But the mare I will not give up': the games in *Iliad* 23", *Classical Bulletin* 74: 159–171
König, J. (2005) *Athletics and Literature in the Roman Empire*, Cambridge.
König, J. (2007) "Greek athletics in the Severan period: literary views" in Swain, S., Harrison, S. and Elsner, J. (eds) *Severan Culture*, Cambridge: 135–45.
König, J. (2009) "Training athletes and interpreting the past in Philostratus' *Gymnasticus*", in Bowie, E. and Elsner, J. (eds) *Philostratus*, Cambridge: 251–83.
Kruger, A. and Murray, W. (2003) *The Nazi Olympics: Sport, Politic and Appeasement in the 1930s*, Urbana.
Kurke, L. (1991) *The Traffic in Praise: Pindar and the Poetics of Social Economy*, Ithaca.

Kyle, D. G. (1983a) "Directions in ancient sport history", *Journal of Sport History* 10: 17–34.
Kyle, D. G. (1983b) "The study of Greek sport: a survey", *Echos du monde classique* 27: 46–67.
Kyle, D. G. (1984) "Non-competition in Homeric sport", *Stadion* 10: 1–19.
Kyle, D. G. (1987) *Athletics in Ancient Athens*, Leiden.
Kyle, D. G. (2007) *Sport and Spectacle in the Ancient World*, Malden.
Kyrielis, H. (2003) "The German excavations at Olympia: an introduction", in Phillips and Pritchard (eds): 41–60.
Lämmer, M. (1993) "The nature and significance of the Olympic oath in Greek antiquity", in Panagiotopoulos, D. P. (ed.) *The Institution of the Olympic Games*, Athens: 141–8.
Large, D. C. (2007) *Nazi Games: The Olympics of 1936*, New York.
Lee, H. M. (1983) "Athletic arete in Pindar", *Ancient World* 7: 31–7.
Lee, H. M. (1984) "Women's athletics and the bikini mosaic from Piazza Armerina", *Stadion* 10: 45–76.
Lee, H. M. (1988a) "The "first" Olympic games of 776 B.C.", in Raschke (ed): 110–18.
Lee, H. M. (1988b) "Did women compete against men in Greek athletic festivals", *Nikephoros* 1: 103–18.
Lee, H. M. (1998) "The ancient Olympic games: origin, evolution, revolution", *Classical Bulletin* 74: 129–41.
Lee, H. M. (2001) *The Program and Schedule of the Ancient Olympic Games*, Hildesheim.
Llewelyn Smith, M. (2004) *Olympics in Athens 1896: The Invention of the Modern Olympic Games*, London.
Lovatt, H. (2005) *Statius and Epic Games: Sport, Politics and Poetics in the Thebaid*, Cambridge.
MacAloon, J. J. (1981) *This Great Symbol. Pierre de Coubertin and the Origins of the Modern Olympic Games*, Chicago.
MacClancy, J. (ed.) (1996) *Sport, Identity and Ethnicity*, Oxford.
McDonnell, M. (1991) "The origin of athletic nudity: Thucydides, Plato, and the vases", *Journal of Hellenic Studies* 111: 182–93.
McPherson, B. (1989) *The Social Significance of Sport. Introduction to the Sociology of Sport*, Champaign.
Mallwitz, A. (1988) "Cult and competition locations at Olympia", in Raschke (ed.): 79–109.
Mandell, R. (1987) *The Nazi Olympics*, Champaign (revised edition; first published in 1971).
Miller, S. G. (2000) "Naked democracy", in Flensted-Jensen, P., Nielson, T. H. and Rubinstein, L. (eds) *Polis and Politics: Studies in Ancient Greek History*, Copenhagen: 277–96.
Miller, S. G. (2004a) *Arete: Greek Sports from Ancient Sources*, Berkeley (third, revised edition; second edition published in 1991; first edition published in 1979).
Miller, S. G. (2004b) *Ancient Greek Athletics*, New Haven.
Miller, S. G. (2004c) *Nemea: A Guide to the Site and Museum*, Athens (second edition; first published in 1990).
Millon, C. and Schouler, B. (1988) "Les jeux olympiques d'Antioche", in *Les sports antiques. Toulouse et Domitien (Pallas* 34): 61–76.
Mitchell, S. (1990) "Festivals, games and civic life in Roman Asia Minor", *Journal of Roman Studies* 80: 183–93.
Moretti, L. (1953) *Iscrizioni agonistiche greche*, Rome.
Moretti, L. (1957) "Olympionikai, i vincitori negli antichi agoni olimpici", *MAL* 8.2: 55–198.
Morgan, C. (1990) *Athletes and Oracles. The Transformation of Olympia and Delphi in the Eighth Century BC*, Cambridge.
Morgan, C. (1993) "The origins of pan-Hellenism", in Marinatos, N. and Hägg, R. (eds)

Greek Sanctuaries. New Approaches, London: 18–44.
Morgan, C. (1994) "The evolution of a sacral landscape: Isthmia, Perachora, and the early Corinthian state", in Alcock, S. E. and Osborne, R. (eds) *Placing the Gods: Sanctuaries and Sacred Space in Ancient Greece*, Oxford: 105–42.
Morgan, C. (2002) "The origins of the Isthmian festival: points of comparison and contrast", in Kyrieleis, H. (ed.) *Olympia 1875–2000: 125 Jahre Deutsche Ausgrabungen*, Mainz: 251–71.
Mouratidis, J. (1985) "The origin of nudity in Greek athletics", *Journal of Sport History* 12: 213–32.
Neils, J. (ed.) (1992) *Goddess and Polis: The Panathenaic Festival in Ancient Athens*, Princeton.
Neils, J. (ed.) (1996) *Worshipping Athena: Panathenaia and Parthenon*, Madison.
Newby, Z. (2002) "Sculptural display in the so-called palaestra of Hadrian's villa at Tivoli", *Mitteilungen des Deutschen Archäologischen Instituts, Römische Abteilung* 109: 59–83.
Newby, Z. (2005) *Greek Athletics in the Roman World: Victory and Virtue*, Oxford.
Newby, Z. (2006) *Athletics in the Ancient World*, London.
Nicholson, N. (2005) *Aristocracy and Athletics in Archaic and Classical Greece*, Cambridge.
Nielsen, T. H. (2007) *Olympia and the Classical Hellenic City-State Culture*, Copenhagen.
van Nijf, O. (2001) "Local heroes: athletics, festivals, and elite self-fashioning in the Roman East", in Goldhill, S. (ed.) *Being Greek under Rome. Cultural Identity, the Second Sophistic and Development of Empire*, Cambridge: 306–34.
van Nijf, O. (2003a) "Athletics, *andreia* and the *askesis*-culture in the Roman East", in Rosen, M. and Sluiter, I. (eds) *Andreia. Studies in Manliness and Courage in Classical Antiquity*, Leiden: 263–86.
van Nijf, O. (2003b) "Athletics and paideia: festivals and physical education in the world of the Second Sophistic", in Borg, B. E. (ed.) *Paideia: The World of the Second Sophistic*, Berlin: 203–28.
van Nijf, O. (2005) "*Aristos Hellenôn*: succès sportif et identité grecque dans la Grèce romaine", *Metis* 3: 271–94.
van Nijf, O. (2006) "Global players: athletes and performers in the Hellenistic and Roman world", in Nielsen, I. (ed.) *Between Cult and Society: The Cosmopolitan Centres of the Ancient Mediterranean as Setting for Activities of Religious Associations and Religious Communities*, Hamburg: 226–35.
Papakonstantinou, Z. (ed.) (2010) *Sport in the Cultures of the Ancient World*, London.
Parker, R. (2004) "New panhellenic festivals in Hellenistic Greece", in Schlesier, R. and Zellmann, U. (eds) *Mobility and Travel in the Mediterranean from Antiquity to the Middle Ages*, Münster: 9–22.
Pemberton, E. (2000) "*Agones hieroi*: Greek athletic contests in their religious context", *Nikephoros* 13: 111–24.
Pfitzner, V. C. (1967) *Paul and the Agon Motif. Traditional Athletic Imagery in the Pauline Literature*, Leiden.
Phillips, D. and Pritchard, D. (eds) (2003) *Sport and Festival in the Ancient Greek World*, Swansea.
Pleket, H. W. (1973) "Some aspects of the history of athletic guilds", *Zeitschrift für Papyrologie und Epigraphik* 10: 197–227.
Pleket, H. W. (1974) "Zur Soziologie des antiken Sports", *Mededelingen van het Nederlands historisch Instituut te Rome* 36: 57–87.
Pleket, H. W. (1992) "The participants in the ancient Olympic games: social background and mentality", in Coulson and Kyrielis (eds): 147–52.
Pleket, H. W. (1998) "Mass sport and local infrastructure in the Greek cities of Roman Asia Minor", *Stadion* 24: 151–72.

Poliakoff, M. (1987) *Combat Sports in the Ancient World*, Yale.
Potter, D. S. (1999) "Entertainers in the Roman Empire", in Potter, D. S. and Mattingly, D. J. (eds) *Life, Death and Entertainment in the Roman Empire*, Ann Arbor: 256–83.
Pritchard, D. (2003) "Athletics, education, and participation in classical Athens", in Phillips and Pritchard (eds): 293–349.
Raschke, W. J. (ed.) (1988) *The Archaeology of the Olympics. The Olympics and Other Festivals in Antiquity*, Madison.
Rausa, F. (1994) *L'immagine del vincitore. L'atleta nella statuaria greca dell' età arcaica all' ellenismo*, Treviso.
Rippon, A. (2006) *Hitler's Olympics: The Story of the 1936 Nazi Games*, Barnsley.
Robert, L. (1940) *Les gladiateurs dans l'Orient grec*, Paris.
Robert, L. (1969–90) *Opera Minora Selecta* (7 vols), Amsterdam.
Robert, L. (2007) *Choix d'écrits* (ed. D. Rousset, in collaboration with Ph. Gauthier and I. Savalli-Lestrade), Paris.
Robinson, R. S. (1955) *Sources for the History of Greek Athletics in English Translation*, Cincinnati.
Rogers, G. M. (1991) *The Sacred Identity of Ephesos. Foundation Myths of a Roman City*, London.
Rutherford, I. (2000) "*Theoria* and *darshan*. Pilgrimage as gaze in Greece and India", *Classical Quarterly* 50: 133–46.
Sansone, D. (1988) *Greek Athletics and the Genesis of Sport*, Berkeley.
Scanlon, T. F. (1983) "The vocabulary of competition: *agon* and *aethlos*, Greek terms for contest", *Arete* 1: 147–62.
Scanlon, T. F. (1984) *Greek and Roman Athletics: A Bibliography*, Chicago.
Scanlon, T. F. (2002) *Eros and Greek Athletics*, Oxford.
Scanlon, T. F. (forthcoming) *Oxford Readings in Greek and Roman Sport*, Oxford.
Seesengood, R. P. (2006) *Competing Identities: The Athlete and the Gladiator in Early Christianity*, London.
Sinn, U. (2000) *Olympia. Cult, Sport, and Ancient Festival*, Princeton (translated by T. Thornton; first published in German in 1996).
Spawforth, A. J. S. (1989) "Agonistic festivals in Roman Greece", in Cameron, A. and Walker, S. (eds) *The Greek Renaissance in the Roman Empire*, London: 193–7.
Spivey, N. (2004) *The Ancient Olympics*, Oxford.
Swaddling, J. (1980) *The Ancient Olympic Games*, London.
Sweet, W. E. (1987) *Sport and Recreation in Ancient Greece. A Sourcebook with Translations*, New York.
Tell, H. (2007) "Sages at the games: intellectual displays and dissemination of wisdom in ancient Greece", *Classical Antiquity* 26: 249–75.
Tyrrell, W. B. (2004) *The Smell of Sweat: Greek Athletics, Olympics and Culture*, Wauconda.
Valavanis, P. (2004) *Games and Sanctuaries in Ancient Greece: Olympia, Delphi, Isthmia, Nemea, Athens*, Los Angeles.
Walters, G. (2007) *Berlin Games: How Hitler Stole the Olympic Dream*, London.
Willis, W. H. (1941) "Athletic contests in the epic", *Transactions of the American Philological Association* 72: 392–417.
Woolf, G. (2006) "Playing games with Greeks: one Roman on Greekness", in Konstan, D. and Said, S. (eds) *Greeks on Greekness: Viewing the Greek Past under the Roman Empire*, Cambridge: 162–78.
Wörrle, M. (1988) *Stadt und Fest in kaiserzeitlichen Kleinasien. Studien zu einer agonistischen Stiftung aus Oinoanda*, Munich.

Young, D. C. (1984) *The Olympic Myth of Greek Amateur Athletics*, Chicago.
Young, D. C. (1987) "The origins of the modern Olympics: a new version", *International Journal of the History of Sport* 4: 271–300.
Young, D. C. (1988) "How the amateurs won the Olympics", in Raschke (ed.): 55–75.
Young, D. C. (1996) *The Modern Olympics. A Struggle for Revival*, Baltimore.
Young, D. C. (2004) *A Brief History of the Olympic Games*, Malden.

Index

Note With occasional exceptions, festivals are indexed by their host cities, not by their titles. For reasons of space, cities and athletes mentioned only once and in passing are in most cases not included in the index.

Achilles, 72, 190
Aelius Aristides, 185
Aeschines, 53, 75, 77, 80–1, 82, 83
age categories, 72, 92, 94, 154, 156, 188
agonothetes, 1, 113–14, 155, 157, 182, 192, 193
Alexander Severus, 259
Alexandria, 109, 117
Alkibiades, 31, 48, 68–9, 162, 170
amateurism and professionalism, 7, 38, 68, 147–8, 152, 161, 167–74, 186–7, 241–2, 251, 265–6, 269–70, 284–311
Anazarbos, 111, 118, 136
Antioch, 107, 121, 156, 159, 179, 258
Antoninus Pius, 112, 123, 257
Aphrodisias, 112, 122
Apollo, 30, 31, 32, 43, 45, 47, 109, 112, 131, 139–40, 152, 181
Appian, 115
Argos, 19, 28, 29, 46, 48, 49, 53, 110, 112, 157, 187, 231
Aristophanes, 31, 73, 75, 77, 81, 82, 305–9
Aristotle, 39, 66–7, 71, 97, 271
Arrichion, 12–13, 165
Asia Minor, 106, 112, 127–8, 136, 179
Asklepios, 113, 114, 115
Astylos of Kroton, 229, 277–8
Athena, 72, 110, 113, 114, 115, 126–31, 140
Athens, 8, 25, 26, 31, 32–3, 44, 45, 47, 48–50, 51, 52, 53, 58, 63–4, 66–86, 94, 110, 112, 119, 122, 124, 125, 126, 127, 129–30, 133, 134, 135, 158, 160, 186, 187, 205, 227, 231
athletic art, 1, 4, 5–6, 11–13, 32, 63, 72–3, 77–8, 202–3, 215–33, 238–62, 296
Augustus, 111, 121, 123, 135, 154, 157, 185
Aurelian, 125, 138, 140
Aurelius Victor, 127
Autolykos, 75, 79

Bacchylides, 9, 70–1, 205, 212, 233, 272
Balboura, 183, 189–90
bath buildings, 241–59
Beamon, Bob, 276–7, 280, 283
benefaction, 1, 14, 65, 73–4, 88–9, 96, 98, 110, 159, 180–2, 191; *see also* agonothetes and gymnasiarchs
Benveniste, E., 205, 206, 211
Beroia, 65, 88, 93, 94–5, 97, 98, 99, 100, 112, 157
Boardman, J., 32
Bohringer, F., 226–7
Brunt, P. A., 172
Byzantion, 133, 135, 136

Caisareia by Mount Argaios (Cappadocia), 133, 135, 136
Callimachus, 228
Capitolia (Rome), 111, 112, 117, 121–2, 123, 126, 127, 129, 133, 135, 137, 139, 185, 202, 238, 248, 252, 257, 258
Caracalla, 136, 137, 138, 180
Carthage, 111, 113–14, 115, 139
Cartledge, P., 177
Cassius Dio, 138–9, 216, 218
Chalkis, 94–5, 100
Chionis of Sparta, 277–8
Christesen, P., 9

Christian responses to athletics, 2, 106–7, 119, 177
Cicero, 171, 238–9
civic life, integration of *gymnasion* and festival activity into, 96–101, 175–97
Claudius, 173
Commodus, 121, 124
Corinth, 19, 26–7, 28, 29, 30, 45, 151, 272
Coubertin, Pierre de, 7, 36–7, 58, 147, 152, 166, 172, 173, 266, 299, 301
Cratinus, 79
Crete, 73, 110–11
crowns, crowning, 78, 108, 120, 121, 148–61, 201, 204–37, 244, 247–51, 254, 256; *see also* sacred games
Crowther, N., 8

Davies, J. K., 230
Day, J., 219
debate over the value of athletics, 10–11, 16
dedications, 5, 23–34
Delorme, J., 149
Delos, 45, 73, 90–2, 97, 115, 159
Delphi *see* Pythian Games
Delphic oracle, 39, 43, 48, 115, 131, 208, 227, 228, 229
Demosthenes, 53, 80, 82, 129
Dio of Prusa, 116, 156, 164, 165, 172, 246, 279
Diodorus Siculus, 87, 208, 209, 213
Diogenes Laertius, 216
Diogenes the Cynic, 216
Dodona, 29, 33, 110
Domitian, 111–12, 121, 137, 139, 185, 238, 248
drawn contests, 190
Dyme, 40, 227

Ebert, J., 8, 160–1, 212, 224
education *see ephebeia*
Egypt, 64, 92
eiselastic contests *see* triumphal entry
Elagabal, 118, 136–40
Elis, 24, 39–55, 73, 165, 208
elite/non-elite involvement in athletics, 23–5, 30–1, 64, 66–86, 98–101, 143–4, 145–97, 232–3, 258
Emesa, 138, 139–40
emperors, 11–12, 184–6; *see also* names of individual emperors
ephebeia, ephebes, 64, 71–2, 74, 75, 92–4, 119, 160, 163, 166, 168, 188
Ephesos, 96, 99, 100, 111, 112, 124, 128, 133, 134, 135, 138, 155, 159, 162, 180, 187, 212
Epidauros, 30, 110, 112
equestrian contests, 9, 31, 47, 49, 68–9, 160, 170, 216, 218, 230, 244–5
Eretria, 95
eroticism, 2, 64, 75–83
euandria, 73, 78
Euphorion, 29
Eupolis, 76, 79
Euripides, 69, 170, 279, 305
Eusebius, 29
Euthykles of Lokris, 225, 226, 229
Euthymos of Lokris, 222, 225, 226, 227, 228, 273
events, 20, 267–83

female involvement in athletic competition /benefaction, 1, 38, 65, 223, 272
festival foundations, 3, 19–20, 23–34, 39, 99, 103–40, 180–2
finances, control over by Rome, 14–16
Fisher, N., 64
Fontenrose, J., 225–6
foundation stories, 27, 28–9, 32–3, 39
Fränkel, H., 205, 211

Galen, 65, 163, 169–70, 171, 270, 279, 305
Gardiner, E. N., 7, 143, 146, 226, 266, 269–70, 276, 279, 284–311
Gardner, P., 299–300
Gauthier, P., 65
gladiators, Roman arena games (*ludi*), 6, 9, 106, 108, 121, 239, 245, 255, 256
Glaukos of Karystos, 68, 69
Gleason, M., 190–1
Gordian, 112, 122, 125–30, 137, 138, 140
Gorgias, 57
guilds (associations), 15, 105–6, 117, 125–6, 163, 168–9, 239, 246, 253, 257
Guttmann, A., 265, 267–8, 269, 276, 280
gymnasia and *palaistrai*, 1, 2, 5, 14–15, 63–101, 119, 149, 162, 163, 188, 238–9, 245, 251, 258; *see also ephebeia*, ephebes

architecture, 88–92
    contests in, 92–3, 94, 96, 98, 188; see also Hermes, Hermaia
    literate education in, 64, 82, 93–4, 96, 98, 100, 182
    openness to non-citizens, 98–101
    regulations, 65, 75, 87, 93, 97–8, 99
gymnasiarchs, 1, 70, 73–4, 78, 88, 89, 92, 93, 94, 95, 97, 98, 99, 101

Hadrian, 112, 121, 123–4, 135, 158, 184–5, 186, 257
Halikarnassos, 95–6, 110
Harris, H.A., 7, 146–7, 161, 269–70, 287
Helios, 114, 128, 138, 139–40
Helix, 138–9, 240, 252–3
hellanodikai, 20, 41, 47, 219, 221
Herakles, 21, 32–3, 46, 94, 98, 112, 164–5, 213, 228, 274
heralds, competition for, 20, 134
Hermes, Hermaia, 88, 92, 93, 94, 98, 100
Hermopolis, 117–18, 255
Herodian, 138
Herodotus, 208–11, 213, 227–8, 231–2
heroes, athletes as, 28, 225–30
Hesiod, 309
Homer, 67, 149, 152, 165, 202, 205, 211, 293, 304, 309
Hornblower, S., 210
Humphreys, S. C., 149

identity, 1, 2, 9, 144, 175–97
Iphitos of Elis, 39, 43
Isokrates, 31, 57, 68–9, 71, 162, 163
Isthmian Games, Isthmia, 19, 21, 25–34, 44, 45, 46–7, 108, 110, 120, 121, 133, 135, 149, 177, 204–5, 212, 218, 223, 273, 275

Johnson, Michael, 276, 282–3
Julius Africanus, 274–5, 280
Juvenal, 238, 239, 241, 245, 259

Kamarina, 204, 211, 213
Kapros of Elis, 274–5, 280
Keos, 92, 97
Kleitomachos of Thebes, 274–7, 280, 282
Kleitor, 110, 151
Kleomedes of Astypalaia, 225, 226, 228

Kleonai, 19, 28, 53
Kleosthenes of Pisa, 39
König, J., 9
Kos, 109, 111, 116
Kroton, 208, 229
kudos, 69, 167, 201, 204–37
Kyle, D., 7, 8, 68, 70, 79, 81
Kylon, 47
Kyniska, 223, 272
Kyzikos, 112, 114–15, 133, 136

Lämmer, M., 10, 21
leisure, 66–7, 166
Leonidas of Rhodes, 278
Lepreon, 48–50
Lewis, Carl, 275, 276–7, 282–3
Libanius, 107
Livy, 291, 309
Lucian, 41–2, 164, 165, 171
Lucius Verus, 125
ludi see gladiators
Lyceum, 73
Lycia, 106, 144, 175–97
Lykourgos, 39, 40
Lysias, 57, 74, 75, 206

MacClancy, J., 9
Macedonia, 53, 54, 57, 88, 100, 109, 177; see also Beroia
MacMullen, R., 166
Magna Graecia (S. Italy), 106, 109, 111, 123
Magnesia on the Maeander, 109, 110, 111, 131
Malalas, 179
Mandell, R., 267, 269
Manetho, 117
Mangan, J. A., 296–7
Mantineia, 48, 49, 53, 110, 114, 124
Marcus Aurelius, 124
Martial, 239, 241
medical writing on athletics, 65; see also Galen
Miletos, 95, 99, 100, 109, 112, 116, 164, 213
military training, 2, 5, 58, 64, 65, 72–3, 92–3, 97, 100, 149, 166, 293–4
Miller, S., 8, 287
Milo, 208, 215, 219, 270, 272

Index

Mithridates, 114–15
modern sport, 1, 5, 21, 265–310; see also Olympics, modern and Sports studies
Moretti, L., 126, 146, 161, 162, 257
Morgan, C., 8–9, 21–2
musical events, 20–1, 134, 144, 158, 181

Naples (Neapolis), 111, 112, 123, 124, 126, 133, 135, 155, 164, 185, 187
Neils, J., 73, 77–8
Nemean Games, Nemea, 8, 19, 21, 25–34, 44, 48, 53–4, 100, 108, 110, 117, 120, 122, 133, 135, 149, 150, 151, 177, 212, 221, 222, 223, 273
neoi, 65, 92, 93, 94, 96, 99
Nepos, 239
Nero, Neronia, 54, 111, 122, 127, 139, 185, 207, 216, 218, 239
New Historicism, 204
Newby, Z., 9, 201–2
Nicholson, N., 9, 201
Nijf, O. van, 106, 144
Nikaia, 14, 112, 133, 135, 136
Nikomedia, 112, 133, 134, 135, 136
Nikopolis (Actian Games), 111, 112, 157, 185
Nilsson, M. P., 92
Nisetich, F. J., 214
nudity, 2–3

Ober, J., 67
Oibotas of Dyme, 225, 226, 227, 229–30
oikoumenikos, 118
Oinoanda, 180–94
Oinomaos, 33
Old Oligarch, 70, 74
Olympic festival (ancient), Olympia, Olympic victors, 5, 6, 8, 11–13, 19–60, 68–9, 105–6, 108, 109, 110, 116, 117, 120, 122, 123, 127, 133, 134, 135, 139, 148–50, 151, 152, 154, 158, 159, 162, 164, 168, 172, 176–8, 179, 185, 204, 207, 209–10, 211–12, 214, 215, 216, 218, 221, 222, 223, 224, 228, 229, 233, 239, 248, 258, 271–9, 291, 293
Olympic truce, 22, 36–60
Olympic victor lists, 9, 21

Olympics (modern), 3, 5, 6–7, 36–8, 55–6, 58–60, 147, 161, 276–7, 281–3
Osborne, R., 71
Ostia, 113, 238–62
Owens, Jesse, 277, 283

paides, 94–6; see also age categories
palaistrai see gymnasia and *palaistrai*
Palmyra, 113
Panathenaia (Athens), 44, 63, 71–4, 81, 112, 151, 156, 186
panhellenism, "panhellenic" festivals 19–20, 21, 39, 50, 51, 57, 71, 108, 110, 111, 177
pankration, 11, 13, 113
Panopeus, 87
Pantakles of Athens, 277
Parke, H., 32
Pausanias, 39, 87, 116, 209, 210, 218, 219, 221, 228, 229–30, 271, 272, 273, 274, 280
Pelops, 21, 32
Peloponnesian war, 45, 48–50, 57
Pergamon, 94, 110, 111, 112, 114, 123, 133, 135, 154, 163
Perge, 112, 131
Perinthos, 113, 114, 133, 136, 137
periodos, *periodonikês*, 8, 19, 21–2, 25–34, 63, 105, 108, 109, 111, 112, 116, 120, 122, 126–7, 135, 149–50, 151, 153, 157, 158, 159, 160, 161, 223, 257
Perpetua, 113
Phanas of Pellene, 277–8
Phayllos of Kroton, 210–11
Pheidon of Argos, 40
Philip the Arab, 112, 125, 127
Philippos of Kroton, 225, 227–8
Philostratus, 11–13, 139, 164, 167, 202, 219, 305
Pindar, 9, 25, 27, 31, 32, 47, 70–1, 75, 148, 150, 151, 153, 161, 162, 163, 164, 165, 166, 167, 168, 201, 204–5, 207, 211, 212, 213–14, 233, 272, 273, 296, 304–5
Plataiai, 116
Plato, 71, 72, 75, 77, 82, 83, 269, 305
Pleket, H. W., 7–8, 143–4, 275–6, 286, 287
Pliny the Elder, 228

Pliny the Younger, 13, 64, 117, 239, 259
Plutarch, 33, 53, 115, 206–7, 209, 216
Polites, 268, 270, 279, 280
Polybius, 40, 54
Polydamas of Skotusa, 225, 226, 228
Priene, 94, 110, 114
Pritchett, W. K., 149
prizes, 68, 69–70, 71, 72, 73, 74–5, 94, 113–14, 116–17, 143, 148–61, 177–9, 181, 243, 244, 246–51; see also crowns
professionalism see amateurism
Puteoli, 112, 123–4, 126, 133, 135
pyrrhic dances, 72
Pythian festival, Delphi, Pythian victors, 19–22, 23–34, 44, 45, 48, 87, 89–90, 108, 109, 112, 114, 120, 122, 131, 133, 135, 138, 139, 149, 152, 177, 179, 207, 211, 212, 214, 223, 231, 271, 273

records, 13, 167, 265, 267–83
religion, 5, 20, 114–15, 129–31, 139–40, 152
Rhegion, 43, 51, 227
Rhodes, 94, 100, 109, 114, 159, 168
Riefenstahl, L., 3, 5
Robert, L., 7–8, 100, 101, 105–7, 143, 146–8, 155, 165, 170–1, 179, 213, 275
Rogers, G., 193
Roman responses to Greek athletics, 5–6, 13–16, 202, 238–62
Rome, 66, 106, 111, 112, 114, 117, 120–40, 154, 163, 238–62
Rougement, G., 42
Roussel, P., 109, 131

sacred games, distinction from local games, 108, 120–1, 143, 148–61, 177–9
 authorisation of, 109, 111, 120–1, 137, 150, 179
Sardeis, 112, 114, 117, 138
Scanlon, T., 8, 9
Schelsky, H., 55
Schiller, F., 47
Sekunda, 71–2
Seneca, 241
Septimius Severus, 111, 113, 125, 136, 137

Sestos, 93, 94–5
Sicily, 109, 111
Side, 112, 131, 159
Sidon, 112, 117
Simonides, 68, 212
Sinis, 33
Sinope, 112, 125, 127
Smyrna, 112, 117–18, 122, 133, 135
Socrates, 73, 74, 75, 79
Solinus, 27
Solon, 75, 149, 164, 231–2
Sparta, 24, 39–40, 43, 45, 48–50, 51, 52, 53, 54, 58, 63, 110, 124, 186, 206, 207, 208, 210, 211, 223, 227, 272, 278
spectators, 11–12, 20, 41, 64
sports studies, sport history, 9, 37, 145–6, 284–6
Strabo, 39, 40
Stratonikeia, 115
Suetonius, 121, 207
Sulla, 54
symposia, 64, 67, 68, 77–8, 83

Tarsos, 118, 136, 137, 159, 179–80
Tegea, 110, 114, 151
Teisamenos, 208–9
Teos, 96, 99, 116
Termessos, 182, 188, 189
Tertullian, 111, 113, 115, 116
Thebes, 45, 112, 133, 135, 221–2
Theogenes (or Theagenes) of Thasos, 153, 168, 225, 226, 227, 270, 272–4, 277, 280
Theognis, 75
Theophrastos, 74, 82
theôroi, 41, 42, 54, 109, 110, 111, 120, 179
Theseus, 32–3
Thessalonike, 112, 114, 131
Thucydides, 38, 45, 48–50, 210, 227, 232
Thyateira, 137, 138, 159
Tiberius, 185
Tod, M. N., 270, 271, 276
Toner, J., 66
torch races, 63, 72, 74, 91, 93, 97
trainers, 75, 77, 95, 162, 170–1, 188
Trajan, 14, 64, 117, 125, 154, 155
Tralles, 92, 110, 112, 114
Tréheux, J., 90

triumphal entry (of athletic victors to their home cities), 15, 116–18, 120, 154, 207, 213
trumpeters, competition for, 20, 134

Veblen, T., 66, 166
Vernant, J.-P., 224–5
Versnel, H. S., 207
Vespasian, 186
victory, financial rewards for, 15–16, 116–17, 143, 148–61, 187–8, 215, 299
idealisation of, 1, 11–13, 38, 116, 164–74, 201, 204–37, 267–83
Vienne, 239
violence, 5–6, 13, 38, 106
Virgil, 202, 291, 309

Visconti, C. L., 243
von Reden, S., 77–8

Weber, M., 230–1
Weiler, I., 146, 147, 166–7, 287
Winkler, J., 81

Xenophanes, 231, 232–3, 305
Xenophon, 51, 52, 72, 73, 74, 75, 79

Young, D., 7, 68, 143–4, 265, 287, 299

Zeus, 20, 28, 31, 33, 39, 41, 43, 49, 50, 52, 58, 109, 110, 152, 154, 165, 204, 216, 272
Zosimus, 129